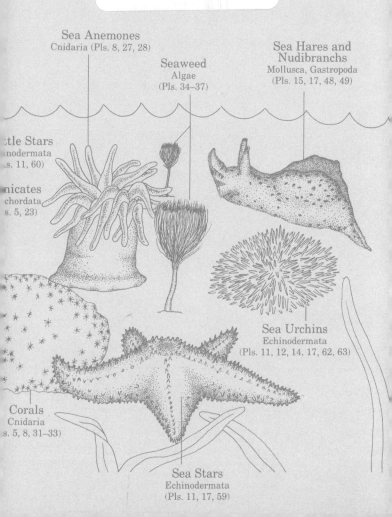

Sea Anemones
Cnidaria (Pls. 8, 27, 28)

Seaweed
Algae
(Pls. 34–37)

Sea Hares and
Nudibranchs
Mollusca, Gastropoda
(Pls. 15, 17, 48, 49)

ttle Stars
nodermata
s. 11, 60)

nicates
chordata
s. 5, 23)

Sea Urchins
Echinodermata
(Pls. 11, 12, 14, 17, 62, 63)

Corals
Cnidaria
s. 5, 8, 31–33)

Sea Stars
Echinodermata
(Pls. 11, 17, 59)

THE PETERSON FIELD GUIDE SERIES
Edited by Roger Tory Peterson

1. Birds—*R. T. Peterson*
2. Western Birds—*R. T. Peterson*
3. Shells of the Atlantic and Gulf Coasts and the West Indies—*Morris*
4. Butterflies—*Klots*
5. Mammals—*Burt and Grossenheider*
6. Pacific Coast Shells (including shells of Hawaii and the Gulf of California)—*Morris*
7. Rocks and Minerals—*Pough*
8. Birds of Britain and Europe—*R. T. Peterson, Mountfort, and Hollom*
9. Animal Tracks—*Murie*
10. Ferns and Their Related Families of Northeastern and Central North America—*Cobb*
11. Trees and Shrubs (Northeastern and Central North America)—*Petrides*
12. Reptiles and Amphibians of Eastern and Central North America—*Conant*
13. Birds of Texas and Adjacent States—*R. T. Peterson*
14. Rocky Mountain Wildflowers—*J. J. Craighead, F. C. Craighead, Jr., and Davis*
15. Stars and Planets—*Menzel and Pasachoff*
16. Western Reptiles and Amphibians—*Stebbins*
17. Wildflowers of Northeastern and North-central North America—*R. T. Peterson and McKenny*
19. Insects of America North of Mexico—*Borror and White*
20. Mexican Birds—*R. T. Peterson and Chalif*
21. Birds' Nests (found east of Mississippi River)—*Harrison*
22. Pacific States Wildflowers—*Niehaus and Ripper*
23. Edible Wild Plants of Eastern and Central North America—*L. Peterson*
24. Atlantic Seashore—*Gosner*
25. Western Birds' Nests—*Harrison*
26. Atmosphere—*Schaefer and Day*
27. Coral Reefs of the Caribbean and Florida—*Kaplan*
28. Pacific Coast Fishes—*Eschmeyer, Herald, and Hammann*
29. Beetles—*White*
30. Moths—*Covell*
31. Southwestern and Texas Wildflowers—*Niehaus, Ripper, and Savage*
32. Atlantic Coast Fishes—*Robins, Ray, and Douglass*
33. Western Butterflies—*Tilden and Smith*
34. Mushrooms—*McKnight and McKnight*
35. Hawks—*Clark and Wheeler*
36. Southeastern and Caribbean Seashores—*Kaplan*

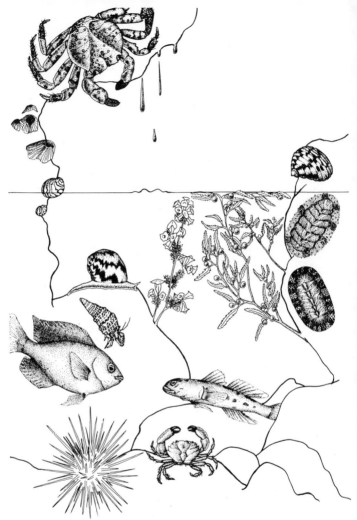

Caribbean tidepool scene at low tide (*clockwise, from top*):
Hanging from rock above waterline is a Sally Lightfoot crab.
Opposite, above waterline, is a Four-toothed Nerite. Beneath the
nerite, submerged, are a Fuzzy Chiton, West Indian Chiton,
Frillfin Goby, Mud Crab, Red Rock Urchin, Dusky Damselfish,
and a Stocky Cerith shell containing a Three-colored Hermit
Crab. Above the hermit crab is a Magpie or West Indian Top
Snail. At water's edge are Zebra Nerites, above which are Ribbed
Barnacles. The seaweeds in the pool are (left) Three-cornered Hat
Algae and Sargassum Weed.

THE PETERSON FIELD GUIDE SERIES

A Field Guide to
Southeastern and Caribbean Seashores

Cape Hatteras to the Gulf Coast, Florida, and the Caribbean

Eugene H. Kaplan

Drawings by
Susan L. Kaplan

*Sponsored by
the National Audubon Society
and the National Wildlife Federation*

HOUGHTON MIFFLIN COMPANY · BOSTON
1988

Contributing Authors

C. Dennis Adams
Richard D. Bray
A. Ralph Cavaliere
Sara Davison
Paul G. Johnson
Frank Maturo

Kaniaulono B. Meyer
Richard Mulstay
Craig W. Schneider
Gordon Taylor
Malcolm Telford
Barry Vittor

Photography Editor

Seymour Leicher

Copyright © 1988 by Eugene H. Kaplan

Library of Congress Cataloging-in-Publication Data

Kaplan, Eugene H. (Eugene Herbert), 1932-
A field guide to southeastern and Caribbean seashores.
(The Peterson field guide series)
"Sponsored by the National Audubon Society and the National Wildlife Federation."
Bibliography: p. 393
Includes index.
1. Seashore biology—Southern states—Guide-books.
2. Seashore biology—Gulf Coast (U.S.)—Guide-books.
3. Seashore biology—Caribbean area—Guide-books.
4. Seashore biology—Atlantic Coast (U.S.)—Guide-books.
I. National Audubon Society. II. National Wildlife Federation. III. Title. IV. Series.
QH104.5.S59K37   1988   508.75   87-27514
ISBN 0-395-31321-X
0-395-46811-6 (pbk.)

Printed in the United States of America
V 10 9 8 7 6 5 4 3 2 1

Contents

Plates

(following p. 198)

Credits

Photographs are by the author except as credited below. Italicized numbers are plate numbers.

C. Dennis Adams: *18* (3), *19* (5,8), *24* (11)

Robert Barker: *15* (6), *16* (2, 7)

C. H. Bigger: *27* (5)

Bill Bird: *50* (3,10), *59* (6)

James Bohnsack: *15* (7, 9), *22* (10), *23* (1,7,8,10,11), *27* (1,3), *29* (9), *30* (7), *51* (2,6), *52* (5,8), *53* (8), *54* (4), *56* (5), *57* (2), *60* (8) *61* (4); Fig. 158

Debra Bradley: *27* (6,9), *28* (1,7,8), *52* (1), *55* (5), *60* (5,6,9,10)

Janet Carl: *15* (8), *25* (9)

Carolina Biological Supply Co.: *27* (2)

Chesapeake Biological Laboratory, M. J. Reber: Fig. 90 (left)

Ralph Cavaliere: *34* (6–8), *35* (1–5), *36* (1,3,5), *37* (4,6,7)

Ralph Cavaliere: *34* (1–5), *36*(2), *37* (1,5). Reprinted, by permission, from *Field Guide to Conspicuous Flora and Fauna of Bermuda* by A. R. Cavaliere, R. D. Barnes, and C. B. Cook. 1987. Special Publication No. 28, Bermuda Biological Station for Research.

Drew Ferrier: *15* (3)

James Fuller: *17* (5)

Jo Furman: *31* (1), *32* (1,5)

Ray Granade: *15* (4), *23* (4), *26* (1,3–5), *51* (3)

Charles Jabaly; *9* (4–6), *10* (4–6)

Dan Harding: *17* (2,4,6,8), *23* (4), *25* (2,5,7), *29* (1,3,4,8), *49* (8), *50* (11), *60* (1)

Peggy Howland: *29* (5)

Breena Kaplan: *1* (1–9), *2* (1–8), *3* (1–8), *4* (1–8), *5* (1–8), *6* (1–8), *8* (1–9), *12* (4), *14* (4,5), *18* (2,3,6–10), *19* (1,3,4,6,7,9), *20* (1–10), *21* (1–11), *22* (3,4,8), *23* (2), *24* (1–10), *30* (6), *52* (2,4,6), *55* (7), *57* (6–8); Figs. 13, 18, 21, 22, 33, 34, 69, 83, 107, 139, 152

Don Keith: *53* (3,4,7), *54* (5–8)

Alice Kesler: *16* (4), *28* (2), *30* (1,2,8), *47* (1–12), *50* (2,8,12), *55* (3)

Don Kissling: Fig. 143

Seymour Leicher: *19* (6), *29* (2), *38* (1–18), *39* (1–21), *40* (1–19), *41* (1–22), *42* (1–20), *43* (1–20), *44* (1–19), *55* (6)

Steve Lucas: *28* (3,4,9), *49* (5), *50* (1)

Mike Marshall and Charles Jabaly: *7* (6–8)

Frank Maturo: *9* (1–3), *10* (1–3)

Chuck McCormick: *60* (4)

Kani Meyer: *48* (1–10), *49* (1–3,6,7,9,10)

John Morrissey: *12* (3)

Richard Mulstay: *57* (3,4)

Joe Nicosia: *17* (7)

Melvin Pavalow: *17* (9), *62* (7)

Marsha Ratner: *17* (10), *29* (7), *51* (4), *55* (4), *60* (3)

Margaret Caldwell Ryan: *58* (2)

Susan Sadoff McCormick: *52* (3), *60* (7)

Nancy Sefton: *23* (3,9)

Duane Stauffer: *17* (3), *28* (10)

Jean Strongin: *22* (1)

Herb Taylor: *26* (2,7), *51* (1)

Vance Vicente: *25* (6,7)

Wometco/Miami Seaquarium: *26* (6,8), *27* (8), *51* (9,10), *59* (2,3,11), *61* (6), *65* (7)

Figs. 121, 122, 124, 130, 136, and portions of 123, 126–128, 132, and 137 were drawn by Susan Richter, courtesy of Malcolm Telford.

Editor's Note

This Field Guide by Dr. Eugene Kaplan takes the beach walker from the Carolina Capes to the Gulf Coast and the Caribbean, covering a total distance of more than 7000 miles.

Beach walkers tend to be generalists. If they are ornithologically inclined they may spot the shorebirds, gulls, and terns and then consult their *Field Guide to the Birds* for their names. Those few flowers that invade the dunes or salt marshes above the line of sea-wrack can be found in one of their flower guides. On the other hand, this Field Guide introduces them to the many other forms of life that live in the intertidal zone along the edge of the sea, as well as some of the denizens of deeper waters that are often cast ashore by the waves, such as certain mollusks which are also covered by Percy Morris in *A Field Guide to the Shells*.

Kenneth Gosner in his *Field Guide to the Atlantic Seashore* has already taken us by the hand from the Bay of Fundy to Cape Hatteras, introducing us not only to the seaweeds but also to 19 major groups or phyla of invertebrates found in the intertidal zone, some of which—sea anemones, sand dollars, crabs, and barnacles—are rather familiar, and others—bryozoans, amphipods, tunicates, medusae, and comb jellies—which are not.

However, until now there remained a great void between the Carolina Capes and the Caribbean, a lack of coverage between the area of Gosner's guide and the ecosystem treated in an earlier book by the Kaplans—*A Field Guide to Coral Reefs* (1982). This gap has now been filled.

In his book on coral reefs Professor Kaplan took us beyond the sandy beaches out to the white breakers and into the clear blue water where another world, a vastly different environment, the coral reef, can be explored by simply donning a snorkel, face mask, and flippers.

The text and illustrations in the present Field Guide, which describe and illustrate the incredible variety of treasures to be found in the tidepools and intertidal flats, have demanded a staggering amount of field work by Eugene Kaplan and his associates. But do not be an armchair marine biologist and be satisfied with merely thumbing through the color plates and drawings, attractive as they are. Take the book with you on your seashore sorties and use it. There are things to be found at all seasons.

In the various Field Guides everything now comes together. Not only can we name most things, but we also have a tool for understanding the overall environment that separates land from sea. We learn how its components fit together, how the various living organisms interact for survival.

There has been a breakthrough in environmental awareness in recent years. The problems of survival of whales, porpoises, and seals are easily dramatized; they are "PR" animals and a number of new conservation organizations have arisen to publicize their plight. But the lesser organisms of the tidal pools and the shore are no less important in an evolutionary sense, and they are no less vulnerable. They send out signals when the sea is abused by pollution, exploitation, or some other form of neglect. Inevitably the beachcombing naturalist becomes a monitor of the marine environment.

ROGER TORY PETERSON

Preface

This book describes the ecology and common organisms of sea-shores from North Carolina through Florida, the Gulf Coast, and the Caribbean. The total distance, not counting numerous inlets and other irregularities, is in excess of 12,000 km (7500 mi.) and encompasses two major faunistic provinces, the Carolinian (East and Gulf Coast warm-temperate) and West Indian (tropical west Atlantic).

It is an ambitious project, a fact brought home innumerable times during the 14 years it has been in the process of development. Why did I attempt it? First, because the current Peterson *Field Guide to the Atlantic Seashore* covers the coast only as far south as Cape Hatteras. Second, the shores of our southern coast have been neglected except for a few excellent, but narrowly restricted, books that are not generally available to the public. Yet the region abounds with interesting organisms and with fascinating ecological relationships. With substantial local exceptions, this book should make it possible to visit any seashore from Cape Hatteras south and feel comfortable in the knowledge that you will have an idea of what is going on ecologically and which organisms are swimming, crawling, or simply washed up on the beach.

Finally, this book and its predecessor, A *Field Guide* to *Coral Reefs of the Caribbean and Florida,* together constitute a textbook in warm-temperate and tropical marine biology. It is my hope that these books will provide an impetus for the creation of field courses to the regions described.

This book is designed to be your companion as you walk the beaches or swim in the shallows. It will help you identify many of the exquisite seashells strewn carelessly over the beach by the tides, the delicate and symmetrical sea-urchin tests, the worms and sea slugs crawling on seaweed. It will explain the never-ending battle between shoreside plants and the sea: sprawling vines and grasses attempting to conquer the arid, inhospitable sand, only to be thrown back by tides and spray. In short, this book attempts to point out what is happening around you in the multiplicity of biological communities whose variety and color lend beauty to the seashore.

A book of this scope requires knowledge too vast for a single mind. I relied on the experience and counsel of a number of experts who shared their expertise willingly and enthusiastically. In addition to the authorities and institutions acknowledged in *A Field Guide to Coral Reefs,* I thank the following contributors: Eveline du Bois-Reymond Marcus, Ivan Goodbody, Dennis Crisp, Marian Pettibone, Amy Edwards, Kenneth Sebens, Don Keith, Bob Johnson, and Fred Wolfe.

Once again Seymour Leicher has acted as photography editor, contributing many photographs and developing and printing most of the prints used in the black-and-white plates.

Photographs were contributed by SCUBA divers and by underwater and nature photographers. Their names are acknowledged on a previous page, but I must add my gratitude here. This book could not have been produced without them. Kani Meyer, Frank Maturo, and Ralph Cavaliere contributed many of the photographs for their sections. James Bohnsack and Alice Kesler provided outstanding photographs of less common organisms and biological interrelationships.

In the course of researching this book, I visited a number of marine laboratories and field stations. At each destination warm hospitality was extended and I was taken by boat, car, and on foot to view representative habitats. My deepest gratitude is extended to: Frank Maturo, director of the University of Florida Marine Laboratory; Mike Marshall of the same institution; David Gillespie of the University of Georgia Marine Institute at Sapelo Island; Amy Edwards, formerly of the Sapelo Island laboratory and naturalist at the Hofstra University Marine Laboratory in Jamaica; Charles ("Chip") Biernbaum of the Grice Marine Laboratory, Charleston, S.C.; Ann and Jack Rudloe of the Gulf Specimen Company, Panacea, Florida; and the staff of the Duke University Marine Laboratory.

My family has contributed most profoundly to this book. Not satisfied with buoying me up with their confidence, each member offered concrete assistance: daughter Julie typed the manuscript, daughter Susan contributed the drawings, and wife Breena took many photographs (spending innumerable hours kneeling in the mud of Georgia marshes and enduring the searing heat of Caribbean seashores) and did the layout work for the plates.

The late Jess Perlman spent hundreds of hours editing this book to make it more comprehensible to the layman.

Special thanks to the wonderful staff at the Houghton Mifflin Company who saw both this Field Guide and its predecessor through the rigors of production. Cope Cumpston, Peggy Burlet, Harry Foster, Anne Chalmers, and Austin Olney were pillars of strength and kindness as we grappled with problems of reducing both books to manageable length. To Barbara Stratton, whose tact, humanity, and editorial skills saved my sanity, goes my warmest gratitude.

This book is dedicated to the memory of Jess Perlman, and to the participants of my field courses, now all friends, who tramped the beaches and snorkeled the lagoons with me.

Eugene H. Kaplan

1

How to Use This Book

This book is divided into two parts. Part I provides an overview of the different environments you will encounter along the shore or beneath the sea from Cape Hatteras to the Florida Keys, the Gulf Coast, Bermuda, the Bahamas, the West Indies, and the Caribbean coasts of Central and South America. This part focuses on habitats and the interrelationships between the plants and animals that inhabit them. The effects of winds and tides are also discussed. Part II describes the common animals you will find in each habitat, with an emphasis on field marks that will help you identify each organism.

How will you know where to start? Look toward the sea. Are there crashing combers? If so, turn to the section on exposed beaches (Chapter 4). Are you walking on a moonscape of jagged, pitted, highly eroded gray rock? Beneath your feet may lie the fascinating ecological communities of fishes, urchins, snails, crabs, and algae that live out their lives within the confines of a meter-wide tidepool. Consult Chapter 5 on rocky shores for more information. Look into the water close to shore. Do you see the broad leaves of Turtle Grass? If so, turn to Chapter 6, which describes the inhabitants of this biome.

In the U.S., most states have national parks with museums and rangers on duty to help explain seashore animal and plant communities, or university marine laboratories that may sponsor field trips or courses for laymen. In the West Indies, in cities such as Port-of-Spain, Trinidad, and Kingston and Montego Bay, Jamaica, there are active nature study clubs. A phone call may result in an invitation to join one of their field trips. Ask the tourist bureau for help in locating the telephone number.

Read the appropriate chapter carefully before you embark for the shore. Take this book along and look for landmarks—typical zonation or characteristic species of animals and plants. After you walk along the shore, reread the chapter. Patterns will become clear.

General organization: Once you have become somewhat familiar with a particular animal or plant community, one kind of animal might particularly fascinate you. To learn more about it, follow these steps:

1. Look at the endpapers inside the front cover to determine what kind of animal your organism is.

1

2. Once you know the phylum (Echinodermata, for example) turn to the chapter (Chapter 15) describing that phylum in Part II of this book.

3. Read about the general characteristics of the phylum in the chapter. Perhaps you will find all you want to know in the general discussion. If not, you will probably need to know the class of the organism. (A sea urchin, for example, is in Class Echinoidea of Phylum Echinodermata.) You will find the description of each class in the chapter on the phylum. Once you have discovered the class, you can either turn to the species descriptions in the section devoted to that class, or turn to the center of the book and thumb through the plates until you come to those depicting sea urchins; look for your urchin there.

You might enjoy specializing in the study of one type of organism each day. One day you might concentrate on seashells and beach plants and never get your feet wet. The next day you might want to search for sea cucumbers; this will require snorkeling in the Turtle Grass bed.

Bear in mind that this book does not cover all organisms in a particular habitat. We have room for only the most common species. Several phyla, especially those containing concealed or camouflaged wormlike animals, have been left out completely, since few of these organisms are noticed by anyone but scientists.

A field library of selected references that will augment this book can be found on p. 393.

Common and scientific names: A common name is provided for most organisms described. Many of these names have been created for this book, as many species had simply never been recognized by laymen before. In some cases an animal has a different name on every island, in Papiamento, French, Spanish, and English. We have tried to use the local name whenever possible, if it is used over a wide area.

The scientific name consists of two words (both printed in italics)— the genus (first Latin name) and species (second Latin name) of an organism. The genus name is always capitalized; the species name appears in lower case. For example, the scientific name of the Long-spined Black Urchin is *Diadema antillarum,* meaning "diadem (jewel, crown) of the Antilles." Subsequent references to this urchin may be shortened to *D. antillarum,* or even *Diadema.*

Don't be put off by scientific names. Common names are often confusing, as the same name may be applied to several different organisms. After a little practice you will find Latin names rolling off your tongue as if you were an expert. Once someone says, "Don't step on that *Diadema,*" you will never forget its meaning. By the time that person could have said, "Long-spined Black Urchin," you might have already stepped on it.

Organization of chapters: The first section of each chapter on a phylum (Chapters 10–16) describes the anatomy and some behavioral and ecological characteristics of the phylum in general. The next section describes individual species. Illustrations of most of the animals described in Part II (Chapters 10–16) can be found on the color and black-and-white plates at the center of the book; additional illustrations are distributed throughout Parts I and II.

Organisms may resemble one another closely, so do not use illustrations alone for identification; use the field marks (distinctive characters) given in the detailed species description (in Part II) as the final arbiter. Each species description includes information concerning the range where an organism is found. Do not take this too literally, however, as many organisms that have not been described for a particular island or part of the coastline may abound there. Some organisms are expanding their range; others may never have come to the attention of scientists.

Illustrations: There are 65 plates of photographs in the center of the book. In most cases, each is devoted to members of one class or phylum. If the specimen you are trying to identify seems to match one of the photographs, consult the legend page opposite the plate. Further descriptive information will be provided. Then turn to the description of the organism in the appropriate chapter of Part II for final identification.

Often a photograph of a preserved specimen does not resemble the organism when it is swimming or crawling in the sea. For this reason, most photographs (except for seashells) depict living specimens. To aid in field identification we have provided a series of scenic photographs, showing living organisms in situ, and line drawings depicting field marks.

Technical terms: Every effort has been made to make this book useful to the layman. The few necessary anatomical and ecological scientific terms included are defined in the glossary, which begins on p. 381. Many anatomical terms are illustrated in text figures.

Measurements and abbreviations: All measurements have been given in metric units and then in U.S. equivalents. A metric rule is shown on the edge of the back cover. The symbol ‰ means parts per thousand and is the usual measure of salinity: seawater has 35 ‰.

Collecting: This book contains few instructions for capturing, anesthetizing, and preserving living organisms. It is our hope that you will content yourself with watching or photographing rather than collecting. In the first place, many animals grow

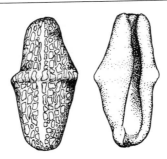

Fig. 1. Flamingo Tongue snail. *Left:* mantle covers shell; *right:* snail dead, mantle retracted.

slowly, and a souvenir wrenched from the bottom will leave a lasting scar on the environment and modify its ecology. Second, the exquisite colors of your specimen may soon fade. By the time you reach home with your trophy it will look like a shadow of its former self and will smell bad. The Flamingo Tongue snail (Fig. 1) is a case in point. Living, it is a blaze of orange and black against the Purple Sea Fan on which it feeds. Preserved, it is an innocuous elongate shell; death has drawn its beautiful leopard-spotted covering out of sight.

Field equipment: Snorkel, face mask, and fins are standard equipment for field work in southern Florida and Caribbean waters. Purchase a plain snorkel without pleats. Try on several face masks until you find one that is comfortable. If you wear glasses most SCUBA shops can supply you with a mask that has the faceplate ground to your prescription. Do not buy a face mask with a purge valve—it will only leak after a while. Fins may be full-foot or "rocket" type. For simple snorkeling purchase full-foot fins. Be sure to allow room for thick gym socks, which prevent chafing. Rocket-type fins must be worn with SCUBA booties and are advised only for divers and serious snorkelers.

If possible, bring along a weight belt with about 5 kg (11 lb.) of weights. Adjust the amount of weight until you are slightly negatively buoyant (sink very slowly). This makes it easier to dive down and remain near the bottom for a few seconds longer when you are snorkeling.

Old sneakers are useful for wading in the shallows. A simple hand lens or jeweler's loupe will help you identify small organisms. The best are of the doublet type, with two lenses delivering 10 and 20 power. Protect your hand lens from sand and salt water. Ordinary cotton gardening gloves will protect your hands until you learn enough about the area to avoid contact with dangerous organisms. Bring a hat and a small medicine kit containing a topical anesthetic, Band-Aids, sunscreen, an antiseptic, and some meat tenderizer to put on stings. **Caution:** The sun is so hot in the tropics that it is advisable to wear a long-sleeved turtleneck shirt and jeans or leotards when you wade or snorkel, at least for the first few days of a visit. Use No. 15 sunscreen liberally; do not rub it in—smear it on.

Area covered: The region encompassed by this book begins just below Cape Hatteras, where the area covered by Kenneth Gosner's *Field Guide to the Atlantic Seashore* ends. Together the two books cover the whole Atlantic, Gulf, and Caribbean coasts. Live animals, of course, are dynamic. Although Cape Hatteras is an important point of demarcation between cold- and warm-temperate regions, it is not an absolute temperature barrier. Many northern species venture southward beyond Cape Hatteras and invade the warm-temperate waters of the Carolinian Faunal Province, which extends from North Carolina to south Florida and the northern Gulf of Mexico. It is certainly a surprise to find the Brown Rock Urchin, so common on rocks on Massachusetts shores, to be equally at home on Texas jetties. It is equally surprising to find sea whips—soft corals associated with the tropics—washing up on North Carolina shores. Nevertheless, there is surprising uniformity within the two major faunistic zones covered by this book. You will find familiar animals and plants when you go on vacation, whether to the Outer Banks of North Carolina, the Florida Keys, Mexico, or the West Indies.

The purpose of this book: This book is meant to be a beach-walker's companion. It is not an exhaustive treatise on the entire flora and fauna of the shores of the southeastern U.S. and the Caribbean. Encyclopedic coverage of such an immense shoreline would make this book a massive tome. Instead, it is hoped that the visitor to southern and Caribbean seashores will find this book useful in orienting himself or herself toward some of the ecological processes characterizing each natural community, and an aid in the identification of the common organisms inhabiting these communities. Coverage includes descriptions of common shoreside plants, explaining their role in stabilizing and building the beach; zonation of rocky and sandy beach communities; and the role of seagrass beds and mangrove swamps in stabilizing shorelines.

Certain animal and plant groups are described in more detail than others; in-depth coverage is necessitated in some cases because some phyla or classes are poorly covered elsewhere. For example, nudibranchs (and other sea slugs) and crabs occupy proportionately more space in this book than do seashells. It is assumed that serious shellers will have field guides devoted exclusively to shells. This book will be useful to them in an ecological context, since there are notes on mollusk behavior and natural history that may not be found in shell guides. For the average beachcomber, who simply wishes to explore the beach for whatever wonders are to be discovered, many of the common seashells to be encountered in a day's search are depicted in the seashell section (Plates 38–44).

This guide also focuses on biotic communities and concepts that are not described in most other books written for the lay reader, including succession in a mangrove swamp and the Red Mangrove root community (Chapter 9), tidepools (Chapter 5), and shallow-water plant communities, including seagrasses and seaweeds (Chapter 7).

Certain organisms, especially echinoderms, are distributed more or less evenly from shore to reef. Thus a small amount of material from *A Field Guide to Coral Reefs* is also covered in this book.

PART I

Plant and Animal Communities

2

Seashores from Cape Hatteras to Cape Canaveral

Two mighty forces, and a host of lesser ones, shape the edge of the sea from Cape Hatteras to Cape Canaveral. From the south, squeezing through the narrow Florida Straits, a huge aquamarine river of warm, salty water flows northward. It skirts the Florida Keys and then, following the edge of the Continental Shelf, begins to separate from shore. By the time it reaches Georgia, the Gulf Stream has meandered 96 to 113 km (60–70 mi.) from the coast. From time to time it hurls huge water masses, miles across, toward the land. These slowly whirling circular masses of tropical water, called *gyres,* carry with them eggs and larvae of tropical animals, and the seeds and spores of tropical plants, which settle along the shore.

Northern cold-water currents reach Cape Hatteras, but they soon veer offshore. The main shore-building influence from the north is a slow, imperceptible movement of sand, the longshore drift. This southward migration of sediment is fundamentally a local phenomenon. Wind-driven currents, surf, and waves pick up particles at one point and drop them an almost imperceptible distance away. The prevailing winter winds—often the products of storms—are from the north, and hence over a year or a century the net movement of sediment along the shore is southward.

A third factor affecting the nature of southeastern U.S. shores is the relative shallowness of the Continental Shelf. In some places water depths of only 15m (60 ft.) can be found as far as 32 km (20 mi.) offshore and the 100-fathom line is more than 80 km (50 mi.) out. This flat platform is inundated with silt and clay washed from local bays and rivers. Thus, especially off Georgia and South Carolina, the shallow muddy shelf, constantly churned by wind, yields a brown, silty sea. Off North Carolina, where there are fewer rivers, the water is somewhat clearer. The presence of so much silt and clay in the water has a profound effect on inshore plants and animals.

THE CAROLINIAN FAUNAL PROVINCE

Warm offshore water and cool longshore currents create a special intermediate or warm-temperate faunistic zone, generally considered to extend from Cape Hatteras to Cape Canaveral and throughout the northern Gulf of Mexico. Northern currents sweep southward, carrying animals and plants common off coasts as far north as Massachusetts and even Maine. The Gulf Stream brings tropical flora and fauna. These mix comfortably in the Carolinian Faunal Province, a region edged by long, dune-draped sandy beaches and barrier islands, behind which are thousands of square kilometers of salt marshes. There is little rock to hinder the movement of the sand—a few manmade jetties and walls impede the flow momentarily, but the steady southward migration of sand continues and the wind-roiled sea adds fine silt to the mix. Drumstick-shaped barrier islands are sculpted by the longshore currents; their northern ends are constantly eroded away and their southern ends become elongate spits, as sediment is removed from one end and deposited at the other (Fig. 2, p. 11). As the dark, rich waters flow through narrow inlets between barrier islands and over shallow seagrass beds, current velocities are reduced to almost nothing and even tiny particles drop out. Thus, behind each barrier island clay and silt are dominant. Over thousands of years, the mud (combination of silt and clay) has piled up enough to reach the surface, making it possible for land plants to colonize the mudflats. Salt grasses grow densely there and help form one of the most productive communities on earth, the Southeast coastal salt marsh.

Geological History of Barrier Beaches and Islands

Barrier islands dominate much of the shoreline of our area. There are 23 in North Carolina, 35 in South Carolina, 15 in Georgia, and 80 in Florida. Georgia's short coastline is almost completely dominated by its "sea islands," with a total acreage of 67,045 hectares (165,600 acres), second only to Florida's 189,356 hectares (467,710 acres).

To understand the creation of barrier islands we must look back 50,000 years or more, during the Pleistocene Epoch, to a time before the last great glacial period. The climate was colder than it is now, and vast ice caps began forming at the north and south poles, extending across much of North America, locking in much of the water of the earth and shrinking the oceans. The sea level descended 91–152m (300–500 ft.) lower than it is today. The Atlantic shores of the United States lay about 80 km (50 mi.) further east (seaward) than they do now.

About 18,000 years ago the glaciers began to melt and the sea rose, covering the old shores and creating a vast Continental Shelf 113 km (70 mi.) or more wide. Today, the shelf remains, submerged under shallow muddy seas. The sediment covering the shelf is composed of tiny particles left over from ancient times when the sea level was comparatively stable. During these periods of stability, called still stands, deposition of sediments and reworking by waves and currents resulted in the formation of barrier islands and marshes. In areas of relatively high wave energy, sand was built up, forming islands. In regions of low energy, smaller particles—silt and clay—were deposited. These ancient sediments are constantly being reworked to form present-day islands and marshes. The Gulf Stream acts as an outer boundary to this system, marking the edge of turbid water from river run-off that has spread sand and mud along the coast and on the shelf, defining the environment to which all seashore life in this region is exposed.

The rate at which the glaciers melted varied. At first the sea rose rapidly, but there is evidence that about 4,000 to 5,000 years ago the sea level's ascent was reduced to 10–15 cm (4–6 in.) per century. Winds and currents have been piling up sediment against the shore throughout the post-glacial period. The result is the formation of two adjacent sets of islands: an older (Pleistocene) group and a more recent (Holocene) series of islands, which are still forming. These newer islands, spawned in the past few thousand years from the more slowly rising sea, are constantly being pushed landward by prevailing winds and storms. In areas where large rivers pour sediment into the sea, the Holocene islands are distinctly separated from the Pleistocene islands. But in the absence of major rivers and their immense load of sediment, the new islands have fused with their older counterparts.

The sea has apparently begun to rise at a faster rate again. At present the rate is 30–35 cm (12–14 in.) per century. There is evidence that man may have had a hand in accelerating this increase. So much carbon dioxide has been produced by the combustion of fuel to produce steel, run factories, and move vehicles, that its level in the atmosphere is increasing. Many scientists believe that the high level of carbon dioxide is making the atmosphere more impervious to heat loss. In effect, less of the excess heat of our planet is able to radiate out into space. This phenomenon is called the "greenhouse effect," likening the carbon dioxide-rich atmosphere to the glass of a greenhouse that allows the sunlight in, but prevents its heat from radiating out.

The end result of this warming of our atmosphere is an increase in the melting of the polar ice caps, and a commensurate, almost imperceptible, rise in sea level. But the flat marshy shores and low islands of our region are sensitive to even the slightest fluctuation in sea level. Most coastal geologists believe that within the next 50 years many barrier islands and even low areas of coastal cities may be inundated.

Sediment generally flows southward along the coast. It accumulates at obstructions such as barrier islands (Fig. 2), and flows around them. The northern boundaries of an island, then, extend outward in shallow shoals that act as reservoirs of sand. After every northeaster, some of this sand has moved along the shore to accumulate in curving ridges called longshore bars. These bars appear to be anchored in the northern shoals that spawned them. They swing around, echoing the refraction of the waves, to lie parallel with the shore. As the ocean waves break upon one offshore bar after another, their energy is reduced, protecting the beach.

Pick a day when there is a strong offshore wind at low tide. Look seaward and you will see the surf crashing over five or six parallel

Fig. 2. A mesotidal barrier island. A reservoir of sand at the north end of the island is the source for long, parallel, submerged sand bars along the island's seaward shore. North-south longshore drift (arrows) erodes north face of island and deposits sand in a curved spit at the southern tip. Reflected currents slow down behind island, depositing fine sediment, which becomes marsh. Dark lines on island are dunes and heavy stippling at north end is forested upland, often of glacial origin.

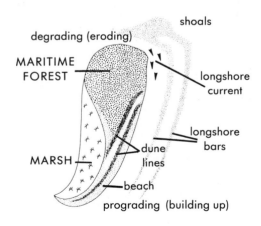

shoals

degrading (eroding)

MARITIME
FOREST

longshore
current

longshore
bars

dune
lines

MARSH

beach

prograding (building up)

Fig. 3. Relic or ghost forest at northern tip of Georgia sea island.

bars, each lying seaward of the next, perhaps for 1600 meters (a quarter mile) or more.

As the sand continues to move along the shore, it reaches the southern end of the island. The waves bend around the tip, carrying the sand with them. This refraction causes the formation of a recurved spit, as the currents swing around the island carrying the sand back and around. The area landward of the spit is protected. Only the smallest particles, silt and clay, can be carried by the now-sluggish currents. The particles settle out, and a marsh forms in the bay landward of the islands.

The recurved spit at the southern end of a barrier island is constantly being renewed. This area tends to be sandy and dominated by pioneering plants. The older, northern end of the island is often heavily forested, but erosion takes its toll and as the shore crumbles, the trees are washed out or inundated by salt water, which kills them. Sometimes the sand of the dunes covers part of the forest and then marches on, leaving behind a once-smothered relic or "ghost" forest of dead Live Oaks and other trees (Fig. 3). Their gnarled, blackened trunks project from the beach sand in mute testimony to the erosive force of the sea.

Barrier islands are dynamic structures, rarely constant in shape. Storm waves surge over the beach, washing out dunes and sweeping sand in washover fans behind the dunes. Longshore currents remove sand and sweep it toward inlets, where it is carried into the lagoons and embayments behind the islands. The combination of longshore and incoming tidal currents at flood tide sweeps sand into the inlet. The ebb tide lacks the strength to remove much of the sand, so there is a net movement of sand into the inlet, where it spreads out behind the island. The combination of erosion of the front of the island and filling in behind results in the gradual movement of some barrier islands shoreward. The converse is true if river effluvium is available, causing barrier islands to prograde, or build up, on the seaward side, becoming larger over time (Fig. 4).

Tides have fundamental effects on island development. Regions with a small (microtidal) tidal range (less than 2m—7 ft.), such as are found in North Carolina and Florida, produce relatively narrow beaches. Often the sand available for dune construction is modest, and dunes are relatively undeveloped. In South Carolina and Georgia tidal ranges are greater, between 2 and 4m (7 to 14 ft.). In such mesotidal areas beaches are wider, dune formation more pronounced, and shores more stable. However, when the stabilizing influence of a substantial dune line is modified by man through the use of dune buggies or the creation of networks of footpaths, even the most stable shoreline is rendered vulnerable. This is especially true if foredunes are leveled for housing sites. Once the protection of beachgrass roots is removed, wind blows the sand away and low spots, or blowouts, are created. These provide passages for washover channels (Fig. 5). The next storm will wash through the low spots, eroding the beach and enlarging

Fig. 4. Incoming tidal currents flow rapidly through narrow inlets carrying heavy sediment load. Currents slow down in broad embayments behind barrier islands, depositing sediment. Outgoing tidal currents flow slowly in embayments. Result: a tendency toward deposition behind barrier islands.

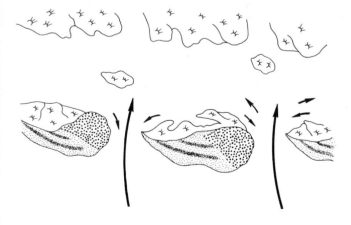

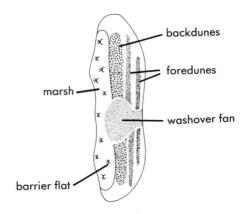

Fig. 5. Washover fan results from erosion of sand due to loss of beach grass.

the newly created blowout boundaries. Sometimes this may provide a channel where the sea can break through the island completely, creating a new inlet. Occasionally a storm piles water up behind the island to such a height that existing inlets are not enough and the overflow spills through the blowout from behind, again creating an inlet.

The Outer Banks of North Carolina are typical microtidal islands. The low tidal range produces relatively narrow beaches and only moderate dune development. Frequent storms often cause overwash and sand is carried behind the dunes and deposited on the landward marsh. On Cape Hatteras National Seashore, attempts were made to prevent overwash by stabilizing and enlarging the dunes. Beachgrass was planted on dune faces to trap windblown sand. The plan was effective and the higher dunes largely prevented the natural overwash characteristic of these microtidal islands. But the end result was surprising: Storms were unable to carry the beach sand over the dunes and the high storm-generated surf and fast longshore currents eroded the beach, making it even narrower. When storm surges flowed inland through existing inlets they spread out behind the islands and further eroded them. Now the islands were being eroded from both shores, so the Park Service had to reverse the process, reducing dune height and allowing some overwash to nourish the marshes behind the islands.

In contrast to the long, narrow Outer Banks, the sea islands of South Carolina and Georgia are rounded islands that tail off to curved spits at their southern extremities. Their origin is complex: Cumberland and Sapelo islands are erosional remnants of the coastal plains. They are projecting Pleistocene beach ridges up to 100,000 years old, overlain with recent sands on their seaward sides. Other islands are simply overgrown sand bars and remains of sand spits that evolved at the southern extremities of remnant islands. Ossabaw, Skidaway, and Hilton Head islands are long, thin sand ridges of relatively recent origin. They are composed of sand laid down seaward of the remnant islands, but are now separated from them by shallow lagoons. St. Phillip's Island in South Carolina consists of a series of low, wide, well-vegetated beach ridges surrounded by marshes, even on the seaward side. This suggests that another barrier island, seaward of the present island complex, was completely eroded away, leaving its landward marsh.

Microtidal conditions occur along the east coast of Florida, and long, narrow sandy barrier islands similar to those of the Outer Banks of North Carolina now reappear. Some of these narrow islands are separated from the mainland only by a narrow lagoon. This lagoon forms part of the Intracoastal Waterway. Cape Canaveral, a large barrier island, was formed by the convergence of longshore currents that deposited sand on ancient (Pleistocene) coral reefs.

Capes can also form as cuspate forelands—huge continental features many miles across. These crescent-shaped projections are produced by longshore currents and erosion of sediment, which is swept southward in some areas and northward in others, forming a long, thin chain of barrier islands. These project out to sea and reach a point or cape, beyond which the land falls away, eroding back until enough has accreted to form another cape. A classic example, perhaps the most extensive cuspate forelands in the world, is the sequence of Cape Hatteras, Cape Lookout, and Cape Fear in North Carolina (Fig. 6, p.16).

Barrier Island Ecology

Barrier islands are spawned by the sea. Most of the plants and animals on these islands bear the mark of the marine environment. Only beyond the dunes on well-developed mesotidal islands in Georgia and South Carolina, on relatively high Pleistocene remnants, does the coastal scrub forest give way to plant assemblages closely resembling continental forests. Here wild turkeys and deer thrive, and in the stillness of the forest one may momentarily forget the sea surrounding the island.

On virtually all barrier islands sand from an extensive beach blows landward to form a series of dunes. On mesotidal islands

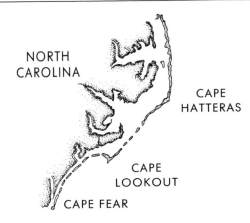

Fig. 6. Cuspate forelands of North Carolina.

(Fig. 7), dune development can become elaborate, with a seaward foredune area progressing to a longitudinal valley or swale zone (often referred to as a dune meadow and carpeted with flowers). The interdune swale zone is followed by one of several backdune areas progressing, especially on large islands, to a barrier flat, covered with coastal scrub forest. Landward of the forest the island slopes downward to merge with extensive salt marshes, sloughs, tidal flats, and sometimes large lagoons or

Fig. 7. Profile of a well-developed mesotidal island, showing topographical and vegetation zones.

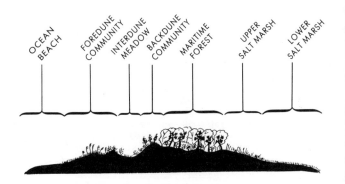

embayments separating the barrier island from continental shores.

On long, narrow microtidal barrier islands dune development is less complex. Sometimes only one line of poorly developed dunes forms, with little or no scrub forest behind it.

Barrier Island Beaches

Beaches in our region are composed primarily of relatively fine, uniform quartz fragments derived from continental rocks worn down by the sea. As one progresses southward, a component of chalklike calcium carbonate, consisting of fragments of marine animals and plants, becomes more significant until, in southern Florida, the carbonate component becomes so important that beach sand looks and feels like talcum powder.

The sand is constantly shifting and flowing as particles are moved by surf and tides. The scene is one of total activity, as waves constantly pick up sand grains and move them down the beach. Each sand grain movement describes a spiral movement, essentially of two complementary circles (Fig. 8). One circle is vertical, as the sand grain is lifted, swings around, and falls landward. The other circle is horizontal, as the grain moves southward (if wind and seas are from the north) as part of the longshore drift.

Where waves break offshore, parallel sand bars and ridges form the primary sand reservoir for the beaches. A *bar*, by definition, is always submerged; a *ridge* projects from the water's surface at low tide. Often bars become ridges; ridges may move shoreward and merge with the beach. Sand is carried from these offshore features and deposited on the beach by the surf. A *runnel* is a depression that runs landward to, and parallel to, a ridge. When you see a water-filled longitudinal depression at low tide on the beach, it is a runnel and the beach region seaward of it is a ridge in the process of coalescing with the original beach (see Fig. 9).

When a wave breaks on the shore, most of its energy is dissipated and it drops its load of sand particles. But some energy

Fig. 8. Horizontal and vertical movement of a sand grain.

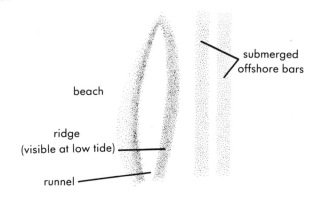

Fig. 9. Ridge-and-runnel system.

remains and is translated into a thin sheet of water that splashes up the beach a short distance. This thin sheet of water is called *swash*. Tiny sand particles and bits of organic matter are so light that they can be carried by the swash. This makes the swash zone (Fig. 10) more habitable than the surf zone. Wave action is much reduced, the suffocating sand has been deposited behind the swash, and tiny particles of organic detritus are available to be filtered from the water. A few animals, such as the Coquina clam (p. 256) and mole crabs (p. 314), constantly position themselves in the swash zone of relatively high-energy beaches, filtering out the detritus in the swash. But the surf in our region is relatively modest. The average height of breaking waves on the Georgia coast is only 23–30 cm (9–12 in.), the lowest recorded along the Atlantic Coast. This means that the swash zone will be narrow, usually less than 1m (39 in.) wide.

Fig. 10. Swash zone of a sandy beach.

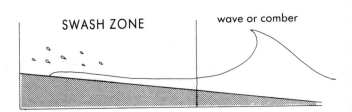

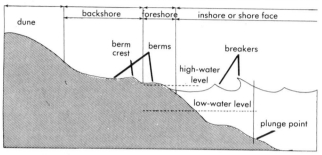

Fig. 11. Profile of a sandy beach.

The constant movement of sand by the waves results in deposition of particles high on the beach, especially in summer, when seas are relatively calm and storms infrequent. A relatively flat sand terrace known as a *berm* is created (see Fig. 11). Its edge, the *berm crest,* sharply falls to the more steeply sloping foreshore in a scarp that may be 30 cm (1 ft.) high. The foreshore is the region affected by tides. In short, while the tides sculpt the foreshore into a more or less gentle slope, the region beyond ordinary tidal influence is left dry and winds blow the sand flat, making a more-or-less level plain called the berm. Since summer is characterized by few storms, the berm remains stable or extends seaward during that period. During winter storms the berm may be washed away or it moves up the beach, so that the berm crest and scarp are usually found higher up on the beach in winter. The berm extends from the intertidal zone to the base of the foredunes.

Dune Formation

While water is the primary means of sand movement on the beach, wind is the source of energy for the accretion of sand into mounds, or dunes, just beyond the influence of winter waves. Seeds of pioneer plants such as Sea Oats (Fig. 22, p. 45) or American Beachgrass (Fig. 18, p. 33) wash up on the shore or drop from distant plants. The seeds germinate and produce mature plants, which then reproduce vegetatively, producing a clump of stalks. As the wind sweeps loose sand landward it catches in the clumps of grass. Gradually, as the sand accumulates, the plants become buried. But both of these pioneer plants have the unique ability to grow upward, even if completely buried under the sand.

Soon new shoots project from the little hillock. Eventually nearby hillocks, formed the same way, coalesce, and a dune is born. Such dunes, facing the sea, are the *primary dunes* or *foredunes*. The sand-catching ability of the plants is necessary at all times to maintain the dune. If the plants are removed the sand will blow away. On some barrier islands wild horses graze on beach grasses of the dune faces, thus destabilizing the dunes. On most barrier islands there are long-term management programs to keep herds at levels that do not interfere with the natural system which stabilizes the dunes.

Gradually other plants move in behind the grass, especially on the less exposed rear (leeward) slope of the dune, and a whole community of wind- and salt-resistant plants appears. In North Carolina and northern South Carolina the dominant dune builder is American Beachgrass; south of this region, Sea Oats and other beach grasses predominate. Woody evergreen shrubs soon appear on the lee slope of the dunes. They are resistant to salt spray, but cannot survive being buried in sand.

The dune grows to its maximum height; prevailing winds can carry sand only so high. New dunes then form windward (towards the sea). Thus the largest dunes are to be found inland.

On more complex islands, such as the sea islands off Georgia and South Carolina, the initial dune line is succeeded by an interdune valley, or swale, and then an area consisting of huge, somewhat more protected, well-vegetated backdunes (see Fig. 7, p. 16).

These large masses of sand actually move over time so that in areas with strong offshore winds, such as Cumberland Island in Georgia, the dunes migrate inland, sometimes burying maritime forest trees in their path.

Beyond the last line of secondary dunes is the barrier flat, which on narrow islands soon merges with the bay shore and salt marsh. On more fully developed islands, the dunes merge with the maritime forest.

Animals of the Barrier Islands and Coastal Beaches

As you walk the broad expanse of a barrier island beach at low tide, you will be struck by the apparently barren appearance of the grayish or olive-colored sand before you. Seaward, a gentle surf breaks on shore, its swash zone not more than a meter wide. Landward, the intertidal zone is marked by the sharp berm crest and scarp. Offshore, four or five longshore ridges break the force of the waves, reducing the crashing combers considerably by the time they reach the beach.

But the barren-appearing, moist sand of the intertidal zone is alive with organisms. The spaces between the sand grains contain a jungle of microscopic animals, collectively called the meiofauna. These tiny organisms are too small to be considered here. But their presence is symbolized by broad, green-tinged patches of sand. When you come across such a patch of greenish, damp, intertidal sand at low tide place a shoe or shovel on the sand. It will either become a darker green in the shadow of the shovel, or lose its color altogether, bleaching or darkening to outline perfectly the shape of the shovel. Myriads of greenish flagellates migrate upwards or downwards in the surface sand layer, exposing their chloroplasts to the sun's rays — but only under low-light conditions, since the sun's brightest rays are too intense and hot.

Beyond the most seaward ridges, in water about 2 meters (7 ft.) deep, large populations of Five-holed Keyhole Urchins abound (p. 354). These flattened, disk-shaped sea urchins — often called sand dollars — live just beneath the sediment surface. Their short bristles are constantly moving, covering them with camouflaging sand. The urchins eat detritus mixed in among the sand grains. Every once in a while a strong comber will scour the bottom, lifting the animals and threatening to wash them ashore. But the five holes (lunules) in the disk-shaped test act as spoilers, and instead of skimming along with the wave, the sand dollar tilts and falls to the bottom. It can disappear beneath the surface in a few seconds by working its bristles and tube feet back and forth, descending vertically beneath the sand. Occasionally a winter storm can be so intense as to dislodge the sand dollars and thrust them onto dry land in great numbers, but normally only an occasional dried-out test is evidence of large populations offshore.

The swash zone is the most habitable part of the beach for a truly aquatic animal. The weak swash carries its meager burden of detritus up and back, providing food for crabs and other organisms. Buried beneath the sand, facing seaward, are large populations of the Cuban Mole Crab (Fig. 128, p. 315). This squat, lavender, cigar-shaped animal extends its long, curved, hairy antennae and uses them to strain detritus from the water as it drifts seaward in the backwash of the swash. Only the crab's eyes and second antennae extend above the sand's surface, almost invisible except to sharp-eyed wading birds such as the Ibis and herons. The mole crab's legs are modified into a paddle form, which helps it burrow backward rapidly to keep up with the swash zone as it moves up and down the beach with the tides. The similar but less common Purple Surf Crab (Fig. 39, p. 83) is both a filter feeder and a scavenger, using its small, sharp claws to tear chunks from dead organisms. Almost identical is Webster's Mole Crab (Fig. 12), which can be differentiated from the Purple Surf Crab by the fact that it lacks spines on its front margin.

The beautiful Coquina clam (p. 256) has delicate tooth-edged

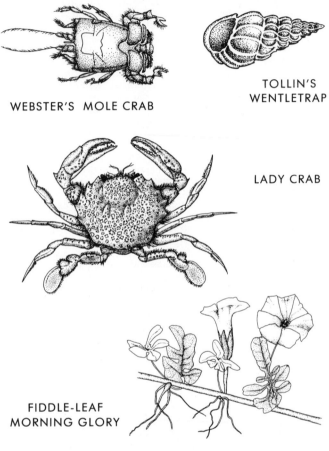

WEBSTER'S MOLE CRAB

TOLLIN'S WENTLETRAP

LADY CRAB

FIDDLE-LEAF MORNING GLORY

Fig. 12. Animals and plants of barrier island shores.

valves (shells) with angular front margins. This wedge-shaped animal is usually 2 cm (¾ in.) long. It can be white, yellow, pink, or purple, sometimes with rays of dark purple or blue. Coquinas are filter feeders, sucking in detritus through short, forked siphons, but otherwise they are distinctly un-clamlike—they are constantly active, moving up and down the beach within the swash zone, sometimes in aggregations of hundreds of clams. How can a clam, normally the epitome of sluggishness, remain in the swash zone, a relatively dynamic, turbulent area? The process is as complex as it is unique: first the clam burrows upwards to the sediment surface. It then relaxes and is swept landward until the swash weakens to a point where it can no longer push the clam. The animal rapidly burrows into the sediment, extending short siphons into the backwash, sucking in life-sustaining oxygenated water together with its burden of detritus. As the tide pushes the swash zone up or down the beach, the Coquinas release their hold in the sand and are carried, like human surfers, along with the swash.

When the tide is at its lowest, in fine sands that reflect the protection provided by extensive offshore bar-and-ridge systems, dense worm populations may be found. On southeastern U.S. coasts these are usually composed of Plumed and Onuphis worms (p. 288). The Plumed Worm's distinctive tube projects about 5 or 6 cm (2–2⅜ in.) from the sand (Pl. 4). It is woven of sand, shells, and a tough mucuslike substance secreted by the worm. Sometimes an upper bend makes the tube appear like a periscope, but most often the tube is straight and about 1 cm (⅜ in.) in diameter. The Onuphis Worm makes a thinner, translucent or tan tube that projects about 2 cm (¾ in.) high and is about 4 mm (⅛ in.) wide. The upper portion is covered with sand; the rest is plasticlike (translucent). On some Georgia beaches, windrows of these 15-cm (6-in.) long tubes, looking like masses of drinking straws, can be seen on upper beaches—or hundreds of them wash back and forth, sometimes to be stranded, at the tide line.

Look among the tubes of Onuphis and Plumed worms for meandering burrows just beneath the sand's surface, usually ending in a tiny hillock of disturbed sand. Follow the bulging burrow to its abrupt end and dig in with your finger. You will come up with the small, plump Dwarf Surf Clam (Pl. 44), usually about 1 cm (⅜ in.) long. Lay the clam on its side and watch. In a moment or two it will extend its foot to burrow in the topmost layer of wet sand. Unlike the Coquina clam, it is not usually exposed, but tends to move just beneath the surface, making meandering hillocks of sand. It feeds by filtering detritus and phytoplankton from the water when it is submerged. In Georgia and South Carolina, the Dwarf Surf Clam often replaces the Coquina clam as the dominant intertidal clam of the open beach.

On beaches of really fine sand, about 3 m (10 ft.) from the lowest tide line, look for thick-walled, gray, clayey tubes about 2 cm (¾ in.) in diameter (see Pl. 4). These are the homes of Ghost Shrimps (p. 310). The tubes often begin about 1 cm (⅜ in.) beneath the sediment surface. Thus, to find Ghost Shrimp colonies, look for round holes in the wet sand, beneath which are the characteristic tubes. The Ghost Shrimp is also a detritus feeder. Its color, like that of many subterranean animals, is a ghostly white. Don't try to dig one up unless you are feeling strong—you will find that the tubes penetrate the sand to a depth of almost a meter. Sometimes, especially along protected Georgia and northern Florida beaches,

Ghost Shrimp colonies may be so large that the distinctive fecal pellets (Pl. 4), which look like chocolate sprinkles on an ice cream cone, may form dense, brown, sticky masses underfoot.

On a well-sorted beach (one with finer sands closest to land and coarser sands closest to the sea), you will find Onuphis Worm tubes near the low-tide line. These worms prefer fine sand grains for their tubes. Mixed in among the uppermost Onuphis tubes are the holes and tubes of the Ghost Shrimp. Landward of these, still well into the lowest tidal zone, are the rough-looking tubes of the Plumed Worm.

Search among the Onuphis tubes near the water's edge for the exquisite tubes of the Ice Cream Cone Worm (Fig. 118, p. 286). One of these delicate masterpieces is a rare find; most of the tubes are destroyed over only one or two tidal cycles because of their delicate nature. Look for a cornucopia about 5 cm (2 in.) long, made of individual sand grains cemented together into a single-layered cone. You may find an inhabited tube, its lower, wider opening protected by a door of golden slivers (setae) projecting across the front of the worm.

As you dig among the worm tubes, your shovel may uncover a flaccid, fleshy, flattened worm up to 2 cm (¾ in.) across and over a meter (39 in.) long. The body is thick and whitish, and the worm is impressive in its length, if one sees the whole animal. But if you try to pick it up or even uncover it, it will immediately autotomize—break up into many small pieces. The head of this huge Milky Ribbon Worm (Pl. 2) is featureless except for two lateral swellings called cephalic lobes, which contain slits with olfactory (smelling) organs. At the tip of the head is a hole from which the worm can "shoot" a long hollow proboscis (reaching at least a quarter of the length of the worm) that it wraps around sandworms or other small prey, pulling its victim to the mouth located beneath the proboscis pore. Hunting occurs at night, when the worm leaves its subterranean haven and undulates over the sand.

As the tide comes in, tiny seashells are deposited among the ripple marks on the middle beach. Coquina and Egg Cockle shells are scattered like snowflakes. The tiny Dwarf Razor Clam (p. 260) abounds in the sediment, but only the fragile, elongate shells, usually no more than 3 cm (1¼ in.) long, are visible on the surface. If you dig up a living razor clam, place it flat on the sand, preferably at the upper edge of the swash, and watch it for a moment. Soon the clam's fleshy, pointed foot will extend from the hind end of the shell to probe the sand. Once a soft spot is found, the foot will be thrust deeply into the sediment. Its end inflates with blood, forming an anchor. The tautly stretched muscles of the extended foot, now buried deeply in the sand, will contract, jerking the razor clam erect. Two or three repetitions of this extension-contraction process and the clam will be buried. The whole process will have taken seconds. In North Carolina the similar but larger (to 20 cm — 8 in.) Northern Razor Clam (p. 260) will be more common.

If the sea is calm and the water not too turbid, you can wade knee deep and look for a Sea Pansy (Fig. 29, p. 63). It looks like a purple mushroom with a thin, flexible stalk. Look at it closely and you will see that it is composed of one huge polyp, measuring about 7.5 cm (3 in.) across its flattened top, with many tiny, translucent daughter polyps scattered across its surface. It is surprising that this fragile-appearing colony can survive in the turbulent, silty nearshore environment. Tiny calcareous spicules buried inside the colony toughen it, and it is one of the few sessile animals that can resist burial by sand. Although it is a colony of more-or-less independent animals, it can move about as if it were just one individual, by detaching itself and allowing the current to sweep it elsewhere, then reanchoring.

As you wade about, watch for the rapidly swimming portunid crabs that abound in sandy shallows. The king of portunids is the Common Blue Crab (Fig. 133, p. 321), an animal of legendary ferocity. It will normally choose to flee as you approach, but if cornered it will assume a classical stance, rear pressed against the sand, claws widely outstretched, able to make lightning-fast, tearing jabs at your fingers. Recently a colleague attempted to show me the tiny hairs edging the last pair of paddle-like legs, which are adapted for swimming in all portunids. These hairs change color when the crab is about to molt, from white (one week from molting) to pink (three days) to red (one day), making it possible for commercial crabbers to ship them to market knowing they will arrive in the valuable molted condition to be sold as "shedders" or soft-shelled crabs. My friend was an expert at analyzing the status of the hairs, but it had been a long time since he had handled a crab. He never showed me the crab's condition because he never finished wrestling with the vicious animal; he simply flung it back into the water with a pained expression on his face and almost every finger bleeding profusely.

A similar, almost as fierce, swimming crab is the Speckled Crab (Pl. 53). It buries itself just under the surface of the sand and pounces on whatever passes by. The third nasty portunid, more common as one goes north, is the so-called Lady Crab (Fig. 12, p. 22). The name is certainly a misnomer — this crab is no lady, as you will find if you try to pick one up. Approach, and it will assume the "portunid stance" with outstretched claws. Its back is covered with attractive dots that look like tiny leopard spots.

In early spring, especially on a full-moon tide, you may see hundreds of paired Horseshoe Crabs (Fig. 13) coming inshore to spawn. The ripe female exudes a substance called a pheromone, which is most alluring to the male. Next, the female moves to the highest point of the tide and uses her telson and other appendages

Fig. 13. *Left:* mating Horseshoe Crabs; *right:* bluish gray Horse-shoe Crab eggs.

to dig a hole about 15 cm (6 in.) deep. Then she begins to extrude up to 200 tiny, blue-gray eggs. The male, stimulated by yet another pheromone released with the eggs, expels his sperm. This synchrony, while obviously less effective than internal fertiliza-tion, assures that most eggs are fertilized. The female then shuffles off, leaving the eggs to be covered by shifting sands. A month later, at the next full-moon spring tide, the newly hatched eggs will again be inundated, and the larvae will burrow to the surface to be washed out to sea. When an onshore wind and spring high tide coincide, conditions are perfect for egg laying and the beach may be littered with mating Horseshoe Crabs. Wait for a day when the water reaches 21°C (70°F) for the first time in the spring to view the fantastic spectacle of this mass-mating ritual. Others will view the scene with equal interest: crabs, fishes, and especially birds, wait for the females to ponderously move out to sea as the tide ebbs. Then the birds descend on the partially exposed egg masses in a frantic, shrieking horde, gorging them-selves on Horseshoe Crab caviar. Sandpipers, plovers, and other shorebirds, usually content to pluck tiny animals from the sand, rush in to partake of the feast. Red Knots seem to gauge their spring migration to coincide with the availability of Horseshoe Crab eggs.

Large, bottom-dwelling, deep-water animals are often washed up after storms. You can find them well up on the beach in the flotsam and jetsam of the high-tide line. Among the most distinc-tive are the soft corals, yellow or purple, lacy, fanlike or flat bushy sea fans (Pl. 32). A deep-water bushy soft coral with finger-thick, bright orange or pinkish red branches may wash up after a particularly severe storm. Orange Bush Coral (*Titanideum grauenfeldii*, Pl. 31) normally lives in water 18–30 m (60–100 ft.) deep, on sand-covered limestone. By the time its remains reach shore only one or two "fingers" are left. This is one of the few soft corals that is more common off the Southeast coast than in the Caribbean.

Three species of jellyfish wash up on shore, especially in spring. It is surprising to realize that jellyfishes are members of that diverse group of animals called zooplankton. When thinking of plankton, one usually visualizes microscopic organisms. But plankton, by definition, includes all organisms that cannot swim against wind-driven currents. No matter how big the jellyfish, the feeble pulsations of its bell cannot prevent it from being driven up on the beach by an onshore wind. The large, firm, almost spherical jellyfish that may wash ashore by the hundreds is the Cannonball Jellyfish (Fig. 91, p. 209). Moon Jellies (p. 207) and the stinging Sea Nettle (p. 209) are often washed ashore. Periodic blooms of Sea Nettles may cause the closing of beaches, especially farther north, in Chesapeake Bay.

At night the sea may deposit blobs of jelly that glow with a bright greenish flash for a few moments and then fade. By the next morning the blob will have begun to disintegrate, and soon it will be a dry stain on the sand. This is a comb jelly or sea walnut (p. 220). Thousands may appear suddenly during the warm summer months, glowing brightly as they are touched by an oar, or tumbling backwards in a glowing spin as they are caught in a boat's propwash. In the daytime they can be captured in cupped hands. Their eight rows of ciliated combs are visible as iridescent lines running from the huge mouth at one end to meet at the other. Comb jellies are not jellyfishes, but members of a related phylum called Ctenophora. They swim by beating their combs of cilia in unison, mouth forward, gulping in any smaller planktonic animals in their path. A bloom of comb jellies is an ephemeral thing. The water may be thick with them one week and all may be gone the next, perhaps for the season. They reappear in huge numbers again when unknown conditions stimulate quiescent eggs, lying innocuously on the bottom, to develop.

As mysteriously as a bloom of ctenophores, masses of black, hairy, pear-shaped animals may appear one day on the beach, thrown up by a fall storm. Thousands of these mud-dwelling Hairy Sea Cucumbers (Pl. 65) lie on the sand, unable to propel themselves back into the sea with their ineffectual tube feet.

Sea stars that wash up are usually Forbes' Sea Stars (Fig. 14). This common animal may be seen in calm, shallow water, even in low-salinity estuaries, eating oysters and snails. Its color is variable—usually purple-brown, with a bright orange, dotlike madreporite near the center of the top (aboral) surface.

There are three cold-tolerant corals whose skeletons may be stranded on the beach. Small white clumps of 5–15 cups are the

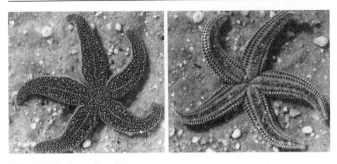

Fig. 14. Forbes' Sea Star.

remains of Northern Cup Coral (Pl. 5). Each cup is about 4 mm (¼ in.) wide. These corals are unable to build reefs, but their skeletons grow so thickly on rocks or wrecks that they give the appearance of a reef. Two other non-reefbuilding corals are Ivory Bush Coral (Pl. 33) — white or, when alive, olive, 10- to 15-cm (4- to 6-in.) long branches with widely spaced cups, and Tube Coral (Pl. 5), which forms masses of white tube-like cups about 3.5 mm (⅛ in.) wide and about 8 mm (³⁄₁₀ in.) long. All three species can survive in relatively silty, inshore waters.

Fig. 15. Egg cases of whelks. Channeled Whelk egg cases (above) have sharp edges. Knobbed Whelk egg cases (below) have flat edges. Size: about 2.5cm (1 in.) wide.

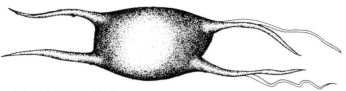

Fig. 16. Mermaid's Purse—a skate egg case.

Sometimes whole windrows of distinctive whelk egg cases (Fig. 15) can be seen on the upper beach. If you cut open the tough covering of a fresh egg case, out will pour dozens of tiny, perfect replicas of an adult whelk. A real find is a skate egg case or Mermaid's Purse (Fig. 16), a rectangular, shiny black, pillowlike structure about 7.5 cm (3 in.) long, with a curved tendril at each corner. The tendrils are attached to seaweed or other bottom features by the female skate. If you find a fresh one torn from its moorings in spring cut it open; inside may be a juvenile skate with a large yolk sac. When placed in a dish of seawater the young skate will thrash about, unable to swim easily because of the burden of the yolk sac, but provided with enough food inside the sac to live for a long time if you change the water frequently.

The Upper Intertidal

Well seaward of the upper beach berm you will find several lines of flotsam and jetsam denoting the various high tides of the day, month, and year (see p. 88 for an explanation). Sometimes broken seagrass blades (Turtle and Manatee grass in Florida; Eelgrass north of this region) will form a distinct line several centimeters thick and wide. In this moist, organic mass, called wrack, can be found delicate seashells, tests of sea urchins, and other fragile collectibles, protected from the surf. As you kick aside the dead brown grass, hundreds of small "beach fleas" will leap out in all directions. These are not really fleas, which are insects, but small crustaceans called amphipods (p. 300). They survive inside dark crevices in masses of seagrass or algae, eating decaying plants and "breathing" the humid air resulting from a daily soaking at high tide. Seaweeds above the mean high-water mark may retain so much moisture that amphipods can survive for long periods of time without daily inundations.

The most striking seashells scattered on the beach are the arks and cockles. Four species are common: the Blood, Incongruous, and Ponderous arks (Pls. 40, 44), and the huge Giant Atlantic Cockle (Pl. 44), which may reach 10 cm (4 in.) across. Arks and cockles are similar in that they bear inflated (bulbous) oval shells with deeply incised grooves running from the edge of the shell to the pointed beak or umbo. The flattened disk shells (p. 256), and the Jingle Shell (p. 254) are also common. Two beautiful snails found off Florida's east coast and Georgia are the Lettered Olive snail (p. 237) and Tollin's Wentletrap (Fig. 12, p. 22). Sand collars, the egg masses of the Moon Snail, are perfectly symmetrical, rubbery, ring-shaped aggregations of sand grains and eggs embedded in a gelatinous medium (Pl. 47).

Among the ripples and runnels of the beach are areas where surf-driven currents form eddies, dropping tiny shells in snowlike heaps. These are usually Coquina and Egg Cockle shells, but mixed in may be small snails such as Common Augers or bivalves such as the Dwarf Surf Clam (p. 258), the Purplish Tagelus and Stout Tagelus (p. 260), and fragile Tellins (p. 260). See Plates 42–44 for photographs of some common shells of the southeastern coast.

Sand-dwelling crabs that frequently wash ashore dead are the Purse Crab and the Shamefaced Crab (Fig. 130). The former, named after the mythical Queen of Hades, Persephone, is almost perfectly circular, except for the front end, which projects as a short cylinder. The latter, locally called the Calico Crab, is known more widely as the Shamefaced Crab because of its habit of covering its "face" with its huge claws when picked up. Examine the right claw carefully and you will find that the lower finger has a massive tooth. Like a can opener, this can be inserted in a snail's shell, providing leverage for the upper finger to pry the shell open. The Flaming Shamefaced Crab, with a flame-like pattern of dark lines on its back, is the largest and most common inshore species.

Sponges which wash up on the beach are usually the Yellow Boring Sponge and the Red Beard Sponge (Pl. 5). Both sponges become dull brown when dry. The Sulfur Sponge looks and feels like a piece of wood, but can be recognized as a sponge by the myriad holes piercing its surface.

One of the more puzzling discoveries of the beachcomber is a dark grayish or brown, translucent, branched, fleshy colony that resembles neither sponge nor soft coral. It has polyps, but not the distinctive arrangement of cups and the internal brown skeleton of soft corals. It is soft, but not spongy. You have come upon some representatives of a relatively obscure phylum—one that is surprisingly well represented on our coasts, where it usually forms dime-sized crusts on seashells or rocks, but is so unspectacular as to be rarely noticed. This phylum is Bryozoa (see Chapter 16), and the colony is the Rubbery Bryozoan (Fig. 30, p. 64). When living, the gelatinous branches are covered with tiny, polyplike zooids, each with a ciliated crest called a lophophore. The colony, perhaps 25 cm (1 ft.) high, was probably ripped from its attachment on a sea whip by a storm.

Just above the day's high-tide mark are a profusion of burrow openings in the sand, ranging from 1 cm (⅜ in.) to more than 2.5 cm (1 in.) in diameter. They are inhabited by Ghost Crabs (Fig. 39, p. 83), legendary grayish white animals with black eyes on long vertical stalks. These crabs can sometimes be seen during the day, especially in early morning, but hordes of them come out at night. They will stand frozen in the beam of your flashlight, but all you will see in the moonlight is a momentary flash of white as the crabs dart, wraithlike, toward their burrows at your approach.

Ghost Crabs are scavengers, eating any sort of rotting plant or animal detritus, but they are formidable predators also. They can crush a Coquina clam or even an Egg Cockle easily, picking out the tissues and discarding the broken shells.

Rock jetties and wooden piers are ideal habitats for the large brown Sea Roach or Beach Slater (p. 302). This isopod, a close relative of the pillbug or ballbug, requires 100% humidity to survive. Its respiratory apparatus is primitive and it cannot leave its moist crevice for long. At your approach, dozens of Sea Roaches will scatter before you, each seeking its own crack or the shadowy, algae-covered dark side of a rock. Sea Roaches live near the mean high-water mark and eat plant detritus. In order to mate, the male must carry the female about until the precise moment when she molts. Only then can he deposit his sperm packs (spermatophores) on the female's now-exposed sexual openings.

Beach and Dune Plants

The pioneer plants of the beach and their successors that carpet the dunes live at the very edge of survival. Their environment is alternately inundated with seawater or salt spray, washed with pure rainwater, or dried out in the intense sun. Storm waves come crashing out of the sea, ripping out chunks of vegetation, and the wind creates abrasions in leaves and breaks off twigs. Much of the beach and foredune area is in the spray zone, so-called because droplets of salt water are blown onto this area adjacent to the sea. The droplets evaporate, leaving a thin, virtually invisible film of salt on everything. Salt crystals may act as miniature magnifying glasses that concentrate the sun's rays and burn tiny holes in leaves. Heavy winds move the shifting sand, sometimes burying the plants. Surprisingly, although salt is deposited on the sand, rain leaches it away rapidly so that dune-face sediments are not particularly salty.

Plants that grow defiantly toward the sea must have mechanisms to prevent the salt water from drying out their cells. They are usually grasses, succulent herbs that can conserve fresh water in thick leaves and stems, or low-lying vines with shiny, waxy, salt-resistant leaves.

Foremost pioneers are the dark green Sea Rocket (see Fig. 17); the whitish green, powdery-looking Beach Croton (Fig. 77, Pl. 19), with its spherical, berry-like fruits; and Orach (Fig. 76), with its arrowhead-shaped, gray-green leaves and red stems. Each of these plants may be found growing bravely beyond the plant line on the berm, projecting from the shifting sands in splendid isolation. A salt-resistant seed has germinated. If a storm spring tide does not rip the plant out it will mature, scatter its seeds, and reproduce vegetatively to create a dense, single-species colony. Usually the Sea Rocket is most aggressive in the establishment of these peripheral colonies.

The grasses are also pioneers, especially Sea Oats (Fig. 22, p. 45) in Florida, Georgia, and South Carolina, and American Beachgrass (Fig. 18) in upper South Carolina and much of North Carolina. They create a dense turf that stabilizes the sand. Other pioneering grasses, such as Beach Sandspur and Saltmeadow Cordgrass (p. 172), aid in the dune-stabilization process.

Seaside Purslane (p. 168), with its reddish stems, elongate succulent leaves, and tiny pink starlike flowers, may form dense colonies close to the sea, especially in the more southerly states. Two species of morning glory send vines seaward, sometimes to the very crest of the berm. The Fiddle-leaf Morning Glory (Fig. 12, p. 22) has white, yellow-throated flowers and elongate, sometimes lobed, dark green leaves. The Beach Morning Glory (Pl. 18) has

Fig. 17. Sea Rocket—isolated colony near high-tide mark.

Fig. 18. *Left:* American Beachgrass, forming hillock of sand; *right:* Prickly-pear Cactus and grasses seaward of Spanish Bayonet plants.

typically purple, morning glory-like flowers; its shiny leaves are deeply indented at the stalk (petiole) and look like the imprint of a goat's hoof. The Fiddle-leaf Morning Glory is more common north of Florida, while the Beach Morning Glory is more common in southern Florida and the Caribbean.

Beach Peas (Fig. 75, p. 162) are vines with typical pea-like, pinkish purple flowers and thick, light green pods to 12 cm (4¾ in.) long, with brown beans inside.

Plants of the Foredunes

The foreslope and crest of the foredunes receive the greatest intensity of salt spray. The flattened and prostrate viny beach plants previously mentioned are common, but a number of bushy plants appear. Marsh Elder (Fig. 72, Pl. 21, p. 166) is a succulent perennial with woody stems. Its light green, pointed, often toothed lower leaves are opposite, but the leaves near the tips of stems are alternate. It is a bushy plant reaching over 1 m (39 in.) in height. Caribbean Sea Spurge (p. 156) and Inkberry (Fig. 71, p. 152) bushes are similar in size to Beach Elder. Inkberry bushes have shoehorn-shaped leaves and yellow-throated pinkish white flowers that are split in a fan shape.

Scattered among the bushy plants is a grass that reaches its greatest concentration on the dunes rather than the beach. Dune Panic Grass (Fig. 78, p. 170), with broad, alternate, blue-green leaves up to 2 cm (¾ in.) wide, grows in scattered clumps, with scraggly, often reclining stems and drooping leaves. Seacoast Bluestem contrasts with the wide-leaved, often drooping Panic Grass. Clumps of this grass are composed of 25-cm (1-ft.) high, erect stems with many small, silvery blue leaves. In late summer its seedheads are covered with dense silvery hairs.

One plant that seems most appropriate in the dry, shifting sands of the dunes is the Prickly-pear Cactus (Fig. 18; see also p. 159). Look for light green, flattened, vertical spiny lobes, up to 25 cm (6 in.) long. Yellow flowers can be found along the edges of the lobes in early spring and summer. The dull red, pear-shaped or oval, pulpy fruit is sweet. **Beware:** Do not bite the fruit until you have singed or peeled it first, or you will have a lipful of almost invisible, but painful spines for your trouble. The fruit will be ripe when it is dark purplish red and soft. You might find this cactus at the very front of the foredunes, not because it originated there, but more likely because it remained in place as the dune swept landward. The Prickly-pear, then, is not so much a pioneer as a relic of a past, more protected site.

A lovely little plant often growing in scattered mats is the Beach Pennywort (Fig. 75, p. 162). Its flat, circular, dark green leaves are appressed to the sand or on short stems growing along rhizomes. Clumps of tiny, nondescript flowers grow on their own stems from the same rhizome.

Russian Thistle (Fig. 77) is a spiny, branching, low herb with succulent leaves and star-shaped flowers. In the northern part of our region, it may be seen far out on the berm, well seaward of the other plants.

Plants of the Interdune Meadows

Here, in the protected hollow between the fore- and back dunes, is an area of gentler climate and respite from salt spray. Lovely wildflowers form a carpet on the sand. Butterfly Pea vines (Fig. 75, p. 162) have large, purple, pea-like flowers and pods spring through fall. Seaside Primrose (Fig. 72, p. 153) is a prostrate herb with deeply notched leaves and primrose-like, pink and yellow flowers in spring and fall. Grassleaf Golden-aster (Fig. 77, p. 167) looks like grass but has groups of three or four asterlike flowers in summer. In fall, Camphorweed (p. 166) has similar yellow flowers on a rough, hairy, bushy plant to 120 cm (4 ft.) tall, with triangular leaves. Firewheel (Fig. 76, p. 165) is a striking herb with large red and yellow flowers.

Beware the Spurge Nettle (Fig. 74, p. 157), which is armed with both nettles and spines. The leaves have three to five distinct lobes and a full complement of spines running along the axial rib. Admire the small, white, five-petaled flowers from afar.

The most spectacular plant of the interdune meadow and seaward slope of the rear dunes is the Spanish Bayonet or Yucca (see Fig. 18 and p. 161). A clump of 30-cm (1-ft.) long, light green, thick, pointed leaves gives rise to a stalk of white, pendulous, bell-shaped flowers in summer. Another summer-flowering plant, Seaside Goldenrod (Pl. 21), adds brightness to the interdune meadow with typical yellow spikes of tiny flowers.

Shrubs and Vines of the Rear Dunes

Trees and large shrubs begin to dominate on the windward side of the rear dunes, where salt spray is mitigated somewhat by distance and protection by the foredunes.

Shrubs and trees exposed to the salt spray and wind have a characteristic growth habit with a sheared-off look on the seaward side. It looks as though someone has cut off the exposed side of the tree so that the crown of leaves forms a wedge shape, wide end landward. The leaves and branches facing the sea are killed as salt gets into abrasions opened by the wind. The chloride ions of the salt cause tissue death in leaves and accumulate in twigs, destroying them also. But the salt is not carried to the leeward part of the tree; it grows normally, hence the pruned appearance.

Amid the Sea Oats or American Beachgrass and other particularly wind- and spray-resistant plants (testifying to the still-severe nature of the habitat) grows a mixed scrub or maritime forest composed of Live Oak, Wax Myrtle, Juniper, Yaupon Holly, Cabbage Palm, Sun Palmetto, and Groundsel Tree.

Two small trees distinguished by dense, large thorns are Buckthorn and Hercules Club (Fig. 72, p. 153).

As one travels north from Georgia, Live Oak trees become less dominant in the coastal scrub community and eventually disappear. On the relatively narrow barrier islands of North Carolina, dune formation becomes less complex and dunes are often low. Small, windswept trees and shrubs are often entangled in masses of thorny vines, especially Catbrier or Greenbrier (Fig. 75, p. 162). These vines may grow densely, festooned from trees or rising from the ground as high as a man's head. They have shiny green, deeply veined, triangular leaves and short tendrils on the stem that can wrap themselves around any stationary object. Farther south, a more benign vine, Muscadine Grape (Fig. 75), is common. It too is festooned from shrubs and trees in dense masses. It has typically grape-like, broad, serrated leaves and, in fall, purple, tasty, sourish grapes.

Succession: From Sand Dune to Forest

Visualize the creation of a barrier island. A small spit of land emerges from a bar—or a long sand spit extending from an existing island is cut off by a storm. Wind- or seaborne seeds wash up on the inhospitable bare sand, taking root and producing deeply rooted pioneer plants. Sand accumulates around stems, forming hillocks. Eventually the hillocks coalesce to form small dunes. These migrate away from the sea, pushed by prevailing winds and built up by drifting sand from the now well-developed beach. The pioneer plants prosper; their yearly cycle of death and rebirth leaves shed leaves and dead stems to disintegrate on the sterile sand, enriching it. As the sediment becomes enriched with humus, other plants are able to survive. The pioneer plants are adapted to the most stressful environments. Now that conditions are more or less stabilized, the pioneers are at a disadvantage. Other plants, better adapted to the higher humus content of the soil and the moisture retained by that humus, replace them. These plants also can resist the salt spray and harsh winds. Eventually the highly specialized foredune community is established. But the dune continues to move landward. Soon its original place is taken by new foredunes. Wind and spray are diminished behind the new foredunes, but are still important factors in the environment. The original dune—now a back dune—accumulates more sand and becomes higher. New plants begin to grow on its somewhat-protected front and crest. Trees take hold, their seaward branches and leaves sheared by the combined forces of wind and salt. On the more protected lee slope a whole community of trees, shrubs, herbs, and grasses takes hold. Eventually a maritime forest is established. Finally, after hundreds of years this succession ends. A relatively permanent plant-based community is established—soils and other environmental factors are more or less permanently stabilized. The climax forest, perfectly balanced with a relatively unchanging environment, is the culmination of the phases of succession.

As you walk from sandy beach inland, you will see stages representing hundreds of years of succession taking place within, perhaps, a hundred meters. Watch the prostrate or low-growing pioneer grasses, vines, and herbs give rise to the foredune community dominated by low shrubs. Pass the protected interdune meadow and notice the resurgence of the most salt-resistant plants on the foreslope of the rear dunes, amidst small, gnarled trees. Stand on the crest of the rear dune and watch the shoreside plants give rise to the scrub community or maritime forest. Finally, if you are on one of the well-developed remnant islands of Georgia or South Carolina, you can follow the path of succession inland, through the stillness of a Live Oak-dominated climax forest.

MUD FLATS AND SALT MARSHES

Stillness. That is the prevailing feeling in the salt marsh. The tidal flow meanders through innumerable channels and sloughs, alternately exposing vast flat muddy plains edging the marsh, or submerging them. The rising tide encroaches on the marsh beyond the mud flats, inundating the grasses with salt water, sometimes until only leaf tips are visible. The tides are the major structural force in the marsh. There is no surf. In some places, where water piles up at the confluence of a number of tidal streams, relatively strong currents are created as the tides flow through restricting channels, scouring the bottom. But for the most part, the gentle rising and falling of each 12-hour tidal cycle is imperceptibly slow. The full force of the sea has been spent on shores of barrier islands and beaches seaward. The sand burden has been dropped as current velocities declined. Here, in the vastness of the marsh, only the tiniest particles of sediment remain suspended. They fall to the bottom and mix with organic detritus produced by the death and decay of innumerable salt grass plants, forming a fine, blackish mud.

Freshwater streams flow into marshes on the landward side, eventually diluting the seawater, creating a gradient of fresh to brackish to full-strength seawater that prevails along the width of the marsh, so that organisms at the seaward margin live in virtually oceanic salt water and those at the landward margin live in almost pure fresh water.

The aforementioned environmental factors—the highly organic muddy substrate, the absence or diminution of surf and oceanic currents, the variable salinity of the water—all affect the distribution of plants and animals. There are typical inhabitants of the mud flats that differ from those in the neighboring low marsh. Low-marsh organisms are separate from high-marsh inhabitants.

The sediment of the marsh is rich and black: rich with nutrients released when uncountable stalks of grass die seasonally and rot in place, and black with populations of decay-producing bacteria and their byproducts. A centimeter or two under the surface the sediment smells of rotten eggs, an indication of the presence of hydrogen sulfide. This gas is produced by bacteria that metabolize sulfur compounds in the absence of oxygen. You know you have uncovered a region of decay, where oxygen is lacking, every time your shovel frees this gas. The sediment presents a set of contradictions: it is rich with detritus, but just beneath its surface, life-sustaining oxygen is absent. Innumerable bacteria in the first inch or so of sediment have used up all the oxygen as they metabolized the detritus, and the fine sediment presents a densely packed impediment to the diffusion of new oxygen. How can any other organism compete with the bacteria for the almost limitless food available on the floor of the marsh? One way is to stay on the surface of the mud, where oxygen is plentiful. But predators are plentiful too. Herons, egrets, and other wading birds have sharp eyes and beaks; raccoons and opossums have intelligence and long teeth. No, except for a few species of mollusks with heavy shells (and even these are vulnerable to sea gulls, which drop them from on high, or raccoons, which beat oysters and mussels with rocks to break their shells), life is too dangerous on the surface. But to live under the surface means suffocation in the anoxic (oxygen-depleted) zone. However, there is an answer. The worms, mollusks, crustaceans, and other animals of the marsh have learned how to live in the mud and survive. They build burrows or tubes and create their own life-giving flow of oxygenated water which allows them to live deep beneath the sediment surface.

The classic example is the Parchment Worm (Fig. 19). This bizarre-looking worm builds a U-shaped tube of whitish, plasticlike protein. Both ends extend from the sediment surface a substantial distance—perhaps 5 cm (2 in.) or so. The body of the worm is modified so that three sets of parapodia form fanlike structures that beat water through the inlet and out the posterior end. Plankton and detritus are caught by a web of mucus stretched across the tube; the web is periodically rolled into a ball and swallowed, together with its complement of plankton.

Fiddler crabs use another technique. They build wide burrows—wide enough to allow oxygenated air—or water—to diffuse in. They hide in these burrows until the tide is low. Then they gather at the surface, especially at the shore edge, in

Fig. 19. Parchment Worm in its tube. Note the three enlarged parapodia used to pump water through the tube.

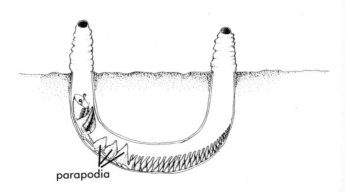

parapodia

tremendous numbers, to pick tiny morsels of detritus from the sediment. On a still day you can stand a few meters away and hear thousands of tiny claws picking away at the mud. Approach the crabs and they will scuttle toward their burrows. In a few moments, where there were thousands of crabs visible, not one will be seen.

The Structure of a Salt Marsh

The prevailing feature of the marsh is its flatness. It arose from the deposition of tiny particles from the sea in flat layers. When enough sediment accumulated for marsh plants to colonize, the flatness was slightly modified by accumulated plant detritus. After hundreds of years of accumulating sediment and detritus the marsh assumes a gentle slope, with the oldest, most landward portion highest. The higher one goes the more compacted the sediment gets, until, near the landward margin of the marsh, so much dead plant material has piled up that, through pressure and time, it has turned into peat. This reddish, clayey substance can be chopped out of the marsh, dried, and burned like coal. Peat underlies the whole marsh, but it is thickest on the older, higher landward portion.

When the tide is out the seaward edge of the marsh is visible as extensive mud flats.

At the edges of tidal streams, where flow is substantial, sharp-edged banks appear and there are no mud flats. The marsh grass grows right to the edge of the channel. But in protected places, the mud flats are dominant. Landward of the flats is an intertidal zone which is inundated daily. Only one marsh grass can withstand this daily inundation, where 90% of the spaces between mud particles are filled with salt water. It is Smooth Cordgrass (Pl. 21). This plant can grow to 1 m (39 in.) or more in height. Its presence indicates daily immersion and the region it dominates is called the low marsh. Smooth Cordgrass grows most luxuriantly and reaches its greatest height close to the banks of tidal channels.

As the land slopes upward, perhaps just a few centimeters in the vertical plane, but many meters horizontally on the very gently sloping marsh, a zone of lesser submergence is reached. This is the high marsh, where inundation comes only during spring tides, perhaps six days a month. Lighter green, thin-leaved Saltmeadow Cordgrass dominates here, covering the marsh for as far as the eye can see, to be replaced, sometimes kilometers landward, by a freshwater-dominated marsh covered with long green stalks of Needle Rush. The rounded leaves of this grass look like long knitting needles. The Needle Rush marsh is always tinged with brown from last year's dead leaves. Individual plants of Needle Rush are much taller, thicker, and darker green than Saltmeadow Cordgrass. In Georgia many marshes have such a shallow slope that tall Smooth Cordgrass gives rise to short Smooth Cordgrass inland, and there is a disproportionately small area of Saltmeadow Cordgrass.

The Mud Flats

In most cases the "mud" of the mud flats is really muddy sand—that is, a combination of small sand grains mixed with detritus and very tiny clay and silt particles. Thus the mud is relatively firm underfoot. When exploring the flats it is best to wear sneakers, even if you like the sensation of mud squishing up between your toes, because sharp oyster and mussel shell fragments are usually embedded in the sediment. Muddy sand is particularly suitable as a habitat because there is enough sand to permit oxygenated water to percolate relatively deeply beneath the surface, yet much food—detritus—is mixed in also.

Animals of the Mud Flats

Near the water's edge at low tide are the burrows of various worms. Some burrows appear as holes about 1 cm (⅜ in.) in diameter. They are surrounded by a coiled gray mound of feces so that the hole may be invisible until you remove the fecal casts. It is difficult to dig up the inhabitants of these burrows, as the burrows do not have distinct walls and will crumble as you dig. They are also at least 30 cm (1 ft.) deep and are U-shaped, with the funnel-shaped front end sometimes a meter (39 in.) from the posterior end with the fecal casts. But the casts are the clue. Pick them up and rub them between your fingers. A strong odor of iodine will assail your nostrils. You are in the presence of a most esoteric animal—the Southern Acorn Worm (Pl. 3). This animal uses a whitish muscular proboscis and collar to burrow into the sand, dragging behind its flaccid gray body. Acorn worms are deposit feeders. They simply eat the sediment and digest the detritus mixed in with it, spewing copious amounts of newly clean muddy feces out of the posterior opening of the burrow. The iodine-like odor is caused by the presence of the compound 2,6-dibromophenol, but no one knows the compound's biological significance. Perhaps it simply is a means of warding off predators. It is effective in the sense that when a person or predator digs to find the worm, the exposed burrow literally reeks of iodine, driving off less than enthusiastic collectors.

The Southern Acorn Worm lives only in clean, unpolluted water, and its range is diminishing. The Northern Acorn Worm may be found in North Carolina. It differs from the grayish white southern species by its orange-yellow collar and pinkish proboscis.

Another unusual worm produces a similar U-shaped burrow. The Lugworm (Fig. 62, p. 122) looks like a brown or greenish cigar, with tufts of reddish gills on either side of its body. In the spring the female releases thousands of eggs in an elongated transparent plume of mucus, which is extruded from the burrow (see Fig. 63, p. 125). This small worm, usually no larger than 25 cm (10 in.) long, can produce a gelatinous plume several meters long. While the northern species of this worm produces coiled fecal casts (which do not smell of iodine), the Southern Lugworm simply pours a formless mass of waste on the surface.

The tubes of the Plumed and Onuphis worms (Pl. 4) are mixed in with the burrows of acorn worms and Lugworms. In North Carolina a third species of worm — the Bamboo Worm — produces a thin, sandy, easily broken tube (Pl. 4). The Bamboo Worm (Fig. 120, p. 289) looks like a yellow bamboo twig with red joints. The tail (pygidium) is crownlike. Two other worms that eat detritus are the Fringe-gilled Mudworm and the Ornate Worm (Fig. 20).

Do not forget to look for the distinctive tubes of the Parchment Worm. If you are lucky, you will see a small, whitish pea crab (p. 280) that lives in Parchment Worm tubes almost exclusively. The crab lives in the upper reaches of the incurrent tube, usually in mated pairs, and feeds on detritus and plankton sucked in by the current created by the worm's modified parapodia. At maturity the crabs may become too large to escape through the opening of the tube.

Fig. 20. *Left:* Fringe-gilled Mudworm (p. 282); *right:* Ornate Worm (p. 281).

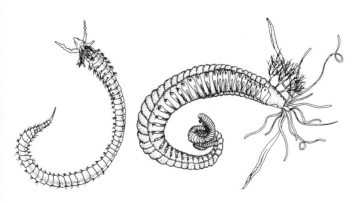

Further up on the flats, in the mid-intertidal zone, are the complex burrows of the Mud Shrimp (Fig. 126, p. 307). The openings of the burrows are not distinguishable from those of burrowing worms, but when uncovered are revealed to be thick cylinders of gray clay, 2.5 cm (1 in.) wide. They may be more than 30 cm (1 ft.) deep and contain several chambers and as many as eight openings. One adult male and a harem of females and juveniles occupy the burrow system, along with a tiny translucent shrimp, *Leptalpheus forceps,* no more than 8 mm (⁹⁄₁₀ in.) long. This tiny shrimp probably lives in Ghost Shrimp burrows also. Mud Shrimps may be differentiated from Ghost Shrimps by habitat (Ghost Shrimps prefer clean sand) and by the surface of the head region. (Mud Shrimps are "hairy"; Ghost Shrimps are "bald.") Finally, Mud Shrimps lack the large claws of Ghost Shrimps.

Three large snails dominate the flats. One burrows beneath the surface and two plough through the upper centimeter or so, like a bulldozer. The Baby's Ear Snail has a flat white shell with a low spire and huge body whorl (Pl. 42). Although the earlike shell reaches 4 cm (1½ in.) in width, it is completely hidden inside the mantle of the snail. Plate 1 shows the mound of sand thrown up by the passage of the snail and its flat, featureless body uncovered. The snail looks like a fleshy blob, but if placed underwater a pair of short, curved tentacles are revealed to project from what appears to be the middle of the dorsal surface.

The Southern Moon Snail (Pl. 3) is also called Sharkeye because of the eye-like design of its shell. Although empty shells are common on the beach, the live animal is less frequently seen because it is often buried in the sediment at low tide. On rare occasions a storm will wash thousands of these globose snails ashore, revealing their true numbers. The Moon Snail is a formidable predator. If you find a live one, place it in a container of sea water and get ready for an extraordinary sight. Out of the shell (which is 5–7.5 cm or 2–3 in. long) will extend a body perhaps four times the diameter of the shell. Once extended, the animal will move off at a speed that seems impossible for a snail. The combination of speed and a sharp radula (rasplike tongue) makes the Moon Snail an effective hunter. It drills circular, beveled holes in the shells of oysters and other mollusks, using the radula to make the hole and to rasp out the flesh of its prey.

Another predatory snail, this one subtidal, is the beautiful Tulip Snail (p. 234). This animal has a lovely symmetrical, banded shell and red flesh. It feeds on other snails and soft-bodied animals, but does not drill through shells. It is a rapidly moving, fierce predator. Look for it just below the low-tide mark on beaches from South Carolina southward. The Striped Hermit Crab often sports the beautiful shell.

The Knobbed Whelk (p. 230) is the largest shallow-water snail of the Southeast coast above Florida. Plate 45 shows a specimen about 30 cm (1 ft.) long. This sluggish, black-bodied predator crawls on its broad foot bearing the shell with its canal extended upward and forward. The head projects from beneath the canal, carrying a pair of stout, tapering tentacles, each topped by an eye. Even large oysters fall prey to the Knobbed Whelk, but its sluggishness makes this snail relatively unimportant on the list of oyster predators.

One of the most dangerous enemies of oysters is the Oyster Drill (p. 241). This small gray snail is also sluggish, but it makes up in numbers for whatever it lacks in activity. In spring look for the Oyster Drill's tiny flat-sided, vase-shaped egg cases, 1–2 mm (to ⅛ in.) tall, festooned in rows and bunches on shells and other hard objects (see Fig. 24, p. 49).

The most common snail on the mud flats is the Mud Snail (Pl. 42). If you drop a piece of bread or meat on the mud, inside of five minutes it will be invisible under a mound of writhing black snails (see Pl. 45). These 2-cm (¾ in.) long animals have a cylindrical shell, often worn at the spire, and a gray body. They have an excellent olfactory apparatus and can smell rotting carrion from a long distance. The Mud Snail is the host to at least six different species of parasitic flatworms (digenetic trematodes or flukes), which spend a larval period developing inside the snail's liver and gonads. One of these worms is a bird schistosome. Although it belongs to a family of flatworms that causes much human anguish in Africa, Asia, and some Caribbean islands, this species is a parasite of birds—it will not develop in humans. When its larva penetrates human skin the necessary cues for further development are missing, and it wanders around under the skin for a few days and then dies. In individuals sensitized to the worm, a rash develops, characterized by intensely itching raised welts. The disease is called "Swimmer's Itch" or "Clammer's Itch," and it can be quite uncomfortable. If you are a wanderer of mud flats inhabited by Mud Snails you might pick up the disease, revealed by a network of red, itchy lines on the back of your hand, arm, or legs. See a physician for medication to relieve the itching. The disease will run its course in a week or two and is not transmissible.

Mud Snail shells are often inhabited by the small Long-clawed Hermit Crab (Pl. 7). Less than 2 cm (¾ in.) long, these active little crabs take the place of the Three-colored Hermit of the Caribbean as the most common crab of the shallows in the Carolinas, Georgia, and n. Florida. Thousands of these tiny tan crabs battle each other over the snail shells that are so important to their survival. Their abdomens are soft and vulnerable, and unless they can move into a vacant shell, they will soon be eaten by predatory fishes or birds.

On South Carolina, Georgia, and Florida flats the much larger Green-striped Hermit Crab (Pl. 52) is common. It may reach 7.5 cm (3 in.), including claws, and has bold longitudinal green stripes on its legs and spooned fingertips on its claws. It commonly uses Moon and Tulip snail shells as its home.

A third common shallow-water hermit is the Flat-clawed Hermit Crab (Pl. 7). It is large, reaching 7.5 cm (3 in.) in total length, and has broad, rounded claws. In the Carolinas and Georgia its color is similar to that of its close relative, the Long-clawed Hermit; both are tan or lavender-tinged gray.

Muddy sand in calm shallows is the habitat of a most extraordinary sea anemone, the American Tube-dwelling Anemone (Pls. 2, 28). At low tide you may see a tuft of brown tentacles lying flaccid on the sand, at the mouth of a burrow. But when the tide comes in, especially at night, the tuft becomes a mass of long, pale tan, streaming tentacles. Look closely and you will see a second ring of thin, incurving tentacles surrounding the mouth. If you disturb the animal it will simply disappear, rocketing down to the bottom of its gray, velvety tube.

Bivalves of the Mud Flats

One of the distinctive animals of the mud flats is the Stout Tagelus (p. 260), which seems to prefer transitional regions where muddy sand grades into sandy mud.

Tiny, yellow-brown, shiny, seedlike clams can be found quite deep in a shovelful of black muddy sand. These are the oval, elongate Awning Clams (Pl. 1). They are active swimmers and have a powerful foot ending in an oval, ridged disk. They inhabit muddy sand that is coarse enough not to have a shallow anoxic zone, so that they may burrow deeply. Awning clams are primitive forms midway between the ancient deposit (mud-eating) feeders and modern filter-feeding bivalves. To this day they have simple gills similar to those found in fossil clams.

Buried in the mud of the marsh, especially in banks and edges, is the large Ribbed Mussel (Fig. 21). Animals such as raccoons eat this large mussel, and its shell has been found in quantity in kitchen middens of long-gone Indians. I have never met anyone who has eaten one, and rumor has it that they are poisonous. However, Euell Gibbons has stalked this mussel and pronounced it "simply not as good as the Blue Mussel"—but perfectly edible.

The Salt Marsh
Plants of the Salt Marsh

Life in the salt marsh is predicated upon the death of the dominant plants, the cordgrasses. It is interesting to note that over the thousands of square kilometers of salt marshes, two plants, Smooth and Saltmeadow Cordgrass, have become so well

Fig. 21. *Left:* Ribbed Mussel partly buried in mud of Smooth Cordgrass flats.

Fig. 22. *Center:* Sea Oats (p. 172); *right:* Salt Reed (*Phragmites,* p. 171).

adapted to the complex environment that only a few competing species, relegated to peripheral regions, can take hold. And no wonder—what other land plant can withstand daily or monthly immersion in salt water with its roots in fine-grained suffocating, almost oxygenless mud?

Sometimes depressions form in the flat surface of the marsh. These become basins where seawater remains after a spring tide. But there is an interval of two weeks between spring tides. The water is not replenished and it stagnates and evaporates. As the seawater evaporates it leaves salt behind. Gradually the salinity of the remaining water increases and a hypersaline pool evolves. The salinity can rise to twice that of the surrounding seawater (about 60 ‰). Now the cordgrasses are not able to compete, and Southern Glasswort (Pl. 18) and Saltwort (Fig. 74; Pls. 19, 24) colonize the area. It takes on a bright green color from the rubbery vertical stalks of the Glasswort and the light green, bunched leaves of the Saltwort.

Around the periphery of the marsh, and in slightly higher elevations, Seashore Saltgrass (Fig. 78, Pl. 21) with short, spiky leaves around an erect stem, abounds.

Where dredge spoil has been deposited or where some other human modification of the marsh floor has raised the level beyond a point where frequent inundation can occur, Salt Reed (Fig. 22) dominates. It grows higher than a man's head and has lovely purplish plume-like flowers that turn grayish in the fall. But it has relatively little significance as food or habitat and indicates the deterioration of the marsh through human intervention. It has become all too evident in the Northeast, but is less common in the less disturbed southeastern marshes.

At the seaward edge of marshy islands the halophytic (salt-tolerant) plants previously described as bordering open beaches can be found. A touch of color is provided by the Sea Daisy (Pl. 20). This low, erect shrub has thick, gray-green, opposite leaves and bright yellow flowers.

Tiny purple flowers on long, thin, sparsely leaved, wiry stems characterize Sea Lavender (Pl. 21), a perennial herb.

Animals of the Salt Marsh

The most important food source in the salt marsh is not the cordgrass itself, although pioneers fed cattle on Saltmeadow Cordgrass and wild horses left to fend for themselves on barrier islands will survive on it. *The detritus remaining after the death of the plants is the potent food.* It is reduced by bacterial action (decay) to the elements and compounds which comprise its very protoplasm, and these atoms and molecules float freely in the water, washing in and out with the tides. Or, the detritus breaks down into tiny, bite-sized chunks. The bacteria that thrive on the detritus are often the most useful component of the detrital food chain, since many detritivores eat them rather than the hard-to-digest cellulose of plant cells. Much of the nutrients and detritus are exported out to sea to support the growth of fish and invertebrate larvae, especially those of commercial shrimp.

Some of the detritus remains on the floor of the marsh. It is eaten by myriad detritivores such as fiddler crabs. Even filter feeders such as clams obtain some nourishment from the freed molecules, if not from the detritus itself.

The most obvious detritivores are the fiddler crabs (Pl. 57). Various species of fiddlers have divided up the marsh into microhabitats. Nearest to the sea, in more sandy areas, the Sand Fiddler (Fig. 139, p. 336) dominates. In muddier areas further landward the Mud Fiddler (Pls. 6, 57) can be found. Closest to land, the much larger Red-jointed Fiddler (Fig. 139) holds sway in the Needle Rush-dominated freshwater margin of the marsh.

Only the male fiddler has a large claw. The female is a "two-fisted" feeder—she uses both claws to pick up detritus. The Sand Fiddler actually places sand into its mouth and, using spoon-shaped, hairlike setae on its mouthparts, scrapes the algae and detritus from the sand grains. The remaining newly cleaned sand grains are formed into "feeding balls" or "pseudo feces" and left outside the burrow opening.

Perhaps the most common marsh animal is the Marsh Periwinkle (Pl. 21). This globose snail is a member of a family found in intertidal environments all over the world. Although these snails have gills, they prefer to remain above the water level as much as possible. The Marsh Periwinkle, for example, crawls up cordgrass stems to wait for low tide, when it descends to glide over the mud and eat detritus.

Another snail that *must* remain out of the water is the Eastern Melampus (Pl. 42) or, in mangrove swamps, its close relative, the Coffee-bean Snail (Pl. 22). These snails have evolved that last step toward a truly terrestrial life, and are true air breathers. They use a tiny hole, the pneumostome, as a nostril and suck air into an internal, lunglike chamber lined with blood vessels. If a Melampus were unable to crawl up the cordgrass stems and if it were covered with water from the rising tide, it would drown. The Eastern Melampus has a fragile shell. It occurs by the thousands on the mud surface and is an important food for ducks and other marsh birds.

Another snail used as food by wild ducks is the Olive Nerite (p. 237). This globose snail has the wide aperture typical of a nerite. It is found in the lower, intertidal marsh and in tidepools and can withstand both low and high salinities. The shell is greenish brown, usually with many transverse, wavy dark lines. This snail produces tiny, white, oval egg capsules, no more than 1 mm (1/16 in.) wide, each with 60–80 eggs inside. The egg capsules are glued to submerged hard objects and cordgrass stems.

A number of tiny snails, usually no more than 4 mm (1/7 in.) long, belong to the family Hydrobiidae. They are elongate, with distinct whorls piled upon one another. Most are tan or brownish; they are found in the lower intertidal on silt and mud or in tidepools, often by the thousands (Fig. 23).

The horn snails are distinctive because of their augerlike shape and distinct vertical ridges. The Ladder Horn Snail (p. 232) is found in the upper intertidal zone, often among melampus snails, while the Costate Horn Snail (p. 232) is found somewhat lower, throughout the whole intertidal. The Ladder Horn Snail reaches 3.2 cm (1¼ in.) in length and occurs from Georgia southward; the Costate Horn Snail is more tropical, but occurs in Florida.

The Bulla Melampus (Pl. 39) is small (to 1 cm — ⅜ in.) and oval, resembling the other melampus snails, but is darker brown.

Fig. 23. Marsh Hydrobiid Snail (*Littorinidops palustris*). Tiny — to 4.5mm (⅙ in.) tall.

Restricted to low-salinity marshes and Needle Rush marshes, it can occur in huge numbers, providing food for crabs, fishes, ducks, rails, and rats.

Several kinds of clams and mussels inhabit southern salt marshes. The most common clam in the intertidal zone is usually the bulbous, symmetrically oval, blackish Carolina Marsh Clam (Pl. 43). This clam reaches 4 cm (1⅗ in.) in width and is found buried in the mud of the intertidal. In low-salinity Needle Rush marshes it may occur in large numbers. Do not confuse this clam with the Wedge Rangia (Pl. 43), which usually has a similar dark brown or blackish outer covering. Although both clams are similar in size and shape, the Wedge Rangia is usually found in very low-salinity water and is subtidal, while the Carolina Marsh Clam is usually found in the intertidal zone. Live specimens of the Rangia usually have wrinkled, corroded umbos (beaks), worn white. These clams have been abundant for thousands of years and their ancient shells are buried under much of the upland surrounding the marsh. The shells are mined and used as the base of roadbeds in some states, notably Louisiana.

The Florida Marsh Clam is small (1 cm or ⅜ in. long), thin-shelled, and fragile. It may be abundant in brackish marshes, buried in mud or muddy sand, or under mats of filamentous algae or detritus. This clam broods its young, releasing larvae rather than eggs.

Oyster Bars

Oyster larvae need a hard, clean surface upon which to settle. In the absence of a proper settling spot they die after a few days. Studies have shown that oyster shell is preferred by the larvae, and once oysters are present in a marsh they themselves provide the necessary substrate for larval settlement. Massive reefs, some kilometers long, build up as subsequent generations use their predecessors as a foundation for survival. But one wonders how the original larvae found a place to settle in the soft, muddy marsh. In any event, many oyster shells now permeate the marsh, so settling surfaces abound — and so do oysters.

One look at an oyster bar will reveal its suitability as a habitat for other animals. Numerous folds in shells and spaces between the shells provide habitats for worms, crabs, and many other animals (see Fig. 24, p. 49).

Most oyster species are protandrous hermaphrodites — that is, all are born males and then, after reaching sexual maturity and pouring sperms into the water, gradually (over a period of about two years) become females. This is logical from the oyster's point of view, as sperm production is not as biologically demanding as the production of millions of relatively large eggs, and can be handled by the smaller, younger animals. The Eastern Oyster (p.

256) has evolved two separate sexes and most do not undergo a sequential sex change.

All oysters respond to invasion by foreign organisms or even grains of sand by surrounding the irritating object with nacre, the mother-of-pearl inner lining of the shell. Unfortunately, Eastern Oysters do not make the lovely spheres produced by Pacific pearl oysters. They do, however, produce interesting, minute lumpy chunks of nacre, which are good for souvenirs, if nothing else.

As one moves farther south, the oysters seem to change habitat. In the plankton-impoverished tropical seas oysters survive best in mangrove swamps, where they grow on Red Mangrove roots, festooned in 30-cm (1-ft.) thick colonies. Southern Florida's mangrove swamps are rich with immense numbers of Eastern Oysters, but in the Caribbean the almost identical Mangrove Oyster takes over.

Oysters grow best in brackish water but can survive throughout the full salinity range. If it were not for their ability to live in almost pure fresh water, they would be in danger of extinction. Every few years a parasitic disease called MSX decimates oyster populations in terrible epidemics. But the parasite cannot survive in fresh water and oyster recovery depends on the millions of fertilized eggs floating downstream from rivers and freshwater marshes.

Oyster bars are primarily intertidal. They can be likened to

Fig. 24. Some animals living on oysters.

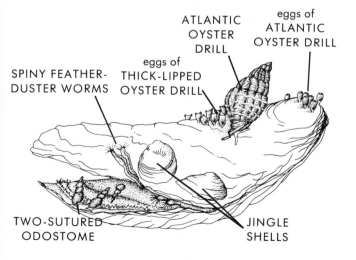

ATLANTIC OYSTER DRILL

eggs of ATLANTIC OYSTER DRILL

eggs of THICK-LIPPED OYSTER DRILL

SPINY FEATHER-DUSTER WORMS

TWO-SUTURED ODOSTOME

JINGLE SHELLS

apartment houses; sometimes almost every crevice contains a crab, worm, anemone, mussel, or barnacle.

Two kinds of mussel live among the oysters. You will have to concentrate to see them, as their dark blue color blends into the shadows in crevices among the oysters. The Hooked Mussel (p. 257) is dark brown or grayish, with a purplish interior. Distinct rounded ribs radiate from a slightly hooked, pointed umbo (beak); the shell is up to 6 cm (2⅜ in.) long. Smaller, but otherwise similar, the Scorched Mussel (Fig. 32, Pl. 49) is more common in the Caribbean. It reaches only 4 cm (1⅗ in.) and is usually dark brown.

Four species of barnacles form grayish encrustations of miniature volcanic cones on oyster shells. These remarkable animals are crustaceans. Their miniature jointed appendages reach out into the water from the safety of the rocklike fortress of plates or scutes that the animal secretes around itself. As soon as the tide recedes, the barnacles become quiescent—their metabolism slows and they hunker down to wait out the dry period until the next high tide covers them, allowing them to once again filter plankton from the water and respire. Some barnacles live so high above the sea that they are inundated for only a few hours each month, yet they seem to "prefer" infrequent functioning to the dangers that come with inundation: crabs, fishes, and other predators with sharp teeth that could scrape them off rock, oyster, or mangrove root.

The Fragile Star Barnacle (Fig. 115, Pl. 16) forms grayish encrustations on oyster shells. The barnacles are so small—only 6 mm (¼ in. wide)—that it is difficult to see the starlike shape of each individual animal. There are often so many that they form a distinct crust. The Bay Barnacle (p. 299) and the Ivory Barnacle (Fig. 32) are both ivory white. The Ivory Barnacle is larger, however, reaching 2.5 cm (1 in.) to the Bay Barnacle's 1.3 cm (½ in.) width. The Striped Barnacle (Fig. 86, p. 192) is midway between the other species in size and is easily recognized by its purple vertical stripes.

The ubiquitous Blue Crab (Pl. 53; Fig. 133, p. 321) may be seen swimming around the oysters, searching for black-fingered mud crabs to devour. At low tide, examine the crevices among chunks of back-to-back oysters for these small, active mud crabs. The Common Mud Crab (Pl. 56) is one of the largest species, reaching 3.5 cm (1⅖ in.). It can be recognized by the presence of a large white tooth on the cutting edge of its upper finger. This crab is usually found with the smaller Depressed Mud Crab (Fig. 128), which lacks the white tooth. Its minor chela (smaller front claw) is spooned. These crabs excavate shallow burrows at the base of the oyster bar, or live in crevices. They feed on young oysters, juvenile snails, and so on.

On the banks of the marsh, among the blades of cordgrass or in the mud near the oyster bars, are burrows of several other small crab species. Two have white claws. The smaller Harris' Mud Crab (p. 326) never grows longer than 1.5 cm (⅗ in.) and has a brown carapace. The Mangrove Mud Crab (Fig. 127) is often almost twice as large. Its carapace is often brilliant purplish blue, dark gray, or black, and the upper half of the upper finger of the claw may be pink or purple.

Harris' Mud Crab is often active at low tide and may be found in freshwater streams at the head of the marsh as well as in estuarine waters near the sea. It is omnivorous and eats detritus as well as small crustaceans such as amphipods. The Mangrove Mud Crab lives in burrows slightly below the high-tide mark that are partly filled with water. It is active at high tide or when the sky is cloudy.

Small, square-bodied crabs under layers of dead grass or other detritus are the Common Marsh Crab and its smaller relative, the Gray Marsh Crab (Pl. 57). These crabs may be found in long, shallow burrows in the upper intertidal zone or above the high-tide mark. Both have light-colored claws and are scavengers, but the Marsh Crab feeds primarily on cordgrass shoots. The burrows of both species are communal, containing one or two males and several females in separate chambers. The burrows permit oxygen to penetrate deep into the mud, tilling the marsh. The Marsh Crab also benefits the marsh by returning 47% of the energy in its food to the sediment surface, where it is exported on the next high tide.

Do not mistake these square-backed crabs for female fiddler crabs, which can easily be differentiated by their long-stalked eyes. In fiddler crabs the eyes originate from the center of the front, rather than the corners.

3

Seashores of the Gulf of Mexico

The Gulf of Mexico (Fig. 25) is a veritable sea, a thousand miles across at its widest point. Its entrance, from the Caribbean Sea, is the 161-km (100-mi.) wide Yucatan Passage; its exit, the narrower Straits of Florida opening into the Atlantic Ocean.

The South Equatorial Current crosses the Atlantic at the Equator and splits; its north branch, driven by the trade winds, piles water into the more or less enclosed Gulf. To escape, the water must pour through the Straits of Florida as the Florida Current, the major component of the Gulf Stream, the most rapid of all ocean currents. The water entering the Gulf has been recruited from equatorial and Caribbean sources and is warm, salty, and tropical. Little of the Gulf's cooler and less saline water circulates out with the Gulf Stream, so that the Gulf of Mexico has its own distinct water characteristics. These are influenced by two major factors. Most profound is the flow of the Mississippi River on the north, bringing in fresh water as it drains almost half of the United States. In addition to the billions of gallons of fresh water pouring into the Gulf each day, the Mississippi brings the pollution from half a continent—the chemicals and industrial wastes from hundreds of cities and towns, the fertilizers and insecticides from thousands of farms—and *two million tons of silt every day*. The biological effects of the river's effluent are profound. The silt load is distributed throughout the Gulf by longshore currents and gyres, giant whirlpools miles across, creating a predominantly soft bottom throughout the region. The admixture of the river's fresh water in such voluminous quantities with the Gulf's seawater produces brackish or estuarine conditions throughout most of the Gulf. However, at its two outer edges, the Mexican coast and Cape Sable off Florida, tropical or desertlike conditions prevail and salinities are at oceanic levels.

The Mississippi's daily influence is compounded by seasonal effects. In the spring, when the river is in flood, salinities throughout the Gulf are drastically reduced. In fall and winter minimal flow from the river and evaporation caused by the hot sun produces an increase in salinity. The variation over a few days may reach 19 ‰ (The scale ranges from 0‰ to 35‰, with zero representing fresh water and 35 ocean salinity)—more than half the total possible range.

Temperatures also vary considerably. In the summer temperatures along the shore may reach 30.5° C (87° F); in the winter ice may form a thin layer on the water's surface and temperatures decline to near freezing. The average temperature range of the Gulf as a whole is 11° C (52° F) to 30° C (86° F).

The short-term and seasonal variations in salinity and temperature can be drastic, making biological conditions in the Gulf of Mexico stressful. Sediments are predominantly suffocating silt and other small particles brought in by the Mississippi River over thousands of years. While the greatest water depth in the Gulf is about 4000 m (13,000 ft.) the depth of sediment on the bottom is greater than 9100 m (30,000 ft.)—*sediment depth is greater than water depth*. Nearshore the sediment is constantly suspended by waves, making the water murky and cutting down light penetration.

On the other hand, the constant introduction of minerals from the central U.S. dissolved in the Mississippi's water adds nutrients to fertilize the water, bringing about rich plankton growth.

Fig. 25. Surface currents in Gulf of Mexico, September to November. Thickest arrows indicate velocities of more than 24km (15 mi.) per day; medium arrows 13–22km (8–14 mi.) per day; thinnest, 8–11km (5–7 mi.) per day.

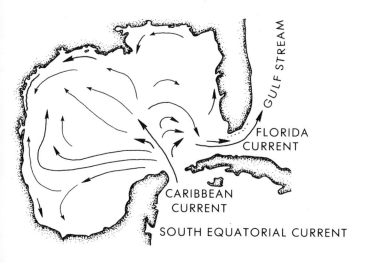

Add to this the products of the decay of marsh grass from the Mississippi delta and the peripheral marshes of the Gulf, *in toto* one of the largest salt marshes in the world, and you get a picture of intense fertility. So, for the organisms that can withstand extreme variations in salinity, temperature, and turbidity, the Gulf of Mexico provides lavish sustenance.

Characteristics of Gulf Shores

The tributaries of the South Equatorial Current enter the Gulf off the Yucatan Peninsula and then fork. A major component flows northward through the Straits of Florida as the Florida Current. The rest of the flow creates a complex series of currents and eddies resulting in a predominantly northward and westward flowing nearshore current along the shores of Texas and eastern Mexico as well as the shores of western Florida and Alabama. Currents along the Mississippi and Louisiana shores are influenced seasonally by the Mississippi River's flow; sometimes they shift eastward and sometimes westward.

Tides are likewise complex. In general, tidal range in the Gulf is small, from less than 60 cm (2 ft.) to 106 cm (3½ ft.). However, the effect of the tides is magnified by the extremely gradual slope of the shore. In some places the slope is so shallow that it approaches 30 cm (1 ft.) per kilometer, so that 32 km (20 mi.) from shore, depths are only about 6 m (20 ft.). The average slope is considerably greater than this. Beaches and marshes with such gradual slopes have extensive intertidal zones, so that even with a vertical movement of less than a meter, an intertidal zone 20 m (65 ft.) or more wide may be created. Tides are additionally complicated in that at certain times and places there may be a semidiurnal pattern (two high tides and two lows daily) and at other times or places, a diurnal pattern (one tide daily). Furthermore, wind patterns and the effects of the spring and fall equinoxes change the average tidal range so that highest sea levels occur during September and October and again during April and May.

A peculiar aspect of the tidal picture is the occasional "vanishing tide." Sometimes the complex interaction of the mixed pattern results in the superimposition of a high low tide over a low high tide (Fig. 26). The result is a very high tide that remains for a whole day, or for several days in bays where tidal action is exaggerated.

In order to choose the most auspicious time to wander the intertidal, consult local newspapers for the time of the major of the two tides in a semidiurnal environment, since it will have the lowest low of the day. Since the modest tides have relatively small

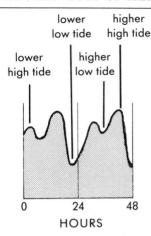

Fig. 26. Mixed tides in Gulf of Mexico. When a high low succeeds a low high, both can be of same height and a constant high-water condition remains over a tidal cycle, resulting in a "vanishing" tide.

effects on the amount of shore exposed, wind direction and strength often have a more important influence. In general, maximum shore exposure occurs in winter during major low tides that correspond with storms from the north.

Much of the Gulf shoreline is marshy. The south and mid-Florida Gulf shore has long sandy beaches and sandy barrier islands that are famous for good shelling. More or less tropical conditions prevail, and beaches are composed of fine calcareous sand. The shores of northern Florida, Alabama, and Mississippi are fringed with extensive marshes and are often protected by sandy barrier islands seaward. Louisiana shores seem to merge with the sea imperceptibly, as marsh extends into Gulf. Some of these marshes contain substantial forests of Black Mangroves. This is the northern limit of the range of these trees. Every 20 years or so a winter freeze kills most of the trees, but recolonization commences almost immediately, so that the vast expanses of brown, dead trees are soon replaced.

To the west of the Mississippi delta are found narrow nearshore sandy islands called cheniers. A chenier plain extends along the western portion of the Louisiana coast. Cheniers are low, narrow, flat ridges of sand located between mud flats, both landward and seaward (Fig. 27). A chenier never rises higher than about 5 m (16 ft.) above sea level and is only 50–500 m (164–1640 ft.) wide and up to 15km (6.2–9.3 mi.) long. The word chenier comes from the

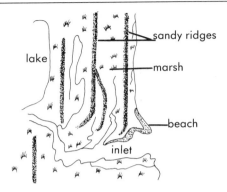

Fig. 27. A chenier island. Lower than a true barrier island, a chenier is really a marshy strandplain with sandy ridges that are often overgrown with oak trees.

French word *chêne,* meaning "oak," because these sandy ridges are dominated by stands of oak trees. The narrow ridges were formed by the westward transport of sand, silt, and clay from the Mississippi delta. As the mouth of the Mississippi changed its position over the years, the river's sediment tended to be deposited either more profusely as the mouth migrated west, or less profusely as it moved east. When the river mouth moved east, deposition stopped and the sediment was reworked by waves. During this time silt and clay were moved seaward and sand was left, forming the beach and sand ridges. Eventually the ridges rose above sea level. Cheniers are not true barrier islands because their position is more or less fixed and they do not migrate shoreward as do true barrier islands. Landward, one frequently finds ponds or lakes, as cheniers block the course of streams.

To the west of the chenier plain, beyond the influence of the Mississippi and its sediment deposits, lie the classical microtidal barrier islands of Texas. It has been said that Galveston Island is one of the finest examples of a barrier island; unfortunately, it is vulnerable to massive oil spills. Padre Island, at 180km (112 mi.), is the longest barrier island in the world. Though generally low, some of these islands rise to 80m (262 ft.). Grass-covered dunes lie parallel to wide sandy beaches, often with a 46-m (150-ft.) wide foreshore and an extensive backshore. Because of a low tidal range, a correspondingly reduced sand budget, and minimal wave action, a beach scarp and berm do not always form and the edge of the intertidal zone is simply marked by lines of flotsam and jetsam. The beach gently slopes up to the toe of the foredunes.

Large islands, such as Padre, have wide, wind-deposited flats landward; sand was blown from the island and settled in its lee. These flats lie just above the high-water mark and are inundated only during storms. There is enough moisture to sustain the growth of filamentous algal mats. In some places the green-covered flats stretch for kilometers.

Ancient barrier islands, laid down during the high-water level preceding the last period of glacial cold (about 25,000 years ago), lie parallel to present barrier islands. Some have, by this time, merged with the continental shore. Thus the coast (if you look seaward) consists of sandy dunes and hills, then extensive lagoons, and finally, thin, long, low, microtidal barrier islands that shelve off into sandy shallows.

The low barrier islands of the Gulf of Mexico are particularly vulnerable to storms. Hurricanes are frequent. Washover is common and inlets appear and disappear with frequency. Large inlets that are relatively stable are called "passes." Stability is due primarily to dredging and the construction of jetties to impede longshore sand movement. With the exception of a handful of passes, inlets are transient. During Hurricane David, in 1979, 40 new inlets were cut in Texas barrier islands.

Offshore, a series of bars form parallel to shore. Usually there are three bars. The outermost or largest lies about 300 m (1000 ft.) from shore. Its crest is about 1.8–2.4 m (6–8 ft.) below mean low water and the accompanying trough (to landward) is about 3.6–4.6 m (12–15 ft.) deep. The two inner bars are rarely less than 1.8 m (6 ft.) from the surface, so that one usually cannot stand on them. These bars may be more than a kilometer long. Each trough provides a secure habitat for shallow-water organisms such as the Five-holed Keyhole Urchin (Pl. 63).

Near-tropical conditions prevail during summer. But winter freezes bring reminders of the temperate latitudes of the Gulf. As a consequence of unique climatic conditions, Gulf of Mexico shores, excepting those of southern Florida and much of the Mexican coast, are considered warm-temperate. Thus the Carolinian Faunal Province, which extends from Cape Hatteras to Cape Canaveral, resumes again from around Cedar Key, Florida, throughout the rest of American Gulf shores.

A constant influx of tropical animals enters through the Yucatan Passage. Temperate forms are relics of past high stands when Florida was submerged and the Atlantic flowed freely across the whole area. Thus the Zebra Periwinkle (Pl. 12), the ubiquitous tropical snail of rocky shores, coexists on Texas rock jetties with the Marsh Periwinkle (Pl. 21), which has migrated from nearby marshes. The large Knobbed Whelk (Pl. 45), at the southern limit of its range here, coexists with a variety of tropical cockles, on which it feeds. And the Brown Rock Urchin (Pl. 14), so common on Massachusetts rocks, turns up frequently on jetties and even shelly mud flats in the Gulf. But the Common Mole Crab (p. 314) has been replaced by its tropical relative, the Puerto Rican Mole Crab (Fig. 40).

For the most part, Gulf inhabitants must be hardy. Temperature extremes seem to be the major limiting factor. Hardiness in this case does not have to be the ability to resist the infrequent freezes. Many inshore organisms migrate to deeper waters with more constant temperatures during winter, avoiding maximum stress from cold periods. Tropical species may flourish during summer, or even throughout a year or two if there is a mild winter. But their inability to migrate—there is no need to adapt to seasonal changes in the relatively constant tropics—eventually causes their downfall. Although summer populations of one or another tropical animal occasionally can become quite large under favorable Gulf conditions, they do not persist over the long term.

In short, the Gulf shoreline is inhabited by organisms characteristic of the disjunct Carolinian Faunal Province, except for southern Florida and Mexico, which are part of the tropical West Indian Faunal Province. Carolinian organisms are described in more detail in the previous chapter; subsequent chapters provide more information on West Indian organisms.

Animals of Sandy Beaches

Most of the animals found on Gulf shores have already been discussed under Atlantic beaches (p. 20). Those few found only in the Gulf (about 10% of all Gulf species) and others of particular interest will be covered below.

Gently sloping beaches of fine sand are bordered by low grassy dunes. Gentle waves, with small tidal range, lap the shore. Sometimes a ridge-and-runnel system develops, with a low ridge near the water line and a shallow pool behind it. The ridge is locally called a "swash bar."

The dominant animal of the upper beach is the Ghost Crab (Pl. 58). It is capable of bursts of speed up to 30 mph for short distances. This scavenger/predator will crush a Coquina clam in its claws or carry carrion back to its burrow just beyond the high-tide mark. If the decayed remains are too large, the crab will move in underneath its windfall. Dozens of Ghost Crabs once fled from their shallow burrows when the remains of a small whale were removed.

The Ghost Crab must return to the water within 48 hours to wet its gills. When engaged in this process the crab does not submerge itself. Instead, it tilts its body so that one side is immersed, crouching in readiness to dart up the beach at the approach of a predator from the sea.

At the water's edge are "herds" or "colonies" of Coquina clams, sometimes numbering in the thousands, all energetically burrowing or riding up or down with the swash (see p. 256). The sharply elongate gray Sallé's and Black auger snails (Fig. 29, p. 63) prey on the Coquina, along with any other animal that can reach the swash zone. The Lettered Olive snail (Pl. 42) will emerge from the sand, enfold a Coquina in the hind quarter of its foot, and burrow under, taking the hapless clam beneath the sand to eat. The two common swimming crabs, the Blue Crab (Pl. 53) and the Speckled Crab (Pl. 53), lie in wait for Coquinas at the seaward edge of the swash zone.

Animals living in the sand of offshore bars or in the protection of troughs between them are difficult to observe alive due to the murkiness of the water. Specimens may be washed ashore alive after storms, but more often only shells or other hard parts of nearshore animals give testimony to their numbers, which are often considerable. Common seashells of the northwestern Gulf Coast are listed below:

Common Bivalves of the Gulf Coast

Transverse Ark (*Anadara transversa*, p. 254)
Giant Atlantic Cockle (*Dinocardium robustum,* Pl. 43)
Elegant Disk Clam (*Dosinia elegans,* Pl. 41)
Atlantic Bay Scallop (*Argopecten irradians,* Pl. 43)
Channeled Duck (*Raeta plicatella,* Pl. 44)
Lined Tellin (*Tellina alternata,* Pl. 41)
Say's Tellin (*T. sayi,* p. 260)
Tampa Tellin (*T. tampaensis,* p. 260)
Texas Tellin (*T. texana,* Pl. 44)

Common Snails of the Gulf Coast

Scotch Bonnet (*Phalium granulatum,* Pl. 43)
Lettered Olive (*Olive sayana,* Pl. 42)
Lightning Whelk (*Busycon contrarium,* p. 231)
Apple Murex (*Chicoreus pomum,* Pl. 38)

The west coast of Florida produces an unusual abundance of seashells. Whole books have been written about the shells of Sanibel Island, for example. Most of the common shells will be covered in this volume, but the serious sheller should consult the Field Library section on p. 393 for a listing of comprehensive seashell field guides.

Many Florida Gulf beaches are narrow, relatively steep and with a conspicuous scarp, sometimes 30 cm (1 ft.) high, separating the fore- and back beaches. At the base of the scarp are deposits of shells, primarily cockles, up to 20 cm (8 in.) thick. In the swash are the ubiquitous Coquinas and way back on the berm one often can find what appears to be a zone of tan plastic objects. These are primarily Parchment Worm tubes, Onuphis Worm tubes, and disklike whelk egg cases. There is often a substantial runnel, sometimes hip-deep, on the forebeach. Live Egg Cockles may be found here.

Take the time, early one morning, to look at the predatory birds which are neatly zoned along the beach. The White Ibis is a large, goose-sized wading bird with a curved bill. It stands ankle-deep in the water, preying on small fishes and swimming and mole crabs and ignoring the abundant Coquinas just landward. The medium-sized Willets stand in the swash zone, eating innumerable Coquinas, and the small sandpipers run comically up and down the beach, apparently trying to avoid getting their feet wet, eating amphipods and other small crustaceans above the tide line and making a row of dashes in the wet sand with their beaks. Occasionally one will be unable to resist picking up a Coquina in its beak, but the clam is too large and is immediately dropped.

At low tide the sharp-eyed observer will see what appears to be an impression of disks—some up to 7.5 cm (3 in.) in diameter—lying flat on the sand, lapped by the edge of the sea. Closer examination will reveal individuals or groups of four or five Gray Warty Anemones (Pl. 8). Poke one on its oral disk and it will disappear under the sand with a squirt. This anemone eats mole crabs, Coquinas, and whatever else it can catch. The Onion Anemone (Pl. 8) is a similar predator on beaches of the northern Gulf.

The Puerto Rican Mole Crab (Fig. 40, p. 84) does not occur in the Gulf in the abundance characteristic of the Common Mole Crab on the Atlantic Coast, but it can be found in the swash if you search for it. The specimens you will find will be 2.5-cm (1-in.) long females. The male is tiny and clings inconspicuously to the female, eventually mating with her. Bright orange eggs may be seen on the female's abdomen in spring. Webster's Mole Crab (Fig. 12, p. 22) shares the swash habitat and lifestyle with the Puerto Rican Mole Crab. It is square-bodied and looks like the Purple Surf Crab but lacks the front claws and is exclusively a filter feeder.

Snails of the sandy beach include three carnivorous species precisely adapted to life in shifting, abrasive, surf-borne sand. The Southern Moon Snail (Pls. 3, 41) and the Lettered Olive snail (Pl. 42) both extend a disproportionately large foot to glide smoothly over the sand's surface or burrow beneath it. Both partially cover the shell with the fleshy, mucus-producing mantle, providing a slippery surface that helps the snail slide through

Fig. 28. A clump of Slipper Snails with a female on bottom and a male on top; others are changing sex.

the sand. The Olive burrows deeply and is rarely seen at the surface. Its polished, cylindrical, streamlined shell is adapted for burrowing. The Black Auger Snail also has a large foot for plowing through the sand, but it uses its foot also as a sail. The foot is expanded, flattened and placed in the backflow of the swash, which washes the snail into deeper water.

A peculiar filter feeder is the Common Slipper Snail (Fig. 28). It neither looks nor acts like a snail. The shell is a flattened oval with an inner shelf. The animal rarely moves. It attaches itself by its broad, flat foot to a rock or shell and pumps water past its gills, filtering out plankton. It is common on the northeast Atlantic Coast, where populations sometimes become so dense as to cover a rocky shore completely. In the muddy Gulf, these snails are at a disadvantage since they will smother unless they find a clean hard surface. Once a Slipper Snail finds a seashell or rock, it provides a home for the survival of smaller members of the species—on its back. But there is more than physical survival at stake: on a large Slipper Snail (3.8 cm — 1½ in. long) may be found four or five smaller specimens, each in a different phase of sex change. The largest member, a female, is always at the bottom of the pile. On her back are one or two medium-sized snails whose gonads are undergoing a transition from male to female. The topmost snail is the smallest—a male. This phenomenon of change of reproductive roles, protandrous hermaphroditism, produces females from males.

Living in discarded snail shells are the hermit crabs. The Long-clawed Hermit (Pl. 7) and the Green-striped Hermit (Pl. 52) are replaced on beaches by the Hairy Surf Hermit, which can be recognized by its hairy antennae and equal-sized claws. This hermit may be found in shallow water at low tide, among the tubes of Plumed and Onuphis worms.

The Sea Pansy (Fig. 29) looks like a purple mushroom. It attaches itself by inserting the tip of its peduncle (stalk) into the sand. It can inflate the peduncle, jamming it into the sand as an anchor while deflating its disk, reducing resistance to currents and remaining in place, even during rough weather. It can escape from its enemy, the Beaded Sea Star, by releasing its hold on the bottom, allowing the colony to be swept away by the next wave.

Two animals live in association with the Sea Pansy, crawling on its upper surface among the translucent polyps. The Twelve-scaled Worm (Fig. 120) is a commensal. It finds protection on or under the Sea Pansy, but is not harmful. Look for it also in the shell of the Flat-clawed Hermit Crab. The Sea-pansy Nudibranch (*Arminia*) actually feeds on the polyps of the Sea Pansy and can be considered a predator or a parasite.

Animals Washed Up on Shore

Animals that live in the troughs and sediments of offshore bars and beyond are rarely seen alive except when a fresh specimen is thrown up onto the beach after a storm. Scotch Bonnets (Pl. 43) have lovely whitish shells up to 10 cm (4 in.) long. These snails feed on Five-holed Keyhole Urchins. When you find a keyhole-urchin test with a 2-mm (1/16-in.) diameter hole neatly bored into it, you will know its demise was brought about by a Scotch Bonnet.

Sea Stars washed up on the beach include the Limp, Netted, and (off Florida) Nine-armed sea stars (Pl. 59) and the Spiny Beaded Sea Star (Pl. 59).

The two species of Sea Whip (Pl. 8) may be found cast up on the beach after storms.

As you walk the sandy intertidal zone you may see, bobbing in the water, what appears to be an onion. Close to a city, in polluted water, it may really be an onion, but more than likely it is the Onion Anemone (Fig. 29). When disturbed, the translucent animal withdraws its tentacles and inflates itself with water, allowing the current to move it over long distances. When near shore it may settle on the bottom and bury its column, leaving just the oral disk and its peripheral tentacles showing.

Two species of coral are sometimes washed up on Gulf beaches. Northern Cup Coral (p. 212) forms small colonies of up to 20 cups about 5 mm (1/5 in.) wide. The polyps are often extended during the daytime, and when seen underwater appear translucent whitish or pink. The closely related Rosebud Coral has larger cups up to 1 cm (3/8 in.) wide, and deep pink polyps. These corals need a hard, clean surface to grow on. In the more or less rock-free muddy Gulf,

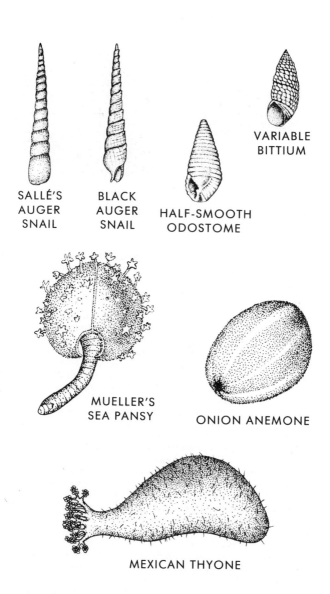

SALLÉ'S
AUGER
SNAIL

BLACK
AUGER
SNAIL

HALF-SMOOTH
ODOSTOME

VARIABLE
BITTIUM

MUELLER'S
SEA PANSY

ONION ANEMONE

MEXICAN THYONE

Fig. 29. Animals of Gulf shores.

Fig. 30. *Left:* Rubbery Bryozoan (p. 368); *right:* Common Bugula (p. 368).

only discarded seashells can provide a suitable substrate. Since they are not attached, storms wash up the shells with their corals. Along with the corals another group of animals with hard skeletons can be found randomly strewn above the low-water line. They look something like corals, but are different enough to be puzzling. Some look like delicately arranged, thin leaves of a plasticlike material; others have short branches; still others produce masses of rubbery, fingerlike branches. A hand lens reveals microscopic zooids, polyplike animals, each in a chamber of its own making. The complex skeletons and colonies are members of a phylum called Bryozoa (see Chapter 16). Off southern Atlantic and Gulf coasts the Rubbery Bryozoans (Fig. 30) are often cast ashore in colonies large enough to require two hands to lift. The colony is composed of grayish, often translucent flexible branches. The Bushy Bugula (Fig. 30) forms bushy, tufted, brown or orange colonies with branches only 1.6 mm (¹/₁₆ in.) thick. This species is difficult to differentiate from seaweed.

The bright orange Gulf Staghorn Bryozoan (Pl. 10) forms colonies of short, thick, abortive-looking branches, each with a hole at its end. Clumps reach 10 cm (4 in.) in diameter. A fresh colony, placed in a dish of seawater, will reveal a veritable jungle of worms, small crustaceans, and anemones living among the branches. Four million years ago this genus was a major contributor to the Miami Limestone formation underlying south Florida.

Small colonies, (7.5-cm—3-in.—wide) of curled, vertical leaflets wash up on the beach and dry out in the sun. When picked up they feel like fine sandpaper. These are colonies of the Lettuce Bryozoan (Pl. 10).

One of the strangest objects the beachwalker comes across in the fall is a flattened, lobate, amorphous mass of tissue that has the consistency of fresh liver. It can be more than 30cm (a foot) across and 2.5 cm (1 in.) thick. This is the compound tunicate (sea squirt) called Sea Pork (Pl. 5). It may be pink, red, slate blue, or dull gray. A hand lens may reveal many microscopic individual animals called zooids, in circular systems of 16–20, invisible to the casual observer. Some colonies may weigh 20 kilos (44 lb.). Many a beachcomber has come upon this nondescript animal and, in the quest to identify it, dredged from the inner recesses of his mind a memory of "whale vomit" or ambergris. When he remembers that ambergris is worth hundreds of dollars an ounce to the perfume industry because a tiny amount will help the perfume to retain its aroma for long periods, he stuffs the dead colony into a bag and attempts to peddle the smelly stuff! Unfortunately the perfume industry is not interested in rotting Sea Pork.

Gulf Salt Marshes and Mud Flats

Gulf Mud Flats

Mud-flat inhabitants along the Gulf include most of those discussed under Atlantic mud flats (pp. 37–39). A few tropical organisms persist along the Gulf, however. Most striking of these are the Great Land Crab (Pl. 58) and the Black Land Crab (Pl. 58). Both are confined to the southern extremities of Gulf shores: south Florida and south Texas and Mexico.

Various small transparent shrimps can be found in pools in the flats and among cordgrass stalks. These are Grass Shrimps (Pl. 7), which reach a maximum size of 5cm (2 in.). Juvenile commercial shrimp use Gulf marshes as nurseries before they reach adolescence and migrate into the open Gulf. Young American Pink Shrimp and White Shrimp (Fig. 126, p. 307) can be differentiated from adult Grass Shrimp by the shape of the abdomen. If the abdomen appears humped the animal is a Pink Shrimp or White Shrimp. If the abdomen is straight in profile it is a Grass Shrimp.

One of the triumphs that makes slogging through the mud flats worthwhile is the discovery of an Angel Wing clam, so named because the spiny valves (shells), when attached to each other at the hinge and spread apart, look remarkably like white angel's wings (see Pl. 43). The shells are huge (to 20 cm — 8 in. — long) but fragile. Their beauty is so great that they are prized by collectors, so discovery of a specimen is cause for celebration. But capture of a *living* Angel Wing is the real challenge. Walk the flats at low tide, close to the water's edge, and look for the striped opening of the clam's siphons (see Pl. 4). Once you have made this difficult discovery, kneel in the mud and gently dig down alongside the siphon, being careful not to touch it. Sooner or later, perhaps when your fingers are down 15 cm (6 in.) or so, you will inadvertently brush up against the siphon, which will immediately retract and disappear with an audible squishing sound. Now you feverishly dig with both hands, trying to follow the hole left by the retracted siphon. You will know you have succeeded if you feel the hole distinctly widen into a chamber wide enough for your whole hand. Grope a little further and you will find the soft retracted siphon and mantle and the hard spiny shell of the clam. By this time your arm will be extended into the mud to your armpit and, as you remove the clam in triumph, you will realize you are covered with mud from head to foot. You can celebrate your success by eating the clam, as is done in the West Indies, or by simply admiring it and replacing it in its burrow.

The common clam of salty bays in the northwestern Gulf and Florida is the Constricted Macoma (Pl. 41), a tropical species. It is a deposit feeder: it eats the mud and extracts nutrients from it.

A clam that looks like the edible hardshelled clam of the North, and is closely related to it, is the Southern Quahog (Pl. 44). It usually lacks the purple inner border found in the Northern Quahog, but otherwise looks similar to its northern counterpart. It is not usually abundant enough to make commercial clamming worthwhile.

In low-salinity bays, the Wedge Rangia (Pl. 43) is the most common clam. It has a brown periostracum (thin "skin" on the shell).

The common mud snail of the Gulf Coast is the Mottled Dog Whelk (p. 235). It becomes more and more common as one goes south from Cape Hatteras, gradually replacing, in the Gulf, the northern Mud Snail, whose habits it emulates (see p. 234).

Worms buried in the muddy sand include the ubiquitous Lugworm (Fig. 62, p. 162). The predatory sandworms, Culver's Sandworm, the Southern Clamworm (Fig. 120, p. 289), and the Long-palped Sandworm (p. 284) attack smaller worms. The prey is grasped with the "jaws" (horny denticles) projecting from the sandworm's muscular pharynx, which is everted and distended for the attack. It is then withdrawn into the digestive cavity by inverting the pharynx.

The yellow Eteone Worm (Fig. 120) reaches a length of 9 cm (3½ in.). It lacks jaws and is a deposit feeder. Another common deposit feeder is the blood-red, opportunistic Capitellid Threadworm (Fig. 120), which resembles an earthworm in appearance and habits. It is able to colonize disturbed areas and reproduces so rapidly that it is one of the first animals to appear in numbers on dredged sites or after an oil spill. Its presence, therefore, is useful in indicating when damaged habitats are beginning to return to normal.

A versatile worm is the Roofing Worm (Fig. 120). This animal lives in fine sand, below the lowest tides. It constructs a long tube, using flat, light-colored sand grains, arranging them like overlapping roof tiles with the free edges facing upward. The anterior end (head) of the worm is crowned with eight multibranched lobes that secrete mucus. Plankton sticks to the lobes and is channeled to the mouth. But the worm also places its feeding crown on the surface of the sediment to feed on detritus.

The most common scaleworm found on shells and in the crevices between them is the Boa Scaleworm (Fig. 120, p. 289). It has a double row of tan or brown fringed plates (actually overgrown setae) protecting its back. It attacks small crustaceans and worms, using its short, blunt proboscis (pharynx).

The mud flats do not reveal the multitudes of organisms beneath the surface. Huge colonies of Burrowing Brittle Stars (p. 347) live deep beneath the surface. At low tide there is no way of knowing they are underfoot. When the tide sweeps in, the brittle stars' thin, stringy arms slide up from the sediment, forming a forest of vertical threads undulating in the currents or lying on the surface of the mud. They are so common in South Carolina and Florida Gulf muddy sand flats that a few minutes of digging near the low-water mark will reveal several of these brittle stars, sometimes enmeshed in one another's long arms. The five arms are often 10–20 times as long as the diameter of the tiny disk, and about 1 mm ($\frac{1}{24}$ in.) thick at their bases. The arms pick up detritus or plankton on the surface and transport it to the mouth by cilia in a groove in each arm. If you place one of these brittle stars on the sediment it will literally disappear from view without moving its arms, as its modified tube feet excavate beneath it.

Seagrass Meadows

Tropical Turtle Grass invades the Gulf, all the way to its northern shores. But cold winters kill the erect blades, leaving only their underground rhizomes, which produce new leaves in spring. Thus Turtle Grass becomes deciduous in the northernmost part of its range. Shoal Grass (p. 142) and Widgeongrass (p. 142) may produce beds of their own—the Shoal Grass in the shallows and the Widgeongrass in brackish-water environments.

A host of shrimps live among the grass blades. These include juvenile Pink, White, and Brown commercial shrimp, Arrow Shrimp, Snapping Shrimp, Broken-back Shrimp, and the Grass Shrimp.

Spider crabs (Fig. 131, p. 317) are common, as are hermit crabs in the shallows. Off Florida two tiny hermits compete with the Long-clawed Hermit close to the water's edge. These are the Bonaire Hermit and the Banded Dwarf Hermit (p. 313).

The common clam of Gulf Turtle Grass beds is the Thick or Jamaica Lucine (Pl. 41). This heavy, solid, circular, yellowish clam reaches 5 cm (2 in.) in diameter. It is tolerant of a broad range of salinities and you will find its shell along the margins of extremely salty lagoons as well as brackish bays. Another common clam, the Cross-barred Venus (Pl. 44), has a distinctive lattice-like pattern on its shell.

Greedy Dove Snails (Fig. 32) are tiny, slender, glossy, and elongate, to 1 cm (⅜ in.) long, often with thin, wavy, tan, vertical lines on their shells. They may be found crawling up Turtle Grass blades or hanging from them by a thin strand of mucus. A similar small snail living on seagrass is the Variable Bittium (Fig. 29, p. 63).

The Virgin Nerite (Pl. 42), found in pools in salt marshes, is common on blades of Turtle Grass. It is more easily found at night or on cloudy days, when it is most active. You will know it is in the region at any time, however, since its shell is a favorite home for small hermit crabs, which are always knocking about at the edge of the sea.

Three large, predatory whelks take over from the Channeled and Knobbed whelks of the Atlantic shore. Unlike most snails, which have shells that coil to the right, the shell of the Lightning Whelk (Pl. 42) almost always winds to the left. To determine the direction of coiling hold the snail vertically, spire up. If the aperture facing you is to your left, the shell is left coiling (sinistral); if the aperture is to your right, the shell is right coiling (dextral). The Perverse Whelk (p. 231) is perverse because it may coil either way. It can be recognized by the large, triangular spines on the shoulder of the body whorl, and its black body. The Fig or Pear Whelk (Pl. 42) has a smooth, pear-shaped, inflated shell that always coils to the right. Its body is pale orange with black tentacles. Whelks do not drill holes in the shells of the clams they prey on. Instead, they wedge open the clam's valves with their own shell, insert the radula, which is located on a long proboscis, and rasp away the clam's flesh.

Sea cucumbers of the Gulf are easily overlooked when in their natural habitat. Only when many are washed up after a storm does one have an inkling of their abundance. The "hairy pear" of the Atlantic Coast has a small relative common in Turtle Grass beds of Texas. The Mexican Thyone (Fig. 29) reaches a maximum size of only 3 cm (1⅕ in.) and is much smaller than the Hairy Sea Cucumber (Pl. 65), which is common in the eastern Gulf as well as along the Atlantic Coast. On rare occasions you may see a tuft of feathery tentacles projecting from the sediment, picking up detritus and plankton in sticky mucus threads. Most of the time the animal is discovered accidentally, when digging for clams or worms.

A common inhabitant of seagrass beds is the Short-spined Brittle Star (Pl. 11). All brittle stars shun the light, and hide during the day. To find one, drop a piece of clam among the Turtle Grass roots and wait. Soon several of these gray-brown animals will slither up to the bait and cover it with their disks. Commercial crabbers consider them a nuisance, since hundreds of them crawl into the crab traps, attracted by the bait.

A small sea star is one of the few animals that is native only to the Gulf. The Brown Spiny Sea Star (Pls. 11, 59) often has orange spines on a brown background. Sometimes hundreds of quarter-sized juveniles will dot the Turtle Grass beds. Adults eat clams and snails.

Oyster Reefs

Conditions under which oysters flourish exist in Louisiana, Texas, and less frequently in other Gulf states. Under optimal circumstances, with regular influxes of fresh water to reduce salinities, subtidal oyster bars grow into massive reefs extending from land and growing across prevailing longshore currents. Where conditions are not optimal oysters will remain in scattered clumps or bars.

Over time the oyster reef can become so extensive that it creates a damming effect, diverting the longshore current seaward, stimulating growth at the seaward end. This causes branching at the outer end, but deprives nearshore oysters of plankton carried by the diverted current. Eventually the nearshore oysters die, leaving the reef separated from shore. Most reefs are spindle-shaped (tapered at each end) and "hogbacked" or mounded in the center. Eventually sediment accumulates on top of the mound and an oyster island is born.

The fauna of oyster reefs varies depending on salinity and temperature levels. While animals abound in the nooks and crannies provided by the irregular oyster shells glued one to another, population sizes and individual species are variable.

Brittle stars are cryptic animals; they thrive in situations where there are dark places to hide. The most common brittle star of the oyster reef is the Angular Brittle Star (Fig. 31), which can be recognized by the profusion of long, glassy spines extending from each arm like stiff hairs.

The Pale Anemone (Pl. 27) grows in fuzzy colonies of small individuals, none larger than 5 cm (2 in.). Close examination with a lens will reveal alternating long and short, transparent tentacles ringing the outer edge of the oral disk.

The small, brown Striped Sea Cucumber (Pl. 11) and the Scorched Mussel (Pl. 40) are dark colored and, though common, are hard to see. In low-salinity areas the Hooked Mussel replaces the Scorched Mussel.

The Smooth Porcelain Crab (Pl. 52), a small, olive-green crab with disproportionately large flat claws, will attempt to escape if you shake a clump of oysters.

Snails of the reefs include drills such as the Florida Rock Snail (Pl. 38), and Hays' Rock Snail (p. 69), and the Cross-barred Spindle (Pl. 42). Look for a tiny parasitic snail that attaches itself

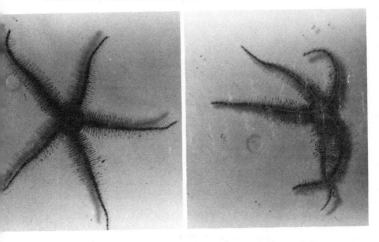

Fig. 31. Angular Brittle Star (p. 349). *Left:* Upper (aboral) surface; *right:* oral surface.

to the edge of the oyster shell and inserts its proboscis into the oyster's mantle cavity, feeding on tissues. When the oyster opens its valves to feed, it becomes vulnerable to the tiny parasite. There are two species of this snail in the eastern U.S. One, the Half-smooth Odostome (Fig. 29, p. 63) parasitizes mature oysters in the Gulf region. The other, the Two-sutured Odostome (p. 230) parasitizes mainly juvenile oysters in the Northeast.

The Common Slipper Snail takes advantage of the hard surface of oyster shells, and small mounds of these snails may frequently be found (see Fig. 28, p. 61).

Flatworms are among the most important oyster predators. They feed by sucking up oyster spat with a tube-like pharynx everted from the midventral surface. When juvenile oysters are not available, flatworms will eat tiny worms and other defenseless prey. The Zebra Oyster Flatworm (Fig. 157, p. 377), may be identified by horizontal brown crossbands on a tan background. The Oyster Flatworm (p. 377) is similar but lacks the stripes.

Larvae of the Yellow Boring Sponge (Pl. 5) settle on the shells of oysters and other bivalves. Each surviving larva becomes the progenitor of a large sponge. As the sponge grows it becomes a yellow-brown crust, but its main mass is inside the shell, lining holes it bores. Some Yellow Boring Sponges grow to be larger than a man's head, but deep inside you will always find the remains of a shell or other hard substrate. Shells riddled with holes are all that remain of the victims of these sponges (see Fig. 33).

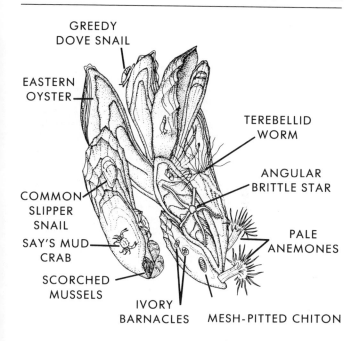

Fig. 32. Animals living on oysters from Gulf of Mexico. 1. Pale Anemone (p. 213), 2. Scorched Mussel (p. 257), 3. Angular Brittle Star (p. 349), 4. Common Slipper Snail (p. 233), 5. Mesh-pitted Chiton (p. 264), 6. Ivory Barnacle (p. 299), 7. Greedy Dove Snail (p. 230), 8. Terebellid worm (p. 281), 9. Texas Mud Crab (p. 324), 10. Eastern Oyster (p. 256).

Gulf Salt Marshes

The shores of the Gulf of Mexico are dominated by the silty mud brought down the Mississippi River for centuries and deposited in the delta and throughout the Gulf. Waves rework this fine sediment, depositing it behind barrier islands, cheniers, and along the continental shore. When the sediment lies below sea level seagrass beds appear. Their vertical leaves, fuzzy with tiny animals and plants adapted to spend their lives on the softly waving leaves, act as a giant filter, slowing the currents. Suspended sediment drops to the bottom. Eventually the sediment level rises until it lies above sea level. Land plants are able to colonize the exposed mud. At the water's edge Smooth Cordgrass survives daily inundation. Inland, Saltmeadow Cordgrass forms immense light green fields. But the river's influence permeates the region and, for vast areas, the dominant plant is the Needle Rush (p. 171), which thrives in brackish to fresh water.

The bayous of Louisiana and Mississippi are narrow, canal-like channels through the dun and green Needle Rush. One may paddle a small boat for hours, seeing nothing but walls of grass. Stand up in the boat and the scene of flat, meter-high grass is still unrelieved, except for occasional hummocks rising above the water, resplendent with Live Oak draped with Spanish Moss, barely able to wrest the tiny speck of upland from the marsh.

The bayou is shallow, rarely more than a meter deep, and the water is thick with aquatic plants. There is rarely a time when you do not see a V-shaped wake crossing from one side to the other. Usually it is created by the tip of the nose of a nutria, a large, muskrat-like animal reaching almost 23 kg (50 lb.), a foreign usurper that was introduced for its fur and has pushed out the native American muskrat. Often the sinuous, sinister wake of a water moccasin or a black water snake breaks the placid surface. Occasionally your paddle will disturb a 1.8-m (6-ft.) long Alligator Gar sunning itself just below the surface, camouflaged among the water plants. Startled, the huge primitive fish will explode through the water, rocking your canoe. Turtles and an occasional alligator sun themselves on the banks. As you pass under a small wooden bridge, the people lining its edges will lift their butcher-twine fishing lines to let you pass. At the end of each line is a chicken neck. The technique is to drop the tethered piece of chicken to the bottom. Almost immediately the line will grow taut. The fisherman slowly pulls in the line. As the end appears he slips a net under it and scoops up a Blue Crab. Even in the virtually freshwater marshes a hundred miles from shore, the Blue Crab thrives.

The salt water of the Gulf floats on the fresh water of the Mississippi River, creating a salt lens for a hundred miles inland. This salty water overflows into the marshes, creating brackish water conditions well away from the coast and spreading across the flat marsh, perpetuating an environment most suitable for the growth of Needle Rush. Over the year the grasses die and decompose into detritus. Some animals, such as commercial shrimps, frequent the marsh only as juveniles, using it as a nursery. Others, such as fiddler crabs, remain in the marsh their whole lives. Some eat the detritus, some the bacteria feeding on the detritus; some eat the tiny worms and crustaceans in the mud, others are predatory on larger organisms. A complex food web is created—all based on the grasses, their decomposition products, or algae that grows on the mud.

Fig. 33. *Left:* Clam shell riddled with holes produced by Yellow Boring Sponge; *right:* Two Florida Crown conchs lie among oysters, their prey. Gray mud covers their beautiful glossy brown-and-white shells. A Ribbed Mussel lies below snails.

In pools of water that are made hot by the sun, where evaporation can cause the salinity to rise to 40 ‰ (three times that of the surrounding brackish water)—and in the freshwater puddles left after the rain—you will find the Olive Nerite (p. 237). This snail can live in any habitat rich in detritus throughout the marsh. It is virtually heedless of salinity and temperature variations.

Tiny, elongate gray or tan snails of the family Hydrobiidae (Fig. 23) often appear, dotlike, in marsh pools, feeding on detritus. They are rarely more than 5mm (⅕ in.) long and consequently are eaten by killifishes, Blue Crabs, mud crabs, ducks, etc.

The ceriths, or horn snails, are represented by three species in Gulf marshes: the Plicate, Ladder, and Costate horn snails (p. 232). These may reach 2.5cm (1 in.) in length and are easily identified by the many vertical ridges covering each whorl of the elongate shell. All three species can coexist with Melampus snails on the marsh floor, eating detritus.

The globose Marsh Periwinkle (Pl. 21) can be found throughout our area, except for south Florida. These familiar gray snails may be festooned on grass stalks or, at low tide, may be seen scavenging for detritus on the marsh floor.

The Florida Crown Conch (Fig. 33) is a large, attractive, intertidal snail much prized by shell collectors. It may reach 10 cm (4 in.) in length and has a prominent crown of wide, flat, incurved spines on the shoulder of the body whorl, and horizontal brown bands on the shell. One usually see several at the edge of an oyster bar, covered with gray mud, looking little like the cleaned and polished shells for sale in shell shops. In fact, despite their large size they must be searched for diligently amid the welter of shapes of the oyster bar. Crown Conchs are sluggish predators of oysters. One study reported that a conch moves an average of 30–60 cm (1–2 ft.) per day, remaining quiescent when the tide is out. They are found primarily in Florida and have not been reported west of Alabama. A Caribbean relative, the West Indian Crown Conch (p. 236), is larger, more lustrous, and even more beautiful.

The Eastern Melampus (Pl. 42) is common on the floor of Gulf salt marshes under detritus where the air is saturated with moisture, and on grass stems. The Coffee-bean Snail (Pl. 22) may be found in south Florida mangrove swamps, often under litter around Red Mangrove trees. A third member of the family, the Bulla Melampus (Pl. 39), is smaller than the others and prefers Needle Rush marshes rather than cordgrass marshes—that is, it favors less saline water. It may appear on the mud in great numbers—one observer estimated populations to be 4 billion per square mile of marsh.

Four clams divide up the available habitats in the marsh. The Carolina Marsh Clam and the Wedge Rangia (Pl. 43) favor brackish water, but the Rangia is almost invariably found subtidally and the Carolina Clam is common intertidally, especially in Needle Rush marshes. The Florida Marsh Clam (p. 259) prefers sandy areas and higher salinities. It is one of the few animals able to tolerate high-salinity pools near the shore, inhabited by Saltwort and Glasswort. The Little Florida Marsh Clam is the smallest (to 1 cm—³⁄₈ in. long) and most delicate clam. It lives under decaying vegetation or mats of algae near the surface in brackish marshes. It might be mistaken for juveniles of the Florida and Carolina Marsh clams, but they have thicker shells.

The most common mussel found in the marsh is the Ribbed Mussel (Fig. 21, p. 45), partially buried in the mud everywhere. Juveniles attach themselves to the roots of marsh grasses.

Crustaceans of Gulf Salt Marshes

The shrimp and crab species discussed under seagrass and Atlantic marsh inhabitants also move into the Gulf marsh at high tide, dig burrows in soft mud, or find dark, moist environments under algal mats or layers of detritus.

Juveniles of commercial shrimp and adult Grass Shrimp are common, as are the Striped Hermit Crab and the Blue Crab. Black-fingered and white-fingered mud crabs and marsh crabs honeycomb moist areas with their burrows.

The evolution of the fiddler crab has reached its American

Fig. 34. Balls of sand around burrow of Sand Fiddler Crab.

zenith in the mud and sand of Gulf marshes. No fewer than eight species have been described from our region. Some have extended their range from the tropics, some are more northern species, and a few seem to be local variants found nowhere else but in small areas of Gulf marshes.

Sand fiddler crabs (p. 337) can be identified from afar by balls of sand around their burrows (Fig. 34). These are remnants of past meals, where the sediment was strained to removed its detritus, which was then digested, leaving balls of cleaned sand.

The Panacea Sand Fiddler was described in 1974. It is similar to the Sand Fiddler and their ranges overlap in western Florida. Panacea, a small fishing village below Tallahassee, has both species, but further west, in Alabama and beyond, the Panacea Fiddler alone dominates all sandy marsh habitats. Differentiation between the two species is difficult. To the expert such differences as the manner in which the male waves its large claw to attract the female before mating delineate each species.

The Gulf Mud Fiddler (p. 337) is smaller than the Sand Fiddlers and lives in muddy areas. It can be differentiated from the Spiny-fingered Fiddler (p. 337) on the basis of the appearance of the male's large claw. In the Gulf Mud Fiddler the upper, movable finger is straight. The Spiny-fingered Fiddler's movable finger forms a distinct arc. Both species have two vertical ridges of tubercles on the inner palm of the large claw. The Sand Fiddlers lack both ridges. The Red-jointed Fiddler (p. 334) is at least one-third larger than the other species. It is found on mud in freshwater upper reaches of tidal marshes or along the banks of rivers. The joints of all legs have distinct red bands.

The Gulf Mud Fiddler (p. 337) has a green-tinged blue stripe on the front margin of its carapace. It is able to tolerate a wide range of salinities and may occur with the other fiddlers in nearly fresh to salty habitats. It is the most common species in Mississippi and Alabama salt marshes.

Rock Jetties and Wharf Pilings

Hard surfaces are at a premium in the muddy Gulf. Manmade substrates have made it possible for animals formerly confined to occasional seashell habitats to have a population explosion. Organisms that were once rare are now abundant on the rocks of jetties and on wharf pilings.

A whole succession of animals appears on pilings soon after they are erected. First come the barnacles: the Fragile Star Barnacle (Pl. 16) forms a gray crust in the upper intertidal; individuals of the Ivory Barnacle (p. 299) spread over the mid- and lower intertidal like pox. Oyster spat settle and soon a dense thicket of oysters and Hooked Mussels covers the piling. Feathery hydroids, bushy Bugula bryozoans (Fig. 30), and Pale Anemones (Pl. 27) colonize the surfaces of the oysters, softening their shapes into a fuzz-covered, sometimes indistinct, gray and brown mass.

Dominant on the subtidal areas of pilings, floating docks, and boat slips are the amorphous masses of the Pleated and Sandy sea squirts or tunicates (p. 375). Both are tan lumps crowded together into dense masses, often as many as 50 animals to a clump. Each is a sac with two siphons protruding upward, one (the incurrent siphon) sucking water in and the other (the excurrent siphon) acting as an exhaust port. Specimens are easily ripped from the piling. They live up to their name when disturbed—the body contracts and a stream of water squirts out the posterior siphon. To differentiate between the two tunicates, feel their surface. The Sandy Sea Squirt looks and feels as if it were made of sandpaper and often has encrusting animals attached to it, obscuring its shape. The Pleated Sea Squirt feels slippery and looks shiny. Vertical brown bands become visible at the entrance to its siphons when they open (see Fig. 84, p. 185).

White crusts strikingly interspersed among the dun-colored tunicates are a close relative, the White Spongy Tunicate (Fig. 85). The brown, purple, or black Variable Encrusting Tunicate (p. 190) and the chocolate-brown marbled crusts of the Bermuda Encrusting Tunicate (p. 190), cover hand-sized areas of piling.

Crawling on the solitary sea squirts is the orange or pink Sea-squirt Flatworm (p. 377). It seems to prefer feeding on old, weakened sea squirts and may reach 2.5 cm (1 in.) in length. Four or five of these flatworms will be revealed if you break up a clump of 20 or 30 tunicates. Sea-squirt Flatworms are found only in the northeast Gulf.

If you snorkel around pilings, be wary of the fuzzy hydroids covering everything. In the winter the Bushy Hydroid (p. 205) lends a pinkish color to oysters, mussels, and the piling itself. In the summer it is replaced by the Fern Hydroid (Pl. 15). This featherlike colony of polyps will release thousands of nematocysts when you brush by, causing considerable pain and raising red welts, so be especially wary during the summer.

Sponges add to the lumpy profile of the pilings. The Garlic Sponge (Pl. 5) smells strongly of garlic if a piece is broken off. Other sponges, such as the Yellow Boring Sponge, the Red Beard Sponge, and the tan, yellow, brown, or olive Crumb-of-bread Sponge (Pl. 5), often are so abundant that they seem to smother other attached organisms.

The flowerlike American Warty Anemone (Pl. 28) is common in the lower intertidal and subtidal zones. It has a thick column with scattered orange dots and three rings of greenish tentacles around the margin of the 5-cm (2-in.) wide oral disk.

With the advent of shore management, rock jetties have become substantial, long-term habitats. Animals and plants find protected niches among the rocks, but they are subject to wave shock, scouring, sudden variations in salinity, and low winter temperatures.

Two tropical snails reach their northern limits on Gulf rock jetties. The Striped False Limpet (p. 241) looks like a Chinese peasant's hat with brown stripes radiating from a pale gray crown. It is considered "false" because it breathes air, using a lunglike apparatus instead of gills. It will drown if submerged for long periods and thus is to be found high in the intertidal zone. The ubiquitous Zebra Periwinkle (Pls. 12, 39) also inhabits crevices in the upper intertidal, blending into the gray crusts of Fragile Star Barnacles (Pl. 16). During the day the periwinkles seek moist crevices and become widely dispersed. They feed at night. In early morning, before the sun's rays cause them to disperse, you will find them forming a narrow band just above the water line.

There is usually an empty zone of at least 30 cm (1 ft.) below the upper intertidal. Then, just above the low-water mark, oysters and their predators, the Florida and Hays' rock snails (p. 240), form dense masses. Both of these predatory snails look alike, but Hays' Rock Snail can be immense, reaching almost 13 cm (5 in.) in height. Dead oysters, each with a neat hole drilled in its shell, are evidence of the destructive power of these voracious snails.

Among the colorful tufts of Sea Lettuce (Pl. 34), Graceful Redweed (Fig. 67), and Petticoat Algae (Pl. 37) may be found the flowerlike American Warty Anemone (Pl. 28) and the spiny Brown Rock Urchin (Pl. 14). Crawling on the rocks near the water's edge are the Common Shore Crab (Pl. 56) and the brown, shiny, insectlike Sea Roach or Beach Slater (Fig. 123, p. 301). The Rock Anemone (Pl. 27) forms small colonies just below the low-tide line, often among clumps of Hooked Mussels (p. 257).

4

Caribbean and
Southern Florida Beaches

THE WEST INDIAN FAUNAL
PROVINCE

This chapter is designed to lead you from the Beach Grape and Manchineel trees on shore, beyond the high-water mark and across the beach, to the Turtle Grass beds of the lagoon.

Characteristics of Tropical Shores

Sand is the habitat of most beach organisms; as such it is the primary determinant of beach populations. But the sand itself is the product of the sea and marine life. In tropical areas, beach sand consists primarily of broken pieces of coral and calcareous algae, plus the tests (shells) of microscopic protozoa and much calcareous detritus, such as the spines of sea urchins.

Examine a pinch of sand in a dish of seawater under a hand lens. Among the tiny pieces of coral and calcareous algae you will see tiny, snail-like tests of amoebas called foraminiferans. This sand will look very different from the squarish quartz particles— remnants of surf-worn rocks—of northern beaches. Rocks of tropical shores, formed from ancient coral reefs, dissolve rapidly and contribute little to tropical beach sands.

The beach is divisible into two zones, a *foreshore* and a *back-shore* (see Fig. 35). The foreshore begins at an intertidal region, usually a small slope interrupted by a depression where waves break, called the *plunge point*. This depression moves up and down the beach depending on the tide and type of surf; on rough days it will be found farther up the beach than on calm days. The foreshore also includes the *swash zone*—the region where the weak outwash of the surf (swash) spends itself. There is a point at which the gentle rise of the beach levels off. This is the *crest of the berm*. Beyond this crest the beach becomes flat, although sometimes ridges (minor berms), formed during past storms, may be discerned landward. The zone from the crest of the berm to the

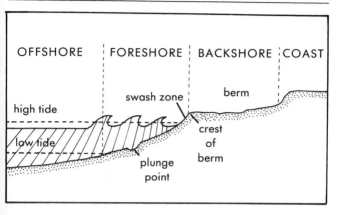

Fig. 35. Terminology of beach profile.

region where terrestrial plants and animals have formed a relatively stable community is called the *backshore*.

Sand can be an inhospitable environment. Where there is surf, strong currents constantly shift the sediment, threatening to suffocate any organism that stands fast to defy the surf. Or, unless it is a strong swimmer, it may be buffeted by the waves. Few species are able to challenge the powerful surf of an *exposed beach*. On the other hand, some beaches are protected by fringing or barrier-type reefs that break the force of the waves. Other beaches may be on the lee side of an island. Many beaches on the western shores of Caribbean islands are protected from the easterly trade winds. These beaches may be expected to have relatively little surf, since surf is primarily a function of wind-driven surface currents. Such low-energy areas are called *protected beaches*. Thus the leeward shore of an island usually is characterized by fine sandy beaches deposited by slowly moving currents, while the windward side often has exposed beaches and/or coral-fringed shores. Figure 36 shows the effects of trade winds on an island.

The fine particles that make up a protected beach are stabilized by mats of filamentous algae, preparing the surface for colonization by seaweeds and seagrasses. Red Mangrove trees often grow on protected beaches. Their root systems further reduce current velocity, producing an even finer sediment. The lagoons of barrier-type reefs are floored with fine sand because the currents are slowed down as they flow over the reef. Turtle Grass grows in these protected areas; it too reduces current velocity and acts as a sediment trap. The sediment also includes organic detritus— pieces of organisms (primarily plants) that have died and broken

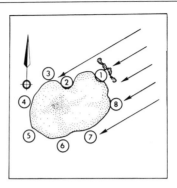

Fig. 36. Effects of prevailing winds on beach types. 1. Medium and fine sand in area protected by coral reef offshore. 2. Medium and fine sand in protected inlet. 3., 8. Coarse sand, deposited as unprotected coast bears full brunt of wind-driven currents. 4., 7. Coarse to medium sand and longshore currents set up by wind scour bottom. 5., 6. Medium to fine sand, as deposited longshore currents slow down, dropping tiny particles.

up. These decaying particles are so buoyant that they will not be deposited except by the slowest of currents. Thus the protected beach is rich in organic matter, providing much food for detritus feeders such as the thousands of Three-colored Hermit Crabs, which live in the elongate shells of horn snails (ceriths). You can watch these small crabs pick up tiny pieces of detritus with their claws.

But the very richness of this habitat threatens the inhabitants of the protected beach. The tiny particles of detritus are decomposed by bacteria, creating an anoxic zone just beneath the surface (see p. 37). Few organisms can survive in this oxygen-deficient zone, except for tube-dwelling and burrowing forms that can reach the surface to obtain oxygen or pump oxygen-rich water through their burrows.

The *semiprotected beach* has a small surf that infrequently shows substantial wave action, often only during storms. Such beaches are situated obliquely to wind and waves, or face the wind, but are partially protected by an incomplete coral reef barrier. Since wave strength on a semiprotected beach is greater than on a protected beach, sand grains will be more varied in size and particles will be more well sorted. There is a good supply of detritus and more oxygen is available to burrowing forms. As a result, this is usually the most highly populated beach type. There may be much overlap between types of organisms on different beaches, however, since most inshore organisms can adapt to a relatively wide range of environmental conditions. The boundaries of tolerance an organism is capable of in its adaptation to changes in the environment is called the organism's range. Animals and plants capable of withstanding a wide latitude of environmental variation usually have the prefix *eury* (from the Greek word *eurys,* meaning "wide") in front of each factor for which they exhibit high tolerance. For example, *euryhaline* means having the ability to withstand considerable variation in water salinity. *Eurythermal* means having the ability to withstand a wide range of temperatures. *Steno* (from the Greek *stenos,* meaning "narrow") means that the tolerance range is limited; *stenohaline* and *stenothermal* mean having narrow ranges of tolerance for salinity and temperature, respectively. Most organisms of the open ocean are stenohaline and stenothermal, living in very narrow ranges of salinity and temperature, around 35‰ (35 parts per thousand) salinity and 23° C (72° F). Most organisms inhabiting the tidepools and mud or sand flats are euryhaline and eurythermal, since a sudden rain squall may dilute the seawater, decreasing the salinity of the pool or flat to 15‰, and the noonday sun may heat the water trapped in a tidepool to 32° C (90° F). If you walk the flats in the afternoon, your feet will feel so warm that you will ask yourself how the animals you see around you can avoid being cooked.

The Landward Margin: The Fringes of the Beach

Stand on the beach and look seaward. Is there a roaring surf crashing on the beach? Is the surf about 20 cm (8 in.) high, or just a few shallow ripples? Determine which beach type (exposed, semiprotected, or protected) you are dealing with.

Walk along the vegetation-fringed upper edge of the beach. The short, gnarled trees with broad, plate-like leaves are Sea Grapes (Pl. 19). The tree with green fruit resembling miniature apples may be a Manchineel tree (Pl. 19). Its fruit is called the "death apple." If it looks like rain, don't seek shelter under this tree, as the runoff might absorb enough toxin to cause a skin rash (see p. 158).

Among the roots of the trees behind the beach are large burrows. On continental shores such burrows would be made by rodents or rabbits. But most Caribbean islands have reduced populations of vertebrates, either because they were never introduced to the islands or because in many cases not enough water is available to sustain them. On many Caribbean islands (such as Jamaica and the U.S. Virgin Islands), poisonous snakes were a problem, so mongooses were imported. They fulfilled their responsibilities well—too well! They ate all the snakes, and then went

Fig. 37. Trail of Soldier Crab in sand.

on to less exotic fare—birds, rodents, and everything else small enough to fit between their jaws. Now on islands such as St. John there are mongooses everywhere . . . and few other vertebrates except some nervous chickens.

Among the largest animals that occupy the niches that might have been filled by vertebrates are the crabs. The Soldier Crab (Pl. 58) is a large hermit crab with strong purple claws. Like other hermits, it can block the opening of its shell with its claws when it is disturbed (Fig. 38). This hermit often lives in the black-and-white shell of the West Indian Top Snail. As it drags the shell along, the crab leaves a characteristic trail in the sand (Fig. 37). Resist the temptation to keep one of these crabs as a pet. I once kept a pair in a glass tank and hand-fed them lettuce (they are vegetarians). They do not have the most amenable of dispositions and would "growl" at us when we approached. The mechanism used for sound production is unknown.

Fig. 38. *Left:* Soldier Crab in Magpie Snail shell; *right:* Crab withdrawn, large purple claw closes off aperture of shell.

Fig. 39. *Left:* Purple Surf Crab (p. 314); *right*: Ghost Crab (p. 333).

Soldier Crabs can live far from the water's edge. I have come across them on mountaintops a mile from shore. In fact, I claim the record for Soldier Crab altitude: I found one in the moist forest atop Sage Mountain, Tortola, at an altitude of 550 m (1800 ft.). These crabs must, however, return to the sea to spawn. The adults are nocturnal, but their young are active in the daytime, just above the strandline of the beach. The juveniles are about 1 cm (⅜ in.) long and live in nerite shells.

The Great Land Crab (Pl. 58) is a huge tan animal that lives in large burrows among the trees behind the beach. The burrows are deep enough to reach water and may measure 30 cm (1 ft.) across. If you peer into a burrow, you may see a male with a formidable claw 15 cm (6 in.) long. This crab is uncommon on highly populated islands because it is edible and used as the major ingredient of crab-back soup and other popular West Indian dishes. Any good restaurant in Puerto Rico will feature this crab in a dish called *juey* or *cangrejo*. From June through September the females migrate to the shore to spawn in the shallows, sometimes in a mass migration called a *corrida* in Puerto Rico. Each female can carry thousands of eggs under her distended abdomen.

Further toward the sea, beyond the vegetation but often just above the high-water mark, are conspicuous holes about 4 cm (1½ in.) or smaller in diameter. These are the homes of the pale gray Ghost Crab (p. 333). Look for tiny balls of sand at the burrow entrance, signifying an occupied burrow. This crab has black eyes on long erect stalks (Fig. 39 and Pl. 58). At night, you may see movement out of the corner of your eye. When you focus on it, it has disappeared, like a ghost.

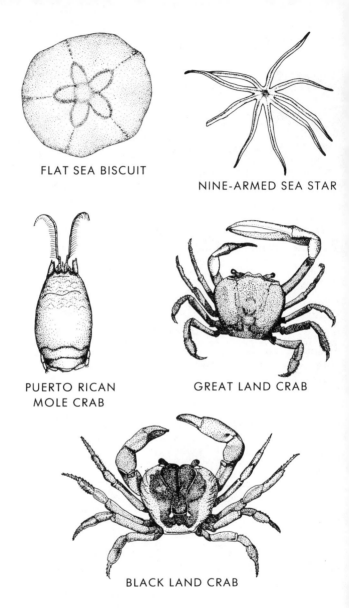

FLAT SEA BISCUIT

NINE-ARMED SEA STAR

PUERTO RICAN
MOLE CRAB

GREAT LAND CRAB

BLACK LAND CRAB

Fig. 40. Crabs and echinoderms of sandy shores.

Exposed Beaches

Crashing combers and swirling clouds of sand in each receding wave give testimony to the difficulty of surviving in this habitat. There are certain animals, however, that seem to thrive on this kind of stress; indeed, they cannot live anywhere else.

Two kinds of mole crabs live in the shifting sands at the edge of the surf line. They migrate up and down with the tide and are always found in the swash zone. If you dig where the waves barely wash over your foot, you may feel a squirming sensation in your hand as you move it under the sand. Strain the sand through your fingers and you may find one of these crabs.

The brown and white Cuban Mole Crab (Fig. 128, p. 315) is less than 2.5 cm (1 in.) long. It feeds on organic matter, living or dead, in the swash. Its body is oval and its flattened legs can be tucked underneath, so at rest it presents a smooth, streamlined surface to the rush of sand grains and water. The grayish Puerto Rican Mole Crab (Fig. 40) is similar. Instead of capturing food with its claws, it uses its long bristly second antennae to filter out organic detritus washing back to sea in the receding waves.

Rarer than the mole crabs is the Purple Surf Crab (Fig. 39). It also buries itself in the sand at the water's edge and forages for organic matter. Beware of its small, sharp claws and the nine marginal spines that extend from the orbit (socket) of each eye.

Mollusks of the exposed beach are the small, carnivorous, drill-shaped Gray Auger Snail and two small clams, the Caribbean Coquina and the Trigonal Tivella (all in Fig. 41). The

Fig. 41. Snails and clams of sandy shores.

GRAY AUGER SNAIL

CARIBBEAN COQUINA

TRIGONAL TIVELLA

STOCKY CERITH

wedge-shaped, 2.5-cm (1-in.) long Coquina may be found in "flocks" surfing up the swash and briefly burrowing into the shifting sand. The Trigonal Tivella is more sedentary. It can be recognized by its elongate, triangular shape and the purple blotch under its beaks.

Beyond the breakers Five-holed Keyhole Urchins abound. On Cuba, Jamaica, and other islands, a close relative, the Six-holed Keyhole Urchin (Pl. 64), takes its place. Both tan, fuzzy, flat urchins are pierced by holes called lunules that reduce the likelihood of surfing into the shore in the wash of a strong wave. Nevertheless, dead "sand dollars," as they are sometimes called, are strewn over the beach after storms, usually denuded of their tiny bristles.

The Nine-armed Sea Star (Pl. 59) also lives beyond the breakers. It has nine arms (not the usual five) covered with purple, velvety bristles.

Semi-protected and Protected Beaches

Semi-protected and protected beaches will be discussed together, since many animals that inhabit one type will inhabit the other. As you wander along the beach, linger where you find rocks and stones awash. If you turn over a rock, you may find a veritable jungle of animals on the underside, including brittle stars, worms, sea urchins, crabs, shrimps, and snails. Sand flats are another distinct habitat type, often part of protected beaches. These extensive shallow areas are common in Florida, the Bahamas, and tropical continental shores. They are relatively rare around Caribbean islands, which tend to shelve sharply into the depths, since they are the remains of volcanic cones.

Just below the waterline on a protected or semi-protected beach, the dominant form is usually the tiny Three-colored Hermit Crab (Pl. 52), which can be recognized by the bright blue-and-orange joints on its legs and by its brown-and-white spotted claws. The closely related, somewhat larger Antillean Striped Hermit (p. 311) has brown stripes down its legs and olive claws with white spines. The snails that most commonly contribute their shells as a home for the hermit crabs are the Middle-spined Cerith, the Stocky Cerith (Fig. 41), and the Black Horn Snail (Pl. 39). Only a few of the hundreds of elongate snail shells you find in the shallows will be inhabited by snails; most will be the adopted homes of hermit crabs.

As you walk the shallows, you may startle a crab, causing it to swim off rapidly. It will be the edible Blue Crab (Pl. 53) or a relative. These crabs have bright blue claws and an oval body terminating in lateral spines. The last pair of legs is modified into

Fig. 42. Shamefaced Crab.

flat, oarlike blades, used for swimming. When cornered, this crab assumes a fierce stance with wide-open claws, facing its antagonist. It is capable of rapid movement, so don't be its antagonist.

Two other crabs that lurk partly buried in the sand, waiting for prey, are the Speckled and Shamefaced crabs. The Speckled Crab, similar in shape and habits to the Blue Crab (see Pl. 53), swims in the shallows and often chases its prey, small fishes and worms. The Shamefaced Crab (Fig. 42) is more sedentary. Instead of fleeing when discovered, it will cover its head and protect itself with its massive claws, armed with a palisade of spines along the edge of each claw. It eats snails, crushing the shells efficiently with a can-opener arrangement on one claw.

Partly buried under the sand of the flats, with detritus on its upper surface for camouflage, is the Inflated Sea Biscuit (Pl. 62). It is heavy, thick, and round, about 10 cm (4 in.) wide, and covered with short, fuzzy spines. Bleached tests, with their huge, five-petaled echinoderm symbol, are found cast up on the beach or in souvenir shops. The less common Flat Sea Biscuit (Fig. 40, Pl. 62) is often only 2.5 cm (1 in.) thick, and has smaller petals.

Walking Along the Beach

A few inquiries will provide you with enough information to find long, secluded, palm-fringed beaches, ideal for shelling and exploration. As you prowl these beaches look for signs of the interaction between land and sea. Seeds will be washed ashore—

a coconut from some far-off place may have nurtured inside its fibrous husk a seed destined to begin populating an island. It may have lived for a year and floated hundreds of miles before fulfilling its destiny. Sea beans and other seeds (Fig. 69, p. 146) will be found among the flotsam and jetsam washed up on shore. The distinctive Sea Pencil, the elongated seedling of the Red Mangrove tree, sprouts wherever its pointed tip can gain purchase on sea-washed sand flats (see Chapter 9).

Look carefully along the upper edge of the beach. Notice the brown clumps of long-dead Turtle Grass festooned over the shoreside plants. There may be as many as four parallel ribbons of dead seagrass blades along the beach, separated by expanses of sand at least 30 cm (1 ft.) from each other. These ribbons of grass blades and other detritus demark the furthest reaches of the tides. The faded brown leaves among the shoreside plants were deposited by the highest tides of all, the storm spring tides—those tides which occurred during a new or full moon that coincided with a storm. Huge waves burst upon the shore, washing anything moveable up the beach into the terrestrial vegetation. If you examine this strandline you may find large seashells such as conchs and whelks, along with pieces of coral and other heavy objects that can be moved only by the strongest of the sea's thrusts.

The next row of leaves seaward denotes this month's highest spring tide. Then comes today's high-tide mark. Here the seagrass pieces may still be fresh and green.

Finally, at the water's edge, a faint accumulation of detritus moves up the beach with the rising tide, eventually to be deposited at the highest point reached by today's tides.

If you are shelling, you can adjust your search pattern to coincide with the tide lines. Look for delicate shells such as tellins (Pl. 41), coiled Spirula shells (Fig. 112, p. 270), or the sun-bleached tests of sea urchins (Pls. 63, 64) by walking along the tide line closest to the water, for thin-walled shells are easily destroyed and must be found soon after they are washed up on shore. If, however, you are looking for more robust shells, such as conchs or Turkey Wings (Pl. 40), or for sea beans (Fig. 69), walk along the upper strandline. They will most likely be found by poking among the detritus and terrestrial plants high up on the beach.

5

Rocky Shores of
Southern Florida
and the Caribbean

Rocky shores may vary from precipitous cliffs with huge vertical walls of rock to gentle slopes that seem to merge with the sea. Beautiful ocher and umber veins often run along the edges of high cliffs. Gnarled turrets and pinnacles, eroded by constant wave action, form grotesque shapes. On low, flat islands such as the Florida Keys, Bermuda, and Cozumel, Mexico, the predominant formations are highly dissected platforms of gray rock, often awash or splashed with spray.

Virtually all of the Caribbean islands originated through volcanic activity, but the igneous rock formed from molten lava lies buried under hundreds of meters of oolitic limestone, made up of the skeletons of coral animals and calcareous plants deposited over millions of years of submersion beneath the sea.

Few signs are left of the original volcanic activity. Here and there flat sheets of lava are seen congealed in their descent to the sea. At the western edge of Virgin Gorda are the mysterious house-sized boulders known as the Baths, a local curiosity. These are granite and were probably belched from some long-extinct volcano. They are geological incongruities, since the surrounding islands are composed primarily of limestone. There are other variations in the almost uniform covering of Pleistocene reef-limestone. Much of the eastern side of Barbados, for example, consists of exposed sedimentary rocks laid down as the mud and sand bottom of an ancient ocean. The covering of limestone has eroded away.

Most rocky shores, however, are the remains of ancient coral reefs filled in by pieces of calcareous algae and the skeletons of microscopic amoebas, the foraminiferans, all cemented together by intense pressures over time. The resulting limestone is highly soluble. It dissolves readily as the warm seas dash against it, as the pure rainwater runs down its sides, as the boring sponges and sea urchins grind holes into it. The result is a pitted, gouged surface, weathered gray and so eroded that it is often hard to stand on, with channels, gulleys, and pools that swell with water at each surge of the sea.

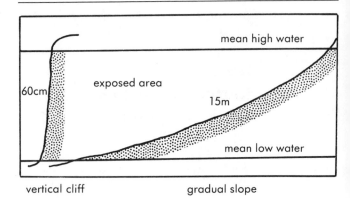

Fig. 43. Comparison of amount of shore exposed during tidal cycles. Vertical cliff (less than 1m — 3¼ ft. — exposed), compared with gradual horizontal slope (15m — 49 ft.) exposed.

The most important factors determining the nature of the substrate and its inhabitants are the tides. These can be *diurnal* (one high and one low tide per day), or *semi-diurnal* (two highs and two lows, or a 12-hour cycle), with a range, in the tropics, of about 60 cm (2 ft.) or less. This compares with a range of about 2.1m (7 ft.) in Long Island Sound, New York, and even greater ranges in more northern latitudes. But the small tidal range of equatorial seas does not mean that there cannot be extensive areas of shoreline uncovered with each tidal cycle. On the contrary, on flat, low-lying islands and coral cays of the Bahamas, Florida, and Central America, the gently sloping shores mean that the tides cover a wide horizontal range despite their limited vertical range. Figure 43 shows how a small vertical tidal movement can expose a wide area of shore.

As the drawing illustrates, the 60- cm (2-ft.) area of vertical cliff exposed in one tidal cycle corresponds to the exposure of 15m (50 ft.) of horizontal slope. Note that there is an additional increase in tidal range resulting from spring tides. The term *spring tide* is an unfortunate misnomer referring to extensive tidal movements that occur for a few days each month, corresponding to periods of full and new moon. At these times the sun, moon, and earth are more or less aligned, so the gravitational force of both sun and moon is maximal, pulling the oceans to their highest levels. The opposite effect, when tidal range is minimal (because sun and moon are at right angles to each other, partially canceling out each other's effects) is the *neap tide*.

The highest of all tides occur when storms or strong winds

coincide with spring tides. Then tides can be one to several feet above normal, inundating a relatively large expanse of gently sloping shelf and pushing the line of flotsam to its highest point on the shore. Terrestrial plants and animals touched by the salty water will die unless they can compensate for the additional salt. Thus, a very specific sort of maritime ecosystem has evolved in these particular ecological circumstances. The fringe of this region that is only occasionally wetted, rarely reached even by spring tides, forms the *white zone* (see below). Here the terrestrial plants and animals constantly encroach on the maritime organisms, but are held back by occasional inundations of seawater.

The rest of the slope is more regularly exposed to alternate wetting and drying. During low tides the intertidal organisms must withstand very hot temperatures (tidepool temperatures have been recorded at over 43° C — 110° F — at noon), intense sunlight, inundation with fresh water during rainstorms, and land predators. At high tide the ever-constant sea covers the organisms, and temperature and salinity are stabilized. But the crushing combers of storms and hordes of fishes, crabs, and other predators rush in to present their own dangers.

Differences among the various levels of the intertidal zone, from the area wetted only by spray to the region rarely exposed to air, result in corresponding zones of animals and plants, depending upon distance above sea level and degree of inundation. All rocky tropical shores have a similar pattern of habitation, which is depicted in Fig. 44.

There are three major ecological divisions of the rocky shore:

(1) The *upper platform* extends from the edge of the land vegetation toward the sea. The tides reach the upper part of this region only a few days a month, sometimes only once or twice a year. The most seaward edge is covered by tides part of every day.

(2) The *lower platform* is usually covered by a few centimeters of water and is rarely exposed.

(3) The *reef flat* is an area under shallow water and is almost never exposed to air. It slopes to depths that are never influenced by even the lowest tides.

The Upper Platform

The White Zone: This area goes far beyond the true intertidal zone, as its upper region may be wetted by the sea only a few times a year, during storm-spring tides. The flotsam line, which marks, with the sea's detritus, the furthest incursions of the highest tides, delineates the upper margin of the white zone. Here the land animals meet those whose evolutionary patterns of survival have driven them beyond the reach of marine predators to an amphibious existence. They live beyond even the spray of the surf,

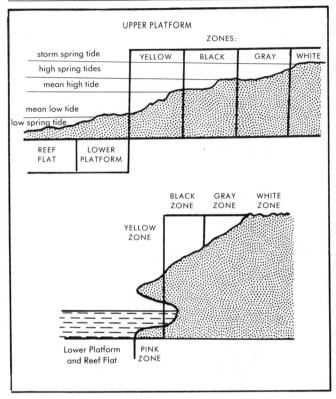

Fig. 44. Zonation of a rocky shore. *Upper drawing:* gradual slope; *lower drawing:* relatively vertical shore, showing undercut yellow zone.

yet they must return to the sea. Some, like the bizarre purple-clawed Soldier Crab, return only at egg-laying time. Its eggs and larvae require immersion in salt water for their survival. Others, notably the white Knobby Periwinkle (Pl. 39), visit the wetted regions of the intertidal zone at night when they feed; during the day, this snail finds protection several meters above the high-water mark. Together with the Soldier Crab and Knobby Periwinkle may be found ants, earwigs, scorpions, and spiders, the pioneers at the frontier of a truly terrestrial existence.

The most distinctive animal living in and above the white zone is the huge Great Land Crab (Pl. 58), which digs massive burrows among the trees and shrubs near shore. It has already been mentioned as an inhabitant of the beach fringe (see Fig. 40, p. 84). Another common crab is the Black Land Crab (Pl. 58), recognized by an irregular dark purple blotch covering most of its carapace.

Plants of the white zone are similar to those of the strandline at the edge of beaches. The White Mangrove tree is common. It can live farther away from total immersion than the Black Mangrove, which may be found here also but which is more abundant along the water's edge in muddy areas. Other trees that can withstand the salty exposure are the Gray Mangrove or Buttonwood (Pl. 24), and the Seaside Maho (Pl. 19), an evergreen tree reaching 9 m (30 ft.) in height, with large, bell-shaped flowers and heart-shaped leaves. The Sea Grape tree (Pl. 19) is a gnarled reminder of the force of sea winds. Its plate-sized, yellow- or red-veined leaves stream backwards away from the constant onshore breezes. On the exposed limestone platform these trees become low, prostrate shrubs. Only their leaves and flowers link them to the taller forms inshore.

The rock is least discolored here and is a weathered white or light gray. As the rest of the platform descends toward the sea, various agents act to discolor the surface or to cover it with distinctively colored growth, providing the basis for distinguishing several other zones. Going seaward from the white zone are the gray, black, and yellow zones.

The Gray Zone: This is usually the widest of the zones above the intertidal. Its upper portion may remain dry for days on end; its lower margin is close to the intertidal, and receives almost daily immersion. Some of the maritime plants of the white zone may be found here, as well as another species of mangrove. The Red Mangrove tree (Pl. 22), lives closest to the sea. It can form colonies that overgrow the gray rock, with its prop roots straddling outcroppings to reach the sea. Its long seedlings (Sea Pencils) hang from branches or grow from between rocks (see Fig. 79, p. 174). At the lower edge of the gray zone appear the hardiest marine algae, especially blackish Sea Moss, which grows in hollows and on the roots of mangrove trees (Pl. 36). Some of the animals of the gray zone are no longer dependent on the sea for daily immersion. Those that are will usually be found closer to the water's edge. Many animals migrate up to the gray zone, where they remain quiescent during the daytime, feeding at night. This, then, is a region of great stress for marine organisms that have forsaken the sea. They live in a lunar landscape of eroded, pitted gray rock, baked by the sun, battered by sudden rainstorms—but safe from the predators threatening them from the sea below.

The small snails are most distinctive. The Zebra Periwinkle (Pls. 12, 39) is about 1 cm (3/8 in.) long, with a pointed spire and gray zigzag lines on a gray-white shell. A snail that looks like a dingy brown Knobby Periwinkle is the Common Prickly Winkle

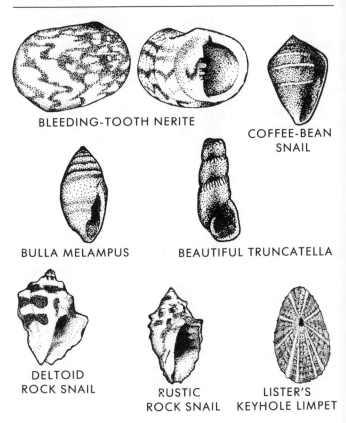

BLEEDING-TOOTH NERITE

COFFEE-BEAN SNAIL

BULLA MELAMPUS

BEAUTIFUL TRUNCATELLA

DELTOID ROCK SNAIL

RUSTIC ROCK SNAIL

LISTER'S KEYHOLE LIMPET

Fig. 45. Snails of rocky shores.

(Pl. 12). The False Prickly Winkle is also grayish brown with a series of beads and sharp nodules. But the smaller, more common Prickly Winkle has nodules in neat rows, while the False Prickly Winkle has scattered nodules.

The Bleeding-tooth Nerite (Pl. 12, Fig. 45) has a tan shell flecked with red and black and two characteristic "teeth" surrounded by a reddish stain along one edge of the large aperture. The Four-toothed Nerite (Pl. 12) is mottled white with streaks of black and red, and its four teeth are squared-off bumps on the margin of the aperture. You can recognize the levels of the gray zone by identifying the nerites. The Bleeding-tooth lives farthest from the sea, often reaching the upper gray zone; the Four-toothed is an indicator of the middle and lower gray zones; and the small, black-and-white Checkered Nerite (Pl. 39) is to be found in the lower gray and black zones, usually at the water's edge.

The snails mentioned above forage mostly at night, when they move downward toward the intertidal. During the day they retain moisture by closing their shells off with a horny operculum, which protects them from heat and desiccation. To see an operculum, remove a nerite from a rock and look for the hard black disk closing off the aperture.

Other animals have found a habitat that is dark and humid even in daytime. They live under rocks. Turn over a few and you will find many flattened "bugs" scurrying away, seeking darkness with what appears to be a sense of urgency. These are isopods, usually Beach Slaters (Fig. 123, p. 301). They are flesh-colored or brown. Although they are sometimes called Sea Roaches, they are not insects but rather crustaceans, related to the pillbugs you find under boards in terrestrial environments.

Together with the isopods are the air-breathing or pulmonate snails. These animals have a hole in their sides which permits entry of air into a moist chamber, a pseudo-lung. This is a fairly effective respiratory organ but it requires a humid habitat. The thin-shelled, olive-colored Eastern Melampus (Pl. 42) lives under rocks in Florida. Its close relative, the Coffee-bean Snail (Fig. 45 and Pl. 22) inhabits the roots of mangroves. The tiny Beautiful Truncatella (Fig. 45) is also found under rocks of the gray zone. It reaches a maximum length of 6mm (¼ in.).

Two types of dark, square-bodied crabs that are common under gray-zone rocks are the marsh crabs (p. 330) and the Round Shore Crab (Fig. 137, p. 332). Both measure about 1 cm (⅜ in.) across the carapace.

The Black Zone: This zone is wetted completely during spring tides and some high tides, but during much of the month it remains dry except for spray. There are usually cracks and fissures in the rocks and these are more often inundated. The color is not really black—it is more like a dark yellowish gray, probably due to an overgrowth of microscopic algae forming a film on the surface. This narrow zone may be only 21 cm (8¼ in.) vertically, or, on gentle slopes, as much as 5m (16 ft.) wide.

All of the previously discussed organisms can be found here, except for the Knobby Periwinkle. The Bleeding-tooth and Four-tooth nerites (Pl. 12) are less common, but a third species, the black-and-white Checkered Nerite (Pl. 39), becomes abundant. Two new snails are the tiny Lined Planaxis (Fig. 47) and the Black Horn Snail (Pl. 39). Both can be abundant, especially in tide pools, virtually covering the bottom. Isopods and the centimeter-long mottled gray, square-backed Common Shore Crab (Pl. 56) may be found under rocks.

Tiny, temporary tidepools have their own fauna. A beautiful small snail is the Zebra Nerite (Fig. 47, Pl. 13). Its maximum size is only 1 cm (⅜ in.), but its zebra-like black-and-white stripes and yellow aperture make it easily visible. The White-spotted Latirus Snail is 2 cm (¾ in.) long and has a thick, knobby shell. It is dark brown with eight large, white, rounded nodules at the periphery of each whorl. During periods of neap tide and drought, shallow pools can dry out, stranding thousands of Black Horn Snails. Their bleached shells, long emptied of living snails, are mute testimony to the vicissitudes of tidepool life.

The Yellow Zone: This is the truly intertidal zone. It is inhabited by many exclusively marine rather than amphibious organisms. Here you will find a steep slope that includes the seaward margin of the platform, and a more or less vertical or undercut ledge that marks the edge of the surf line. At the base of this wave-cut ledge is the lower shelf, a region of almost continuous immersion.

The powdery yellow-gray color is probably due to a diminution of the algae that darken the black zone. The algae of the yellow zone tend to be short, mosslike forms. If the slope is gentle and sunny the number of species may be small, due to the intense drying effect of the sunlight. On steep or overhanging platforms where there is more shade, filamentous fuzzy algae appear, especially Banded Weeds (p. 140) and red *Polysiphonia* algae (p. 140). Blackish Sea Moss algae (Pl. 36) is common, especially in fissures.

Tiny Fragile Star Barnacles (Pl. 16) appear as grayish spots, coalescing to form a gray-white bumpy crust on the rocks.

As you approach the lower, moister areas of the yellow zone two dominant colonial organisms make their appearance. A green alga that forms sheets of bubble-like cells is Encrusting Bubble Alga (*Valonia ocellata*, p. 134). Be careful not to step on these green crusts—they may be slippery. The other dominant form in some areas is the unusual tube-dwelling Irregular Worm Snail, which lives in calcareous gray-brown tubes. Its wormlike tubes are intertwined and cemented together to form 30-cm (1-ft.) high masses covering the rocks, protecting them from erosion. In more northerly subtropical waters, where coral does not compete with them, these mollusks form huge banks called vermetid reefs. Worm snails feed by entrapping plankton on retractable mucus threads.

The Ribbed Barnacle (Pls. 13, 16) first appears in the lower yellow zone. It looks like a miniature volcano. The lines (sutures) separating the plates in other barnacles are absent. Instead, a network of deep fissures runs from top to bottom. Each grayish cone may be 2.5 cm (1 in.) high and wide, much larger than the tiny Fragile Star Barnacle. The two species appear together (see

Pl. 16) where the tide wets the yellow zone relatively frequently; eventually the Star Barnacle, which first makes its appearance near the black zone, is superseded. Stands composed exclusively of Ribbed Barnacles mark the lowest margin of the yellow zone. When barnacles are submerged, their jointed arms extend from the top and sweep plankton from the water. Don't try to pry a barnacle from its rock with a knife; barnacles attach themselves with a glue so strong that several corporations have spent years trying to analyze it for commercial purposes.

In the yellow zone, the Checkered Nerite becomes dominant, the Bleeding-tooth disappears, and the Four-toothed Nerite appears infrequently. Black Horn Snail shells will often contain Three-colored Hermit Crabs, especially in tidepools.

Limpets—snails with conical rather than spiral shells—press themselves against the rock. Some are pulmonate (air breathers); the rest have gills and require water for respiration. Keyhole limpets, named after the shape of the opening at the apex of the cone, propel a stream of water over their gills and out the top opening. Lister's Keyhole Limpet (Fig. 45, p. 94) is about 2.5 cm (1 in.) long and has rough ribs radiating from the apex. The Knobby Keyhole Limpet (Pl. 39) has even coarser, nodulated ribs, and the Barbados Keyhole Limpet (Pl. 39) has fine ribs and a round apical hole surrounded by a green ring inside the shell. These limpets are hard to find on seaweed-covered rocks because they are covered with a dark, fuzzy periostracum.

Medium-sized snails, collectively called "drills" because of their style of predation, make their appearance on rocks in the lower yellow zone. The Rustic Rock Snail (Fig. 45) is about 3.7 cm (1½ in.) tall with a gray-brown shell and two spiral rows of blunt spines. The Florida Rock Snail (Pl. 38) and Deltoid Rock Snail (Fig. 45, Pl. 38) feed on mussels, oysters, and barnacles by boring a hole through their shells. The Tinted Cantharus snail (Pl. 12) has a smaller, smoother shell. The coarse blunt spines of the rock snail shells are mere nodules in this yellow-brown or blue-gray species.

The Dwarf Periwinkle is sometimes very common but may remain unnoticed because of its small size, although rocks may be peppered with this snail. Look carefully among the algae of wave-washed rocks for 6-mm (¼-in.) long, globose, shiny gray snails with revolving dark lines on their shells.

The common brown Scorched Mussel (Fig. 47) has finely radiating ribs and reaches 1.9 cm (¾ in.) in length. In the drier portions of the zone it can be found lining cracks in the rock. Lower down, it forms sheets covering the sides of boulders. Sometimes mixed in with the mussels, sometimes in colonies of its own, is the small, dark-edged Flat Tree Oyster (Pl. 40). The irregular, purple-brown shells may have a rippled outer margin; inside, a blue-white pearly layer does not extend to the margins. While mature specimens can reach 7.5 cm (3 in.) in length, smaller specimens, often with brown-rayed yellowish shells, are more common.

The first of the common chitons appears in the hollows and tidepools of the middle yellow zone. Chitons are the last word in sluggishness; compared to them a snail is a speedster. Chitons in a meter-square box drawn on a rock were still located within the perimeter of the square after a month. There is little need for speed, because chitons are well protected; they have a flexible suit of armor, formed of eight calcareous plates intermeshed in tough tissue. The loaf-shaped body is edged with a scaly or bristly girdle which is applied to the rock surface. This, together with the broad foot, can arch, creating a suction-cup configuration, effectively sealing the chiton to the rock if attacked. A chiton under stress can crawl so fast you can actually see it move. Chitons feed by means of a file-like "tongue" called the radula, which scrapes off algae covering the rocks.

The Fuzzy Chiton (Fig. 47) is so called because its black-and-white striped girdle is covered with bristles, distinguishing it from the other two common intertidal chitons which have scaly girdles. These are the West Indian Chiton and the Marbled Chiton (Pl. 16).

The Common Shore Crab (Pl. 56) is the 1-cm (⅜-in.) long, square-bodied gray crab, found in abundance under rocks in the black zone as well as here. Sally Lightfoot (Pl. 56) is a larger crab, up to 7.5 cm (3 in.) wide, with a squarish, brown, flattened carapace dotted with red and yellow spots. It can be seen on the sides of boulders and when disturbed will run with incredible speed across the rocks to hide in a crevice. Its range extends into the black zone, and it does not usually allow itself to be submerged. One often finds a molted exoskeleton of this crab on a rock (Fig. 46), looking for all the world like a living crab. Only when you laboriously sneak up and pounce on it do you find that the living crab has slipped out of its shell to grow a new, larger one, leaving the paper-thin molt behind to be crushed by your over-eager grasp.

The Surf Zone and Boulder-strewn Beaches: On exposed shores a surf zone extends from the mean low-water mark to the mean low water of spring tides. It is almost never dry, being wetted by the breakers if not completely inundated.

Boulder-strewn beaches offer sheltered, perpetually moist environments beyond the thrust of the surf even at the lowest tides, in the form of miniature pools and watery depressions under the rocks. The under-rock environment offers new opportunities to hunt for organisms. A special prize is the Brown Rock Sea Cucumber (Pls. 14, 61). It is usually hidden among the seaweeds in groups of as many as twelve, clinging to the sides of rocks. Its sausage-like body is a uniform light brown to black, and it has

Fig. 46. Molted skeleton of Sally Lightfoot crab.

large, densely branched black tentacles at the front. This sea cucumber is found only in wave-splashed areas. The yellowish green, sluglike Spotted Sea Hare (Fig. 47 and p. 247) is slightly longer — it commonly reaches 15 cm (6 in.) in length. It has black, leopardlike, circular spots on its skin, and two rabbit-ear-like rhinophores on its head, with which it smells the water. During the daytime these striking animals hide under rocks; at night they browse on algae in the shallows.

The Deltoid Rock Snail, as previously mentioned, prefers heavy surf and exposed rocky beaches.

Near the low-water mark, large boulders lie partially buried in the sand in a band about 2 m (6½ ft.) wide. This stabilized area forms the major habitat of boulder-strewn, surf-washed beaches. Under the boulders can be found a distinct fauna. The common West Indian Chiton and the Brown Rock Sea Cucumber adhere to the sides of the rocks. A crab that specializes in living under boulders is the pink or red Red Beach Crab (Fig. 134, p. 323); when frightened, it will stop moving, feigning death.

Many small snails live under the rocks. The Green-based Tegula (Pl. 39) has a smooth, round, cone-shaped shell about 2 cm (¾ in.) high, with an iridescent green tinge surrounding the large umbilicus and aperture. Black and Lined planaxis snails (Fig. 47) are tiny — to 1 cm (⅜ in.) long. The more common Black Planaxis has a large aperture, the outer lip of which has five faint grooves running backward over part of the last whorl. The Lined Planaxis is narrow, with brown bands on a tan background. White-spotted (Pl. 39) and Smooth dove snails are also about 1 cm (⅜ in.) tall, with glossy, spindle-shaped shells.

SCORCHED MUSSEL

FUZZY CHITON

ZEBRA NERITE

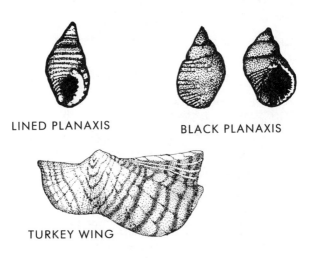

LINED PLANAXIS

BLACK PLANAXIS

TURKEY WING

SPOTTED SEA HARE

Fig. 47. Mollusks of rocky shores.

Gobies and blennies are small fishes that will slither away when you turn over a rock. Two common gobies are the large (to 15 cm—6 in.) Frillfin Goby (Fig. 51), a drab, blunt-faced fish with pelvic fins that form a sucking disk, and the smaller Bridled Goby, which has an orange streak extending backward from the eye and a vertical dusky bar at the base of the tail. Gobies are carnivorous. Many blennies have a gargoyle-like, blunt face; the mouth points downward, so the front of the head is almost vertical from eye to mouth.

The Pink Zone: Immediately below the lower yellow zone on vertical rock faces there is sometimes a zone of encrusting pink algae known as the pink zone or coralline lip. It is usually a white to bright pink band about 15 cm (6 in.) wide, composed of a smooth crust of encrusting calcareous red algae (p. 140), which projects several centimeters from the vertical surface. If this band exists, it will be easy for you to determine the upper boundary of the lower platform, for the bottom of the pink zone marks the level of the lowest spring tides. Only close examination of the pink crust with a lens reveals cells invested with chalky calcium carbonate. Some species form tiny cones or thin, cylindrical branches that bleach white when thrown up on the beach, and are mistaken for corals. A common branched coralline alga is *Goniolithon strictum* (Fig. 48). See p. 140 for a discussion of these unusual and important algae. Their remains contribute to the composition of coral sand, and they protect the shore by preventing erosion beneath the rock-hard pink crust.

Tube-building organisms are often dominant forms in the pink zone. The Horned Christmas-tree Worm (Pl. 26) forms bluish white calcareous tubes, sometimes in small groups, often overgrown by coralline algae so that only the six or seven red, white, and blue whorls of gills are visible projecting from the rock. When the worm is approached, the gills suddenly disappear, leaving only a reddish, two- or three-spined "trap door" or operculum visible to the careful observer. The other dominant animal of the

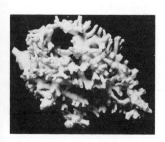

Fig. 48.
A pink coralline alga,
Goniolithon strictum.

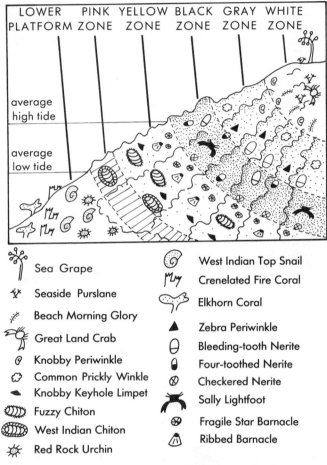

Fig. 49. Patterns of habitation on Caribbean rocky shores.

pink zone is the tube-building Irregular Worm Snail, described above as an inhabitant of the yellow zone. Other snails are the Knobby Keyhole Limpet, the White-spotted Latirus, and the Florida Rock Snail.

Bright yellow or green mats of Sun Anemones (Pl. 28) may cover intertidal or subtidal rocks, and three species of small, solitary sea anemones can be found in crevices extending upward to the yellow zone and down into the lower platform and deep water. They are the Rock, Maroon, and Red Warty anemones (Pls. 27, 28). Colonies of Pale Anemones (Pl. 27) sometimes cover the side of a rock (see pp. 213–214 for descriptions).

Along the outer margin of the zone, just at the upper edge of the surf, or in crevices constantly inundated by surges, are a number of animals that have wandered here from the zones above and below. These include the Red Rock Urchin (Pl. 62), the reddish brown Sargassum Anemone, the Barbados Keyhole Limpet, Three-colored and Smooth-clawed hermit crabs, and the Calico Crab. This small crab, about 2.8 cm (1 1/10 in.) long, is covered with brightly colored spots (p. 327). The Wide-mouthed Rock Snail (Pl. 15) extends its range from above.

Tidepools: A tidepool is a marine environment of maximum stress—a small, almost self-contained world at the mercy of both terrestrial and marine forces. The almost closed, highly competitive environment reminds one of an inner city slum. The crowded, impoverished, limited nature of the tidepool makes it necessary for many of its inhabitants to delineate a territory and defend it. The algal turf comprising the territory of a damselfish is as ardently defended as the inner city "turf" of a street gang.

Tidepools can be divided into two types: gray-zone pools with limited access to the sea, where replenishment with fresh seawater occurs infrequently, often only during spring tides; or yellow-zone pools, where frequent—usually daily—inundations are the rule. Normally fissures between rocks or low spots permit surges of seawater to enter at high tide. This highly oxygenated, turbulent flow maintains some semblance of the constancy of the open sea beyond. The degree to which the pool maintains its stability determines the stress to which its inhabitants are exposed.

A gray-zone tidepool (Fig. 50) may not be replenished with fresh seawater for days. During this time of isolation, evaporation causes the salinity to increase or torrential rains may dilute the seawater, reducing its salt content to brackish levels. The intense tropical sun causes daily changes in temperature rivaling those in salinity. A string of hot days can raise the pool's temperature to 49° C (120° F) and a series of cool nights can lower the water temperature to 15.5° C (60° F). Limited availability of food presents another problem. The number of niches available to tidepool inhabitants is reduced from that in the open sea, causing the ecological web to become a tangled mass of interdependencies. A classic study was done on a northern tidepool whose dominant carnivore was a species of sea star. All sea stars were removed by the experimenter. The result was not the expected increase in the number of species, now that the pool was freed of a major predator. Instead, one species, in this case a mussel, was freed from the pressures of predation; it reproduced so rapidly that it crowded out the other sessile (attached) forms, drastically reducing the species diversity of the pool.

Fig. 50. Gray-zone tidepool.

Conditions are so stressful in gray-zone tidepools that only the most flexible organisms can survive. The beautiful, 6-mm (¼-in.) long Zebra Nerite (Fig. 47, Pl. 13) is often the only inhabitant of tiny tidepools. The snails are crowded around the edges of the pool, sometimes in a thick ring. Black Horn Snails (Pl. 39) are commonly seen in shallow pools. Sometimes their dead, bleached shells litter the bottom, mute testimony to a drought or other natural disaster that pushed conditions in the pool to intolerable levels. Sometimes the tiny Dwarf Periwinkle *(Littorina mespillum)*, no more than 6mm (¼ in.) wide, is able to survive in great numbers. It is globose, smooth, whitish or pale brown, sometimes with rows of black dots. In pools where infrequent inundations with seawater allow fine mud to settle at the bottom, a number of algae take hold, including the fragile, beautiful Umbrella Alga (Pl. 34).

Yellow-zone tidepools can be several meters deep and wide. Rushing through a narrow inlet, the seawater scours the pool clean and strong currents may buffet the tidepool inhabitants. Small fishes dart to and fro, attaching themselves to the walls with suction disks to prevent being washed away. These are gobies, blennies, and clingfishes—torpedo- or tadpole-shaped predators with bulging eyes placed far forward on bulldog faces so that they have binocular vision. They press themselves against a vertical rock wall or sit on the bottom, propped up on stiff pectoral fins, so that they appear alert and ready for movement. And ready they are: when a small fish or crab approaches, the goby or blenny attacks. It is common for a goby to try to engulf a fish almost its own size. The prey fish struggles but the goby holds on; yet it

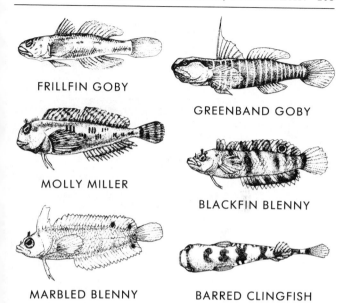

FRILLFIN GOBY

GREENBAND GOBY

MOLLY MILLER

BLACKFIN BLENNY

MARBLED BLENNY

BARRED CLINGFISH

Fig. 51. Tidepool fishes (1).

cannot swallow such large prey and after several long minutes the goby lets go and its would-be meal swims off, unharmed.

The Frillfin Goby (Fig. 51) reaches 15 cm (6 in.) in length, but is usually much smaller. It has two distinct dorsal fins and is drab tan, often with five broad dark bands crossing its back. A special find is the tiny — to 4.3 cm (1⅔ in.) long — Greenband Goby (Fig. 51). This beauty has bright green stripes on an olive background with a horizontal red bar running through the eye.

Gobies are among the few species of fishes that will spawn in large tidepools. The male digs a burrow under an empty seashell. If another male approaches, the first male exhibits a threat display, turning dark and extending its fins at right angles to its body. This same display attracts a female, which deposits her eggs, often upside down on the underside of the shell. The male then chases her away and guards the eggs, ventilating them with his fins, until they hatch after a few days.

Most tidepool blennies can be distinguished from gobies by the dorsal fin, which has either three parts or is one long single fin in blennies; gobies have two dorsal fins, the rear one being longer. One of the most common blennies, however, has such a deeply notched dorsal fin that it looks like a goby. The Pearl Blenny reaches 10 cm (4 in.) and has six pairs of dark vertical stripes on its sides. Rows of pearly white spots appear between the stripes. Tiny, feathery, antlerlike cirri project upward from between the eyes. If there is an additional fringe of cirri, extending from between the eyes backward toward the dorsal fin, the blenny is a Molly Miller (*Scartella cristata,* Fig. 51).

A common, tiny clinid is the Blackfin Blenny (Fig. 51). Its face is less blunt than that of the others and it is smaller overall, reaching a maximum size of 5 cm (2 in.). Its tail is transparent, so that in the water it appears tailless. Its long, single dorsal fin may have a black dot with a blue center, surrounded by an orange ring. Other tidepool blennies are the Coral Blenny *(Paraclinus cingulatus)*, the Puffcheek Blenny *(Labrisomus bucciferus)*, the Mimic Blenny *(Labrisomus guppyi)*, and the Marbled Blenny (Fig. 51). Most of the smaller species eat tiny crustaceans, such as isopods and amphipods, which abound in the algal mats on the walls of the pool.

Clingfishes resemble gobies in that they are tiny, tadpole-shaped fishes with sucking disks. But in clingfishes the sucking disk is a separate structure, not formed by the junction of the pelvic fins as in gobies. The dorsal fin of a clingfish is small and located toward the rear, unlike the long fins of gobies and blennies. The Barred Clingfish (Fig. 51) is about 3 cm (1¼ in.) long and has hourglass-shaped bars across its back. The color is variable, but is usually olive, black, pink, and white. The brown-and-white Padded Clingfish (Fig. 52) can be 7.5 cm (3 in.) long. It is large enough to swallow crabs, limpets, and chitons whole, and may be the dominant carnivore in a tidepool. The Red Clingfish (Fig. 52) is common in tidepools on exposed, windward shores. Its back is covered with reddish brown stripes and its ventral surface is pale red.

Damselfishes are the most common larger tidepool fishes. They are especially adapted to this environment because of their opportunistic, omnivorous food preferences. They will eat tiny planktonic animals drifting by, or small crustaceans, or even algae. Consequently, they have no trouble finding food—unless their population becomes too large for the pool. Each damselfish stakes a claim to a portion of the pool as its territory. Every square foot of pool is defended to the death. The territory supplies both food and egg-laying surface, and without its territory, a damselfish could not survive. Watch the damselfish population in a large pool. So much time is spent chasing other damselfishes that one wonders when feeding occurs. There is a constant flashing of dark flanks as the fishes perform threat displays or actually attempt to slash each other with their dorsal fins.

The Dusky Damselfish (Fig. 52) may reach 10 cm (4 in.) in length. This pugnacious, blackish, full-bodied fish will sometimes attack your toes if you dip them into the pool. A delicately lavender damselfish is the Beaugregory (Fig. 52). Tiny blue dots

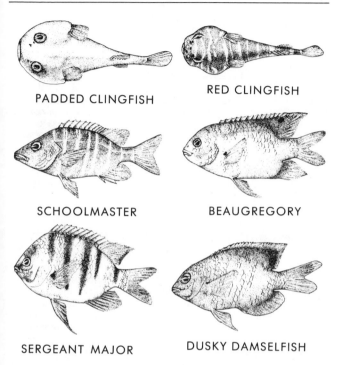

PADDED CLINGFISH

RED CLINGFISH

SCHOOLMASTER

BEAUGREGORY

SERGEANT MAJOR

DUSKY DAMSELFISH

Fig. 52. Tidepool fishes (2).

in rows line the rear half of the head and back. Sergeant Majors (Fig. 52) are common everywhere. Their yellow upper bodies crossed by five dark bars make them distinctive. These are shoaling fishes. They travel and feed together and are less territorial than the solitary species of damselfish. Groups of eight or ten tiny (2.5-cm—1-in. long) Sergeant Majors lend color to the pool. Larger ones leave for the open sea.

The most devoted territorial defender is the Schoolmaster (Fig. 52). It has a yellow body with a gray back crossed by a series of pale, narrow, vertical bars. It feeds at night, and spends its days attacking any animal that approaches the invisible boundary lines of its territory. A 7.5-cm (3-in.) specimen, placed in an aquarium, attacked the other inhabitants with such single-mindedness that they all perished. Only juveniles live in tide-pools; specimens larger than 10 cm (4 in.) are rare.

Sometimes small Ocean Surgeonfishes (with a broadly crescent-shaped tail) or Doctorfishes (with stripes and an almost straight tail) can be seen plucking algae from the walls of large tidepools.

The Red Rock Urchin (Pl. 14) and the West Indian Top Snail (Pl. 15) graze on rock walls near the water's surface. The Wide-mouthed and Florida rock snails (Pl. 38) commonly feed on the Star and Ribbed barnacles coating the intertidal portion of the pool's walls. Both the Black Horn Snail (Pl. 39) and ceriths may be found on the bottom; usually their shells are inhabited by Three-color or Antillean hermit crabs. If there is a well-defined entrance to the pool, chitons may wander in. The Fuzzy Chiton (Pl. 14) will be close to the surface, while Marbled and West Indian chitons may be seen if you peer into the lower depths.

Most large tidepools are surrounded by a fringe of brown algae. Sargassum, Three-cornered Hat, and Petticoat algae (Pl. 37) line the walls of intertidal areas. At greater depths the rocks are often grazed bare.

The Lower Platform and Submerged Rocky Shores

The lower platform is a region of almost perpetual inundation. It is fully exposed to the air only at low water of the major spring tides. Exposure occurs for two hours or so, around slack low tide. This means that the area will be a truly marine environment throughout the month except for, at most, two to four hours a day for perhaps six days a month. Some tides do not have equal cycles and some months have relatively weak spring tides, so total exposure is even less frequent.

If the coast is a gently sloping platform, sharply cut off in the lower yellow zone to form an undercut or vertical wall, the lower platform is usually a flat shelf beginning at the base of that wall. If the coast consists of vertical rock walls, the lower shelf is a narrow, vertical transitional region (see Fig. 44, p. 92).

The Red Rock Urchin and the edible whelk or West Indian Top Snail abound just below the surface on rocky shores. The urchin resembles a round, 5-cm (2-in.) wide pincushion, with a red test (body) visible between its robust spines (Pl. 62). It browses on algae and seeks protection in crevices, sometimes remaining in them for long periods, gouging out depressions as a result of its confined movements.

The West Indian Top Snail (Pl. 38) is an ingredient in chowders throughout the Caribbean and is sometimes uncommon because of overexploitation as a source of protein. The handsome black-and-white shell may be 10 cm (4 in.) high with a broad base. This snail has been extinct in Florida and Bermuda for the past 200 to 300 years.

The ark shells or bearded mussels are attached to the undersides of rocks by many strands of threadlike byssus. A brown hairy coat or periostracum covers the shells of living specimens. All shells are elongate with a long narrow hinge line and distinct ribs radiating from the umbo (beak); most shells are brown. The Turkey Wing (Fig. 47, Pl. 40) is the largest of the three arks, reaching 7.5 cm (3 in.) in length. It has zebra-like brown stripes. In Bermuda this edible bivalve is minced and baked in a piecrust with raisins, potatoes, carrots, and curry powder.

Irregular Worm Snails line the upper rocks with their sinuous tubes. Wide-mouthed Rock Snails produce a purple dye when handled (see p. 229). The snail's shell is dull gray, with a very wide, brown-rimmed aperture (Pl. 15). Hermit crabs abound at the landward edge of the platform, usually inhabiting shells of Black Horn Snails or Stocky or Ivory ceriths.

The conical star snails are unusually beautiful. The aperture faces down and is part of the iridescent or silvery base of the shell. The operculum is a convex white dimpled disk. The Imbricated (Pl. 38) and American star snails reach 3 cm (1¼ in.) high and have distinct white ribs on the shell. The Carved Star Snail (Pl. 38) has a blue-gray shell with hollow, folded-over spines extending from each whorl. The exquisite Long-spined Star Snail has a flattened, iridescent and white shell, with radiating spines and a silvery aperture.

Green and tan colonial anemones are among the marine organisms invading the lower platform at its seaward margin. The Green Colonial Anemone (Fig. 53, Pl. 29) forms green mats of

Fig. 53. *Left:* Green Colonial Anemones (p. 218); *right:* Ringed Anemone (p. 214).

fingerlike polyps, each with a fringe of tiny tentacles intermeshing with its neighbors' tentacles. Tan or whitish leathery mats are produced by the Encrusting Colonial Anemone. Each small polyp is only 1 cm (⅜ in.) wide, but the colony may cover a boulder. Polyps have fringes of tiny tentacles around each oral disk when expanded; when contracted they become slitlike (Pl. 29).

In knee-deep water you will begin to find the solitary Beaded, Ringed, and Giant Caribbean anemones (Pl. 28). The Beaded Anemone is so called because it has a flat, beaded oral disk surrounded by a fringe of many short, thick, pointed tentacles. It may be buried in sand or may be seen extending from a crevice. The Ringed Anemone (Fig. 53) has long, thin, tan, almost transparent tentacles encircled with white spirals. The tentacles are often seen extending in a large tuft from a crevice, but the body is invariably hidden. The spectacular Giant Caribbean Anemone can be 30 cm (1 ft.) across, with long, thick, tan tentacles tipped with pink or purple. Its body is usually orange, but may be purple or green.

A distinctive identifying feature of the lower platform is the yellowish green carpet of Laurence's Weeds (Fig. 67, p. 139) covering the rocks. Each branch has sub-branches with short, pale yellow to olive green, leaflike or tubercle-like projections. In protected areas the plants can grow to 10 cm (4 in.) tall, but here they form low, rubbery mats. At the seaward border of the yellow zone it mixes with the fuzzy filamentous algae.

The large algae of the lower shelf are usually golden green. Sometimes, however, tan Petticoat Algae (Pl. 37) covers rocks in sheets with its flat, pleated thalli, each banded with white calcium carbonate ribbons. Three-cornered Hat Algae (Pl. 37) forms bushes of vertical stalks of tricornered, golden, beadlike leaves, spotted with brown. Sargassum Weeds (Fig. 66, p. 135) have dark golden brown, elongate leaves that form bushy plants about 25 cm (10 in.) high. Many species have a profusion of small round bladders (see Fig. 66 and Pl. 37). Forked Sea Tumbleweed (Pl. 37) forms tan, filmy bushes and may be recognized by its bluntly forked leaves. Iridescent Banded Alga (Pl. 37) can form clumps of light brown, squared-off, elongate blades with iridescent green bands. Leathery Lobeweed can form a turf to 6 cm (2½ in.) high with its broad, light brown blades.

Flat sheets of Encrusting Bubble Alga extend down from the lower yellow zone. Clusters of miniature green grapes or tufts of pale green feathery branches, the Grape and Feather algae (Pl. 35), add interest to the algal turf.

The truly marine calcareous green algae so characteristic of tropical shallow waters, the Merman's Shaving Brushes (Pl. 34, Fig. 57), Hard and Soft fan algae (Pl. 35, Fig. 62), and Disk Algae (Pl. 34) begin to appear in deeper regions of the lower shelf, growing in sandy areas interspersed among the rocks.

Fig. 54. *Left:* Flat-topped Fire Coral, with Blue Chromis and Staghorn Coral in background; *right:* Elkhorn Coral.

Corals invade the deeper portions of the lower terrace. Crenelated and Flat-topped Fire Coral (*Millepora,* Pl. 33) form yellow, smooth, castle-like structures where depth permits vertical growth. Otherwise they form a bumpy tan crust on the rocks, with short vertical elements. On exposed coasts of the Bahamas and West Indies they can be so abundant as to color the shallows yellow, giving an alternate name to the region, the Millepora Terrace. Among the first true corals to appear is Shallow-water Starlet Coral (Pl. 33). It forms domed or flat colonies on rocks, less than 30 cm (1 ft.) wide, with evenly spaced, dotlike cups. Sometimes Elkhorn Coral (Fig. 54) survives so close to shore that parts of the colony are awash. Its thick, orangish, flattened branches can, together with fire corals, form an almost impenetrable barrier, preventing passage to the sea. Both corals can be bothersome; fire corals cause on irritating burnlike wound if you rub against them, and Elkhorn Coral can scratch your leg with its sharp edges.

6

Turtle Grass Beds of Southern Florida, the Gulf, and the Caribbean

Turtle Grass (Fig. 55) grows wherever there is protection from wind-driven currents and surf. It is abundant in tranquil lagoons protected by coral reefs and in coves. Its broad leaves reduce the velocity of the slowly flowing currents to almost nothing and even the tiniest particles, no longer buoyed up by the water's movement, drop to the bottom. In this manner, Turtle Grass beds act as huge filters, removing particles from the water and depositing them as a fine sediment. Many other plants find the calm water and soft bottom a suitable environment. In the shallows, often awash at low tide, Shoal Grass (Fig. 68, p. 143) becomes dominant. Creeping rhizomes give rise to short, erect stems bearing 1–4 thin flat leaves at each joint. The leaves are usually broken at their tips where they reach the water's surface. A parasitic fungus, *Plasmodiophora diplantherae,* commonly causes a swelling between the joints of the stem, giving it the appearance of a string of beads.

Shoal Grass cannot compete with the other grasses beyond the intertidal zone; it is replaced in knee-deep water by broad-bladed Turtle Grass or the thin, rounded blades of Manatee Grass (p. 142). Manatee Grass is usually found mixed in with Turtle Grass, but it is able to dominate in brackish water. In bays that have freshwater runoff or that receive the outflow of streams, dense, pure beds of Manatee Grass cover the bottom. In water more than ten meters (33 ft.) deep it sometimes forms extensive meadows.

Turtle Grass, however, is the dominant seed-bearing plant of the shallows. Its leaves can be 1.2 cm (½ in.) wide and present a suitable surface for colonization by other organisms. No fewer than 113 different species of algae are known to grow on Turtle Grass leaves, and numerous encrusting animals, including sponges, hydrozoan polyps, flatworms, and tunicates, spend their lives on the gently undulating blades, suspended above the danger of a bottom-dwelling existence (see Fig. 55). Plants that live attached to other plants are called *epiphytes;* animals so attached are called *epizoites.* The general term for organisms (plants or animals) living on the surface of plants is *epibionts.*

Fig. 55. Scene from Turtle Grass bed. Note Sea Egg urchin at lower left. Leaves of Turtle Grass are fuzzy with tiny animals and plants.

It is hard to believe that underwater plants can have flowers, but although it is capable of spreading by means of rhizomes, Turtle Grass has not forsaken sexual reproduction and the flowers that are its sexual organs. Pale white flowers less than 2.5 cm (1 in.) wide are produced in spring and summer. Only 1–5% of the plants have flowers, so finding them can be difficult. You must swim with your nose almost touching the leaves. The structures that look like spidery petals are really the stamens or stigmas. There are no true petals. Push the leaves aside and look near the base of the plants; male flowers are borne higher on the plant than female ones.

The algae growing among the grasses are among the most exotic and beautiful marine plants. Two fan-shaped algae project from the bottom on short stalks. Hard Fan Algae (Fig. 62, Pl. 35) has a thin, wrinkled, light green fan. It is highly calcified and moves stiffly in the slow currents. Soft Fan Algae (Fig. 62, Pl. 35) is sometimes heart-shaped, with a relatively thick, flat blade of spongy texture.

Merman's Shaving Brushes (Fig. 57, Pl. 34) are conical, flat-topped, or round-headed algae. Sometimes these species dominate the narrow transitional zone between the Shoal Grass and the deeper, Turtle Grass-dominated areas.

The most important algae here, as well as on the reef, are the Disk Algae (Fig. 62, Pl. 34). One species grows in prostrate, dark green mats, sometimes covering the bottom for several meters, excluding even the Turtle Grass. Fanworms, especially the Black-spotted Fanworm (p. 276), find refuge here, and the many spaces between the algal disks are havens for small crustaceans, worms, and sea slugs. Other species produce small, trilobed disks crowded onto several branches growing in one plane, or elongate, beadlike segments.

Grape and Feather algae belong to the genus *Caulerpa,* which has evolved an extraordinary array of shapes, including clusters of miniature grapes, Indian headresses, and so forth (Pl. 35). In Florida, the Bahamas, and the northern Caribbean the distinctive Ripweed (Fig. 56) is often mixed in among the other green calcareous algae. It has a short stalk topped by a columnar mass of small, vertical, scale-like plates.

Snorkeling over Turtle Grass can be exciting, as many exotic animals are found here. These "meadows of the sea" support innumerable browsers that eat the Turtle Grass itself or the detritus produced as the plants complete their life cycles and die. Even the rich, highly organic sand is eaten for its organic particles. There appear to be relatively few predators to mar the tranquility of this pastoral scene. Occasional flashes of light reflected from the flank of Great Barracuda (Fig. 59) signal the

Fig. 56. *Left:* Ripweed (*Rhipocephalus phoenix*).
Fig. 57. Merman's Shaving Brush (*Penicillus dumetosus*).

DUSKY ANCHOVY

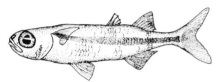

REEF SILVERSIDES

REDFIN NEEDLEFISH

BALLYHOO

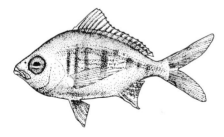

YELLOWFIN MOJARRA

Fig. 58. Fishes of the Turtle Grass bed (1).

death of a member of the clouds of Reef Silversides, Dwarf Herrings, or Dusky Anchovies (Fig. 58). The slender, silvery Ballyhoo and the long-jawed Redfin Needlefish (Fig. 58) patrol the area in small schools just under the water's surface. At night, they appear quite fierce in the beam of a flashlight, although they generally do not grow more than 30 cm (1 ft.) long.

Some fishes are capable of extracting food from the sand, taking in mouthfuls from which they strain the small bottom-dwelling animals. After each mouthful of sand has been gleaned of its inhabitants, it is released through the fish's gill openings. The Yellowfin Mojarra (Fig. 58) is the most common sand-eating species, reaching 38 cm (15 in.) in length. It is silvery and wide-bodied, with puckered lips and a deeply forked tail, and swims in small schools.

Usually there are small outcroppings of finger coral or Stag-horn Coral in the Turtle Grass bed. Around these you will find Sergeant Majors (Fig. 52, p. 107) and other damselfishes (p. 106), wrasses, such as the Slippery Dick (Fig. 59) or the Puddingwife, and juvenile French Grunts (Fig. 60, Pl. 25). The Spotted Goatfish (Fig. 60) may be seen feeding on small organisms buried in the sand, using the pair of barbels under its chin to stir up the bottom.

If you are lucky you may see schools of silvery, disklike Palometas or juvenile Permits in the shallows, or even the grotesque Lookdown, another silvery disklike fish, easily distinguished by its immensely elongated face.

A "tame" fish, which can be approached—but not touched—is the Porcupinefish (Fig. 60). It is fearless, for obvious reasons. If disturbed, it not only raises its long, sharp spines, but inflates to the size of a balloon, presenting the very picture of invulnerability. Its beaklike jaws are adapted for crushing snails. Two other fishes that can be approached in Turtle Grass beds are the Goldspotted Eel (Fig. 59), which has a creamy sinuous body covered with dark-rimmed gold spots, and the camouflaged Peacock Flounder (Fig. 60), whose iridescent blue-rimmed spots give it away to the observant snorkeler.

One of the most interesting fishes of the Turtle Grass bed is the Southern Stingray (Fig. 59). This flattened, slate-gray or brown fish has no bones and thus is a close relative of the sharks. It lies hidden under a thin coat of sand, with just its eyes and spiracles (gill openings) visible. It eats crabs, small fishes, and worms. If disturbed, it undulates the edges of its body in graceful, rippling movements as it glides away from you. If you step on it, it may embed its long, poisonous spine in your leg. But this rarely happens, as the fish usually retreats at the first sign of your presence.

The most dramatic bottom-dwelling animals of Turtle Grass beds are the Cushion or Reticulated Sea Star (Pl. 17) and the Donkey Dung Sea Cucumber (Pl. 61). Both animals are large: the

GREAT BARRACUDA

GOLDSPOTTED EEL

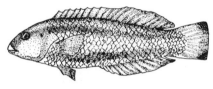

SLIPPERY DICK

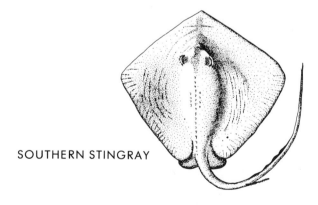

SOUTHERN STINGRAY

Fig. 59. Fishes of the Turtle Grass bed (2).

SPOTTED GOATFISH

PORCUPINEFISH

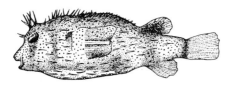

FRENCH GRUNT

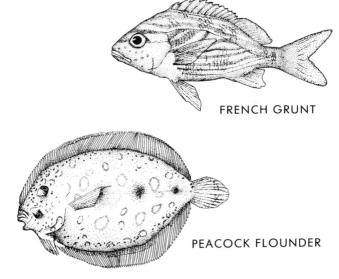

PEACOCK FLOUNDER

Fig. 60. Fishes of the Turtle Grass bed (3).

tan-orange sea star reaches a diameter of 41 cm (16 in.); the sea cucumber sometimes exceeds 51 cm (20 in.) in length.

The Reticulated Sea Star has a thick body covered with a netlike pattern of tubercles on its upper surface. Its young are olive-green. Although it is huge, its primary source of food is bacteria and other microscopic animals that live on sand or sea grass leaves. Most sea stars feed by turning inside out part of the stomach and extruding it out of the mouth over the prey. Digestive juices are secreted, dissolving the food which is then absorbed through the stomach wall. The Reticulated Sea Star gathers grass blades and scours them clean with its stomach, eating everything on the blades, then releasing them. Thus one of the largest inhabitants of the Turtle Grass bed feeds primarily on the smallest, bacteria. Only about 10% of the sea star's food consists of Sea Egg urchins and other large animals, which it pursues and envelops with its large arms.

The Donkey Dung Sea Cucumber looks for all the world like evidence of an indiscreet horse or donkey. It has a few warts on its ocher-yellow to dark brown upper surface. The deep rose (sometimes white) bottom or sole is flat. The anterior (oral) end is ringed with many short, tan tentacles with brushlike ends, used to shovel sand into the mouth.

Sea cucumbers have a fascinating lifestyle: they are deposit feeders, taking in sediment through the mouth in the center of the tentacular ring. Once in the gut, the sand is flooded with enzymes and its organic detritus is reduced to molecules that are absorbed through the gut wall. The remains, mostly shell fragments and sand grains, are released through the anus as distinctive, tubular fecal casts, visible behind most cucumbers.

If a sea cucumber is subjected to stress it will resort to an unusual defense mechanism: it will eviscerate, that is, eject its internal organs through its anus in one repulsive, rapid movement. If a predator attacks a sea cucumber it will trigger the evisceration process. Thus, the attacker is presented with a substitute meal (the entrails of the cucumber), and while it is distracted with consuming this easily obtained feast, the deflated sea cucumber is able to slink off to a hiding place in the Turtle Grass, there to regenerate new insides.

The Three-rowed Sea Cucumber and Five-toothed Sea Cucumber are also large, but they can be differentiated from one another as follows: hold the cucumber gently just beneath the water's surface and examine the flattened sole. The Donkey Dung Cucumber usually has a rose-colored or white ventral surface with contrasting dark brown, scattered podia (tube feet). The Three-rowed Cucumber has three distinct rows of brown podia, the central row widest. The Five-toothed Cucumber has numerous scattered, tan tube feet and, of course, five square teeth around its anus (see Fig. 146, p. 357).

The Three-rowed Cucumber is the common large species off Bermuda. The Donkey Dung Cucumber dominates Turtle Grass beds throughout the Caribbean and Florida Keys, although a similar, slightly smaller species, the Florida Cucumber, is abundant in southern Florida. The Five-toothed Cucumber is most common in the Bahamas. It offers a special surprise. If placed in a bucket of water that is frequently changed, it can be kept alive overnight. The next morning you might be one of the lucky few to see an iridescent Pearlfish (Fig. 149), which sometimes lives inside the cucumber. The fish escapes every night to feed and returns to its haven every morning, worming its way inside the cucumber, past the teeth and through the anus.

The Sea Egg (Pl. 62, Fig. 55) is a large black sea urchin covered with short, harmless white spines. Its eggs are eaten by West Indians, who have spread far and wide the tale of their value as an aphrodisiac. The procedure for preparing this healthful and stimulating food, should you feel the need, is to remove the eggs of several urchins and place them into half the test (shell) of a large specimen. Bake for 10 minutes at 205° C (400° F.), and garnish with lime slices.

Turn a live specimen over and look at the five white teeth at the center or oral area. They are attached to a complex structure of white bone-like struts called Aristotle's lantern, in the shape of an old-fashioned five-sided lantern. Thus the sea urchin is the first invertebrate to have invented "bones." The struts function in the same manner as do our bones: the muscles that move the teeth are attached to and pull against this structure, giving the tooth muscles the leverage needed to grind up Turtle Grass leaves. The similar, smaller Green Sea Urchin (Pl. 62) is usually green and white but can be pure white or tinged with red or purple.

The Long-spined Black Urchin (Figs. 61, 62) is king of the Turtle Grass bed. Although the test is smaller, this appears to be the largest of the four common urchins, because its very long spines give it an aspect of great size and ferocity. This urchin is truly fear-inspiring—its black, needle-sharp spines sometimes project more than 30 cm (1 ft.) from the test. The hollow spines have barbs, and should your hand be impaled on a spine, the pain would be like that of a hornet's sting. As if that were not enough, the mucus on the spines contains a poison and the tips of the spines break off in the wound. But these are absorbed after a few days and the pain disappears after about half an hour in most cases. The spines can be rotated by the urchin and will point at you if you hover nearby. All this notwithstanding, the urchin is virtually stationary, and it is easy to avoid.

Usually the Long-spined Black Urchin can be found in groups of ten, twenty, or more, in depths beyond 2m (6½ ft.) in daytime (see Fig. 61). One possible explanation for this "schooling" behavior relates to their search for shelter. Perhaps the urchins perceive black shadows and move toward them at daybreak, after a

Fig. 61. A group of Long-spined Black Urchins forming the characteristic daytime phalanx or triangle pattern.

night's grazing. These shadows represent the shelter of crevices in the reef, but as the urchin draws near, the shadow turns out to be another Long-spined Black Urchin, whose formidable spines provide precious little shelter. So they spend the rest of the day jockeying for position around each other, seeking shelter where there are only spines. Other urchins, in their daily migration back to the reef, are drawn to the scene by the double black shadow and join the group; soon there is a herd of urchins in a sandy area. All this maneuvering without real eyes! Furthermore, when we netted 50 of these urchins and dumped them on a pier, they all moved off in the direction whence they came. All this movement in one direction, by animals without a head!

You will not find Long-spined Black Urchins on some Turtle Grass beds, probably because they require a coral reef nearby where they can hide during the daytime. The fourth common sea urchin on Turtle Grass beds is the Club Urchin (Pl. 63), whose thick, blunt spines, draped with filamentous algae, project from under a rock or other shelter.

Two species of coral live on the sandy bottom of the lagoon, unattached. Neither participates in reef building. Ivory Bush Coral (Pl. 33) forms small, creamy white or olive drab, branching colonies projecting from or lying on the sand.

Common Rose Coral (Pl. 33) forms a small flat oval, about 5 cm (2 in.) long, with a tan or brown undulating rim. The polyps live inside the border. On the bottom of each colony is the remnant of a white calcareous stalk, attached to the bottom when the colony was young. At maturity the stalk breaks off and the coral lies free among the blades of Turtle Grass. Living on the bottom without a stabilizing attachment is dangerous, since waves can overturn these small colonies, threatening the polyps with suffocation in the sand. But they have evolved a defense mechanism. The polyps

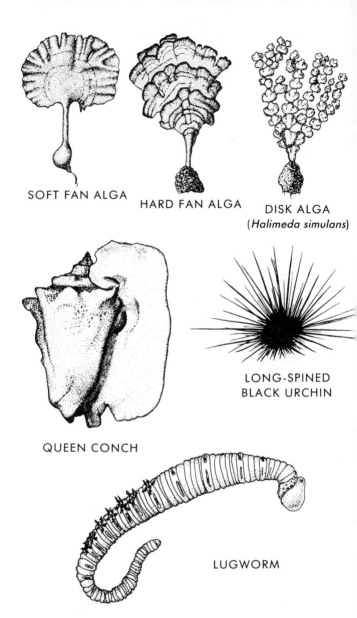

SOFT FAN ALGA

HARD FAN ALGA

DISK ALGA
(*Halimeda simulans*)

QUEEN CONCH

LONG-SPINED
BLACK URCHIN

LUGWORM

Fig. 62. Plants and animals of the Turtle Grass bed.

absorb water and forcefully eject it in unison, undermining the bottom and tilting the overturned colony. Extending their bodies and pushing on the sand, the polyps cause the whole colony to rock back and forth, eventually turning upright!

Fire coral is usually found on reefs or rocky areas. It is mentioned here because it often attaches itself to any hard object on the bottom and may be found in Turtle Grass beds in water less than waist deep, covering a discarded bottle, can, or a rock. It is important to recognize this coral because to brush against it means instant pain and a whiplash-like welt. It may be identified by its deep tan or yellow color, which contrasts with the white edges of its flat, vertical plates. It resembles a flattened sand castle with its battlements bleached white. If you suspect that a coral near you is a species of fire coral examine it closely with your mask on; if it is fire coral it will appear not to have the cups that are present in true corals.

In protected areas young colonies of Shallow-water Starlet Coral may be found among the Turtle Grass blades. They appear as 2.5-cm (1-in) wide balls with dotlike cups. This coral is capable of shedding silt, preventing the suffocation of its polyps.

A dramatic denizen of the Turtle Grass bed is the Queen Conch (Fig. 62), a large snail that reaches 30 cm (1 ft.) in length. The interior of the aperture is bright glossy pink and the shell is yellowish brown. Mature specimens have a thick, flared lip extending from the aperture. This conch is uncommon on the more populated islands because its meat is widely eaten and its shell is sold to tourists. In the Bahamas the shell is exported for cutting into cameos because of its smooth iridescent inner surface. Semiprecious pearls are occasionally found inside the mantle fold. Off Anegada in the British Virgin Islands, and some other "undiscovered" islands, these snails abound, but in Bonaire, Turks and Caicos, and some Bahama islands it has become necessary to establish conch hatcheries to attempt to reestablish decimated conch populations.

A shock is sometimes in store for collectors of Queen Conchs. When you turn the shell over, you may be confronted with the largest hermit crab of the West Indies, the Red Hermit (Pl. 52), thrashing its red claws covered with white-tipped tubercles. It can be up to 15 cm (6 in.) long, but is harmless and soon withdraws into its shell when handled.

Other mollusks inhabit Turtle Grass beds. Pen shells (Pl. 40) look like large arrowheads (15 cm — 6 in. — long) embedded in the sand. These bivalves will be half-buried, with the wide end gaping, facing upward. The shells are sharp and delicate, so be careful not to step on one. Buried beneath the surface, among the intertwined roots, are many kinds of clams, the largest and most common of which is the Tiger Lucine (Pl. 41). You will probably find its 5-cm (2-in.) long shell on the beach.

The Tulip Snail (p. 234, Pl. 45) is a cannibal, gliding over the sand in search of other snails. The smooth, graceful shell can reach a length of 15 cm (6 in.), and the snail has red flesh.

Holes in the Bottom: One cannot fail to be puzzled by the mysterious holes, ridges, and mounds scattered throughout the Turtle Grass bed. Any ridge or ripple in the sediment forms an inviting haven for a bottom-dwelling animal; eyes, antennae, or tentacles are usually visible at the edge of the darkness of that haven.

Burrowing forms make their own safe shelters, often living in colonies of mounds or burrows. Hover for a while over such a colony. You may see puffs of sediment periodically emitted from the top of a cone, like smoke from a semidormant volcano. These are the wastes of the inhabitant, a worm or shrimp, which reverses its position so that its posterior faces upward, defecates, and then quickly resumes its normal head-upward stance.

The Lugworm (Fig. 62) resembles a brown or green blunt cigar with many tufted red gills running down each flank. It favors sandy mud in shallow water. In spring, long gelatinous streamers of eggs extend from shallow depressions atop low mounds (Fig. 63), making identification easy. In the absence of these, gently disrupt the surface around the burrow opening with your hand. When the sand settles, if you do not find fecal casts and clearly defined mud walls, the mounds have probably been produced by Lugworms.

If the top of the cone is covered with tiny, brownish, longitudinally striated, rod-shaped fecal pellets, this indicates that the burrow was made by the Ghost Shrimp (Pl. 4). If you disturb the mound you will find branching tunnels lined with limy mud. The Ghost Shrimp prefers sandier sediments than the Lugworm.

As suggested by its name, the Ghost Shrimp (Fig. 126) is white; the absence of pigment is common among subterranean animals. The first pair of legs have claws, one longer than the other. The second and third pairs dig, drawing the sandy mud backward into a receptacle formed by another pair of legs or leglike mouthparts. When enough sand has been collected, it is dumped outside the burrow. The tunnels are complex and intertwined, and the work of extending and cleaning them is never ending. One researcher found that these shrimps are so highly adapted to living in burrows that if they do not feel walls around them they will die within a few hours. The shrimps eat mud, extracting bacteria and detritus as food. A number of "boarders" use the burrows of Ghost Shrimps as adopted homes, coexisting in the labyrinth of tunnels with the shrimp. The similar, less abundant Mud Shrimp (Fig. 126) may be found in the same area. Its body is hairy.

Throughout much of the West Indies and Bahamas, colonies of sand mounds 30 cm (1 ft.) high are built by the Burrowing Sea

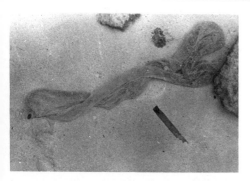

Fig. 63. Gelatinous egg mass streaming from Lugworm burrow at left. Mass is doubled on itself.

Cucumber (Pl. 61). This animal is tan with paired blotches of brown on its back. Its cone is often topped with the distinctive feces of sea cucumbers, cylindrical casts of sand grains and mucus (Pl. 17).

None of the aforementioned animals can be extricated from its burrow under water except through extraordinary effort. At low tide Ghost Shrimps and Lugworms can be dug up with a shovel, even though their burrows may be 60 cm (2 ft.) deep.

The Flats at Night: Walk in the shallows at night and you will be startled by some lively nightlife not mentioned in your hotel brochure. The flats become alive with animals that were invisible during the day. In water just a few centimeters deep along the shore is a sandy area populated in the daytime by tiny hermit crabs, horn and cerith snails, and a few other animals. At night your flashlight choreographs a grotesque dance as you sidle along, trying to avoid stepping on a carpet of anemones. These were either indistinguishable lumps of drab jelly during the day or they had withdrawn beneath the sediment surface. Now the anemones flaunt long, brown-and-white striped tentacles flowing in the currents. Look closely at the center of the disk. If there are many small tentacles surrounding the mouth, the animal is probably the Banded Tube-dwelling Anemone (Pl. 28) or the similar American Tube-dwelling Anemone (Pl. 28), which lacks stripes on its marginal tentacles. Touch a tentacle and the anemone will disappear, retreating into its now-obvious tube.

True sea anemones common on sand flats near shore are the Beaded Anemone and the Collared Sand Anemone. The Beaded Anemone (Pl. 27) has a thick fringe of short, dark, tan-and-white striped tentacles, with rows of tiny, white tubercles covering the oral disk. The Collared Sand Anemone (Pl. 27) has about 20 long, tan, translucent tentacles around the mouth; tubercles cover the rest of the olive and tan, scallop-edged disk.

As you continue your walk, various crabs will scuttle from one hiding place to another. A voracious enemy of the crabs is on the prowl: the Briar Octopus, or more rarely, the larger Common Atlantic Octopus (see Pl. 46).

The body of the Briar Octopus, about the size of a tennis ball, is perched alertly on its eight flexible arms. Your light stuns it. Now is your chance to capture a prize specimen! Simply grasp it by its body. This part is easy—what to do next is the problem. The octopus will suddenly awaken from its trance and wrap all eight sucker-covered tentacles around your arm. Its body will seem to shrink, eluding your grasp, and its slippery skin will become almost impossible to hold. Suddenly it is you who will be defenseless, and the octopus will press its advantage by crawling up your arm. Visions of it reaching your armpit will cause you to involuntarily flex your arm, and the octopus will sail off into the distance, landing with a splash. It is just as well, because octopods have small, upside-down beaks, used to bite and inject poison into their prey.

One of the most exciting nocturnal events to watch for in the shallows is the swarming and mating ritual of the Luminescent Threadworm (Fig. 117, p. 285). The female secretes a halo of bioluminescent mucus that surrounds her in an aura of brightly glowing greenish white light about 30 cm (1 ft.) wide. Within this ring she glows as an even brighter, undulating sliver of light. Male worms rush to this display, for it is over in less than 15 minutes. The ritual occurs just after the full moon from March through October—the second and third nights after full moon are most important. Swarming peaks 1¼ hours after sunset, when as many as six or eight luminescent females will be visible at any given moment.

Hidden under rocks during the daytime, Spotted Sea Hares (Pl. 49) may sometimes be found by the dozens out in the open at night, their 20-cm (8-in.) long, olive and black-spotted bodies glowing in the beam of your light. Some of us feel that you haven't lived until you have performed the ritual of picking up a 450-g (1-lb.) specimen to feel its Jello-like consistency and watch its harmless purple defense secretion run down your hands.

7

Seaweeds and Seagrasses

SEAWEEDS

The Marine Algae of the Southern States and Caribbean

A. R. Cavaliere and C. W. Schneider

Algae are almost endlessly diverse in size, shape, complexity, and color. Their names—green algae (Division Chlorophyta), blue-green algae or cyanobacteria (Division Cyanophyta), brown algae (Division Phaeophyta), and red algae (Division Rhodophyta) — give no indication of the possible variations that occur in the color of these plants.

Algae can be single-celled (floating freely as members of the plankton); grouped in colonies; simple, unbranched or branched filaments; or complex and elaborate plants having blade-like or tree-like forms. The difference between these and the higher plants is that the algae lack true roots, stems, and leaves. Some algae may be 45 m (150 ft.) long, yet there is usually or specific means of carrying food or other important substances from end to end. Often, each cell survives as an individual. The marine algae have adapted in various ways to this; in some attached forms there is a great distance from the leaflike to the rootlike structures, and as a result of this length large numbers of chlorophyll-bearing cells are exposed to light.

Algae thrive in definite zones along the shore; however, conditions at various levels favor one species over another. Each algae is adapted to meet two important environmental conditions: space utilization and exposure to the air. Some algae live completely uncovered and are wetted only by spray. Others are uncovered twice a day as a result of tidal movements. Many subtidal algae are never exposed unless they are torn free from their holdfasts and swept ashore by waves.

Because temperature changes occur slowly in the sea, climate generally does not play a major role in the distribution of algae. Shore conditions, the physical nature of the substrate, water depth, and the influx of fresh water contribute substantially to the presence or absence of seaweeds in an area. Algae that grow in the intertidal zone must be capable of surviving periods of exposure. The clearly visible zonation of seaweeds in the intertidal is really determined by the capability of particular algae to withstand regular periods out of water.

Zonation: Rocks in the intertidal zone are the most suitable habitat for most algae and usually harbor the greatest number of species. Many species may be crowded together. Others layer themselves like plants in a forest, with canopy and undergrowth forms.

The most terrestrial of the algae are those that occupy the upper intertidal zone. Most of these species are small, cropped short by grazing animals during spring tides. They have little competition due to the rigorous environmental conditions. The upper intertidal zone is itself separated into at least two zones based on color and type of algae present. Uppermost is the *black zone,* which is composed of microscopic blue-green algae, mixed with a few unicellular or filamentous green forms. The next zone ranges from green to green-brown or purple-brown in color and is composed of several red and green algae and, occasionally, a few species of brown algae.

Below, in the rest of the intertidal zone, is an entirely different group of algae, marked by an increase in diversity. Most of the surface is occupied by one species or another, each location offering suitable environmental conditions for a particular species. In many cases, a small holdfast is attached to the substrate while the major portion of the algal fronds, blades, or bladders floats in the water at high tide.

A third zone of algae, populated by all groups found in the other two zones, occurs below the low-tide mark. Here in the *subtidal zone* the algae are usually attached to hard surfaces, but some can survive on soft, sandy, or shelly bottoms. The number of algal species decreases on sand because of the difficulty the plants have in anchoring, coupled with the shifting nature of the sand.

The depth at which algae can grow is ultimately determined by the amount of light penetrating the water. The depth of light penetration differs locally and geographically. The less turbid an area, the clearer the water and the greater the penetration of light. Usually algae are more abundant—both in number of individuals and number of species—above a depth of 50 m (165 ft.). Although red and blue-green algae are physiologically best suited for life at the greatest depths, green algae occasionally break from the classical zonation pattern and are found at depths greater than 100 m (330 ft.) in warm seas, far beyond the range of red and blue-green algae.

Many algae, especially the reds, are epiphytic: that is, they are attached to other algae or to seagrasses. Most epiphytes are not anchored but are only superficially attached to their hosts. In many cases, a single host can harbor a dozen species of epiphytes, usually small, delicately branched algae.

Coralline algae: These algae do not look much like plants at all, more like crusts, scabs, and knobs. They grow on hard surfaces below the water's surface. Their shades of pink, rose, red, purple, or white remind one of paint capriciously daubed by some creative child. The corallines, which are red algae, contribute to the protection and maintenance of the reef by filling in and cementing spaces between coral heads. If it were not for these algae, some reefs would be continuously reduced to rubble by the destructive forces of boring animals and wave action. In some areas encrusting algae have probably contributed more to the build-up of coral reefs than have the corals themselves.

Many forms of green and a few red algae produce jointed, external or crystalline internal skeletons of calcium carbonate or silicate. When they are broken apart or eaten by herbivores, these algae become a major component of the fine sandy sediment upon which later generations of the same algae grow.

Algae are divided into four groups: green algae (Chlorophyta, below), brown algae (Phaeophyta, p. 134), red algae (Rhodophyta, p. 136), and blue-green algae or cyanobacteria (Kingdom Monera, Division Cyanophyta, p. 141).

Unless otherwise indicated, algae described below will be found in south Florida and the Caribbean. Many species extend their range to the Gulf and southeastern U.S., but extensive sandy areas and turbid water reduce their numbers and variety.

Macroalgae

Usually complex; branching, sheetlike, spherical. May have leaf-like, stemlike, or rootlike structures, but no true roots, stems, or leaves. Species of three divisions (phyla) are described below.

Green algae: Division (Phylum) Chlorophyta. Typically grass-green or yellowish green; structure variable. Chlorophyll is the dominant pigment. Not all green-colored algae are chlorophytes; some species of red and brown algae also appear green. Chlorophytes can be small, epiphytic, simple filaments, massive filamentous forms, or large blades.

Green Macroalgae

MBRELLA ALGAE *Acetabularia* species **Pl. 34**
Looks like *tiny umbrella*. Partially or wholly calcified. May be white, usually green. A thin stalk arises from lobed rhizoidal base, with parasol-shaped cap composed of a whorl of fingerlike branchlets. Cap to 2 cm (¾ in.) wide. Whole plant is a single cell.

A. crenulata is found in sheltered water on rocks.

LEAFY ALGAE   *Anadyomene stellata*
Bright green, crisp and leafy, translucent. *Fanlike ribs* formed by branched filaments barely visible to naked eye. *A. stellata* is common on hard substrates in protected shade where water circulation is good. To 10 cm (4 in.) tall and wide.

SOFT FAN ALGA   *Avrainvillea nigricans*   **Fig. 62, Pl. 35**
Flat, *fan-shaped head* arising from stalk. Fan composed of many dichotomously branched, usually uncalcified filaments. *Soft spongy texture.* Occasionally stalk and/or head may be calcified. *A. nigricans* is common on soft, sandy bottoms. To 15 cm (6 in.) tall.

GREEN HORSETAILS   *Batophora oerstedi*   **Fig. 64**
Clusters of soft green branchlets of two types: (1) wider fuzzy branches composed of *hairlike* or *feathery whorls;* (2) naked stems, upper third of each becoming a *long, darker green tuft,* sometimes covered with massed spheres. *B. oerstedi* in warm, sheltered areas just below low-tide level. To 10 cm (4 in.) tall.

GRAPE and FEATHER ALGAE   *Caulerpa* species   **Pl. 35**
Horizontal branching stolons attached primarily in sand, occasionally on hard substrates. *Erect branches* of various types arise from stolons. (1) In **Feather Alga** (*C. sertularioides*) erect branches have flattened lateral branches resembling feathers. (2) **Grape Alga** (*C. racemosa*) forms grape-like clusters. Many other shapes; branches to 15 cm (6 in.) long.

GREEN FLEECE   *Codium* species   **Fig. 64, Pl. 34**
Large, forked branches, with a felty or rubbery texture. *Each branch rope-like,* made up of tightly interwoven microscopic filaments; forked branching repetitive, terminating in blunt or rounded forks. Hard bottoms. Four common species: (1) *C. intertextum,* (2) *C. isthmocladum,* (3) *C. decorticatum,* and (4) *C. fragile,* which grows to 28 cm (11 in.) tall.

TUFTED JOINTWEED   *Cymopolia barbata*   **Pl. 35**
Bushy, partially calcified, with flexible, jointed branches. Each branch ends with a *tuft of bright green, hairlike filaments.* Usually grows on rocky or calcareous bottoms, especially in Bermuda. To 20 cm (8 in.) tall.

SQUIRRELTAILS   *Dasycladus vermicularis*   **Pl. 34**
Short, dark green, *columnar,* stiffly flexible, spongy. On rocks in sandy shallows, tidepools. Often partly submerged in sand. May form dense colonies on partially buried objects, often in surf near low-tide level. To 6 cm (2³/₁₆ in.) tall.

ROUGH BUBBLE ALGAE   **Fig. 64, Pl. 34**
Dictyosphaeria species
Subspherical, hollow, convoluted or irregular in shape. Forms mounds 2–12 cm (³/₄–4³/₄ in.) wide. Consists of a *single peripheral layer of large cells* (distinguishing these algae from *Valonia*). Two common species: (1) *D. cavernosa* (Pl. 34) and the smaller, less widespread (2) *D. versluyii,* which is attached to hard bottom in shallow water. *D. cavernosa* reaches 5 cm (2 in.) tall.

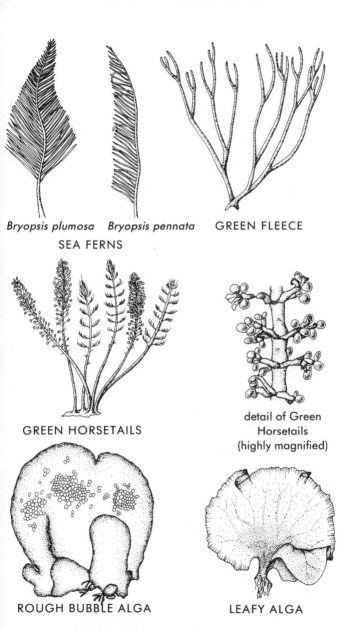

Bryopsis plumosa   *Bryopsis pennata*   GREEN FLEECE
SEA FERNS

GREEN HORSETAILS

detail of Green
Horsetails
(highly magnified)

ROUGH BUBBLE ALGA   LEAFY ALGA

Fig. 64. Green algae (1).

HOLLOW GREEN WEEDS *Enteromorpha* species **Fig. 65**
Light green, tubular filaments up to 30 cm (1 ft.) tall, usually with same diameter throughout. Usually with *Ulva, Chaetomorpha,* or *Cladophora.* Extremely variable in length and diameter of tubes, which may be constricted at intervals. *E. intestinalis* is common in tidepools and quiet water on hard bottoms.

COMMON DISK or SEGMENTED ALGAE **Fig. 65, Pl. 34**
Halimeda species
Erect, from fibrous holdfast. Branches with *flexible, jointed segments.* Usually dichotomously branched along more than 1 plane. On sandy bottoms or in crevices in reef flats. (1) *H. incrassata* (Pl. 34), to 24 cm (9 in.) tall; segments *flat, lobed,* occasionally ribbed. (2) *H. monile* has short segments, *cylindrical,* or slightly flattened. (3) *H. tuna* has padlike, kidney-shaped segments, like those of Prickly-pear Cactus; it grows in coral crevices. (4) *H. opuntia* forms low-growing colonies with *crowded, kidney-shaped, fluted or round disks* covering sediment in sandy areas of lagoon.

THIN and TUFTED SEA LETTUCES *Ulvaria* species
Sheetlike, resembling *Ulva.* Although difficult to discern in field, *Ulva* is two cell layers thick; *Ulvaria* is a single layer. *U. oxysperma* is thin, transparent, and usually *attached in tufts;* common on hard bottoms in quiet water or isolated pools. Usually to 10 cm (4 in.) tall; reaches 60 cm (2 ft.) tall in pools.

SPINDLEWEEDS *Neomeris* species **Fig. 65, Pl. 37**
Small, gregarious, *spindle-shaped,* about 1 cm (⅜ in.) high; partially calcified, tipped with *cluster of bright green filaments. N. annulata* is common on rocks and soft calcareous bottoms in quiet shallow areas.

MERMAN'S SHAVING BRUSHES **Fig. 57, Pl. 34**
Penicillus species
Stalked, bushy. Green, flexible or calcified stalk terminates in *brushlike tuft of filaments.* Stalk usually extends into head. (1) *P. capitatus*—to 15 cm (6 in.) tall—and (2) *P. dumetosus* are abundant; (3) *P. pyriformis,* with a somewhat larger brush, is less common. Along with *Halimeda* (disk algae), abundant in lagoons and Turtle Grass beds.

RIPWEEDS *Rhipocephalus* species **Figs. 56, 65**
Usually cylindrical, sometimes expanding into oval head resembling a Merman's Shaving Brush *(Penicillus)*—see Figs. 56 and 57. *R. phoenix* to 12 cm (4¾ in.) tall, with *light green, squarish, calcified, vertical plates* surrounding stalk. In shallow water among *Halimeda* and *Penicillus;* often in Turtle Grass beds.

HARD FAN ALGAE *Udotea flabellum* **Pl. 35**
Stalked, calcified green algae resembling *Avrainvillea. Fan more solid* and compact, sometimes split, proliferated. Concentric calcification zones may appear like lighter arcs across fan. Grows on sandy bottoms and rock crevices in shallow to deep water. To 20 cm (8 in.) tall.

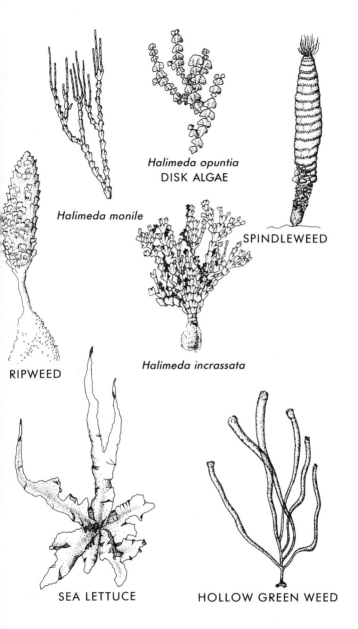

Halimeda monile

Halimeda opuntia
DISK ALGAE

SPINDLEWEED

RIPWEED

Halimeda incrassata

SEA LETTUCE

HOLLOW GREEN WEED

Fig. 65. Green algae (2).

SEA LETTUCE *Ulva* species **Fig. 65, Pl. 34**
Sheetlike, simple or broadly lobed; shiny bright green. On hard surfaces or free-floating in tidal shallows. *U. lactuca* has 1 to several broad blades arising from a basal holdfast and is one of the best-known seaweeds. To 3m (10 ft.) long.

SMOOTH BUBBLE ALGAE *Valonia* species **Pl. 34**
(1) *V. ventricosa* (Pl. 34) is a *single spherical* or subspherical translucent *cell,* to 4 cm (1½ in.) wide. Looks like a *large green bubble.* Main sphere may have smaller ones attached at base. On hard surfaces. One of largest single-celled organisms. (2) **Encrusting Bubble Alga** (*V. ocellata*) forms a 5-mm (¼-in.) thick crust of *tiny green bubble-like cells,* on intertidal and subtidal rocks.

Brown algae: Division Phaeophyta. Brown, yellow-brown, or olive-green; structure varies from branched and filamentous to bushy and thick to flattened branches. Although this group possesses chlorophyll, a number of xanthophyll (yellow-brown) pigments may mask the green to produce various shades of olive-green to brown. The brown algae produce the most complex thalli (plant bodies) among the algae, having leaflike, stemlike, and rootlike structures. With few exceptions, they are usually large, fleshy, and attached to hard bottoms.

Brown Macroalgae

BROWN BUBBLE ALGAE *Colpomenia* species **Fig. 66**
Thallus yellowish brown, sessile, hollow, spherical, somewhat *crinkled and irregular* in shape, like a *ball* or small balloon; usually clustered. *C. sinuosa* grows on rocks, oyster beds, reefs. Occasionally found floating free. To 12 cm (4¾ in.) wide.

RIBBED BROWN ALGAE *Dictyopteris* species **Fig. 66**
Large, leafy, with a substantial holdfast. Branches flat, strap-shaped, dichotomous. Edges of blades ruffled, toothed, or entire. *A pronounced rib on each blade.* On rocky shores and reefs. *D. justii* forms tufts to 40 cm (15½ in.) tall; blades to 8 cm (3¼ in.) wide.

FORKED SEA TUMBLEWEEDS *Dictyota* species **Pl. 37**
Filmy, light brown; bushy with flattened fronds. No midrib; *branches usually dichotomous.* Three common species: (1) *D. dichotoma,* largest with broader fronds; (2) *D. bartayresii,* and (3) *D. linearis,* smaller and more delicate. All 3 grow on hard surfaces below intertidal zone, often floating free in clumps on bottom; *D. bartayresii* and *D. dichotoma* common in sheltered areas, where they grow to 20 cm (8 in.) high.

LEATHERY LOBEWEEDS *Lobophora* species **Fig. 66**
Leaflike and expanded, resembling *Padina* but with a leathery texture. Faint *concentric rings* or zones without calcification. *L. variegata* grows on intertidal rocks.

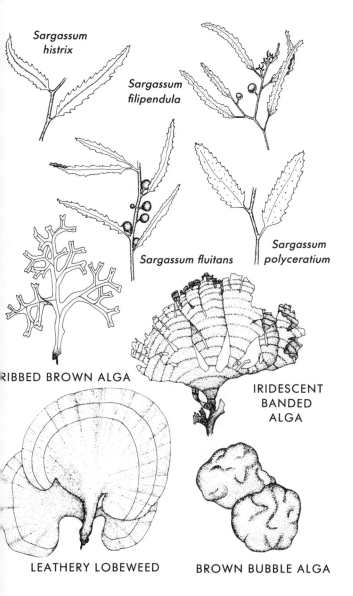

Sargassum histrix

Sargassum filipendula

Sargassum fluitans

Sargassum polyceratium

RIBBED BROWN ALGA

IRIDESCENT BANDED ALGA

LEATHERY LOBEWEED

BROWN BUBBLE ALGA

Fig. 66. Brown algae.

PETTICOAT ALGAE *Padina* species **Pl. 37**

Leafy, low-growing; fronds fanlike or funguslike, resembling wood shavings or petticoat with horizontal lacy bands. *Distinct concentric zonation* having various degrees of calcification forming *broad whitish bands.* On rocks and dead coral heads in intertidal or below. *P. sanctae-crucis* (Pl. 37) is common in Caribbean; to 9 cm (3½ in.) wide. *P. vickersia* is common in se. U.S. and Caribbean.

GULFWEED or SARGASSUM WEED **Fig. 66, Pl. 37**
Sargassum species

Fronds differentiated into stem and leaflike structures. Leaves of various species broad or narrow, sessile or attached by minute petioles, and with smooth or toothed margins. Some species pelagic, others subtidal, attached to hard bottoms. Attached forms to 45 cm (18 in.) tall, or more. (1) *S. polyceratium* and (2) *S. filipendula* (Pl. 37) are the commonest attached forms. Leaves of *S. polyceratium* short; those of *S. filipendula* long — many times longer than broad. (3) *S. bermudense* is the common attached species in Bermuda; leaf blades have distinct midrib. (4) *S. hystrix* is a less common attached species. (5) *S. fluitans* and (6) *S. natans* are the commonest free-floating forms; often washed ashore. Bladders of *S. fluitans* have *needle-like projections.*

The free-floating species of Sargassum are often associated with the Sargasso Sea, off the southeastern coast of the U.S., seaward of Gulf Stream. The sea results from ring of currents that enclose a great eddy approximately 5.2 million sq. km, which rotates clockwise under the influence of the Earth's rotation. Sargassum Weed accumulates in sea due to the influence of the eddy. It is believed to live a free-floating existence and is never attached.

IRIDESCENT BANDED ALGAE **Fig. 66, Pl. 37**
Stypopodium species

Erect, flat, leafy. Older plants are bushy and split into segments. *S. zonale* is magnificent, its large blades *transversely banded and iridescent green.* Plant blackens upon drying. On subtidal rocks, reefs. To 36 cm (14 in.) long.

THREE-CORNERED HAT ALGAE **Pl. 37**
Turbinaria species

Fronds differentiated into stems and trumpet-shaped (turbinate) leaves. Similar to *Sargassum.* *T. turbinata* has distinctive *pyramid-shaped leaves;* usually attached in intertidal zone along rocky shores, occasionally free floating. Leaves *yellowish with brown dots.* To 40 cm (15¾ in.) tall.

Red Macroalgae

Red Algae: Divison Rhodophyta. Usually some shade of red or olive-red; may be pink, purple, or olive-green (for positive identification red pigments can be leached in boiling water). Two pigments, phycoerythrin and phycocyanin, in combination with chlorophyll, are responsible for the various colors. Olive or green species are often mistaken for green algae. Several species become heavily calcified and turn white when old or dried. Form varies: may be branching, bushy, bulbous, blade-like, or even rocklike. Red algae develop elaborate plant bodies, many very small or microscopic. Almost exclusively marine; common in tropical and subtropical waters. Abundant in intertidal and subtidal zone. Larger species grow attached to hard surfaces; smaller forms are epiphytes on other, larger algae or attached to animals.

SPINY SEAWEEDS Pl. 36
Acanthophora species
Pale pink or buff, with soft, flexible branches. *Short branchlets with spines.* A. *spicifera* common along most beaches, on hard substrates, including Red Mangrove roots. Often harbors filamentous algae. To 25 cm (9½ in.) long.

BRANCHING CALCIFIED ALGAE Pl. 36
Amphiroa and *Jania* species
Fragile, white or *pink;* repeatedly branched, *calcified.* Branches dichotomous, fine, circular in cross-section, jointed at forks. *Jania* species are usually smaller and more delicate than *Amphiroa.* **Similar species:** A red, Brillo-like calcareous alga, *Coelothrix irregularis,* has outer branches colored with *blue-purple iridescence,* which differentiates it from the red matting A. *fragilissima.* Both grow on hard substrates in lagoons in clumps to 4 cm (1½ in.) tall.

LARGE SEA GRAPES *Botryocladia* species Fig. 66
Rosy red to olive-green, multibranched stems with numerous *mucilage-filled, oval bladders* to 1 cm (⅜ in.) long. *B. occidentalis* produces clusters of bladders resembling a clump of grapes. To 25 cm (10 in.) tall.

RED SPIKEWEED *Bryothamnion* species Pl. 36
Reddish or brownish purple bushy plants, to 25 cm (10 in.) tall. Two species, both with a *spiky appearance. B. triquetrum* (Pl. 36) has short stalks, then branches irregularly, with pointed branchlets 2–3 mm (1/12–⅛ in.) thick. On rocks and dead coral in shallow, moderately exposed areas and deep reefs.

CHAMPIA *Champia* species Fig. 67
Small, multibranched, with *constricted pink or red filaments. C. parvula* grows on hard bottoms or is epiphytic on other algae; to 10 cm (4 in.) long.

CHENILLE WEED *Dasya* species Fig. 67
Bushy; main axis or branches with several delicate lateral branches, forming a *featherlike, soft, fluffy* plant. Ultimate branchlets look like hair to naked eye. Pink or rosy red. Attached to hard surfaces or epiphytic on other algae. Many species; some more than 20 cm (8 in.) long.

BONE ALGAE *Galaxaura* species   **Pl. 36**
Terete or rounded, occasionally jointed stems; usually calcified, firm, dichotomously branched. Ends of branches truncate or *depressed at tips;* may look like bones. Pink or buff. In shallow water, rock crevices, on dead coral. *G. obtusata* grows in hemispherical clumps to 10 cm (8 in.) tall.

GRACEFUL REDWEED *Gracilaria* species   **Fig. 67**
Deep red, maroon, or purplish. Several species with rounded and strap-shaped branches. In some species entire plant consists of slender, terete branches that constrict slightly at their point of attachment. In others, main branches strap-shaped, branchlets strap-shaped or terete (round in cross section). Intertidal and shallow subtidal zone, on hard bottom. To 30 cm (1 ft.) long.

HOOKED WEEDS *Hypnea* species   **Pl. 36**
Bushy, with spine-like lateral branches; rosy red. Terminal branches often *curved or hook-shaped.* In quiet, shallow water. *H. musciformis* (Pl. 36) to 20 cm (8 in.) tall.

LAURENCE'S WEEDS *Laurencia* species   **Fig. 67**
Bushy; cartilaginous or crispy, greenish or pinkish. *Short branchlets with blunt or sharp tips.* Some species totally pink, some yellow, most with reddish tips. *L. papillosa* is one of most common species on hard surfaces in intertidal zone.

SPAGHETTI WEEDS *Liagora* species   **Fig. 67, Pl. 36**
White, brown, light buff, pinkish; may calcify into coral-like or rope-like structures, often appearing banded. Branches cylindrical; they form multiaxial filaments with dispersed calcification. Texture of *soft, tangled yarn or white spaghetti.* (1) *L. farinosa* (Pl. 36) is a loose, widely branching, tangled mass; common along bottoms; calcified, partially calcified, or uncalcified; uncalcified portions pink or reddish; in tangled masses to 12 cm (4½ in.) long. (2) *L. valida* is stiff, wholly calcified; terete (round).

LAVER *Porphyra* species   **Fig. 67**
Resembles Sea Lettuce (*Ulva,* Fig. 65) but is red or purple. Blades extremely thin, flat; several may grow from a common base. Margins of blades *ruffled or fringed. P. rosemurtii,* to 30 cm (1 ft.) long, is found in intertidal or in shallow subtidal zone. Other species are harvested in California and cultivated for food (*nori*) in Japan. Commercially rolled and dried; may be eaten directly or used as seasoning in meat dishes and soups.

Microalgae

Either encrusting or filamentous. Although some filamentous forms are large, microscopic examination is necessary for identification to genus.

Antithamnionella species and *Callithamnion* species
Red algae. Two of many genera composed of tufted, delicate, uniseriate filaments. Branched, with fine, opposite, alternate, or

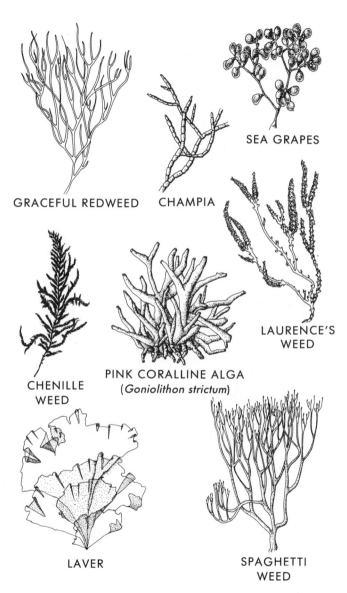

GRACEFUL REDWEED CHAMPIA

SEA GRAPES

CHENILLE
WEED

PINK CORALLINE ALGA
(*Goniolithon strictum*)

LAURENCE'S
WEED

LAVER

SPAGHETTI
WEED

Fig. 67. Red algae.

whorled filaments. Usually rose to pink. In *Antithamnionella*, branching opposite, tufted more densely at tips. *Callithamnion* usually alternately branched, with densely crowded spirals of filaments around each branch. Both are common on hard surfaces and *epiphytic on larger algae*. Tufts to 5 cm (2 in.) long.

SEA MOSSES *Bostrychia* species **Pl. 36**
Red algae. *Feathery,* with erect branches arising from stolons. Terminal portions composed of recurved branchlets. Plants red, purple, brownish, or black. (1) *B. tenella* and (2) *B. binderi* form *feltlike mats* on rocks; conspicuous in upper intertidal zone. (3) *B. montagnei* forms a dark felt mat on mangrove roots, exposed at low tide. To 7.5 cm (3 in.) tall; mats to 2 cm (¾ in.) thick.

BANDED WEEDS *Ceramium* species
Red algae. Very small, fine filaments. Microscopic, evenly branched, uniseriate filaments; light translucent red. Each filament has transverse binding, or ring, of darker corticating cells at cell junctions. Ends of branches often terminate in *forceplike tips,* resembling pincers. Most species are epiphytic on larger algae; also common on hard bottoms. Dense tufts to 8 cm (3¼ in.) tall.

Fosliella species
Red algae. White or pinkish, *calcareous, encrusting* algae, 1 or 2 cell layers thick; spherical or semispherical in outline when sparse, otherwise merging into a *thin white crust*. Common on Turtle Grass blades; often totally encrusting coral heads with thin, hard film.

CORALLINE ALGAE or ENCRUSTING **Figs. 48, 67**
CALCAREOUS RED ALGAE *Goniolithon* species
LITHOTHAMNIOIDS *Lithophyllum, Lithothamnion* species
Red algae. Shape variable but all thick, *encrusting and calcified;* shelflike, fanlike, or branched. Some species circular or disklike; light pink, lavender, or purple. These algae do not resemble seaweeds—they look like *spots or spills* of paint on rocks, dead corals, or shells, or form massed *branches of pink or white calcium carbonate*. **Pink Coralline Alga** (*G. strictum*, Figs. 48, 67) forms branched masses to 6 cm (2½ in.) thick.

Polysiphonia species
Red algae. Delicate red, pink, occasionally brown or black. Erect, with alternate or dichotomous branches. Major branches polysiphonous, with jointed microscopic tubes or siphons extending length of plant. *Epiphytic on hard animal parts* or on other marine plants.

Spyridia species
Red algae. Small, feathery, branched thallus. Rosy red *branch-*

lets, often recurved. Some species in algal mat on exposed shores, others in quiet waters near low-tide level.

Ectocarpus and *Giffordia* species

Brown algae. Filamentous, small; yellowish, brownish, or olive; *epiphytic* on other algae, seagrasses, shells, dead coral. Filaments regularly septate, opposite or alternately branched; many filaments bearing oval, *conical or ellipsoid spore-bearing structures (sporangia)*. Ruglike, in tufts 30 cm (1 ft.) tall.

SEA FERNS *Bryopsis* species Fig. 64

Green algae. Feathery or bushy, with plume-like branches. Fronds *fernlike;* stiff, coarse branches extend from main axis. Sea ferns often resemble upright portions of *Caulerpa* but are much finer in texture. In quiet waters in tidepools. To 7 cm (2¾ in.) long.

Chaetomorpha species

Green algae. Light green unbranched filaments with irregular-sized cells, each containing many chloroplasts. Most have a *dry, not slimy, texture.* (1) *C. aerea* forms tufts or mosslike mats in areas with heavy surf. (2) *C. brachygona* occurs as long strands in quiet water.

Cladophora species

Green algae. Branched, filamentous, with many chloroplasts per cell, giving it a dark green color. Similar to *Chaetomorpha* but mostly *slimy and branched.* Some forms occur as *lemon-sized balls* at surface or below sand. Tidepools, rocky bottoms.

Cladophoropsis species

Green algae. Filaments massive, branched, often entangled. Resemble *Cladophora* but filaments and individual cells much larger, some plants *free-floating. C. membranacea* common in shallow, calm pools as *rolling balls.* Other species form tufts to 5 cm (2 in.) tall.

Blue-green Algae or Cyanobacteria: Kingdom Monera, Division Cynaophyta. Bluish green single cells, globose colonies, or microscopic filaments, often producing thin, flat mats on the surface of mud or fine sand or black bands on intertidal rocks. Cells lack a discrete nucleus. When found along the shore, these algae are usually slimy.

Lyngbya species

Blue-green algae. Similar to *Oscillatoria* (below) but filaments encased in *mucilaginous sheath.*

Oscillatoria species

Blue-green algae. On most surfaces usually appear as short encrusted filaments; also epiphytic. *Blue-green color* distinguishes these algae from filamentous green, red, and brown algae.

SEAGRASSES AND OTHER AQUATIC FLOWERING PLANTS

A number of true flowering plants (spermatophytes) have successfully invaded the sunlight-drenched shallows. Instead of propagating by bee- or wind-induced pollination, these plants rely on water currents to carry pollen to ovule. Insect-attracting petals are unnecessary, and flowers are often spiderlike aggregations of elongated pistils or stamens. Much reproduction is asexual, with dense mats of rhizomes consolidating and stabilizing the sediment. Each rhizome gives rise to new plants every few centimeters, so that in sheltered bays seagrasses densely cover the bottom.

SHOAL GRASS *Halodule wrightii* **Fig. 68**
Clusters of flat, grasslike leaves to 40 cm (15¾ in.) long; usually broken at tips. Long stalk may branch into several leaves to 1.2 cm (½ in.) wide. In shallow beds, *rarely beyond knee depth,* often landward of Turtle Grass; S. Florida, Caribbean.

DWARF SEAGRASS *Halophila decipiens* **Fig. 68**
Tiny; many thin stems arising from rhizome, each with *2 small, broadly ellipsoid leaves* with conspicuous midrib. Leaves to 2 cm (¾ in.) long. **Related species: Six-leaved Dwarf Seagrass** (*H. engelmanni*) with 10-cm (4-in.) long stems bearing terminal whorls of 4–8, usually 6, *fleshy ellipsoid leaves.* Both species in brackish, muddy, protected areas and salt ponds; S. Florida, Caribbean.

WIDGEON GRASS *Ruppia maritima* **Fig. 68**
Long, dark green stems with 5- to 10-cm (2- to 4-in.) long, flat, single-veined, grasslike leaves with long slender tips. *First fifth of leaf broad, tapering rapidly to narrow flat blade.* Rhizomes have few roots at each stalk junction. Prefers very low salinities (almost fresh water), but will survive in brackish estuaries. *Only common seagrass with many leaves extending from single stalk.* East and Gulf coasts.

MANATEE GRASS *Syringodium filiforme*
Long, thin, round, vermicelli-like, stiff, light green blades to 30 cm (1 ft.) long, arising from a 5-cm (2-in.) long sheath. Flowers inconspicuous, tiny; fruit beaked, flat, oval, to 6.5 mm (¼ in.) long. Leaves extend from extensive rhizomes. Common among Turtle Grass blades or in separate meadows; s. Florida, Caribbean.

TURTLE GRASS *Thalassia testudinum* **Fig. 55, Pl. 17**
Clumps of broad, flat blades to 30 cm (1 ft.) tall or higher and 1.8 cm (¾ in.) wide, arising from dense rhizome system. Flowers with curved whitish pistils or stamens low on stalk. Usually no

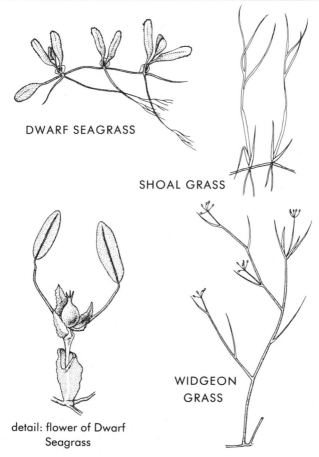

DWARF SEAGRASS

SHOAL GRASS

WIDGEON GRASS

detail: flower of Dwarf Seagrass

Fig. 68. Aquatic flowering plants.

more than 5–10% of plants flower at one time, usually in spring and summer. S. Florida, Gulf, Caribbean. **Similar species: Eelgrass** (*Zostera marina*) is narrower than *Thalassia*—to 1.2 cm (½ in.) wide—and usually longer—to 1.2 m (4 ft.). Flowers small, green, sheathed. Greenland to n. Florida.

8

Beach-Plant Communities

Sara Davison and C. Dennis Adams

Nowhere is the struggle of the sea against the land fought more fiercely than at the boundary between the beach and its shoreside vegetation. Terrestrial plants grow in finger-shaped colonies, grasping for more and more land. The sea fights back, ripping up shrubs and flinging them back against the shore. Occasionally a gnarled tree withstands the onslaught, its branches streaming backward toward the protection of the land.

As you wander along the beaches you will often find that one beach does not resemble another, and that the vegetation is not uniform throughout an individual beach. Instead, you will find aggregations of distinct plant communities. But within each type of plant community there is often a remarkable similarity wherever you go. For instance, mangrove communities of the Florida Keys are similar to those in Puerto Rico or even in far-off Trinidad.

Tides in our area generally have little amplitude, and beaches are often narrow. Wave-washed beaches are normally devoid of plant life, at least to high-tide levels. Above these, salt levels gradually diminish, and the sediment changes from pure mineral matter saturated with seawater to less barren soil types. The vegetation inland usually becomes progressively taller because of the improved soil and because the sheltering effects of the foremost shrubs lessen the force of the wind. Thus, regardless of geology and climate, seaside plant communities are always zoned parallel to the shore, creating a striking contrast between neighboring plant communities. The sparse, low, herbaceous plants of the sand beach contrast strongly with the shrubby dense thickets covering and hedging the dunes.

Many of the factors that affect beach vegetation zonation are not the same as those that influence the zonation of inland plants. For example, salt tolerance greatly affects beach flora. Beach plants have evolved special adaptations to cope with the high salinity of beach soils, and plants growing closest to the high-tide line have developed a greater salt tolerance than those growing higher on the beach. Seaside Purslane, growing within reach of the salty spray of breaking waves, and Red Mangroves, whose roots are always partly submerged under seawater, are examples of particularly salt-tolerant plants. Other factors that affect not only zonation but also the shape and size of beach plants are the high temperatures and strong winds of the tropics. The almost incessant trade winds buffeting Caribbean islands exert a strong drying effect on plants. This, plus periods of drought, has caused the beach plants to evolve xerophytic (water-conserving) characteristics.

Also important in determining the type of vegetation is the physical nature of the beach itself. A beach is a transient environment. Wind and wave action, carrying sand from one location to another, constantly changes the appearance of the beach. In turn, the vegetation is altered.

A beach dune, with its massive size, may appear to be a permanent feature, but in reality it is in a constant state of flux. Those dunes farthest inland are the oldest, whereas those nearest the sea are new and active. A dune is built by waves and wind. Vegetation is a crucial factor in the maintenance and building of the dune; plants soon colonize the shifting surface. The Sea Grape tree (Pl. 19), with its spreading roots and large, flat, wind-catching leaves, is an important dune-building species. The rapidly spreading Seashore Dropseed grass (Pl. 18) is an effective ground cover and helps preserve the dune. As the dune becomes well established, the Sea Grape loses its importance as a colonizer and is replaced by other plants.

Beaches with little wave action may not develop dunes. The beach vegetation reflects this protected state. For example, inlets and bays usually are not fringed with thickets of Sea Grape. Instead, these plants grow as isolated shrubs, unable to dominate the less stressful environment where competition with other plants is keener.

As the environment affects the nature of its vegetation, so do the plants affect the physical character of the beach in a complex interrelationship. The Sea Grape and grasses are dune builders. Mangrove roots collect sediment carried by currents and gradually form new land. Once new soil has been deposited, the mangroves extend seaward, allowing other species to move in behind (see Chapter 9). Conversely, the sediment can regulate the distribution of plants. Sea Rocket (Figs. 17, 76) grows only in loose sand near the high-tide line, whereas the Gray Nickerbean vine (Fig. 69) needs a pulverized limestone soil and grows behind the dunes, where such soil has accumulated in a more permanent environment. Rocky beaches present a hard, impenetrable surface that often defies plant colonization. Sea-washed sand may be silica derived from pulverized rocks or a smooth fine "talcum powder" composed of the remains of corals, sea urchins, and calcareous algae. Other beaches are made of broken coral cast up by storms; still others are composed of black lava and volcanic ash particles.

Plants that can endure permanent existence on the beach are usually adapted to carrying out their life functions with high

Fig. 69. Sea Beans. *Upper left:* True Sea Bean; *upper right:* Sea Heart; *bottom left:* Sea Coconut; *bottom right:* Gray Nickerbean— pod and "beans."

concentrations of salt in their cells. Others resist the entry of salt through physiological mechanisms. Some, such as the Black Mangrove (p. 178), secrete salt from their leaves (Pl. 24).

Although habitats near the sea are essentially watery, the presence of salt renders fresh water scarce, and the adaptations of seaside plants are frequently similar to those of plants in dry or desertlike environments. These modifications include succulence—the presence of water-storage tissues in stems—and simple thick leathery leaves. Waxiness and thick cuticles on leaf surfaces resist excessive water loss. Small leaves, as in Acacia trees, or even the total absence of leaves, as in cacti, serve the same ends. Water is stored in stems or extensive root systems.

Typical species of the strand—the seaward edge of the vegetation—are low, trailing, and multirooting plants with extensive horizontal shoots. This growth habit offers the least resistance to wind and blown sand, and frequent rooting enables the plant to overcome the limited availability of certain mineral nutrients in the sand. These pioneer communities are always shifting and are referred to as open (not covering the ground completely).

The wind-trimming effect often seen in thickets near the sea is caused by the mechanical damage to leaves and buds by wind and by the deposition of salt spray on leaves. When salt crystals form on immature leaves, sunlight may be optically concentrated (like hundreds of tiny magnifying glasses), causing damage to the tissues. The net effect of these factors is to give a sloping shape to the vegetation, the most salt-encrusted seaward edge of the plant being the lowest-growing. The commonest and most frequently encountered zones, starting at the seaward edge, are (1) the beach community, (2) the dune community, and (3) the scrub and thicket community.

Where coastal vegetation is invading new land, such as may occur in river estuaries, this sequence may be repeated in a succession of developmental stages, one community replacing another on the same spot over a period of time (see p. 35).

The beach community: The first vegetation zone above the high-tide line is occupied by the beach community. Permanent vegetation is impossible here because this zone is frequently disturbed by storms. Such an unstable environment can support only sparse growth. The plants found here are called coastal pioneers and are characterized by low creeping growth habits. Their capacity to establish themselves very rapidly is the key to their survival. Some of these colonizers are grasses such as Sandbur (Fig. 78), Seashore Paspalum, and Seashore Dropseed (Pl. 18). Other more conspicuous colonizers are the prostrate fleshy species such as Seaside Purslane (Pl. 18), with its bright pink flowers, and the Seaside Heliotrope (Fig. 77). Caribbean Sea Spurge is fleshy but grows erect in loose clusters. The creeping runners of Beach Morning Glory and Seaside Bean (Pl. 18) intermingle with these plants and also form dense single-species carpets. Both vines are common and have shiny green leaves and purple flowers.

While you explore the beach community an added delight is the search for drift seeds and fruits, such as sea beans (Fig. 69). Whole fruits or seeds travel down streams and rivers, eventually reaching ocean currents. They are often collected and polished for trinkets and jewelry.

Floating Seeds

One cannot walk the beaches of the Caribbean or Florida without encountering distinctive sea beans or other seeds that wash up on shore. All share common characteristics: they contain air-filled spaces, which provide buoyancy, and a resistant coat, which isolates the embryo and its food from the salt water. All can survive long voyages on the currents, usually for at least a year, and still retain their viability. All provide a mechanism for dispersal, so that the species can invade new niches or at least spread into hospitable environments even thousands of miles away. All of the species mentioned, except the coconut, have been found on the shores of Ireland and England, carried there by the Gulf Stream from the Caribbean. The Gulf Coast and southeastern beaches to Cape Hatteras occasionally receive floating seeds.

## TRUE SEA BEAN or HORSE-EYE BEAN	Fig. 69
Mucuna sloanei

Round seed, to 4 cm (1½ in.) in diameter and 2 cm (¾ in.) thick. Dark brown or reddish brown, sometimes mottled with black; lustrous. *Black band (hilum) around edge* of seed bordered by yellowish margin (sometimes pale, rarely absent). **Similar species:** (1) **Fawcett's Sea Bean** (*M. fawcettii*) is similar but somewhat more compressed in cross-section. Black hilum broader — to 1 cm (⅜ in.), compared to a maximum of 6 mm (¼ in.) for True Sea Bean. (2) *M. urens,* a third sea bean, is rare; seed is reddish or grayish brown with a grayish border around hilum. Plants producing seeds are climbing vines with bright yellow flowers, often found on trees along stream banks and woodland margins. Seeds in a pod to 18 cm (7 in.) long.

## SEA HEART	*Entada gigas*	Fig. 69

Round seed, to 6 cm (2⅓ in.) in diameter and 2 cm (¾ in.) thick, with a distinct *notch in margin.* Dull or slightly lustrous dark chocolate to mahogany brown, smooth. Seeds produced by a climbing vine to 15 m (49 ft.) long, on trees along river banks and in wet areas. Leaves compound, with 4–5 pairs of leaflets; flowers greenish yellow, numerous. Fruit is among the longest of all fruits — a twisted pod to 2 m (6½ ft.) long and 12 cm (4¾ in.) wide, containing 10–15 seeds, each in an individual compartment.

## SEA COCONUT	Fig. 69
Manicaria saccifera

Almost spherical seed, except *region near scar becomes angular.* To 5 cm (2 in.) in diameter. Brown, gray, or white; often brown, shading to gray near scar. Thin, hard skin, often cracked. Fruit has facets on surface like a pineapple; may be spherical, two- or three-lobed. Fruit is produced by a palm tree but is not a close relative of the true coconut. Tree unique because it possesses the largest entire leaf blade of any plant. Grows in colonies near seashore. Specimen shown is covered with Goose Barnacles (p. 300), testifying to fact it has been floating for a long time.

## COCONUT	*Cocos nucifera*

Oval fruit to 40 cm (15¾ in.) long, tapering to narrow base bearing prominent terminal scar. Fruit has *fibrous, buoyant husk* covered by tan lustrous coat (exocarp). Inner layer of fruit (endocarp) hard, dark brown, fibrous, bearing *3 basal pores* that are smooth, dark brown circles. Seed inside endocarp covered by thin brown seed coat, then white, watery endosperm (food) that becomes solid when mature. Fruit is borne in clumps on tall palm trees near or on beaches (p. 149). Most coconuts fall from tree between 2 A.M. and 5 A.M.

GRAY NICKERBEAN *Caesalpinia bonduc* **Fig. 69**
Round or oval seed, to 2.5 cm (1 in.) in diameter. Olive, silver gray or grayish yellow, with smooth surface bearing numerous faint *concentric fracture lines*. Hilum a conspicuous brown area. Fruit produced by a spiny shrub (p. 161) living just beyond high-tide mark. Seeds are used as marbles; in fact, another name for marbles is nickers.

The dune community: The dune plant community is characterized by thickets of both herbaceous and woody plants that have largely replaced coastal pioneers. You can find an occasional runner of the Beach Morning Glory or Seaside Bean here but not the dense carpet of these plants characteristic of the beach community. Since the dune is a site where soil accumulates, it provides a more stable environment than that of the shifting sands of the beach. As a result of the stability of the dune, larger shrubs and small trees can grow.

Of the herbaceous plants, grasses are most important. Seashore Paspalum and Seashore Dropseed grasses (Pl. 18) prevent erosion with their multirooting runners. The fragrant white Spider Lily (Pl. 18) may often be found in a sheltered nook. Inkberry (Fig. 71), a plant with waxy, shiny, thick green leaves, is one of the larger herbaceous plants found here.

Although grasses may be useful in this zone, what is most distinctive about the dune community is the littoral hedge or dune thicket. You will find here plants that are predominantly woody, ranging from 50 cm (20 in.) to 3 m (10 ft.) high and clustered in a hedge running parallel to the sea. Sometimes this littoral hedge consists of a single species, as is often the case with Sea Grape (Pl. 19). Or it can also be a tangled mixture of Sea Grape; West Indian Sea Lavender (Pl. 19), a fine, silky shrub with silvery white leaves; and Bay Cedar (Pl. 21), with its clustered orange-green leaves. The bright yellow flowers of the Sea Daisy (Pl. 20) distinguish this species from the others in the littoral hedge. Break one of its succulent light green leaves and you will smell a delightful pungent fragrance.

Also a member of the dune community is the omnipresent Coconut palm (Pl. 19). What beachcomber has not sat under one of these graceful palms, one of man's 10 most useful trees? Although the Coconut palm is often planted by man, it grows naturally on many beaches. The Australian-pine (Fig. 73) is another species often planted near beaches. This tree, originally introduced from Australia, has spread naturally, bordering many beaches in the Bahamas and West Indies. Its needle-like branches and scale-like leaves have such a small surface area that little water is lost and the tree is well suited to the arid shore.

The scrub and thicket community: This plant community, the farthest inland of the three, is characterized by woody shrubs and

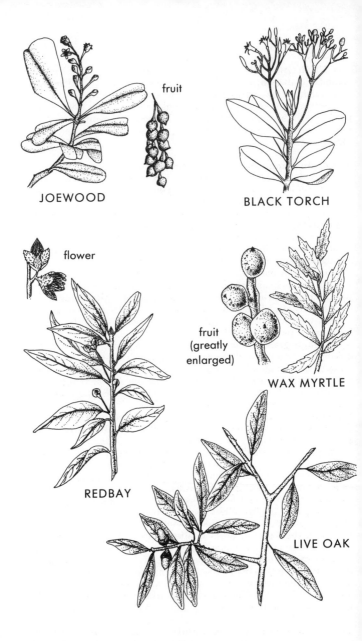

Fig. 70. Seaside shrubs and trees (1).

trees. Left undisturbed, this scrubby thicket might eventually become a forest; but all too often it is considered choice real estate and becomes greatly altered by man.

Many species found in the dune thicket can also be found here: Sea Grape, Sea Lavender, Sea Daisy, and Bay Cedar. Many new species of shrubs appear. Black Torch and Joewood (Fig. 70) are common, often growing in rocky soil. The small, whitish, fragrant flowers of the Joewood attract numerous insects. The Coco Plum (Fig. 71) grows in abundance in the scrub and thicket zone, as does the prickly Gray Nickerbean.

Trees often mix with the shrubs, creating a forestlike environment. The Geiger Tree and the Seaside Maho (Fig. 71) both have buoyant fruits and are among the few coastal trees with showy flowers. The Shortleaf Fig is one of the largest coastal trees and is distinctive for its size and its hanging aerial roots. Another large tree is the poisonous Manchineel tree (Pl. 19). The milky sap from its twigs, leaves, and green, apple-like fruit, is irritating to the skin and poisonous if consumed. Even though it is more commonly associated with mangrove forests, the Buttonwood tree (Pl. 24) is often found in coastal thickets as well. Look for the gnarled and twisted trunks of older trees.

Where rainfall is very low, you may find a drier cactus-scrub thicket. There are three distinctive types of cactus: the Prickly-pears (Fig. 77), the Barrel Cactus, and the tall Organ-pipe Cactus (*Cephalocereus royenii*). The Sweet Acacia tree (Fig. 73), with its sharp spines and round yellow flower clusters, is commonly found in this cactus-scrub thicket.

The salt-marsh and salina (salt-pond) community: Salt marshes are most commonly found near calm water where the soil has stabilized. Tidal inlets, bays, and mangrove margins are the most likely locations. At first glance they may appear as a uniform stretch of low-growing grass, but coastal salt marshes are an interesting mixture of grasses, sedges, and dicotyledonous plants. Marsh-loving trees and mangroves often border these low stretches.

Southern Glasswort (Pl. 18) is one of the commonest species; its reddish yellow stems and flower spikes add color to the salt marsh. It grows in extensive dense mats, as does another common salt-marsh species, Saltwort (Fig. 74), especially along the margins of salinas or salt ponds. Amid these dense mats, the bright yellow Sea Daisy (Pl. 20) and the Tropical and Caribbean sedges (Pl. 18) abound. Slender Cordgrass is an important member of this coastal salt-marsh association. Like Glasswort and Saltwort, this grass grows in dense meadows, not scattered clumps, like the sedges and Sea Daisy.

The beach, dune, littoral hedge, scrubby thicket, mangroves, and salt marsh sustain distinct, easily recognizable plant communities. Man's effect on these communities is all too often

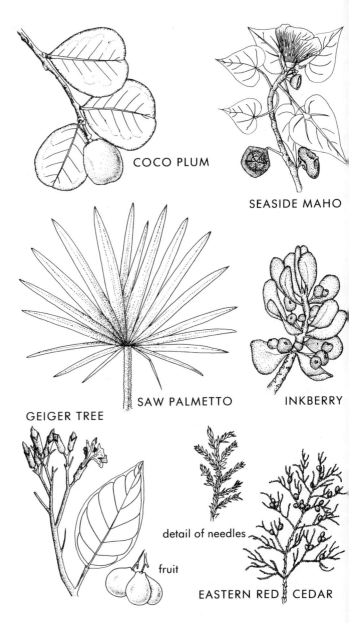

COCO PLUM

SEASIDE MAHO

SAW PALMETTO

INKBERRY

GEIGER TREE

detail of needles

fruit

EASTERN RED CEDAR

Fig. 71. Seaside shrubs and trees (2).

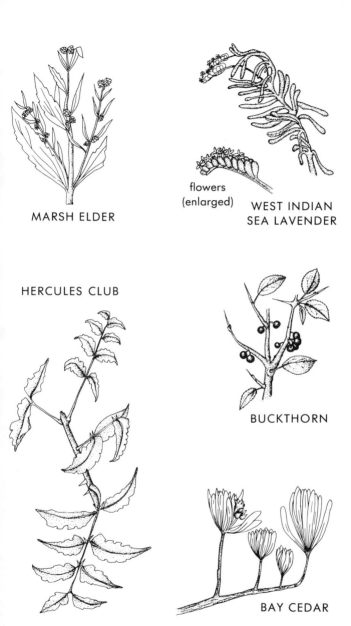

MARSH ELDER

flowers
(enlarged)

WEST INDIAN
SEA LAVENDER

HERCULES CLUB

BUCKTHORN

BAY CEDAR

Fig. 72. Seaside shrubs and trees (3).

destructive. If you expect to find sand dunes and a littoral hedge near a hotel you may be disappointed. When the natural vegetation is disturbed, weedy species infiltrate. When this disturbance continues over a long period, weedy herbs and shrubs gain ascendancy and eventually the original vegetation is unable to compete with them.

Descriptions of mangroves and associated plants will be found in Chapter 9. Bear in mind, however, that mangroves are often important constituents of beach communities.

Trees and Shrubs

SWEET ACACIA *Acacia farnesiana*   **Fig. 73**
A small tree with *paired whitish spines* and delicate twice-pinnate leaves to 10 cm (4 in.) long. Fragrant yellow flowers in *round fuzzy heads,* to 1.5 cm (½ in.) wide. Fruit is a pod to 7 cm (3 in.) long; green, turning brown. Dry coastal limestone thickets; Florida, Caribbean. Deciduous; flowers Nov.–Feb. Flowers often used for perfume.

GROUNDSEL TREE *Baccharis halimifolia*   **Pl. 21**
Shrub or small tree, to 4.5m (15 ft.) tall. Leaves broad; *upper* ones *toothless, small*—to 2.5 cm (1 in.) long; lower ones to 6.3 cm (2½ in.) long, with few irregular teeth. Separate sexes. Flowers beige to yellow; *seeds with white bristles.* In summer upper plant with clusters of tiny buds on long stems. Edges of salt marshes, dunes, often surrounded with sea's debris; Massachusetts to Florida and Gulf, Caribbean. Commonly found with Marsh Elder (Pl. 21).

SALTWORT *Batis maritima*   **Fig. 74; Pls. 19, 24**
Spreading small shrub with ascending shoots. *Aromatic, fleshy leaves,* to 3 cm (1¼ in.) long. Small flowers in dense spikes, 1 cm (⅜ in.) wide. Roots and main stem can be woody. Low saline ground, especially salt marshes and mangrove swamps; Florida, Caribbean. Flowers spring and summer.

BUCKTHORN *Bumelia lycioides*   **Fig. 72**
Shrub or small tree, to 20m (65 ft.) tall, with milky sap. Leaves alternate, often in clumps, oval to elongate, to 12 cm (4¾ in.) long. *Large thorns on stem often longer than leaves.* Branches cracked and rough, often inhabited by lichens, moss. Flowers in groups of 3 to many; five-petaled; white. Shrub zone of dunes; Virginia to Florida; Gulf to Texas. Flowers all year.

AUSTRALIAN-PINE   **Fig. 73, Pl. 18**
Casuarina equisetifolia
Conical tree with slender trunk, to 25m (83 ft.) tall. Leaves reduced, in whorls around modified needle-like twigs; *pine-tree-like.* Male flowers in spikes to 5 cm (2 in.) long; female flowers in globose heads, to 2 cm (¾ in.) wide. Woody, cone-like fruit. Sandy coastal areas; often planted as windbreak. Florida, Bahamas, Caribbean, naturalized from Australia. Flowers all year.

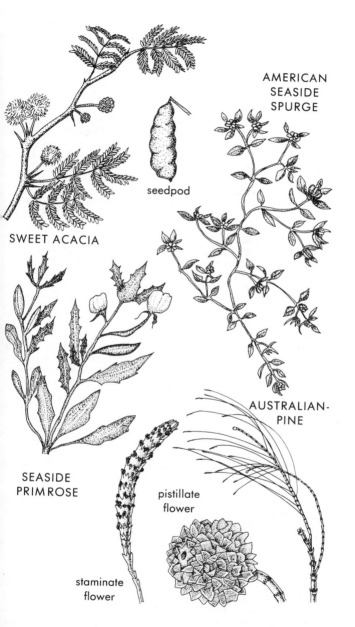

AMERICAN
SEASIDE
SPURGE

seedpod

SWEET ACACIA

SEASIDE
PRIMROSE

AUSTRALIAN-
PINE

pistillate
flower

staminate
flower

Fig. 73. Seaside shrubs and trees (4).

SPURGE NETTLE *Cnidoscolus stimulosus* **Fig. 74**

Shrub with milky sap, *stems with stinging hairs,* leaves with fewer stinging hairs; stem and leaves with spines. Leaves to 22.5 cm (9 in.) long, with 3–5 elongate, toothed lobes, each with *2–3 long spines pointing upward from midvein.* White, trumpet-shaped flowers in small groups with 5 oval, flat, petal-like sepals. Fruit an oval capsule. Interdune meadow, Virginia to Florida; Gulf to Texas. Flowers March to Sept.

SEA GRAPE *Coccoloba uvifera* **Pls. 18, 19**

Spreading shrub or tree, to 6m (20 ft.) tall. Round, rubbery, bright green leaves to 27 cm (11 in.) long, with *red or yellow veins.* White flowers in spike-like clusters, to 30 cm (12 in.) long. Green or dark reddish *fruit in grape-like clusters,* edible, often used in jellies. Sandy beaches, dunes; solitary or thicket-forming; Florida, Caribbean. Flowers spring, fall.

COCONUT PALM *Cocos nucifera* **Pl. 19**

Palm tree with slender, often leaning trunk, enlarged at base, to 20m (60 ft.) tall. Drooping compound leaves to 5 m (15 ft.) long; linear leaflets. Whitish flowers at leaf base. Buoyant three-sided fruit—*the coconut*—to 30 cm (12 in.) wide. Spreads naturally along shores, often planted. Florida, pantropical. Flowers all year.

COCO PLUM *Chrysobalanus icaco* **Fig. 71**

Shrub or small tree, to 6m (20 ft.) tall. Roundish, thick, dark green leaves to 8 cm (3¼ in.) long, *turned upward on twig.* Small white flowers with 5 petals in round clusters, to 6 cm (2½ in.) wide. Fruit edible but tasteless, often fed to pigs. Forms thickets on beaches; Florida, Caribbean. Flowers all year. Icaco Cay off Puerto Rico named after this tree.

GEIGER TREE *Cordia sebestena* **Fig. 71**

Small tree, to 15m (50 ft.) tall. Slightly hairy oval leaves; *flowers in showy orange-red clusters* of 5 or 6. Hard, egg-shaped fruit. Dry coasts; also planted. S. Florida, Caribbean. Flowers and fruits all year.

BLACK TORCH *Erithalis fruticosa* **Fig. 70, Pl. 20**

Compact rounded shrub, to 3m (10 ft.) tall. Dark green, leathery, elliptical leaves, to 9 cm (3½ in.) long; small, tubular, fragrant white flowers to 1 cm (⅜ in.) wide, in terminal clusters. *Furrowed round black fruit* 6mm (¼ in.) wide. Near beaches in coastal thickets; Florida, Caribbean. Flowers all year.

CARIBBEAN SEA SPURGE

Euphorbia mesembrianthemifolia

Much-branched shrubby herb, sometimes woody at base, to 1m (3¼ ft.) tall. *Fleshy, purplish red stems;* fleshy oblong leaves, pointed at tips, to 12mm (½ in.) long. Flowers reduced to a fleshy bud 1.5mm (¹⁄₁₆ in.) wide. Small smooth fruit, 3mm (⅛ in.) wide. Sandy beaches; Florida, West Indies. Flowers all year. **Similar species: American Seaside Spurge** *(E. polygonifolia,* Fig. 73) is a prostrate, creeping, small-leaved plant on dunes and beaches.

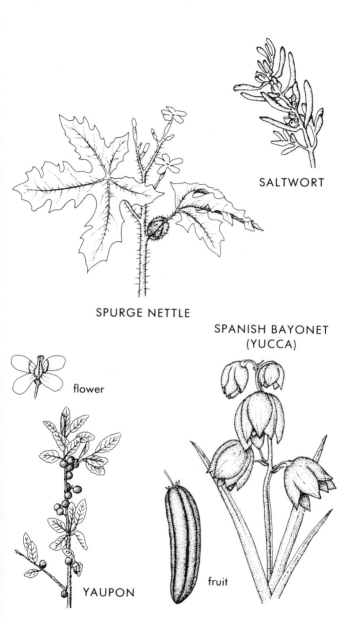

SALTWORT

SPURGE NETTLE

SPANISH BAYONET
(YUCCA)

flower

fruit

YAUPON

Fig. 74. Seaside shrubs (5) and an herb.

Many roots along creeping stems keep plant flat, reducing wind abrasion. Tiny, round, six-sided fruit, to 1.2 cm (½ in.) wide; flowers inconspicuous. *Milky sap.* Quebec to Georgia.

SHORTLEAF FIG   *Ficus citrifolia*

Spreading tree, to 12m (40 ft.) high, with *hanging aerial roots* often fusing with main trunk. Smooth, leathery, elliptic leaves, to 15 cm (6 in.) long, with pointed tips. Smooth, spherical, *yellow fruit with red protuberance;* 12mm (½ in.) wide. One of the largest trees in seashore thickets. Florida, Caribbean. Flowers and fruits most of year.

MANCHINEEL   *Hippomane mancinella*   **Pl. 19**

Spreading tree, to 9m (30 ft.) tall. Shiny dark green leaves with rounded base and pointed tip, to 10 cm (4 in.) long. Flowers lack petals; in inconspicuous green spikes to 10 cm (4 in.) long. *Round fruit resembles an apple*—green or yellow, sometimes with a reddish cheek; 3 cm (1¼ in.) wide. Fruit sweet-scented, palatable, but *very toxic.* The native antidote for poison is arrowroot, and poultices of arrowroot starch and water are used for Manchineel burns in the Grenadines. In 1884, 54 German seamen were poisoned in Curaçao; 5 died. Many recent cases, including a member of the 1970 Danish gymnastic team visiting St. John, have been saved by stomach pumps in hospitals. Irritating milky sap in leaves, twigs, and bark. Sap may wash off leaves, so do not stand under Manchineel tree when it rains. Coastal thickets, mangrove margins; Florida, Caribbean, Galápagos. Flowers spring to Oct.; fruit matures a year later.

YAUPON HOLLY   *Ilex vomitoria*   **Fig. 74**

Shrub or small tree, to 8m (26 ft.) tall, with elongate evergreen leaves and clusters of red berries. Separate male and female plants, both with tiny greenish white flowers: male flowers in stalked clusters of 3–9; female ones unstalked, 1–3, with 4 petals. Leaves leathery, finely toothed, smooth, dark green above, lighter below. *Red translucent berry,* 5mm (⅕ in.) wide. Shrub zone of dunes; Virginia to Florida and Gulf to Texas. Flowers March–May. Berries used by Indians to induce vomiting.

JOEWOOD   *Jacquinia arborea*   **Fig. 70, Pl. 20**

Shrub or tree, to 5m (18 ft.) tall, with pale bark. Glossy yellow-green, leathery, spoon-shaped leaves to 5 cm (2 in.) long. Fragrant white or *pale yellow, bell-shaped flowers* 1 cm (⅜ in.) wide, in dense clusters at ends of twigs. Clusters of smooth, round, orange fruit with pointed tips; each fruit 1 cm (⅜ in.) wide. Coastal thickets; Florida, West Indies. Flowers all year.

EASTERN RED CEDAR or JUNIPER   **Fig. 71**

Juniperus virginiana

Small columnar tree, to 15.2m (50 ft.) tall, shrubby on dunes. Leaves of two types: dark green scales about 1.6mm (¹⁄₁₆ in.) long, in 4 rows pressed on one another; young leaves light green, elongate, pointed "needles"; upper surface of "needles" silvery white. Flowers of each sex on separate trees; male flowers golden brown, female ones purplish. *Cones berry-like, dark blue,* to 8mm (⅓ in.) wide. Bark fibrous, reddish brown. Shrub zone of dunes; Canada to Florida.

AX MYRTLE *Myrica cerifera* **Fig. 70**

Evergreen shrub or small tree, to 8m (26 ft.) high, usually with several trunks. Bark pale brown, conspicuous whitish lenticels on twigs; leaves alternate, elongate, coming to blunt point; lower leaves larger, to 10cm (4 in.) long, irregularly toothed on upper edges. Upper leaves (near branch tips) smaller, often reddish. *Crushed foliage aromatic.* Male and female plants separate; female plants produce *waxy gray berries,* clustered along stems, that can be melted to produce candles. Mangrove swamp edges, shrub zone of dunes; S. Carolina to Texas, Bermuda, W. Indies. Flowers most of year.

IVE OAK *Quercus virginiana* **Fig. 70**

Can be huge tree, to 15.2m (50 ft.) tall, with trunk to 1.2m (4 ft.) wide above buttressed base, with thick, low, wide-spreading branches. Shrubby on dunes. Leaves elongate, alternate, evergreen (but falling in spring after new foliage appears); to 12.7cm (5 in.) long, dark green; shiny above, pale and hairy below. Flowers in 7.5-cm (3-in.) long catkins or spikes. *Acorns in long-stalked clusters* of 3–5. Shrub zone of dunes; Virginia to Florida, Gulf to Mexico, Cuba.

RICKLY-PEAR CACTUS *Opuntia* species **Fig. 77**

Flat, blade-like branches, to 2.5cm (1 in.) thick and 25cm (10 in.) long, attached to one another, giving plant a jointed appearance. Often prostrate near sea. Branches covered with few solitary 2.5-cm (1-in.) long *spines.* Yellow flowers, to 5cm (2 in.) wide, with 8–10 petals, followed by pear-shaped, 2.5- to 5-cm (1- to 2-in.) long fruit, which ripens to a purple color. Fruit edible, but covered with tiny spines that must be carefully brushed or singed off, or peel to eat. Many species on beaches, dunes; Canada to Texas and Mexico, W. Indies. Flowers in spring and summer.

EDBAY *Persea borbonia* **Fig. 70**

Evergreen tree, to 21.3m (70 ft.) tall, with a straight trunk; shrubby on dunes. Leaves alternate, elongate, *aromatic when crushed;* 10cm (4 in.) long, pointed, bright green; shiny above, paler, wooly below. Petioles 1.3cm (½ in.) long, red-brown. Flowers in small groups, yellow or creamy white, six-lobed. *Blue-black oval berry with large pit, on orange stem.* Shrub zone of dunes; Delaware to Florida, Gulf to Texas. Flowers in spring. Leaves, called "bay leaves," used as spice.

EASIDE ROCK SHRUB *Rachicallis americana* **Pl. 20**

Shrub, to 120cm (47 in.) tall, usually much lower, almost prostrate in exposed areas. *Tiny oval, shiny, fleshy, light green leaves covering branches in clusters.* Yellow waxy flower with 4 tiny petals on tube 6mm (¼ in.) long. Fruit a seven-sided capsule 3mm (⅛ in.) wide. On coastal limestone bare rocks; W. Indies (especially Jamaica), Bahamas, Cayman I. Flowers all year.

CABBAGE PALM   *Sabal palmetto*   **Pl. 21**
Branchless, columnar, gray-tan trunk with a crown of *large, fanlike leaves* to 3m (9⅘ ft.) long, each with a prominent midrib. Small creamy flowers in large *drooping clusters* on crown, followed by black fruits 8mm (⅓ in.) wide. Shrub zone of dunes; N. Carolina to Florida; W. Indies. Flowers in summer. Official state tree of Florida.

SAW PALMETTO   *Serenoa repens*   **Fig. 71**
Shrub with *main stem prostrate,* creeping; bright green, *palmlike, circular leaves* notched into many points. Leaves to 1m (39 in.) wide, on long, slender, three-sided, spiny petioles. Flower white, fragrant; bluish black berry, to 2cm (¾ in.) long, juicy. Shrub zone of dunes; N. Carolina to Florida. Flowers in summer.

SEASIDE STRUMFIA   *Strumfia maritima*   **Pl. 20**
Many-branched shrub, to 1m (39 in.) high. Tiny, narrow, pointed leaves in whorls of 3, hairy beneath, to 2cm (¾ in.) long. *Flower with pink petals.* White berry, about 3.5mm (⅛ in.) wide. On coastal limestone bare rocks; Florida, W. Indies, Mexico. Flowers Dec.–March, June.

BAY CEDAR   *Suriana maritima*   **Fig. 72; Pls. 19, 21**
Branching shrub or small tree, to 8m (27 ft.) tall. Broadly linear, *hairy, yellow green, clustered leaves,* to 4cm (1½ in.) long. Inconspicuous small yellow flowers, solitary or in small clusters. Hairy fruit at leaf bases, to 5mm (¼ in.) wide. Coastal beaches and dunes, often part of littoral hedge; Florida, W. Indies. Flowers all year.

SEASIDE MAHO   *Thespesia populnea*   **Fig. 71, Pl. 19**
Dense, spreading shrub or tree, to 9m (30 ft.) tall. Dark green, shiny, heart-shaped leaves, to 20cm (8 in.) long. Large *bell-shaped flower* with 5 petals, 5cm (2 in.) wide; yellow, turning purple inside. Fruit round, slightly flattened, green or brown, five-ridged, hard; 3cm (1¼ in.) wide. Coastal thickets, mangrove margins; Florida, W. Indies, pantropical. Flowers and fruits in spring and fall. Flowers reportedly eaten. A related tree with larger yellow flowers, also known as Seaside Maho, is *Hibiscus tiliaceus;* it grows on the landward side of mangrove swamps throughout the tropics.

WEST INDIAN SEA LAVENDER   **Fig. 72, Pl. 19**
Mallotonia gnaphalodes
Stocky shrub, to 2m (6½ ft.) tall. *Silvery greenish white, silky, hairy, broadly linear leaves,* to 10cm (4 in.) long. Small white flowers in dense, one-sided, slightly curved clusters. Small black fruit, 5mm (¼ in.) in diameter, with pointed tips. Sandy beaches, rocky areas; solitary or hedge-forming. Florida, W. Indies, Mexico. Flowers all year.

HERCULES CLUB   *Xanthoxylum clava-herculis*   **Fig. 72**
Shrub or small tree, to 17m (55 ft.) tall, with *sharp spines* on trunk, branches. Compound leaves, to 30cm (1 ft.) long, each

consisting of 5–19 opposite leaflets, often with *paired spines at junction.* Leaflets to 5 cm (2 in.) long. White or greenish white flowers of separate sexes in large groups; 5 petals. Berry 5 mm (⅕ in.) long, in 2–3 sections. Dune shrub zone; Georgia to Florida; Gulf to Texas. Flowers all year.

ꟼANISH BAYONET or YUCCA   **Fig. 74, Pl. 19**
Yucca aloifolia
Upright perennial, to 7.6 m (25 ft.) tall. Leaves hairless, elongate, *swordlike, sharply pointed;* to 35 cm (13¾ in.) long and 4 cm (1½ in.) wide, in clusters around a single light green stem. *Spike of waxy, white, bell-shaped flowers,* to 7.5 cm (3 in.) wide. Fleshy black fruit, to 9 cm (3½ in.) long; seeds black, shiny. Dunes; S. Carolina to Texas; W. Indies. Flowers in spring.

Vines

ꞄAY NICKERBEAN   *Caesalpinia bonduc*   **Fig. 69**
Sprawling vine with *vicious spines.* Compound leaf, to 60 cm (2 ft.) long; twice pinnate, 5–9 pairs of pinnae, 5–7 pairs of leaflets. Leaflets oval, to 4 cm (1½ in.) long. Dark brown *prickly pod,* to 8 cm (3⅕ in.) long, contains buoyant smooth gray seed commonly washed up on beaches (see p. 146). Limestone thickets. Widely distributed in tropics and subtropics. Flowers and fruits Aug.–April. Seeds used in jewelry.

ꞄASIDE BEAN   *Canavalia maritima*   **Pls. 18, 20**
Trailing vine, to 10 m (35 ft.) long. Trifoliate, smooth, dark green leaves. Showy *rose-purple flower,* to 3 cm (1⅕ in.) across. Thick pod, to 10 cm (4 in.) long; becomes woody with age; several brownish "beans" inside pod. Coastal strands. Widely distributed throughout tropics. Flowers all year. Beans can be eaten if boiled for a long time and outer skin removed.

ꞄTTERFLY PEA   *Centrosema virginianum*   **Fig. 75**
Vine with climbing stems and twining branchlets. Leaves alternate, divided into 3 elongated leaflets, each 6.3 cm (2½ in.) long. Flower to 3.8 cm (1½ in.) wide, violet, with broad *petal-like standard facing down, narrow keel facing up.* Pod to 12 cm (4¾ in.) long. Dune meadows; New Jersey to Florida, Gulf to Texas. Flowers summer. **Similar species: Blue Pea** *(Clitoria mariana)* climbs higher; leaves similar, fruit a flattened pod to 5 cm (2 in.) long. Pink flower with *petal-like standard facing up, keel pointing down.* Dune meadows; New York to Florida, Gulf to Texas. Flowers in summer.

ꞄACH MORNING GLORY   *Ipomoea pes-caprae*   **Pl. 18**
Long prostrate runner, to 6 m (20 ft.) long. Roundish or notched, smooth, rather succulent shiny green leaves, to 10 cm (4 in.) long. *Funnel-shaped purple flowers,* to 5 cm (2 in.) wide, solitary or in

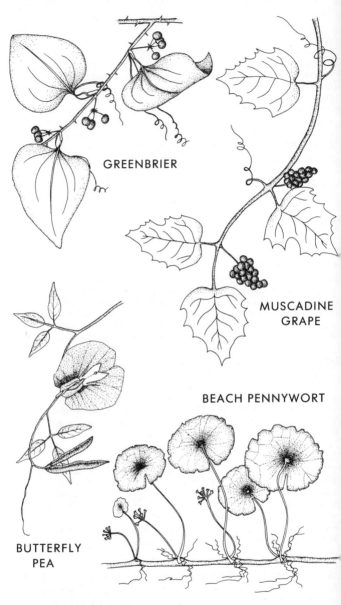

GREENBRIER

MUSCADINE
GRAPE

BEACH PENNYWORT

BUTTERFLY
PEA

Fig. 75. Seaside vines and a viny herb.

small clusters. Brown, buoyant seed covered with pale hairs. Forms carpets on sandy beaches. Pantropical, Florida. Flowers and fruits most of year.

DDLE-LEAF MORNING GLORY Fig. 12
Ipomoea stolonifera

Vine with dark green, shiny leaves, variable in shape— elongate-oval, some deeply lobed at base. Leaves to 10 cm (4 in.) long, on petioles as long as leaf. *Flower white with yellow throat.* Beaches; N. Carolina to Florida, Gulf to Mexico; Caribbean. Flowers all year.

UBBER VINE *Rhabdadenia biflora*

Smooth shrubby vine with soft flexible stems. Dark green oval leaves, pointed at tips, to 9 cm (3½ in.) long. *Pinkish white, tube-shaped flower with yellow eye,* solitary or in small clusters, to 6 cm (2½ in.) wide. Fruit slightly curved, slender, elongate, to 14 cm (5½ in.) long. Mangrove communities, coastal areas; Florida, Caribbean. Flowers all year.

REENBRIERS *Smilax* species Fig. 75

Thorny vines with light green, broad, *oval, heavily veined, leathery, glossy leaves* and small, white, *three-petaled flowers.* Green stems with tendrils; small berries in clusters. **Similar species:** Many. (1) **Common Greenbrier** *(S. rotundifolia)* has broad oval leaves and bluish black berries. Stems and branches with stout flattened spines. (2) **Coral Greenbrier** *(S. walteri)* is similar but with *red berries* that persist over winter. (3) **Catbrier** *(S. bonanox)* has some leaves with *lobes at base,* dark-tipped spines on stems, black berries with one seed, and *four-angled stems.* (4) **Wild Bamboo** *(S. auriculata)* has narrow, elongate leaves that are usually lobed near base, *zigzag branchlets,* and black berries. All species densely cover trees to 5m (16 ft.), in rear and shrub zones of dunes; Canada to Florida, Gulf to Texas and beyond. Flowers May–June.

USCADINE GRAPE Fig. 75
Vitis rotundifolia

Deciduous vine, often climbing on trees, with *purple-black to bronze grapes* to 2.5 cm (1 in.) across, few per bunch. Long tendrils; opposite leaves on long petioles. Leaves *not lobed,* shiny, irregularly toothed; broad, to 12 cm (4¾ in.) long and wide. Groups of tiny greenish flowers with 5 fused petals. Dune shrub zone; Delaware to Florida, Gulf to Texas. Flowers in summer.

EST INDIAN CREEPER or CREEPING DAISY Pl. 18
Wedelia trilobata

Prostrate vine with bright green opposite leaves at about 10-cm (4-in.) intervals. Leaves have *long central lobe and a reduced lobe on either side.* Small yellow flower with 8–13 petals. Sandy beaches behind spray zone; Florida, Bahamas, Caribbean. Flowers all year. Called Beach Marigold in W. Indies, where its leaves are used to make medicinal tea.

Herbs

ORACH or SPEARSCALE *Atriplex arenaria* **Fig. 76**
Annual herb, alternate leaves elongate or arrowhead-shaped, silvery gray, *scaly beneath;* branches sprawling, weak, causing plant to appear broad, flattened. Flowers spike-like; fruits broad, with 3–5 teeth across top; seeds reddish brown. Beaches, dunes, edge of salt marshes; New Hampshire to Florida, Gulf to Texas, W. Indies. **Similar species: Northern Orach,** *A. patula* var. *hastata.* Lower leaves opposite and *triangular;* upper leaves alternate and elongate; green or purplish green. Canada to S. Carolina. Edible—tastes like its relative, spinach. Flowers in late summer.

SEA DAISY *Borrichia arborescens* **Pl. 20**
Bushy, to 1m (3¼ ft.) tall, with *silver-green, aromatic, fleshy, pointed, elliptical leaves* to 6cm (2¼ in.) long. Cheery *yellow flowers in solitary heads.* Salt marshes, mangrove swamps, beaches, and dunes; Virginia to Florida and Gulf, Caribbean. Flowers in spring, summer.

SEA ROCKET *Cakile edentula harperi* **Figs. 17, 76**
Succulent annual herb, with much-branched stem, to 50cm (20 in.) tall. Leaves dark green; spatulate or elongate, coarsely lobed or toothed, narrowed at base; to 15cm (6 in.) long near bottom of plant, smaller on branches. Tiny flowers pale purple, whitish, 5mm (⅕ in.) wide with *4 petals.* Fruit a cylindrical pod with 2 swellings; upper fruit segment eight-ribbed. Sandy beaches; Maine to Florida. Flowers fall. **Similar species: Caribbean Sea Rocket** *(C. lanceolata)* is similar to *C. edentula,* except often prostrate with long branches, to 50cm (20 in.) in length; *leaves less toothed, often narrow,* with few lobes. Beaches; Florida, Caribbean to Brazil, W. Indies. Flowers all year.

BEACH CROTON *Croton punctatus* **Fig. 77, Pl. 19**
Whitish green, feltlike perennial herb to 1m (39 in.) tall, with a woody base; often prostrate. Oval leaves to 5cm (2 in.) long, thick, covered with white fuzz, on long petioles. Spike-like male flowers to 2cm (⅔ in.) long, in tiny groups; female flowers below male ones on spike, in groups of 1–3. Berry to 8mm (³⁄₁₀ in.) long. Dunes, beaches; N. Carolina to Florida, Gulf to Texas. Flowers all year. **Related species: Shore Croton** or **Rosemary** *(C. linearis,* Pl. 20) is a small, aromatic shrub to 3m (10 ft.) high (usually less than 1m—39 in.—tall), with elongate, narrow, glossy green leaves; *upper leaves often bright red.* Male and female plants separate; male flower tiny, white, with 12 stamens; fruit is a berry 5mm (⅕ in.) long. Florida, Bahamas, West Indies.

FIREWHEEL or INDIAN BLANKET **Fig. 76**
Gaillardia pulchella
Herb with branching hairy stems bearing solitary flowers with

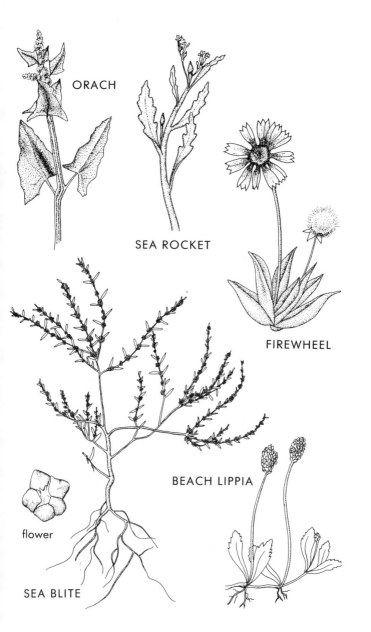

ORACH

SEA ROCKET

FIREWHEEL

BEACH LIPPIA

flower

SEA BLITE

Fig. 76. Seaside herbs (1).

brick red, triple, yellow-tipped petals. Flowers to 7.5 cm (3 in.) wide; leaves to 7.5 cm (3 in.) long, fuzzy or hairy, lower bluntly lobed, upper elongate. Stem to 40 cm (16 in.) tall. Interdune meadows; Virginia to Florida and Gulf to Texas, Mexico. Flowers in summer.

GRASSLEAF GOLDEN-ASTER
Heterotheca graminifolia
Herb with *alternate, grasslike leaves,* to 25 cm (10 in.) long, covered with silvery hairs. Small, *yellow, asterlike flowers* in groups of 3 or more, to 1.5 cm (⅗ in.) wide, with many petals. Interdune meadows; Delaware to Florida, Gulf to Mexico. Flowers fall. **Similar species:** (1) **Camphorweed** *(H. subaxillaris),* to 1 m (39 in.) tall, with alternate oval leaves to 7 cm (2¾ in.) long; lower ones with lobes or toothed, *upper ones clasping stem.* Bright yellow flowers, to 2 cm (¾ in.) wide, with 15–30 petals, on long hairy stems. Beaches, interdune meadows; Delaware to Florida, Gulf to Texas and Brazil. Flowers in fall. (2) **Salt-marsh Aster** *(Aster tenuifolius,* Fig. 77, Pl. 19), to 60 m (2 ft.) tall. Scraggly, many branched, with few *white or purple-petaled, daisy-like flowers* to 2.5 cm (1 in.) wide, with yellow centers. Leaves fleshy, round, narrow, tapering at both ends. Brackish marshes; New Hampshire to Florida, Gulf to Mississippi. Flowers in fall.

BEACH PENNYWORT or DOLLARWEED   **Fig. 75**
Hydrocotyle bonariensis
Prostrate perennial herb with umbrella-shaped leaves to 10 cm (4 in.) wide, extending from a slender prostrate stem that roots at nodes. Groups of tiny whitish green flowers, on long stems originating at nodes together with leaf stem. Fruit with flattened sides, about 3 mm (⅛ in.) wide, ribbed. Moist sand above beach; N. Carolina to Florida; Gulf to Texas to Brazil, W. Indies. Flowers all year. May grow in mats on sand or water.

SEASIDE HELIOTROPE   **Fig. 77**
Heliotropium curassavicum
Branched, spreading, prostrate, with ascending shoots. Often woody at base, to 50 cm (20 in.) tall. Gray-green, almost linear, fleshy leaves, 5 cm (2 in.) long. Small white odorless *flowers with yellow eye, in linear clusters at ends of stems, curling at apexes.* Tiny depressed fruit, 2 mm (1/12 in.) long. Sandy or gravelly places near sea; Florida, Caribbean. Flowers most of year.

SPIDER LILY   *Hymenocallis latifolia*   **Pl. 18**
Herb arising from a large, papery-coated bulb to 10 cm (4 in.) wide. Many broadly linear, *shiny bright green leaves,* to 60 cm (2 ft.) long. Stout stem bearing *fragrant white flowers* to 16 cm (6¼ in.) wide, with narrow, often drooping petals. Upper sandy and limestone beaches; Florida, W. Indies. Flowers sporadically.

MARSH ELDER   *Iva frutescens*   **Fig. 72, Pl. 21**
Woody, rather succulent herb to 1 m (39 in.) tall. *Lanceolate, often sharply toothed, light green leaves,* to 10 cm (4 in.) long. Small, yellow-white flowers clustered into a small arch alternating

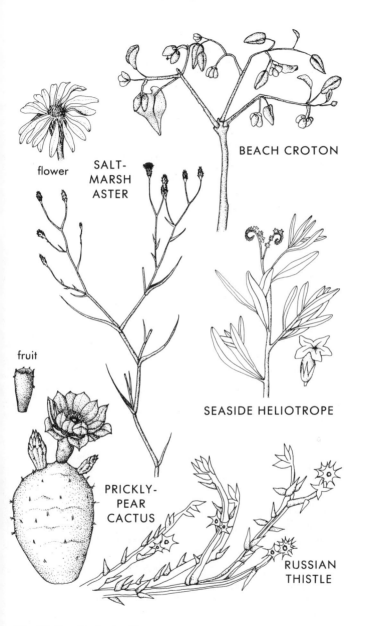

flower

SALT-
MARSH
ASTER

BEACH CROTON

fruit

SEASIDE HELIOTROPE

PRICKLY-
PEAR
CACTUS

RUSSIAN
THISTLE

Fig. 77. Seaside herbs (2).

between leaf pairs. Beach thickets and salt marshes; Canada to Florida, Gulf, W. Indies, Mexico. Flowers summer to fall.

SEA LAVENDER *Limonium carolinianum* **Pl. 21**

Perennial woody herb with much-branched stems, to 60 cm (2 ft.) tall. Basal leaves narrow to oval, to 17.5 cm (6⅘ in.) long; upper leaves reduced or absent, giving plant a *wiry appearance*. Groups of tiny, tubular, *lavender flowers* with 5 petals on one side of stem; fruit a capsule to 6mm (¼ in.) wide. Salt glands on leaves and stems allow plant to withstand submersion in salt water. Salt marshes; Canada to Mexico, W. Indies. Flowers all year.

BEACH LIPPIA *Lippia nodiflora* **Fig. 76**

Weedy, creeping herb with ascending shoots, to 1m (39 in.) long. *Spoon-shaped, partly serrated leaves* to 6 cm (2¼ in.) long. Purplish white *flowers clustered into dense, cylindrical heads* 12mm (½ in.) long. Sandy beaches, salt marshes; Florida, Caribbean. Flowers all year.

SEASIDE or DUNE PRIMROSE **Fig. 73**
Oenothera humifusa

Perennial herb with woody, often prostrate stems branching from base; leaves to 3 cm (1⅕ in.) long, elongate, may have toothed edges; leaves and branches covered with silky hairs. Bright *yellow or pink and yellow primrose flowers open near sunset; fruit an elongate hairy capsule* 3 cm (1⅕ in.) long, slightly curved; seeds brown. Interdune meadows, beaches; N. Carolina to Florida, Gulf to Louisiana, W. Indies. Flowers in spring and fall.

SOUTHERN GLASSWORT *Salicornia perennis* **Pl. 18**

Erect, branched, fleshy herb, to 30 cm (1 ft.) tall. Main stem often woody; leaves reduced to minute scales on jointed stem, resembling thin asparagus. Minute flowers sunken into greenish yellow spikes to 4 cm (1½ in.) long. *Stems often yellow-red.* Forms mats in salt marshes, mangrove marshes, salinas. Near sea throughout our area. Flowers all year. Several similar species in our area.

RUSSIAN THISTLE *Salsola kali* **Fig. 77**

Annual bristly, branching herb with linear, succulent, *thornlike leaves, each with a spine at tip.* To 60 cm (2 ft.) tall, with alternate leaves and spiny, pinkish or purplish flowers to 1 cm (⅜ in.) wide, in groups. Beaches; Canada to Florida, Gulf to Louisiana. Flowers in summer.

INKBERRY *Scaevola plumieri* **Fig. 71**

Succulent, erect, glossy herb to 1.5m (5 ft.) tall. *Yellowish, scarred stem* with oval, bright green leaves tapering at base, to 6 cm (2¼ in.) long. Pinkish white, open-tube flower to 3 cm (1¼ in.) long. Black pulpy fruit to 1.5 cm (⅝ in.) wide; has 2 seeds. Sandy beaches and dunes; Florida, W. Indies. Flowers all year.

SEASIDE PURSLANE *Sesuvium portulacastrum* **Pls. 18, 19**

Prostrate fleshy herb. Stems often reddish with green, broadly linear leaves to 5 cm (2 in.) long. *Star-shaped, deep pink, solitary flowers,* 1 cm (⅜ in.) wide. Ovoid fruit 7mm (⁵⁄₁₆ in.) wide. Forms dense cover on beaches and dunes; often most seaward plant.

Florida, W. Indies, Central America. Flowers all year. Leaves
edible.

SEASIDE GOLDENROD   **Pl. 21**
Solidago sempervirens
Woody stems to 1.8m (6 ft.) high with elongate leaves to 7.5 cm (3
in.) long. *Typical goldenrod flowers* above leaves in fall. Sandy
beaches, dunes; Canada to Florida, Gulf to Texas and beyond.

SEA BLITE   *Sueda maritima*   **Fig. 76**
Annual herb, often much branched, often forming mats, with
spiny stem to 60 cm (2 ft.) tall. Alternate, cylindrical, pointed
leaves to 5 cm (2 in.) long; tiny flowers in clusters of 3–5
surrounding leaf bases and half encircling stem. Tiny fruit to
2 mm (¹⁄₁₀ in.), a transparent sphere enclosing 1 horizontal, shiny
black seed. Salt marshes, beaches; Canada to Florida. Flowers in
summer. **Similar species: Common Sea Blite** *(S. linearis)*
grows to 1 m (39 in.) tall. Leaves dark green; *stems not spiny.* Fruit
resembles irregular star with unequal sepals. Salt marshes,
beaches; Florida to Texas, W. Indies. Flowers in spring, fall.

Grasses

AMERICAN BEACHGRASS   **Fig. 18, Pl. 21**
Ammophilia brevigulata
To 1m (39 in.) tall, with extensive rhizomes and long, narrow
leaves extending primarily from sheaths at base of plant. *Panicle
(seedhead) to 30 cm (1 ft.) long,* nearly cylindrical; becomes pale
tan in fall. Covers dunes and upper beaches; Canada to N.
Carolina.

SANDBUR   *Cenchrus tribuloides*   **Fig. 78**
Branching tufts of 1 cm (³⁄₈ in.) wide, elongate blades, to 18 cm (7
in.) long. *Bur with many spikes,* to 2 cm (³⁄₄ in.) wide. Bur green in
June, tan later. Plant to 45 cm (1½ ft.) tall, on secondary dunes
and rear of primary dunes; New York to Gulf, tropical America.

BERMUDA GRASS   *Cynodon dactylon*   **Fig. 78**
Weedy grass 10 cm (4 in.) high. Leaves to 6 cm (2¼ in.) long,
growing from creeping rhizomes. *Minute flowers in 3–5 spikes
radiating out like fingers* at tips of stems. Dry disturbed areas,
tropical. Flowers April–Nov.

CARIBBEAN SEDGE   *Cyperus ligularis*   **Fig. 78, Pl. 18**
Forms large clumps to 1m (39 in.) wide. Pale green leaves with
rough edges; triangular stems. *Cluster of dark, coppery brown
spikes.* Salt marshes, mangrove swamps; Florida, Central America. Flowers most of year.

SEASHORE SALTGRASS   *Distichlis spicata*   **Fig. 78, Pl. 21**
Light green, with *overlapping narrow leaves pointed diagonally
upward.* Leaves thin, less than 15 cm (6 in.) long; plant to 80 cm
(32 in.) tall, usually less than 30 cm (1 ft.) tall. Inflorescence
stalked, to 6 cm (2⅓ in.) long, pale or greenish, composed of

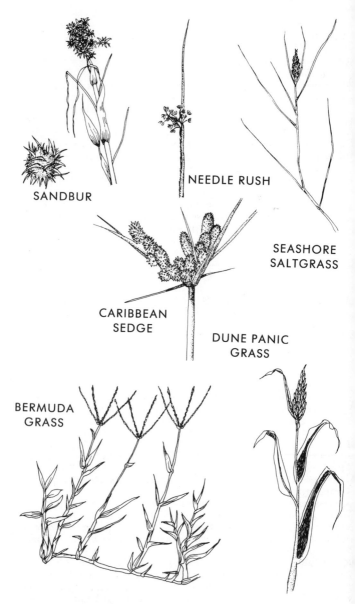

SANDBUR

NEEDLE RUSH

SEASHORE
SALTGRASS

CARIBBEAN
SEDGE

DUNE PANIC
GRASS

BERMUDA
GRASS

Fig. 78. Seaside grasses.

spikelets to 1 cm (⅜ in.) long. Vertical stems on underground rhizomes. Forms light green meadows or mats on edges of cordgrass marshes, salt flats, beaches; Canada to S. America, W. Indies. Flowers in summer.

ROPICAL SEDGE *Fimbristylis cymosa* **Pl. 18**
Slender, stiff stem arising from flat spreading leaves, to 40 cm (16 in.) tall. *Dark brown head of dense spikes.* Swamps, mangrove swamp margins, coastal areas. Pantropical. Perennial. Flowers all year.

EEDLE RUSH or BLACK RUSH **Fig. 78**
Juncus roemerianus
To 1.5 m (5 ft.) tall. Leaves rigid, *needle-like;* in tufts, on scaly rhizomes. Leaf tips pointed, penetrate clothing. Flowers in clusters, tiny with green centers, maturing to *flat brown capsules,* each 3 mm (⅛ in.) wide, *on short stems, partway up plant.* Forms extensive colonies landward of cordgrass marshes in brackish to fresh water. Needle Rush marsh is tan-brown all year, distinguishing it from cordgrass marsh in areas where they meet. Atlantic and Gulf coasts. Flowers in early spring and fall.

UNE PANIC GRASS *Panicum amarum* **Fig. 78**
Scraggly, often *drooping blue-green leaves,* in tufts to 40 cm (16 in.) tall. Leaves to 2 cm (¾ in.) wide. Inflorescence sparse, narrow, nodding, composed of spikelets to 7 mm (³⁄₁₆ in.) long. Beaches and dunes; N. Jersey to Florida, Gulf to Mexico, Bahamas, Cuba. Flowers in spring and summer.

:ASHORE PASPALUM or SEASIDE MILLET
Paspalum distichum
Creeping grass with brown rhizomes. Leaf blades to 15 cm (6 in.) long, rather stiff. *Minute flowers clustered on 1 side of each raceme* of 7.5-cm (3-in.) long, *forked floret.* Moist sandy soil near sea. All warm coasts. Flowers sporadically.

ALT JOINTGRASS *Paspalum vaginatum*
Creeping perennial grass to 60 cm (2 ft.) tall; blades flat, to 8 mm (3/10 in.) wide and 15 cm (6 in.) long. Flower consists of *2 racemes forking at tip of stem in V-shape,* each 5 cm (2 in.) long. Forms mats on dunes, sand; N. Carolina to Texas, Mexico to Brazil. Flowers in fall.

ALT REED or REED GRASS **Fig. 22**
Phragmites australis
Tall—to 4 m (13 ft.)—*with fuzzy brown or tan inflorescence* to 30 cm (1 ft.) long and 7.5 cm (3 in.) wide. Inflorescence fades to tan or bluish in fall and winter. Forms meadows on disturbed, sandy areas adjacent to salt marshes. Common in Northeast, spreading throughout southern and Gulf coasts. Flowers July–Sept.

:ACOAST BLUESTEM *Schizachyrium scoparius*
Silver-blue hairy leaves curve off stems at right angles, giving tufted appearance; stems to 30 cm (1 ft.) high. Inflorescences at tips of slender stems which are interspersed among leaves, so that *flowers appear as tiny clusters up and down plant.* Beaches, dunes;

East and Gulf coasts, W. Indies. Flowers in early summer; seed-heads covered with silvery hairs in late summer, fall.

SMOOTH CORDGRASS   *Spartina alterniflora*   **Pl. 21**
Stem to 2.5m (8⅕ ft.) tall, usually spongy at 1-cm (⅜-in.) thick base. Leaf blades smooth, flat, to 1.5 cm (⅝ in.) wide. Flowers on spike to 15 cm (6 in.) long, hairy. Forms dense colonies of dark green, wide leaved plants in lower marsh; grows where subject to almost *daily inundation with salt water.* Canada to Texas. Flowers summer. **Similar species: Saltmeadow Cordgrass** (*S. patens*) is slender and shorter—to 1m (39 in.) tall; pale green, in dense colonies produced by slender rhizomes. *Leaf blade less than* 3mm (⅛ in.) wide; flower a pale spike to 5 cm (2 in.) long. Forms extensive meadows in salt marshes higher than Smooth Cordgrass, and on sand, dunes, where inundated several times a month or subject to intense spray. Canada to Bahamas, W. Indies, Texas. Flowers in summer.

SEASHORE DROPSEED   *Sporobolus virginicus*   **Pl. 18**
Creeping grass that forms large colonies; roots at nodes. Erect stems, to 40 cm (16 in.) tall. Sheathed leaf blades to 5 cm (2 in.) long. Flowers clustered into *slender spikes* to 10 cm (4 in.) long. Saline and brackish sands. Warm coasts of both hemispheres. Flowers in summer.

SEA OATS   *Uniola paniculata*   **Fig. 22, Pl. 21**
Tall grass, to 1.5m (5 ft.) high. Lower leaves numerous, elongate, to 40 cm (16 in.) long. Flowers in long, drooping, purplish spikelets to 3 cm (1⅕ in.) long, in clusters to 40 cm (16 in.) long; *fruit oval, flat, disklike,* to 1.5 cm (⅗ in.) long; *tan on tan stalk.* Dunes; Virginia to Florida, Gulf Coast to Texas. Flowers June–July.

9

Mangrove Communities of Florida and the Caribbean

Like the many-armed Hindu god Siva, the Red Mangrove tree squats in the mud and creates land out of the void. Its many prop roots reach out into the water, and tiny motes of sediment fall at its feet. The mystical belief in the cyclical nature of creation and destruction is also fulfilled, for the very nature of its creative role seals the doom of this unusual tree.

The Red Mangrove is virtually unique in its ability to live with its roots bathed in the saltiest of seawater. This ability and the fact that it nurtures its young (seedlings) longer than do most other plants, together make the Red Mangrove a pioneer plant in the ecological sequence called succession.

Succession is the sequence of events by which a biotic community constantly changes in composition until it achieves near-perfect balance with its environment. This complex web of interdependence between animals, plants and their physical environment eventually produces a relatively unchanging biological unit, the climax community. The process is subtle. For example, it may take hundreds of years to go through the stages of succession from sand dune to forest. First, pioneer plants, such as grasses, stabilize the dune. Their rotting leaves provide organic matter that begins to change the sand to soil. When sufficient moisture and organic matter have accumulated, shrubs appear, then trees. As the plant cover changes, so do populations of animals dependent on the plants. Ants and spiders, among the few animals capable of eking out an existence on the almost bare dunes, must eventually, as grasses and then shrubs appear, share their habitat with grasshoppers, beetles, and other animals. When the soil becomes richer and the shade dense, other animals invade the virgin habitat, soon crowding out its original inhabitants. As the forest replaces the scrubland, new animals appear, adapted to life in the trees and in the dense shade below them. Once the climax forest biome is reached, unless a fire or storm intercedes, no further succession occurs and the composition of the climax forest will remain more or less constant.

Man and fire, however, have had a profound influence on the climax forest. Only on a few mountainous Caribbean islands can one gain a glimpse of the original forests. Even these are not virgin forests of exclusively native trees, for many exotics from Africa and Asia have been introduced. These trees often lack natural enemies in their new habitat and may displace native plants, so the original climax forests will never again appear as they were before the islands were burned over for sugar and tobacco plantations. Tobago, that wonderful Gauguinesque island with its richly forested mountains, was a sea of sugar cane two centuries ago, with only the tops of mountains too rugged to be deforested. It is shocking to learn that the tall jungle now covering the island is perhaps a hundred years old or less, and that its most beautiful trees, the Immortelles, with their huge canopies of orange flowers, were brought from South America to provide shade for cocoa plantations.

Succession in the Mangrove Community

You can still see mangrove forests edging the land, sometimes as extensive as they were hundreds of years ago. The doctor on Columbus' ship off Hispaniola reported in 1494 that the mangroves were "so thick that a rabbit could scarcely walk through." The mangroves may look the same today, a wall of bright green along the shore, but their location is not the same. During several hundreds of years the mangroves have extended the edges of the island a mile or more in their determined march toward the sea.

Mangroves specialize in land reclamation. The process begins with the yellow waxy flower, which soon becomes a brown, cone-shaped fruit that contains an embryo. In most fruits the tiny

Fig. 79. Red Mangrove leaf and seedling.

embryo is buried within the seed and surrounded by food. No further development occurs until the seed is covered with suitable moist soil. But the Red Mangrove embryo grows to 30 cm (1 ft.) in length before it drops off the tree into the seawater. A seed is vulnerable. That is why plants expend so much energy producing huge numbers of them, in anticipation that only a few will survive. But the Red Mangrove retains its young until they develop into seedlings, juvenile plants, before releasing them into the cruel world. The elongate seedling floats. After a few days the pointed end absorbs water, becomes heavy, and sinks; the waxy fruit end repels the water and floats, so the seedling bobs along pointed end down. Sometimes a few leaves sprout from the upper end and roots from the lower. The seedling can survive in this state for a year. If, during that time, the young plant floats to a shoal or the shallows of a sand island, it will penetrate the sediment and take root. Often this occurs offshore, out of sight of land, as ocean currents pile up sand within a few centimeters of the water's surface.

In a year the plant grows to 1 meter (39 in.) tall. Within three years it has produced many prop roots, which look like pendulous branches growing down into the water. If it is rooted near other young mangroves, then in five years, barring a hurricane, a diminutive forest will have been created (see Fig. 80, Pl. 23). The maze of prop roots slows down the currents, and tiny suspended particles sink to the bottom. The sandy sediment that the mangroves originally invaded becomes mixed with these tiny particles and turns to muddy sand. The leaves of the trees drop into the water and become trapped among the roots. It has been estimated that an acre of Red Mangroves sheds more than 3 tons of leaves per year. Bacteria and molds, invading the area in incredible numbers, begin to decompose the leaves, breaking them down into tiny fragments of highly organic detritus. This mixes with the muddy sand to form a rich, densely packed sediment. The first stage in succession has been completed: the composition of the bottom has been altered.

The fertile mud is invaded by algae, whose green filaments cover exposed surfaces in the intertidal zone, stabilizing the mud. In the shallows distinctive large algae appear. The Merman's Shaving Brushes and hard and soft fan algae (Plate 35) grow in profusion. The many forms of *Caulerpa* (bunches of tiny green grape-like spheres or horizontal rows of feathery blades) are also pioneers. A disk alga, *Halimeda opuntia* (p. 132) forms dense green colonies that cover the bottom in patches, disintegrating after a time into calcareous sand.

Now the intertidal shallows are invaded by the thin, stiff, rounded leaves of Shoal Grass (Fig. 68). These form dense mats in the lower intertidal that extend outward into deeper water. As time goes on, however, the dominant seagrasses invade the now-receptive environment, replacing the Shoal Grass except in

Fig. 80. Seedlings of Red Mangroves colonizing sandy shallows.

the intertidal. Turtle Grass, its broad, fuzzy leaves slowing the water and filtering out even the smallest particles of sediment, takes over in water 30 cm (1 ft.) deep, and the foundations of the Turtle Grass biome are laid (see p. 112).

Meanwhile the rich mud has become thicker under the Red Mangroves. The bacteria in the upper few centimeters of sediment use up the available oxygen, and the dense mud inhibits oxygen penetration. The layer below the surface becomes black and smells of rotten eggs, a sign of oxygen deficiency and an anoxic environment. As the sediment builds up, the roots of the Red Mangrove become too high to be perpetually bathed in seawater. The mangroves can survive, since their roots reach down into the water layer beneath the sediment surface, but the slight increase in sediment height has permitted a competitor to appear. The Black Mangrove (p. 178) is adapted to living a few centimeters higher than the Red. It solves the problem of obtaining oxygen in the anoxic mud by extending from its roots pencil-shaped, gray, knobby, air-breathing rootlets called pneumatophores (Fig. 81). These rootlets grow vertically at intervals along the length of the root in a straight line. Near the tree the pneumatophores are crowded together; but you can trace the roots along the periphery by following the pneumatophores as they grow outward in single rows.

Fig. 81.
Pneumatophores
of Black
Mangrove tree.

In the mature mangrove swamp the succession to dry land may be observed. Beyond the canopy formed by the Red and Black mangroves are the White Mangrove (p. 179) and the Buttonwood, or Gray Mangrove (p. 178). They form a mixed forest several meters back from the water's edge, on relatively high ground. As the leaves fall from these trees the sediment becomes thicker and dryer, and the true dry-land plants appear.

One of the first of the low-growing ground cover plants to appear in the transition area of salty, partly dry mud is Saltwort (p. 154). This spreading, prostrate shrub has pale green leaves and crunches underfoot. It can form an underbrush among the White and Gray mangroves, but is especially noticeable around salinas—shallow ponds of very salty water near the mangroves—together with the Southern Glasswort (p. 168), which forms mats of reddish stemmed, thin, asparagus-like plants.

Colonies of beautiful Mangrove Ferns edge the swamp with their glossy, dark green leaves up to a meter (39 in.) long and as wide as your hand. They can grow as well in fresh water as in salty mud, and often line roads near mangrove swamps.

The Mangrove Swamp

There are two approaches to studying the mangrove swamp. You can walk along the shoreline until you come across the distinctive Red Mangrove with its prop roots plunging into the sea. Or you can rent a boat and penetrate the swamp from its landward edge. If you rent a boat without a guide, don't wander from the main channel. It is easy to get lost in the sameness of the swamp. You can be only a few dozen meters from the channel and find yourself just as isolated as you would be on a mountaintop. Bring your snorkeling mask and place it at the water's surface so that you can see the bottom (as if through a glass-bottomed bucket).

Descriptions of each of the mangroves may be found below.

The leaves of all four mangroves have a heavy waxy cuticle. One usually associates this kind of covering with desertlike conditions, since the cuticle prevents evaporation from inside the leaf, thus conserving water. But here we have swamp plants whose roots are submerged, yet have evolved a water-conserving mechanism. Why is this necessary?

The mangrove has an even more desperate need to conserve water than many desert plants. Water molecules are constantly moving in and out of plant cells. The number of water molecules inside the cell is greater than the number in the salt water outside (per unit of volume), so that more water molecules diffuse through the cell membrane to the outside than move in from the salt water. The more salt water the plant takes in, the drier its cells become. (The same thing would happen to us if we were to drink seawater.)

The mangroves have evolved mechanisms to pump the salt out while retaining the water molecules. This unique ability has ensured their survival. They have become effective halophytes (salty environment plants). The mechanism varies with the species. The Black Mangrove, for example, excretes the salt through its leaves, which taste salty.

Mangrove Trees and the Mangrove Fern

Leaves alternate on stem; not opposite one another.
BUTTONWOOD or GRAY MANGROVE Pl. 24
Conocarpus erectus
Leaves long, pointed at both ends. Brown (last year's) or green, spiny-appearing, berrylike fruit 1.2 cm (½ in.) wide, in clusters on long stem. Bark dark brown to nearly black, broken into branching ridges by irregular fissures. Shrub or tree reaches 18m (60 ft.), grows almost prostrate on rocky shores.

Next 3 species: *Leaves opposite each other on stem.*
BLACK MANGROVE *Avicennia germinans* Pl. 24
Leaves narrowly elliptical. Upper surface green, shiny; lower gray-green, coated with fine hairs. Both surfaces often with scattered salt crystals, leaf salty to taste. Clusters of white stalkless flowers in season; flowers 6mm (¼ in.) long, 1 cm (⅜ in.) wide. Base of tree surrounded by many gray, pencil-shaped, knobby wooden pneumatophores extending more than 7.5 cm (3 in.) from mud. Bark dark brown, with longitudinal and horizontal

Fig. 82. *Left:* Leaves and fruit of White Mangrove tree; *right:* Mangrove Fern.

fissures creating squarish blocks. Shrub or tree reaching 21 m (70 ft.).

WHITE MANGROVE   Fig. 82; Pls. 19, 24
Laguncularia racemosa
Leaves rounded, broadly oval, borne on reddish or pink stalks (petioles). Leaves yellow-green; bark gray-brown, rough, fissured on trunk of tree. Clusters of small whitish flowers in season. Fruit velvety, gray-green, pear-shaped; flattened on sides, with ridges; to 2 cm (¾ in.) long. Shrub or tree to 18 m (60 ft.) tall.

RED MANGROVE *Rhizophora mangle*   Pl. 22
Leaves shiny, broad, dark green, rhododendron-like. Reddish prop roots arch from trunk into water; old trees may have aerial roots hanging from branches. Yellow, waxy, stalked flowers in groups of 4 in season. Seedlings (sea pencils) to 25 cm (10 in.) long hang from branches much of year. Fruit a leathery brown, conical berry about 2.5 cm (1 in.) long. Tree reaches 6 m (20 ft.) in Florida, 24 m (80 ft.) in W. Indies.

Leaves notched, fernlike.
MANGROVE FERN *Acrosticum aureum*   Fig. 82, Pl. 24
Dark green, glossy leaves; to 1 m (3¼ ft.) high, in clumps. Bases of leaves (and sometimes whole leaves) yellowish or brown. In mud of mangrove swamps, sometimes in large colonies.

Animals of the Mangrove Community

The most important contribution of the mangrove swamp is invisible. The tons of rich organic detritus produced every day form the bottom of an elaborate food web. Bacteria, molds, and tiny crustaceans such as copepods feed on the minute particles of detritus. So do larval shrimps and fishes. Adult mullets are among the few mature fishes that can utilize the bottom of the food web directly, by straining detritus and tiny plants from mouthfuls of the mud. Many other animals, such as wading birds and ducks, feed on the next level, eating small, shrimplike animals living in the mud. It has been estimated that 75% of all American Pink Shrimp, an important commercial species, undergo larval development in Gulf Coast mangrove swamps. Innumerable fish and crustacean larvae in the waters around the mangrove roots reveal the important role of the mangrove swamp as a nursery. The destruction of the mangroves for condominiums and hotels will cause far-reaching damage to migratory species as well as to local forms. The extensive destruction of mangroves in southern Florida has already resulted in reduced animal populations. For example, the American Pink Shrimp, usually netted about 160km (100 mi.) south of Florida, has experienced a drastic decline in numbers, as evidenced by the incredibly high prices charged for this shrimp in the fish market.

Animals on the prop roots of the Red Mangrove: The prop roots are important animal habitats. Even the region above the water has its inhabitants. The two most distinctive animals of the upper prop roots are the Mangrove Periwinkle (p. 235) and the Mangrove Crab (p. 331). The periwinkle is a robust brown snail 2 cm (¾ in.) high, with dark brown markings and a pointed spire. The Mangrove Crab is squarish, about 2.5 cm (1 in.) wide, and brown or greenish. Its wide-set eyes are located at the front corners of its body.

Another crab found on the prop roots is the Spotted Mangrove Crab or Tree Crab (Pl. 22). It looks like a dark reddish brown enlarged version of the Mangrove Crab, but has bright red legs and white spoon-shaped claws that stand out against its dark body. You must be fast to catch mangrove crabs. Upon your approach they will run up the prop root and just when you think you have one cornered, it will drop into the water and disappear.

Animals on the mud: The Coffee-bean Snail (Pl. 22) is caught between two worlds. It is a pulmonate (air-breathing) snail, and will drown if submerged. So it wanders up the prop roots as the tide comes in, and returns to feed on detritus on the mud at low tide. Look for a tiny hole in its side that appears and disappears with each breath. Its 1.2-cm (½-in.) long brown shell is decorated with three orange or cream bands.

Two other snails often found in abundance on the mud are the elongate yellow-brown Costate Horn Snail (*Cerithidea costata*) and the rough gray Pitted Murex (*Favartia celluosa*).

The dominant animal of the mangrove mud is the crab. It browses on the rich deposit of detritus and algae covering the black mud, and for protection, burrows into its soft recesses.

Hordes of fiddler crabs riddle the mud flats with their burrows. At low tide, when they are feeding, the observer will hear the sound of thousands of tiny claws picking away at the mud's surface. Crabs commonly found on the mangrove mud flats are described below and in Chapter 14.

Crabs of Mangrove Roots and Mud Flats

Red Mangrove prop roots—an underwater habitat: Red Mangroves at the very edge of the land, directly challenging the sea, are exposed to a harsher environment than those occupying the older portions of the swamp farther inland. Yet both face the possibility of destruction. The pioneers at the shore are often buffeted by waves; they will be the first to be uprooted by a storm. The inland trees live in perpetual tranquility in the still, dark swamp. They have created this habitat; even the water itself is stained a transparent brown from the tannin in their bark. (Extracting tannic acid from Red Mangrove bark for tanning purposes was a major industry in the Florida Keys.) Yet these trees face the insidious danger of land encroachment as they trap particles and raise the level of the sediment.

As you walk along the shore skirting the edge of the mangroves in water up to your knees, do not be startled as the bottom slopes down in front of the trees. You will find a shallow depression, usually less than 1m (39 in.) deep, seaward of each tree; storms and currents have scooped out these deeper areas. They become soft-bottomed as a layer of detritus accumulates.

As you approach, you may see a V-shaped wake move rapidly

seaward. If you move carefully you may catch the maker of this wake feeding. A strong crescent tail protruding from the water denotes the presence of a Bonefish, one of the most sought-after game fishes of our region. It feeds by rooting out small crustaceans with its mouth, so it assumes a vertical position, with its tail often protruding from the water. Small schools feed on sand flats and in shallow pools at the base of Red Mangroves. If you startle a school the fishes will flee seaward in a hysterical explosion of spray.

A frequent inhabitant of the flats and pools near the mangroves is the Common Blue Crab (Fig. 133, Pl. 53). The last pair of legs is flattened for swimming; the crab glides, half scuttling, over the bottom. When startled, it will sidle off toward deep water, its claws raised in a menacing position. If you corner one, with visions of boiled crab in your head, remember that this animal is capable of lightning-quick thrusts with its claws and delivers a mean pinch.

The roots of the Red Mangrove facing the sea are often relatively bare, with just a few tiny Gray Star Barnacles (Fig. 115) forming a prickly zone in the upper intertidal. There are too many stresses here, preventing most mangrove inhabitants from settling successfully. As you penetrate the swamp the picture changes. The prop roots abound with organisms. Even the species of barnacle changes. The Mangrove Star Barnacle (*Chthamalus rhizophorae*) appears, especially in the Antilles; but in muddy areas you are more likely to see the Two-striped Star Barnacle (*C. bisinuatus*). Living among the star barnacles at the water's edge are a variety of small, globose, brown-and-black striped snails with large apertures. Some, such as Clench's Nerite (*Neritina clenchi*) and its close relative, *N. piratica,* prefer brackish or fresh water. Others, such as the Virgin Nerite (*N. virginea)* are found closer to the sea.

Swim, wade, or paddle a boat into protected channels. Here you will find a complex and crowded community of animals and plants living on the Red Mangrove roots extending from the upper reaches of the highest tide to the muddy bottom.

The uppermost animals are the star barnacles. These are exposed for most of the day, covered only by the highest point of the tide. Below them are larger barnacles, some more than 1.2 cm (½ in.) wide, resembling miniature white cones. You can see that the exoskeleton (shell) of these animals is made up of plates (scutes). The large barnacles are the Ivory Barnacle (Fig. 84) or a related species. Observe those barnacles that are underwater. You will see the top open periodically. Jointed translucent appendages will extend like tiny hands sweeping plankton into the mouth hidden inside the shell.

The presence of the Mangrove Oyster (Fig. 85) marks the midtidal zone. These relatively thick, gray oysters are crowded together and often have Ivory Barnacles growing on their elon-

Fig. 83. Young Florida Crown Conch. Larger specimens usually have curved spines projecting vertically from the shoulder.

gate shells. They extend into the lowest intertidal, almost disappearing from view as they become smothered with an array of exotic animals and plants. Sometimes the prop roots will have mixed colonies of several species of oysters; sometimes one species will dominate a root, a tree, or a whole area. The Flat Tree Oyster (Fig. 85) and its relative, Lister's Tree Oyster (Pl. 40), are thin-shelled, delicate, and very flat. In Florida the familiar Eastern Oyster (p. 256) is the common species.

There are a number of oyster drills and other snails that prey upon the oysters. The West Indian Murex (*Chicoreus brevifrons*) is a large, brown, thorny-spined snail. It eats barnacles, oysters, and mussels. The large, beautiful West Indian and Florida crown conchs (Fig. 83) also feed on oysters. They are usually dark brown with spiral bands; pointed conical spines project upward from the shoulder of their glossy shells.

The Florida Rock Snail (Pl. 38) drills through oyster and mussel shells, extracting the soft tissues through a neat round hole.

The familiar blackish purple Sea Moss (p. 140) alga grows throughout the intertidal zone of the prop root, giving the area a hairy appearance. Sometimes it colonizes the upper part of a root so rapidly and thoroughly that it excludes all other forms by denying them surface to settle on. But more often it grows between organisms, filling in every bare spot. Usually two similar intertidal red algae are mixed together on the prop root to form the foundation of an ecological grouping called the Bostrychietum community. The dominant algae in this community are the blackish purple Sea Moss and the transparent purple alga *Caloglossa leprieurii*. The former resembles miniature fuzzy pine trees no taller than 5 cm (2 in.). *Caloglossa* has broad, flat branching thalli resembling purple macaroni about 5 cm (2 in.) long, with tiny forked tips. A similar dull purple seaweed on intertidal prop roots is *Catanella,* which looks like a string of elongate beads.

In the mid and lower intertidal the mussels appear. The common Scorched Mussel (Fig. 84, Pl. 40) lives among the oysters, sometimes in large clumps. Its larger relative, the Hooked Mussel (p. 257) is more common in some areas—it can be recognized by its larger size (greater than 2 cm —¾ in.) and its pointed umbo or beak. The much larger, yellow-brown, smooth Tulip Mussel (Pl. 40) may be found in Florida and the northern Caribbean; the dark purplish brown Guyana Mussel is its counterpart in the southern Caribbean and South America.

Among the mussels and oysters in the lowest intertidal appear colonies of 2.5-cm (1-in.) long Pale Anemones (Pl. 28), enhancing the fuzzy appearance of the root well into the subtidal.

The subtidal region of the prop roots: In this region of perpetual submersion an entirely new group of animals and plants appears. Organisms that can resist predators but which require permanent submersion take the place of the intertidal inhabitants. Lift the root out of the water and examine it. Be careful—it will be brittle. Closely examine the myriad organisms crowded together into a confusing mass. Let the root fall back into the water and don your mask, fins, and snorkel and float so as not to disturb the muddy bottom. Hold on to adjacent roots and watch the living subtidal community as it functions in its natural state. Notice the peculiar baglike organisms attached to the root, each with two siphons extending outward. If you pluck one from the root, it will expel a stream of water at you. You have discovered one of the dominant animals of the prop root, the sea squirt or tunicate.

Tunicates are lumpy, baggy, often translucent animals with only one distinctive external feature: two siphons protruding from an otherwise nondescript round body. They are sessile (attached) in all cases and are often covered with seaweed. The only common northern species, the Manhattan Sea Grape, is a

Fig. 84 (opposite). Red Mangrove root intertidal and subtidal community. 1. Seedlings of Red Mangrove trees colonizing beach near prop roots of larger trees. 2. Tiny (2 mm—³⁄₃₂ in. tall) zooids of Green Colonial Tunicate (p. 188) form a gelatinous mass on roots. 3. Roots covered with Striped Barnacles (p. 299). 4. Close-up of a Striped Barnacle. 5. Ivory Barnacles (p. 299) are common in intertidal zone. 6. Scorched Mussels (p. 257) compete with oysters and are often found among them. 7. Rock Anemones (p. 214) often colonize subtidal zone. 8. Close-up of siphon of Pleated Sea Squirt (p. 375), showing brown stripes inside. 9. Clump of Pleated Sea Squirts, with siphons closed and puckered.

nuisance along the East Coast of the U.S.; large colonies foul boat bottoms. Individuals resemble rubbery grayish bubbles. See p. 371 for a discussion of the phylum.

There are three types of tunicates: solitary forms, in which each animal is distinct and unconnected to its neighbors (although they may crowd together in clumps); colonial forms, attached to each other by a rootlike stolon; and compound forms, flat jelly-like or crustose masses, often with no individuals visible to the naked eye. Actually, in many cases there are no complete individual animals; instead several zooids share an opening, usually an excurrent pore. Sometimes the zooids form a flattened, flowerlike grouping, each radiating out from a common central excurrent opening. In some crustose forms, the zooids may be forced to lie at an angle or on their sides by the flatness of the crust.

Some common species of tunicates found on Red Mangrove roots are described below.

Common Tunicates on the Roots of Red Mangrove Trees

Next 10 species (solitary tunicates): *Saclike, with 2 siphons. Over 2.5 cm (1 in.) long.*

BLACK TUNICATE   *Ascidia nigra*   **Fig. 85**
   Black. Siphons often elongate, with fringed edges, round openings. Common also on wharf pilings. Large—to 15 cm (6 in.) tall.
ORANGE TUNICATE   *Pyura vittata*   **Pl. 23**
   Bright *orange, red, or yellow-red;* color often deepening at siphons. Surface around siphons bumpy, with very fine spines. Apertures diamond-shaped; siphons may be elongate. To 5.5 cm (2¼ in.) tall.
EXASPERATING TUNICATE   *Microcosmus exasperatus*
   Red, red-purple, orange, or pink; inside of apertures pearly gray. Body often elongate, with siphons widely separated; surface rough. Apertures round. To 5.5 cm (2¼ in.) tall.

Fig. 85 (opposite). Red Mangrove root subtidal community (2). 1. Flat Tree Oysters (p. 257) in lower intertidal zone. On lower right, in subtidal zone, is a Divided Tunicate (p. 188). 2. A mass of Flat Tree Oysters covered with Ivory Barnacles (p. 299); a Mangrove Crab (p. 331) has wandered from above at low tide. 3. Banded Fanworm (p. 276) and a White Spongy Tunicate (p. 189); at lower left is a clump of Rock Anemones (p. 214). 4. Close-up of Rock Anemones being overgrown by White Spongy Tunicate. 5. Tunicates. *Upper:* Black Tunicate (p. 186); *lower:* Orange Tunicate (p. 186). 6. Black and Orange tunicates among branches of Spiny Seaweed (p. 137).

PINK TUNICATE *Herdmania momus*
Pink or pinkish gray; skin (test) smooth, soft. Interior of siphons iridescent green and pink. To 5.5 cm (2¼ in.) tall.

CURVED TUNICATE *Ascidia curvata*
Yellow to orange. Body tall, elongate. Anterior siphon to center of top, posterior siphon far down on side and sometimes pointing slightly downward; apertures round, with fringed edges. Common in Bermuda. To 6.5 cm (2½ in.) tall.

DIVIDED TUNICATE *Styela partita* **Pl. 23**
Gray or yellow, becoming brown, purple, or red near siphons. Apertures occasionally with white and purple stripes or triangles—purple ones pointing toward opening, white ones pointing inward. Skin rough, often overgrown (compare with Encrusted Tunicate, below). To 3 cm (1¼ in.) tall. Often in crowded clusters.

INTERRUPTED TUNICATE *Ascidia interrupta*
Gray-green; skin pliable, soft. Distal (top) part of animal usually long, narrow, terminating in eight-lobed opening of siphon; atrial opening six-lobed, far back on side. To 5 cm (2 in.) tall.

WESTERN or SANDY SEA SQUIRT
Molgula occidentalis
Gray, dingy yellow, sandpapery surface, usually covered with mud. Apertures round, sometimes deep red. Siphons not very far apart on top; posterior siphon has small, chimney-like constriction on top. Animal globular and easily plucked from root. To 6.5 cm (2½ in.) tall. Common in Florida.

ENCRUSTED TUNICATE *Polycarpa obtecta*
Yellow-gray, darkening to red, brown, or purplish brown around apertures. Apertures conspicuously four-sided (diamond-shaped). Skin wrinkled, rough, warty, often encrusted with sand and shell fragments, but may be soft and thin if growing in mud. Strongly attached; grows singly, not in clusters. Commonest species in Caribbean. To 5 cm (2 in.) tall.

PLEATED SEA SQUIRT *Styela plicata* **Fig. 84, Pl. 23**
Surface *tan;* smooth, but may have cobblestone-like appearance; often wrinkled, slippery. Apertures large, surrounded by 4 lobes with radiating purple-brown lines. To 7.2 cm (2¾ in.) tall. Commonest species in Gulf.

Next 6 species (colonial tunicates): *Zooids transparent, vase-like, crowded together in a mass, attached by rootlike stolons at bases; each zooid distinct.*

GREEN COLONIAL TUNICATE *Perophora viridis* **Fig. 84**
BERMUDA GREEN TUNICATE *P. multiclathrata*
Both species visually indistinguishable from each other. Zooids tiny, not more than 5mm (⅕ in.) high. Colony a gelatinous-looking mass with a tinge of *yellow-green.* In patches on shells and around roots in colonies 5 cm (2 in.) long.

NKLIN'S COLONIAL TUNICATE *Ecteinascidia conklini*
Zooids club-shaped, transparent, with gray-green line and tinge;
thin red line around siphons. To 2 cm (¾ in.) tall. Bermuda only.
Replaced in Caribbean by *E. styeloides.*

Next 3 species: Transparent or whitish, usually with pastel-colored vertical visceral mass visible as an internal curved line.

INTED TUNICATE   *Clavelina picta*   **Pl. 23**
Zooids clustered, transparent, with carmine or purple band
around upper end. Test may be *purplish white or transparent.*
Zooids to 1.9 cm (¾ in.) tall. Colony may surround root for length
of 30 cm (1 ft.), containing as many as 1000 zooids.

ANGROVE TUNICATE   *Ecteinascidia turbinata*   **Pl. 23**
Internal *orange or pink vertical, curved line.* Zooids club-shaped,
about 2.5 cm (1 in.) high, in colonies often surrounding root for
distance of 15 cm (6 in.).

LONG TUNICATE   *Clavelina oblonga*
Internal parts form a *brown mass;* zooids club-shaped, with 2
openings clearly visible on top; in groups of 6–7 on thick stolons.
Colonies small in spring, but become a mass of as many as 40 by
late summer. May have white spots around apertures. To 1.6 cm
(⅝ in.) tall.

*Next 9 species (compound tunicates): These form a crust a few
millimeters thick, a gelatinous mass, or a spherical, sponge-like
colony. Zooids often indistinct or appear in flower-shaped,
branched, or star-shaped pattern of holes or dots.*

ITE SPONGY TUNICATE   **Fig. 85**
Didemnum conchyliatum
Flat, *white, yellow-white, or reddish,* chalky or shiny crust. Can
form rounded, thick, ball-like masses but most often forms crust
on shells or around root. In thin colonies tiny zooids may be
visible, sometimes in a radiating pattern. Large colonies may be
wrinkled or flat and are usually featureless. Can be mistaken for
a sponge. Most abundant compound ascidian. Five almost identical species in our area.

IVE GELATINOUS TUNICATE   **Pl. 23**
Eudistoma olivaceum
Olive-green, yellow-olive; olive-brown to blackish tops. Thick
colony of numerous small zooids to 8 mm (⁵⁄₁₆ in.) across, to 1 cm (⅜
in.) high. Flat-topped masses taper to thick stalks. Colony covered
with a *gelatinous,* translucent test.

ARRED GELATINOUS TUNICATE
Polyclinum constellatum
Deep red or green. A single *gelatinous mass* attached by a large
base. No prominent stalks. Zooids barely visible except for outline
of system of channels leading to common exhalent openings.

GREEN ENCRUSTING TUNICATE   Pl. 23
Symplegma viride
Purple, black, or dark green thin crust covered with *gelatinous* test. Tiny ring of white, pale green, salmon, or yellow around each opening. Sometimes colony yellow or salmon-pink with a red line around each opening. Zooids randomly distributed; each has 2 openings.

BERMUDA ENCRUSTING TUNICATE   Pl. 5
Distaplia bermudensis
Chocolate-brown, marbled with olive, violet-black, and red; rubbery. Forms round head or flat crust. Test translucent, surface dull. Zooids visible through test, arranged in rows or circles; tiny white circles around openings. Colony 1.6 cm (⅝ in.) high, 2 cm (¾ in.) wide. **Related species: Raspberry Tunicate** (*Distaplia stylifer,* Pl. 23) looks like a purple raspberry; common on reef.

BLACK ENCRUSTING TUNICATE   Pl. 23
Botrylloides nigrum
VARIABLE ENCRUSTING TUNICATE   Pl. 23
Botryllus planus
These two tunicates are difficult to distinguish visually from one another. Brown, purple, or black, often surrounding root. Crust can be flat when on rocks, to 10 cm (4 in.) wide. Rings around openings visible as circular or star-shaped, white, green, or orange dots. Zooids have 1 opening, and are visible as crowded black dots, often in branching, tree-like or starlike pattern.

SAVIGNY'S ENCRUSTING TUNICATE
Trididemnum species
Surface smooth, glossy, slimy. Colony to 3mm (⅛ in.) thick, to 9 cm (3¾ in.) across; dark smoky brown. Usually on deepest part of mangrove root. Several similar species.

LISTER'S ENCRUSTING TUNICATE
Diplosoma listerianum
Transparent, jelly-like. Zooids clearly visible through test as small, irregularly distributed black dots, some with a yellowish tinge. On upper root just below low-water mark. Zooids very small—to 1.6mm (1/16 in.). **Related species:** *D. glandulosum* cannot be differentiated from *listerianum* in the field.

The subtidal region of the mangrove root so abounds with organisms that there is little room for newcomers. Indeed, space is the limiting factor in this food-rich microhabitat. If a larva cannot find solid footing on a root within a few days of its birth it falls into the silty sediment and is smothered. Sponges sometimes find room on the roots. The Fire Sponge (Pl. 25) is common in most shallow water tropical habitats. It forms rough bright orange crusts with occasional openings (oscules). The Chicken Liver Sponge (Pl. 25) grows in slimy brown mottled sheets, sometimes surrounding a root. It is hard to differentiate from the Black

Encrusting Tunicate, which also forms brown slimy masses. But the tunicate is distinguished by tree-like patterns of black dots (zooids) on a brown background and it does not have oscules.

To observe the organisms of the prop-root community properly, let the root hang undisturbed for a few minutes. Soon a forest of miniature fans will slowly appear among the oysters and tunicates. These are fanworms. They live in parchmentlike (Family Sabellidae) or calcareous tubes (Family Serpulidae), entwined among the other animals. Often the tubes are covered with a thin coat of sediment or seaweed and are invisible until the exquisite feathery fan of the worm is extended.

A common sabellid is the Black-spotted Fanworm (p. 276). It produces a whorl of brown, feathery gill-tentacles less than 2.5 cm (1 in.) wide. Bring your finger toward the tiny black eyespots on the gills. As your finger comes within a centimeter of the gill, the whole feather duster will disappear as the worm instantly withdraws into its tube.

The sinuous white calcareous tubes of serpulids are sometimes visible on dead shells. Whether or not the tube can be seen, the two Christmas-tree-like sets of gills of the Horned Christmas-tree Worm (Pl. 26), and the whorl of orange gills of Spiny Featherduster Worms (*Hydroides*, Fig. 115, p. 277) are brightly colored reminders of their presence.

There are a number of other species of polychaete worms that live out their lives hidden in dark crevices among other animals on the root. You may see a worm 10 cm (4 in.) long with two undulating or coiling tentacles projecting from its head. This is a species of *Polydora* (p. 282). Small threadworms with more than two antenna-like tentacles are members of Family Syllidae (p. 292).

Don't confuse the sea anemones with the fanworms. The anemones on mangrove roots do not live in a tube. They are usually crammed in among other organisms and they can slowly creep over the root to find an appropriate niche. A ring of relatively thick tentacles distinguishes the anemones from the feathery fringed fanworms.

The most common anemones are the Rock and Pale anemones (Pl. 27, Fig. 86), already mentioned as inhabitants of the lower intertidal zone. They can be found throughout the subtidal, also. The Stinging Anemone (Pl. 27) is brown, with a dense fringe of long and short white-tipped tentacles. The short tentacles are forked. Be careful not to touch these camouflaged animals, as their sting results in painful welts. Mangroves that border the sea may be inhabited by anemones commonly found in the lagoon, such as the purple-tipped, orange Giant Caribbean Anemone and the brownish, translucent, long-tentacled Ringed Anemone (Pl. 27).

Green filamentous algae, such as *Chaetomorpha* (p. 141), give the root a hairy, disheveled appearance, especially when the

Fig. 86. Red Mangrove root subtidal community (3). *Top to bottom (clockwise):* Ivory Barnacles (upper right), siphon of Sandy Sea Squirt, Black Tunicate, wrinkled tube of sabellid worm, colony of Pale and Rock anemones, Keyhole Limpet on Flat Tree Oyster, crust of White Spongy Tunicate, and sabellid worms (see feathery gills).

strands are covered with silt. Matted cushions or clumps of green filaments belong to the ingeniously named genus *Boodleopsis*. These algae are not to be mistaken for the darker Sea Moss, which is more often found in the intertidal zone.

In brackish bays look for bristly-looking reddish Spiny Seaweed (Pl. 36 and 10-cm (4-in.) tall clumps of the fuzzy Green Horsetail algae (Fig. 64). Creeping over the roots just below the low-tide mark is the deep purple seaweed *Murrayella periclados;* from its threadlike stolons arise hairy stems about 4.5 cm (1¾ in.) long.

The red-and-white striped Banded Coral Shrimp (Pl. 51) sometimes wanders from its usual habitat, the coral reef, to grace the otherwise grubby-looking living mass on the mangrove root. Small swimming crabs resembling young Blue Crabs are probably species of *Portunus* (Pl. 53).

If you are walking along the shore don't be surprised if you discover what appears to be a real treasure: a group of young Spiny Lobsters (Pl. 51) hiding among the prop roots. They are usually below legal size, so do not attempt to gather them for dinner.

Fuzzy-looking ark clams that sometimes gain a foothold in the highly competitive subtidal root zone are the Turkey Wing (Pl. 40) and the Eared Ark (p. 253).

Channels between the mangroves—the deep sublittoral: Most mangrove swamps are dissected by innumerable mud-bottomed channels, most less than 9m (30 ft.) across. Often tidal currents will scour away the bank, leaving an overhang of mud and interlaced roots. Many animals find shelter here, but fishes dominate. In the Florida Keys schools of Mangrove Snappers (Fig. 87), Schoolmasters (Fig. 52), and Mutton Snappers lurk under the overhangs. Every cast of a shrimp will catch you one, or you can use your mask to view the large schools among the roots.

Keep looking as you drift down a tidal stream. In Florida you might see large, ponderous Redfish or Red Drums or schools of Spotted Sea Trout. At the mouth of the stream you may hit the jackpot and see young (30-cm or 1-ft. long) Tarpon chasing minnows.

Once, in the Nariva Marsh in Trinidad, we discovered the strangest fish I have ever seen. It was utterly transparent, with no visible internal organs, no red blood, no gills. The eyes looked like tiny bubbles. The 2.5-cm (1-in.) long fish was a larval Tarpon. This species, eels, and a few others produce larvae called leptocephali—leaflike transparent young that bear little resemblance to the adults.

Look for a shallow, tranquil inlet. Test the bottom gingerly as the silt may be more than knee-deep. It will pay to snorkel rather than walk, even if the water is less than 60 cm (2 ft.) deep. The bizarre, 30-cm (1-ft.) wide Upside-down Jellyfish (Fig. 88) will be

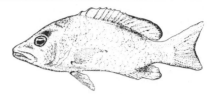

Fig. 87. Mangrove Snapper.

gently pulsating on the bottom, mouth facing upward. Several species of sea stars are able to sidle over the suffocating mud on hundreds of flat-bottomed tube feet. In Bermuda you will find the Purple Sea Star, which reproduces by fragmenting its body into two or more sections, each of which regenerates into a new animal. In the process, it seems to lose count, and six-, seven-, eight-, or even nine-armed specimens may be found. In Florida look for the more conventional Brown Spiny Sea Star (Fig. 88, Pl. 59), often strewn in considerable numbers on the mud.

The lovely Umbrella Alga (Pl. 34) grows in the mud; its 2.5-cm (1-in.) tall body consists of only one cell.

Birds

Deep in the silent swamp the tranquility is broken by the flapping of what appears to be huge birds, just barely visible among the mangrove leaves. Often these birds are herons or egrets. Occasionally they may be the long-necked, fish-eating Snakebird or Anhinga, high up on a sun-drenched branch, hanging their wings out to dry, like laundry on a line. Most birds produce oil to coat

Fig. 88. Animals of muddy mangrove bottoms. *Left:* Upside-down Jellyfish (p. 207); *right:* Brown Spiny Sea Star (p. 342).

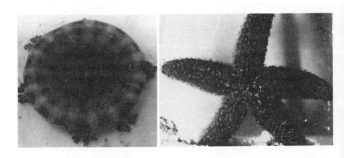

Fig. 89. Egret tree at sunset.

their feathers, making them waterproof; the Anhinga does not. Perhaps this deep diver would be too buoyant to reach its prey, so it soggily swims below the surface, barely able to keep its snake-like neck above water.

Although a detailed discussion of the birds of the mangrove swamp is beyond the scope of this book, one experience must be recommended. Ask the local people if they know of an egret tree. A huge Red Mangrove tree stands alone on a beach at Pear Tree Bottom, about 20 km (12 mi.) west of Ochos Rios, Jamaica. At dusk flocks of white Cattle Egrets fly toward the tree from their posts close to the cattle, where the birds have been waiting for their large friends to scare up insects and lizards as they browse. As it grows darker, more and more arrive until hundreds of birds glide in together to land on the branches. Soon the tree has turned into a white pulsating hemisphere, and rasping sounds of quarreling birds create quite a din. It looks as though the branches will snap under the weight of thousands of birds. The eye is overwhelmed. Yet new flocks of tens, fifties, and hundreds of birds continue to arrive. Their appearance is greeted by hoots, jeers, and considerable restlessness on the part of their already roosting relatives. Then, as if by a signal, the whole flock rises and wheels in the air in a massed arc, the sun's last rays gleaming from thousands of white wings. After several repetitions, the flock settles in for the night, but the hooting, rasping and jeering goes on until total blackness obscures the scene.

A panorama rivaling the one described has become a tourist attraction in Trinidad. Every day at 3 P.M. large open boats penetrate into Caroni Swamp. The boats anchor along the edge of a wide lake. Soon thousands of Cattle Egrets begin to arrive. But this is only half the show, for among the pure white flocks sparks of flame begin to appear. As you look excitedly through your binoculars you will focus on bright red, goose-sized birds with long curving beaks. Scarlet Ibises are arriving! Soon two or three huge hemispheres of white (the egret trees) are flanked by flaming masses of Scarlet Ibises — and more and more birds keep coming, creating one of the most spectacular natural events still available to us.

The Future of the Mangrove Swamp

I attended a conference on man's influence on the environment, and saw aerial photos of a mangrove swamp in Vietnam that had been defoliated by a single application of defoliant during the war. There was a clear line of green off in the distance, marking the edge of the sprayed zone. It was as if a giant had stepped on the land, crushing it and making it bare. The lecturer remarked on how susceptible the mangroves were, to succumb to only a single spraying.

I took consolation in the fact that mangroves are such good colonizers, and told the lecturer not to worry, for new mangrove seedlings would soon fill the region with green again. He looked sadly at me and pointed out that his pictures were taken 14 years after the defoliant had been administered and there was not a sign of green anywhere, not even a fringe along the shore. The land had been poisoned for mangroves for a long time. He did not know for how long. No one knows.

Oil spills have a particularly harmful effect on mangroves. The gentle slope of the mangrove shoreline means that the oil will be spread maximally as the tide moves in and out. The fact that a mangrove-fringed shore acts as a giant filter means that almost every drop of oil will be removed from the water. Here is an extract from a scientific report of an oil spill on the Caribbean shore of Panama:

> The wide intertidal mud flats were more or less thickly covered with oil. Every footstep . . . released large quantities of oil from the substrate. The pneumatophores of Black Mangrove trees . . . were covered with a mixture of oil and mud. The stilt roots of the Red Mangroves . . . had a thick layer of pure oil on their mesolittoral (intertidal) sections . . .

The majority of young seedlings . . . were killed . . . A strong reduction of the fiddler crab population could be observed . . . The characteristic intertidal algal community "bostrychietum" on the *Rhizophora* stilt roots was practically eliminated . . . as were the sedimentary animals of this zone, such as oysters . . . mussels . . . barnacles . . . sponges, tunicates and hydrozoans.

We have observed dead and dying sea turtles . . . on mangrove beaches . . . A number of oil-smeared herons and one dying cormorant were observed.[*]

Marginal organisms such as mangroves are finely adapted to their environments. This is both a strength and a weakness. Although they are able to adjust to a stressful environment, they expend so much energy in coping with their highly saline habitat that they have little energy left for defense. The mangrove has few enemies; the tannin in its bark makes its leaves unpalatable, and the harsh intertidal, highly salty habitat eliminates most competition. So the mangroves have existed for millennia—kings of their environment, like the dinosaurs, and, also like the dinosaurs, highly susceptible to change.

The pneumatophores of the Black Mangrove allow the roots to obtain oxygen. What happens when these pneumatophores are covered with oil? The oysters, mussels, and tunicates living in the intertidal are all filter feeders, straining plankton from the water. What happens when even small quantities of oil irritate their surface membranes, causing them to drown in the mucus they produce in response to the irritation? The mangrove community is unable to cope with oil spills and is destroyed.

Mangroves are builders. They create new land along the shore. They filter the water and buffer the effects of hurricanes. They are the nurseries of many species of fishes, shrimps, crabs, and other animals, even those that migrate along the shore or out into the ocean as adults. Yet the trees are bulldozed and smothered with mud to build condominiums and hotels. They are poisoned, polluted, harvested for their tannic acid, and burned as firewood.

When the huge mangrove swamps are gone, the effect on the marine ecosystem will be devastating.

Reutzler, K. and W. Sterrer, "Oil Pollution Damage Observed in Tropical Communities along the Atlantic Seaboard of Panama," *Bioscience* 20 (4) February, 1970): 222–224.

PLATE 1

Sand and Mud Dwellers
of Southeastern and Gulf Shores (1)

1–4. Razor Clam (p. 260) removed from sediment and placed on surface of sand. (1) Pointed foot almost immediately is extended. (2) Foot probes surface and penetrates deeply. Tip of foot swells with blood, forming anchor. (3) Muscles of extended foot contract, jerking clam erect; 2 or 3 more contractions and clam pulls itself under surface. (4) Clam almost buried.

5. Track about 3.2 cm (1¼ in.) wide on surface of muddy sand.

6. Region at right end of track excavated, revealing **Atlantic Baby's Ear Snail** (p. 239).

7. Close-up of Baby's Ear Snail shows little. Wide-mouthed shell (Pl. 43) is buried inside hump in mantle on left. Two small, retractible tentacles are sometimes visible. Animal glides on mucous trail.

8. AWNING CLAM *Solemya velum* p. 259
Tiny—usually 1.2 cm (½ in.) long. Shell covered with shiny brown periostracum with yellow rays. Buried deep in intertidal mud.

9. Awning Clam with powerful foot extended, showing fringed disk at bottom. Disk forms anchor when digging.

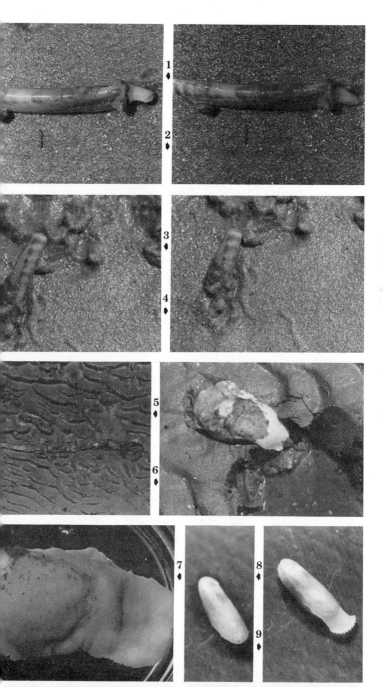

PLATE 2

Sand and Mud Dwellers of
Southeastern and Gulf Shores (2)

1. One end of U-shaped tube of **Parchment Worm**. Note inner parchment lining extending from rough outer portion.

2. **Parchment Worm** (p. 280) removed from tube. Note blunt head and 3 enlarged parapodia, which constantly beat water through tube.

3. **Ornate Worm** (p. 281). Note swollen thorax and thinner abdomen. Tuft of white tentacles barely visible above red gills at head end.

4. Anterior of **Plumed Worm** (p. 288), showing 2 paired tentacles and central, single tentacle extending from prostomium (head), and fir-tree-like gills along sides.

5. **Mud Brittle Star** (p. 347) lies buried in sandy mud, sometimes at depths to 12.7 cm (5 in.). Long, threadlike arms remove detritus from mud.

6. **American Tube-dwelling Anemone** (p. 219) removed from its smooth gray tube, which lies coiled below. When disturbed, wormlike anemone descends to bottom of lengthy tube, deep beneath surface of mud.

7. Extended anterior of **Milky Ribbon Worm** (p. 376). When contracted, head is pointed, with lateral swellings. A long, threadlike proboscis shoots out of a special opening above mouth, entrapping polychaete worms, the Ribbon Worm's prey.

8. A section of pinkish white, fleshy body of **Milky Ribbon Worm**. Flaccid body may be 1 meter (39 in.) long and is rarely removed from mud intact.

PLATE 3

Sand and Mud Dwellers
of Southeastern and Gulf Shores (3)

1. Extensive mud flats lie inshore of barrier islands and along Gulf Coast. Despite generally small tidal range, flats may extend ½ km (³⁄₁₀ mi.) or more offshore at low tide.

2. **Sand Collar** is, in reality, an egg case of moon snails. Tiny eggs are interspersed among sand grains and bound together with tough, gelatinous secretion.

3. **SOUTHERN MOON SNAIL** *Polinices duplicatus* p. 238
Dark callus obscures umbilicus. Operculum plasticlike, ocher or tan, with coiled line. See also Pls. 42, 47.

4. **Southern Moon Snail** with foot extended. Mantle partially covers shell. This snail can move with great rapidity on copious mucus secreted by its foot.

5. **ANGEL WING** *Cyrtopleura costata* p. 256
To 20 cm (8 in.) long, covered with gray periostracum. Removed from burrow about 2.5 cm (1 in.) wide at top and 60 cm (2 ft.) deep. Foot and visceral mass at front (left end); siphon retracted.

6. **Angel Wing** with siphon extended. Siphon may be over 30 cm (1 ft.) long.

7. **SOUTHERN ACORN WORM** p. 371
Ptychodera bahamensis
To 1 m (39 in.) long. Worm shown in mucus-lined burrow. Coiled fecal casts (Pl. 4) smelling of iodine serve to identify posterior opening of burrow. Odor becomes stronger as burrow is excavated.

8. Flaccid posterior of **Acorn Worm** is usually all that a digger can retrieve. Note gray body with whitish bands. Anterior (front end) has large gill slits and pronounced winglike genitalia.

PLATE 4

Burrows and Tubes
of Southeastern and Gulf Shores

1. Fecal casts of **Southern Acorn Worm** (p. 371) dot mud flats at low tide. Smelling strongly of iodine, fragile casts wash away with each high tide. Beneath coiled mass is posterior opening of U-shaped tube of this worm.

2. **Onuphis Worm** (p. 288) tube made of fine sand grains. Beneath surface of sediment sand grains on wall of tube become sparse, revealing flexible, plasticlike section. Where worm is present in abundance, 6-mm (¼-in.) wide tubes may wash up on shore in quantity, looking like masses of plastic drinking straws.

3. U-shaped tube of **Parchment Worm** (p. 280), seen in silhouette at low tide on mud flats among seagrass leaves. Distance between "chimneys" about 40 cm (16 in.). Tubes are tan, tough. Worm lies near one end and pumps water through tube with specially modified parapodia, filtering plankton and detritus from water with mucous net.

4. Tube of **Bamboo Worm** (p. 281), similar to that of Onuphis Worm but narrower and usually found in groups. Tubes rarely project from sediment; more often seen when digging in sand. Tube has no plasticlike lining and crumbles when squeezed.

5. Thick, clayey, gray lining of **Ghost Shrimp** (p. 310) burrow usually does not reach surface of sand and is revealed only by 1-cm (⅜-in.) wide hole. Burrow walls sometimes become visible when upper centimeter or so of sand is washed away by a wave.

6. Opening of **Ghost Shrimp** burrow surrounded by fecal pellets, which are released periodically as shrimp moves to surface, reverses, and defecates. On beaches with large populations fecal pellets are so abundant as to form sticky masses underfoot.

7. Tube of **Plumed Worm** (p. 288), about 1 cm (⅜ in.) wide; and may reach 1.5 m (5 ft.) in length. This tube is ornamented with bits of seashell. Found somewhat higher on beach than Onuphis Worm tubes, in sandy intertidal zone.

8. Siphon of **Angel Wing clam** (p. 256) at surface of muddy sand flat at low tide. Opening of burrow often more than 2.5 cm (1 in.) wide. Plankton- and bacteria-rich water is sucked into incurrent siphon at left and filtered by mucus-covered gills of clam, then expelled from striped excurrent siphon. Burrow expands to 7.5 cm (3 in.) wide and arm's length.

PLATE 5

Sponges, Corals, and Tunicates
Washed Up on Southeastern and Gulf Shores

1. **YELLOW BORING SPONGE** *Cliona celata* p. 222
Live sponge is bright sulfur yellow with brownish tinges; pores surrounded by pimple-like areas, scattered over surface. Dead specimens become woodlike; smooth, tan with brown pores. Irregular, moundlike, never spongy to touch. To 30 cm (1 ft.) or larger.

2. **RED BEARD SPONGE** *Microciona prolifera* p. 223
Red or orange when alive; dead specimens brown. Begins as a scablike crust; enlarges to become branched or even fanlike (shown). Thin, gnarled fingers about 6 mm (¼ in.) thick with inconspicuous oscules (pores); whole sponge to 20 cm (8 in.) high. On rocks and shells, in lower intertidal or shallow subtidal zone.

3. **CRUMB-OF-BREAD SPONGE** p. 222
Halichondria bowerbanki
Yellow, gold, or brown; crustose to moundlike, lobed and irregularly branched, often with interconnected fingers. Oscules to 3 mm (⅛ in.) across, scattered on surface of 7.5-cm (3-in.) high to 15-cm (6-in.) wide sponges. Contains symbiotic algae and may have greenish cast.

4. **GARLIC SPONGE** *Lissodendoryx isodictyalis* p. 223
Live sponge whitish, bluish, or greenish; moundlike with lobed edges. Firm, brittle; overgrown with marine organisms. Tube-like papillae covered with pores project from surface. Oscules to 1 mm (¹⁄₁₆ in.) across, scattered over surface. To 20 cm (8 in.) high; on rocks, pilings. When cast ashore becomes brown, smells pungently of garlic.

5. **NORTHERN CUP CORAL** *Astrangia danae* p. 212
Up to 30 cups, each less than 6 mm (¼ in.) wide, in a calcareous, grayish white, lumpy, rocklike clump. Polyps translucent white; do not contain zooxanthellae. Subtidal; often washes up on beach in colonies about 2.5 cm (1 in.) in diameter.

6. **TUBE CORAL** *Cladocora arbuscula* p. 212
Mass of up to 15 small, white, tube-like branches; to 1.2 cm (½ in.) long, about 3.5 mm (⅛ in.) in diameter. Branches have fine longitudinal ridges.

7. **SEA PORK** *Amaroucium stellatum* p. 374
Compound tunicate. Smooth, liverlike; color variable—colony shown is brick red. To 30 cm (1 ft.) across. Zooids in circular pattern, often not visible.

8. **BERMUDA ENCRUSTING TUNICATE** p. 374
Distaplia bermudensis
Similar to Sea Pork, but more jelly-like; brown, violet-black, or red. Surface dull; zooids sometimes visible through translucent test, arranged in rows or circles.

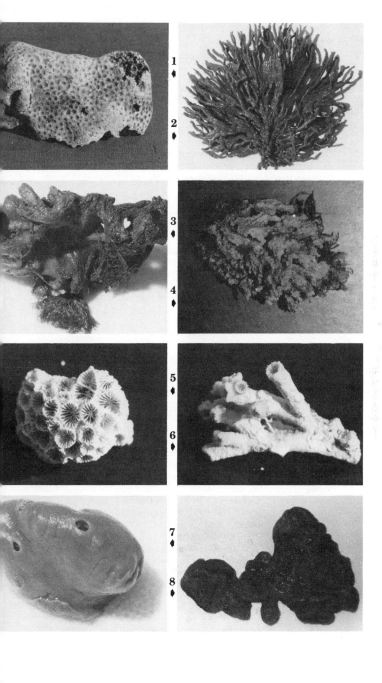

PLATE 6

Crabs and a Shrimp
of Southeastern and Gulf Shores

1., 2. Male (left) and female **Mud Fiddler Crabs** (p. 337). Front of carapace is iridescent blue.

3. LESSER BLUE CRAB or GULF CRAB p. 321
Callinectes similis
Carapace green, with iridescent edges. Claws white outside; blue to fuchsia inside, with fuchsia tips. Walking legs blue with fuchsia tips. Lateral spines curve slightly forward. Common.

4. COMMON BLUE CRAB *Callinectes sapidus* p. 322
Differs from *C. similis* in that carapace is proportionately wider and as much as ⅔ larger. Claws tipped with red in males, purple in females. Note small clumps of **Crab Barnacle** (*Chelonibia patula,* p. 299) along front edge of carapace.

5. COMMON SPIDER CRAB *Libinia emarginata* p. 318
Nine tubercle-like spines run along midline of back; rostrum minutely forked. Yellowish brown to dark brown. Claws often white.

6. ATLANTIC GHOST SHRIMP p. 310
Callianassa atlantica
Translucent white. Males lack large tooth on inner margin of upper finger of large claw. To 6.8 cm (2⅝ in.) long. In burrows in intertidal mud (see Pl. 4).

7. LADY CRAB *Ovalipes ocellatus* p. 322
Yellowish gray with reddish purple, leopardlike spots. Last pair of legs paddle-like. Often buried in sand with eyes exposed. Handle with care—vicious.

8. GULF CALICO CRAB *Hepatus epheliticus* p. 317
Red, dark-edged, irregular spots scattered over graying carapace. Edge of carapace irregularly serrated. Often buried in sand with eyes exposed. Docile, easily handled.

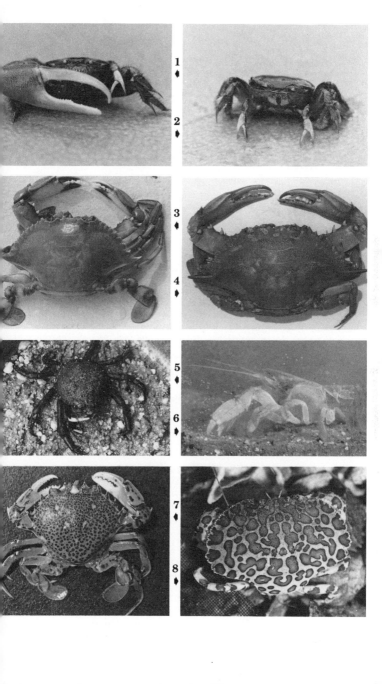

PLATE 7

Hermit Crabs and Small Shrimps
of Southeastern and Gulf Seagrass Beds

1. **FLAT-CLAWED HERMIT CRAB** p. 313
   Pagurus pollicaris
   Large; inhabits shells of whelks and moon snails (shown). Tan or light brown except in Florida, where claws are whitish.

2. **COMMON or BIG-CLAWED SNAPPING** p. 305
   SHRIMP *Alpheus heterochaelis*
   To 5 cm (2 in.) long. Dark, translucent green, with a purple sheen on sides. White markings on chelipeds; walking legs pale red. Tips of uropods (tail) blue with orange border.

3. View of **Flat-clawed Hermit Crab,** showing rounded, serrated claws and quadrangular lower finger of major claw.

4. **AMERICAN PINK SHRIMP** *Penaeus duorarum* p. 308
   Large—females may reach 28 cm (11 in.) long; males much smaller. Rostrum not upturned at tip and slightly arched above eye, with 7–10 sharp teeth above, 2–3 below. Juveniles gray or reddish brown, with a dark spot at juncture of third and fourth abdominal segments. Adults red, pinkish, bluish, or white; abdominal spots reddish, brownish, or lacking. A commercial shrimp.

5. **LONG-CLAWED HERMIT CRAB** p. 313
   Pagurus longicarpus
   Tiny; occupies shells of Mud Snails and other small snails. Right claw elongate, smooth; much larger than left claw. Tan with cream markings; lighter in w. Florida than on east coast. Major claw white, with light brown stripe. Walking legs cream, with brown stripes on edges and across some joints.

6. **ARROW SHRIMP** *Tozeuma carolinense* p. 308
   Straight, elongate, thin, and transparent. Swims with body in a vertical position. Small—to 5 cm (2 in.) long—and narrow; well camouflaged on seagrass blades. Rostrum sharp; untoothed above and curved upward near tip. Assumes color of background.

7. **EELGRASS BROKEN-BACK SHRIMP** p. 308
   Hippolyte zostericola
   Tiny—to 1.8 cm (7/10 in.) long. Abdomen sharply flexed, giving it a hump toward rear. Rostrum with 2 upper and 1–4 lower teeth. Brown-red or bright green. On seagrass.

8. **FLORIDA GRASS SHRIMP** *Palaemon floridana* p. 308
   To 5 cm (2 in.) long. Transparent, with dark lines encircling body and running diagonally on sides toward rostrum. Claws on first 2 pairs of legs; second pair largest. On seagrass.

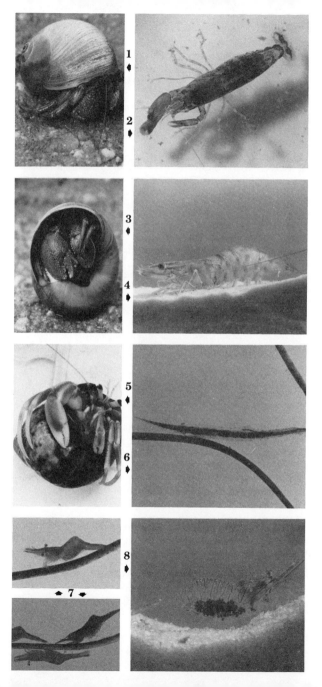

PLATE 8

Sea Anemones and Soft Corals
of Southeastern and Gulf Shores

1. **SEA WHIP** *Leptogorgia virgulata* p. 210
   Long—to 91 cm (3 ft.) tall. Branches with tiny, evenly distributed cups on both sides. Purple, yellow, red, orange, or tan.

2. **Sea Whip** colony.

3. **ORANGE BUSH CORAL** *Titanideum frauenfeldii* p. 27
   Pinkish red, orange, or, rarely, white branches; each to 8 mm (⅓ in.) thick. May form colonies with fingerlike projections and no branches. Cups scattered on branches. In deep water; frequently washed up on southeastern beaches.

4. **ONION ANEMONE** *Paranthus rapiformis* p. 215
   Medium-sized. Column smooth; grayish white or cream, translucent. Tentacles transparent or green. Oral disk green, transparent, splotched with orange, green, and/or white spots. Specimen shown was disturbed to demonstrate its ability to distend its body, which makes it resemble an onion.

5. **MUELLER'S SEA PANSY** *Renilla muelleri* p. 211
   Purple, jelly-like. Umbrella-shaped frond broader than long; polyps scattered, not in rows. Stalk short, thin, stringlike.

6. **TEXAS WARTY ANEMONE** *Bunodactis texaensis* p. 214
   About 96 translucent, greenish tentacles with dark gray streaks. Column light gray, with vertical lines of darker tubercles. On rocks, jetties.

7. **AMERICAN WARTY ANEMONE** p. 215
   Bunodosoma cavernata
   About 96 short, tapering, olive-green tentacles. Column rust red. A fringe of white, bubble-like vesicles at edge of collar beneath tentacles. Column covered with scattered warts. On jetties, rocks. *Foreground:* A **Five-toothed Sea Cucumber.** Seashell to right of cucumber is a **Baby Bonnet** (see p. 234).

8. **GRAY WARTY ANEMONE** *Anthopleura carneola* p. 214
   Large—to 7.5 cm (3 in.) across gray oral disk. Over 100 stubby, pinkish or yellowish, white-flecked, translucent tentacles. Column translucent, whitish, covered with vertical lines of warts; column buried beneath sand near low-water mark.

9. View of oral disk of **Gray Warty Anemone,** showing translucent, white-flecked tentacles. When touched, disk folds up and is withdrawn beneath surface of sand.

PLATE 9

Branching and Bushy Bryozoans
of Southeastern and Gulf Shores

1. COMMON SHEEP'S-WOOL BRYOZOAN   p. 367
Amathia convoluta
Bushy, straw-colored; about 7.5 cm (3 in.) tall. Branches rather stiff. Each branch appears twisted into an elongate spiral.

2. DELICATE SHEEP'S-WOOL BRYOZOAN   p. 367
Amathia distans
Bushy, densely branched; about 3.5 cm (1¼ in.) tall. Branches not very stiff; zooids mostly in short spiral clumps on branches.

3. MUDDY-TUFT BRYOZOAN   *Anquinella palmata*   p. 368
Resembles tufts of mud-coated algae. About 3–5 cm (1½–2 in.) tall.

4. HAUFF'S ALCYONIDIUM   *Alcyonidium hauffi*   p. 368
Grayish or translucent whitish. Forms fleshy, gelatinous, finger-like colonies on dead stems of the **Sea Whip** (*Leptogorgia virgulata,* p. 210). When cast up on beach, the Sea Whip may have been torn away or eroded.

5. SAUERKRAUT BRYOZOAN   p. 368
Zoobotryon verticillatum
Vine-like, transparent masses resembling sunbleached seaweed or sauerkraut. Limp when out of water.

6. COMMON BUGULA   *Bugula neritina*   p. 368
Reddish brown or reddish purple, plantlike tufts.

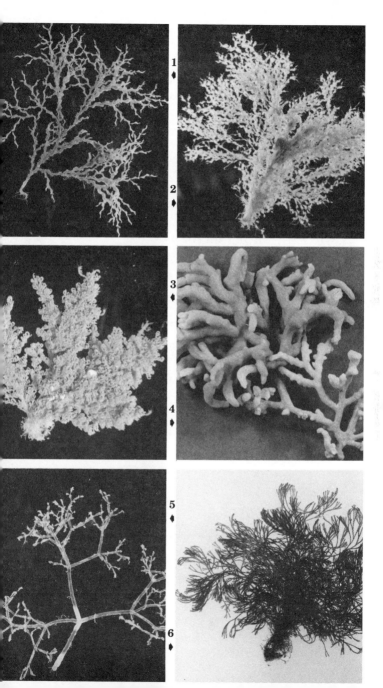

PLATE 10
Encrusting, Leafy, and Branching Bryozoans of Southeastern and Gulf Shores

1. **COMMON SEA MAT** *Membranipora tenuis* p. 368
White lacy crusts on shells or rocks.

2. **SARGASSUM SEA MAT** p. 368
Membranipora tuberculata
White lacy crusts on Sargassum Weed (p. 136).

3. **LETTUCE BRYOZOAN** p. 369
Thalamoporella gothica floridana
Two-layered, crinkled sheets, usually forming fragile, calcareous balls of leafy, sandy-looking plates. Whitish or straw-colored.

4. **GULF STAGHORN BRYOZOAN** p. 369
Schizoporella pungens
Coral-like colonies with hollow-tipped branches. Live colonies bright orange, dark reddish brown, or purplish black.

5. **TEXAS LONGHORN BRYOZOAN** p. 369
Hippoporidra calcarea
Forms spiny, spindle-shaped house for hermit crab.

6. **SPINY TOOTHED CRUST BRYOZOAN** p. 370
Parasmittina echinata
Knobby, calcareous, spindle-shaped crust on narrow-bladed seagrasses. Yellowish or tan.

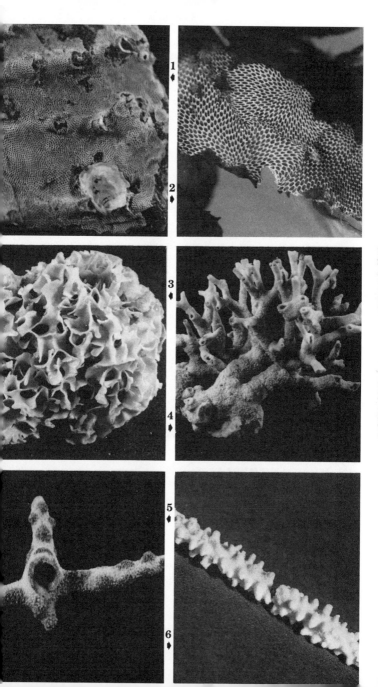

PLATE 11
Echinoderms of the Gulf of Mexico

1. SPINY BEADED SEA STAR   p. 342
Astropecten duplicatus
To 20 cm (8 in.) in diameter. Reddish, brown, or tan, with contrasting beads and spines along lower margins of arms. Has pointed podia (tube feet), used to feel deeply into sediment for buried mollusks.

2. BROWN SPINY SEA STAR   *Echinaster spinulosus*   p. 342
To 16 cm (6¼ in.) wide. Found only in s. and w. Florida and Alabama. Brown or purple; spines and podia often orange.

3. SHORT-SPINED BRITTLE STAR   p. 348
Ophioderma brevispinum
To 1 cm (⅜ in.) across disk. Light green, with arms banded in green or orange and gray. Arm spines so short that arms appear serrated. Each interbrachium has 4 genital slits.

4. FIVE-HOLED KEYHOLE URCHIN   p. 354
Mellita quinquiesperforata
To 10 cm (4 in.) wide. Covered with short, tan bristles, which can move sand to cover upper surface. Five lunules.

5. STRIPED SEA CUCUMBER   *Thyonella gemmata*   p. 363
To 15 cm (6 in.) long, with dark brown and tan stripes. Tube feet in double rows. Ten dark brown tentacles.

6. NETTED SEA STAR   *Luidia clathrata*   p. 343
To 30 cm (1 ft.) across. Tan with brown or black wavy lines running length of arms. Velvetlike spines.

7. Contracted **Striped Sea Cucumber**—podia and stripes not visible.

8. MEXICAN THYONE   *Thyone mexicana*   p. 363
To 5 cm (2 in.) long. Usually grayish, with 10 dark tentacles.

PLATE 12

Caribbean Rocky Shores (1):
Snails of the Gray Zone
and Other Inhabitants of Rocky Areas

1. Uppermost snail is a **Bleeding-tooth Nerite** (p. 237)—tan or gray with black, purple, and red zigzag blotches. Inhabits the upper and middle gray zones, along with the **Zebra Periwinkles** (p. 235) in photo 3 below.

2. **TINTED CANTHARUS** *Pisania tincta* p. 238
   To 3.8 cm (1½ in.) tall. Pale reddish brown with bluish gray and white markings. Four spiral cords cross 13–14 rounded vertical ribs. Outer lip has strong ridge inside. This snail feeds on barnacles, worms, and small mussels on or under rocks.

3. **Four-toothed Nerites** (p. 237), larger snails with strongly corded shells and red, yellow, and black markings, live in the middle and lower gray zones. The gray-brown snail covered with rows of rounded tubercles at lower left is a **Common Prickly Winkle** (p. 234), found in greatest abundance in the uppermost, driest part of the gray zone, usually with **Zebra Periwinkles.** To the right of the Prickly Winkle (see inset) is a **Scorched Mussel** (p. 257), which can be found in moist crevices in the lower gray and black zones, and covering rocks in large colonies in the yellow (intertidal) zone.

4. **MAGNIFICENT SPINY URCHIN** p. 353
   Astropyga magnifica
   Spines long, but shorter than in juvenile Long-spined Black Urchins. Spines white with red-brown, dashlike spots, not bands. Spines less than 3 × diameter of test; test to 7.5 cm (3 in.) across. Subtidal, usually in deep water.

5. **SPONGE CRAB** *Dromia erythropus* p. 316
   To 13 cm (5 in.) long, covered with dark brown rough hairs. Carapace wider than long, with 4 conical teeth along front margin. Last pair of legs longer than penultimate pair and reflected over back, where they hold sponges, tunicates, or colonial sea anemones on carapace. Crab obtains protection and camouflage from organisms on its back, while they benefit from being moved from place to place, instead of being completely sessile (attached to bottom). This photo shows the underside of a female.

PLATE 13

Caribbean Rocky Shores (2)

1. RIBBED BARNACLE p. 300

Tetraclita squamosa stalactifera

Large—to 3 cm (1¼ in.). Grayish white, with vertical grooves running from aperture to base. Most barnacle skeletons consist of a few fused plates with clearly defined edges. This species lacks visible plates, clearly differentiating it from *Balanus* barnacles (p. 299). In yellow (midintertidal) zone, Ribbed Barnacles are sometimes mixed with tiny **Fragile Star Barnacles** (p. 299), as seen here. Farther down in the intertidal zone the gray crust of star barnacles disappears, leaving pure stands of Ribbed Barnacles.

2. KNOBBY PERIWINKLE *Tectarius muricatus* p. 239

White or blue-gray; robust, globose. Covered with spiral rows of white beads. Found high up on shore, often above head level. These snails were clustered on a branch of a dead tree several meters above the high-tide mark.

3. Gray-zone tidepool. These snails were gathered at the rim of the pool, at water's edge. The larger snails at top are **Checkered Nerites** (p. 237), to 2 cm (¾ in.) long. Shell deeply corded and checkered in black and white. Aperture toothless, or with 2 tiny teeth. The smaller, globose snails with a regular, black-and-white dotted pattern are **Melancholy Nerites** (*Puperita tristis*), which reach only 8 mm (⅓ in.) in length and have a bluish aperture. The two boldly striped snails near the bottom are **Zebra Nerites** (p. 238). Less than 1 cm (½ in.) long; found only in tidepools. Aperture suffused with bright yellow.

4. Yellow-zone (intertidal) scene. At center, a **Fuzzy Chiton** (p. 263), recognized by its coarsely bristled girdle with black-and-white stripes. Note the tiny rods, feces of this chiton, at its posterior end. Just above feces is a **Checkered Nerite.** The deeply corded globose snail at the front of the chiton is a **Four-toothed Nerite** (p. 237). Four strong teeth project into aperture; shell whitish, with flecks or zigzag bars of red and black. Above front of chiton and in upper right-hand corner are **Zebra Periwinkles** (p. 235)—do not confuse them with Zebra Nerites (above). Shell elongate, with a sharp spire; whitish, with black herringbone lines. To 2.5 cm (1 in.) long; often much smaller. Note: The Zebra Periwinkles and Four-toothed Nerite have migrated down from the gray zone at low tide in this unusual photo.

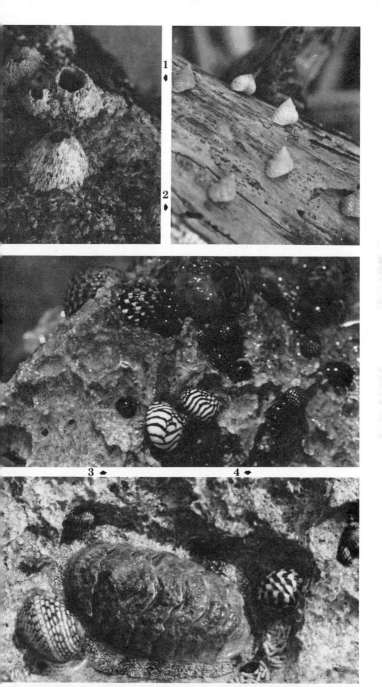

PLATE 14

Caribbean Rocky Shores (3)

1. **Gray zone** of coastal shelf composed of eroded gray limestone, the remains of ancient, once-living coral. Cups of ancient corals would be visible on close examination of rocks. *Foreground:* **Yellow-zone** (intertidal) tidepool has daily supply of seawater through fissure barely visible at upper central margin of pool. One would expect to find Fuzzy and West Indian chitons in this pool, as well as Wide-mouthed and Florida rock snails. Schools of tiny juvenile Sergeant Majors and a few Beaugregories and Schoolmasters compete with gobies and blennies for food. *Background:* Waves erode rocks, creating an overhang beneath which are the **black zone,** with walls overhung by masses of blackish sea moss (*Bostrychia*), a red alga, and the **yellow zone.** Overhang visible in inlet just above tidepool. Rocks at left, covered with short fuzzy seaweed exposed by waves, are at lowest level of intertidal zone, revealing that this photo was taken at low tide.

2. **Squamose Chiton** (p. 263) and **Fuzzy Chiton** (p. 263) on a rock in mid-intertidal zone.

3. **Brown Rock Sea Cucumber** (p. 361), often found in groups on rocks in heavy surf among seaweeds. Body color varies from tan to blackish, but tentacles always black.

4. **Red Rock Urchin** (p. 353), common on rocky shores just below intertidal zone. Black to bright red, but even black specimens show some red on test. In crevices in rock.

5. **Brown Rock Urchin** (p. 353) occupies same niche as Red Rock Urchin but is found only on continental shores (not W. Indies). Common on jetties in Gulf. Brown test with grayish brown spines.

PLATE 15

Caribbean Rocky Shores (4):
Intertidal and Subtidal Organisms

1. Awash at low tide, these rocks are covered with yellow or tan **Sun Anemones** (p. 216), forming a mat more than a meter square. Where rocks are not colonized by anemones, **Red Rock Urchins** (p. 353) abound.

2. **Red Foram** *Homotrema rubrum*
Red blotches on rock are tests (shells) of microscopic amoeboid foraminiferans—protozoans that settle on any hard, clean, underwater surface. The organism dies when washed up on shore, but its test stays red. Remains of millions of tests color some beaches pink.

3. **ATLANTIC UMBRELLA SEA SLUG**   p. 248
Umbraculum umbraculum
To 15 cm (6 in.) long. Pale orange body, covered with low tubercles. Oval, calcareous shell, about the size and thickness of a silver dollar, lies at apex of tapered body. Note 2 small, retractible tentacles just in front of disk.

4. **PURPLE STYLASTER**   *Stylaster roseus*   p. 206
Purple, pink, red, or white. Delicate; multibranched in 1 plane, rarely more than 10 cm (4 in.) long or high. Tiny polyps live inside pinholes in calcareous skeleton. End branches wavy.

5. Pink zone. **Fuzzy Chitons** (p. 263) surround a **Knobby Keyhole Limpet** (p. 242).

6. **WEST INDIAN TOP SNAIL**   *Cittarium pica*   p. 233
To 10 cm (4 in.) tall. Shell heavy, with black zigzag markings, pearly white aperture, circular olive operculum with black concentric lines. At or just below waterline.

7. **THREE-COLORED HERMIT CRAB**   p. 311
Clibanarius tricolor
Tiny—carapace to 9 mm (⅜ in.) long. In auger and cerith snail shells, in tidepools and on intertidal and subtidal rocks.

8. **WIDE-MOUTHED ROCK SNAIL**   *Purpura patula*   p. 239
Dull gray; 6–7 rows of sharp nodules. To 9 cm (3½ in.) high. In yellow (intertidal) zone. Produces purple stain that smells of garlic.

9. Plume-like hydrozoan colony. Related to jellyfishes and corals, these colonies consist of polyps distributed on branches. Most colonies are fuzzlike and few are taller than 15 cm (6 in.). This colony is a **Fern Hydroid** (*Halocordyle disticha*). Each white dot is a polyp with a whorl of long, thin tentacles below short, knobbed tentacles surrounding bulbous tip. Many species deliver a short-lived, strong sting.

10. **CANCELLATE FLESHY LIMPET**   p. 242
Lucapina suffusa
Round hole at apex, slightly forward of middle of shell. Strong radiating ridges extend from hole. Interior white, with bluish ring around hole. Yellow zone.

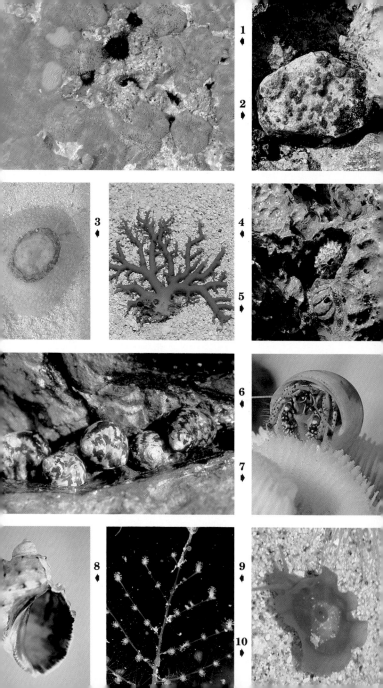

PLATE 16
Caribbean Rocky Shores (5):
Zonation, Tidepools, and Chitons

1. The **white zone,** wetted infrequently during the year, often supports salt-resistant terrestrial plants that seem to grow directly from the rock, such as this **White Mangrove.** The relatively sharp slope of this rocky shore produces narrow zones: the gray and yellow zones together extend less than 1 m (3¼ ft.) up the shore.

2. This deep, **yellow-zone** tidepool has relatively stable conditions because seawater enters daily at high tide. Thus organisms used to almost constant inundation survive alongside more resistant intertidal animals. Bright yellow and brown rock at left is above waterline. In upper right corner are **Ribbed Barnacles.** Tiny, gray and white spots around and beneath them are **Fragile Star Barnacles.** Halfway down the right side is a mass of **Scorched Mussels.** To left of mussels, beneath water's surface, are many **Red Rock Urchins** and a **West Indian Top Snail.** On bottom of pool is a small, almost indistinguishable, eroded head of **Shallow-water Starlet Coral,** p. 213.

3. **WEST INDIAN CHITON**   *Chiton tuberculatus*   p. 263
Valves (plates) smooth in center, then covered with curved riblets; sides of valves with a distinct triangle composed of elongate beads. Girdle scaly, with alternating areas of whitish, green, and black. To 7.5 cm (3 in.) long.

4. **FUZZY CHITON**   *Acanthopleura granulata*   p. 263
Valves usually eroded; easily recognized by black-and-white fuzzy girdle. Upper yellow zone. To 7.5 cm (3 in.) long.

5. **MARBLED CHITON**   *Chiton marmoratus*   p. 263
Valves shiny, smooth; marked with dark brown or olive stripes. To 7.5 cm (3 in.) long.

6. **ROUGH-GIRDLED CHITON**   *Ceratozona squalida*   p. 263
Valves usually eroded. Girdle leathery, not striped, covered with thick, flat, yellowish hairs, often partially obscured by algae. To 5 cm (2 in.) long.

7. **SQUAMOSE CHITON**   *Chiton squamosus*   p. 263
Valves smooth, with no curved riblets; beaded triangle along edges less pronounced than in West Indian Chiton. Girdle broad, strongly scaled, with alternating stripes of grayish green and grayish white. Upper yellow zone, usually below Fuzzy Chiton. To 7.5 cm (3 in.) long.

8. **PURPLE SLENDER CHITON**   p. 264
Stenoplax purpurascens
Narrow—about 3 times as long as wide. Valves roundly arched; whitish, green, olive, buff. Central area has fine, smooth, longitudinal riblets. Girdle appears smooth but is covered with minute scales. To 5 cm (2 in.) long.

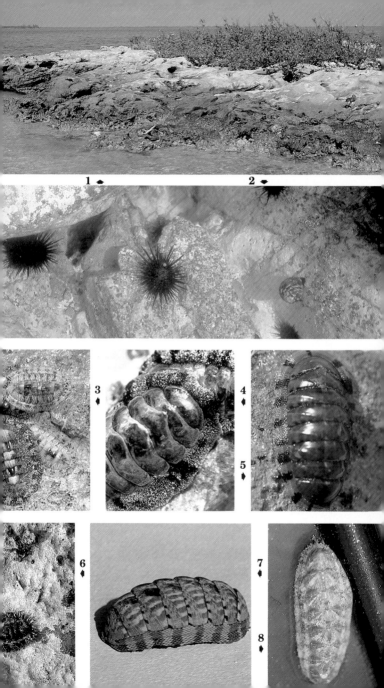

PLATE 17
The Turtle Grass Bed Community

1. A clump of **Thin Finger Coral** (p. 213) among broad green leaves of **Turtle Grass** (p. 142). Note that leaves are encrusted with minute plants and animals. Just above Finger Coral is a clump of tan **Forked Sea Tumbleweed algae** (p. 134). Dark green plant in upper right corner is **Soft Fan Alga** (p. 130).

2. Common sea urchins. *Bottom:* **Sea Egg urchin** (p. 356) has short, white, harmless spines. Above Sea Egg are 2 **Long-spined Black Urchins** (p. 353).

3. **YELLOWFIN MOJARRA** *Gerres cinereus*   p. 116
To 38 cm (15 in.) long. Grayish, silvery, with bluish gray vertical bars on sides. Anal and pelvic fins yellow. Ingests sand; extracts and digests small animals and expels sand through gills.

4. **GOLDSPOTTED EEL** *Myrichthys oculatus*   p. 116
Pale tan to greenish brown, with dark brown rings enclosing gold spots. Eats crabs, shrimps. Sluggish, may be picked up by hand. Excellent for aquaria. To 96.5 cm (38 in.).

5. Fecal casts on top of sand mounds indicate the presence of the **Burrowing Sea Cucumber** (p. 361).

6. **SPOTTED GOATFISH** *Pseudupeneus maculatus*   p. 116
Pale tan, with 3 square black spots. A pair of barbels under chin used to stir up sand and expose small animals, which are eaten. To 25 cm (10 in.) long.

7. **SOLITARY PAPER BUBBLE SEA SLUG**   p. 246
Haminoea solitaria
Tan or gray, with tiny brown dots. Head with 2 eyes and lateral swellings. Large swelling on back contains thin, glassy shell. To 2.5 cm (1 in.) long.

8. **CUSHION or RETICULATED SEA STAR**   p. 343
Oreaster reticulatus
Large—to 50 cm (20 in.) wide; thick. Juveniles green; adults yellow, orange, and/or tan, with a network of contrasting tubercles.

9. **RAGGED SEA HARE** *Bursatella leachii pleii*   p. 247
To 25 cm (10 in.) long. Tan with brown spots. Flattened, forked papillae extend from back. Often seen among **Forked Sea Tumbleweed algae** (p. 134), which its papillae resemble.

10. **ANTILLEAN LIMA or INFLATED FILE CLAM**   p. 257
Limaria pellucida
Thin, inflated white shell, to 2.8 cm (1⅛ in.) long; surface sculptured with fine lines. Swims by sharply opening and closing valves, jetting water from between them. Under rocks.

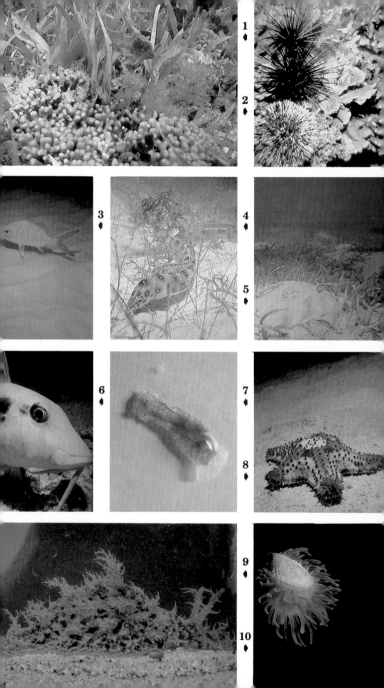

PLATE 18
Seashore Plant Communities (1):
Pioneer Beach Plants

1. Beach and strandline vegetation. Three distinct layers of dead Turtle Grass mark levels of previous tides. Most seaward layer was washed up by that day's highest tide. Next landward line indicates furthest point of the month's spring high tide. The third line, almost at the base of the shoreside plants, was created when a storm combined with a spring tide to push the debris to its maximum height up the beach.

   The vertical, pencil-shaped projections in the water are pneumatophores of the **Black Mangrove** tree behind them (center). To its right is a broad-leaved **Sea Grape** tree. Another Sea Grape is at far right. Towering above it is an **Australian-pine.** Other trees in background are **White** and **Gray mangroves.**

2. **BEACH MORNING GLORY** *Ipomoea pes-caprae*   p. 161
   Vine grows to water's edge. Notched leaves, like the cloven hoof of a goat; purple flowers like those of the Morning Glory.

3. **SPIDER LILY** *Hymenocallis latifolia*   p. 166
   Broad, shining, dark green leaves; fragrant white flowers.

4. **WEST INDIAN CREEPER** *Wedelia trilobata*   p. 163
   Leaves to 10 cm (4 in.) long; light green with a long central lobe and a reduced lobe on either side. A prostrate vine; small yellow flowers with about 7 trilobed petals.

5. **SOUTHERN GLASSWORT** *Salicornia perennis*   p. 168
   Fleshy vertical stems on long runners; leaves reduced to minute scales. Forms mats in salt marshes near the sea. Edible.

6. **SEASIDE BEAN** *Canavalia maritima*   p. 161
   Beanlike flower on trailing vine; forms pods. Often mixed with Beach Morning Glory, but lacks notch in leaf.

7. **SEASIDE PURSLANE** *Sesuvium portulacastrum*   p. 168
   A prostrate herb with thick, fleshy leaves about 2.5 cm (1 in.) long. Tiny, star-shaped, pink flowers. Forms thick carpets.

8. **SEASHORE DROPSEED** *Sporobolus virginicus*   p. 172
   Erect stems to 40 cm (16 in.) tall with alternating short, sheathed blades to 5 cm (2 in.) long. Forms dense colonies.

9. **CARIBBEAN SEDGE** *Cyperus ligularis*   p. 169
   Cluster of dark, coppery seedheads at apex of plant with 6 or more long, grasslike leaves extending from cluster. Stem bare.

10. **TROPICAL SEDGE** *Fimbristylis cymosa*   p. 171
    Vertical stem arises from basal mass of elongate, flat, spreading leaves. At apex of stem is cluster of brown seedheads.

PLATE 19
Seashore Plant Communities (2)

1. **Rocky shoreside community.** *Center foreground:* **Seaside Purslane** (p. 168) forms a mat, giving way on left to **West Indian Sea Lavender** (p. 160) with clumps of succulent, whitish green leaves. On lower left are arched masses of its tiny white flowers. *Left background and right side:* **Bay Cedar shrubs** (p. 160). Behind Bay Cedar on right are the plate-like, glossy, red-veined leaves of a prostrate **Sea Grape** tree (p. 156).

2. **SEASIDE MAHO** *Thespesia populnea*   p. 160
To 9 m (30 ft.) tall. Dark green, shiny, heart-shaped leaves and yellow, purple-throated flower.

3. **SALT-MARSH ASTER** *Aster tenuifolius*   p. 166
White or faintly magenta, daisy-like flowers on upper branches. Long, narrow, alternate, thick leaves on lower third of stem.

4. **Succession on a West Indian shore.** Sandy beach closest to sea is being colonized by pioneering **Seaside Bean** (p. 161) and **Beach Morning Glory** (p. 161) vines. Behind them, grasses take hold. Higher up, in background, detritus from pioneering plants enriches sand, creating an environment suitable for **White Mangroves** (p. 179) and **Coconut Palms** (p. 156).

5. **The edges of a Red Mangrove swamp.** *Foreground:* **Saltwort** shrubs (p. 154) cover low-saline area. *Background:* On left are the rhododendron-like leaves of the **Red Mangrove** (p. 179). On higher ground to the right are **Buttonwood** trees (p. 178).

6. **SPANISH BAYONET** *Yucca aloifolia*   p. 161
Cluster of broad, thick, sharply pointed, smooth leaves to 35 cm (13¾ in.) long. Spike of waxy white flowers in season. Another species, *Y. filamentosa*, has fraying whitish threads along leaf margins, giving it a hairy appearance.

7. **SEA GRAPE** *Coccoloba uvifera*   p. 156
Tree or prostrate shrub growing near shore. Plate-like, shiny leaves to 27 cm (11 in.) long, with red veins. Edible, purple, grape-like fruit has large pit. In green clusters when unripe.

8. **MANCHINEEL** *Hippomane mancinella*   p. 158
To 9 m (30 ft.) tall. Dark shiny leaves and apple-like fruit. **Toxic.** Don't eat sweet-smelling fruit or stand under tree when it rains.

9. **BEACH CROTON** *Croton punctatus*   p. 164
Whitish green, velvety leaves. Berry to 8 mm (³⁄₁₀ in.) wide. Grows among Sea Rocket and Sea Oats on open beach or foredunes.

PLATE 20
Seashore Plant Communities (3):
Plants of Caribbean Rocky Shores

1. *Left:* **Sea Daisy** (p. 164) shrub with bright yellow flowers and whitish, elongate leaves. *Right:* Shrubby **Sea Grape** tree (p. 156) with broad, yellow- or red-veined leaves.

2. Yellow flower and whitish green leaves of **Sea Daisy**.

3. *Left:* **West Indian Sea Lavender** (p. 160), with silvery, greenish white clumps of leaves. *Right and foreground:* **West Indian Creeper** (p. 163), a vine with trilobed leaves and yellow flowers.

4. Close-up of **West Indian Sea Lavender,** showing clumps of elongate, greenish white, thick leaves.

5. **SHORE CROTON**   *Croton linearis*   p. 164
Small shrub with glossy, dark green, narrowly elongate leaves that often turn reddish or brownish near tips. Tiny white flowers.

6. **Shore Croton,** showing berry-like fruit, mixed with a **Seaside Bean** vine (p. 161). The broad leaf of Seaside Bean lacks a notch at petiole, differentiating this vine from Beach Morning Glory.

7. **BLACK TORCH**   *Erithalis fruticosa*   p. 156
Small shrub; dark green, leathery, almost round leaves. Tiny white, six-petaled flowers, in clusters at ends of branches.

8. **JOEWOOD**   *Jacquinia arborea*   p. 158
Shrub or tree, to 5 m (18 ft.) tall. Glossy, yellow-green, blunt leaves. Clusters of orange, berry-like fruit with pointed tips. This plant is growing on a bare rock at water's edge.

9. **SEASIDE STRUMFIA**   *Strumfia maritima*   p. 160
Low-growing shrub found on shoreside rocks. Small, narrow, profuse leaves; branches with dark, radial ridges. Tiny pink flower. White, waxy, berry-like fruit (shown).

10. **SEASIDE ROCK SHRUB**   *Rachicallis americana*   p. 159
Prostrate shrub with tiny, oval, glossy, bright green leaves growing in clusters. Minute, waxy, four-petaled yellow flowers. May be the dominant plant on exposed rocky shores.

PLATE 21
Seashore Plant Communities (4): Dune and Salt-Marsh Plants of the South and Caribbean

1. Dunes, constantly moving landward, are overtaking a stand of **Cabbage Palms** (p. 160) on a barrier island. Cabbage Palm has a crown of fanlike leaves atop a gray, columnar trunk.

2. View from interdune trough (swale) between sparsely vegetated foredunes and heavily vegetated reardunes. *Center background:* Clump of **Sea Oats** (p. 172), behind which are areas colonized by pioneering grasses.

3. **SEASHORE SALTGRASS** *Distichlis spicata* p. 169
Light green with overlapping, V-shaped, narrow leaves that are pointed diagonally upward and arranged in 1 plane on opposite sides of stem. Seedhead compact; whitish green, turning tan.

4. **AMERICAN BEACHGRASS** p. 169
Ammophila brevigulata
Clumps of long, narrow leaves extending from sheaths at base of 1 m (39 in.) tall plant. Seedhead to 30 cm (1 ft.) long.

5. **SMOOTH CORDGRASS** *Spartina alterniflora* p. 172
Broad, flat, dark green leaves, to 1.5 cm (⅗ in.) wide; plant often 1 m (39 in.) tall or taller. At seaward edge of low salt marsh; inundated daily by tides. **Marsh Periwinkle** (p. 235) climbs plant during high tide, descends to feed at low tide.

6. **GROUNDSEL TREE** *Baccharis halimifolia* p. 154
Shrub to 4.5 m (15 ft.) tall. Leaves alternate; upper leaves narrow, with no teeth; lower leaves broadly oval, toothed. Flowers beige; seeds (shown) in clusters, have white bristles in fall.

7. **MARSH ELDER** *Iva frutescens* p. 166
Bushy, to 3 m (9½ ft.) tall. Often found with Groundsel Tree in "saltbush community" at edge of marshes. Leaves toothed, thicker than on Groundsel Tree, and opposite. Berry-like green fruits in clusters at ends of branches; fruits turn brown in fall.

8. **SEASIDE GOLDENROD** *Solidago sempervirens* p. 169
Tall, with long, arched leaves to 7.5 cm (3 in.) long. Leaves grow along entire length of stem.

9. **SEA LAVENDER** *Limonium carolinianum* p. 168
Clump of smooth leaves (to 17.5 cm—6⅘ in. long) gives rise to wiry, much-branched, bare stems covered with tiny lavender flowers.

10. **BAY CEDAR** *Suriana maritima* p. 160
Shrubby—to 8 m (27 ft.) tall, but usually stunted from exposure on rocky shores. Clumps of light green leaves on short secondary branches and main branches.

11. Small flower of **Bay Cedar,** to 1.2 cm (½ in.) wide.

PLATE 22
Red Mangrove Community (1)

1. **RED MANGROVE** *Rhizophora mangle* p. 179
Prop and aerial roots descend from trunk and branches respectively, plunging into seawater. Note accumulated dead leaves and debris filtered from water by roots, building up sediment and paving the way for succession by Black Mangroves.

2. Close-up of welter of prop and aerial roots. Note seedling at base of roots.

3. Seedlings of the **Red Mangrove tree** are retained on tree until well developed. These juvenile plants (30 cm — 1 ft. — long) can float for a year in the open sea. Note pointed brown hydrophilic end and the remains of the fruit, a brown oval at opposite end. Leathery, glossy, opposite, rhododendron-like leaves retain fresh water, an aid in maintaining water balance.

4. Note yellow, waxy, four-petaled flowers on long stalks, in groups of 2 or 3. Petals hairy on inner surface. There are 8 stamens.

5. **Collared Sand Anemones** (p. 216) with columns buried in sand, among Red Mangrove roots. Olive, with radial lines on oral disk.

6. **STINGING MANGROVE ANEMONE** p. 215
Bunodeopsis antilliensis
Tiny, column to 3.8 cm (1½ in.) tall, with 20–40 transparent tentacles. Mass of green or brown, tiny, bubble-like or fingerlike vesicles at base. Nocturnal; stings.

7. **SPOTTED MANGROVE CRAB** p. 331
Goniopsis cruentata
To 6.3 cm (2½ in.) long. Eyes on red stalks at front corners of carapace, separated by 4 blunt, shallow teeth. Carapace brown with lighter reticulations. Legs red with white or yellow spots; larger white spots along edges of carapace. Claws white.

8. **MANGROVE PERIWINKLE** *Littorina angulifera* p. 235
Tan or brown with darker oblique markings. Sharp apex; thin shell with 6–7 whorls. On undersides of mangrove prop roots.

9. **SEAWEED CUCUMBER** *Synaptula hydriformis* p. 359
To 7.5 cm (3 in.) or longer. Two color morphs — green or brown. Found entangled among seaweeds on subtidal Red Mangrove roots. Transparent; jelly-like when root lifted from water. Must be gently pulled from seaweed or will fragment, releasing dozens of juveniles from body cavity. Skin sticky.

10. **COFFEE-BEAN SNAIL** *Melampus coffeus* p. 236
To 1.2 cm (½ in.) tall. Smooth; pale brown, often with 3 creamy bands. Inner lip with 2 white folds. Snails are eating detritus on mud at base of Red Mangrove tree at low tide.

PLATE 23
Red Mangrove Community (2):
Tunicates (Sea Squirts)

1. **DIVIDED TUNICATE** *Styela partita* p. 188
   Apertures of both siphons with purple stripes or triangles. To 3 cm (1¼ in.) tall. Skin rough, often overgrown.

2. **PLEATED SEA SQUIRT** *Styela plicata* pp. 188, 375
   Surface tan, slippery. Apertures four-lobed, edged with purple-brown lines. Often in large clumps of many unattached individuals. To 7.2 cm (2¾ in.) tall.

3. **GREEN ENCRUSTING TUNICATE** p. 190
   Symplegma viride
   Tiny zooids, to 1 cm (⅜ in.) tall, olive green to yellowish. Forms thick, cushion-shaped or lobed, encrusting colonies, often obscured by gelatinous, translucent test. Individuals randomly scattered; visible to naked eye only as 2 white, yellow, or green rings, one around each siphon.

4. **PAINTED TUNICATE** *Clavelina picta* p. 189
   Colonial. Carmine or purple band around apertures. To 1.9 cm (¾ in.) tall. Zooids attached by stolon at base; crowded.

5. Clump of *Clavelina* **colonial tunicates** surround end of Red Mangrove root. Bright red **Fire Sponge** (p. 223) at right.

6. **RASPBERRY TUNICATE** *Distaplia stylifer* p. 190
   Colony of purplish zooids in an oval mass to 2.5 cm (1 in.) wide, on thick stalk. Common offshore and on coral reefs.

7. **BLACK ENCRUSTING TUNICATE** p. 190
   Botrylloides nigrum
   Compound tunicate, forming a brown or black, hard crust to 1 cm (⅜ in.) thick. Aperture of buccal (incurrent) siphon often surrounded by white ring. Many zooids share and surround 1 large excurrent siphon.

8. **MANGROVE TUNICATE** *Ecteinascidia turbinata* p. 189
   Orange or orange-brown, club-shaped zooids, attached by a thin, vine-like stolon. Internal orange or pink, vertical, curved line (intestine). To 5 cm (2 in.) tall. Forms grape-like clusters to 15 cm (6 in.) wide around mangrove roots.

9. Another color form of **Mangrove Tunicate** or a closely related species. Note thin stolons wrapped around root.

10. **Crozier's Flatworm** (p. 378), feeding on **Mangrove Tunicates.**

11. **VARIABLE ENCRUSTING TUNICATE** p. 190
    Botryllus planus
    A compound, encrusting sea squirt. Color variable—may range from black to cream, often with zooids of contrasting colors. Another **waxy tropical flatworm** (p. 378), possibly *Pseudoceros aurolineata,* is crawling across surface.

PLATE 24

Red Mangrove Community (3):
Black, White, and Gray Mangrove Trees and the Mangrove Fern

1. **BLACK MANGROVE** *Avicennia germinans* p. 178
   To 21 m (70 ft.) tall. Leaves opposite, elliptical; upper surface dark green, lower surface lighter, somewhat fuzzy. Note halo of 10-cm (4-in.) long pneumatophores on sand.

2. Close-up of pneumatophores. Note that those at edges of mass extend in straight lines, delineating root beneath sand. Do not confuse these with pneumatophores of White Mangrove, which are sparser and knobbier.

3. Flowers of **Black Mangrove** have 4 petals and are borne in short, spike-like clusters at ends of branches.

4. Fruit of **Black Mangrove** is laterally compressed and fuzzy; to 3.8 cm (1½ in.) long and 2.5 cm (1 in.) wide.

5. Fruit and leaf of **Black Mangrove.** Note white salt crystals on leaf surface.

6. **WHITE MANGROVE** *Laguncularia racemosa* p. 179
   Leaves opposite, broadly elliptical, light green; borne on short, thick, red petioles. Note pair of slitlike glands on petiole adjacent to leaf.

7. Fruit of **White Mangrove** is oval, leathery, and ten-ribbed, arranged in clusters at ends of branches. Each fruit contains a dark red seed. To 1.2 cm (½ in.) long.

8. **SALTWORT** *Batis maritima* p. 154
   Forms mats on saline edges of mangrove swamps. Stems arching; small leaves to 3 cm (1¼ in.) long. Flowers in spikes.

9. **BUTTONWOOD or GRAY MANGROVE** p. 178
   Conocarpus erectus
   Leaf elongate, pointed at both ends. Spiny-appearing, berry-like, green fruit, 1.2 cm (½ in.) wide, in terminal clusters. Mature fruit brown. Leaves alternate. Often prostrate on rocky shores.

10. Close-up of **Buttonwood** fruit.

11. **MANGROVE FERN** *Acrosticum aureum* p. 179
    Dark green, glossy leaves, to 1 m (39 in.) long; deeply notched. Often upper portion or whole leaf turns brown or yellow. In pure stands in sunny clearings or along roads in mangrove swamps.

PLATE 25
Caribbean Shallow-water Sponges

1. COMMON LOGGERHEAD SPONGE   p. 223
Spheciospongia vesparium
Barrel-shaped, gray, with a cluster of large black holes in center of flat top. Groups of pinhole-size ostia on sides. To 60 cm (2 ft.) across top. Branches of **Staghorn Coral**, above sponge, and yellow **Crenelated Fire Coral** (p. 204), below, provide havens for a school of **French Grunts.**

2. STINKING VASE SPONGE   *Ircinia campana*   p. 223
Vase-shaped. Brown, reddish, and/or grayish. Surface with pointed warts. Black oscules (pores) inside central depression. To 60 cm (2 ft.) across. At base of sponge is a **Bicolor Damselfish** swimming over a **Red Boring Sponge** (*Cliona deletrix*) covered with *Parazoanthus* colonial anemones. A spherical head of greenish **Boulder Coral** is visible below and to left of Vase Sponge. A branch of **Red Finger Sponge** (p. 222) is at far right.

3. YELLOW TUBE SPONGE   *Aplysina fistularis*   p. 222
Bright yellow, thick-walled tubes, fused at bottom; tubes turn black when removed from water. May have thin, fingerlike projections near top of tubes. Shallow to deep water.

4. PILLOW STINKING SPONGE   *Ircinia strobilina*   p. 223
To 46 cm (18 in.) tall and wide. Gray when mature; covered with large, pointed warts. If cake-shaped, black holes on top are scattered, not clustered in center as in Common Loggerhead Sponge. If pillow-shaped, large black oscules are lined up on narrow edge of top of sponge. Crab is **Green Reef Crab** (p. 320).

5. FIRE SPONGE   *Tedania ignis*   p. 223
Red crust on rocks, walls, dead corals. A few large, raised, scattered oscules. Causes rash and pain when touched. Note **Cardinalfish** between valves of **Rough Lima** clam (p. 257).

6. VARIABLE SPONGE   *Anthosigmella varians*   p. 221
Flat amorphous crusts on sand or hard objects, taking the shape of the object covered. Light-rimmed oscules, raised on chimneys, often project from crust. Rubbery when alive, woodlike when dry.

7. CHICKEN LIVER SPONGE   *Chondrilla nucula*   p. 222
Flat, shiny brown crust on sand, rocks, dead coral. Oscules scattered, dark, close when sponge is touched. Liverlike consistency. Specimen shown has encrusted a tree root.

8. BLUE-GREEN FINGER SPONGE   p. 223
Amphimedon viridis
Thick, green fingers, to 30 cm (1 ft.) tall; may form thick crusts, hemispheres, or cockscomblike structures. Oscules large; flush or raised, conical. Soft, limp, spongy, easily torn; leaves sticky, slimy feeling on hands when touched.

9. RED FINGER SPONGE   *Amphimedon compressa*   p. 222
Brick-red. Thick, lumpy, crooked fingers, to 5 cm (2 in.) wide, or a thick crust (shown). Scattered oscules to 5 mm (⅕ in.) wide, flush with surface or slightly raised. See above (photo 2) for fingerlike form.

PLATE 26

Segmented Worms

1. **HORNED CHRISTMAS-TREE WORM**   p. 279
   Spirobranchus giganteus giganteus
   Paired, yellow, conical whorls. Red or blue gills extend from
   convoluted, white, calcareous tube, which is usually attached to
   rocks or coral. Tiny pink antlers on operculum. Common.

2. Calcareous tube of **Horned Christmas-tree Worm;** note white
   operculum. Note also lettuce coral at right and Red or Orange
   Coral polyps at left.

3. **RED-BANDED FANWORM** *Potamilla fonticula*   p. 278
   A large feather-duster worm with white or red gills extending
   from a tough, parchmentlike tube, to 15 cm (6 in.) long. Dark red
   band midway along gills.

4. **ELEGANT FANWORM** *Hypsicomus elegans*   p. 276
   Gills usually yellow, banded with purple. Tube parchmentlike,
   long, dark, and tortuous. On calm, shaded reefs or rocky areas.

5. **MAGNIFICENT BANDED FANWORM**   p. 278
   Sabellastarte magnifica
   Large. A brown or red-brown circlet of gills, to 25 cm (10 in.)
   across, usually much smaller. In clumps of many worms, muddy
   tubes project 20–25 cm (8–10 in.) from bottom. Common.

6. **FIVE-SPOTTED FEATHER-DUSTER WORM**   p. 276
   Sabella melanostigma
   Small. Four or 5 pairs of black eyespots along each gill. Tube
   muddy. Often in clumps.

7. **FIREWORM** *Hermodice carunculata*   p. 290
   Large. Olive; edges banded with red and white. White band
   consists of thousands of glassy, needle-like setae; if touched, setae
   become embedded in flesh and cause a hornetlike sting. Common
   and predaceous in Turtle Grass beds, coral reefs.

8. **RED-TIPPED FIREWORM** *Chloeia viridis*   p. 290
   To 30 cm (1 ft.) long, usually smaller. White with brown stripe and
   tan bars. Setae long, numerous, needle-like; can become embedded in skin, causing irritation.

PLATE 27

Sea Anemones

1. **PALE ANEMONE** *Aiptasia pallida* p. 213
   Small—to 5 cm (2 in.) tall. Usually in dense colonies of unattached individuals, on rocks and Red Mangrove roots.

2. Individual **Pale Anemone.** Alternate long and short tentacles.

3. **BEADED ANEMONE** *Epicystis crucifer* p. 216
   Color variable; light and dark stripes and rows of warts radiate from mouth. Disk flat, fringed with about 200 short, tapering tentacles. A sand-dweller. To 15 cm (6 in.) across disk.

4. **MAROON ANEMONE** *Actinia bermudensis* p. 213
   Maroon, with several rows of short, tapering tentacles. Circle of bright blue warts at margin. To 5 cm (2 in.) across disk.

5. **ROCK ANEMONE** *Anthopleura krebsi* p. 214
   Small—to 3 cm (1¼ in.) across disk. Dark gray ring around mouth. On rocks in intertidal zone, often in small colonies.

6. **BLUNT-TENTACLED ANEMONE** p. 216
   Telmactis cricoides
   Orange-brown disk with up to 80 short, blunt, brown-tipped tentacles; innermost largest. To 10 cm (2 in.) across disk.

7. **COLLARED SAND ANEMONE** p. 216
   Actinostella flosculifera
   Olive or greenish brown disk covered with radiating furrows. About 22 long tentacles around mouth, often visible only on cloudy days. Column buried in sand. Intertidal, often among Red Mangrove roots (see Pl. 22). To 8 cm (3¼ in.) across.

8. **STINGING ANEMONE** *Lebrunea danae* p. 215
   Whitish, multiforked false tentacles predominate in daytime; medium-length, greenish or brownish, tapering tentacles predominate at night and when animal is feeding. Stings. To 30 cm (1 ft.) across disk.

9. **RINGED ANEMONE** *Bartholomea annulata* p. 214
   Tentacles brownish, transparent, with spiral white lines of nematocysts. Column usually hidden in crevice, with dense mass of tentacles protruding. To 12.5 cm (5 in.) across disk.

10. **TRICOLOR ANEMONE** *Calliactis tricolor* p. 215
    Tentacles short, thin, furry, light-colored, in a fringe around disk. Column purple or yellow-brown, with 1 or 2 rows of large, dark warts just above base. Lives on snail shells inhabited by hermit crabs, such as this **Star-eyed Hermit** (p. 313).

PLATE 28
True and Tube-dwelling Sea Anemones

1. RED WARTY ANEMONE   p. 215
Bunodosoma granuliferum
Orange or maroon, with 3 rings of short, tapering, olive tentacles
blotched with white. Projecting mouth surrounded by crimson
stain. Vertical rows of light-colored warts on column. To 8 cm (3¼
in.) across disk.

2. AMERICAN WARTY ANEMONE   p. 215
Bunodosoma cavernata
Similar to Red Warty Anemone (abo   ), but lacks white blotches
on tentacles. Warts on column scatte.ed, not in vertical rows.

3. GIANT CARIBBEAN ANEMONE   p. 215
Condylactis gigantea
Purple-tipped, thick, tan tentacles, with a faint ribbed pattern.
Column often orange; purplish in Florida and Bahamas. Here
swollen tips have greenish tinge. Large—to 30 cm (1 ft.) across
disk. **Purple Sea Fan** (p. 210) behind anemone; a few sprigs of
Disk Alga (p. 132) are visible above.

4. Tentacles of **Giant Caribbean Anemone,** showing purple tips.

5. SUN ANEMONE   *Stoichactis helianthus*   p. 216
Disk flat, circular; covered with stubby, yellow, olive, or tan
tentacles. Often many individuals crowded together, resembling
a rug. To 15 cm (6 in.) across. Note **Brown Bubble alga** (p. 134).

6. DUERDEN'S SUN ANEMONE   p. 216
Homostichanthus duerdeni
Large—to 15 cm (6 in.) across disk. Tan or sand-colored; tentacles
stubby, shorter than those of Sun Anemone. Solitary.

7. BROWN-STRIPED SAND ANEMONE   p. 213
Actinoporus elegans
Disk covered with wartlike tentacles; about 7 bands of dark brown
tentacles radiate from central mouth area. Collar of dotlike,
brown or white vesicles in vertical rows. To 5 cm (2 in.) wide.

8. AMERICAN TUBE-DWELLING ANEMONE   p. 219
Ceriantheopsis americanus
Two rings of tentacles: inner ring of short, stubby, incurved
tentacles; outer ring of long, streaming, brown, gray, or tan
tentacles that are not banded. To 2 cm (¾ in.) across disk. Tube,
made of nematocysts, is gray, wrinkled, velvety.

9. BANDED TUBE-DWELLING ANEMONE   p. 218
Arachnanthus nocturnus
Inner ring of tan, incurved tentacles; outer ring of long, streaming, brown-and-cream striped tentacles. In muddy brown tube
projecting from sand. Nocturnal. To 2 cm (¾ in.) wide.

10. **Banded Tube-dwelling Anemone,** with tentacles streaming in
current.

PLATE 29
False Coral and Colonial Anemones

1. ST. THOMAS FALSE CORAL p. 216
Discosoma sanctithomae
Disk, to 10 cm (4 in.) across, covered with tufts of tiny, leaflike, branched tentacles. Tentacles at edge of disk tiny, pointed, unbranched; equidistant, may be expanded into tiny lumps. Naked zone between edge and ring of tuftlike tentacles.

2. Cluster of 3 **St. Thomas False Coral** anemones, showing low collar around disk.

3. RED BALL ANEMONE p. 217
Pseudocorynactis caribbeorum
125–200 long, transparent tentacles, each tipped with an orange or red ball. Nocturnal; specimen only partially expanded.

4. View of **Red Ball Anemone** at night, with tentacles expanded.

5. FLORIDA FALSE CORAL *Ricordia florida* p. 217
Disk covered with iridescent green (rarely orange) warts; one or several mouths appear as larger warts. To 2.5 cm (1 in.) across. In clumps, since they reproduce by fragmentation or budding.

6. UMBRELLA FALSE CORAL *Discosoma neglecta* p. 216
Concave olive disk with distinct, irregular marginal lobes; to 8 cm (3¼ in.) across. Large lobes may alternate with smaller ones. About 200 tiny, tuftlike tentacles, arranged in radial rows on disk. Column brown, disk may have white, brown, or blue stripes.

7. GREEN COLONIAL ANEMONE p. 218
Zoanthus sociatus
Green, mosaiclike mat of crowded polyps; each bright green disk about 9 mm (⅜ in.) across, fringed with tiny tentacles. Fleshy column about 2.5 cm (1 in.) tall. In crevices and rubble.

8. Panoramic view of mat of **Green Colonial Anemones.**

9. ENCRUSTING COLONIAL ANEMONE p. 217
Palythoa caribaeorum
Flat tan crust on rocks, to 1 m (3¼ ft.) wide. Crust consists of many 1-cm (⅜-in.) wide polyps fringed with tiny tentacles. Polyps surrounded by tan matrix so that they are not discrete.

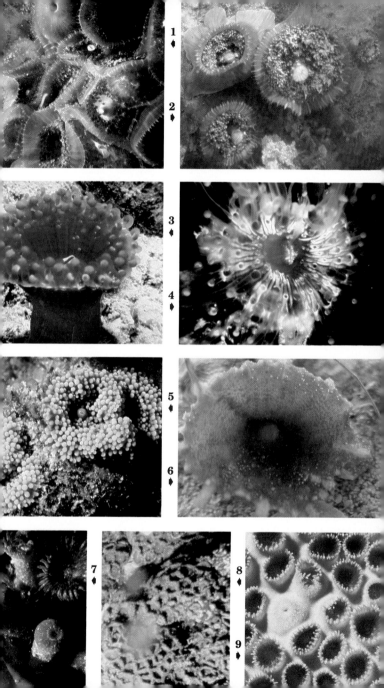

PLATE 30
Jellyfishes and a Hydroid

1. **BLUE BUTTON** *Porpita porpita*   p. 205
Small—to 2.5 cm (1 in.) across, with black margin and dark radiating lines on float.

2. **BY-THE-WIND SAILOR** *Velella velella*   p. 205
Flat disk-shaped float with gelatinous triangular sail. Purplish, to 7.5 cm (3 in.) across. Many small, tentacle-like polyps suspended beneath float. Longest tentacles (around edge) are defensive. Large central mouth is part of feeding polyp. Note **Violet Snail** (*Janthina*) feeding on underside, buoyed up by mucus-covered bubbles to left of snail.

3. **UPSIDE-DOWN JELLYFISH**   p. 207
Cassiopeia xamachana
Large—to 30 cm (1 ft.) across; brown or olive and cream. Underside covered with frilly lappets; multibranched tentacles around lower margin of bell.

4. **Upside-down Jellyfish** swims in normal position, with its mouth down, but rests upside-down. This one is about to land on bottom, and is in the process of turning over.

5. **MOON JELLY** *Aurelia aurita*   p. 207
To 25 cm (10 in.) across. Bluish, transparent. Reproductive tissues arranged in four-leaf clover pattern.

6. **SNAIL FUR** *Hydractinia echinata*   p. 206
Colony of pinkish polyps, usually found on mud or moon snail shells occupied by **Long-clawed** or **Flat-clawed hermit crabs.** Several types of polyps, each less than 1 mm (1/16 in.) tall.

7. **PORTUGUESE MAN-OF-WAR** *Physalia physalia*   p. 205
Iridescent blue, balloon-like pneumatophore, to 30 (1 ft.) long, from which is suspended a colony of polyps. Fishing polyps have long tentacles (to 10 m—33 ft.) with powerful nematocysts. Note black-banded **Man-of-war Fish** (*Nomeus gronovii*) among tentacles.

8. A windrow of **Portuguese Men-of-war** washed up on the beach.

9. Arm of person freshly stung by nematocysts of **Portuguese Man-of-war.** Note raised, whiplash-like welts.

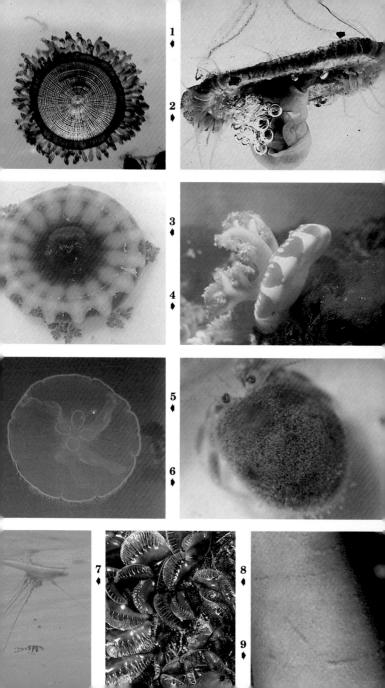

PLATE 31
Shallow-Water Soft Corals (1)

1. **SEA FANS** *Gorgonia* species   p. 210
   Two shallow-water species, both usually yellow or purple. *G. flabellum* inhabits a variety of habitats, from shallow, turbulent subtidal zone to deep water. *G. ventalina* is usually found on coral reefs and in deeper, calmer water, where it may reach more than 1 m (39 in.) in height, as shown.

2. **CORKY SEA FINGERS or DEADMAN'S**   p. 210
   FINGERS *Briareum asbestinum*
   Branches often covered with long brown polyps, even in daytime. Naked branches purplish gray to 1 cm (½ in.) thick and 60 cm (2 ft.) tall.

3. Close-up of **Knobby Candelabrum,** showing tubular cups with rounded lips.

4. **KNOBBY CANDELABRUM** *Eunicea mammosa*   p. 210
   Small tan colony less than 20 cm (8 in.) high, growing on 1 plane.

5. **TAN BUSHY SOFT CORAL** *Plexaura flexuosa*   p. 211
   Bushy, but tends to spread in 1 plane. Cups round, not slitlike. Branches forked; to 4.5 mm (⅙ in.) thick at ends. White, yellow, brown, or tan.

6. **COMMON BUSHY SOFT CORAL**   p. 211
   Plexaura homomalla
   Dark brown to blackish, branches to 5 mm (⅙ in.) thick. Cups round, not slitlike (as in *Plexaurella*); branches in 1 plane.

PLATE 32
Shallow-Water Soft Corals (2)

1. Coral head dominated by colonies of **Smooth Sea Feather** or deep-water **Forked Sea Feather** (*Pseudopterogorgia bipinnata*). Cup-shaped sponge in left foreground is **Tub Sponge** (*Xestospongia muta*).

2. **SEA ROD** *Plexaurella grisea*   p. 211
   Gray, long, smooth, straight branches, usually forked near base; branches to 1.2 cm (½ in.) thick. Cups oval, with long axis running length of branch.

3. **YELLOW SEA BLADE** *Pterogorgia citrina*   p. 211
   Small colonies in rough-water areas. Flat, yellow, purple-edged blades with polyps in cups along edges.

4. **GUADELOUPE SEA BLADE**   p. 211
   Pterogorgia guadelupensis
   Broad (to 10 cm — 4 in. — wide), blade-like branches. Polyps retract into longitudinal grooves along branch edges. Branches in one plane. Usually light purple.

5. **SLIMY SEA FEATHER**   p. 211
   Pseudopterogorgia americana
   Bluish gray, plume-like colonies, to 2 m (6½ ft.) high. Branches thick with mucus; feel slimy to touch.

6. **SPINY CANDELABRUM** *Muricea muricata*   p. 210
   Fan-shaped colonies in a single plane; yellow, brownish, or tan. To 30 cm (1 ft.) tall. Spiny to touch. Branches to 6 mm (¼ in.) thick; ends flattened.

PLATE 33
Shallow-Water Hard Corals

1. **IVORY BUSH CORAL** *Oculina diffusa*   p. 213
   Thin, blunt, horizontal branches with well-spaced, large, protruding (not tubular) cups. When alive, covered with olive-drab tissue. Branches less than 1 cm (⅜ in.) thick. Colonies extensively branched; they may form large beds in sandy areas, especially in Bermuda and Florida north of the Keys.

2. **STAR CORAL** *Favia fragum*   p. 212
   Loaf- or mound-like; colony no longer than 5 cm (2 in.). Yellow or brownish white. Widely spaced, elongate cups separated by thick, dense, flat walls. On rocks in shallow water.

3. **FLAT-TOPPED FIRE CORAL**   p. 204
   Millepora complanata
   An underwater scene showing an extensive colony. Yellow or tan, with flat, white upper edge. Can form a dense zone edging rocky, exposed shores. Stings when touched.

4. **CRENELATED FIRE CORAL**   p. 204
   Millepora alcicornis
   A close-up. Similar to Flat-topped Fire Coral, but upper edge bumpy and/or crenelated, like the battlements of a castle. Stings.

5. Close-up of **Flat-topped Fire Coral.** Note tiny holes into which polyps withdraw. Fire corals seem to lack cups unless viewed from very close range.

6. **DEPRESSED BRAIN CORAL**   p. 212
   Diploria labyrinthiformis
   This large, round head of **Depressed Brain Coral** shows the shallow depressions in "hills." Yellow or greenish tan. Vertical-sided "hills" broader than "valleys." A colony of **Elkhorn Coral** (*Acropora palmata,* p. 212) threatens to overgrow the brain coral. Notice the tubular cups and broad branches that become flattened like moose (not elk) antlers. The white area at the base of the Elkhorn Coral has been damaged by the brain coral in an attempt to resist encroachment by killing all corals of other species within reach of its mesenterial filaments.

7. **SHALLOW-WATER STARLET CORAL**   p. 213
   Siderastrea radians
   Forms a gray or tan crust in rocky shallows, or a marble-sized ball in Turtle Grass beds. Cups dotlike, black, angular, steep-sided. Similar to **Round Starlet Coral** (*S. siderea*), which forms large hemispheres with rounder, wider cups on coral reefs.

8. **COMMON ROSE CORAL** *Manicina areolata*   p. 212
   Juveniles stalked, attached to bottom; older colonies free on sand in Turtle Grass beds. Usually oval, with undulating edges; to 7.5 cm (3 in.) long. Yellow.

PLATE 34
Seaweeds (1): Green Algae

1. **MERMAN'S SHAVING BRUSHES**   p. 132
   Penicillus species
   Tufts of stiff, light green fibers on longish stalks. In *P. dumetosus* (at left) brushlike tuft expands to a flattened top surface. *P. capitatus* (at right) has a smaller, tight, oval tuft. Both species grow on sandy bottoms and Turtle Grass beds. To 20 cm (8 in.) tall.

2. **SEA LETTUCE**   *Ulva lactuca*   p. 134
   Bright green, flat, sheetlike. Has a stalk and holdfast, but they are usually not visible. Large sheets of this alga often wash ashore. Can reach well over 1 m (39 in.) in length, but usually smaller.

3. **UMBRELLA ALGA**   *Acetabularia crenulata*   p. 129
   A ribbed, umbrella-shaped disk on a thin stalk. Dull, light green. Disk no larger than 1 cm (⅜ in.) across; stalk to 5 cm (2 in.) tall.

4. **DISK or SEGMENTED ALGA**   p. 132
   Halimeda incrassata
   Dull, light green disks, somewhat trilobed. Heavy stalk may fork 2–3 times. To 24 cm (9½ in.) tall.

5. **GREEN FLEECE**   *Codium decorticatum*   p. 130
   Dark green, ropy; has spongy texture when squeezed. Many short, forked branches. May form bushes over 1 m (39 in.) tall; usually about 20 cm (8 in.) tall. Grows in colonies on rocks in shallow water.

6. **SQUIRRELTAILS**   *Dasycladus vermicularis*   p. 130
   Short, dark green columns, usually in groups on hard surfaces in tidepools or on sandy beaches near the low-tide mark. To 6 cm (2³⁄₁₆ in.) tall.

7. **SMOOTH BUBBLE ALGA**   *Valonia ventricosa*   p. 134
   A green, translucent sphere. Solitary. Usually attached to the bottom in sandy areas and Turtle Grass beds. May be covered with epiphytes, giving it a silvery sheen or fuzzy appearance. To 4 cm (1½ in.) across.

8. **ROUGH BUBBLE ALGA**   p. 130
   Dictyosphaeria cavernosa
   Flattish, irregular, oval, hollow colonies, usually in small groups of different-sized individuals. Grows on rocks and dead corals in intertidal zone and in shallow water. To differentiate this from Bubble Alga, look for individual cells, sometimes 1 mm (¹⁄₁₆ in.) in size (see photo). To 5 cm (2 in.) across.

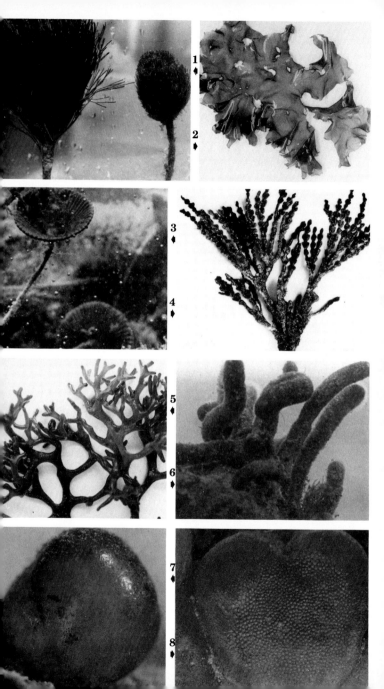

PLATE 35

Seaweeds (2): Green Algae

1. **TUFTED JOINTWEED** *Cymopolia barbata* p. 130
   Bushy, with elongate, beadlike, hard, whitish segments. Bright green tufts of thin filaments. On rocky bottoms. To 20 cm (8 in.) tall.

2. **GRAPE ALGA** *Caulerpa racemosa* p. 130
   A horizontal rhizome with vertical, 10-cm (4-in.) high branches, covered with clusters of light green, grape-like leaves.

3. **VARIABLE CAULERPA** *Caulerpa cupressoides* p. 130
   Long, horizontal rhizomes with crowded branches arising at frequent intervals. Branches usually extensively forked, reaching 7 cm (2¾ in.) in height. Each branch usually has 3 rows of short, pointed leaves; often naked near base. Large colonies in sandy shallows, on sand or on rocks and shells; in sunny tidepools. Has many slight variations in appearance.

4. **FEATHER ALGA** *Caulerpa sertularioides* p. 130
   A horizontal rhizome with vertical, 10-cm (4-in.) high branches. Light green, featherlike leaves.

5. **TUFTED CAULERPA** *Caulerpa verticillata* p. 130
   Thin, horizontal rhizomes with thin, single or multiple-forked branches. Outer branches with many circular tufts of leaves; more or less naked near base. Looks filmy under water. Often forms large mats; to 7 cm (2¾ in.) tall. In shallow, protected, muddy lagoons or at borders of mangrove swamps.

6. **SOFT FAN ALGA** *Avrainvillea nigricans* p. 130
   Thick, spongy, green; fan- or heart-shaped. Surface suede-like. In Turtle Grass beds and on sandy bottoms. Soft, supple, sways with the currents. To 20 cm (8 in.) tall.

7. **HARD FAN ALGA** *Udotea flabellum* p. 132
   A thin, hard, dull green, fan-shaped blade, sometimes with ringlike calcified areas. Stalk rigid, to 2 cm (¾ in.) long. In sandy areas and Turtle Grass beds. To 20 cm (8 in.) tall (including blade).

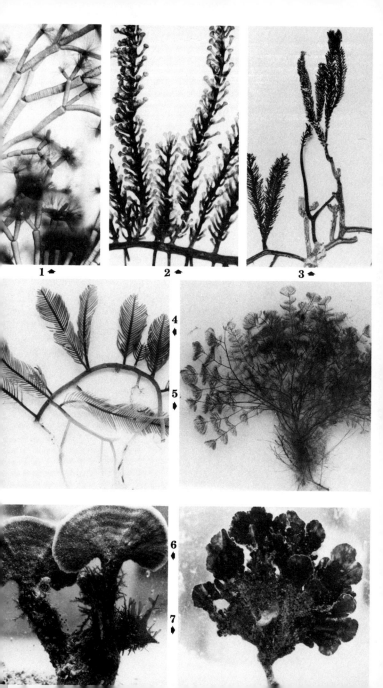

PLATE 36
Seaweeds (3): Red Algae

1. SPAGHETTI WEED *Liagora farinosa*　　　　p. 138
A loose mass of tangled, reddish, soft branches with forked tips. When dead, mass turns white and looks like spaghetti. On rocks and dead coral in shallow, sheltered areas.

2. BRANCHING CALCIFIED ALGA　　　　p. 137
Amphiroa species
Finely branched, rigid, calcified. Pink or rose (white when dead). Erect, often in broad mats or tufts to 3 cm (1¼ in.) tall. On rocks and coral in quiet, shallow water; bleached tufts (see inset) wash up on beaches. If alga is thin enough to look like a tuft of thick hairs with long forks at top, it may be *Jania* (p. 137).

3. SEA MOSS *Bostrychia montagnei*　　　　p. 140
Dull reddish purple or brownish; black when dry. Soft, fuzzy mats, to 2 cm (¾ in.) thick. Festoons Red Mangrove prop roots in the upper intertidal zone. An almost identical species, *B. tenella*, grows in crevices and on rocks and Red Mangrove roots in the upper intertidal zone (upper yellow and black zones and in crevices in lower gray zone).

4. SPINY SEAWEED *Acanthophora spicifera*　　　　p. 137
Pale pink or buff. Attached by a lobed disk to rocks or Red Mangrove roots (see Fig. 85); in shallow water. To 20 cm (8 in.) tall; branches to 3 mm (⅛ in.) in diameter.

5. HOOKED WEED *Hypnea musciformis*　　　　p. 138
Purplish red; bushy, entangled. Branch tips hooked; hooks often encircle objects and act as tendrils. On rocks in sheltered, shallow water. To 20 cm (8 in.) tall. (Pencil point included in photo to show relative size.)

6. BONE ALGA *Galaxaura obtusata*　　　　p. 138
Pink or buff; bushy. Branches round, with short, stubby forks; tips have slight depressions. To 10 cm (4 in.) tall.

7. RED SPIKEWEED *Bryothamnion triquetrum*　　　　p. 137
Red or brownish purple; bushy, spiky looking. Stalk short and irregularly branched, with thick, pointed branchlets to 3 mm (⅛ in.) long. On rocks and dead coral in shallow areas. To 25 cm (10 in.) tall.

PLATE 37

Seaweeds (4): Brown Algae

1. IRIDESCENT BANDED ALGA p. 136
Stypopodium zonale
Bushy, with large, greenish brown, iridescent leaves crossed by thin dark bands. To 36 cm (14 in.) tall. In lowest intertidal zone and shallow water on rocks and dead coral in moderately exposed areas.

2. LONG-LEAVED SARGASSUM WEED p. 136
Sargassum filipendula
Long branches, sparsely forked, with irregularly, lightly serrated leaves. Branchlets bear narrow, alternate, stalked leaves, each with a distinct midrib. Attached to shells, rocks, and dead coral, from just below low-tide line to deep water.

3. THREE-CORNERED HAT ALGA p. 136
Turbinaria turbinata
Leaves tricornered; golden-yellow, with brown dots. On rocks, often in intertidal or shallow subtidal zones. To 40 cm (15¾ in.) tall; leaves to 1 cm (⅜ in.) wide.

4. SERRATED SARGASSUM WEED p. 136
Sargassum platycarpum
Short, stout main branches with slender branches extending from them. Leaves often crowded onto small lateral shoots. Leaves broad, to 1 cm (⅜ in.) wide; margins with coarse, regularly spaced teeth. Leaves taper to a pronounced stalk (petiole). On exposed rocks in shallow water. To 40 cm (15¾ in.) tall.

5. FORKED SEA TUMBLEWEED p. 134
Dictyota dichotoma
Light brown, translucent; bushy, with flattened forked fronds. Leaftips squarish, slightly forked; leaves repeatedly and strongly forked from base. Often detached, rolling with the current. To 10 cm (4 in.) tall.

6. PETTICOAT ALGA *Padina sanctae-crucis* p. 136
Tan, with whitish horizontal stripes. Forms a crust on shallow subtidal rocks, often just below the low-tide mark. Common in tidepools. Prostrate fronds to 15 cm (6 in.) long, but divided into smaller, wrinkled leaflets.

7. TRUMPET PETTICOAT ALGA *Padina pavonica* p. 136
SPINDLEWEED *Neomeris annulata* p. 132
Trumpet Petticoat Alga is similar to Petticoat Alga (above), but has smaller leaves that are clustered and usually partially curved into the shape of a trumpet. The calcified, clumped cylinders are the green alga, **Spindleweed.** Each crowded, spindle- or cylinder-shaped plant is topped with a tuft of thin green hairs. Fine annulations (rings) not visible in photo. Each plant small — to 2.5 cm (1 in.) long. In shallow, sunny places, in tidepools, or on shells on sandy bottom. Note 2 or 3 **Umbrella Algae,** especially visible pointing downward at bottom of photo.

PLATE 38

Seashells (1): Snails

1. **ATLANTIC HAIRY TRITON** *Cymatium pileare* p. 233
   Brown. Outer lip of shell thick, with small paired teeth.
2. **FLAMINGO TONGUE** *Cyphoma gibbosum* p. 234
   Smooth, glossy; pink or purple. Mantle covers shell of live snail
   (see Fig. 1, p. 4).
3. **MUSIC VOLUTE** *Voluta musica* p. 241
   Pink or tan, with brown spots; 2–3 brown spiral bands.
4. **FLORIDA ROCK SNAIL** p. 240
   Thais haemastoma floridana
   Gray or yellow, with brown spots. Outer lip grooved. See also no.
   7.
5. **NETTED OLIVE** *Oliva reticularis* p. 237
   Glossy white, with wavy brown lines. Aperture white.
6. **CARVED STAR SNAIL** *Astraea caelata* p. 230
   Whitish, mottled brown. Pyramidal. Large spines.
7. **FLORIDA ROCK SNAIL** p. 240
   Thais haemastoma floridana
   Alternate body form with pointed nodules; compare with no. 4.
8. **STRIATED BUBBLE** *Bulla striata* p. 230
   Light brown with dark spots. Base grooved.
9. **IMBRICATED STAR SNAIL** *Astraea tecta* p. 230
   Whitish or greenish brown. Pyramidal. No spines.
10. **WIDE-MOUTHED ROCK SNAIL** *Purpura patula* p. 239
    Dull gray. Aperture large, oval. See also Pl. 15.
11. **IVORY CERITH** *Cerithium eburneum* p. 233
    White with brown spots. 4–6 rows of 18–22 beads on each whorl.
12. **APPLE MUREX** *Chicoreus pomum* p. 236
    Cream, tan, or brown. Aperture glossy orange.
13. **DELTOID ROCK SNAIL** *Thais deltoidea* p. 240
    Gray or white, with brown blotches. Body whorl knobbed.
14. **MIDDLE-SPINED CERITH** *Cerithium algicola* p. 233
    White or brownish, 8–9 whorls; pointed spines on midwhorl.
15. **WEST INDIAN TOP SNAIL** *Cittarium pica* p. 233
    Black zigzag splotches on white. Aperture pearly.
16. **COLORFUL MOON SNAIL** *Natica canrena* p. 237
    Shiny. Brown spiral bands; darker lines and blotches. A worn
    specimen shown; color faded. See also Pl. 50.
17. **STOCKY CERITH** *Cerithium litteratum* p. 233
    Whitish, with rows of square brown dots. Spire pointed.
18. **BANDED TULIP SNAIL** *Fasciolaria hunteria* p. 234
    Almost identical to **Tulip Snail** (*F. tulipa*), but bands are more
    distinct.

PLATE 39

Seashells (2): Small Snails and Limpets

1. **ATLANTIC MODULUS** *Modulus modulus* p. 236
   White, flecked with brown. 3–4 whorls. Aperture round.

2. **VARIABLE NASSA** *Nassarius albus* p. 235
   White or yellow; brown spots or bands. Outer lip toothed; ridged.

3. **CHESTNUT TURBAN** *Turbo castanea* p. 241
   Gray or orange; white or brown spots. Aperture pearly.

4. **KNOBBY PERIWINKLE** *Tectarius muricatus* p. 239
   White; apex may be gray. Snail lives above waterline.

5. **COMMON DOVE SNAIL** *Columbella mercatoria* p. 233
   Solid. Usually white or tan and brown. Outer lip thick, toothed.

6. **GREEN-BASED TEGULA** *Tegula excavata* p. 240
   Brown or gray; base pearly green, concave. Conical; whorls flat.

7. **ZEBRA NERITE** *Puperita pupa* p. 238
   White with black stripes; aperture walls yellow. In tidepools.

8. **LINED PLANAXIS** *Planaxis lineatus* p. 238
   Whitish, with brown spiral bands. (See **Black Planaxis,** Fig. 47.)

9. **WHITE-SPOTTED DOVE SNAIL** *Mitrella ocellata* p. 236
   Tan to dark brown; white spots. Aperture long and narrow.

10. **ZEBRA PERIWINKLE** *Littorina ziczac* p. 235
    White; wavy black lines. Larger specimens often gray. See Pl. 12.

11. **EIGHT-RIBBED LIMPET** *Hemitoma octoradiata* p. 242
    White or gray. 8 knobby ribs. No hole at top; notched at front.

12. **DWARF SUCK-ON LIMPET** *Acmaea leucopleura* p. 241
    White, with radiating black lines. Brown, arrow-shaped blotch inside.

13. **CHECKERED NERITE** *Nerita tesselata* p. 237
    Black or checkered. Toothless, or with 2 tiny teeth on outer lip.

14. **BLACK HORN SNAIL** *Batillaria minima* p. 230
    Black, white, or striped. Ribbed; spire pointed.

15. **ANTILLEAN LIMPET** *Acmaea antillarum* p. 241
    White; thin, red or brown rays radiate from summit.

16. **BLEEDING-TOOTH NERITE** *Nerita peloronta* p. 237
    Smooth. Tan, with red and black zigzags; red stain around 2 white teeth in center of parietal wall. **Four-toothed Nerite** (*N. versicolor,* Pl. 12) has deep cords and 3–4 teeth on wall.

17. **BULLA MELAMPUS** *Detracia bullaoides* p. 234
    Brown, with encircling gray lines. Apex blunt.

18. **BARBADOS KEYHOLE LIMPET** p. 242
    Fissurella barbadensis
    White or gray, with brown rays. Green-banded inside. Hole round.

19. **COMMON PRICKLY WINKLE** p. 234
    Nodilittorina tuberculata
    Dull gray. Rows of sharp nodules. Lives above high-water line.

20. **COMMON ATLANTIC MARGINELLA** p. 236
    Prunum apicinum
    Shiny. Yellow to orange-brown. Inner lip has 4 pleats.

21. **KNOBBY KEYHOLE LIMPET** *Fissurella nodosa* p. 242
    White or brownish. Inside white. Hole keyhole-shaped.

PLATE 40

Seashells (3): Bivalves

1. **EARED ARK** *Anadara notabilis* p. 253
Elongate. 25 thick white ribs. Periostracum (outer skin) brown.

2. **INCONGRUOUS ARK** *Anadara brasiliana* p. 253
Oval. 25 ribs crossed by concentric grooves.

3. **TURKEY WING** *Arca zebra* p. 254
White; red-brown zebra-like stripes. Elongate.

4. **ROUGH LIMA** *Lima scabra* p. 257
Dull brown. Surface rasplike. (See Pl. 17 for Antillean Lima.)

5. **TULIP MUSSEL** *Modiolus americanus* p. 258
Shiny, smooth. Yellow-brown. Inside rose-tinted.

6. **BEARDED ARK** *Barbatia cancellaria* p. 255
Oval. Weakly beaded cords radiate from umbo (beak).

7. **MAHOGANY DATE MUSSEL** p. 257
Lithophaga bisulcata
Mahogany-brown, encrusted with gray.

8. **SCORCHED MUSSEL** *Hormomya exusta* p. 257
Yellow-brown. Radiating ribs. On intertidal rocks, crevices.

9. **PURPLISH TAGELUS** *Tagelus divisus* p. 260
Purplish gray. Umbones (beaks) central. Fragile.

10. **YELLOW COCKLE** *Trachycardium muricatum* p. 262
Whitish with brown flecks. 25–30 scaly ribs.

11. **ATLANTIC STRAWBERRY COCKLE** p. 253
Americardia media
White or buff. Posterior slope sharp. 33–37 ribs.

12. **WEST INDIAN CARDITA** *Carditamera gracilis* p. 255
White or gray, with brown blotches. 14 ribs.

13. **BROAD-RIBBED CARDITA** *C. floridana* p. 255
White with brown flecks. Oval. 20 broad ribs.

14. **WINGED PEARL OYSTER** *Pteria colymbus* p. 259
Brownish. Outside eroded; inside (at left) pearly.

15. **STIFF PEN SHELL** *Atrina rigida* p. 254
Tan or brown. 15–25 rows of spines. Large—to 28 cm (11 in.).

16. **CAT'S PAW** *Plicatula gibbosa* p. 259
White with red or gray, dashlike lines. Broad folds.

17. **LISTER'S TREE OYSTER** *Isognomon radiatus* p. 257
Reddish; yellow radiating lines. 4–8 grooves in hinge. Flat.

18. **FLAT TREE OYSTER** *Isognomon alatus* p. 257
Gray or purple. 8–12 grooves in hinge.

19. **COON OYSTER** *Lopha frons* p. 257
Red or brown; inside white. Thin, with folds and ridges.

PLATE 41

Seashells (4): Bivalves

1. **COQUINA** *Donax variabilis*   p. 256
Color variable. Inner edges toothed.
2. **CONSTRICTED MACOMA** *Macoma constricta*   p. 258
Dull white. Periostracum (outer skin) thin, gray.
3. **PENNSYLVANIA LUCINE** *Lucina pensylvanica*   p. 258
White. Periostracum yellow. Deep fold at rear.
4. **CARIBBEAN COQUINA** *Donax denticulata*   p. 256
Brown, violet, or yellow. Inner edges toothed.
5. **SUNRISE TELLIN** *Tellina radiata*   p. 260
Shiny. Bluish or yellow, with red or purple rays.
6. **LINED TELLIN** *Tellina alternata*   p. 260
White, pink, or yellow. Concentric grooves.
7. **WHITE SEMELE** *Semele proficua*   p. 259
White. Inside yellow, shiny.
8. **CROSS-HATCHED LUCINE**   p. 256
Divaricella quadrisulcata
Glossy white. Grooves crossed by wavy lines.
9. **WEST INDIAN POINTED VENUS**   p. 254
Anomalocardia brasiliana
Gray with tan or purple speckles. Concentric ribs.
10. **TRIGONAL TIVELLA** *Tivella mactroides*   p. 261
Tan with brown rays. Inside shiny white.
11. **CALICO SCALLOP** *Aequipecten gibbus*   p. 253
20 ribs. Wings usually larger and equal in size; worn here.
12. **ELEGANT VENUS** *Pitar dione*   p. 259
Squarish spines. Lavender ridges and white grooves.
13. **GAUDY ASAPHIS** *Asaphis deflorata*   p. 254
White with purplish rays or shading. Inside yellow or purple.
14. **ROSY STRIGILLA** *Strigilla carnaria*   p. 260
Pale rose; inside pink. Fine lines on surface.
15. **COMMON EGG COCKLE**   p. 257
Laevicardium laevigatum
Shiny. Tan or yellow; brown-edged.
16. **JAMAICA LUCINE** *Lucina pectinata*   p. 258
Whitish. Heavy concentric ridges; fold at rear.
17. **CALICO CLAM** *Macrocallista maculata*   p. 258
Shiny. Cream or tan with brown squares.
18. **ELEGANT DISK CLAM** *Dosinia elegans*   p. 256
White or yellowish; equidistant concentric ridges. (See Pl. 44.)
19. **BEADED VENUS** *Chione granulata*   p. 255
Yellow or gray, with purple mottling. Inside purplish.
20. **KING VENUS** *Chione paphia*   p. 255
Shiny; white with red-brown flecks. 10–12 heavy ribs.
21. **MOTTLED VENUS** *Chione interpurpurea*
White with purple splotch on inside end. Solid.
22. **TIGER LUCINE** *Codakia orbicularis*   p. 255
White with rose or yellow flush on inside. Common.

PLATE 42

Seashells (5): Snails
of the Southeastern and Gulf Coasts

1. **LIGHTNING WHELK** *Busycon contrarium* p. 231
   Aperture on left. Brown streaks; knobs on shoulders of whorls.
2. **FIG WHELK** *Busycon spiratum* p. 231
   Thin, whitish shell with red-brown streaks; spire flattened.
3. **GIANT EASTERN MUREX** *Hexaplex fulvescens* p. 237
   White, brown, or gray; pointed hollow spines; lower canal long.
4. **VARIABLE DWARF OLIVE** *Olivella mutica* p. 238
   Gray spiral band around body whorl. Brown spot at base of callus.
5. **LETTERED OLIVE** *Oliva sayana* p. 237
   Reddish brown zigzag markings; polished.
6. **SOUTHERN MOON SNAIL** *Polinices duplicatus* p. 238
   Gray; apex coiled. Umbilicus almost covered with brown callus.
7. **COMMON AUGER SNAIL** *Terebra dislocata* p. 240
   Gray, brown, or white; sutures bordered with knobby bands.
8. **MUD SNAIL** *Ilyanassa obsoleta* p. 234
   Dull black shell; spire eroded. Aperture oval; purple inside.
9. **NEW ENGLAND DOG WHELK** p. 235
   Nassarius trivittatus
   Yellowish or tan. Stepped shoulders on whorls; surface beaded.
10. **EASTERN MELAMPUS** *Melampus bidentatus* p. 236
    Brown; thin, translucent. Aperture long; outer wall toothed.
11. **ANGLED WENTLETRAP** *Epitonium angulatum* p. 234
    White. Six whorls; blade-like vertical ridges have blunt shoulders.
12. **HUMPHREY'S WENTLETRAP** *E. humphreysi* p. 234
    White. 8–9 whorls. Thick, round vertical ridges.
13. **BROWN-BANDED WENTLETRAP** *E. rupicola* p. 234
    Pinkish or yellowish white, often with 1–2 brownish bands.
14. **SINGLE-TOOTHED SIMNIA** *Simnia uniplicata* p. 239
    Thin, purple or yellow. Snail lives on sea whips.
15. **COMMON SLIPPER SNAIL** *Crepidula fornicata* p. 233
    Tan or gray, with purple marks; moundlike, with shelf underneath.
16. **VIRGIN NERITE** *Neritina virginea* p. 237
    Dots, streaks, or lines. Tiny, irregular teeth on white or yellow aperture wall.
17. **CROSS-BARRED SPINDLE** p. 238
    Cantharus cancellarius
    Yellowish or reddish brown; surface covered with flattened beads.
    Columellar wall has spiral fold at bottom.
18. **OYSTER DRILL** *Urosalpinx cinerea* p. 241
    Dull gray or tan. Aperture dark purple; outer wall thin.
19. **THICK-LIPPED OYSTER DRILL** p. 241
    Eupleura caudata
    Gray. Outer wall of aperture thick-lipped.
20. **COMMON WORM SHELL** *Vermicularia spirata* p. 241
    Yellowish brown or white, with longitudinal ridges.

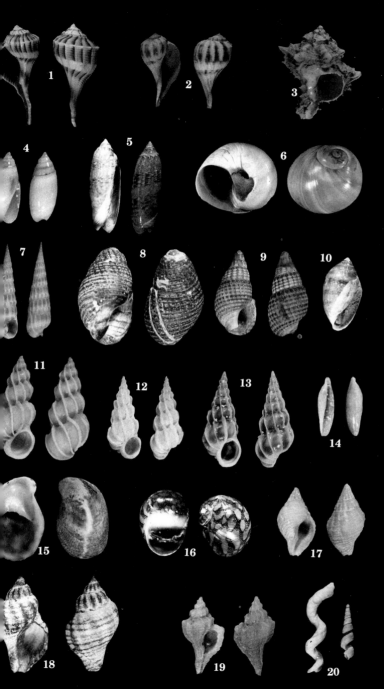

PLATE 43

Seashells (6): Snails and Bivalves
of the Southeastern and Gulf Coasts

1. **PARTRIDGE SNAIL** *Tonna maculosa* p. 240
   Brown, with dark blotches and crescent-shaped white flecks.
2. **GIANT TUN** *Tonna galea* p. 240
   Brown and white. Aperture wall is attached near apex.
3. **ATLANTIC BABY'S EAR** *Sinum perspectivum* p. 239
   White, with fine striations on outer surface; inside glossy.
4. **SCOTCH BONNET** *Phalium granulatum* p. 238
   Globose; yellow-white, with spiral rows of blurry rust or tan spots
   and spiral cords. Outer lip thick; inner edge toothed.
5. **LONG-SPINED STAR SNAIL** *Astraea phoebia* p. 230
   Whitish or silvery; triangular, sawtooth spines on whorl edges.
6. **ROCKING-CHAIR KEYHOLE LIMPET** p. 242
   Fissurella fascicularis
   Rocks when on base. Hole in top long and narrow, with a round
   notch in center. Brownish purple, pinkish, or white.
7. **ROSY CUP-AND-SAUCER LIMPET** p. 241
   Crucibulum auricula
   Grayish; interior pinkish. Cup on underside almost free.
8. **POINTED KEYHOLE LIMPET** *Fissurella angusta* p. 242
   Shell flattened, with irregular edges; one lobe in front longer than
   others. Whitish or brownish, with brown blotches.
9. **CAYENNE KEYHOLE LIMPET** *Diodora cayenensis* p. 242
   Grayish with rough ribs. Dumbbell-shaped hole forward of center.
10. **MOSSY ARK** *Arca imbricata* p. 254
    Purple; mossy brown periostracum. Diagonal lines between um-
    bones.
11. **WEDGE RANGIA** *Rangia cuneata* p. 259
    Tan or gray periostracum. Umbones curved forward, eroded
    white.
12. **CAROLINA MARSH CLAM** *Polymesoda caroliniana* p. 259
    Triangular, with central, eroded umbo. Olive-green or bluish.
13. **ROUGH SCALLOP** *Aequipecten muscosus* p. 253
    Pink, brownish, or yellow. 20 ribs; spiny near edge. Wings un-
    equal.
14. **ATLANTIC BAY SCALLOP** *Argopecten irradians* p. 254
    Orange brown, whitish, or grayish. Wings almost equal.
15. **CANDY-STICK TELLIN** *Tellina similis* p. 261
    Shiny, thin; white or yellowish, with pink flush and pink rays.
16. **WOOD PIDDOCK** *Martesia cuneiformis* p. 258
    Front has sharp ridges; triangular plate over umbones.
17. **JINGLE SHELL** *Anomia simplex* p. 254
    Upper valve inflated. Glossy, wrinkled, gray, yellowish, orange.
18. **ANGEL WING** *Cyrtopleura costata* p. 256
    Chalky; gray periostracum. 30 ribs with sharp teeth at front.
19. **TRUNCATE BORER** *Barnea truncata* p. 255
    Very fragile, thin; white with gray periostracum.
20. **FALSE ANGEL WING** *Petricola pholadiformis* p. 259
    Chalky; front has sharp ridges, which become indistinct at rear.

PLATE 44

Seashells (7): Bivalves
of the Southeastern and Gulf Coasts

1. **SOUTHERN QUAHOG** *Mercenaria campechiensis* p. 258
   Solid, thick; umbones point forward. Heart-shaped lunules in front of umbones. Grayish white; no purple inside shell.
2. **Juvenile Southern Quahog** with thick ridges on surface.
3. **ATLANTIC SURF CLAM** *Spisula solidissima* p. 260
   Shell triangular, with a central umbo (compare with forward-curved umbo of Quahog). Thin, tan or olive periostracum.
4. **TEXAS TELLIN** *Tellina texana* p. 260
   White; iridescent, sometimes faintly pinkish. Tiny.
5. **NARROWED MACOMA** *Macoma tenta* p. 258
   Thin; posterior strongly narrowed and slightly twisted. Grayish.
6. **BUTTERCUP** *Anodontia alba* p. 254
   Dull white; interior yellow to orange. Ligament red when alive.
7. **DWARF SURF CLAM** *Mulinia lateralis* p. 258
   Glossy, white; thin-shelled, inflated.
8. **PURPLISH TAGELUS** *Tagelus divisus* p. 260
   Thin, fragile, elongate. Purplish gray to white; interior purple.
9. **LITTLE GREEN RAZOR CLAM** *Solen viridis* p. 260
   Shell straight. Grayish white with yellow or green periostracum.
10. **DWARF RAZOR CLAM** *Ensis minor* p. 260
    Shell curved. Periostracum light olive-green.
11. **ATLANTIC RAZOR CLAM** *Ensis directus* p. 260
    Dark olive-green periostracum. Shell slightly curved.
12. **CROSS-BARRED VENUS** *Chione cancellata* p. 255
    White with brown rays; strong ribs form rectangles on surface.
13. **DISK CLAM** *Dosinia discus* p. 257
    Sharp umbones point forward; shell thin, almost circular, with concentric ridges on surface (see also Pl. 41).
14. **POINTED VENUS** *Anomalocardia cuneimeris* p. 254
    Glossy, greenish white or brownish white, with heavy concentric ribs and elongate, nearly pointed posterior; interior pale lavender.
15. **CHANNELED DUCK** *Raeta plicatella* p. 259
    Chalky white. Thin-shelled, inflated, with heavy concentric ridges; posterior gaping.
16. **RIBBED MUSSEL** *Geukensia demissa* p. 257
    Strong ribs radiate from inflated umbones. Exterior dark brown; interior silvery, iridescent white.
17. **PONDEROUS ARK** *Noetia ponderosa* p. 259
    Thick; almost rectangular. Exterior has 30 strong ribs covered with velvety blackish periostracum.
18. **Ponderous Ark,** washed up with **Sea Whip** (p. 210) attached.
19. **GIANT ATLANTIC COCKLE** p. 256
    Dinocardium robustum
    Large, much inflated. Exterior has about 35 flat ribs; tan or yellowish brown, with reddish brown spots.

PLATE 45

Snails: Reproduction and Feeding

1. **Tulip Snails** (p. 234) laying eggs. These inhabitants of seagrass beds must find a hard, clean place above the sediment to deposit their eggs; otherwise the developing young might suffocate in silt.

2. Close-up of **Tulip Snail** eggs. To 8 mm (³⁄₁₀ in.) high.

3. Vase-shaped eggs of the **Oyster Drill** have been deposited on the shell of a living **Bay Scallop.** Note tentacles and ring of blue, dotlike eyes on edge of mantle of scallop. Juvenile scallops are active and often swim from place to place by alternately opening the valves of their shells and snapping them shut, propelling themselves with jets of water. Adult scallops are more sedentary and provide **Oyster Drills** with a clean hard surface where their eggs can be laid.

4. **Oyster Drills** (p. 241) near egg mass under rock. Eggs to 3 mm (⅛ in.) high.

5. **Knobbed Whelk** (p. 230) may reach 30 cm (1 ft.) in length. Body black with a thick, rough operculum.

6. **Mud Snails** have such a keen sense of smell that moments after this **Lady Crab** carcass was washed ashore it was covered with a mound of these omnivorous snails.

7. **West Indian Triton** (p. 233) attacking a **Cushion Sea Star.** It took more than 2 days for the snail to reduce the sea star to a dismembered mass of tissue. Tritons are among the few predators of adult sea stars and urchins. When shell collectors selectively remove the beautiful Tritons from an area, an imbalance can occur, possibly resulting in an unnatural increase in sea stars and urchins.

8. **Mud Snail** (p. 234) is often present by the thousands on muddy beaches along the Atlantic Coast to Florida. The siphon is extended like an elephant's trunk to take in water, which then passes over the gills and olfactory organ.

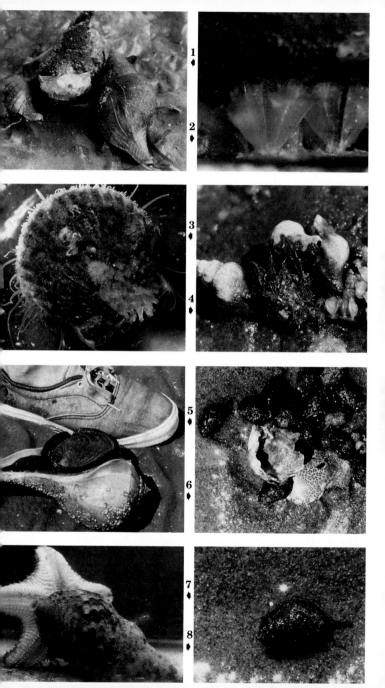

PLATE 46
Squids and Octopods

1. **ATLANTIC OVAL SQUID** *Sepioteuthis sepioidea*   p. 270
Fins run length of mantle (body); squid moves by rippling them.
10 arms short and bunched up, resembling a pointed head. Color
variable when alive, usually purplish. When alarmed, squid
becomes black, or blanches and becomes almost colorless, sometimes with 4 conspicuous spots on body and fins. To 25 cm (10 in.)
long.

2. Underside of **Atlantic Oval Squid,** showing purple spots and
siphon.

3. **PLEE'S STRIPED SQUID** *Loligo pleii*   p. 269
Triangular fins on last third of narrow body; skin covered with
maroon dots; long, narrow maroon bands along sides. To 60 cm (2
ft.) long.

4. Underside of **Plee's Striped Squid.**

5. **BRIEF THUMBSTALL SQUID**   p. 269
Lolliguncula brevis
Short, rounded fins on last third of body form flat round disk.
Upper surface covered with purple dots; underside of fins white.
Body wide, squat; to 25 cm (10 in.) long, including arms.

6. **JOUBIN'S OCTOPUS** *Octopus joubini*   p. 271
Tiny—to 15 cm (6 in.) long, usually smaller. Arms thin, short,
only a little longer than body. Dark or reddish brown with a few
white warts around eyes. If disturbed may turn white.

7. **COMMON ATLANTIC OCTOPUS**   p. 271
Octopus vulgaris
Arms look equal in length and thickness, but front and rear arms
are somewhat shorter than side arms; extensive webs between
arms. Skin smooth, usually bluish green mottled with white or
brown and tan. Largest octopus—to 2.2 m (7 ft.) from tip of longest
arm, across body, to tip of opposite arm.

8. **WHITE-SPOTTED OCTOPUS** *Octopus macropus*   p. 271
Arms long; upper pair longest. Blue-green, brownish, or pinkish;
white spots. When octopus is alarmed, spots become prominent
and skin turns ocher or red. To 1 m (3¼ ft.) across.

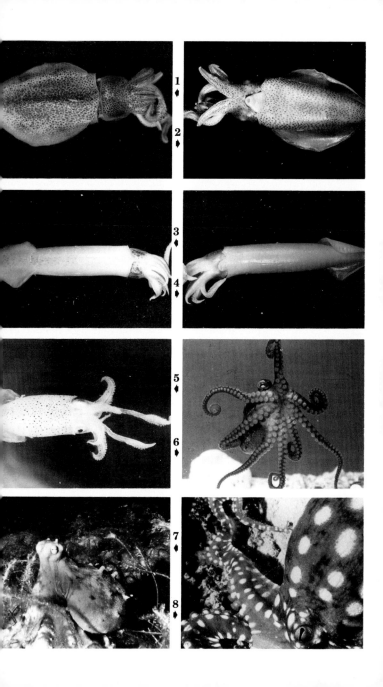

PLATE 47
Mollusk Eggs and Development

1. Tiny **Joubin's Octopus** (p. 271) lays masses of elongate, translucent eggs in bottles or clam shells and under rocks. Eggs to 6.3 mm (¼ in.) long, in clumps of up to 100. Note eyes of embryos visible through egg membrane.

2. **Juvenile octopus hatching from egg.** Note filmy membranes of empty eggs. Female guards eggs, blowing water over them.

3. Juvenile, capable of swimming at birth, enters sponge haven.

4. **Squid** (p. 269) **eggs** are laid in clumps attached to hard object. Eggs transparent, whitish, elongate; divided into long lower and short upper sections by slight constriction. Embryo often visible inside. Up to 5 cm (2 in.) long, depending on species.

5. **Southern Moon Snail** (p. 238) lays thousands of tiny eggs inside gelatinous sand collar (see Pl. 3).

6. **Oyster Drill** (p. 241) lays up to 30 egg capsules singly, or hundreds, when as many as 9 females produce a communal mass. Eggs not hidden; in this case they virtually fill an empty oyster shell. Capsules to 4 mm (³⁄₁₆ in.) long, with a tubular apex covered with a thin membrane that ruptures when larvae escape.

7. **Florida Horse Conch** (p. 238) deposits masses of capsules in seagrass beds on hard objects. Two or 3 females lay a communal egg mass. Capsules to 1.9 cm (¾ in.) long; vase-shaped, narrow, with a frilly "veil" completely surrounding apex.

8. **Tulip Snail** (p. 234) eggs are laid in seagrass beds on hard objects. Two or 3 females produce communal egg mass, each contributing up to 27 capsules. Inside each capsule is a dense mass of albumen containing up to 1200 embryos. Only 5–7 survive and hatch as juveniles. Capsules to 1.6 cm (⅝ in.) long.

9. Several **Apple Murex snails** (p. 236) producing a communal egg mass. Each mass may contain up to 10,000 individual capsules, each containing up to 1500 embryos. As many as 55 spawning females congregate under rocky ledges to produce eggs simultaneously. Capsules to 1.6 cm (⅝ in.) long.

10. **Whelks** (*Busycon* species, p. 231) produce coiled masses of disk-like egg capsules, usually in sandy areas near seagrass. Partly buried in sand, they are often washed ashore. Each string may contain over 100 capsules and over 97,000 embryos. Capsules shown, produced by **Lightning Whelk** (p. 231), have sharp ridges along edges and may reach 3.8 cm (1½ in.) in diameter.

11. **Juvenile Lightning Whelks** in egg capsule.

12. Individuals from capsule, to 6.3 mm (¼ in.) long.

PLATE 48
Nudibranchs and Other Sea Slugs

1. **WARTY BUBBLE SEA SLUG** *Lobiger souverbii* p. 246
Two pairs of large, warty parapodia surrounding a thin, fragile shell incised with fine black lines. To 2 cm (¾ in.).

2. **SMOOTH BUBBLE SEA SLUG** p. 247
Oxynoe antillarum
Body smooth except for tiny papillae on parapodia. Fragile shell almost covered by parapodia. To 3.5 cm (1½ in.).

3. **ATLANTIC PLEUROBRANCH** p. 248
Pleurobranchus areolatus
Back covered with low, rounded, red, cream, or yellow tubercles. Rhinophores emerge from beneath back; gill along right side. To 5 cm (2 in.).

4. **LONG-TENTACLED NUDIBRANCH** p. 250
Phidiana lynceus
Clumps of white-tipped, black or brown cerata. Light orange, white-tipped tentacles, longer than rhinophores. To 2.5 cm (1 in.).

5. **ORNATE ELYSIA** *Elysia ornata* p. 248
Parapodia an elongate fold extending from head to tail. Parapodia and rhinophores green with black and orange edges. To 4 cm (1½ in.).

6. **COMMON GREEN ELYSIA** *Elysia tuca* p. 248
Y-shaped marking on head. Green with a few white spots. Parapodia an elongate fold extending from head to tail. To 4 cm (1½ in.).

7. **BLUE GLAUCUS** *Glaucus atlanticus* p. 250
Cerata project from each side, as inflated fingers. Foot and tips of cerata deep blue. Floats near surface of water, foot upward. Feeds on jellyfish; not found on bottom. To 2.5 cm (1 in.).

8. **LETTUCE SEA SLUG** *Tridachia crispata* p. 248
Parapodia a mass of white-rimmed frills on back. Sole and rhinophores cream colored. To 5 cm (2 in.).

9. **SARGASSUM NUDIBRANCH** *Scyllaea pelagica* p. 250
Cerata are 2 pairs of thick, blunt projections from back. Lives only on Sargassum Weed. Found on fresh Sargassum when washed ashore; matches color of Sargassum. To 5 cm (2 in.).

10. **NEAPOLITAN SPURILLA** *Spurilla neapolitana* p. 250
Cerata white-tipped, keeled, curled toward midline. Cerata often olive-green. On or near sea anemones. To 4 cm (1½ in.).

PLATE 49
Dorid Nudibranchs and Sea Hares

1. **CLENCH'S DORIS**   *Chromodoris clenchi*   p. 249
   Body blue or bluish white, with a mosaic of brick-red lines or spots on back. A circlet of 7–9 white gills with purple tips around anus. To 2.5 cm (1 in.).

2. **KEMPF'S DORIS**   *Chromodoris kempfi*   p. 249
   White, with black spots inside yellow border. Circlet of white, purple-tipped gills around anus. To 2 cm (¾ in.).

3. **KREB'S DORIS**   *Dendrodoris krebsii*   p. 249
   Velvety body may be black, light gr*;*y with black spots, yellow with black spots, or red. Tips of rhinophores and gills white. Circlet of gills around anus. To 5.7 cm (2¼ in.), reported to 17 cm (6¾ in.).

4. **COMMON LEATHER DORIS**   *Platydoris angustipes*   p. 249
   Orange or brownish orange; leathery. Tips of rhinophores brown, gills white. Gills form circlet around anus. Under rocks. To 5.7 cm (2¼ in.).

5. **GREEK GODDESS NUDIBRANCH**   p. 249
   Hypselodoris edenticulata
   Dark blue, streaked with chrome yellow; sides with yellow rings. Gills and rhinophores blue. Gills form circlet around anus. To 5 cm (2 in.).

6. **BAYER'S DORIS**   *Felimare bayeri*   p. 249
   Body bright blue with white, blue, or brown-spotted border. Back covered with yellow network over blue. Circlet of gills around anus (retracted in photo). To 3.4 cm (1¼ in.).

7. **LONG-TAILED SEA HARE**   p. 247
   Stylocheilus longicaudata
   Parapodia cover a slit containing mantle cavity. Within it are a gill and reduced shell. Body gray-brown with dark brown longitudinal stripes. Rhinophores and body covered with long, pointed warts. To 9 cm (3½ in.).

8. **SPOTTED SEA HARE**   *Aplysia dactylomela*   p. 247
   Long, flaplike parapodia partly cover a hump containing a gill and a hatchet-shaped vestigial shell. Olive-drab with black, leopardlike spots. Rhinophores rabbit-ear-like. Common. Large—to 40 cm (15 in.).

9. **WARTY SEA CAT**   *Dolabrifera dolabrifera*   p. 247
   Parapodia inconspicuous, opening only in posterior half of body where gill and reduced shell can be found. Body covered with pointed warts; rhinophores rabbit-ear-like. To 10 cm (4 in.).

10. **ENGEL'S SEA HARE**   *Phyllaplysia engeli*   p. 247
    Parapodia reduced to an inconspicuous slit. Rhinophores not rabbit-ear-like, but covered with tiny white specks. White dots along margin. To 2 cm (¾ in.). Do not confuse with Common Green Elysia (Pl. 48).

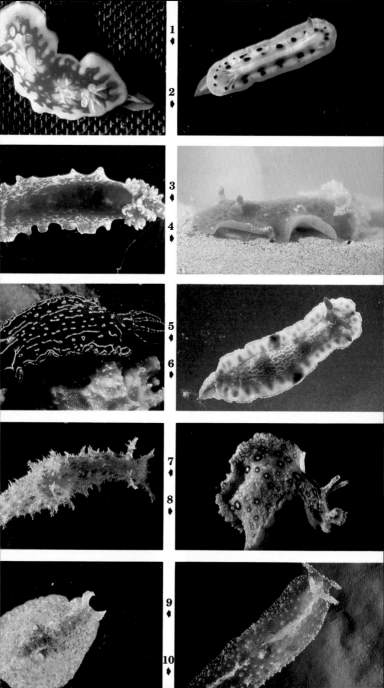

PLATE 50

Conchs, Helmets, and Other Snails

1. **FLAMINGO TONGUE**   *Cyphoma gibbosum*   p. 234
   Shell pink or lavender; elongate, polished, with a narrow aperture and a hump across middle. To 2.5 cm (1 in.) long.

2. **VIOLET SNAIL**   *Janthina janthina*   p. 228
   Thin, fragile; pale violet above, deep purple below. Floats on mass of mucous bubbles. To 3.8 cm (1½ in.) across.

3. **COLORFUL MOON SNAIL**   *Natica canrena*   p. 237
   Glossy; light brown spiral bands alternating with tan bands. Equidistant purplish brown blotches. To 6.4 cm (2½ in.) high.

4. **QUEEN CONCH**   *Strombus gigas*   p. 239
   Short spire with pointed nodules on shoulder of each whorl. Aperture pink; outer lip pink inside and flaring in adults, reduced in juveniles under 15 cm (6 in.). To 30 cm (1 ft.) high.

5. **HAWKWING CONCH**   *Strombus raninus*   p. 239
   Horizontally grooved. Inside white; inner wall of columella pink. Grayish stain on upper columella. To 12.5 cm (5 in.) tall.

6. **WEST INDIAN FIGHTING CONCH**   p. 239
   Strombus pugilis
   Outer lip flares outward below, deeply notched just before base. Aperture orange or mahogany. Florida Fighting Conch (*S. alatus*) may lack spines; more common in Florida. Both to 10 cm (4 in.) high.

7. **BABY BONNET**   *Cypraecassis testiculus*   p. 234
   Surface covered with latticework of ribs and grooves. Inside of outer lip tan with whitish folds; columellar shield smooth, glossy, toothed. To 7.5 cm (3 in.) high.

8. **FLORIDA HORSE CONCH**   *Pleuroploca gigantea*   p. 238
   Largest American snail—shell to 61 cm (2 ft.) tall; heavy, thick. Brown, horny periostracum. Shoulders with wide, thick nodules. Columella with 3 pleats; aperture orange-red, canal long.

9. **TRUMPET SNAIL**   *Charonia variegata*   p. 233
   Inner lip brown crossed with white wrinkles; outer lip with squares of brown and white. To 38 cm (15 in.) tall.

10. **KING HELMET**   *Cassis tuberosa*   p. 232
    Three rows of coarse, blunt spines; spire reduced. Outer lip with 3 pairs of dark brown bars; inside of outer lip has 11 teeth. To 35 cm (14 in.) tall.

11. **EMPEROR or QUEEN HELMET**   p. 232
    Cassis madagascariensis
    Similar to King Helmet but inside of outer lip has 10–12 teeth; outline round, not triangular. Upper part of parietal wall not blotched with brown.

12. **APPLE MUREX**   *Chicoreus pomum*   p. 236
    Seven whorls, each with 3 horizontal ridges crossed by vertical ribs. Short, hollow spines or bumps, especially at junctions of ridges and ribs. Canal long, almost closed, sharply curved at end. To 11.5 cm (4½ in.) tall.

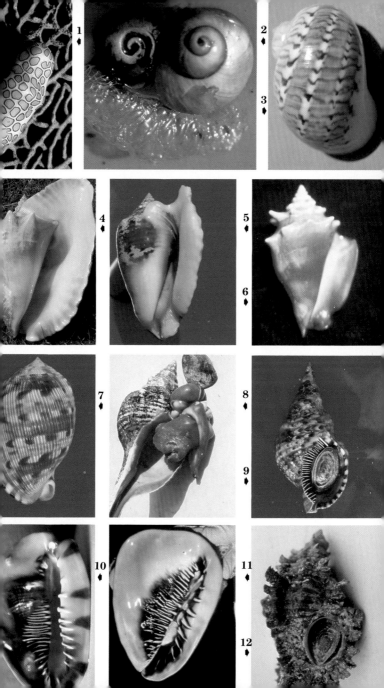

PLATE 51

Shrimps, a Crab, and a Lobster

1. **BANDED CORAL SHRIMP or BARBER-POLE**　p. 309
   SHRIMP *Stenopus hispidus*
   Often perches or "dances" on coral, where it sets up a cleaning
   station. To 5 cm (2 in.) long.

2. **BUMBLEBEE SHRIMP**　p. 306
   Gnathophyllum modestum
   Front blunt, with projecting transparent antennal scales.
   First and second pairs of legs clawed; second pair larger, with 1
   broad band of brown or purple. Brown body stout, covered with
   scattered yellow dots. To 2.1 cm (⅘ in.) long.

3. **SPOTTED CLEANING SHRIMP**　p. 306
   Periclimenes yucatanicus
   White-ringed brown spots. A common cleaning shrimp on Ringed,
   Giant Caribbean, and other anemones. To 2.5 cm (1 in.) long.

4. **PEDERSON'S CLEANING SHRIMP**　p. 306
   Periclimenes pedersoni
   Transparent, with purple bands and spots. Note white eggs on
   underside of this female. Up to 20 individuals live on a Ringed,
   Stinging, or Giant Caribbean Anemone. Shrimp sways back and
   forth, signaling its readiness to clean fishes. To 2.5 cm (1 in.) long.

5. **RED SNAPPING SHRIMP** *Alpheus armatus*　p. 306
   Male's claws larger than female's. To 5 cm (2 in.) long. A mated
   pair (male closer to viewer) commensal with **Ringed Anemone.**

6. **SHORT-CLAWED SPONGE SHRIMP**　p. 306
   Synalpheus brevicarpus
   Major claw smooth, reddish, enlarged, cylindrical. A snapping
   shrimp; when cocked claw is released, it snaps shut with a loud
   popping sound. Lives inside sponges. To 2.5 cm (1 in.) long.
   Female shown; note eggs glued to swimmerets under abdomen.

7. **SPINY LOBSTER** *Panulirus argus*　p. 309
   No claws or rostrum. A hornlike spine arches over each eye. A few
   pairs of white spots scattered over abdomen. To 60 cm (2 ft.) long,
   14 kg (30 lbs.); usually much smaller.

8. **PURPLE SURF CRAB** *Albunea gibbesii*　p. 314
   Purplish, with white grooves crossing back. Eyes on triangular
   stalks jutting forward. Front edges of carapace with 9 tiny spines
   extending from eye to margin. To 5 cm (2 in.) long.

9. **PEPPERMINT or VEINED SHRIMP**　p. 306
   Lysmata wurdemanni
   Longitudinal red lines edged with white. This cleaning shrimp is
   shown on Staghorn Coral. To 4 cm (1⅝ in.) long.

10. **RED-BACKED CLEANING SHRIMP**　p. 306
    or SCARLET LADY *Lysmata grabhami*
    Yellow, with a broad red stripe on back. To 5 cm (2 in.) long.

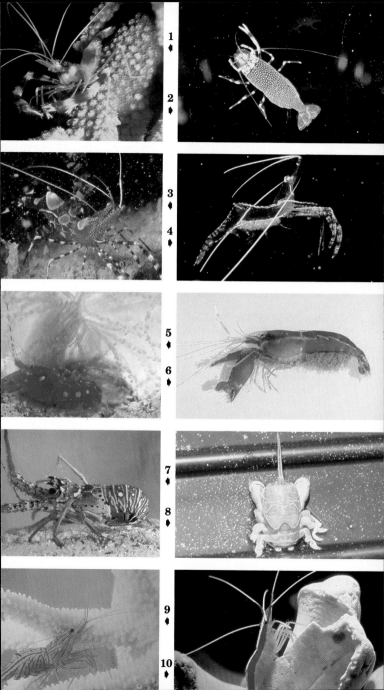

PLATE 52
Hermit and Porcelain Crabs; Mantis Shrimps

1. THREE-COLORED HERMIT CRAB   p. 311
Clibanarius tricolor
SMOOTH-CLAWED HERMIT CRAB   p. 311
Calcinus tibicen
Three-colored Hermit has blue legs with white bands and orange joints. Most common intertidal hermit of Caribbean. Tiny — carapace to 9 mm (⅜ in.) long. **Smooth-clawed Hermit** to 1.2 cm (½ in.) long. Claws maroon or reddish, with white fingertips. Left claw much larger than right.

2. GREEN-STRIPED HERMIT CRAB   p. 311
Clibanarius vittatus
Legs cream with green longitudinal stripes. Both claws same size, with spooned, brown-edged fingertips. Tips of walking legs brown. Shown here in Knobbed Whelk shell. To 7.5 cm (3 in.) long.

3. RED HERMIT CRAB   *Petrochirus diogenes*   p. 311
Red; right claw slightly larger than left; left claw with black, spooned fingertips. Claws covered with groups of white tubercles separated by semicircular fringes of white hairs. The largest Caribbean hermit — carapace to 8 cm (3¼ in.) long. Often in conch, tun, and moon snail shells, with a porcelain crab.

4. BAR-EYED HERMIT CRAB   *Dardanus fucosus*   p. 313
Left claw much larger than right, both claws covered with whitish granules, outlined in a network of fine red lines. Fingers of claws spooned, black-tipped; walking legs banded light red and tan. Pupil of eye bar-shaped. If pupil is star-shaped and crab is found south of Florida, species is **Star-eyed Hermit** (*D. venosus*), a tropical hermit. Carapace to 2.5 cm (1 in.) long.

5. LINED PORCELAIN CRAB   *Petrolisthes galathinus*   p. 313
Small gray crab covered with hairy ridges. Lower finger of claw sinuous. 4–5 large spines on inner margin of wrist. Carapace to 1.6 cm (⅔ in.).

6. SMOOTH PORCELAIN CRAB   *Petrolisthes politus*   p. 314
Olive-colored, with flat chelipeds; claws not sinuous. Three spines on inner margin of wrist. To 1.6 cm (⅔ in.) long.

7. ROCK MANTIS SHRIMP   *Gonodactylus oerstedi*   p. 304
Shrimplike, with enlarged lower finger of "claw" untoothed. Base of lower finger swollen. Color variable, bright green to dark brown. Beware! This shrimp is nicknamed the "Thumb Buster" because it can cut your finger by making a rapid upward movement with its sharp lower finger. To 10 cm (4 in.) total length, usually smaller.

8. COMMON MANTIS SHRIMP   *Squilla empusa*   p. 304
Large, pale white or green; lower finger of raptorial arm has 6 teeth on inner margin. Carapace has a central, deeply grooved ridge and 2 other ridges on either side, making animal look armored. Eyes on long stalks, forming a V. To 20 cm (8 in.) long.

PLATE 53

Swimming Crabs

All crabs on this plate are members of Family Portunidae, characterized by paddle-shaped rear legs.

1. **SPECKLED CRAB** *Arenaeus cribrarius* p. 322
Tan or gray, covered with a network of irregular white spots extending onto claws. Fringe of tiny hairs tends to obscure notches between marginal teeth. To 5 cm (2 in.) long.

2. **COMMON BLUE CRAB** *Callinectes sapidus* p. 322
The common edible crab. Fingers of claws red; palms and chelipeds blue. Spine at lateral apex of margin long and narrow. To 9 cm (3½ in.) long.

3. **PURPLE SWIMMING CRAB** p. 321
Callinectes exasperatus
Lateral spine stout, usually less than twice length of preceding tooth. Granules cover carapace. Upper surface of legs purplish red with orange-red joints. Fingers of claws violet. Near mangroves and river mouths. To 6.7 cm (2⅗ in.) long.

4. **BROWN-FINGERED SWIMMING CRAB** p. 321
Callinectes larvatus
Lateral spine slender, more than twice length of preceding tooth. Last 2 teeth before lateral spine curved forward. Carapace brown with areas of bluish black. Claws brown above; fingers dark. Gulf; in tidepools, sand, mud flats. To 6.7 cm (2⅗ in.) long.

5. **DANA'S BLUE CRAB** *Callinectes danae* p. 322
Lateral spine long, slender; last marginal spine, spines on claw, and lateral spine white-tipped. Tips of claws crossed; upper finger straight-edged. Carapace olive. Claw purple-tinged; other legs blue, grading to olive. Common in Brazil, W. Indies. To 5.8 cm (2¼ in.) long.

6. **SARGASSUM SWIMMING CRAB** *Portunus sayi* p. 322
Lives only on Sargassum Weed, often washed up on shore. Camouflaged to be almost invisible on Sargassum. Wrist has 3 sharp spines pointing toward claw. To 2.5 cm (1 in.) long.

7. **SPINY-CLAWED SWIMMING CRAB** p. 322
Portunus spinicarpus
Long red spine with red hairs along inner margin extends from wrist diagonally toward claw. Eyestalks and tips of paddles have red spot. Carapace grayish green, marbled with brown in life. To 3.4 cm (1⅓ in.) long.

8. **SPOTTED SWIMMING CRAB** *Portunus sebae* p. 322
Long lateral spines and 2 distinct red-brown spots on carapace. To 10 cm (4 in.) long.

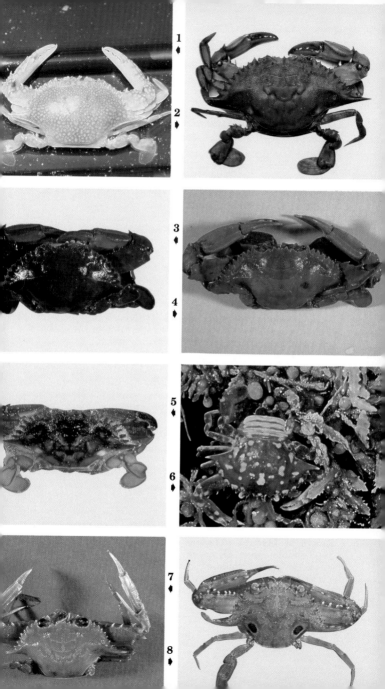

PLATE 54
Mithrax Spider Crabs

All *Mithrax* crabs have spooned fingertips on claws (see p. 318).

1. **GREEN REEF CRAB**   *Mithrax sculptus*   p. 320
   A common small green crab found in coral crevices, rocks. Legs hairy. 4 rounded lobes on margin of carapace; red spot on inner elbow. To 2.5 cm (1 in.) long.

2. **RED SPIDER CRAB**   *Mithrax verrucosus*   p. 320
   Medium-sized. Back paved with flat granules and hairless; wrist has 3 large spines; 8 double or forked spines along front edge of carapace. To 5.1 cm (2 in.) long.

3. **KNOBBED SPIDER CRAB**   *Mithrax caribbaeus*   p. 320
   Four spines on outer edge of coxa of cheliped. Spoon-tipped claws have tiny teeth along inner margins of both fingers. Two parallel rows of small blunt tubercles along rear margin of carapace. Preserved specimen shown; color in life brownish red. To 7.5 cm (3 in.) long. (*M. hispidus* is similar, but lacks teeth on upper finger of claw and tubercles on rear margin.)

4. **SPINY SPIDER CRAB or CABOUCA**   p. 320
   Mithrax spinosissimus
   Six spines along edge of carapace; 8–9 spines on outer edge of coxa of cheliped. Preserved specimen shown; color in life maroon to bright carmine. Large—to 17 cm (6⅝ in.) long.

5. **YELLOW MITHRAX**   *Mithrax pleuracanthus*   p. 320
   Four broad, irregular spines on margin. Preserved specimen shown; in life carapace yellowish white, with blotches of bright red; legs yellowish, blotched or barred with red. Claws light red with pale tips. Often encrusted with algae, bryozoans. To 3.6 cm (1⅖ in.) long.

6. **RED MITHRAX or SPIDER CRAB**   *Mithrax ruber*   p. 320
   Three marginal spines, only 2 distinct. Wrist inflated, smooth; palm without tubercle on outer surface at wrist. Walking legs hairy. Chestnut red, bluish at rear. Tiny—to 1.2 cm (½ in.) long.

7. **CORAL MITHRAX**   *Mithrax coryphe*   p. 320
   Three rounded marginal spines; surface of carapace covered with deep grooves and distinct ridges. Finely mottled green and white. In crevices of corals, rocks, sponges. To 2.2 cm (⅞ in.) long.

8. **ROCK MITHRAX**   *Mithrax forceps*   p. 318
   Four simple spines along margin; first one shortest, the others curved forward. Carapace red, terra cotta, yellowish brown, often with a pale yellow stripe down middle of back. Legs often banded. Rocky shores, under rocks or coral. To 3.1 cm (1⅕ in.) long.

PLATE 55
Spider, Sponge, Calico, and Box Crabs

1. SPONGE SPIDER CRAB p. 321
Macrocoeloma subparallelum
Rostral horns curved inward or straight, with a U-shaped space between them. Tiny eyes on bulging projections. Body covered with stiff, curved hairs. Two large spines on rear edge of margin point backward. To 4.1 cm (1⁹⁄₁₆ in.) long.

2. SPOTTED DECORATOR CRAB p. 321
Microphrys bicornutus
Rostral horns V-shaped, forking outward; may have large spine in front of eye, small spine at rear corner of margin; no tail-like rear spine. Chelipeds spotted gray on cream; back often covered with algae or sponges. To 3.8 cm (1½ in.) long.

3. LESSER SPONGE CRAB *Dromidia antillensis* p. 315
Last pair of legs dorsal, longer than preceding pair. Claw tips crimson. Covered with sponges, colonial anemones, or tunicates. To 7.5 cm (3 in.) long.

4. ARROW CRAB *Stenorhynchus seticornis* p. 317
Rostrum elongate. Legs long, slender; claws bright blue. Carapace gray or tan, with brown and cream stripes in a triangular pattern. To 6 cm (2⅓ in.) long, including rostrum.

5. GRAY PITHO *Pitho aculeata* p. 317
Front broad, blunt, wider than rear; eyes widely spaced, at corners of front margin between 2 long spines. Five marginal teeth; second and third teeth united at base, last one reduced. Carapace white or tan, with gray or olive blotches. Fingers of claws of male spooned; female claws weak. To 2.5 cm (1 in.) long.

6. CORAL CRAB *Carpilius corallinus* p. 323
A large red crab with a white network on carapace. No marginal teeth except for 1 blunt tooth about ⅔ down margin. Fingers of claws brown or black. Among coral rubble and rocks; nocturnal. Largest W. Indian crab—to 12.5 cm (5 in.) long.

7. GULF CALICO CRAB *Hepatus epheliticus* p. 317
Margins of carapace finely toothed; each claw has a three- or four-toothed crest on upper margin. Gray or brownish, with large, rounded, dark-bordered red spots scattered over carapace and legs. Buried in sand in shallow water. Chesapeake Bay to W. Indies, but most common in Gulf. To 6 cm (2⅓ in.) long.

8. YELLOW BOX CRAB or CHICKEN CRAB p. 316
Calappa gallus
Yellow; carapace covered with nodules and ridges. May have red-brown spots on chelipeds and front of carapace. Distinctive palisade of 7 spines forms a crest on ridge of flattened claws. Note "can-opener" arrangement of fingers on right claw, used to pry open snail shells. To 10.6 cm (4⅛ in.) long.

PLATE 56
Mud and Shore Crabs

1. **COMMON MUD CRAB** *Panopeus herbstii* p. 324
Brown or gray. Fingers of claws dark brown with whitish tips;
brown color on lower finger extends a short distance onto palm.
Irregularly distributed brown dots at border between upper gray
and lower white areas on cheliped. To 3.5 cm (1⅖ in.) long.

2. Underside of male **Common Mud Crab,** showing white tips on
claws and enlarged tooth at base of upper finger.

3. **COMMON SHORE CRAB** p. 331
Pachygrapsus transversus
Olive or black; tan striations across back. Long spine at outer
corner of eye, followed by shorter spine. Sides of carapace angular.
Claws equal, spooned, brown-tipped; upper finger sharply bent.
Small—to 1.2 cm (½ in.) long.

4. Underside of female **Common Shore Crab.**

5. **BROWN HAIRY WHARF CRAB** p. 329
Pilumnus dasypodus
Carapace red-brown; front half sparsely covered with hairs, rear
half hairy. Four marginal teeth, counting 1 at edge of orbit (eye
socket); except for orbital tooth, each may have a long brown
spine. Legs covered with white hairs. To 1.4 cm (⅝ in.) long.

6. **SALLY LIGHTFOOT** *Grapsus grapsus* p. 331
Carapace round and flattened, brown with scattered light blue
and cream spots; margins untoothed, blue. Chelipeds light blue,
with rust markings and maroon blotches and stripes. Claws
small; each has a large, flat spine on inner wrist above claw. Runs
rapidly over rocks in spray zone. To 8 cm (3¼ in.) long.

7. **URCHIN CRAB or BANDED SPRAY CRAB** p. 332
Percnon gibbesi
Broad front extends into 3 projections; central one minutely
forked. Legs brown, banded with gold. Eyestalks and claws
orange; underside of body pale blue, legs pale pink. Claws small
in female, large and unequal in male. Juveniles common under
Long-spined Black Urchin, adults under rocks in spray zone.
Similar to Spray Crab, but with 6–7 recurved spines on longest
segment of walking legs. To 3.3 cm (1¼ in.) long.

8. **SPRAY CRAB** *Plagiusa depressa* p. 331
V-shaped notches in front; 4 widely spaced marginal teeth. Flattened, oval carapace brown, covered with flat, scale-like tubercles
among black hairs. Chelipeds have several longitudinal rows of
small black tubercles that form stripes. Often found with **Sally
Lightfoot.** To 4.5 cm (1¾ in.) long.

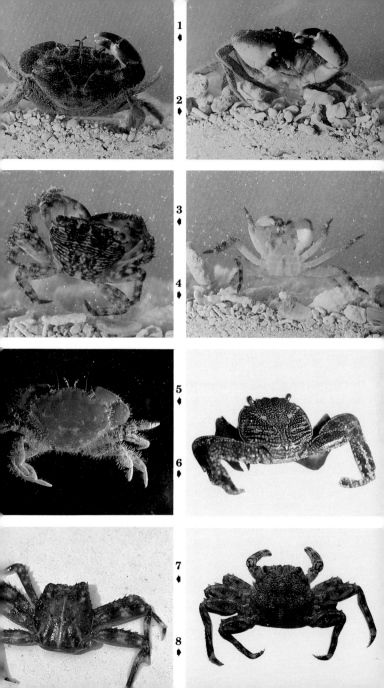

PLATE 57

Marsh and Fiddler Crabs

1. **MARBLED MARSH CRAB** *Sesarma ricordi* p. 330
Color variable, often mottled with brown and cream. One distinct spine at corner of eye. To 2 cm (¾ in.) long.

2. **GRAY MARSH CRAB** *Sesarma cinereum* p. 330
Square carapace is gray, brown, and/or olive, mottled with black. No spines at corner of eye. To 2 cm (¾ in.) long.

3. **PURPLE MARSH CRAB** *Sesarma reticulatum* p. 330
Square carapace dark olive, black, or purple, sometimes with purple or black dots; convex, with scattered clumps of tiny spines on front. Lower surface covered with fuzz. Claws of male robust, somewhat unequal; gaping, tips spooned. Major claw has opposing teeth at base of each finger; upper tooth meshes slightly behind lower one. Palms yellowish or tan, tips of fingers white or yellowish. Last 3 segments of walking legs densely fuzzy. In communal burrows, sometimes with enlarged or hoodlike rim of mud. To 2.5 cm (1 in.) long.

4. **CARIBBEAN MUD FIDDLER CRAB** *Uca rapax* p. 337
Major claw of male has a smooth palm except for a pronounced ridge on palm with large tubercles. This photo shows display (courtship or threat) color phase: carapace is cream with reddish brown markings. No banding on walking legs; major claw whitish. To 2.1 cm (⅘ in.) long.

5. **BURGER'S FIDDLER CRAB** *Uca burgersi* p. 334
Female, showing typical mottled lavender carapace. Two pairs of chocolate-colored arcs or lines along front edge near eyestalks. Brown, H-shaped figure in center of carapace. Legs brown, mottled or banded with cream; no fuzz on manus of second and third walking legs. To 1.2 cm (½ in.) long.

6. Male **Caribbean Fiddler Crab** in brown color phase.

7. **TROPICAL RIVER FIDDLER CRAB** p. 334
Uca mordax
Similar to Burger's Fiddler Crab, but major claw of male slightly larger, less inflated (narrower). Oblique ridge of several rows of tubercles on inner palm near joint. Fuzz covers the manus of second and third walking legs. To 1.6 cm (⅗ in.) long.

8. **MUD FIDDLER CRAB** *Uca pugnax* p. 337
Blue-green or turquoise coloration on front of carapace and eyestalks; often faded in Florida, becoming green on Gulf Coast. To 1.2 cm (½ in.) long.

PLATE 58

Land Crabs

1. **BLACK LAND CRAB** *Gecarcinus lateralis* p. 333
   Carapace with large central area of dark purple. Two lavender spots on either side of sulcus (groove), about ⅓ of distance from rear edge. Small, irregular, cream area beneath outer edge of orbit (eye socket); thin line extends backward to small white dot. Claws somewhat unequal; white, with pointed brown tips. To 4.5 cm (1¾ in.) long. Edible.

2. **MOUNTAIN CRAB** *Gecarcinus ruricola* p. 333
   Carapace variable; often dark purple, with a yellow area at each rear corner. Legs orange or reddish; claws equal, granulated, with slender fingers and yellow tips. Last 2 joints of walking legs are bordered with short spines. Edible.

3. **MANGROVE LAND CRAB** *Ucides cordatus* p. 333
   Large—to 7 cm (2¾ in.) long. One claw larger than the other in males. Carapace purple, edged with yellow; legs bright purple, edged with fringe of silky hair. Inner margin of chelipeds edged with large teeth.

4. **GHOST CRAB** *Ocypode quadrata* p. 333
   Carapace squarish, with sharp front corners; white or yellowish gray. Large black eyes on long perpendicular stalks. Chelipeds covered with tubercles; claws somewhat unequal, inner margins of fingers minutely toothed. To 4.4 cm (1¾ in.). Runs fast.

5. **SOLDIER CRAB** *Coenobita clypeatus* p. 310
   A land hermit crab that occupies empty snail shells. Claws unequal; major claw round, inflated, shining purple. Walking legs reddish, with purple dots and black hairs. Small Soldier Crabs occupy nerite shells; large ones prefer whelk shells.

6. **Soldier Crab** withdrawn into snail shell, closing off aperture with large purple claw.

7. **Great Land Crab** at entrance to 25-cm (10-in.) wide burrow, which extends as much as a meter deep, to water level. This crab is nocturnal and edible.

8. **GREAT LAND CRAB or DUPPY** p. 333
   Cardisoma guanhumi
   Huge—to 9.5 cm (3¾ in.) long. Males have white, unequal claws with slender, gaping fingers; male's major claw may be much longer than carapace. Carapace inflated, oval; pale gray or olive. Walking legs hairless or edged with black spines.

PLATE 59

Sea Stars

1. **LIMP or WEAK SEA STAR** *Luidia alternata* p. 343
   Rays limp, flaccid; will sag or even break off if large specimen is lifted. Tan, with blotchy brown or purple bars across arms. Just under surface of sand. Large—to 36 cm (14 in.) across.

2. **NETTED SEA STAR** *Luidia clathrata* p. 343
   Cream, tan, or bluish gray with a brown stripe on each ray, bordered with wavy dark lines. Velvetlike covering of tiny spines. Under surface of sand. To 30 cm (1 ft.) across.

3. **NINE-ARMED SEA STAR** *Luida senegalensis* p. 343
   Nine purple, velvety, long, narrow arms. Under sand. To 30 cm (1 ft.) across.

4. **BERMUDA SEA STAR** *Coscinasterias tenuispina* p. 342
   Aboral surface purple, with yellow spines. Usually has more (rarely fewer) than 5 arms. Bermuda. To 27 cm (11 in.) across.

5. **CUSHION or RETICULATED SEA STAR** p. 343
   Oreaster reticulatus
   Tan, orange, or brown, with a network of contrasting tubercles. Juveniles green. Thick, large—to 50 cm (20 in.) across.

6. **BEADED SEA STAR** *Astropecten articulatus* p. 341
   Color variable; often brown, purple, or maroon. Marginal plates beadlike; always of contrasting color, often cream or tan. No large erect spines on aboral marginal plates. Pointed podia lack suction disks. Soft bottoms. To 15 cm (6 in.) across.

7. **COMET SEA STAR** *Linckia guildingii* p. 342
   Beige or tan, rarely reddish. Rays long, thin, parallel sided, and rounded, covered with randomly distributed round, smooth nodules. Usually five-armed, but four- and six-armed specimens common. To 23 cm (9 in.) across.

8. **RED FINGER SEA STAR** *Ophidiaster guildingii* p. 343
   Similar to Comet Sea Star but smaller—to 10 cm (4 in.) across. Blotchy tan, purple, pink, or red, with 7 rows of smooth, round nodules running length of each arm on aboral surface.

9. **SPINY BEADED SEA STAR** p. 342
   Astropecten duplicatus
   Preserved specimen—in life it has reddish, brown, gray, or light brown spots on tan. Large spine projects from each marginal plate of oral surface. Marginal plates contrasting, often color of underside. To 20 cm (8 in.) across.

10. **RED SPINY SEA STAR** *Echinaster sentus* p. 342
    Bright red. Rays straight-sided, covered with large, pointed spines. To 15 cm (6 in.) across.

11. **BROWN SPINY SEA STAR** *Echinaster spinulosus* p. 342
    Reddish or greenish brown, tapering rays, covered with short, contrasting-colored spines, often orange. Mangrove swamps in Florida. To 16 cm (6¼ in.) across.

12. A form of *E. spinulosus* common along Florida Gulf Coast.

PLATE 60

Brittle Stars

1. **SPINY OPHIOCOMA**   *Ophiocoma echinata*   p. 347
   Large—arms to 15 cm (6 in.) long. Disk usually dark brown, sometimes mottled brown and cream; spines long, conspicuous. The most common brittle star under rocks in shallows.
2. **RUBY BRITTLE STAR**   *Ophioderma rubicundum*   p. 349
   Disk solid purplish red or mottled with white. Spines flattened against indistinctly banded arms. Medium-sized—to 2 cm (¾ in.) across disk.
3. **OERSTED'S BRITTLE STAR**   *Ophiothrix oerstedii*   p. 350
   Aboral surface of disk gray, bluish gray, or brown, covered with long, barbed spines. Glassy spines on finely banded arms. Longitudinal black stripe on arms. Medium-sized—to 2 cm (¾ in.) across disk.
4. **SLIMY BRITTLE STAR**   *Ophiomyxa flaccida*   p. 349
   Disk covered with smooth, opaque skin. Arms long, slender, with tiny pinnate spines. Feels slimy. To 2 cm (¾ in.) across disk.
5. **LOBATE BRITTLE STAR**   p. 347
   Ophiocnida scabriuscula
   Aboral view: disk covered with small, scattered papillae. Aboral arm plates rectangular; 3 short, blunt, flattened arm spines per segment. Slender arms banded with brown. To 1.2 cm (½ in.) across disk.
6. Oral view of **Lobate Brittle Star.** Disk appears to be mounted on jaw-arm complex.
7. **RETICULATED BRITTLE STAR**   p. 349
   Ophionereis reticulata
   Disk bluish or bone white, with a webbed pattern. Arms banded with brown. To 1.2 cm (½ in.) across disk. Common on clean sand under rocks.
8. An amphiurid brittle star, probably the **Burrowing Brittle Star** (*Hemipholis elongata,* p. 347) or the **Caribbean Mud Brittle Star** (*Ophionepthys limicola*). Many amphiurids live deep in mud and are often white, as are many other cryptic and infaunal (buried) animals. Note small disk in relation to extraordinarily long arms, and fine banding on arms. In *Hemipholis,* aboral disk surface is covered with fine papillae; aboral disk gray or olive, podia red. In *Ophionepthys,* dark stripe runs down arms.
9. **CHOCOLATE BRITTLE STAR**   p. 348
   Ophioderma cinereum
   Brown. Arms about 4× disk diameter. Ellipsoid radial shields; short, blade-like spines pressed against arms. Large—to 3.5 cm (1⅜ in.) across disk.
10. **HARLEQUIN BRITTLE STAR**   p. 348
    Ophioderma appressum
    Olive-green or gray, with white and/or black spots; arms banded green. Cigar-shaped spines pressed against arms. To 2.5 cm (1 in.) across disk.

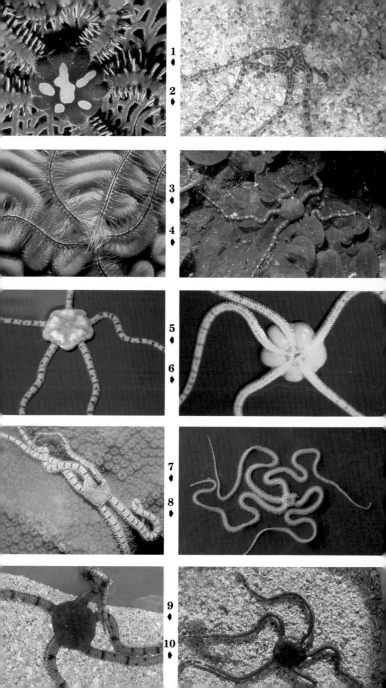

PLATE 61

Sea Cucumbers

1. BURROWING SEA CUCUMBER p. 361
Holothuria arenicola
Tan or gray, with 2 rows of brown blotches on back. Tentacles tan, peltate. Lives deep under sediment in mounds in Turtle Grass beds. To 15 cm (6 in.) long.

2. DONKEY DUNG SEA CUCUMBER *H. mexicana* p. 361
Brown, wrinkled; scattered pointed warts on back. Sole usually pink or rose, sometimes white, covered with scattered brown podia. Tan, peltate tentacles. The commonest form in Caribbean Turtle Grass beds. To 40 cm (16 in.) long.

3. BEADED SEA CUCUMBER *Euapta lappa* p. 360
Body divided into square, beadlike segments. No podia. Large, feathery tentacles. Thin, yellow and black longitudinal stripes. Brown body wall delicate, sticky; can be damaged when animal sticks to your hand. Under rocks. To 1 m (3¼ ft.) long.

4. WHITE SYNAPTA *Leptosynapta inhaerens* p. 360
About the size and shape of a garden worm. Skin sticky, transparent pink or yellow, revealing 5 whitish longitudinal muscle bands. No podia. 12 pinnate tentacles, each with 5–7 branches on opposite sides of stalk. To 15 cm (6 in.) long.

5. BROWN ROCK SEA CUCUMBER p. 361
Holothuria glaberrima
Dark brown, black, or tan. Skin smooth, or with a few pointed warts. Sole covered with dark brown randomly scattered podia. Tentacles dark brown or black, never tan. On or under rocks in surf zone. To 15 cm (6 in.) long.

6. PYGMY SEA CUCUMBER *Pentacta pygmaea* p. 362
Small—to 10 cm (4 in.) long, usually smaller. Chocolate brown, with 3 rows of yellow or pink podia. Back covered with 2 double rows of blunt tubercles. 10 tentacles.

7. THREE-ROWED SEA CUCUMBER p. 362
Isostichopus badionotus
Large—to 45 cm (1½ ft.). Color variable, usually mottled brown or tan. Three rows of podia on sole, middle row split; podia usually brown. Sole flat, bordered by large, double, wartlike projections. The commonest large sea cucumber in Bermuda.

8. GRAY SEA CUCUMBER *Holothuria grisea* p. 361
Gray or mottled gray and pink, covered with small pointed warts. Podia yellow; 23 bushy yellow tentacles. To 20 cm (8 in.) long.

9. FIVE-TOOTHED SEA CUCUMBER p. 361
Actinopyga agassizii
Large—to 30 cm (1 ft.) long. Note 25–30 tan, peltate tentacles visible in this front view. Light tan podia scattered over sole. Five square teeth visible in anus.

10. SURINAM SEA CUCUMBER p. 362
Holothuria surinamensis
Brown or purple; cylindrical, covered with small, dull white, pointed papillae. Whitish podia with yellow tips. 20 pale, peltate tentacles.

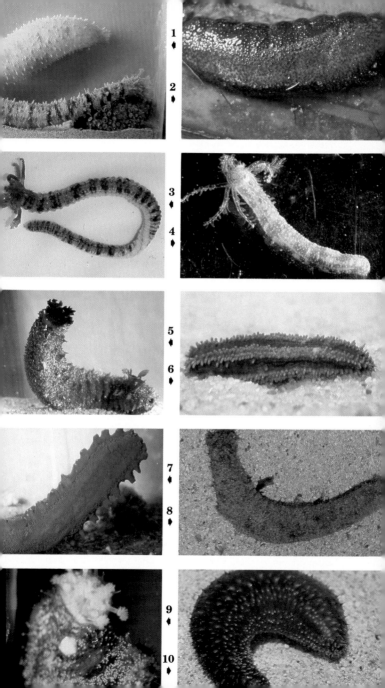

PLATE 62

Sea Urchins

1. SEA PUSSY or CAKE URCHIN p. 355
Meoma ventricosa
Four groove-like ambulacra, angled from center of dorsal surface; the fifth ambulacrum, a depression rather than a distinct groove, runs forward. Reddish brown, bristly. To 12.5 cm (5 in.) long.

2. Lower surface of Sea Pussy, showing bristle tract and tiny white commensal **Sea-pussy Pea Crab** (*Dissodactylus crinitichilis*).

3. RED ROCK URCHIN *Echinometra lucunter* p. 353
Red and/or black; usually some red shows on test. Common under rocks. To 8.5 cm (3¼ in.) wide.

4. REEF URCHIN *Echinometra viridis* p. 354
Spines have white ring at base, then are rose-colored, shading to green; tips brown. Color consistent, distinguishing this urchin from Red Rock Urchin. To 5 cm (2 in.) wide.

5. VARIABLE or GREEN SEA URCHIN p. 354
Lytechinus variegatus
Test green or white; spines short, light green or white (color varies with location. To 7.5 cm (3 in.) wide.

6. WILLIAMS' VARIABLE SEA URCHIN p. 354
Lytechinus williamsi
Two major color variations: (1) white or light green spines with purple podia and pedicellaria, or (2) green spines with purple tips and white podia (shown). Spines longer than in *L. variegatus*, test smaller—to 5.5 cm (2¼ in.) wide.

7. FLAT SEA BISCUIT *Clypeaster subdepressus* p. 353
Flat; a specimen 25 cm (10 in.) long may be only 2.5 cm (1 in.) high. Five small petals extend to less than ½ radius. Covered with short, tan or brown bristles. To 25 cm (10 in.) long.

8. INFLATED SEA BISCUIT *Clypeaster rosaceus* p. 353
Large and thick. Upper surface of test almost completely covered with 5 petals; underside of test deeply concave. Anus at rear, mouth in middle of underside. (Specimen shown with some of bristles removed to show petals clearly.) To 13 cm (5 in.) long.

9. SEA EGG *Tripneustes ventricosus* p. 356
Short white spines on a dark test. The most common urchin on most Turtle Grass beds. Eggs edible. To 12.5 cm (5 in.) wide.

10. GREAT RED-FOOTED URCHIN p. 356
Plagiobrissus grandis
Straw-colored or silvery gray. About 20 dorsal spines near front, to 7.5 cm (3 in.) long, pointing upward and rearward. Mouth and anus on underside; mouth surrounded by jawlike projection. Thick red podia surround mouth and anus. Large—to 23 cm (9 in.) long.

11. MICHELIN'S SAND DOLLAR *Encope michelini* p. 354
Five narrow-petaled ambulacra and 6 lunules. Three lunules along margin near front reduced to notches; rear 2 diagonal, long, and narrow, in an arrangement that causes rear of test to appear tail-shaped. One lunule in center of "tail" not marginal. Shallow water, in Gulf only. To 13.8 cm (5½ in.) long.

PLATE 63
Sea Urchins and Sea-Urchin Tests

1. **FIVE-HOLED KEYHOLE URCHIN**   p. 354
   Mellita quinquiesperforata
   To 10 cm (4 in.) wide. Tan, with short bristles, 5 lunules.

2. **NOTCHED SAND DOLLAR**   *Encope emarginata*   p. 354
   To 14 cm (5½ in.) long. Notchlike lunules; interradial lunule narrow (not distinctly oval, as in *E. michelini,* Pl. 62).

3. **GREAT RED-FOOTED URCHIN**   p. 356
   Plagiobrissus grandis
   Test to 23 cm (9 in.) long.

4. **CLUB or PENCIL URCHIN**   *Eucidaris tribuloides*   p. 354
   Test to 5 cm (2 in.) wide. Brown, blunt cylindrical spines.

5. **HEART or MUD URCHIN**   *Moira atropos*   p. 355
   To 6 cm (2½ in.) long. Ventral view, showing anterior mouth (to right) and blunt posterior.

6. Side view of **Heart Urchin,** showing thin, slitlike ambulacra and grayish, furlike bristles.

7. **LITTLE BURROWING URCHIN**   p. 354
   Echinoneus cyclostomus
   Ventral view of test, showing centrally located mouth and oval anus (periproct) on underside. About 2.5 cm (1 in.) long.

8. Dorsal view of **Little Burrowing Urchin** test, showing 5 ambulacra.

PLATE 64

Sea-Urchin Tests

1. SEA EGG *Tripneustes ventricosus* p. 356
To 13 cm (5 in.) wide, usually bleached white. Somewhat flattened—about half as high as wide. Rows of closely spaced small tubercles form ball joints on which spines are rotated.

2. LONG-SPINED BLACK URCHIN p. 353
Diadema antillarum
To 6.3 cm (2½ in.) wide, with 5 paired, diverging rows of large tubercles. Ambulacra (rows of tiny holes, from which tube feet protrude in living urchins) may be outlined in black.

3. VARIABLE URCHIN *Lytechinus variegatus* p. 354
To 7.5 cm (3 in.) wide. Similar to Sea Egg but smaller. May have a greenish tint if fresh, otherwise white.

4. SEA PUSSY *Meoma ventricosa* p. 355
To 12.7 cm (5 in.) long. Front ambulacral groove reduced; others point diagonally forward or back. Anus on underside, at rear; shovel-shaped mouth on underside, toward front. Shallow geometric groove outlines ambulacra.

5. CLUB URCHIN *Eucidaris tribuloides* p. 354
To 5 cm (2 in.) wide, except in Bermuda and Brazil, where it reaches 7.5 cm (3 in.) wide. 5 diverging paired rows of very large tubercles. Often brown.

6. INFLATED SEA BISCUIT *Clypeaster rosaceus* p. 353
To 12.7 cm (5 in.) wide. Large, petal-shaped ambulacra extend almost to margin, cover more than half of aboral surface. Specimen still retains short spines.

7. A fresh test of a **Sea Pussy** still retains its brown colors.

8. SIX-HOLED KEYHOLE URCHIN p. 354
Leodia sexiesperforata
To 10 cm (4 in.) wide. Fuzzlike spines have fallen off this old specimen, and serpulid worms have colonized surface with calcareous tubes. Five small, petaloid ambulacra and 6 oval lunules, one along midline. Edges of test sharp.

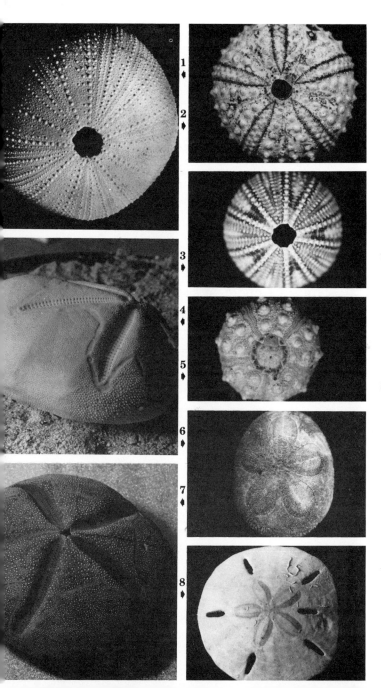

PLATE 65

Sea Cucumbers

1. **Donkey Dung Sea Cucumber** (p. 361), showing fecal casts at right.

2. Oral view of **Three-rowed Sea Cucumber** (p. 362), showing tan peltate tentacles.

3. **Donkey Dung Sea Cucumber** in sandy area of Turtle Grass bed. Lines crossing body are reflections of ripples on water surface. Dots on sand at lower right are **Green Colonial Anemones** (p. 218). At lower left end of cucumber is a **Pencil Urchin** (p. 354); its blunt spines are overgrown with algae. Behind urchin is a tuft of tentacles of the **Ringed Anemone** (p. 214). Each translucent brown tentacle is ringed with white rows of nematocysts (stinging cells). Several small wrasses are swimming above the cucumber.

4. Profile of front end of sea cucumber, showing peltate tentacles.

5. **HAIRY SEA CUCUMBER** *Sclerodactyla briaereus* p. 363
To 15 cm (6 in.) long. Black or brown, densely covered with whitish, translucent tube feet. Ten tentacles; 2 lowest ones smaller.

6. View of underside (sole) of **Three-rowed** (left) and **Donkey Dung sea cucumbers.** Central row of podia of Three-rowed Cucumber split. Sole of Donkey Dung Cucumber cream, pale pink, or rose; covered with scattered brown podia.

7. **THREE-ROWED SEA CUCUMBER** p. 362
Isostichopus badionotus
To 45 cm (18 in.). Large pointed tubercles along lower edge of body; tubercles may be paired. Anus on right is open, expelling stream of water as animal exhales. See also Pl. 61.

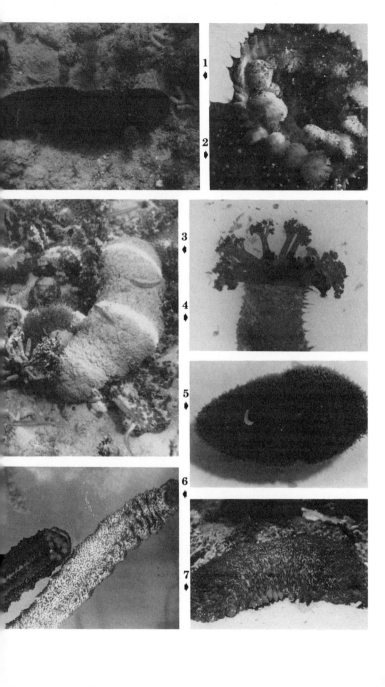

PART II

Common Seashore Animals: Ecology, Natural History, and Identification

10

Corals, Sea Anemones, and Jellyfishes

Living an attached, or sessile, existence requires a host of adaptive strategies. How can an animal that is literally glued to the bottom find food and shelter from its enemies, escape strong currents and storms, and survive the perpetual inundation of sediment constantly threatening to smother it? How can it reproduce if it cannot seek out a mate? These and myriad other problems of survival are solved uniquely by each species. Some adaptive strategies of Phylum Cnidaria, which includes the corals, sea anemones, and jellyfishes, are outlined below.

Radial symmetry: An attached organism does not need a front or back. In fact, to be oriented in a particular direction would be disadvantageous. Instead, many sessile animals have evolved radial symmetry, a pie-shaped body plan whereby the animal can capitalize on food-bearing currents coming from any direction. Radially symmetrical animals often look like undersea flowers: their appendages stream out in every direction, like petals of a daisy.

External fertilization: Attached animals usually do not have sexual dimorphism: that is, both sexes look alike. This is logical, since sexual recognition is not necessary for reproduction. Instead, chemical recognition is often the rule. When water temperature and other conditions are appropriate, the female simply sheds her eggs. A chemical called a pheromone is released at the same time, wafting across the currents like perfume, stimulating the males to release their sperms. This synchrony of egg and sperm production assures that a relatively large percentage of eggs are fertilized. But, of the millions of eggs forming whitish clouds in the water, only a few — usually less than 1% — will reach adulthood. The eggs and larvae are the food of innumerable planktonic and sessile predators. A number of sessile animals have evolved techniques for brooding their young. Corals and sea anemones, for example, hang their eggs on partitions inside their body; the sperms swim into the female's mouth and fertilize the eggs internally. The developing eggs remain protected inside the mother until they escape through the mouth as a cloud of ciliated, football-shaped larvae, having already reached a relatively advanced state of development.

Finding a foothold on the bottom: On rocky shores the main factor limiting the size of a population of attached animals is not food availability and often not even predation; instead, it is lack of living space. Most bottom-dwelling organisms require a clean surface, free of sediment, for survival. The billions of larvae have a few days of free-living existence before they must settle on a suitable surface—or die. But as they approach a rock, its inhabitants reach out in a dense network of entrapping mouths and tentacles. Should a larva escape its enemies long enough to settle on a bare space, it may be inundated with sand and smothered. Corals and anemones have evolved cilia-mucus systems to combat siltation. The silt particles stick to the mucus-covered surface of the animal and are swept off its body by the cilia. But the effectiveness of this system varies with the species. That is one of the reasons why most corals can live only in clear, sediment-free tropical waters.

Once a suitable space is found, however, the larva rapidly metamorphosizes into an adult and soon buds off many exact duplicates of itself, covering the bare surface with its offspring. The young colony is then in a position to compete with its neighbors in the never-ending battle for food, space, light, and the other necessities of life.

Food-getting: Attached animals must wait for food to approach them. Once it approaches within reaching distance, a juvenile fish, tiny worm, or microscopic planktonic animal is doomed. For the members of Phylum Cnidaria have evolved a most effective prey-capturing mechanism: they release clouds of microscopic darts called nematocysts, which stick to, wrap around, and poison their prey.

CORALS, SEA ANEMONES, AND JELLYFISHES

Phylum Cnidaria: Corals, sea anemones, and jellyfishes. Corals resemble rocks, anemones look like flowers, and jellyfishes float through the sea as free-living blobs of jelly. What do they have in common, that they should all belong to the same phylum? All are radially symmetrical, all possess nematocysts, and all have a single central body space called the gastrovascular cavity, which is responsible for both digesting food and distributing it. All have a mouth but no anus. But where are these features in a brain coral or staghorn coral, for example? The answer will become apparent only if you view corals at night, in the beam of a strong light. Only then will you be able to see the tiny translucent polyps that actually form the coral head. Each polyp lives in a cup of its own making, sometimes only a few millimeters in diameter, embedded in the surface of the coral head. The polyp consists of a column topped with a crown of tentacles. Inside the ring of tentacles is a slitlike mouth that can gape widely to ingest the prey. The polyps withdraw during the daytime into the inner recesses of their cups, and are visible only as a sheen of green-brown color coating the coral head. At night each polyp stretches its full length out of the cup, extending its tentacles, capturing planktonic animals as they rise from the depths. The nematocysts are found inside special cells called cnidocytes, which have triggerlike mechanisms. When the trigger is brushed by a tiny copepod, for example, water rushes into the cell, swelling it until the pressure is so great that a door, the operculum, pops open and the threadlike nematocyst unravels and squirts out, ready to ensnare or poison the prey, or both.

Their effectiveness as predators notwithstanding, corals face what appears to be an insurmountable problem: there is little plankton in the water to begin with. Clear tropical seas, with visibility to depths of 30 m (100 ft.) or more, are so transparent because they lack the particulate matter, primarily plankton, which makes more northern seas so densely green. Corals have evolved another source of nutrition that frees them from depending solely on plankton. Over millions of years of parallel evolution, corals have entered into a partnership with microscopic, one-celled plants called zooxanthellae. These algae live inside the polyps and are bathed by the intense tropical sunlight during the day; the light passes right through the coral's skeleton and into each polyp's cup. The zooxanthellae, like other algae, produce food by means of photosynthesis. Recent research has shown that they produce extra food, and share it with the polyps. In turn, the polyps supply the zooxanthellae with shelter, protection, and their nitrogen-rich waste products, providing necessary elements for the manufacture of protoplasm. Thus the coral polyp acts as both plant and animal, trapping plankton when it can, and supplementing its diet with energy-rich food supplied by its internal plants. This extraordinary mutualistic relationship provides the massive quantities of energy needed for the production of coral reefs, which may extend, in some cases, over a thousand miles.

Unlike bank/barrier reefs, which lie offshore, a fringing coral reef begins *at* the shore. Only a few species of coral are adapted to sediment-laden inshore waters. These corals have unique adaptations for preventing suffocation by inundation with sediment.

For example, a young colony of Rose Coral (Pl. 33) lives in Turtle Grass beds, at first attached by a stalk to a solid object on the bottom. But when the colony reaches maturity, the stalk breaks and the colony tumbles free, now susceptible to the buffeting waves. Occasionally the colony is overturned, threatening the polyps with suffocation in the sand. But the Rose Coral can employ a unique defense mechanism: the colony can extend its polyps and imbibe large volumes of water. Then, in unison, the hundreds of polyps expel the water through their mouths, spurting a jet of water sufficient to excavate a depression in the sand. A few more communal bursts of water and the colony has rocked itself right-side up.

Shallow-water Starlet Coral (Pl. 33) forms marble-sized spheres in Turtle Grass beds and small mounds on inshore rocks. Its ability to survive results from a particularly effective cilia-mucus system.

Two coral species that are usually found offshore may be common on exposed rocky shores. If the water is turbulent, fast-moving, and silt-free, the vertical, tan, plate-like fire corals and the huge, tree-like Elkhorn Coral (Pl. 33) may form thickets in shallow water. Both species are adapted to the seaward edge of offshore bank/barrier reefs, where they absorb the full force of the ocean's swells. But exposed rocky coasts on such desertlike islands as Bonaire and Curaçao have low rain runoff and clean rough surf, duplicating conditions on the crest of the bank/barrier reef. Fire corals and Elkhorn Coral can also flourish there.

Taxonomy: There are three classes in Phylum Cnidaria: Hydrozoa, Scyphozoa, and Anthozoa. Class Anthozoa contains both the true corals and the sea anemones. But there are two kinds of true corals, classified on the basis of their skeleton types—hard corals and soft corals. The hard corals and anemones belong to Subclass Zoantharia, and the soft corals belong to Subclass Alcyonaria.

Although anemones and hard corals belong to the same subclass, they differ sufficiently to be placed in separate orders: hard corals belong to Order Scleractinia and anemones to several orders: solitary anemones, Order Actiniaria; colonial anemones, Order Zoanthidia; tube-dwelling anemones, Order Ceriantharia; false corals, Order Corallimorpharia.

Finally, each kind of coral or anemone has its own scientific name, consisting of two Latin names. The genus name comes first and is always capitalized and italicized. The species name is written in lower case and is also italicized. Thus the scientific name for Elkhorn Coral is *Acropora palmata. Acropora,* the genus, is the name of a broader group that includes other closely related species, such as Staghorn Coral (*Acropora cervicornis*), but the name *palmata* is unique within this group, assigned only to the Elkhorn Coral.

The taxonomy of Elkhorn Coral, then, would be:
Phylum Cnidaria
   Class Anthozoa
      Subclass Zoantharia
         Order Scleractinia
            Genus *Acropora*
               Species *palmata*

On the following pages the common shoreside and shallow-water species of corals, anemones, and jellyfishes will be described.

Fire Corals, Siphonophores, and Hydroids

Class Hydrozoa: This class is characterized primarily by colonies of tiny polyps appearing as a fuzzy mass on hard surfaces or on the underside of jellyfish-like floats. Some colonies are candelabra-like; others look like feathers about 5 cm (2 in.) high. There are a number of atypical groups; only four orders common in our region will be discussed.

1. Fire corals: Order Milleporina. Produce hard skeleton superficially resembling that of true corals, but cups not visible. Polyps, located in tiny pinholes, have virulent nematocysts. Brushing your body against a colony of fire coral results in a painful red welt, as the nematocysts inject poison into your skin.

2. Portuguese Man-of-war and other floating colonies: Order Siphonophora. Hollow, air-filled or jelly-like float, from which are suspended polyps of several types—some devoted to capturing prey, others to reproduction or protection. Compare with true jellyfishes (p. 207).

3. Colonial polyps: Orders Athecata and Thecata. Fuzzy masses, tiny candelabra, or feathery colonies—all composed of many tiny polyps.

4. Stylasterine corals: Order Stylasterina. Small, delicate, calcareous colonies, branching in one plane. Polyps in tiny pores. Resemble tiny fire corals but more colorful.

Fire Corals

CRENELATED FIRE CORAL *Millepora alcicornis*   **Pl. 33**
Flat, vertical, yellow-tan plates lacking visible cups. Upper edge of plates bumpy, white-tipped. May form thickets edging exposed shores. Caribbean, W. Indies. **Related species:** (1) **Flat-topped Fire Coral** (*M. complanata*) is similar but tops of colonies are

squared off, not bumpy (Fig. 54). (2) **Encrusting Fire Coral** (*M. squarrosa*) forms purplish, wrinkled crusts on rocks; tops of wrinkles white.

Portuguese Man-of-war and
Other Siphonophores

PORTUGUESE MAN-OF-WAR   **Pl. 30**
Physalia physalia
Bladderlike, iridescent blue float (pneumatophore), from which is suspended a colony of polyps, including feeding polyps (gasterozooids), each with a single branched tentacle, and short, buttonlike reproductive polyps (gonozooids). Transparent tentacles of defensive and food-capturing polyps (dactylozooids) to 10 m (33 ft.) long trail behind float, entrapping small fishes and plankton. Bathers coming into contact with these fishing tentacles are attacked by hundreds of nematocysts, which cause whiplash-like lesions, with intense pain and redness. Children may be seriously injured; adults may experience discomfort for days. For first aid, remove tentacle fragments, apply a topical pain killer, and take antihistamines. Florida, W. Indies, Caribbean.

The small, banded **Man-of-war Fish** (*Nomeus gronovii*) lives among the tentacles and eats leftovers from colony's daily catch.

BLUE BUTTON   *Porpita porpita*   **Pl. 30**
Small—about 2.5 cm (1 in.) wide. Shaped like an ordinary jellyfish, but the float has a *black margin and dark radiating lines*. Horny, chambered pneumatophore (float), with central feeding polyp dangling from underside and tentacle-like fishing polyps hanging from margin. If you find a Blue Button in water, look closely for tiny pelagic sea slugs (**Blue Glaucus,** Pl. 48). Pantropical.

BY-THE-WIND SAILOR   *Velella velella*   **Pl. 30**
About 2.5 cm (3 in.) across. Purplish, with internal, horny, chambered pneumatophore (float), and a *jelly-like sail* extending from aboral (upper) surface. Florida, W. Indies, Caribbean.

Colonial Polyps or Hydroids

Fuzzy masses covering rocks, or minute candelabra or featherlike colonies rarely more than 5 cm (2 in.) high. We have room for only a few common species.

BUSHY HYDROID   *Bougainvillia carolinensis*
Bushy, dense clusters to 30 cm (1 ft.) high. Mouth forms cone above 8–20 thin, long tentacles per polyp. *Reproductive polyps look like bubbles* extending from stalks of feeding polyps. Stalks

greenish; polyps pink. Medusae tiny, oval, with groups of 3–9 stringy tentacles at 4 corners of bell. Mouth, located inside bell, has branching tentacles. To 5 mm (³⁄₁₆ in.). Colonies of polyps common on seaweed and wharf pilings; Arctic to Florida, Gulf, W. Indies, Mexico. A common fouling hydroid of Gulf in winter.

PINK HYDROID *Eudendrium carnaeum*
Plume-like colonies of *red feeding polyps and orange gonozooids,* 20–30 thin tentacles in one whorl around trumpet-shaped mouth region. Grows explosively over pilings in spring and dies off in winter in Gulf. Canada to Brazil.

SNAIL FUR or HERMIT-CRAB HYDROID   **Pl. 30**
Hydractinia echinata
Fuzzy pink coat occasionally found on snail shells—only when occupied by a hermit crab. Commonest on Mud Snail shells occupied by Long-clawed Hermit Crab. In northern part of range colony covers shell completely; off Florida it forms tufts. Has all three types of polyps (feeding, defensive, and reproductive). May have a mutualistic relationship with crab, in which polyps gain mobility in return for protecting crab with nematocysts. **Similar species: Northern Snail Fur** (*Podocoryne carnea*) is similar, but it produces medusae, which can be seen budding from reproductive polyps. Only *two types of polyps,* both of which have 12–16 tentacles. Produces a *spiny fibrous crust* on snail shell, with chambers in which polyps live. On snail shells occupied by hermit crabs and on carapace of Horseshoe Crabs. Arctic to S. America.

FERN HYDROID *Pennaria tiarella*
Feathery plumes with *alternate branches;* to 15 cm (6 in.) high. Polyps extending from these branches have a flask-shaped upper portion, surrounded with 2–3 irregular rows of tentacles, each crowned by a knob of nematocysts. Medusae bud off polyp stems. Colony white to rose colored. *Stings.* Medusae tiny, *cuboidal,* rose or pink, with no apparent tentacles. On seagrass, rocks, and pilings; Maine to Florida, Gulf, and W. Indies. A common fouling hydroid in summer in northern Gulf. **Similar species:** (1) *Macrorhynchia phillipina,* (2) *Aglaophenia allmani,* and (3) *Sertularia speciosa* are other plume-like or fernlike hydroids that sting. These usually grow on rocks in clumps to 7.5 cm (3 in.) tall. Look for white, dotlike polyps on branches that resemble candles in a candelabrum. Florida, W. Indies, Caribbean.

Stylasterine Corals

PURPLE STYLASTER *Stylaster roseus*   **Pl. 15**
To 10 cm (4 in.) wide. *Bright purple* or rose; rarely white with a pink flush. *Branches in 1 plane, terminal branches wavy.* Polyps extend from tiny pores in netlike pattern, effectively trapping plankton. Under ledges or on shaded walls, subtidal zone to deep water; Bahamas, Florida, Caribbean.

True Jellyfishes

Class Scyphozoa: In true jellyfishes, unlike the hollow sipho-nophores (p. 205), the body is filled with mesoglea, an acellular jellylike substance. The technical term for a jellyfish is *medusa,* after the fringe of nematocyst-bearing tentacles resembling the coiffure of snakes worn by a mythological lady with the same name.

The medusa floats through the water, mouth down, propelled feebly by contractions of its bell-shaped body, and trailing a mass of almost invisible tentacles. Despite its size, the medusa lacks the strength to swim against the currents and thus is technically a member of the plankton—even bathtub-sized jellyfishes are plankton.

Medusae and polyps are related through their life cycle. The polyp buds off medusae, and the medusae produce sperms and eggs, which (after fertilization) become polyps. Thus the phylum has the advantage of increased diversity from the sexually repro-ducing medusae (jellyfishes), and easy and plentiful reproduction from the asexually reproducing polyps.

A number of jellyfishes that commonly are blown into bays or that wash up on beaches are described below.

MOON JELLY   *Aurelia aurita*   **Pl. 30**
Body bluish, transparent; to 25 cm (10 in.) across. Reproductive tissue arranged in a *four-leaf clover* pattern. Short, almost invis-ible tentacles around margin. Harmless. Maine to Florida, Gulf, W. Indies, Caribbean.

SEA WASP   *Carybdea* species   **Fig. 90**
Small—to 2.5 cm (1 in.) wide. Body cuboid, with 4 sides and *4 tentacles, one suspended from each corner of body.* Swims rapidly, at up to 6 m (20 ft.) per minute. Found in deep water, except at night, when it is attracted to lights of piers or beaches. Common off beaches in daytime in Jamaica. Long tentacles (30 cm—12 in.—long) have virulent nematocysts and *sting painfully.* Most common species is *C. alata.* Usually found in small schools. **Similar species:** *Chiropsalmus* species have several tentacles, rather than one, dangling from each corner. W. Indies, Caribbean.

UPSIDE-DOWN JELLYFISH   *Cassiopeia xamachana*   **Pl. 30**
Large—to 30 cm (1 ft.) across. Bell brown and white; mouth surrounded by frilly extensions (oral arms) that branch into thousands of lacy extensions (lappets). These resemble the edge of a petticoat and contain thousands of yellow-brown zooxanthellae (mutualistic algae). This jellyfish swims mouth downward, *but flops over when settling on bottom,* exposing its underside (and zooxanthellae) to sun. In muddy areas dozens of these beautiful medusae may cover bottom. **Similar species:** *C. frondosa* differs

from *C. xamachana* in that its underside is so frilly that oral arms are not visible. Oral arms are as long as disk is wide, thus lappets extending from arms are *not visible from above*. *C. frondosa* is more common in Turtle Grass beds; *C. xamachana* inhabits channels in mangrove swamps. Florida, Bermuda, W. Indies, Caribbean.

Look carefully among lappets for the predatory **Jellyfish-eating Nudibranch** (*Dondice parguerensis*). This small—to 4.8 cm (1⅘ in.) long—nudibranch is common on underside of both species of jellyfish from November to March. Up to 75% of jellyfish may be parasitized, with as many as 11 nudibranchs on one jellyfish. Four or five of these sea slugs can denude the *Cassiopeia* of all its lappets in one week. However, one or two slugs will cause no apparent harm to the host, because the jellyfish is able to

Fig. 90. *Left:* Sea Wasp (p. 207)
right: Sea Nettle (p. 209).

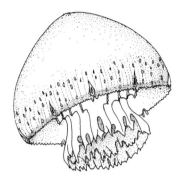

Fig. 91. Cannonball Jellyfish.

regenerate its lappets at the same rate as the slugs crop them. See p. 251 for a description of a related *Dondice*.

SEA NETTLE   **Fig. 90**
Chrysaora quinquecirrha
Aptly named for its bothersome sting. About 10 cm (4 in.) across. Bell milky white or transparent with white spots; sometimes with reddish radiating lines. Usually has 4 tentacles, but larger forms may have as many as 40. *Four simple oral arms* extend from mouth for several body lengths. Virginia to Florida, W. Indies.

JELLYBALL or CANNONBALL JELLYFISH   **Fig. 91**
Stomolophus meleagris
Large, firm, brownish hemisphere, to 25 cm (10 in.) across. Bell is milky bluish or yellowish, *edged with a brown band*. Forked lappets around mouth but no trailing tentacles. Does not sting. Central mouth with 16 slitlike subsidiary mouths. N. Carolina to Florida, W. Indies, Caribbean. Sometimes surrounded by a school of dime-sized, silvery fish—juvenile jacks—which hide inside bell when threatened.

Corals and Sea Anemones

Class Anthozoa: All members of this class are polypoid. Some form colonies that secrete a chalky substance, calcium carbonate, producing a hard colony in shapes of domes, brains, trees, and so forth. Others form flexible, fanlike or bushlike colonies that sway with currents. Still other members of this class exist as solitary, naked polyps, sometimes as large as 30 cm (1 ft.) across.

Soft Corals

Subclass Alcyonaria, Order Gorgonacea: Bushlike, fanlike or rodlike; flexible. Polyps, in scattered cups, have 8 pinnate (feathery) tentacles when seen under lens. Outer crust consists of meshwork of calcium carbonate spicules surrounding brown inner core of flexible protein, gorgonin, a tough, fibrous material resembling wood. All species are found in S. Florida, Bahamas, and Caribbean, except where otherwise specified.

CORKY SEA FINGERS or DEADMAN'S FINGERS   Pl. 31
 Briareum asbestinum
 Sometimes forms a crust, but commonly produces vertical stalks to 3 cm (1⅕ in.) wide and more than 15 cm (6 in.) tall. When extended, long brown polyps give stalks a fuzzy appearance. When polyps are retracted, *reddish branches resemble wart-covered fingers. No axial skeleton;* in cross-section fingers consist of white surface spicules in ring around red core.

BROWN ENCRUSTING SOFT CORAL
 Erythropodium caribaeorum
 Crust often covered with long (to 1.5 cm — ⅝ in.) polyps, giving colony a fuzzy appearance. When polyps are retracted, surface looks reddish brown and shiny, with *star-shaped cups.*

KNOBBY CANDELABRA *Eunicea* species   **Pl. 31**
 Thick branches; light-colored *rounded projection beneath each cup* gives branches a distinct bumpy appearance. Bushy or branching in one plane. *E. mammosa* and *E. succinea* are yellow-brown. *E. tourneforti* is dark brown or black, with few branches arranged in one plane.

SEA FANS *Gorgonia* species   **Pl. 31**
 Purple, green, or yellow. Two species that often grow on rocks or dead coral: (1) *G. ventalina,* with branches *compressed in plane of fan,* and (2) *G. flabellum,* with branches *compressed at right angles to plane of fan.* To 1 m (39 in.) tall. *G. flabellum* is absent from Bermuda.

SEA WHIP *Leptogorgia virgulata*   **Pl. 8**
 To 90 cm (36 in.) high, 1.3 cm (½ in.) wide. Long and whiplike, usually with *several long branches;* grows attached to rocks, shells. Cups in *evenly distributed* multiple series along two sides of branches; *cups do not protrude.* Purple, red, yellow, orange, or tan. New York to Florida, Gulf of Mexico to Brazil. **Similar species: Tall Sea Whip** (*L. setacea*), to 183 cm (6 ft.) high; *unbranched* or with one or two branches. Often unattached. Cups in two rows are crowded and irregularly spaced. Yellow or purple. Chesapeake Bay to Florida, Gulf to Brazil.

SPINY CANDELABRUM *Muricea muricata*   **Pl. 32**
 Flattened colony, branching in single plane. Branches prickly to

touch—*long spicules form scales* into which polyps retract. Yellow, brownish, or tan.

COMMON BUSHY SOFT CORAL Pl. 31
Plexaura homomalla
Brown, bushy. Branches feel soft and exude a brown cloud when squeezed. Terminal branchlets to 10 cm (4 in.) and 5 mm (⅕ in.) wide. Surface nearly smooth. **Similar species: Tan Bushy Soft Coral** (*P. flexuosa,* Fig. 150) has slightly *rough-feeling* branches; usually tan or yellowish, may be purplish.

SEA RODS *Plexaurella* species Pl. 32
Branches thick—to 1.5 cm (⅝ in.) wide. Usually gray or tan. Resemble broom handles; stiff and somewhat brittle. Polyps retract into *slitlike cups.* The **Sea Rod** (*P. grisea*) has long gray branches that usually *fork only once.* The **Double-forked Sea Rod** (*P. dichotoma*) is similar but more frequently branched and light brown or yellow.

SLIMY SEA FEATHER *Pseudopterogorgia americana* Pl. 32
Large, *plume-like* colonies, to 2 m (6½ ft.) tall. When touched, *mucus-covered branchlets feel slimy.* Bluish gray. **Related species: Smooth Sea Feather** (*P. acerosa*) *feels smooth* or slightly sandpapery. Large drooping plumes are grayish, purplish, or yellow.

SEA BLADES *Pterogorgia* species Pl. 32
Guadeloupe Sea Blade (*P. guadalupensis*) has flat, broad branches, to 10 cm (4 in.) wide. Polyps retract into longitudinal grooves *along edges of branches.* **Yellow Sea Blade** (*P. citrina*) forms small colonies in rough-water areas; it has *flat yellow blades* with purplish margins. **Angular Sea Blade** (*P. anceps*) has *three- or four-edged,* blade-like branches; it is purplish, olive, or yellow.

SEA PANSY *Renilla reniformis* Fig. 29, Pl. 8
Purple, gelatinous parasol with stalk to 7.5 cm (3 in.) long and frond (top) to 7.5 cm (3 in.) wide. Top of horizontal frond covered with many translucent polyps of two sizes, none higher than 1 cm (⅜ in.). Each polyp has 8 pinnate tentacles. Strongly bioluminescent when touched at night. Stalk buried in sand, near shore to deep water. N. Carolina to Brazil, but not Gulf. **Similar species: Mueller's Sea Pansy** (*R. muelleri,* Fig. 29) has a somewhat larger frond, with a thin *stalk that is much shorter than diameter of frond.* Gulf to Brazil.

Hard Corals

Subclass Zooantharia, Order Scleractinia: The polyps of hard corals are joined together so that even their digestive-circulatory gastrovascular cavities are interconnected. Thus no one polyp is independent—when one eats, other polyps nearby obtain food also. Together the polyps build a coral head; they secrete calcium carbonate in a pattern dictated by inherited instructions. Each polyp lives in its own self-secreted cup, producing supporting walls (septa) inside the cup that divide it into sections. The septa may radiate out from a central supporting rod (the columella) like spokes in a wheel. When the polyp dies the septa remain. Since they are arranged in a distinctive pattern that varies with the species, the septa are useful in classification. Colony shape, number and arrangement of septa, and presence or absence of a columella are features that help identify corals. All species s. Florida, Bahamas, and throughout Caribbean, except where noted.

ELKHORN CORAL *Acropora palmata*   **Fig. 54, Pl. 33**
  Colonies flattened, branching, resembling *moose antlers;* cups *protruding, tubular.* May form golden brown "forests" in exposed shallows.

NORTHERN CUP CORAL *Astrangia danae*   **Pl. 5**
  Rough, irregular *white clumps of cups.* Each cup to 6 mm (¼ in.) wide; up to 30 cups per colony. Polyps translucent, fuzzlike when extended; polyps often visible during daytime. Subtidal, on wrecks, rocks, in deep water. Dead colonies often wash up on shore. Cape Cod to Florida, Gulf. **Related species: Southern Cup Coral** (*A. solitaria*) forms brownish clumps or isolated cups to 4 mm (³⁄₁₆ in.) wide, each with 36 septa. Under rocks; Bermuda to Brazil.

TUBE CORAL *Cladocora arbuscula*   **Pl. 5**
  Mass of small white tubes, each ending in a cup about 3.5 mm (⅛ in.) wide. Branches have fine longitudinal ridges continuous with septa. About 36 septa per cup. Florida, Gulf, Caribbean to Brazil; in Turtle Grass beds.

SHARP-HILLED BRAIN CORAL *Dipoloria clivosa*
  Usually encrusting, knobby; rarely hemispherical. *Narrow sharp hills; valleys wider than hills.* Brown with greenish valleys to 6 mm (¼ in.) wide. About 35 septa per cm. **Similar species: (1) Depressed Brain Coral** (*D. labyrinthiformis,* Pl. 33) forms large, hemispherical, brown-yellow heads. Hills broad and flat, with distinct *depressions running length of each hill.* (2) **Common Brain Coral** (*D. strigosa*) forms hemispherical greenish brown colonies with rounded *hills that are almost as wide as valleys.* 15–20 septa per cm.

STAR CORAL *Favia fragum*   **Pl. 33**
  Small, yellow-brown, loaf-shaped or hemispherical colonies, on rocks or dead coral in shallow water. Not more than 5 cm (2. in.) wide. *Cups angular, oval,* less than 6 mm (¼ in.) across, widely separated by flat-topped walls. 36–40 septa per cup, with small irregular teeth.

COMMON ROSE CORAL *Manicina areolata*   **Pl. 33**
  Yellow, oval, with undulating edges. *Upper surface flattened.* To 7.5 cm (3 in.) long. Young colonies stalked; older colonies have a *vestige of stalk underneath.* 18 septa per cm. In Turtle Grass beds.

IVORY BUSH CORAL *Oculina diffusa* **Pl. 33**
Lumpy branches; horizontal, never vertical. Covered with olive-drab tissue when alive. Cups far apart, slightly projecting; 24 septa per cup. Colonies extensively branched; branches less than 1.2 cm (½ in.) thick. If branches are more than 1.2 cm thick, species is *O. valenciennesi.* In shallow bays and Turtle Grass beds.

THIN FINGER CORAL *Porites furcata*
Forked, vertically branching; each branch about 1.2 cm (½ in.) wide or less. *Branches not clubbed at ends.* Can form large beds in shallow water. **Similar species: Thick Finger Coral** (*P. porites*) has *clubbed branches* (swollen at tips). Diameter of branches 2 cm (¾ in.) or greater. Forms clumps in sandy or rocky areas and Turtle Grass beds.

SHALLOW-WATER STARLET CORAL **Pl. 33**
Siderastrea radians
Grayish hemispheres with *black, dotlike cups evenly scattered over surface.* Cups angular, deep, narrow; 30–40 septa per cup. Forms round "pebbles" about 2.5 cm (1 in.) wide in Turtle Grass beds; also encrusts rocks.

RED or ORANGE CORAL *Tubastrea coccinea*
Small clumps of orange or red cups, each cup about 1 cm (⅜ in.) wide, projecting from spongy encrusting base. On shaded sides of rocks or dead coral. Polyps large, yellow, often visible during daytime.

Sea Anemones

Subclass Zooantharia, Order Actiniaria: True anemones. Solitary or in groups of unattached individuals. Usually with a thick column and often with tapering tentacles. S. Florida, Bahamas, Bermuda, W. Indies, and Caribbean, unless otherwise noted.

MAROON ANEMONE *Actinia bermudensis* **Pl. 27**
Short, tapering red tentacles in several rings around oral disk. *Whole animal maroon.* Column smooth, with circles of bright blue warts at margin. In caves and under rocks.

BROWN-STRIPED SAND ANEMONE **Pl. 28**
Actinoporus elegans
Disk to 5 cm (2 in.) wide, covered with numerous *wartlike tentacles* distributed in about 96 radial rows. Mouth surrounded by smooth, transparent area. *Seven bands of dark brown tentacles radiate toward mouth.* Column smooth, whitish, with collar of dotlike, brown or white vesicles arranged in vertical rows. Buried in sand near low-water line; withdraws if disturbed. Jamaica, Curaçao, Guadeloupe, Brazil.

PALE ANEMONE *Aiptasia pallida* **Pl. 27**
Small, brownish or whitish translucent column, about 2.5 cm (1

in.) tall. About *100 marginal tentacles of two sizes:* a few long ones interspersed among many small ones. Disk about 1 cm (⅜ in.) wide. Usually in crowded colonies of unconnected individuals on rocks or Red Mangrove roots. Look for a predator, the aolid nudibranch *Berghia coerulescens,* that is almost identical to the anemone; the fingerlike cerata on its back resemble the anemone's tentacles. **Similar species: Ghost Anemone** (*Diadumene leucolena*) has 40–60 tapering tentacles of equal size, and vertical ridges on column. Maine to Georgia.

TEXAS ROCK ANEMONE *Aiptasiomorpha texaensis*
Clusters of *tiny pink anemones,* about 5 mm (⅕ in.) wide and high. 20 long tentacles, length roughly equals diameter of oral disk. Juveniles often bud off column of adult. Subtidal, on oyster bars and jetties; n. Gulf to Mexico.

SARGASSUM ANEMONE *Anemone sargassiensis*
Tentacles of various sizes; length of longest tentacle equal to radius of oral disk. Reddish brown with *dull white radial lines from mouth to base of tentacles.* Oral disk diameter to 4 cm (1½ in.), column height to 2 cm (¾ in.). Soft, flabby, lightly attached. Adults in caves, among boulders and jetties. Young less than 1 cm (⅜ in. long), often on floating Sargassum Weed.

ROCK ANEMONE *Anthopleura krebsi* **Pl. 27**
Length of tentacles equal to radius of oral disk. Tentacles greenish yellow to dull rust red. Column greenish yellow with conspicuous rows of *rust-red warts* (verrucae). Oral disk diameter to 3 cm (1¼ in.); column height a little less. Intertidal, among rocks and in crevices on exposed rocky coasts.

RINGED ANEMONE *Bartholomea annulata* **Pl. 27**
Large; tentacles abundant, very long—to 12.5 cm (5 in.). Tentacles thin and transparent, but with a continuous *spiral band of white batteries of nematocysts.* Column hidden in crevice; thick mass of tentacles projects from crevice. Look for tiny cleaning shrimp (p. 306) on tentacles and Red Snapping Shrimp (p. 306) under tentacles. **Similar species: Knobby Stinging Anemone** (*Heteractis lucida*) also has white nematocysts but in *dotlike* batteries on tentacles rather than in spirals. Stings mildly.

GRAY WARTY ANEMONE **Pl. 8**
Anthopleura carneola
Gray oral disk to 7.5 cm (3 in.) wide, edged with more than 100 stubby, pinkish or yellowish, translucent tentacles, each with a thin longitudinal line. Vertical rows of *whitish warts on column.* If touched, anemone retracts under sand. Column to 30 cm (1 ft.) under surface. On high-energy beaches above and below low-water line; N. Carolina to Texas. **Similar species: Texas Warty Anemone** (*Bunodactis texaensis*) has a gray column with vertical rows of warts and a *ring of spherical warts just beneath tentacles.* Oral disk brownish green with dark gray splotches. Gulf, especially Texas.

STINGING MANGROVE ANEMONE   Pl. 22
Bunodeopsis antilliensis
Column to 3.8 cm (1½ in.) tall, with 20–40 long, thin, transparent tentacles covered with dotlike nematocyst batteries (visible only with a lens). Mass of *brown or green, bubble-like, fingerlike, or stalked vesicles at base of column,* extending halfway up column. Nocturnal, crawls actively. *Stings.* Bermuda, Caribbean; subtidal on Red Mangrove roots, Turtle Grass leaves, rubble, sponges.

RED WARTY ANEMONE *Bunodosoma granuliferum* **Pl. 28**
About 96 short, tapering, olive-green tentacles *splotched with white* and arranged in 5 rings. A fringe of leafy or bubble-like vesicles on collar underneath tentacles. Column covered with *warts in vertical rows.* Mouth area projects from disk and is usually red. Color varies, often brick red; oral disk usually closed during day, resembling a red lump about 3.8 cm (1¼ in.) wide. To 8 cm (3¼ in.) across expanded disk. **Similar species: American Warty Anemone** (*B. cavernata,* Pl. 8) *lacks columns of warts in a striped effect* on column and white flecks on tentacles; it is common on Red Mangrove roots, rocks. *B. granuliferum* is more common in the Caribbean; *B. cavernata* is common in Carolinas, Georgia, Gulf.

TRICOLOR ANEMONE *Calliactis tricolor* **Pl. 27**
On snail shells occupied by hermit crabs. A thick fringe of fuzzlike, white or tan tentacles. Column plum-colored or yellow-brown, with several irregular rows of *dark spots above base.* Usually less than 5 cm (2 in.) across disk.

GIANT CARIBBEAN ANEMONE   Pl. 28
Condylactis gigantea
Large; colorful. Tentacles to 15 cm (6 in.) or longer, thick, tapering; tan, striated, usually *tipped with pink, purple or green bulb.* Column thick; sometimes green, usually orange. In Florida and Bahamas often tinged with purple. Coral reefs and rocky shallows.

STINGING ANEMONE *Lebrunia danae* **Pl. 27**
Oral disk edged with long, tapering tentacles (expanded at night) and shorter, *forked or branched, inflatable false tentacles* (expanded during day), which are actually extensions of margin. Brown and white; may form camouflaged network to 30 cm (1 ft.) across false tentacles. *Stings.*

ONION ANEMONE *Paranthus rapiformis* **Pl. 8**
To 7.5 cm (3 in.) across disk and length of column. Tentacles and smooth column pinkish, translucent. 144 or more short tentacles edging oral disk in 3 cycles. Disk appressed to sand in lower intertidal zone on protected beaches; column buried, with anchorlike swelling at base. When touched, anemone withdraws rapidly, leaving parts of disk exposed. When disturbed, anemone pulls in tentacles and detaches itself, *floating off like a boiled onion.* Massachusetts to n. Florida, Florida Gulf Coast.

COLLARED SAND ANEMONE   **Pl. 27**
Actinostella flosculifera
About 20 long tentacles, originating near mouth; visible on
cloudy days or at night. Ruffled, greenish brown, olive, violet, or
ocher disk, to 8 cm (3¼ in.) across. *Collar of many bubble-like
vesicles at margin of disk.* Column with sticky warts at base.
Buried in sand among Red Mangrove roots or near rocks in
intertidal and shallow subtidal. Common.

BEADED ANEMONE   *Epicystis crucifer*   **Pl. 27**
About *200 tiny tapering tentacles* in several rings around *edge of
oral disk.* Disk covered with warts and lines radiating from
mouth. Color variable—usually olive or brown and white, sometimes reddish. Column buried in sand; withdraws beneath sand
when disturbed. To 15 cm (6 in.) across disk.

SUN ANEMONE   *Stoichactis helianthus*   **Pl. 28**
Short, stubby tentacles, to 1 cm (⅜ in.) long, cover oral disk, *giving
it a ruglike appearance.* Disk pale green or yellowish; to 15 cm
(6 in.) across. Often in groups, covering rocks; often abundant in
lower intertidal. **Similar species: Duerden's Sun Anemone**
(*Homostichanthus duerdeni,* Pl. 28), has more crowded, thinner,
tan tentacles. Solitary rather than in groups. Long column buried
in sand of Turtle Grass beds; not intertidal.

BLUNT-TENTACLED ANEMONE   **Pl. 27**
Telmactis cricoides
Disk to 10 cm (2 in.) across; orange-brown, with up to 80 *blunt,
brown-tipped, tan tentacles.* Tentacles in two innermost cycles
(rings) larger than those close to edge. Inner tentacles have pairs
of brown dots at bases. Column to 10 cm (4 in.) long; irregularly
furrowed, brown or orange-red. Under rocks and coral ledges,
often hanging upside-down; Bermuda, s. Florida, W. Indies.

False Corals

Order Coralliomorpharia: Solitary or colonial. Oral disk covered with buttonlike or wartlike tentacles or with clumps of short,
hairlike tentacles. One or several mouths may project upward on
short, conical papillae from oral disk.

UMBRELLA FALSE CORAL   **Fig. 92, Pl. 29**
Discosoma neglecta
Oral disk concave, olive-green or brown. Thick, *irregular stubby
marginal lobes* of varying sizes projecting outward from edge of
disk. May have radiating white streaks on surface of disk. Tiny
feathery tentacles in clumps on surface of disk to 8 cm (3¼ in.)
across. In clusters of a few individuals or solitary, on reefs
throughout Caribbean; not Bermuda or Brazil.

ST. THOMAS FALSE CORAL   **Pl. 29**
Discosoma sanctithomae
Disk covered with *clumps of tiny, leaflike or hairlike, branched*

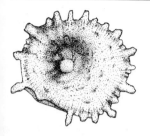

Fig. 92. Umbrella False Coral.

tentacles. Tentacles at edge of disk tiny, unbranched. Olive-green, bluish or purplish pink oral disk may have pale blue lines radiating from central mouth to margin. Edge of column may form a low collar around disk. To 10 cm (4 in.) across. Shallows, coral reefs.

ED BALL ANEMONE **Pl. 29**
Pseudocorynactis caribbeorum
125–200 long, transparent tentacles, each *tipped with an orange or red ball* (acrosphere) of nematocysts. Oral disk translucent, sometimes with patches of cream, white, or green. Mouth often white. Column smooth, brown, maroon, purplish red, divided into two parts—an upper narrow ridge (scapulus) and lower scapus. Scapulus light, with 6 vertical bands. On coral reefs or rocks, in water to 22.5 m (74 ft.) deep. Resembles brown lump during day, expands at night. This anemone is able to detect prey before it touches tentacles. Southern and eastern Caribbean, especially Curaçao, Bonaire, and Puerto Rico. **Similar species: Little Red Ball Anemone** (*Corynactis parvula*) is small—disk to 8 mm (⅓ in.) across—with fewer (no more than 86) tentacles. Tentacles transparent, each tipped with a red, orange, or rose ball. Intertidal and subtidal, under stones; Florida to W. Indies.

LORIDA FALSE CORAL *Ricordia florida* **Pl. 29**
Tentacles *wartlike, iridescent green or orange,* crowded on surface of disk. One or several larger wartlike projections (mouths) usually near center of disk. Individual polyps, each about 2.5 cm (1 in.) across, crowd together on rocks to form a mat, often encrusting young Flat Tree Oysters.

Colonial Anemones

Order Zoanthidia: Usually form mats of interconnecting polyps. Oral disks crowded together, each fringed with a ring of tiny tentacles.

NCRUSTING COLONIAL ANEMONE **Pl. 29**
Palythoa caribaeorum
Forms flat *leathery tan or whitish mat* on rocks or dead coral.

Individuals usually 1.2 cm (½ in.) across. Colony may reach 1 m (39 in.) across, forming an irregular patch on rocks. Many individuals in colony may be retracted into slits, so fringe of tiny tentacles may not be visible in all cases. **Related species:** (1) *P. variabilis* has brown leathery polyps, connected at their bases by tube-like, filamentous stolons; not usually crowded into mats. To 1.4 cm (9/16 in.) across. Sometimes found among mats of Green Colonial Anemone (*Zoanthus*), often buried up to disk in sand. (2) *P. grandiflora* is larger—to 4 cm (1½ in.) wide; its oral disk has white flecks on a blue background.

GREEN COLONIAL ANEMONE *Zoanthus sociatus* **Pl. 29**
Forms *green, mosaiclike mat* on bottom, coral rubble, or in crevices between coral heads. Individuals about 2.5 cm (1 in.) tall, fleshy; *oral disk bright green,* about 1 cm (3/8 in.) wide, surrounded by two adjacent rings of about 30 stubby tentacles. Common on shallow rubble zone of reef crest. **Similar species:** *Z. solanderi* is slightly larger—to 1.2 cm (½ in.) across. Its oral disk has white flecks on a blue background.

DUCHASSAING'S COLONIAL ANEMONE **Fig. 93**
Isaurus duchassaingi and *I. tuberculatus*
Bizarre, elongate polyps that defy classification (even as to plant or animal) when first observed. Only at night are two series of 44–46 short white or brown tentacles extended. During day *clumps of bent, rubbery polyps* are common on wave-washed reef crest and from rocky intertidal zone to deep water. Polyps to 7.5 cm (3 in.) tall and 8 mm (3/10 in.) wide. Brown, tan, gray-green, or yellow, with yellow or white flecks and tubercles on column. Colonies of up to 700 individuals may cover 3 square meters, but usually are in groups of 6–8. These anemones use zooxanthellae (see p. 202) to obtain energy from sunlight, and may live for at least three years without actively seeking food, although they are capable of capturing plankton, especially fish larvae. Nocturnal; by 8 P.M. curved polyps become vertical, expand by about 1 cm (3/8 in.) in height, and extend tentacles.

Tube-dwelling Anemones

Order Ceriantharia: Elongate, wormlike body secretes tube made of nematocysts and sand glued together with mucus. Two sets of tentacles: one short and incurved, around mouth; the other long and tapering (often streaming with currents), originating around edge of oral disk.

BANDED TUBE-DWELLING ANEMONE **Pl. 28**
Arachnanthus nocturnus
Brown tube projects from rubble or sand. Fewer than 100 *brown-and-white banded,* long, streaming marginal tentacles (banding more distinct when tentacles contracted) of several lengths, to

Fig. 93. Duchassaing's Colonial Anemone. *Left:* Individual showing tubercles and white flecks on brown column; *right:* Colony of curved polyps in daytime, tentacles withdrawn.

15 cm (6 in.) or longer. *Inner ring of tentacles* short, incurved. Nocturnal. To 2 cm (¾ in.) across disk.

MERICAN TUBE-DWELLING ANEMONE   **Pls. 2, 28**
Ceriantheopsis americanus
In wrinkled, slippery gray tube, sometimes covered with mud, projecting from sandy bottom. *Outer ring of 100–125 equal-sized tentacles;* usually brown, may be tan, maroon or purple. Inner ring of tan, short, incurved tentacles around mouth. Body elongate, wormlike, to 20 cm (8 in.) long. Usually nocturnal, often in intertidal or shallow subtidal zone. When disturbed, anemone plunges to bottom of 45-cm (18-in.) tube. N. Carolina to Florida, Gulf, Caribbean, W. Indies.

COMB JELLIES

Phylum Ctenophora: Closely related to jellyfishes (p. 207), comb jellies retain a jelly-like mass of acellular mesoglea between their inner and outer skins and look like blobs of transparent jelly. Instead of swimming by contracting a bell, as jellyfishes do, comb jellies use eight rows of ctenes (comblike tufts of microscopic cilia) to propel themselves. Each row of these minute combs is iridescent during day and luminescent at night. Propelled by ctenes, a ctenophore swims through the sea, engulfing plankton with its huge mouth. The comb jellies in one class, Tentaculata, have two tentacles with sticky cells called colloblasts that entrap plankton. The comb jellies in the other class, Nuda, lack tentacles. Once a planktonic animal enters the mouth of a comb jelly it is carried to a blind sac, the gastrovascular cavity, where it is digested. Wandering amoeboid cells carry digested food through a primitive circulatory network of canals throughout the body. Each meridional canal lies under a corresponding row of ctenes. There is no anus.

What makes comb jellies so obvious is their tendency to "bloom." Rarely does one see just a few ctenophores. One week there may be none; the next, thousands seem to have appeared from nowhere. When environmental conditions are right, hundreds of innocuous eggs hatch and rapidly growing comb jellies seem to be everywhere. On summer nights along the Atlantic and Gulf coasts, every stroke of an oar or prop blade produces what appears to be a tumbling row of low-intensity light bulbs, as abundant ctenophores glow in the boat's wake.

Comb jellies are hermaphroditic—both sexes are found in the same animal. Fertilization is external; sperms and eggs are expelled through the mouth and meet outside the body.

BEROE'S COMB JELLY   *Beroe ovata*   Fig. 94
Large—to 11.2 cm (4½ in.) long, usually smaller. Oval, with 8 rows of ciliated combs. Pinkish, brownish, or whitish. *No tentacles.* During day, ciliated rows are iridescent; at night, bioluminescent. Seasonal. Chesapeake Bay to Florida, Gulf, Caribbean.

SEA WALNUTS or LOBATE COMB JELLIES   Fig. 94
Mnemiopsis species
Transparent, body somewhat flattened, with 2 large oral lobes extending beyond huge mouth. Two tiny tentacles, incorporated into *4 ciliated flaps (auricles) surrounding mouth.* A common species is *M. macradyi.* To 10 cm (4 in.) long. N. Carolina to W. Indies, Gulf.

Fig. 94. *Left:* Beroe's Comb Jelly; *right:* Lobate Comb Jelly.

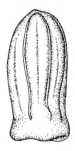
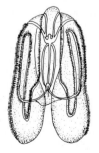

11

Sponges

Sponges, Phylum Porifera, are ancient animals that bridge the gap between colonies of single-celled organisms (protists) and the much more complex jellyfishes. Sponges may be found in a profusion of sizes, shapes, and colors. Some are as big as bathtubs and others have diverse body types ranging from iridescent tubes as long as your arm, to tubs, pillows, or spheres resembling baseballs.

Sponges consist of an outer skin, a central layer of microscopic needle-like or branched spicules, and an inner layer of tubes and chambers lined with special cells called choanocytes, each of which has a hairlike flagellum that beats back and forth, causing currents of water to flow through the sponge. Tiny holes (ostia) in the surface of the sponge allow the water to enter. The flow surges through innumerable channels lined with the choanocytes. A mucus-covered collar on each flagellated cell presents a sticky surface to the flow and traps plankton. These pass into the cell and are digested. Amoeboid cells pick up some food and pass it to the other cells of the body. The water, now devoid of plankton, passes out through larger holes called oscules. These pores are usually clearly visible on the surface of the sponge. There is no excretory system, no circulatory system (except for the wandering amoebocytes), and no respiratory system; indeed, no systems at all. Yet sponges have evolved techniques for survival that allow them to dominate in certain habitats. They will cover pilings in profusion, and deep on coral reefs, at depths which limit life-sustaining light, sponges will reach huge size and great diversity, overpowering the coral itself with their numbers. It has been shown recently that sponges are able to utilize a broader spectrum of food than most filter feeders can; in fact, they often rely heavily on bacteria rather than plankton as their major food source.

Taxonomy: There are four classes of sponges, but only one class, Demospongia, with a skeleton composed of horny proteinaceous fibers, spicules, or both, is likely to be seen in our area.

Most sponges live at depths beyond those covered in this book. However, their distinctive bodies are often strewn on the beach and are thus of interest to us. Those species likely to be found on pilings, in seagrass beds, or washed ashore are covered below.

VARIABLE SPONGE *Anthosigmella varians* **Pl. 25**
Light brown, tan, or greenish, with a smooth velvety surface;

oscular rim paler than rest of sponge. Oscules sometimes *raised in chimney-like or lumpy processes*. Can form patches larger than 20 square meters (215 sq. ft.). Can be massive, amorphous. Rubbery when alive; when dry feels like wood. In lagoons, shallows, and Turtle Grass beds; commonly washed up on shores of Biscayne Bay, Florida. Also in Bahamas and W. Indies.

YELLOW TUBE SPONGE Pl. 25
Aplysina fistularis
Bright yellow, thick-walled tubes, united at bases; to 10 cm (4 in.) tall in shallows, more than 30 cm (1 ft.) tall in deeper water. One form has thin projections, like gnarled fingers, surrounding opening at top. On rocks, coral reefs; Bermuda, Bahamas, Caribbean.

GLOBULAR TUBE SPONGE
Callyspongia fallax form *fallax*
Reddish or bluish purple, short, *globular* tubes, to 15 cm (6 in.) high and 4 cm (1½ in.) wide, united in clusters. In Turtle Grass beds, shallow pools in sand flats, and lagoons; Bahamas, Caribbean.

CHICKEN LIVER SPONGE *Chondrilla nucula* Pl. 25
Thin — to 3 mm (⅛ in.) thick — brown crust on bare sand in Turtle Grass beds or on pilings, rocks, or dead coral. Smooth, slippery *surface resembles fresh liver*. Oscules to 3 mm (⅛ in.) wide, dark; conspicuous only in undisturbed specimens. In lagoons and shallows; s. Florida, W. Indies to Brazil.

YELLOW BORING SPONGE or SULFUR SPONGE Pl. 5
Cliona celata
In life, bright yellow with *pimple-like yellow pores,* brown overtones, hard, not spongy. When washed up on beach and dry, turns woody, brown with dots surrounded by faint circles. Begins life when larva lands on rocks or shells; soon overgrows shell and appears as lumpy mound, sometimes as large as a man's head. Can kill oysters, clams, by *riddling shell with holes* (see Fig. 33). Subtidal; Canada to Gulf.

CRUMB-OF-BREAD SPONGE or BOWERBANK'S Pl. 5
HALICHONDRIA *Halichondria bowerbanki*
Yellow, olive, or beige; irregular, with gnarled, *fingerlike, low branches* projecting from crust. Oscules on tiny conical projections. On pilings, seagrass, and rocks in lower intertidal or subtidal zone; Maine to Gulf. **Similar species: Loosanoff's Haliclona** (*Haliclona loosanoffi*) also forms tan crusts, but with oscules on chimney to 2.5 cm (1 in.) high. Individual sponges to 7.5 cm (3 in.) across, but commonly fuse to form large mats. Under rocks or on seagrass; Cape Cod to Gulf. Mixed colonies of both sponges common on pilings; differentiation difficult without microscope.

RED FINGER SPONGE *Amphimedon compressa* Pl. 25
Brick red, firmly spongy, *erect column* or columns to 45 cm (18 in.) high. *No opening on top,* but conspicuous oscules (to 5 mm — ¼ in.

wide) are scattered over surface or in rows. Turtle Grass beds; s. Florida, Bahamas, Caribbean. Similar species: **Blue-green Finger Sponge** (*A. viridis*, Pl. 25) is green, with shades of blue, brown, or gray. May form an undulating mass, like a cockscomb.

PILLOW STINKING SPONGE   *Ircinia strobilina*   **Pl. 25**
Gray; shaped like a pillow or cake. Covered with *large pointed warts* to 8 mm (⁵⁄₁₆ in.) high. If sponge is cake-shaped, *oscules are scattered over flat top*, not clustered in center. If pillow-shaped, oscules lined up along top edge of pillow. This sponge emits a terrible odor if removed from water. **Similar species: Stinking Vase Sponge** (*I. campana*, Pl. 25) is brown or reddish brown, forming a broad *vase* to 60 cm (2 ft.) high, with oscules inside a central depression. In lagoons, Turtle Grass beds; Bahamas, Caribbean to Brazil.

GARLIC SPONGE   *Lissodendoryx isodictyalis*   **Pl. 5**
Dull yellowish, tan, or green-gray; amorphous, irregular, sometimes rounded. Spongy; when squeezed under water it emits green-gray exudate. Surface usually *smooth, with conspicuous oscules* to 1.5 cm (⁵⁄₈ in.) wide. On pilings or seagrass, where it surrounds each blade, often growing to fist-size. *When broken, this sponge emits a strong odor of garlic.* Subtidal; Cape Cod to Florida and Gulf to W. Indies, Bahamas.

RED BEARD SPONGE   *Microciona prolifera*   **Pl. 5**
Bright red or orange, branching colonies to 20 cm (8 in.) high, growing from a crust on rocks or seashells. Dried specimens on beach are often brown, but distinctive, knobby, multibranched form makes identification easy. Ostia and oscules inconspicuous. Rarely in lower intertidal, primarily in shallow subtidal zone; Canada to Florida and Gulf to Texas.

BLACK CHIMNEY SPONGE   *Pellina carbonaria*
Dark green, but looks black. May be buried in sand. Forms crust from which *long* (to 5 cm — 2 in.) *chimneys* arise. Skin easily detached. In sandy shallows in lagoons; s. Florida, Caribbean.

COMMON LOGGERHEAD SPONGE   **Pl. 25**
Spheciospongia vesparium
Large—to 1 m (39 in.) across. Black or gray, barrel- or cake-shaped; top, flattened, with a *cluster of large black holes in center*. Rubbery, not spongy. Clearly visible clusters of pores in sides; surface lumpy but never cone-shaped. In Turtle Grass beds and shallows (sometimes huge specimens awash); s. Florida, Bahamas, Caribbean to Brazil.

FIRE SPONGE   *Tedania ignis*   **Pl. 25**
Orange or red crust to 1 cm (³⁄₈ in.) thick, or amorphous, spherical masses. Oscules (to 1 cm wide) on cones about 1 cm high, are conspicuous only in undisturbed specimens. Thin, delicate, translucent (sometimes whitish) skin. *Causes rash and burning sensation when touched.* On rocks, dead coral, and Red Mangrove roots; s. Florida, Bahamas, Caribbean to Brazil.

12

Snails, Clams, Squids, Octopods, and Chitons

What could differ more than a clam and a squid? A clam lies inert in its half-shell, its soft body unmoving, uncomplaining, even as it slides down your throat as an hors d'oeuvre. The squid darts through the water so rapidly that it can capture small fishes. Its eyes, near in function and acuity to man's, look out on the undersea world backed by an I.Q. high on the scale of invertebrate intelligence. It invented jet propulsion long before man even appeared on the earth.

The great diversity of Phylum Mollusca (there are 88,000 species) is matched by numbers of individuals which often dominate a habitat. Huge populations of clams can exist on a sand flat with no evidence on the surface except for a few discarded shells. Rocky beaches may be covered with thousands of snails, each species confined to a particular zone, from water's edge to the heights of towering cliffs. No member of one species stays long in a zone dominated by another species. It is as if some invisible barrier has been established.

The lowly chiton lives in a region of great turbulence. Huge waves surge over the algae-covered rocks that it inhabits. The chiton presents its armor-plated back to the sea and defies it, inching its way across a boulder, scraping the algae from the surface, oblivious to wave and current.

The octopus broods its young, hardly eating for more than a month, until, in a cloud of tiny massed tentacles, the infants leave the parental cave, ready for independence. Their adult lives will be dedicated to the pursuit of crabs, their main food (see Pl. 46).

Taxonomy: There are six classes in Phylum Mollusca:

1. Snails, limpets, nudibranchs, and sea slugs (Fig. 95): Class Gastropoda. Most gastropods move along the bottom on a flat foot, usually protected by a spiral or domed shell carried on the back. True nudibranchs have lost the shell completely, but close relatives (sea hares) have a vestigial shell in a small mantle cavity on the back.

2. Clams, oysters, and mussels (Fig. 96): Class Pelecypoda (also known as Lamellibranchia and Bivalvia). This group contains animals with soft bodies enclosed in two shells, or valves.

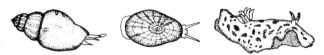

Fig. 95. Gastropods: Snail, limpet, and sea slug.

3. Chitons (Fig. 97): Class Amphineura. Members of this group have a flattened, domed body with a broad foot applied to the surface of rocks. The back is covered with eight jointed plates that form a flexible, armored exterior surrounded by a scaly or bristly girdle.

4. Tusk shells (Fig. 98): Class Scaphopoda. This group is characterized by a soft body inside a shell resembling a miniature elephant's tusk. These animals live buried in the sand and feed by removing detritus with sticky, threadlike tentacles.

5. Octopods and squids (Fig. 99): Class Cephalopoda. This group includes those mollusks that have tentacles extending from the head. Octopods have eight tentacles and squids have ten.

6. Monoplacophorans: Class Monoplacophora. This group was recently discovered. It consists of rare deepwater species available to us only in museums.

Why do we place these very different animals in the same phylum? Three features reveal their common ancestry:

1. All mollusks have a mass of tissue, the mantle, which surrounds the viscera (internal organs).

2. The mantle secretes a shell. The shell may enclose the body or it may be enclosed within the body, as in the case of the relatively inconsequential penlike shell of a squid. With the exception of some nudibranchs and octopods, there is some sign of a shell in or around every mollusk.

3. All mollusks have a foot—a muscular organ usually used for propulsion. The foot can be easily recognized in a snail or a clam but has been employed for different purposes as the phylum has become diversified, and it is sometimes unrecognizable.

Octopods and squids are cephalopods or "head-footed" animals. Their tentacles extend from the head like an Indian's headdress. Each tentacle is soft and muscular. The ventral surface is covered

Fig. 96. Bivalves: clam, oyster, and mussel.

Fig. 97. Chiton.

Fig. 98. Tusk shell.

with round suction cups that are so effective that you might tear off a tentacle before you are able to dislodge an octopus under a rock.

Snails are gastropods, or "stomach-footed" animals. They secrete slime from glands on the bottom of the foot and slide along on this slippery layer in rhythmic undulations.

If left alone in an aquarium, a tightly closed clam will open its valves (shells) after a few moments. Soon the fleshy pointed foot extends from inside to probe the bottom daintily. When a soft spot is found the foot squirms downward, pointed end first, becoming longer and longer. Normally a hatchet-shaped appendage at the edge of the soft body, the foot becomes engorged with blood and expands to many times its original size. Buried deep in the sediment, its tip becomes flattened like an anchor. Finally, with a massive contraction of the muscles (already stretched taut like rubber bands by the pressure of the blood) the foot contracts, pulling the clam upright. Several repetitions of this sequence drag the clam beneath the sand (see Pl. 1).

Most marine mollusks have gills that must be bathed in seawater. A snail that lives on shore traps water inside its shell to facilitate the exchange of oxygen and carbon dioxide. Its metabolism becomes so slow that it approaches a deathlike state for the duration of its isolation from the water. When high tide reaches it or when the cool, humid night air has replaced the burning sun, the snail extends itself and comes back to life. Snails whose lives are fully aquatic use a single gill located behind the head. Some terrestrial snails have evolved lunglike chambers and breathe through a hole, forsaking gills completely (see p. 47).

Mollusks have a three-layered shell. The inner layer, close to the soft body, is the smooth, iridescent, nacreous layer. Nacre

Fig. 99. Cephalods: squid, octopus.

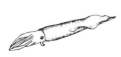

(mother-of-pearl) lines the shell and neutralizes any irritants (sand grains or tiny attacking animals) by coating them. When enough layers build up, eventually a pearl forms. Many mollusks, even mussels, can make pearls. The middle layer of the shell, the prismatic layer, is thick and calcareous. The thin outer layer, the periostracum, is soft and either fibrous or horny. The Mossy Ark shell (Pl. 43), is so called because of its well-developed hairy outer layer. Most shells appear brownish because of this outer covering.

Modes of reproduction in mollusks are almost as diverse as the phylum itself. Fertilization is internal in snails, but many species are hermaphrodites, each individual containing both sexes. When two snails copulate, each inserts a penis into the other's genital opening and cross-fertilization occurs. Many marine snails, however, have separate sexes. In more sedentary mollusks, such as clams and chitons, the male simply casts millions of sperm into the water. There is a statistical certainty that many will be sucked into the genital chamber of the female, where fertilization will occur.

A five-year-old oyster produces millions of eggs, which hatch into the typically motile mollusk larva, the microscopic veliger, with a bilobed, winglike collar called a velum. The ciliated velum enables the larva to swim feebly. Often it is swept by currents over rock or reef where young fishes, worms, coral polyps, and hungry planktonic animals lie in wait to devour it. After a few days of planktonic (free floating) existence, the veliger is carried far from its parent. It sheds the velum and, now a miniature adult, sinks to the bottom.

Octopods and squids, among the most sophisticated of invertebrates, have separate sexes. Many forms have elaborate courtship rituals. Most octopods give excellent postnatal care. Squids produce tough, transparent, whitish egg sacs that are draped over rocks and seaweed (see Pl. 46). Inside the sacs, the young go through their larval development, and eventually emerge as fully formed miniatures of the adult.

Snails, Limpets, Nudibranchs, and Sea Slugs

Many snails are herbivorous (plant eating). They spend their lives scraping algae from rocks with a rasplike radula or tongue (Fig. 100) composed of hundreds of tiny teeth. The carnivorous species have evolved a host of mechanisms for attacking their prey, and the radula is highly modified. The Tulip Snail (Pl. 45) is a fierce predator that even attacks others of its own kind. It inserts its proboscis into the aperture of another snail and rasps away the horny operculum, eventually reaching the soft tissues.

Fig. 100. Radula of snail (greatly enlarged).

By the time the Tulip Snail has devoured its prey, not a shred of tissue is left. Other snails, such as oyster drills, use a chemical secretion and the radula to drill patiently through the shells of barnacles, clams, oysters, and other mollusks until the radula reaches the internal tissue, which is then scraped into the drill's mouth. A round hole in a clam's shell is the telltale sign that it was prey to a drill.

The most bizarre modification of the radula occurs in the carnivorous cone snails. These species have developed a radula that is modified into a poison-tipped dart. The dartlike radula is thrust into the prey (worms, snails, and even fishes), which is paralyzed and swallowed whole. Cones that feed on more active prey, such as fishes, produce a more virulent, fast-acting poison, which (in Pacific species) can kill a man.

Snails that are being overharvested and need to be carefully conserved are the helmet snails of the genus *Cassis,* the conchs of the genus *Strombus,* and the Florida Horse Conch (Pl. 50, Fig. 101). All are large (to 60 cm — 2 ft. — long in the case of the Horse Conch) and all are used for food. Huge mounds of Queen Conch shells are typically found on many Caribbean harborsides, where commercial fishermen pile them after extracting the meat for conch stew and conch fritters (Fig. 101). The situation has become so serious that several conch mariculture facilities have been established. Conchs are vegetarians, but helmet snails are carnivores that eat sea urchins, especially the Long-spined Black Urchin (Fig. 61). It is conceivable that souvenir hunters might so deplete stocks of helmet snails that populations of spiny urchins would correspondingly increase, making swimming and wading hazardous.

One of the most beautiful snails, the Violet Snail (Pl. 50), floats on a cushion of mucus-coated bubbles. When it finds a jellyfish,

Fig. 101. *Left:* The largest Caribbean snail, the Florida Horse Conch (p. 238). Note vertical slot made by a fisherman's screwdriver. One cut at this point frees snail from shell. *Right:* One of 3 huge mounds of conch shells left by fishermen along shores of the Lac, Bonaire.

such as a Portuguese Man-of-war, the snail floats along with it, nibbling away until its prey is no more. This snail floats through life on its bubbles, virtually never touching bottom. Even its eggs are laid in bubbles.

In about 1600 B.C. someone, probably a Phoenician living along the eastern Mediterranean coast, accidentally crushed a *Thais* snail and found his hands stained violet. Soon a commercial process for extracting the dye was developed. The people of the city of Tyre crushed the *Thais* snails to obtain a rich maroon dye and mixed it with the dark violet secretion from Murex snails to produce the favored "royal purple." These snails (now classified in other genera) release a colorless liquid that, when exposed to light, changes from yellow to green to blue and finally to purple. "Wearing of the purple" was declared a royal privilege, to be paid for handsomely. The ancient Phoenicians cornered the market and their Tyrian purple was the keystone of a vast trading empire. In the Caribbean the Indians independently discovered the purple dye. They drew a thread across the mouth of a *Thais* or Murex snail, or, more often, the Wide-mouthed Rock Snail, (*Purpura patula,* Pl. 15). If you hold this snail, you will find your hands blotched with purple and smelling faintly of garlic.

Snails

Photographs of more than 80 of the commonest species appear on Plates 38, 39, and 50. Measurements given are for the distance between the tip of the shell spire and the bottom of the aperture.

For limpets, the measurements are for the length of the shell on its longest axis. Unless otherwise specified, all species are to be found in the Caribbean and s. Florida.

GREEDY DOVE SNAIL *Anachis avara* **Fig. 32**
Tiny—to 1 cm (⅜ in.) high. Shell brownish yellow; thick, with 6–7 whorls. Vertical ridges on all whorls except body whorl. New Jersey to Florida, Gulf.

IMBRICATED STAR SNAIL *Astraea tecta* **Pl. 38**
To 4 cm (1½ in.) tall. Shell whitish or greenish brown; pyramid-shaped, without distinct whorls. No spines. **Similar species:** (1) **Green Star Snail** (*A. tuber*), to 5 cm (2 in.) high, is green and white, mottled with brown; it has distinct whorls and ridges rather than spines. (2) **Carved Star Snail** (*A. caelata,* Pl. 38), to 5.7 cm (2½ in.) tall. Shell dirty white or greenish, mottled with brown; pyramid-shaped, with strong oblique and revolving ribs. Operculum oval, white, finely pimpled. (3) **Long-spined Star Snail** (*A. phoebia,* Pl. 43), to 5 cm (2 in.), is whitish with *long spines;* inside of aperture silvery pearl. Shell flattened.

BLACK HORN SNAIL *Batillaria minima* **Pl. 39**
To 1.2 cm (½ in.) long. Shell elongate, with a sharp apex; network of vertical ribs and horizontal ridges gives appearance of square depressions covering surface. Aperture oval, angled, with notch in upper corner. Black, deep brown, or banded with brown on cream. Common in tidepools and shallows; s. Florida, Caribbean.

VARIABLE BITTIUM *Bittium varium* **Fig. 29**
Tiny—to 1 cm (⅜ in.) long. Shell bluish black or reddish; elongate, with rounded whorls covered with parallel rows of beads. Aperture rounded, *wall translucent;* body wall may have thick rib. Seagrass beds, sandy flats, subtidal; often in great numbers. Maryland to Texas.

HALF-SMOOTH ODOSTOME *Boonea seminuda* **Fig. 29**
Tiny—to 4 mm (1/16 in.) long. Shell white, elongate, covered with *rows of spiral beads.* Aperture oval, lip thin. Parasitic snail inserts long proboscis into mantle of common Slipper Snail, Bay Scallop, or Periwinkle, sucking contents of host. Just below high-tide line; Canada to Texas. **Related species:** (1) **Incised Odostome** (*B. impressa*), to 8 mm (⅛ in.) long. White; elongate, with 6–7 flat whorls and 3 equally spaced spiral grooves. (2) **Two-sutured Odostome** (*B. bisuturalis*) has 2 oblique folds on columella (Fig. 24).

STRIATED BUBBLE *Bulla striata* **Pl. 38**
2–4 cm (¾–1½ in.) long. Light brown with darker spots. Smooth or spirally grooved at base.

KNOBBED WHELK *Busycon carica* **Pl. 45**
Large—to 30 cm (1 ft.) long. Shell gray, with distinct *knobs on ridge of body whorl.* Spire low, with a series of low knobs on edge of each whorl. Shell of live animal covered with *yellowish, bristly periostracum.* Large, disklike egg capsules (see Fig. 15). Body

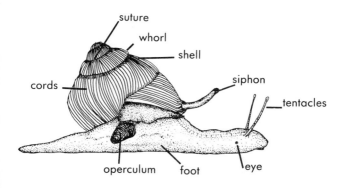

Fig. 102. Anatomy of a snail.

black. Massachusetts to Florida. **Similar species:** (1) **Channeled Whelk** (*B. canaliculatum*) has deep, *squarish channels at sutures.* Uncommon south of Cape Hatteras. (2) See **Lightning Whelk** and (3) **Perverse Whelk** (below).

LIGHTNING WHELK *Busycon contrarium* **Pls. 42, 47**
Large—to 40.6 cm (16 in.) long; small shells have brown vertical streaks on a tan background, large ones become gray. Spire moderately elevated; shell of live animal is covered with gray periostracum bearing minute hairs. Similar to Knobbed Whelk except shell *twisted to left.* Lower intertidal and subtidal on sand; N. Carolina to Florida and Texas. **Related species:** (1) **Perverse Whelk** (*Busycon perversum*) is smaller than Knobbed Whelk—to 20 cm (8 in.) long—with distinct pointed knobs on ridge of body whorl, but is easily differentiated because shell usually is *twisted to left.* However, it sometimes twists to right. In this case, best identifying feature is *swollen wall of columella* projecting into aperture about ⅓ distance from bottom. N. Carolina to Florida. (2) **Fig or Pear Whelk** (*Busycon spiratum*, Pl. 42), to 14 cm (5½ in.) long. Shell thin; *body whorl comprises almost all of shell. Spire flattened;* no knobs. Body whorl has deep channel at suture. Whitish with wavy, reddish brown vertical streaks. N. Carolina to Florida.

SCULPTURED TOP SNAIL *Calliostoma euglyptum*
To 1.6 cm (⅝ in.) high, bottom to 2.5 cm (1 in.) wide; width of bottom exceeds height. Pale yellow or pink, *tip of spire darker.* Each spire whorl with 6 beaded spiral cords; base almost flat, *aperture pearly.* Under rocks at low tide; N. Carolina to Texas, Mexico.

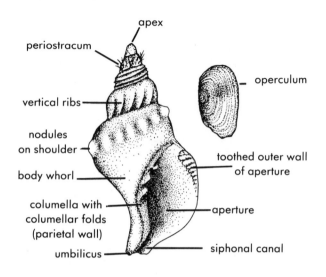

Fig. 103. Parts of a snail shell.

KING HELMET *Cassis tuberosa* **Pl. 50**

Huge—to 22.8 cm (9 in.); heavy, solid. Outside of shell sand colored, tan. *Glossy area around columella triangular,* blotched with dark brown, contrasting with white ridges. Large ridges on inner lip separated by brown markings or streak. **Similar species:** (1) **Emperor Helmet** (*C. madagascariensis*, Pl. 50) is also huge—to 22.8 cm (9 in.); a subspecies reaches 35.5 cm (14 in.). *Glossy area around columella often salmon pink, rounded.* Outer lip has about 10 large teeth edged with dark brown. Outside of shell tan. (2) **Flame Helmet** (*C. flammea*), to 15 cm (6 in.) high. Spire small. *No brown markings between teeth on outer lip.* Glossy area around columella round. Rows of blunt tubercles on body whorl, separated by beaded horizontal lines. Outside of shell *glossy orange-brown.* Not in Florida; found in Bahamas, W. Indies.

COSTATE HORN SNAIL *Cerithidea costata*

Small—to 1.6 cm (⅝ in.) long. Slender, *elongate;* brown with whitish, vertical, crescent-shaped ribs. *Ribs end at bottom of body whorl,* at a spiral cord sharply marking base of shell. **Related species:** (1) **Ladder Horn Snail** (*C. scalariformis*), to 3.2 cm (1¼ in.). Reddish brown, *rounded whorls with distinct sutures.* Grayish ribs; thin brown band around middle of each whorl. Aperture of *C. costata* has sharp edge; that of *C. scalariformis* has flared lip. Both species in upper intertidal zone; S. Carolina, Florida, W. Indies. (2) **Plicate Horn Snail** (*C. pliculosa*), the *only species in Gulf*, ranges from Alabama to Texas, Cen. America, W. Indies. Similar to above but with several distinct, *large yellowish ribs.*

TOCKY CERITH *Cerithium litteratum* **Fig. 41, Pl. 38**
To 2.5 cm (1 in.) long. Whitish, with *brown markings in rows* (like print). Shoulder below each suture has 9–12 sharp nodules. **Related species:** (1) **Ivory Cerith** (*C. eburneum*) is narrower, *lacks sharp nodules.* White or speckled with brown; each whorl has 4–6 rows of 18–22 small rounded beads. (2) **Middle-spined Cerith** (*C. algicola*, Pl. 38) is more elongate than *C. litteratum;* white or yellowish, blotched with brown.

EST INDIAN TOP SNAIL or MAGPIE **Pl. 38**
Cittarium pica
To 10 cm (4 in.) long. Globose, *heavy shell* with *strong black zigzag markings* on whitish background. Aperture round, shell *pearly inside;* umbilicus wide and deep. On rocks just below water's surface. Commonly eaten in "whelk stew."

RUMPET SNAIL or WEST INDIAN TRITON **Pl. 45**
Charonia variegata
Huge—to 38 cm (15 in.) high. Elongate shell, with 8 or 9 whorls. Tan with brown, purple, or red, *crescent-shaped blotches.* Inner lip reflected outward; brown, with white ridges. Outer lip with brown and white squares. Aperture pale orange.

OMMON DOVE SNAIL *Columbella mercatoria* **Pl. 39**
To 2.2 cm (⅞ in.) tall; usually smaller. Tall, pointed spire and triangular body whorl. *Outer wall of aperture thick, toothed;* often with sand grains in *narrow aperture.* Low horizontal cords on shell; color variable—orange, usually brown mottled with cream, or tan.

OMMON SLIPPER SNAIL **Fig. 28, Pl. 42**
Crepidula fornicata
To 3.8 cm (1½ in.) long. Shell oval, inflated, loaf-shaped; tan with purplish marks. Apex turned to side. *Shelf on underside* contains internal organs. Broad, fleshy foot. Found attached to rocks, often in mounds, with oldest (female) on bottom, youngest (male) on top (Fig. 28). Filter feeders. Canada to Gulf. **Related species:** (1) **Flat Slipper Snail** (*C. plana*) is smaller—to 2.5 cm (1 in. long). *White, flat;* found inside apertures of whelk and Moon Snail shells. (2) **Convex Slipper Snail** (*C. convexa*) is even smaller—to 1.2 cm (½ in.) long and more convex; *apex centered.* All three species have shelf on underside and similar ranges, but *C. convexa* ranges southward to W. Indies.

TLANTIC HAIRY TRITON *Cymatium pileare* **Pl. 38**
To 10.2 cm (4 in.) tall. Yellow-ocher to brown. Shell heavy, with thick, reflected lips. Inner lip brown, ridged with white; outer lip

ocher, with *pairs of ridge-like teeth.* Shells of living specimens covered with *hairy periostracum*—hairs in vertical rows.

FLAMINGO TONGUE *Cyphoma gibbosum* **Fig. 1, Pls. 38, 50**
To 2.5 cm (1 in.) long. Living animal found on sea fans and other soft corals. Shell of living snail hidden by fleshy mantle covered with *black, leopard-like spots* (Fig. 1). Shell elongate; white, lavender, or pink, with a slitlike aperture and a *transverse hump halfway along its length.*

BABY BONNET *Cypraecassis testiculus* **Pl. 50**
To 7.6 cm (3 in.) high. Globose shell, with a short spire; outer surface finely ribbed. Gray or orange, with brown streaks, blotches, and horizontal bars. Outer lip with distinct, dark brown, paired bars. Inner margins of columella and *lip with numerous white ridges.*

BULLA MELAMPUS *Detracia bullaoides* **Pl. 39**
To 1 cm (⅜ in.) long. Shell *brown,* with *encircling gray lines.* 5–6 whorls; *apex blunt. Columella with a deep fold.*

FALSE PRICKLY WINKLE *Echininus nodulosus*
To 2.5 cm (1 in.) long. Brownish gray, with spiral rows of *sharp nodules.* **Similar species: Common Prickly Winkle** (*Nodilittorina tuberculata,* Pls. 12, 38). Often smaller; has portion of columella flattened, shelf-like; *tubercles less sharp.*

BROWN-BANDED WENTLETRAP **Pl. 42**
Epitoneum rupicola
To 2.5 cm (1 in.) long. *Pinkish or yellowish white,* often with 1–2 brownish bands. *Sharp vertical ridges* run length of shell; 10 rounded whorls. Sandy intertidal, subtidal; eats small anemones. **Similar species:** (1) **Angled Wentletrap** (*E. angulatum*) is white; it has only 6 whorls. (2) **Humphrey's Wentletrap** (*E. humphreysi*) is white and has 8–9 whorls and *thick round ridges.* (3) **Tollin's Wentletrap** (*E. tollini,* Fig. 12) has 8–10 rounded whorls; pure white shell. To 1.2 cm (½ in.) tall. Gulf. First 3 species Massachusetts to Texas; many others in our area.

TULIP SNAIL *Fasciolaria tulipa* **Pl. 45**
To 23 cm (9 in.) long. Shell smooth; reddish brown to gray, with dark brown, *broken spiral lines.* Body red when alive. In Turtle Grass beds. **Similar species: Banded Tulip Snails** (*F. lilium, F. hunteria,* Pl. 38) have brown spiral lines but they are more distinct and *unbroken. F. tulipa* and *F. hunteria* range from N. Carolina to Gulf; *F. tulipa* extends to Caribbean. *F. lilium* ranges from Florida and Gulf to Yucatan.

MUD SNAIL *Ilyanassa obsoleta* **Pls. 42, 45**
To 2.5 cm (1 in.) long. *Dull black* shell; *apex often eroded. Aperture oval;* purple with glazed inner lip. Lightly incised squares cover shell. Body gray. Active, fast-moving snails extend siphon, which resembles an elephant's trunk; they gather quickly in mounds on carrion (see Pl. 44). This snail is host of at least 5 larval parasitic flatworms (flukes); its shell is used by the Long-clawed Hermit

Crab. Abundant in intertidal and shallow subtidal zone; Cape Cod to Gulf of Mexico. **Similar species:** (1) **Mottled Dog Whelk** (*Nassarius vibex*) is smaller—to 1.9 cm (¾ in.) long—and more oval, with *distinct ribs* on each whorl. Gray; may have red-brown bands. Aperture oval, with *pale, flaring lips;* outer lip toothed. N. Carolina to Florida, Gulf Coast to Mexico. (2) **New England Dog Whelk** (*N. trivittatus*, Pl. 42). *Yellowish or tan,* sometimes with 3 reddish bands on body whorl. *Whorls strongly stepped, beaded. Round projection at upper end of columellar wall.* Body white with pale violet spots. To 2.2 cm (⅞ in.) long. Canada to ne. Florida. (3) **Variable Nassa** (*N. albus,* Pl. 39). To 1.2 cm (½ in.) tall. *White or yellowish* with *brown spots or bands.* Strong axial ribs crossed by spiral cords. *Outer lip toothed; ridged within.* N. Carolina to W. Indies.

MANGROVE PERIWINKLE   Pl. 22
Littorina angulifera
Larger than most periwinkles—to 3 cm (1⅕ in.) long. Yellowish to brown, with dark brown markings; central part of *columella pale purplish.* On prop roots of Red Mangroves, above water line. **Related species: Cloudy Periwinkle** (*L. nebulosa*) is gray, without markings. S. Caribbean.

MARSH PERIWINKLE   *Littorina irrorata*   Pl. 21
To 3.2 cm (1¼ in.) long. Globose; grayish white with thin radial lines. *Callus of inner lip brown.* On cordgrass leaves when tide is high; crawls on mud, eating detritus, during low tide. The common periwinkle of marshes from New York to Florida and Gulf Coast to Texas (except s. Florida, where it is replaced by *L. angulifera*).

ZEBRA PERIWINKLE   *Littorina ziczac*   Pls. 12, 39
To 2.5 cm (1 in.) long. Gray or white, with *zigzag dark lines.* Columella usually dark brown. Above water line on rocks. This snail exhibits such wide physical and ecological variations that it has been divided into as many as 7 species. Most experts accept 3: *L. lineata,* found highest above the water, as much as 4.5 m (almost 15 ft.) above mean low water; smallest and darkest of the 3 species. *L. lineolata,* rarely found more than 2.4 m (almost 8 ft.) above mean low water, has *tan or lavender columella. L. ziczac* (Pl. 38) is largest and lives lowest on rocks, usually within 1 m (39 in.) of water line. Florida's east coast, Texas, Bermuda, W. Indies, Caribbean to Uruguay.

MARSH or GRAY HYDROBIID SNAIL   Fig. 23
Littoridinops palustris
Tiny—to 4.5 mm (⅕ in.) long, elongate. Shell smooth, *translucent;* gray or tan. Abundant on wet mud in tidal marshes (to 10,000 per square meter). Eaten by birds, killifishes, crabs. Gulf of Mexico. **Similar species:** Many; *L. monroensis* lives in Gulf tidal ponds, *L. tenuipes* in marshes on southern Atlantic Coast.

COMMON ATLANTIC MARGINELLA   Pl. 39
Prunum apicinum

To 1 cm (⅜ in.) long. *Shiny yellow to orange-brown;* solid with 3–4 whorls near apex. Outer lip thick; *inner lip with 4 pleats.*

EASTERN MELAMPUS or DUCK SNAIL   Pl. 42
Melampus bidentatus

Small—to 2 cm (¾ in.) long, usually smaller. *Brown,* sometimes banded, delicate shell. Many *sharp white ridges inside outer wall* of aperture. Spire conical; *aperture long—occupies ¾ of length of shell.* On mud of salt marshes and mangrove swamps, upper intertidal zone. A pulmonate (air-breathing snail), so it must climb grass blades to avoid drowning. Present in huge numbers on mud of marshes; important duck food. Canada to Texas, Bermuda, W. Indies.

COFFEE-BEAN SNAIL   *Melampus coffeus*   Pl. 22
Small—to 1 cm (⅜ in.) high. Shell brown, with *3 white horizontal bands.* Aperture long with sharp edge, wrinkled inside; *inner lip with 2 white folds.* Intertidal, primarily in litter under Red Mangroves; Florida to W. Indies.

FLORIDA CROWN CONCH   Figs. 33, 83
Melongena corona

To 20.3 cm (8 in.) high. Large body whorl with *sharp, curved, vertical white spines on shoulder of each whorl.* Brown with white spiral bands; shell glossy. Columella white. Among roots of Red Mangroves and on oyster beds; Florida and e. Alabama. **Similar species: West Indian Crown Conch** (*M. melongena*) has a brown or gray shell with yellow or white bands. Large body whorl with pointed spines on shoulder and sometimes about halfway between shoulder and base. Columella thick, reflected. Often on Red Mangrove roots; W. Indies to S. America.

LUNAR DOVE SNAIL   *Mitrella lunata*
Tiny—to 5 mm (⅕ in.) long. Shell glossy; yellowish tan or white, with *brown, crescent-shaped markings.* Six whorls; outer lip of aperture has 4 small teeth. Eelgrass and Turtle Grass beds; Massachusetts to Florida and Texas to Brazil; W. Indies.

WHITE-SPOTTED DOVE SNAIL   *Mitrella ocellata*   Pl. 39
To 1 cm (⅜ in.) long. Smooth; tan to dark brown with white spots. *Aperture long, narrow. Outer lip notched and toothed within aperture.* Under rocks. **Related species: Glossy Dove Snail** (*Nitidella nitida*) is *glossy white* with yellow or tan markings. Aperture long; outer *lip with 7 white teeth.* On rocks.

ATLANTIC MODULUS   *Modulus modulus*   Pl. 39
To 1 cm (⅜ in.) long. Shell white, flecked with brown. Spire low; 3 or 4 whorls; largest is body whorl, which has a *sloping shoulder* and a *keeled edge. Aperture round.*

APPLE MUREX   *Chicoreus pomum*   Pls. 47, 50
To 11.5 cm (4½ in.) tall. Shell thick, rough; cream, tan, or brown. Interior of aperture glossy tan, yellow, or orange. Usually with *brown spots on upper columella wall.* Turtle Grass beds. This snail

was formerly classifed in genus *Murex*. **Related species:** (1) **West Indian Murex** (*C. brevifrons*) is larger—to 15 cm (6 in.) long—with *long spines*. Often on Red Mangrove roots. (2) **Giant Eastern Murex** (*Hexaplex fulvescens*, Pl. 42) is large—to 17.8 cm (7 in.) tall; shell white, yellowish brown, or gray. Each whorl has 7–9 vertical ridges, each bearing a *pointed, hollow spine*. Aperture white. *Lower canal long*. N. Carolina to Texas; common in Gulf.

COLORFUL MOON SNAIL   *Natica canrena*   **Pls. 38, 50**
To 6.4 cm (2½ in.) long. Shell has eight *brown spiral bands* intersected by *darker brown zigzag lines or blotches*. Operculum hard, white, with about *10 spiral grooves*. (Most of color has faded in worn shells, a common occurrence—see Pl. 37.) Sandy beaches. **Similar species: Atlantic** or **Southern Miniature Moon Snail** (*N. pusilla*) is tiny—to 6 mm (¼ in.) high. Shell white or gray, with faint brown bands. Brown callus in umbilicus. Sandy intertidal or subtidal zone; Massachusetts to Brazil, W. Indies.

BLEEDING-TOOTH NERITE   **Fig. 45; Pls. 12, 39**
Nerita peloronta
The largest nerite—to 3 cm (1⅕ in.). Shell yellowish, with red and black zigzag markings. Inner edge of *aperture stained reddish around 2–3 prominent white teeth*. Intertidal on rocks; higher above water line than any other nerite.

CHECKERED NERITE   *Nerita tessellata*   **Pls. 13, 39**
To 2 cm (¾ in.) long. Shell usually black or checkered black and white. *Toothless*, or with 2 tiny teeth in center. Near water line.

FOUR-TOOTHED NERITE   *Nerita versicolor*   **Pls. 12, 13**
To 2.5 cm (1 in.) long. Similar to *N. peloronta,* but lacks "bleeding" tooth. *Four strong teeth*. On rocks, just below level of *N. peloronta*. Shell corded; black and white with red markings.

VIRGIN NERITE   *Neritina virginea*   **Pl. 42**
To 2 cm (¾ in.) high. *Color variable,* with white spots and streaks, on a black, purple, or red background. Tiny irregular teeth on yellow or white inner wall of aperture. In brackish water, mangrove swamps, mouths of streams; Florida and W. Indies to Brazil. **Similar species: Olive Nerite** (*N. reclivata*) is small—to 1.3 cm (½ in.) long. Shell smooth, shiny; greenish to olive-colored, usually with fine black lines. *Aperture toothless;* operculum black. Brackish water; on grass in marshes and in shallow, low-salinity bays on mud or underwater plants; also in tidepools. Florida to Texas and Brazil, W. Indies.

NETTED OLIVE   *Oliva reticularis*   **Pl. 38**
Glossy white shell with *wavy brown lines; aperture white*. To 4.5 cm (1¾ in.) long. S. Florida and W. Indies. **Similar species:** (1) **Caribbean Olive** (*O. caribaensis*) has *purple aperture.* (2) **Lettered Olive** (*O. sayana*, Pl. 42) has *reddish brown zigzag markings;* 2 broad spiral bands on body whorl. Inner wall of aperture with *4 strong, slanting ridges*. To 7 cm (2¾ in.) tall. N. Carolina to Florida; Gulf to Texas and Brazil.

VARIABLE DWARF OLIVE *Olivella mutica* **Pl. 42**
Small–to 1.6 cm (⅝ in.) long. Looks like a miniature Lettered Olive except that spire is less than one-half of shell length. Callus on inner margin of shell thick, with *brown spot at base. Gray spiral band* around body whorl. No streaks or network of lines. N. Carolina to Florida, Bahamas.

SCOTCH BONNET *Phalium granulatum* **Pl. 43**
Large—to 9 cm (3½ in.) high. Shiny, globose shell; yellow-white, with spiral rows of blurred *rust or tan squarish spots* and spiral cords. Outer lip of aperture thick, with long, parallel, ridge-like teeth. Official seashell of S. Carolina. N. Carolina to Texas, W. Indies, and Brazil.

CROSS-BARRED SPINDLE *Cantharus cancellarius* **Pl. 42**
To 3.8 cm (1¼ in.) tall. Yellowish or reddish brown, with white areas. Shell has 3–5 cords of *white-tipped tubercles* on each spire whorl, 12–14 on body whorl. Edge of outer lip wavy, columellar wall with ascending spiral fold at bottom. Intertidal zone to deep water; west coast of Florida to Texas and Yucatan, Mexico. **Similar species: Tinted Cantharus** (*Pisania tincta,* Pl. 12) also to 3.8 cm (1¼ in.) tall, but lacks white-tipped tubercles. Shell *pale reddish brown,* with *bluish gray blotches and white spots.* Aperture pointed at upper end; outer lip has *strong ridge* inside. N. Carolina to Brazil.

BLACK PLANAXIS *Planaxis nucleus* **Fig. 47**
1 cm (½ in.) long. Shiny, black-brown shell. *Parallel grooves extend from aperture onto back of largest whorl.* At water's edge and under rocks. **Similar species: Lined Planaxis** (*P. lineatus,* Fig. 47, Pl. 39) is 6 mm (¼ in.) long. Shell white or yellowish brown, with *brown spiral bands.* Intertidal on rocks.

FLORIDA HORSE CONCH **Fig. 101; Pls. 47, 50**
Pleuroploca gigantea
Huge—to 48 cm (19 in.) long. Spindle-shaped shell with a narrow, elongate spire. Each whorl has 8–10 *triangular knobs on shoulder.* Whitish, orange, or brown, with a thin brown periostracum. Operculum thick, horny, pointed at one end. This conch eats other snails. On sand below low-tide mark; N. Carolina to Florida and Texas, Yucatan, Mexico.

SOUTHERN MOON SNAIL *Polinices duplicatus* **Pls. 3, 42, 47**
Large gray shell, to 7.5 cm (3 in.) tall. Globose; *apex coiled, resembling eye*—shell sometimes called Sharkeye. *Umbilicus almost completely covered* with dark brown callus (see Pl. 3). **Similar species: Northern Moon Snail** (*Lunatia heros*) *lacks large, dark callus*—umbilicus clearly visible. Both species are predatory; they drill holes in shells of other mollusks. Southern Moon Snail ranges from Massachusetts to Florida and Gulf; Northern Moon Snail from Canada to N. Carolina.

ZEBRA NERITE *Puperita pupa* **Fig. 47; Pls. 13, 39**
White with black zebra-like stripes; *interior yellow.* Tidepools. Tiny—to 1 cm (⅜ in.) wide.

WIDE-MOUTHED ROCK SNAIL *Purpura patula*   **Pl. 15**
Dull gray shell; outer surface has 6–7 rows of *sharp nodules.*
Aperture very large, oval; columella purple. Produces clear fluid
which becomes purple (see p. 229) and smells of garlic. Intertidal,
on rocks.

WEST INDIAN SIMNIA *Simnia acicularis*
To 1.3 cm (½ in.) long. Thin, delicate shell, with an *elongate
aperture.* Purple or yellow; columella has 2 narrow white ridges.
Like Flamingo Tongue snail, *lives on soft corals,* especially sea
whips. Takes on color of host: mantle, covered with camouflaging
brown lines, obscures shell in living animals. N. Carolina to W.
Indies. **Related species: Single-toothed Simnia** (*S. uniplicata,*
Pl. 42) is larger—to 2 cm (¾ in.) long—and has only 1 ridge on
columella. On sea whips; N. Carolina to W. Indies. More common
off U.S. than West Indian Simnia. Males of both species territorial.

ATLANTIC BABY'S EAR SNAIL   **Pls. 1, 43**
Sinum perspectivum
Shell to 5 cm (2 in.) long; living animal to 11.4 cm (4½ in.) long.
Shell flattened, with a *huge body whorl;* white, covered with fine
striations outside; glossy, sometimes purplish inside. *Shell hidden within mantle of snail when alive.* Animal flat, squarish;
appears featureless but close examination will reveal 2 close-set
tentacles. Foot large, used to plane through sand. Animal lives
beneath sand and preys on other snails. Virginia to Florida and
Texas, W. Indies.

QUEEN CONCH *Strombus gigas*   **Fig. 62, Pl. 50**
Large—to 30 cm (12 in.) high. Shell white or tan, covered with a
thin brown periostracum. Aperture and *flaring lip bright pink* in
living specimens. Turtle Grass beds and sandy bottoms. Edible—
used in soups, fritters, ceviche, other dishes; seriously depleted off
many W. Indian islands. **Related species:** (1) **West Indian
Fighting Conch** (*S. pugilis,* Pl. 50) is shiny orange; outer lip of
shell lacks flare near apex and is *notched near bottom.* To 10 cm (4
in.) high. Long spines on shoulders of whorls. Almost identical to
(2) **Florida Fighting Conch** (*S. alatus*), which is more common
from N. Carolina to Florida and Gulf to Texas, Mexico. (3)
Hawkwing Conch (*S. raninus,* Pl. 50) is a gray or whitish shell
with streaks of black or brown. It has spines on shoulder of first
whorl; outside of shell has horizontal ribs. *Outer lip extends
upward higher than spire.* (4) **Milk Conch** (*S. costatus*) is solid
and heavy, with blunt spines. *Aperture and inside of lip glossy
white.* To 17.8 cm (7 in.) tall. *S. pugilis* is eaten in Haiti as stew
called *lambi.*

KNOBBY PERIWINKLE *Tectarius muricatus*   **Pl. 39**
To 2.5 cm (1 in.) tall. Shell white, sometimes tinged with blue-
gray near apex; covered with *spiral rows of white beads.* High
above intertidal, often well above head level on vertical rocky
walls.

GREEN-BASED TEGULA   *Tegula excavata*   **Pl. 39**

To 2 cm (¾ in.) long. Shell brown or gray, with (sometimes indistinct) spiral lines. Umbilicus deep, round. *Base concave; pearly, iridescent green color.* Under rocks. **Similar species:** (1) **West Indian Tegula** (*T. levidomaculata*) lacks iridescent green on base. (2) **Smooth Atlantic Tegula** (*T. fasciata*) is a smooth, reddish brown shell, mottled with red and white; it has 2 white teeth at base of columella. Both snails live under rocks.

COMMON AUGER SNAIL   *Terebra dislocata*   **Pl. 42**

To 4.4 cm (1¾ in.) high. About 15 whorls; sutures appear as *pairs of thin lines,* between which is a *thin, knobby band.* Aperture small, with distinct twist at base of columella. Shell light gray or brown, sometimes whitish. Intertidal on sand and mud; in tidepools, especially at night, from Virginia to Florida and Gulf. **Similar species:** (1) **Black Auger Snail** (*T. protexta,* Fig. 29) has 10–12 whorls; shiny, creamy white or brown shell. To 3.7 cm (1½ in.) long. (2) **Sallé's Auger Snail** (*T. salleana,* Fig. 29) is gray or brown, with purple apex. To 2.5 cm (1 in.) long. (3) **Gray Auger Snail** (*T. cinerea,* Fig. 41) is similar to *T. salleana,* but thicker and without purple tip; 10 flat whorls. To 5 cm (2 in.) long. All 3 species range from N. Carolina to W. Indies.

FLORIDA ROCK SNAIL   **Pl. 38**

Thais haemastoma floridana

To 7.5 cm (3 in.) long. *Shell gray or yellow,* with *brown spots.* Shape variable. Spiral lines, sometimes with 2 or more rows of *small nodules* (see Pl. 38). Many *deep grooves* line *outer lip* of aperture. Interior of *aperture salmon pink;* body whorl lacks knobs. Under or on rocks. **Related species: (1) Rustic Rock Snail** (*T. rustica,* Fig. 45) is similar, but body whorl has 2 spiral rows of knobs. To 4.4 cm (1¾ in.) tall. Gray to dark brown shell with chocolate, vertical, stripe-like markings. *Aperture white, edged with brown lines.* (2) **Deltoid Rock Snail** (*T. deltoidea,* Fig. 45, Pl. 38) is gray or whitish, with thick, *brown horizontal bands or blotches.* To 5 cm (2 in.) tall. *Seven large, pointed knobs on body whorl.* Aperture white; outer lip finely toothed, inner edge blotched with brown. On exposed rocky shores.

GIANT TUN   *Tonna galea*   **Pl. 43**

Large—to at least 15 cm (6 in.) tall. Shell thin, glossy, inflated. Thin *outer wall of aperture inserts near* almost insignificant *spire.* Deeply incised grooves on surface; columella strongly twisted. *Yellowish white to brown* shell, sometimes blotched with *dark brown.* N. Carolina to Texas, W. Indies. **Similar species: Partridge Snail** (*T. maculosa,* Pl. 43) has a wide aperture with thin, scalloped outer edge. Shell glossy *brown,* with *dark blotches* and *white, crescent-shaped spots.* To 15 cm (6 in.) tall. S. Florida to W. Indies.

BEAUTIFUL TRUNCATELLA   *Truncatella pulchella*   **Fig. 45**

To 6 mm (¼ in.) tall. Pale brown to yellow. *White ridge on base of body whorl;* shell covered with vertical riblets. Outer lip thick, flaring at base. N. Carolina to Florida; W. Indies.

CHESTNUT TURBAN   *Turbo castanea*   **Pl. 39**
To 3 cm (1⅕ in.) long. Gray, orange, or brown, with white or brown spots. *Bands of pointed nodules.* Aperture white or pearly. 5 or 6 whorls. Under rocks.

OYSTER DRILL   *Urosalpinx cinerea*   **Fig. 24; Pls. 42, 47**
To 2.5 cm (1 in.) long, rarely to 4.4 cm (1¾ in.) long. Dull gray or tan. Shell has 5 whorls with 12 vertical rounded ribs crossed by horizontal threads. *Aperture dark purple; lip thin.* Sluggish, usually found at base of rocks or on oyster banks. Snail drills round hole in oyster shell, inserts proboscis, rasps flesh of oyster or other bivalve with radula. Intertidal; Massachusetts to ne. Florida. **Similar species:** (1) **Thick-lipped Oyster Drill** (*Eupleura caudata*) has a thick outer lip; aperture is bordered inside with raised granules. (2) **Tampa Oyster Drill** (*Urosalpinx tampaensis*) and (3) **Gulf Oyster Drill** (*U. perrugata*) are found on w. Florida shores.

COMMON WORM SHELL   *Vermicularia spirata*   **Pl. 42**
Wormlike shell; whorls near apex whitish or brown, closely coiled; whorls nearer opening pale yellow to red-brown, uncoiled but irregularly sinuous. Animal inside a true snail with tentacles and eyes. Shells often in clumps, cemented to one another. To 15 cm (6 in.) long. Massachusetts (rare) to W. Indies—common off s. Florida.

MUSIC VOLUTE   *Voluta musica*   **Pl. 38**
To 6 cm (2½ in.) long. *Shell pink or tan,* with 2–3 *brown spiral bands* of fine lines dotted with *brown spots* (*like music notes*).

Limpets

ANTILLEAN LIMPET   *Acmaea antillarum*   **Pl. 39**
To 2.5 cm (1 in.) tall. White shell with *thin, red or brown rays* radiating from summit. Interior glossy white with brown stain at apex. Shell flattened, thin-walled, without hole on top. **Similar species:** (1) **Spotted Limpet** (*A. pustulata*) is white with brown spots. Shell thicker than in *A. antillarum;* knobby ribs radiate from apex. Living animal cream with brown spots; tentacles bright green. (2) **Dwarf Suck-on Limpet** (*A. leucopleura*, Pl. 39) is only 1 cm (⅜ in.) wide; it lives on shells of other snails, usually the West Indian Top Snail. (3) **Striped False Limpet** (*Siphonaria pectinata*) is similar to *A. antillarum* but has a bulge on rear margin. Air-breathing.

ROSY CUP-AND-SAUCER LIMPET   **Pl. 43**
Crucibulum auricula
Low, pointed, cap-shaped shell; rim wavy. *Exterior grayish, interior pinkish;* outer surface with rough, wavy radial ridges that

become more pronounced near edges. *Cup inside shell nearly free;* to 2.4 cm (1 in.) wide at base. S. Florida to W. Indies. **Similar species: Yucatan Cup-and-saucer Limpet** (*C. planum*) is almost identical, but with finer striations. Western and Northern coasts of Yucatan, Mexico.

LISTER'S KEYHOLE LIMPET   **Fig. 45**
Diodora listeri
White, sometimes with dark blotches; heavy, alternating large and small radiating ribs crossed by concentric ridges form square pits. *Opening keyhole-shaped;* black on outside. Shell of living animal covered with thick, hairy, brown periostracum. To 4.5 cm (1¾ in.) long. Intertidal on rocks. **Similar species: Cayenne Keyhole Limpet** (*D. cayenensis,* Pl. 43) is *whitish or gray;* elongate. *Dumbbell-shaped hole* tilts *forward from apex.* Rough, bumpy ribs; every fourth one larger. Sculpturing less coarse than on *D. listeri.* On intertidal, subtidal rocks; Maryland to Florida and Brazil. Most common keyhole limpet north of Florida.

KNOBBY KEYHOLE LIMPET   **Fig. 49; Pls. 15, 39**
Fissurella nodosa
Shell *brown or white; interior white. Hole keyhole-shaped.* Edge of shell ridged with 20–22 coarse, knobby ribs. To 3 cm (1¾ in.) long. **Similar species: (1) Barbados Keyhole Limpet** (*F. barbadensis,* Pl. 39) is *white or gray,* with *brown spots or rays;* ribs lower and less regular than in *F. nodosa.* Inside of shell white. Opening *round,* not keyhole-shaped; opening *surrounded by a green band* edged in red. Both species intertidal on rocks; shells covered with hairy periostracum. **(2) Rocking-chair Keyhole Limpet** (*F. fascicularis,* Pl. 43) is brownish purple, pinkish, or white, sometimes with reddish rays. *Interior white, flushed with pink* at hole; hole *elongate,* with a *round notch* at center. Ends of shell raised so that shell rests on its sides and *rocks on its base.* To 3.2 cm (1¼ in.) long. **(3) Pointed Keyhole Limpet** (*F. angusta,* Pl. 43) is a *flattened* shell with irregular edges and a lobate *point at front;* 10 knobby ribs. Whitish to brownish, with reddish brown blotches. Interior greenish; pale brown around hole. To 2.5 cm (1 in.) long. S. Florida to S. America.

EIGHT-RIBBED LIMPET   **Pl. 39**
Hemitoma octoradiata
White or gray shell; *notched at front. Eight evenly spaced, knobby ribs.* No hole on top. Living animal bright green, edged in iridescent red. To 2.5 cm (1 in.) long.

CANCELLATE FLESHY LIMPET   **Pl. 15**
Lucapina suffusa
Low, oval shell, narrower at front; oval hole forward of middle. *Radial ribs* crossed by concentric threads, creating sculpture of tiny boxes. Margin finely toothed. Exterior whitish to purplish gray; *interior white,* often with a *bluish ring* around hole. To 3.8 cm (1½ in.) long. On or under rocks at low-tide line.

Nudibranchs and Other Sea Slugs

Kaniaulono B. Meyer

It seems remarkable that the sea slug has given up the safe haven of its ancestral shell, and that it has survived competition with the heavily armored snails that occupy the same environmental niches. True, to relinquish the thick shell means greater mobility and speed; but anyone who has seen a sea slug slithering along realizes that although it seems somewhat more responsive than conventional snails, it would still not win any invertebrate Olympics.

The sea slugs have assembled an array of protective devices and can survive handily in the undersea jungles. Defense mechanisms include smelly or bad-tasting glands, purple dye, and white nauseating secretions. Remarkably, a sea slug can even swallow the nematocysts of its prey—jellyfishes, anemones, or hydroids—and use them for its own protection. Some slugs are camouflaged; others, especially the nudibranchs, are the gaudy butterflies of the gastropod clan.

Nudibranchs are among the most beautiful animals in the sea. Their name is derived from their "naked" gills (*nudus* means "naked," and *branch* means "gill"). The gills are upward-projecting branches of the body wall, usually finger-shaped appendages or posterior feathery tufts. Blood flows through these thin-walled structures. Oxygen is absorbed and wastes pass out through them. Adaptations for respiration take a variety of forms. In many sea slugs the whole body surface is used for gas exchange; no specialized organ has been developed for that purpose. The sea hares, however, have a single gill, which lies between the parapodia (body flaps). Some nudibranchs (aolid nudibranchs, p. 249) have numerous fingerlike projections called cerata on their backs; others (dorid nudibranchs) have a circlet of gills surrounding the anus.

Nudibranchs and sea slugs have unique sense organs called rhinophores—a pair of retractile, tentacle-like structures that project from the head like horns. These are olfactory (smelling) organs. (Rhinophore, from *rhino,* means "of the nose," and *phorous* means "bearing"; thus, "nose-bearing.") In some groups the rhinophores are rolled and have a ciliated inner surface to aid the passage of water over the sensory surface. Sometimes a pair of true tentacles used for touching is also present. Eyes consist of brown-pigmented dots at the base of the rhinophores; these primitive eyes permit the nudibranchs to sense gradations in light intensity. Many nudibranchs seek dark areas for protection.

Some nudibranchs feed by grazing on colonies of fuzzlike

hydroids. The toothed radula effectively scrapes hydroid polyps into the nudibranch's mouth. Other prey species include sponges, soft corals, and sea anemones. Many sea slugs eat algae.

The ingested food passes into the digestive tract. In some groups there is a unique structural arrangement in the midgut. The intestinal wall extends (in the form of long, pocketlike projections) all the way to the back, where food is visible inside fingerlike extensions called cerata that project from the back. The tips of these extensions contain stinging cells (cnidocytes), from polyps that were eaten. These cells are removed, undigested, from the prey polyps and stored just under the surface of the cerata in a functional state! When a predator attacks, the borrowed nematocysts are discharged, repelling the enemy in a broadside of poison darts.

The ultimate example of "not wasting a drop" of prey is exhibited by the Lettuce Sea Slug (Pl. 48). This beautiful green-mottled animal feeds on algae. It sucks chloroplasts out of the plant cells and deposits them beneath its skin, at the base of the frilly parapodia. The chloroplasts perform photosynthesis under the translucent skin of their new host. Some of the food produced is taken up by the tissues of the slug, which has set up an internal algae farm.

Many nudibranchs release repugnant secretions from special skin glands. The sea hares also secrete blobs of viscous purple dye if attacked. The blob contains mucus and remains more or less intact as it floats above the sea hare. The predator is confused about which target to attack: the purple mass seductively undulating with the currents, or the camouflaged, unmoving sea hare beneath.

Although sea slugs are hermaphrodites, reproduction is accomplished by cross-fertilization between two individuals. Sea hares usually copulate in chains, in which each member acts as a male to the preceding sea hare and as a female to the succeeding one. The first animal in the chain functions only as a female and the last only as a male. Resourceful sea hares close the chain as a circle. Eggs are laid in gelatinous strings, often in spiral patterns. One species produces a string of eggs at a rate of 5 cm (2 in.) an hour. One string may contain a million eggs.

Most sea slugs detect food primarily by touch, although their rhinophores are quite responsive to odors. Some kinds of nudibranchs eat only one species of hydroid polyp. Not only can they differentiate this hydroid from other hydroids, they can even distinguish it from other species of the same genus. Another nudibranch eats soft corals of one species only. But that species has two varieties, an orange variant and a white one. The nudibranch eats only the polyps of the white coral, rejecting the orange. Another nudibranch feeds only on one species of sea anemone. It selects only damaged, young, and expanded specimens and can even distinguish between water that has passed over anemones and water that has not.

Members of two of the sea slug groups (Order Anaspidea and Order Sacoglossa—see below) are mainly herbivores, feeding by rasping or piercing algae with their radular teeth. Two of the sacoglossans are carnivores, however; they feed on the eggs of other sea slugs, cephalopods, or fishes.

One common nudibranch, the Blue Glaucus (Pl. 48), has evolved appendages resembling short arms and legs with large flat fingers. These are used as an aid in floating. Since it can hang suspended near the water's surface, it has no need to compete for bottom-dwelling polyps. Instead it chases jellyfish, especially the Portuguese Man-of-war (see p. 205). A few of these blue and silver nudibranchs can surround and destroy a large colonial jellyfish, just as a pack of wolves can kill a huge moose.

Common sea slugs in lagoons and Turtle Grass beds are the Lettuce Sea Slug and the large Spotted Sea Hare.

The Lettuce Sea Slug (Pl. 48) is often visible festooned over a clump of algae. Its green and cream blotches and frilly greenish parapodia provide excellent camouflage, but if that fails, a predator will spit out the slug after tasting the secretions of its repugnatorial glands.

The Spotted Sea Hare (Pl. 49) can grow to 30 cm (1 ft.) or longer. It is not a nudibranch, since it has a reduced mantle, a small true shell, and a gill, all missing from true nudibranchs. It resembles a huge, olive drab, shell-less snail with two distinct flaps running the length of its back. Its two large erect rhinophores resemble rabbit ears, hence the name sea hare. It will discharge its purple dye if gently squeezed.

Another sea hare is the Warty Sea Cat (Pl. 49), common in Turtle Grass beds in the West Indies. It is bright green or brown, with tiny pointed warts and white spots. Another relative is the Ragged Sea Hare (Pl. 17). It reaches 10 cm (4 in.) long and is greenish gray with brown spots. Long, pointed or straplike, forked extensions from its body give it a leafy appearance similar to the Forked Sea Tumbleweed on which it grazes.

One of the best ways to find the cleverly camouflaged sea slugs is to look for their food instead. Take a clump of algae or a hydroid colony, place it in a glass bowl filled with seawater, and leave it in the dark. After an hour a variety of sea slugs may be seen crawling up the side of the bowl or floating upside down on the water's surface.

Taxonomy: All sea slugs belong to the diverse gastropod subclass Opisthobranchia. Of the nine orders, only the four that are most likely to be found in shallow water are described here:

1. Order Notaspidea (= Pleurobranchomorpha). Flattened, elongate, with rhinophores emerging from beneath the back (not

through it, as in the similar dorid nudibranchs) and a gill along the right side, between the foot and back (*Pleurobranchus areolatus*, p. 248).

2. Order Sacoglossa or Ascoglossa. Leaflike or elongate forms; most often green but sometimes brown or black. Some (*Lobiger, Oxynoe*) have an external shell; some (*Cyerce*) have leaflike projections from their backs. Most are herbivores.

3. Order Anaspidea or Aplysiacea. The sea hares (*Aplysia, Bursatella*). Large and bulky, with two rabbit-ear-like rhinophores and a hump containing a thin hidden shell and a gill, concealed between two flaps (parapodia). All are herbivores.

4. Order Nudibranchia. True nudibranchs, with no shell. Three main body types: (1) The aolids have clusters of fingerlike extensions (cerata) on their backs containing branches of the digestive system. (2) The dorids are flattened and oval when viewed from above, with rhinophores near the front (head) and a circlet of gills surrounding the anus. No cerata. (3) The dendronotids are elongate and have fewer cerata on their backs; cerata paired, not clustered. Fine gills are associated with cerata. Rhinophore stalked; elaborate (*Scyllaea*).

Although the classification of nudibranchs and sea slugs (opisthobranchs) is largely based on internal characteristics, for field identification they are grouped below according to external features. This is an artificial system and, for the most part, does not reflect true taxonomic relationships. Unless otherwise specified, all species are found in s. Florida and the Caribbean.

Next 3 species: *These sea slugs have a shell (hidden or partially hidden).*

SOLITARY PAPER BUBBLE SEA SLUG　　　　Pl. 17
Haminoea solitaria

To 2.5 cm (1 in.) long. Tiny, yellowish or bluish, *translucent shell* with spiral grooves, *hidden inside* the *gray, sluglike animal*, which burrows in sand, feeding on worms, other small animals, and algae. Shell to 6 mm (¼ in.) long. Sand flats, Eelgrass beds; Maine to S. Carolina. **Similar species: Channeled Barrel Bubble** (*Acteocina canaliculata*) has a white, solid, cylindrical internal shell 5 mm (⅕ in.) long, with a *moderately elevated spire.* (Paper Bubble's shell has no visible spire.) On underside of dead shells, shell rubble; Canada to Mexico. Order Bullomorpha.

WARTY BUBBLE SEA SLUG　　*Lobiger souverbii*　　Pl. 48

Internal shell thin, fragile, incised with fine black lines. Body yellowish green, with *4 large, warty parapodia* extending upward from back. Tail long, warty. Body may have a red-purple or orange-brown tinge. On algae (*Caulerpa* and *Halimeda*). To 2 cm (¾ in.). Order Sacoglossa.

SMOOTH BUBBLE SEA SLUG   *Oxynoe antillarum*   **Pl. 48**
Light to dark green with white spots. Body smooth except for tiny papillae on edge of parapodia that almost cover shell. Rhinophores large, smooth; dotted with white and blue spots. *Tail more than one-half body length.* On algae (*Caulerpa* and *Halimeda*). To 3.5 cm (1½ in.). Order Sacoglossa.

Next 4 species: Parapodia cover a hump containing a gill.
SPOTTED SEA HARE   *Aplysia dactylomela*   **Pl. 49**
Body olive drab with *black, ringlike spots.* May be large — to 40 cm (15 in.). Emits a cloud of purple mucus when disturbed. Usually found browsing on algae in Turtle Grass beds; young may be under rocks. **Similar species:** (1) **Black-rimmed Sea Hare** (*A. parvula*) is much smaller — usually about 3.5 cm (1½ in.) long. Has a *black rim on parapodia* and around opening above shell between parapodia. (2) **Black Sea Hare** (*A. morio*) has a *black body* with olive or golden overtones. No spots. To 30 cm (12 in.). (3) **Willcox's Sea Hare** (*A. willcoxi*) has a dark brown body with *darker bars* and *no spots.* To 23 cm (9 in.). (4) **Juliana's Sea Hare** (*A. juliana*) has an olive body with irregular buff spots, and a *sucker at each end of foot.* To 10 cm (4 in.). Order Anaspidea.
WARTY SEA CAT   *Dolabrifera dolabrifera*   **Pl. 49**
Body stout. Color varies from mottled light green with tan spots to dark green, tan, and black. Sole light green with tan spots. Body covered with pointed warts. Parapodia inconspicuous, consisting of a *groove running toward rear, with an opening only in the rear half of body.* Under stones; in tidepools. To 10 cm (4 in.). Order Anaspidea.
RAGGED SEA HARE   *Bursatella leachii pleii*   **Pl. 17**
Body stout; covered with *elongate, often flattened papillae,* giving animal a hairy or woolly appearance. Color variable, usually tan with black or brown spots. Among algae, on mud or sand. To 25 cm (10 in.). Order Anaspidea.
LONG-TAILED SEA HARE   *Stylocheilus longicauda*   **Pl. 49**
Body slender; light gray-brown with *dark brown longitudinal stripes.* Tiny spots on parapodia vary in color — blue circled in orange, or orange circled in black. Rhinophores and body covered with pointed warts. Under stones, among algae, on pilings. To 9 cm (3½ in.). Order Anaspidea.

Next 4 species: Cylindrical or flattened with no apparent parapodia, or with fused parapodia appearing as a slit on back.
ENGEL'S SEA HARE   *Phyllaplysia engeli*   **Pl. 49**
Color variable — green, gray, or white, with red-yellow or brown dots; usually green with lighter longitudinal lines. *White specks cover rhinophores.* Warty or smooth. Generally flattened. On Turtle Grass or algae such as *Padina.* To 2 cm (¾ in.). Order Anaspidea.

BOSIELLA SEA SLUG *Bosiella mimetica*
Minute green slug with *no apparent parapodia.* Commonly found on *Halimeda* algae. To 6 mm (¼ in.). Order Sacoglossa.

Parapodia extend to tail; hump absent. Animal elongate and cylindrical.

ATLANTIC ELYSIAS *Elysia* species   **Pl. 48**
(1) **Pimpled Elysia** (*Elysia cauze*). Body yellow-green to gray-green; covered with tubercles. *Parapodia frilled and dark-edged,* covered with pointed tubercles, white papillae, and small black rings. *Rhinophores elongate, brown.* Head and parapodia may be brown. To 2 cm (¾ in.) long. On algae (*Caulerpa*). (2) **Papillate Elysia** (*Elysia papillosa*). Similar to *E. cauze* but body covered with longer, *conical papillae.* Parapodia not dark-edged. Body dark green, obscured by a powdering of opaque white. To 1.2 cm (½ in.) long. On *Halimeda* algae. (3) **Ornate Elysia** (*Elysia ornata,* Pl. 48). *Parapodia and rhinophores green with a black and orange edge.* Dusted with black and white specks. To 4 cm (1½ in.) long. (4) **Common Green Elysia** (*Elysia tuca,* Pl. 48). Papillae on tips of rhinophores only. Distinctive *Y-shaped marking on head.* Green with a few white spots. To 4 cm (1½ in.) long. On algae (*Halimeda* and *Caulerpa*). Order Sacoglossa.

LETTUCE SEA SLUG *Tridachia crispata*   **Pl. 48**
Parapodia a mass of *white-rimmed frills covering the back.* Body usually green (sometimes blue), with cream-colored spots. Sole and rhinophores cream. On algae (*Halimeda, Caulerpa,* and *Penicillus*); often in Turtle Grass beds. To 5 cm (2 in.) long. Order Sacoglossa.

Next 2 species: Rhinophores emerge from beneath back; gill along right side between foot and back.

ATLANTIC PLEUROBRANCH   **Pl. 48**
Pleurobranchus areolatus
Back covered with *low rounded bumps;* some red, others cream or yellow. Background color deep orange to tan. To 5 cm (2 in.) long. Order Notaspidea.

ATLANTIC UMBRELLA SEA SLUG   **Pl. 15**
Umbraculum umbraculum
Large—to 15 cm (6 in.) long. Foot broad; deeply slit at front. Pale orange or yellowish brown, tubercle-covered body. Head, bearing 2 short, conical tentacles, projects slightly beyond *flattened, glossy, whitish, oval shell,* which has radiating lines like rings in a tree trunk. Thin brown periostracum extends as a fringe around shell. Subtidal, in holes in rocks; Bermuda, W. Indies. Order Notaspidea.

Next 6 species (dorid nudibranchs): Rhinophores emerge through back; gills in a circlet around anus.

'OMMON LEATHER DORIS   **Pl. 49**
Platydoris angustipes
Body orange or brownish orange; leathery. Tips of rhinophores brown, gills white. To 5 cm (2 in.) long. Order Nudibranchia.

.REB'S DORIS   *Dendrodoris krebsii*   **Pl. 49**
Body smooth, *velvety.* Body black or light gray with black spots, yellow with black spots, or red with a few darker spots. *Tips of rhinophores and gills white.* Intertidal or subtidal, under stones. To 5.7 cm (2¼ in.) long, rarely to 17 cm (6¾ in.). Order Nudibranchia.

LENCH'S DORIS   *Chromodoris clenchi*   **Pl. 49**
Body blue, with a mosaic of brick red lines or spots forming a mesh over back. A thin red line along margin. Rhinophores purple or white with purple tips. *7–9 gills; white with purple axes and tips.* Usually subtidal; may occur intertidally, under rocks. To 2.5 cm (1 in.) long. **Related species:** *C. kempfi.* Back mostly white, with a *broad yellow border* and black spots arranged along inner side of border, leaving midline of back white. Foot, rhinophores, and gill tips purple. To 2 cm (¾ in.) long. Order Nudibranchia.

AYER'S DORIS   *Felimare bayeri*   **Pl. 49**
Body narrow and elongate; *bright blue with a white border* containing dusky spots. Back darker toward center, with a loose yellow network of lines and scattered dark spots. To 3.4 cm (1¼ in.) long. Order Nudibranchia.

REEK GODDESS NUDIBRANCH   **Pl. 49**
Hypselodoris edenticulata
Similar in body form to Bayer's Doris, but larger—to 5 cm (2 in.) long. Gills blue. *Back dark blue, streaked with chrome yellow. Sides with yellow rings.* Sole of foot bright blue. Usually subtidal. **Related species:** *H. ruthae.* Back deep blue with white border. Gills and rhinophores white with blue tips. *Three continuous or intermittent gold lines run down back;* gold lines also on top border of foot and along midline of projecting tail. To 2 cm (¾ in.) long. Order Nudibranchia.

OUGH-BACKED DORIS   *Onchidoris verrucosa*   **Fig. 104**
Dull orange, with numerous *large, rounded tubercles scattered on back;* may have small brown spots on edge of mantle. Posterior tuft of gills whitish; rhinophores small. To 3.8 cm (1½ in.) long. On pilings, sponges, and seagrass; Chesapeake Bay to Florida. Order Nudibranchia.

Next 6 species: *Extensions (cerata) on back.*
NTILLEAN CYERCE   *Cyerce antillensis*
Cerata flattened, leaflike. Rhinophores forked. Drab brown to tan, with a red spot near base and one near tip of each ceras. To 3.5 cm (1¼ in.) long. **Related species:** *C. cristillana.* Similar to *C. antillensis* but with crimson markings on a white background. On algae (*Halimeda* and *Caulerpa*). Order Sacoglossa.

Fig. 104.
Rough-backed Doris
(preserved specimen).

SARGASSUM NUDIBRANCH *Scyllaea pelagica* **Pl. 48**
Cerata are 2 pairs of thick, blunt projections from back. Rhinophores flattened, broader near tips. Body cream to orange-brown, with brown and white patches and flecks of red-brown. Blue spots on sides. Matches Sargassum Weed, on which it lives; found only when Sargassum is washed ashore by storms. To 5 cm (2 in.) long. Order Nudibranchia.

BLUE GLAUCUS *Glaucus atlanticus* **Pl. 48**
Cerata arranged laterally, as inflated fingers. Body silver and deep blue. Foot and tips of cerata deep blue. Floats foot upward. Feeds on jellyfish such as *Physalia, Velella,* and *Porpita.* To 2.5 cm (1. in.) long. Order Nudibranchia.

LONG-TENTACLED NUDIBRANCH **Pl. 48**
Phidiana lynceus
Cerata pointed, elongate ovals, *appearing in clumps;* black or brown with white tips. Animal slender. Back with orange tinge, blue-white stripe down middle. *Tentacles long;* reddish orange with white tips. Rhinophores shorter than tentacles; ringed with numerous folds, reddish with lighter tips. Under stones, among algae, or on mangrove roots. To 2.5 cm (1 in.) long. **Related species:** *Dondice occidentalis* is similar to *P. lynceus,* but *tip of foot is angular and drawn out at front* (not rounded as in *P. lynceus*). White with red stripe along head and sides. *Orange ring on cerata.* To 3 cm (1¼ in.) long. Order Nudibranchia.

BULB-BEARING NUDIBRANCH *Favorinus branchialis*
Cerata brown with white specks and tips. *Rhinophores dark brown with 2–3 swellings and white tips.* Body color variable; 1 brown horizontal stripe. On mud, algae (Sargassum Weed, *Padina*). To 1.5 cm (¾ in.) long. Order Nudibranchia.

NEAPOLITAN SPURILLA *Spurilla neapolitana* **Pl. 48**
Cream to pink, with red-brown or olive-green cerata. Cerata white-tipped, *keeled and curled toward midline of back.* White spots on cerata, back, and head. Rhinophores with folds toward tip. Feeds on sea anemones. To 4 cm (1½ in.) long. Order Nudibranchia.

Clams, Oysters, and Mussels

In bivalves (members of Class Pelecypoda) the two shells are hinged, held together by an adductor muscle. Most bivalves live buried in sand or attached to rocks. An exception is the Rough Lima (Pl. 39), often seen swimming near coral reefs. It is startling to come upon one of these clams flapping along, its valves (shells) alternately opening and closing, expelling powerful jets of water to propel itself on an erratic, purposeless little trip of a few meters. It gives the appearance of ghostly castanets suspended in the water, silently clicking as if to some Spanish melody. When the clam lands it opens, revealing blood-red tissue and a mass of long, delicately streaming tentacles. This flamboyant traveler bears little resemblance to the workaday clams buried in sand.

Clams have sacrificed much for the relative safety of underground life. Sometimes they must obtain food and oxygen while buried in oxygen-deficient mud. Some clams can eat the mud, extracting organic material from it. Most, however, must pump gallons of water through their bodies, filtering out phytoplankton. They extend from between their valves a double siphon: one tube (the incurrent siphon) draws in water, the other (excurrent siphon) expels it. A pair of flat, leaflike gills is covered with millions of cilia embedded in a thin film of mucus. The incessant beating of the tiny, hairlike cilia sets up a substantial flow of water, enough to pump several gallons over the gills every day. Anything small enough to be caught in the current sticks to the mucus-covered gills. Tracts of cilia sort the particles. The small ones are carried to the mouth; the large ones are swept back to the incurrent siphon, where they are expelled in occasional bursts when the cilia beat in a reverse direction.

The multipurpose siphons, which can be up to 30 cm (1 ft.) long, provide the buried clam with its only access to the outer world. Through these siphons water containing food and oxygen is drawn in and wastes are released; sperms are ejected in the outflow and are drawn into the body of the female in the incurrent flow. The ciliated larvae are released to the outside through the excurrent flow.

Living in the sand beneath the matted Turtle Grass roots is the Tiger Lucine clam (Pl. 41). It is unique in that its siphons are conveyed to the surface by the foot and thus project upward and forward rather than to the rear as in other clams. This clam feeds not on phytoplankton, which is sparse in tropical seas, but on bacteria, which are abundant on the rotting remains of dead Turtle Grass.

Remarkable bivalves, found partially buried among the Turtle Grass leaves, are the pen shell clams (Pl. 40). Pen shells look like large arrowheads (15 cm—6 in.—long) embedded in the sand. The paper-thin, serrated edges of the valves are usually open to allow entry of water. Don't step on one, as the edges of the valves are sharp.

Mussels are also bivalves. Each mussel is forever attached to its rock by brown threads called byssus. These are glued to the rock by a fabulous glue, resistant to most environmental stresses. Some day, if dental researchers can uncover the secret of this glue, cavities in your teeth may be filled with it.

The commonest mussel of intertidal rocky shores is the Scorched Mussel (Pl. 40) and its relatives. These mussels cover rocks or are crowded into moist cracks between boulders. Below the mussels, still in shallow water and attached to rocks by byssus, are the arks. Commonest are the Turkey Wing and Mossy Ark (Pls. 40, 43). A hairy periostracum (outer layer) often obscures their shells, but the distinct brown, zebra-like stripes of the Turkey Wing will allow you to identify it.

Red Mangrove roots make excellent habitats for oysters. The Mangrove Oyster has given rise to century-old stories told by seamen about lush Caribbean islands where oysters grew on trees. In Florida the similar Eastern Oyster takes the place of the Mangrove Oyster.

More than 70 of the commonest bivalves in southeastern U.S. and Caribbean waters are depicted on Pls. 40–44 and are de-

Fig. 105. Anatomy of a clam.

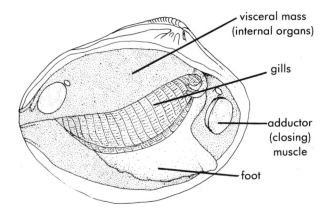

visceral mass (internal organs)

gills

adductor (closing) muscle

foot

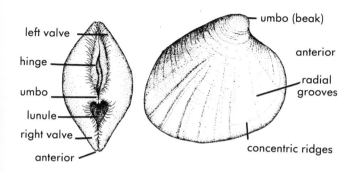

Fig. 106. Anatomy of a clam shell.

scribed below. Unless otherwise specified, all species are found in s. Florida and the Caribbean.

Size is measured from front to back — that is, across the width of the shell when the umbo (beak) is uppermost.

COMMON ATLANTIC ABRA *Abra aequalis*
Small—to 1 cm (⅜ in.) long. Globose, pale brown; smooth, polished, with minute concentric ridges near margins. N. Carolina to Texas; W. Indies.

CALICO SCALLOP *Aequipecten gibbus* **Pl. 41**
Surface often rough, with about 20 rounded, radiating ribs; wings of hinge of about equal in size. Color pattern variable, often with maroon flecks. To 5 cm (2 in.) long. **Similar species: Rough Scallop** (*A. muscosus,* Pl. 43) has unequal wings. Surface rough, with about 20 strong ribs; sharp scales on lower region of ribs. Shells pinkish red, brown, or bright yellow. To 5 cm (2 in.) long.

ATLANTIC STRAWBERRY COCKLE **Pl. 40**
Americardia media
White with orange-brown flecks; 33–37 scaly radial ribs. To 5 cm (2 in.) long. **Similar species: Guppy's Cockle** (*A. guppyi*) has 26–28 ribs. To 1.5 cm (⅝ in.) long.

INCONGRUOUS ARK *Anadara brasiliana* **Pl. 40**
White; about 25 ribs crossed by equidistant lines and a row of comblike teeth that are smallest at center. To 5 cm (2 in.) long. **Related species:** (1) **Eared Ark** (*A. notabilis*) is larger—to 9 cm (3½ in.) long—and thicker. Front end of shell short, rounded; rear end long, squarish. About 25 thick ribs crossed by thin lines; white with silky brown periostracum. (2) **Blood Ark** (*A. ovalis*) has a white shell with hairy brown periostracum covering its

lower half; 26–35 ribs. Body red (contains hemoglobin). To 5.7 cm (2¼ in.) long. (3) **Transverse Ark** (*A. transversa*) is oblong; umbones (beaks) incurved and set close to front end of shell. 12 ribs. White with a dark brown hairy periostracum. To 2.5 cm (1 in.) long.

BUTTERCUP   *Anodontia alba*   Pl. 44
Dull white, with an orange or yellow interior. Shell inflated, almost circular, with a notch near pointed umbones; smooth except for faint growth lines. To 6.4 cm (2½ in.) long. N. Carolina to W. Indies.

WEST INDIAN POINTED VENUS   Pl. 41
Anomalocardia brasiliana
Yellowish gray, with tan or purple speckles. Heavy concentric ribs. Posterior squared off, flared. To 3 cm (1¼ in.) long. **Similar species: Pointed Venus** (*A. cuneimeris,* Pl. 44) is smaller — to 2 cm (¾ in.) long — and thinner. Florida.

JINGLE SHELL or MERMAID'S TOENAIL   Pl. 43
Anomia simplex
Upper shell inflated, irregular, lumpy; glossy, translucent gray, yellowish, or orange. Similar in thickness and texture to a large toenail; to 5 cm (2 in.) long. Flat lower valve (shell) is cemented to rock, consequently rarely found. Canada to W. Indies.

TURKEY WING   *Arca zebra*   Pl. 40
White or tan, with reddish brown, zebra-like stripes. Periostracum is brown, fuzzy. To 7.5 cm (3 in.) long. Found on subtidal rocks. **Similar species: Mossy Ark** (*A. imbricata,* Pl. 43) is purplish white inside and out, but outer surface is covered with brown, thick, mosslike periostracum. Umbones widely separated, often with a pattern of diagonal lines between them. To 6.3 cm (2½ in.) long.

ATLANTIC BAY SCALLOP   *Argopecten irradians*   Pl. 43
To 7.5 cm (3 in.) long. *About 21 squarish ribs.* Both wings of hinge nearly equal in size. Two southern subspecies: (1) **Southern Bay Scallop** (*A. irradians concentricus*) is squarish; orange-brown to bluish gray. Lower valve usually grayish. New Jersey to Florida. (2) **Gulf Scallop** (*A. i. amplicostatus*) has *12–17 ribs.* Mottled gray and black; lower valve white. Gulf of Mexico. All species have rows of blue eyespots along edge of mantle. Capable of swimming by clapping valves together, using the single adductor muscle (the part of the scallop we eat).

GAUDY ASAPHIS   *Asaphis deflorata*   Pl. 41
To 6 cm (2½ in.) long. White with purplish rays. Inside yellow, stained with rose or purple. Outside of shell sculptured with *low radial threads.*

STIFF PEN SHELL   *Atrina rigida*   Pl. 40
HALF-NAKED PEN SHELL   *Atrina seminuda*
To 28 cm (11 in.) long. Light brown or reddish shells with 15–25 rows of *tube-like spines.* Virtually identical, but Half-naked Pen

Shell is absent in s. Florida. Both species are generally found buried with posterior (wide) end projecting from sand and usually gaping. **Similar species: Amber Pen Shell** (*Pinna carnea*) is translucent, orange or yellow. It has only 8–12 ribs with *scale-like rather than tubular spines.*

TRUNCATE BORER   *Barnea truncata*   **Pl. 43**
Shells thin and fragile, with *sharp ridges and scales at front. Posterior almost vertical.* White with gray periostracum. To 7 cm (2¾ in.) long. Deep in mud or peat; Maine to Texas, W. Indies.

BEARDED ARK   *Barbatia cancellaria*   **Pl. 40**
To 5 cm (2 in.). Weakly beaded dark brown surface, often covered with hairy brown periostracum. **Similar species:** (1) **Reticulate Ark** (*B. domingensis*) is white with a brown, fuzzy periostracum covering deep grooves in surface. To 2 cm (¾ in.). (2) **Bright Ark** (*B. candida*) is similar to *B. domingensis* but larger and more elongate, with *very prominent posterior ribs.* All 3 species live on and under rocks.

WEST INDIAN CARDITA   *Carditamera gracilis*   **Pl. 40**
To 3 cm (1⅕ in.) long. White or gray, with a gray periostracum. *Umbo set far to the front,* with 17 smooth ribs. Muscle scar may be dark brown. **Similar species: Broad-ribbed Cardita** (*C. floridana*) has heavy, rounded, beaded radial ribs with brown flecks. Shell oval. To 3 cm (1⅕ in.). Common on Florida and Mexican beaches; absent from W. Indies, where *C. gracilis* is found.

JEWEL BOX   *Chama macerophylla*
To 7.5 cm (3 in.) long. Pink, yellow, or flesh-colored; irregularly rounded. Covered with short spines when fresh, but usually found eroded, as a *thick disk with a shallow depression on underside.*

CROSS-BARRED VENUS   *Chione cancellata*   **Pl. 44**
To 4.5 cm (1¾ in.). White, with brown, blotchy rays. Strong, concentric and vertical ribs form *rectangles over surface.* Interior white, sometimes with purple blotch or tinge. **Similar species:** (1) **Beaded Venus** (*C. granulata,* Pl. 41) is a slightly smaller yellow shell with purple mottling and less distinct concentric lines; surface beaded. (2) **King Venus** (*C. paphia,* Pl. 41) is white, mottled with red-brown; it has 10–12 heavy concentric ribs. (3) **Gray Pygmy Venus** (*C. grus*) is small—to 1.3 cm (½ in.) long. Shells ovate; gray-white or pinkish. Concentric ridges are crossed by axial riblets, but not pronounced enough to produce distinct rectangular units as in Cross-barred Venus. Purple stain along hind margin. Sandy subtidal; N. Carolina to Florida and Texas.

TIGER LUCINE   *Codakia orbicularis*   **Pl. 41**
To 9 cm (3½ in.) long. White, with *a rose or yellow flush inside shell and at margins.* Surface covered with numerous lightly beaded radial ribs. Usually the commonest shell near Turtle Grass beds. **Similar species:** (1) **Dwarf Tiger Lucine** (*C. orbiculata*) is smaller—never more than 2.5 cm (1 in.) long. Lacks rose or yellow flush inside; beaded ribs on exterior more prominent. (2)

Costate Lucine (*C. costata*) is even smaller—to 1 cm (⅜ in.) long—and more circular. Ribs flatter, less beaded.

EASTERN OYSTER   *Crassostrea virginica*   **Figs. 32, 33**
To 20 cm (8 in.) long. Oval, narrow at upper end, bumpy, wrinkled; irregular right valve flatter than left. Interior white with a *purple muscle scar near hind margin.* Intertidal or subtidal, in masses, bars; shells often attached to each other. Prefers low salinities. Canada to Texas, W. Indies. **Similar species:** (1) **Mangrove Oyster** (*C. rhizophorae*) is almost identical; it is found especially on Red Mangrove roots in Caribbean. S. Florida to Brazil, W. Indies. (2) **Crested Oyster** (*Ostrea equestris*) is small—to 8.3 cm (3¼ in.) long—and round or triangular. Whitish, covered with brown or purplish scaly periostracum. Interior lacks purple muscle scar. Low-tide line to deep water; prefers high salinities. Maryland to W. Indies.

ANGEL WING   *Cyrtopleura costata*   **Pls. 4, 43**
Large—to 20 cm (8 in.) long. White with a thin, gray periostracum. Each valve has *30 strong radial ribs* covered with tubercles that become sharp, *pointed teeth at anterior end.* Siphons long, fused; openings with brown-and-white stripes. Siphons cannot be fully withdrawn inside valves. Intertidal near low-water line or subtidal in sandy mud flats, clay, or peat; Cape Cod to Gulf; W. Indies to Brazil.

GIANT ATLANTIC COCKLE   *Dinocardium robustum*   **Pl. 44**
Our largest cockle, to 13.3 cm (5¼ in.) long. Exterior of inflated shell tan with brownish blotches consisting of *vertical bars on adjacent ribs.* Ribs on front third of shell rounded, with scales; posterior ribs flat-topped. Interior pale reddish, purplish, or brown, white toward front. N. Carolina to n. Florida, Gulf.

CROSS-HATCHED LUCINE   **Pl. 41**
Divaricella quadrisulcata
To 2.5 cm (1 in.) long. Glossy white; 3–4 concentric grooves crossed by *wavy lines.*

CARIBBEAN COQUINA   *Donax denticulata*   **Pl. 41**
To 2.5 cm (1 in.) long. Color variable—usually white with brown and orange rays. *Interior purple.* Wedge-shaped; blunt posterior sharply inturned. *Surface has distinct radial grooves.* Sandy intertidal. Edible. **Similar species:** (1) The **Coquina** (*D. variabilis*, Pl. 41) has a shiny surface with less distinct riblets. *Interior whitish,* tinged with yellow, red, or light purple. Both species have toothed margins. (2) **Texas Coquina** (*D. texasiana*) lacks rays of color on shell and tends to be yellowish; it is smaller and blunter than *D. variabilis.* Texas Coquina is found in subtidal; Coquina (*D. variabilis*) lives in swash zone. Caribbean Coquina is found in W. Indies; Coquina from Virginia to Florida, Gulf to Texas. Texas Coquina is found in Gulf off Texas.

ELEGANT DISK CLAM   *Dosinia elegans*   **Pl. 41**
To 7.5 cm (3 in.) long. White or yellowish white shell; looks as if it has been lacquered. Covered with *uniformly spaced thin ridges.*

W. Florida to Texas. **Similar species:** (1) **West Indian Disk Clam** (*D. concentrica*) is almost identical, but concentric lines are closer together. Throughout W. Indies. (2) **Disk Clam** (*D. discus*, Pl. 44) is similar, but ridges not as distinct. *D. elegans* has 8–10 lines per cm; *D. discus* has 20. Sand, mud in lower intertidal; Virginia to Florida, Texas, Bahamas.

RIBBED MUSSEL *Geukensia demissa* **Pl. 44**
Large—to 12.7 cm (5 in.) long. Yellowish green, bluish green, or brown shell, inflated at umbo, with *strong radiating ribs.* Interior silvery white, iridescent. Partly buried in mud of marsh, sometimes attached to pilings. Canada to n. Florida.

SCORCHED MUSSEL *Hormomya exusta* **Fig. 32, Pl. 40**
To 2 cm (¾ in.) long. Brown to yellow-brown shell with a metallic *purple interior.* Surface covered with radial grooves. Commonest mussel in the Caribbean intertidal. **Similar species:** (1) **Hooked Mussel** (*Ischadium recurvum*) is larger, with a distinct *curve along each margin* and a pointed umbo (beak). (2) **Yellow Mussel** (*Ischadium citrinus*) has a yellow periostracum. 30 tiny teeth border ligament.

FLAT TREE OYSTER *Isognomon alatus* **Pl. 40**
To 7.5 cm (3 in.) long. Gray or purplish; *very flat.* Hinge has 8–12 parallel grooves. Colonies on Red Mangrove roots. **Related species: Lister's Tree Oyster** (*I. radiatus*, Pl. 40) is smaller and more elongate, yellowish with reddish radial markings; *4–8 widely spaced grooves in hinges.* Both species on rocks and Red Mangrove roots.

EGG COCKLE *Laevicardium laevigatum* **Pl. 41**
To 3.8 cm (1½ in.) long. Glossy white shell; *much inflated,* with swollen umbones curved under, not visible when viewed from above. Interior margin scalloped. Fresh shells have *rusty, wavy horizontal lines.* Shell stained brown at hinge. Uses foot to leap about. Sand or mud, subtidal; N. Carolina to W. Indies, Brazil.

ROUGH LIMA or FILE CLAM *Lima scabra* **Pl. 40**
To 7.5 cm (3 in.) long. Periostracum brown; shell has *file-like or rasplike surface.* When alive, bright red or orange flesh with numerous long tentacles protrudes from gape in shells. Under rocks; sometimes seen swimming. Commonest of our 3 *Lima* species. **Similar species: Antillean Lima** (*Limaria pellucida*, Pl. 17) is smaller—to 2.8 cm (1⅛ in.) long. Delicate, glassy, *translucent white,* oval shell, with 2 tiny ears at blunt umbo. Edges of valves scalloped by threadlike riblets. N. Carolina to Brazil.

MAHOGANY DATE MUSSEL *Lithophaga busulcata* **Pl. 40**
To 3 cm (1⅕ in.) long. Mahogany brown, often encrusted with gray. *Bores holes in rocks.* **Similar species: Black Date Mussel** (*L. nigra*) is black outside, iridescent inside. In holes in coral.

FOON OYSTER *Lopha frons* **Pl. 40**
To 5 cm (2 in.) long. Reddish, maroon, or red-brown. Interior white, often with violet margins. On Red Mangrove roots.

PENNSYLVANIA LUCINE   *Lucina pensylvanica*   **Pl. 41**
To 5 cm (2 in.) long. White, with a yellowish periostracum when fresh. *Deep fold* extends from tip of umbo to rear edge of shell. Surface *has widely separated concentric ridges*. **Similar species: Jamaica Lucine** (*L. pectinata,* Pl. 41) is yellow-white with yellow interior edges. Heavy, with fine concentric ridges.

CONSTRICTED MACOMA   *Macoma constricta*   **Pl. 41**
To 6 cm (2⅓ in.) long. Dull white, with a thin, gray periostracum. Hind end blunt, indented, *twisted slightly to right.* Fine concentric growth lines. **Similar species:** (1) **Tagelus-like Macoma** (*M. tageliformis*) is also dull white, but periostracum is thin and brown around edges. More elongate; hind end gently rounded. (2) **Narrowed Macoma** (*M. tenta,* Pl. 44) is oval, smooth, slightly iridescent; hind end strongly narrowed and slightly twisted. To 2 cm (¾ in.) long. Canada to Florida, Gulf, W. Indies.

CALICO CLAM or CHECKERBOARD   **Pl. 41**
Macrocallista maculata
To 7.5 cm (3 in.) long. Cream or tan, with a *checkerboard pattern* of red-brown or buff squares. Surface glossy; interior shiny white.

WOOD PIDDOCK   *Martesia cuneiformis*   **Pl. 43**
To 2 cm (¾ in.) long. Pear-shaped, with a gaping hind end (almost closed by callus in adults). *Sharp ridges at front end;* round, smooth ridges at hind end. Grayish white. **Similar species: Striated Wood Piddock** (*M. striata*) is larger — to 4.1 cm (1⅝ in.) long, with sharp, file-like ridges. Both animals bore into wood by rotating, causing substantial damage to marine structures. Easily differentiated from Shipworms (p. 261) by larger diameter of burrow in wood. N. Carolina to Brazil.

SOUTHERN QUAHOG   *Mercenaria campechiensis*   **Pl. 44**
Large — to 15 cm (6 in.) long. Almost identical to commercial hardshell clam of northern waters, but larger and heavier. Exterior grayish when alive, white when bleached by sun. Shells of young clams (less than 2 cm — ¾ in.) long have *strong concentric ridges* (Pl. 44); those of adults have fine ridges. Interior white; usually *lacks purple area* near hind end that characterizes Northern Quahog. Not often present in commercial quantities. New Jersey to Florida and Texas; Mexico.

TULIP MUSSEL   *Modiolus americanus*   **Pl. 40**
To 10 cm (4 in.) long. *Yellowish brown; shiny, smooth. Interior rose-tinted,* iridescent. Thin; may have purplish rays on outside. May be covered with a hairy brown periostracum.

DWARF SURF CLAM   *Mulinia lateralis*   **Pl. 44**
Small — to 1.9 cm (¾ in.) long. Fragile, white, inflated; surface *polished,* with a fibrous yellow periostracum. Umbones large; located a little forward of center. Sand and mud, subtidal and intertidal; Maine to Florida and Texas. **Related species: Puerto Rico Surf Clam** (*M. portoricensis*) is larger — to 3.8 cm (1½ in.) long. Front end rounded, hind end pointed.

PONDEROUS ARK   *Noetia ponderosa*   **Pl. 44**
To 7 cm (2¾ in.) long. Thick; quadrate, *almost rectangular*. Strong whitish ribs radiate from umbo. Ribs become more densely covered with feltlike periostracum toward margin of shell. Animal has red blood. Near surface of sand; Virginia to Florida and Texas.

FALSE ANGEL WING   *Petricola pholadiformis*   **Pl. 43**
To 4 cm (1⅗ in.) long. Chalky white, with numerous *sharply scaled ridges on front*. In clay and peat, sometimes riddling clay banks with holes in which hind end of clam is visible; Canada to Florida and Gulf.

ELEGANT VENUS   *Pitar dione*   **Pl. 41**
To 3 cm (1¼ in.) long. Lavender or white; covered with deep grooves. *Spines* (in intact specimens) *long and tapering, squarish*. **Similar species: Purple Venus** (*P. circinata*) lacks spines.

CAT'S PAW   *Plicatula gibbosa*   **Pl. 40**
To 2.5 cm (1 in.) long. White, with reddish or gray lines; fades to dull white. *6–7 broad folds* radiate from beak.

CAROLINA MARSH CLAM   *Polymesoda caroliniana*   **Pl. 43**
To 4 cm (1⅗ in.) long. Oval, with projecting umbones (beaks). *Inner surface often pale blue;* outer surface covered with brown periostracum, which is usually worn away on umbones—often *scarred white* (as in *Rangia*). Usually intertidal in mud; especially common in low-salinity Needle Rush marshes. Virginia to n. Florida, Gulf to Texas. **Similar species: (1) Wedge Rangia** (*Rangia cuneata*, Pl. 43) is almost identical but has a thicker shell and more pointed umbones (beaks), which are widely separated. Occurs subtidally in brackish bays; rare in intertidal marshes. (2) **Florida Marsh Clam** (*Pseudocyrena maritima*) is smaller—to 1.2 cm (½ in.)—and more elongate; less robust than Carolina Marsh Clam. Outer surface of shell light purple; *inner surface dark purple*. Lacks brown periostracum. In salt marshes and mangrove swamps, in relatively high-salinity mud; s. Florida, Gulf Coast to Mexico; rare in Alabama, Mississippi.

WINGED PEARL OYSTER   *Pteria colymbus*   **Pl. 40**
To 7.5 cm (3 in.) long. Brownish purple; *interior pearly*. Usually attached to Sea Fans.

CHANNELED DUCK   *Raeta plicatella*   **Pl. 44**
To 8.3 cm (3¼ in.) long. *Thin-shelled;* inflated, with *heavy concentric ridges*. Front end narrow. In sandy shallows; N. Carolina to Florida and Gulf, to south Brazil.

WHITE SEMELE   *Semele proficua*   **Pl. 41**
To 3 cm (1¼ in.) long. Creamy white, sometimes with faint pink rays; periostracum thin, brown. Exterior covered with thin, fine, concentric lines; *interior pale yellow, polished*.

AWNING CLAM   *Solemya velum*   **Pl. 1**
Tiny—may reach 2.5 cm (1 in.) in length, but usually half that size. Fragile, shiny; often with *yellowish rays on brown periostracum,* which extends beyond shell margins as a fringe. Swims.

Lives in U-shaped burrows in muddy intertidal sand. Many may be found in a spadeful of sand, dig about 10 cm (4 in.) deep. Canada to Florida.

LITTLE GREEN RAZOR CLAM *Solen viridis*   **Pl. 44**
Thin, small—to 6.7 cm (2⅝ in.) long. Grayish white, *squared-off* shell covered with thin, pale yellowish or greenish periostracum. One central tooth in each valve. Intertidal in sandy bays and inlets; Rhode Island to Florida and Louisiana. **Similar species:** (1) **Atlantic Razor Clam** (*Ensis directus,* Pl. 1) is much larger— to 20 cm (8 in.) long. It has a *low, flat ridge running from umbones (beaks) to hind end;* 2 small, vertical central teeth in left valve. Edible. In intertidal sand; Canada to S. Carolina. (2) **Dwarf Razor Clam** (*E. minor,* Pl. 44) may reach 10 cm (4 in.); it is usually curved more than other razor clams. (Those in genus *Solen* have the straightest shells). Florida to Texas.

ATLANTIC SURF CLAM or SKIMMER CLAM   **Pl. 44**
Spisula solidissima
Large—to 17.8 cm (7 in.) long. Looks like a thinner-shelled version of Quahog, but *umbo is centered,* not obviously turned forward. Smooth, grayish white shell with grayish yellow periostracum. Common in offshore beds, where it is harvested mechanically to be made into fried clam strips. Intertidal and subtidal; Canada to S. Carolina.

ROSY STRIGILLA *Strigilla carnaria*   **Pl. 41**
To 2.5 cm (1 in.) long. Pale rose; interior pinkish. Covered with extremely fine radial lines that become *oblique and wavy over hind end.*

PURPLISH TAGELUS *Tagelus divisus*   **Pl. 44**
To 4.1 cm (1⅝ in.) long. Thin, fragile, elongate. White when worn, purplish gray when fresh. *Interior deep purple;* exterior smooth, shiny, covered with thin, yellow-brown periostracum. Umbo (beak) nearly central. **Related species: Stout Tagelus** (*T. plebeius*) is larger—to 9.5 cm (3¾ in.) long—and thicker; interior not deep purple. Both species range from Massachusetts to Florida, Gulf, W. Indies.

TELLINS *Tellina* species   **Pls. 41, 43, 44**
A family of flattened, oval, shiny, delicate shells, often of great beauty. *Many petal-like.* It is impossible to do them justice here. Seven most common species: (1) **Lined Tellin** (*T. alternata,* Pl. 41) is usually white, but may be pink or yellow. To 7.5 cm (3 in.) long. (2) **Sunrise Tellin** (*T. radiata,* Pl. 41) is similar in size to *T. alternata.* Shiny bluish white, rayed with red, purple, or yellow. Interior yellowish, umbones red. (3) **Caribbean Tellin** (*T. caribaea*) is 2.5 cm (1 in.) long. Thin; glossy white, pink, or orange. (4) **Watermelon Tellin** (*T. punicea*) is red inside and/or outside. To 5 cm (2 in.) long. (5) **Rose-petal Tellin** (*T. lineata*) is whitish or reddish (color less pronounced than on Watermelon Tellin). To 3 cm (1¼ in.) long. (6) **Texas Tellin** (*T. texana,* Pl. 44) is iridescent

white or pinkish. To 1.2 cm (½ in.) long. Gulf of Mexico. (7)
Candy-stick Tellin (*T. similis,* Pl. 43) is shiny, thin-shelled;
exterior white or yellowish, flushed with pink—pink rays often
extend from umbo to edges of valves. To 2.8 cm (1⅛ in.) long. S.
Carolina to Brazil.

SHIPWORM   *Teredo navalis*   **Fig. 107**
An elongate, *wormlike bivalve that burrows in wood.* Found in
pieces of driftwood riddled with holes about 6 mm (¼ in.) wide.
Surface of wood may have smaller holes, but calcareous linings of
burrows easily visible. Use knife to open burrow, revealing 2
white, calcareous, arc-shaped shells used to grind wood. Living
clam can be 30 cm (1 ft.) long. Animals mate in burrows and never
leave wood. They destroy millions of dollars' worth of ships and
piers every year. Subtidal; Canada to Fla. and Tex., W. Indies.
Similar species: (1) The **Gribble** (*Limnoria tripunctata*) also
destroys pilings. It is not a mollusk, but a crustacean (see p. 302),
with *7 pairs of jointed legs.* Produce tiny burrows, 1.6 mm (¹⁄₁₆ in.)
wide by 1.2 cm (½ in.) deep, usually running with grain of wood;
burrows gradually erode surface, exposing deeper layers of wood.
Gribbles damage wood incidentally; they actually eat a wood-
dwelling fungus. Subtidal; Rhode Island to Caribbean. (2)
Gould's Shipworm (*Bankia gouldii,* Fig. 107) has a small
shell—to 1.3 cm (½ in.) long—at front end of wormlike bivalve,
which may be more than 1 m (39 in.) long. In limy burrows
riddling wood. Spiny shells are rotated to bore through wood. New
Jersey to W. Indies, Gulf. (3) See also **Wood Piddock,** p. 258.

TRIGONAL TIVELLA   *Tivella mactroides*   **Fig. 41, Pl. 41**
Tan with brown rays; interior white with purple under umbones.
To 3 cm (1¼ in.) long.

Fig. 107. Shipworms. *Left:* Wood riddled by the Shipworm, *Teredo navalis; right:* Limy tube of Gould's Shipworm, *Bankia gouldii.*

YELLOW COCKLE *Trachycardium muricatum* **Pl. 40**
Yellowish white, sometimes with brown flecks. *Interior yellow.*
20–30 scaly ribs, but central rib smooth near umbo. **Similar species: Prickly Cockle** (*T. egmontianum*) is also yellow but has pronounced brown blotches; spines much larger than in *T. muricatum*. 31–37 ribs. Interior of shell salmon-colored.

Chitons

Chitons belong to Class Amphineura. These mollusks are protected by eight calcareous plates, edged by a fleshy girdle. A broad flat foot clings with such tenacity to the surface of a rock that it must be pried loose.

Chitons are sluggish animals, often taking months to traverse a boulder. They use a toothed radula to scrape algae from the rock's surface. The underside of the animal is equipped with the large foot, a mouth, and a pair of small tentacles. Two narrow slits, the mantle grooves, run the length of the organism, along its margins between the foot and the edge of the mantle. These slits are ciliated and contain 2–40 small gills. The cilia create a current and the chiton simply raises the edges of its girdle at several points to let water flow in and out.

The eight-piece shell has many eyes, which are sensitive to light and let the plodding animal know when it is in the dark safety of a crevice.

Chitons have separate sexes. Sperms are sucked into the female's mantle chamber in the incurrent flow of water, fertilizing the eggs. The female releases ciliated balls of cells, trochophore larvae, which (if not eaten) develop directly into miniature adults and settle on the surface of a rock.

The Fuzzy Chiton (Pl. 16) is common in the Caribbean upper intertidal, often awash at low tide. Its bristly, brown or black and tan girdle encircles blotchy brown eroded valves. Two large chitons live in the lower intertidal. Unlike the Fuzzy Chiton, both have a black-and-white-striped scaly girdle. The West Indian Chiton (Pl. 16) features olive-green plates with a central ridge. Beautiful lightly sculptured chevrons run toward the girdle, so each valve is embossed with an elongate diamond-shaped design. The Marbled Chiton, with its glistening dark brown marbled plates, lives alongside the West Indian Chiton.

In the descriptions below, size is measured from front to rear of the animal. The habitat is always on or under rocks, usually in the intertidal zone or just below it. Unless otherwise specified, all species inhabit Caribbean and s. Florida waters.

GLASS-HAIRED CHITON *Acanthochitona spiculosa*
Narrow and elongate; to 3 cm (1¼ in.) long. Girdle naked, covers valves; lower edge has fringe of brown or blue bristles. Valves

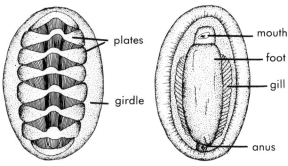

Fig. 108. Anatomy of a chiton.

bluish green and gray, with a distinct central ridge. *Four tufts of long glassy spicules near anterior valve,* 1 tuft on each side of other valves. **Similar species: Dwarf Glass-haired Chiton** (*A. pygmaea*) is smaller—to 2 cm (¾ in.) long. *Dorsal ridge less distinct; more triangular, grooved.* On rocks, dead shells at low-tide line.

UZZY CHITON *Acanthopleura granulata*   **Pl. 16**
Broad. To 7.5 cm (3 in.) long. Girdle bristly; ashy-white, striped with black bands. Valves eroded white; unworn edges brown. Commonest chiton in upper intertidal.

HUTTLEWORTH'S CHITON *Callistochiton shuttleworthianus*
Small—to 1.4 cm (¾ in.). Girdle wide, covered with tiny orange-yellow or rust scales. Valves rust-colored, with a *sharp central ridge* and sloping sides. Valves strongly sculptured. Subtidal, under rocks.

OUGH-GIRDLED CHITON   **Fig. 109, Pl. 16**
Ceratozona squalida
To 5 cm (2 in.). *Girdle leathery;* yellowish brown, not striped; covered with *flat yellowish hairs* rather than bristles. Valves usually eroded—they appear whitish gray with green mottlings on sides. *Foot bright orange.*

ARBLED CHITON *Chiton marmoratus*   **Pl. 16**
To 7.5 cm (3 in.). Girdle banded with greenish white and dark brown. Valves shiny, smooth; *marbled with dark brown or olive with brown zebralike stripes.* Absent in Florida.

QUAMOSE CHITON *Chiton squamosus*   **Fig. 109, Pl. 16**
To 7.5 cm (3 in.). Girdle has alternating pale stripes of grayish green and white. Valves dull gray or tan, with irregular brown longitudinal stripes. Rear edges of valves have small brown squares; sides have diagonal rows of bumpy ridges running toward center.

EST INDIAN CHITON *Chiton tuberculatus*   **Pl. 16**
To 7.5 cm (3 in.). Girdle has alternating areas of whitish, green, and black. Valves grayish green or green-brown. Wide, *flattened,*

diamond-shaped pattern on each valve, made up of beaded tubercles. Commonest chiton on wave-dashed rocky shores.

HEMPHILL'S CHITON *Craspedochiton hemphilli* **Fig. 109**
To 3 cm (1¼ in.) long. Girdle naked, rusty brown, covers most valves; *lower edge has fringe of spines.* Valves heart-shaped, red, occasionally white-spotted. Four tufts of *long glassy spicules* near anterior valve, 1 tuft on either side of other valves. Below intertidal, on dead Finger Coral.

MESH-PITTED CHITON *Ischnochiton papillosus* **Fig. 32**
Small—to 1.2 cm (½ in.) long; girdle narrow with alternating bars of white and greenish brown. *Valves whitish,* mottled with olive-green or brown. Under rocks; Florida, Gulf, W. Indies.

FLORIDA SLENDER CHITON *Stenoplax floridana* **Fig. 109**
Elongate—length about 3 times width. To 3 cm (1¼ in.) long. Girdle appears smooth and naked but has fine striated scales, marbled in bluish and gray. Valves roundly arched; whitish with olive or black markings. Diagonal rows of *beaded riblets run posteriorly from edge of valves toward center.* **Similar species:** (1) **Purple Slender Chiton** (*S. purpurascens,* Pl. 16) is similar to *S. floridana* but riblets not beaded and plates buff, gray-green, or purplish. To 5 cm (2 in.) long. Wave-swept rocky intertidal; Florida, Bermuda, W. Indies. (2) **Ashy Slender Chiton** (*S. erythronota*) has a brown girdle with green spots and tiny scales. Elongate *valves with sharp ridges on top.* Ash gray or brownish, may have 2 longitudinal green streaks or may be mottled green or brown. To 3 cm (1¼ in.) long. (3) **Slug-shaped Chiton** (*S. limaciformis*) has a creamy girdle with marbled green and white flecks and tiny beaded scales. *Valves rounded,* with *no central ridge;* grayish green with flecks of dark green and white. To 2.5 cm (1 in.) long. Under rocks.

SCHRAMM'S CHITON *Tonicia schrammi* **Fig. 109**
To 2.5 cm (1 in.) long. Girdle naked, fleshy; brownish to flesh-colored. Valves glossy, brownish red to buff with dark brown specks. Beaklike central ridge on each valve overlaps next valve to the rear. Intertidal in W. Indies; absent in Florida.

Tusk Shells

These animals are mollusks that belong to Class Scaphopoda. Their shells have long been used for jewelry by primitive people. Archaeologists use this fact as proof that trade existed among ancient peoples as long as 20,000 years ago, as inland tribes buried their dead with frontlets of tusk shells, which could only have been obtained by barter with coastal tribes.

The shells of these fragile secretive animals resemble miniature elephant tusks. The living animals lie buried with the narrow tip of the shell projecting from the surface of the sand. The

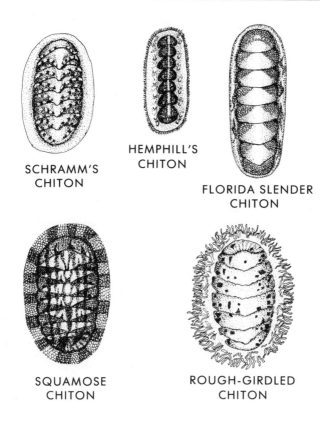

Fig. 109. Some common chitons.

shells of dead scaphopods may be found enmeshed in the seaweed along the strandline of the beach. They are soon crumbled by the surf, so finding a tusk shell is a matter of luck; your best chance is after a storm.

Most scaphopods are small. They have no gills and must absorb oxygen through the body surface. Blood is circulated by rhythmic movements of the foot, which is also used for burrowing. Sexes are separate and fertilization is internal. Sticky, threadlike tentacles called captacula are extended from the head into the sand; the plankton and detritus adhering to them are brought back to the mouth. A current is created by cilia lining the mantle cavity, and water is sucked through the small hole in the top. Every few minutes the current is reversed, and waste-laden water is blown out through the same hole.

The common Flattened Tusk (Fig. 110) is slightly flattened on two sides, and shiny white. The tiny Slender Cadulus has minute white bands encircling the translucent shell.

SLENDER CADULUS *Cadulus acus*
Tiny—to 1.2 cm (½ in.) long; slender, slightly curved. Translucent, usually covered with opaque white bands of varying widths. *Apex simple, no slits.* Slight swelling near aperture; apical end usually sculptured with fine lines running around shell. Common in W. Indies; absent in Florida. **Similar species:** (1) **Four-toothed Cadulus** (*C. quadridentatus*) has *well-defined slits* near apex, giving it a four-toothed appearance. (2) **Tetrodon Cadulus** (*C. tetrodon*) is similar to *C. quadridentatus*, but has a *swelling in center,* not near tip, and tapers slightly toward both ends.

FLATTENED TUSK *Dentalium didymum* **Fig. 110**
To 2.5 cm (1 in.) long, glossy white, no ribs. Slightly curved; *sides slightly flattened,* especially toward convex side. Common in Yucatan, Puerto Rico, Barbados. **Similar species:** (1) **Reticulated Tusk** (*D. ceratum*) is glossy *yellow,* becoming white on front half. Nine primary ribs on apex, increasing to 18; these disappear, leaving front half, which is smooth. *No slit at apical end.* (2) **Ivory Tusk** (*D. eboreum*) is similar but glossy ivory white to pinkish. *Deep apical slit on convex side.* 20 fine longitudinal lines near apex. To 6 cm (2½ in.) long. (3) **Paneled Tusk** (*D. laqueatum*) is opaque white, with *splotches of translucent gray.* Nine primary ribs, increasing to 12 near middle and 24 near aperture. Round. (4) **Half-scratched Tusk** (*D. semistriolatum*) is similar to *D. eboreum* but more curved. Translucent white with milky patches, sometimes reddish at apex. *One thin apical slit on each side.*

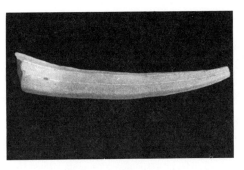

Fig. 110.
Flattened
Tusk.

Octopods and Squids

These dramatic animals, members of Class Cephalopoda, are among the most exciting in the sea. Stories of huge squids rising to the surface at night to terrorize sailors are true. There is a deepwater species, *Architeuthis,* that reaches at least 15 m (50 ft.) in length.

Octopods (octopuses) exhibit emotions and actually turn red with pleasure or in anger. They are surprisingly intelligent and have been trained to perform tricks. From a laboratory in Florida comes this remarkable story: an octopus, kept in an aquarium, secretly stole out of its tank every night and raided a nearby tank containing crabs, returning to its own aquarium before dawn. The owner of the crabs was becoming paranoid. Who could be stealing his animals? Hiding himself in the laboratory one night, he saw the thief in action. The octopus extended its boneless body through a tiny feeding hole, tentacle by tentacle, until everything was outside except its bulging eyes. With an audible pop each was pulled through the hole.

Both octopods and squids have a beak shaped like a hawk's except that it is inverted, with the longer half underneath. Many species of octopods inject poison as they bite, paralyzing their prey. The favorite food of most octopods is crabs. The octopus descends on them and enmeshes them in the webs between its tentacles. One quick bite behind the eyes and the crab is immobilized. Squids eat small fishes and have been caught on hook and line, as they will attack minnow bait. Most squids swim in schools; most octopods are solitary.

Cephalopods have a muscular mantle that alternately relaxes and contracts to force water into the mantle cavity, bathing the gills. An elaborate circulatory system with a heart and auxiliary pumping stations drives the blood through the body rapidly enough to support a relatively high rate of metabolism.

Squids usually swim headfirst by gently rippling their lateral fins. Octopods crawl along the bottom in their never-ending search for crabs. When startled or attacked they change color, often turning black, perhaps to frighten the predator. If this doesn't work, a squid will instantly become virtually transparent, almost invisible in the water. The octopod becomes camouflaged, matching the bottom. If the predator advances further, the cephalopod (squid or octopod) gives it the old one-two: a cloud of black dye is released, simulating another prey animal and confusing the attacker. At the same time the squid or octopod rapidly contracts its mantle, forcibly ejecting a stream of water through its siphon, jetting backward with great velocity under cover of the dye.

These animals can almost instantly match the color of the environment by sending nerve messages to cells in the skin called chromatophores. These contain bags of dye in three primary colors. When the bags are expanded the color becomes intense. When contracted, the cells become nearly colorless as the dye is reduced to a tiny dot. Camouflage is achieved by expanding some chromatophores and contracting others until the color of the background is matched.

The eye of a cephalopod is much like ours in its ability to focus and form images. But the lens, like that of a camera, moves back and forth, rather than changing its shape as a human lens does.

During courtship, the male, using a specially adapted tentacle, removes a packet of sperms from its own body and places it inside the female's mantle cavity. Squids lay chains of egg capsules in festoons over the bottom. Octopods lay eggs in caves; the female broods them, blowing oxygenated water over them with her siphon (see Pl. 47). Recent studies of the Seaweed Octopus have revealed that the female spawns only once in her life. While brooding her young she eats little and her feeding habits change. Instead of boring a hole in snails to remove the tissue, she wrenches the animal from its shell, often not eating it after all her work. About ten days after her eggs hatch she dies. What is so exciting to scientists is the fact that a gland in the female's eye socket seems to be responsible for her rapid aging and death. If the gland is removed the octopus resumes her normal habits and lives for many months. The optic gland has been compared to the human pituitary. Is this a clue to the possibility that we may be able to prevent or attenuate aging?

Squids have a thin, plasticlike internal shell called a pen. Most octopods have lost the shell completely. A deepwater squid, the Common Spirula, has embedded in its body a coiled, gas-filled shell that gives it buoyancy (Fig. 112). When the animal dies and decays, the shell floats to the surface and drifts ashore, to the delight of shell collectors. Look for the shell in seaweed on the beach.

The Atlantic Oval or Reef Squid (Pl. 46), because of its gregarious and fearless habits, provides much joy to snorkelers and divers. Small schools of this wonderful animal appear suddenly in the corner of your eye as you swim over lagoon or reef. You are startled, not so much by their sudden appearance as by the realization that they are staring at you with as much interest as you are exhibiting toward them. Approach slowly and they will hold their ground, staring all the more intently. When you are about 1.5 m (5 ft.) away they will swim slowly backward in unison, with their fins rippling and their tentacles bunched up. Swim faster and they will match your velocity, keeping the same precise distance. Stop and they will stop too. This game can go on for 15 minutes or more, until one of the parties tires.

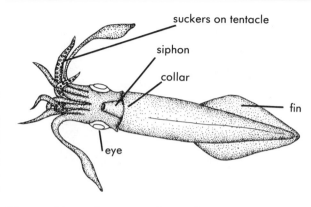

Fig. 111. External anatomy of a squid.

The Briar or Reef Octopus reaches 50 cm (20 in.) in length. Its skin is a smooth pinkish brown or reddish color. It sometimes invades the intertidal zone, where it hides under rocks or in tidepools, surprising the barefoot wader who suddenly finds his ankle caught in the animal's cold embrace.

Joubin's Octopus (Pls. 46, 47) is small, rarely reaching 15 cm (6 in.) overall. Females are sometimes found brooding their eggs inside clam shells or in tin cans or bottles.

Four squids and five octopods are commonly found in shallow water in s. Florida, the Gulf, and the Caribbean. Squids have ten arms, a long tapered body, and are pelagic (free swimming). Octopods have eight arms, a bulbous body, and are most often seen scuttling from one hiding place to another in rocks or reefs.

Squids

LEE'S STRIPED SQUID *Loligo pleii* **Pl. 46**
To 75 cm (2½ ft.) long, including arms. Body elongate, slender, with long, narrow, slightly wavy, *dark maroon bands along sides; rest of body covered with maroon dots. Triangular fins on last third of body.

BRIEF THUMBSTALL SQUID *Lolliguncula brevis* **Pl. 46**
To 25 cm (10 in.) long, including arms. Short, rounded fins on last third of body form a *flat round disk*. Upper arms very short; upper surface covered with purple dots. Underside of fins white. S. Carolina to Florida, Gulf, Caribbean. **Similar species: Pickford's Squid** (*Pickfordiateuthis pulchella*) is tiny—to 4 cm (1½

Fig. 112. Internal shell of Common Spirula.

in.) long. Body broad, with 2 small, round, *disklike fins that are separated from each other, not joined at rear.* Eyes large. Over Turtle Grass beds in shallow water.

ATLANTIC OVAL or REEF SQUID   **Pl. 46**
Sepioteuthis sepioidea
To 25 cm (10 in.) in length. *Long, oval fins that start just behind mouth.* Purplish or yellowish with purple dots. Swims with short tentacles bunched, appearing like part of head. Conspicuous fins have rippling movement used for propulsion. In schools of 4–6 in back reef area, lagoons.

COMMON SPIRULA *Spirula spirula*   **Fig. 112**
Fragile white shell is chambered cone *coiled in flat spiral,* usually less than 2.5 cm (1 in.) wide. Each chamber divided from the next by a shiny white, concave, fragile wall with a tiny dot in the center. Shell develops inside body of small, short-armed, deepsea squid. When animal dies and decays, air-filled shell floats to surface and is washed ashore. N. Carolina to Caribbean.

Octopods

BRIAR or REEF OCTOPUS *Octopus briareus*
To 54 cm (1½ ft.) long. Arms thick at bases; *longest arm about 5 times body length.* Pinkish or greenish to red-mottled. Intertidal, subtidal under coral heads.

SEAWEED or FOUR-EYED REEF OCTOPUS
Octopus hummelincki
Small—to 20 cm (8 in.) long. Covered with flat, blade-like, fuzzy-ended papillae. Eyes project conspicuously from body. A *round pale blue to purplish blotch or circle next to each eye.* These false

eyespots may be vivid, making identification easy. When crawling, animal reddish, yellow-brown, or whitish, mottled with yellow; when swimming, changes to light brown. Beds of sargassum and other brown algae.

JOUBIN'S OCTOPUS *Octopus joubini*   **Pls. 46, 47**
Small—to 15 cm (6 in.) long, with *short arms* that are only slightly longer than body. Skin smooth, with few warts. Brownish, blackish. Often within bivalve shells.

WHITE-SPOTTED or GRASS OCTOPUS   **Pl. 46**
Octopus macropus
To 1 m (3¼ ft.) long, including longest arm. Blue-green, brownish gray, or pinkish orange, with *large white spots.* When disturbed, becomes brick-red and spots become prominent. First arm longest.

COMMON ATLANTIC OCTOPUS *Octopus vulgaris*   **Pl. 46**
Largest of shallow-water octopods, with maximum radial spread to 2.2 m (7 ft.), including longest arm, which is about 4× body length. *Front and rear pairs of arms shorter than side arms.* Skin smooth; usually white, mottled with bluish green.

13

The Segmented Worms

Barry A. Vittor and Paul G. Johnson

The word "worm" evokes something less than the image of a multicolored flower, but just such a picture often rewards the careful observer of coral reefs and underwater ledges. Among the segmented worms (Phylum Annelida), the feather-duster worms are certainly the most conspicuous and attractive of tropical animals (see Pl. 26). They are indeed similar to flowers: some have long stalks topped with brightly colored fan-shaped massed tentacles; others are crowned with Christmas-tree-like structures.

The polychaetes (Class Polychaeta), the bristle-bearing annelid worms, are among the most important sources of food for bottom-dwelling fishes and arthropods. There are probably at least 8000 species in the oceans of the world, most of which are adapted to a burrowing existence in reefs or sediment.

Most people are more familiar with earthworms (Class Oligochaeta) than with the polychaetes. Earthworms may reach lengths of more than 1 m (3¼ ft.) but most are less than 15 cm (6 in.) long. Tropical polychaetes also vary in size, with some species in Family Eunicidae attaining a length of 3 m (10 ft.).

Polychaete worms are found on rocky shores, sand flats, and beaches. Some are burrowing scavengers in soft bottoms, some tube-dwelling filter feeders on the surfaces of reefs and sand flats; others are crawling scavengers and carnivores.

There are three classes of annelids in addition to Polychaeta: Oligochaeta, Hirudinea (leeches), and Archiannelida. Each is represented in the marine environment by relatively few species. Oligochaetes look much like some of the polychaetes, but generally have fewer bristles and seldom have a well-developed head. Leeches may be parasitic on fishes but are not usually seen inshore. Archiannelids are primitive segmented worms, numerous in beach sands and soft bottoms offshore. They can be identified only with a microscope.

Polychaetes

Class Polychaeta is divided into two groups of families: the Errantia, or free-moving forms, and the Sedentaria, or burrowers and tube-dwellers. These categories are artificial and thus hard to relate to the ecology and phylogeny (evolution) of the group.

Figure 113 depicts a generalized polychaete. The head is of particular importance since its appearance, including appendages, serves to identify many species. The head is termed the prostomium and includes the eyes, antennae, and palps. The mouth is on the underside and may be equipped with an armored pharynx, jaws, and teeth. The peristomium, or first body segment, often carries tentacles or other filamentlike appendages. The anus is found at the end segment, or pygidium. Hairlike setae are found on most segments and are arranged in varying numbers and kinds. Each of these principal morphological characteristics exhibits major differences from one species to the next. Unfortunately, our "typical" polychaete is representative of only a handful of families.

Polychaetes generally have a pair of lateral appendages, or parapodia, extending from each body segment (see Fig. 113). The degree of development of the parapodia varies greatly from family to family and is thought to reflect the mobility of the species. Scaleworms, for example, have well-developed parapodia and are highly mobile. The capitellid worms, on the other hand, generally lack parapodia and are nearly stationary burrowers.

Some species of worms have evolved flattened, paddle-like parapodia. Most are among the several pelagic families repre-

Fig. 113. Anatomy of a polychaete worm.

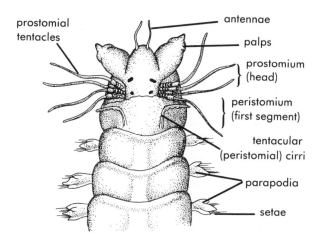

sented in our area. Others, such as the Phyllodocidae, are bottom-dwellers that use their parapodia for crawling. Families Nereidae and Eunicidae include many species that develop flattened parapodia during spawning season. Swimming epitokes (worms modified for reproduction) leave the bottom in great numbers, making the water seem alive with undulating, ribbonlike worms.

The parapodia carry a variety of setae. These small hairs are nearly invisible to the unaided eye in the feather-dusters and other tube-dwelling worms but are conspicuous in other groups. The setae may serve a protective function in one group while being used for locomotion in another. The Sea Mouse (p. 286) has extremely long setae that cover the entire back of the worm. Protection from predators, including man, appears to be the function of the tubular, poison-bearing setae of the fireworms. The sting of the setae may result in extreme pain and swelling for the careless observer.

Many polychaetes have branchiae (gills) on certain segments. These may have a respiratory and/or food gathering function. Some polychaetes display plate-like scales, elytra, on their segments, which may cover the sides of the worms or completely conceal the back. Elytra provide protection for the scaleworm, acting as both shield and camouflage. Scales of the Rough Scaleworm (Fig. 117) are often covered with algae, hydrozoans, and debris, allowing the worm to blend in with its surroundings.

One of the most striking characteristics of some polychaetes is the arrangement of feeding tentacles. This is especially true among the feather-dusters. Plate 26 shows the color patterns and delicate beauty displayed by these worms. The branched tentacles, or radioles, are used to catch food particles brought by water currents. This mode of feeding is known as filter feeding and is similar to that displayed by a less spectacular worm, the Medusa Worm (Fig. 114). This polychaete has long, retractile, filamentous tentacles that it lays on the sand. Food that is picked up from the bottom in the form of tiny pieces of disintegrating plants or animals is carried to the mouth by tiny cilia. This mode of feeding is called detritus feeding.

Polychaetes inhabit a variety of homes (Fig. 115). Sabellid feather-dusters build leathery tubes that stand above the bottom, while serpulids secrete stony tubes on hard surfaces. The Medusa Worm and other members of Family Terebellidae are secretive and are normally found between rocks, in dead sand dollars, or in other cavities. Exquisite sand-grain tubes are created by the Royal Trumpetworm, which is generally found on sand flats. The Sponge Threadworm (Fig. 115) is found inside living sponges. It is only 6 mm (¼ in.) long, but its numbers more than compensate for its small size. Thousands may inhabit a single fist-sized sponge.

Polychaetes can be hard to identify in the field. Only those varieties that are most frequently encountered and that can

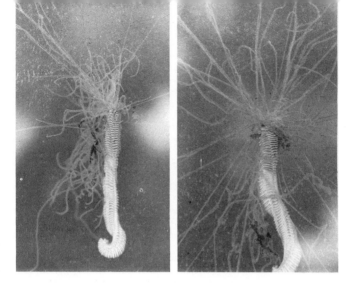

Fig. 114. Medusa Worm climbing aquarium wall using sticky tentacles.

be identified on the basis of obvious external characteristics are covered in this guide. Tube type, coloration, length, unusual appendages, unique habitat, and other criteria may be used to establish at least the family of the worms included here.

Polychaetes are divided into two groups:

1. Sedentary Polychaetes: Worms adapted to existence in one place. Usually build tubes or burrows. Often have elaborate fanlike or elongated tentacles. Body often divided into 2 or 3 distinct regions. Parapodia and setae often reduced.

2. Errant Polychaetes: Free-living worms that move about, usually in search of food. Predatory. Most have well-developed parapodia to aid in swimming or burrowing. Usually have a toothed, eversible pharynx used to capture worms or small invertebrates.

Sedentary Polychaetes

Fanworms and Christmas-tree Worms: Families Sabellidae and Serpulidae

BLACK-SPOTTED FANWORM
Branchiomma nigromaculata
Small—rarely exceeding 2.5 cm (1 in.) long. *Body speckled with dark spots;* branchiae (gills) have many *minute black eyespots.*

Cannot be differentiated from juvenile *Sabellastarte magnifica* in the field. Mangrove roots, coral reefs; Caribbean. Family Sabellidae.

GULF FANWORM *Eupomatus dianthus*

Tiny—to 2.5 cm (1 in.) long. Under a hand lens operculum is seen to have lower disk of 30–36 sharp spines, ventralmost longest. Upper disk has *10–12 inward-pointing spines.* Produce sinuous white calcareous tubes on surface of old seashells, sometimes in clumps on boat bottoms. Intertidal and subtidal; sw. Florida to Texas. Family Serpulidae.

SPINY FEATHER-DUSTER WORMS   **Fig. 115**

Hydroides species

10–15 species throughout our area. Many have immigrated from Europe aboard hulls of ships. To 4 cm (1½ in.), usually smaller. Stout white calcareous tube; rough, often irregularly coiled, and attached to surface of shells or rocks. Branchial plumes (gills) orange, fanning out to either side of opercular stalk. Operculum ornate; has *10–11 large, equal-sized horny spines,* all curving inward and ending in sharp points. Spines mounted in depression of a basal funnel of fused, radially symmetrical, toothlike structures. Bases of large spines hinged, so when worm withdraws into tube, opercular spines expand out into a *circle of daggerlike projections,* protecting tube entrance. Common species include *H. uncinata, H. crucigera,* and *H. elegans.* Cape Cod to Brazil; W. Indies. Family Serpulidae.

BANDED FANWORMS *Sabella* species   **Fig. 85, Pl. 26**

Thick-bodied worms that occupy rocky habitats on leeward side of coral reefs or protected tidepools. (1) *S. melanostigma* has regular arrangement of *4–5 pairs of black eyespots* along length of each tentacular filament. Spots easily visible to unaided eye (see Pl. 26). Body yellowish brown, with a distinctive pattern of *black spots arranged in double rows* on either side (pattern most noticeable on anterior segments). Expanded branchial crown brown at base, grading to uniform yellow toward end of filaments. Unlike most sabellids, *S. melanostigma* will leave its tube quickly if disturbed and build a new mucus-silt tube elsewhere. (2) *S. micropthalma* has more numerous eyespots irregularly distributed along filaments. Filaments not banded in either species. Body pale yellow, *without paired spots.* S. Florida, Bermuda, W. Indies. Family Sabellidae.

ELEGANT FANWORM *Hypsicomus elegans*   **Pl. 26**

Body pale purplish brown, darker along middorsal line. Membrane at base of tentacular crown usually purple. *Branchiae yellow,* occasionally spotted or banded with purple. White, yellow, purple-spotted, and red forms have also been found. To 6 cm (2½ in.) long, 1.8 cm (¾ in.) of which forms the branchiae. Oblique lateral row of setae on collar, just below tentacular crown. Parchmentlike tube dark, tough, sometimes long and tortuous, pene-

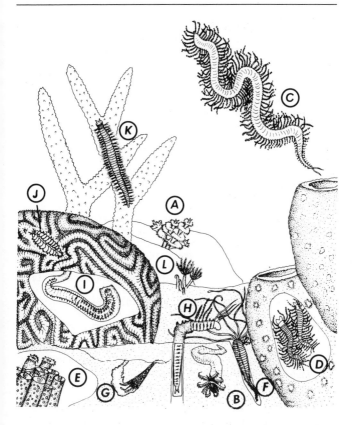

Fig. 115. Polychaete worms inhabiting coral reefs and sand-flat communities in s. Florida and Caribbean. (Scale of worms exaggerated to show characteristic structures.) (A) Horned Christmas-tree Worm (*Spirobranchus giganteus,* p. 279), (B) Feather-duster Worm (*Hydroides* species, p. 276), (C) Zebra Worm (*Trypanosyllis zebra,* p. 292), (D) Sponge Threadworm (*Haplosyllis spongicola,* p. 292), (E) Gulf Honeycomb Tubeworm (*Phragmatopoma lapidosa,* p. 282), (F) Medusa Worm (*Loimia medusa,* p. 281), (G) Royal Trumpet Worm (*Cistena regalis,* p. 280), (H) Plumed Worm (*Diopatra cuprea,* p. 288), (I) Atlantic Palolo Worm (*Eunice schemacephala,* p. 291), (J) Fringed Scaleworm (*Lepidonotus variabilis,* p. 288), (K) Fireworm (*Hermodice carunculata,* p. 290), (L) Magnificent Banded Fanworm (*Sabellastarte magnifica,* p. 278).

trates clumps of shells or rocks. Most common on older parts of reef where there is little living coral or on underside of loose rocks on shallow landward side of reefs. Prefers well-shaded areas. Se. U.S., Bermuda, and W. Indies, in rocky and reef habitats. Family Sabellidae.

STAR CHRISTMAS-TREE WORM *Pomatostegus stellatus*

Similar to *Spirobranchus giganteus,* but identifiable by its distinctively shaped operculum consisting of a series of *3–5 disklike horny plates* mounted one on top of the other on a hollow central axis. Under each plate are rows of starlike diverging spines and a circle of spines. Branchiae spiraled, about a turn and a half; bright rose to chocolate brown in color, barred lightly with white. Body flesh-colored, with yellow cross-stripes that shine like silk when held to light. Tube hard and calcareous. Caribbean and s. Florida. Family Serpulidae.

RED-BANDED FANWORM *Potamilla fonticula* **Pl. 26**

Large tube-dwelling feather duster — about 7 cm (2¾ in.) long, 3 cm (1¼ in.) of which forms the tentacular crown, which is white or red, with a *dark red band midway along branchial filaments*. Row of minute eyespots on most branchiae, not visible without magnification (hand lens). Bases of branchiae united by a delicate low, weblike membrane. Body flesh-colored, with *2 brown ventral stripes* running length of worm. About 20 thoracic segments in adult. Tube tough and horny for most of its 15 cm (6 in.) length; greatest width 1.5 cm (¾ in.). Free end of tube tapered; consists of fine mud incorporated with mucus, allowing for flexibility. Among loose rocks or in clumps in quiet water; Florida Keys, Virgin Islands, Puerto Rico. **Similar species:** *P. reniformis* has 1 pair of eyes at base of tentacular crown. Family Sabellidae.

MAGNIFICENT BANDED FANWORM **Fig. 115, Pl. 26**
Sabellastarte magnifica

A common and strikingly colored fanworm. Body about 12 cm (4¾ in.) long, including 9 cm (3½ in.) tentacular crown, which is made up of numerous closely set filaments and may have a spread of 20–25 cm (8–10 in.). *Shades of brown* with several series of color spots arranged in bands. Colors include brown banded with light tan spots, chocolate-brown banded in white, dark purple with brown spots, and dark mahogany-red banded with light brown. A few are almost white with indistinct barring like watered silk. Mucus and mud tube cylindrical, lined internally with hardened mucus. Clumps of tubes consolidate and thus stabilize sediment down to a depth of 19 cm (7½ in.), protecting bottom from erosion by storm surges. In clumps near leeward side of rocks or on floor of small protected tidepools. The many expanded branchial crowns resemble a field of flowers when animals are undisturbed. However, the slightest water movement or shadow results in a speedy retreat into the tubes. S. Florida, W. Indies to Brazil. Family Sabellidae.

ORNED CHRISTMAS-TREE WORM   **Fig. 115, Pl. 26**
Spirobranchus giganteus giganteus
The largest and most visible serpulid; common name derives from
shape of its expanded branchial crown. Body to 12 cm (5 in.) long,
divided into thorax and abdomen, housed in a sturdy convoluted
calcareous tube attached to rocks, coral, or other hard object.
Protruding from tube are the paired whorls of the branchial
crown, as well as a plate-shaped operculum mounted on a fleshy
stalk. Branchial crown important in respiration and food gathering, filters organisms from water. Operculum armed with 2–3
branched, antlerlike processes that project in a defensive manner.
When disturbed, worm quickly withdraws into tube, sealing
entrance with operculum.

Tube smooth and porcelainlike inside; deep lavender, shading
to white at rim. Outside chalky white, rough, irregular; often
encrusted with marine organisms. Antlers deep carmine-red;
operculum yellow; body flesh-colored; spectacular crown yellow,
red, or blue. The variety of possible color combinations may be a
specialized adaptation to confuse predatory fishes and reduce
their ability to home in on a given color pattern. *S. giganteus* is
usually solitary on rocks or reef face, where currents provide a
continuous supply of plankton. Shallow water; s. Florida, W.
Indies, Caribbean.

Threadworms:
Families Capitellidae and Orbiniidae

APITELLID THREADWORM   *Capitella capitata*   **Fig. 120**
Thin, *earthwormlike;* to 10 cm (4 in.) long. Parapodia reduced,
appearing to be absent. *Reddish purplish* at anterior, sometimes
becoming lighter and yellowish at posterior. Body divided into
slightly swollen thorax and narrower, longer abdomen. Intertidal
and subtidal mud; Arctic to N. Carolina, rare in Gulf, Texas,
especially common in polluted water near sewage outfalls; also in
dredged channels. Family Capitellidae.

ED THREADWORM   *Scoloplos rubra*   **Fig. 119**
Small, slender, *red, threadlike* worm, to 7 cm (2¾ in.) long by 1
mm (1/24 in.) thick. Prostomium pointed; body divided into thick,
flattened or oval thorax and cylindrical abdomen—division
abrupt at segment 24 or 25. Middle third of body often greenish.
In mud or sandy mud in lower intertidal or subtidal zone in poorly
drained parts of marshes and brackish water. Virginia to W.
Indies, Gulf. **Similar species:** (1) Many other worms in this
family are similar; lens and patience are necessary for differentiation. (2) Three capitellid threadworms—*Capitella capitata,
Notomastus latericeus,* and *Mediomastus californiensis* (Fig.
119)—are similar and may be so common that each spadeful of

mud reveals dozens. Especially common on disturbed bottoms, they will colonize dredged channels before any other species. Family Orbiniidae.

LUGWORM   *Arenicola cristata*   **Figs. 63, 120**

Brown or green; cigar-shaped, thick-bodied. *11 pairs of coiled, tuftlike, reddish brown gills extend along sides of trunk.* Three body regions: trunk, which has small parapodia and gills that start roughly ⅓ of the way back from head; tail, which lacks parapodia and setae; and head, which is small and lacks appendages. Builds mounds of sediment with U-shaped burrows open at both ends. Intertidal mud (see Fig. 63); Cape Cod to Caribbean; Gulf. Family Arenicolidae.

ICE CREAM CONE or TRUMPET WORMS   **Figs. 115, 118**
Cistena gouldii and *C. regalis*

Cone-shaped tube built of single layer of sand grains or similar particles, cemented together as if by stone mason. Sand grains selected for tube construction are stored in pouch behind head. Tube open at both ends; smaller end opens to surface, so worm faces down in sand. There it gathers food particles using grooved buccal tentacles surrounding mouth. Head equipped with row of heavy, forward-directed *golden setae,* used both for digging and as operculum to seal entrance of tube. Worm moves freely; carries sand grain home from place to place in search of food-rich sediments. Conical body with few segments divided into thorax, abdomen, and shovel-shaped front end consisting of 6 segments without parapodia. **Ice Cream Cone Worm** (*C. gouldii*) common from Cape Cod to Florida, Cuba, Jamaica, Puerto Rico; **Royal Trumpet Worm** (*C. regalis*) found in Antilles, Bermuda, Florida Keys. Family Amphictonidae (Pectinariidae).

PARCHMENT WORM   **Fig. 19, Pl. 4**
Chaetopterus variopedatus

Thick; to 25 cm (10 in.) long. Flabby, flesh-colored, with body divided into 3 sections; midsection has 3 large, fanlike parapodia. Builds tan, whitish, U-shaped tube measuring about 30 cm (1 ft.) from end to end across U, with tips projecting about 5 cm (2 in.) from surface of muddy sand flats. Worm assumes position near front end of tube and flaps *large, fanlike segments* (14, 15, and 16) to pump water through tube. Winglike appendages on segment 12 and cuplike segment 13 spread mucous net across tube to catch plankton, detritus. Periodically mucous net and food are rolled into a ball and passed up food groove to shovel-shaped head, thence to mouth. Lower intertidal or subtidal; Cape Cod to Gulf, rare in W. Indies. Family Chaetopteridae. Tube often contains Parchment-worm Crab (*Pinnixa chaetopterana*) or Gibbs' Parchment-worm Crab (*Polyonyx gibbesi*). *Pinnixa* is smaller, whiter, and narrower than *Polyonyx,* which reaches 1.6 cm (⅝ in.). *Polyonyx* has flat, S-shaped claws and a broadly oval carapace. Both species rarely leave tube.

Long-tentacled or Ornate Worms:
Family Terebellidae

ORNATE WORM   *Amphitrite ornata*   **Fig. 20, Pl. 2**
Thick; to 15 cm (6 in.) long. Elaborate crown of numerous *long yellowish tentacles* and *3 pairs of short, red, fuzzy gills.* Reddish brown body divided into 2 parts: thick thorax and thin, tapered abdomen; setae on 50 segments. Lives in a thick-walled, gray, clayey burrow topped by a low mound in shallow, muddy bays near low-tide line. Worm extends crown of tentacles over surface to pick up detritus. Commensal **Many-scaled Worm** (*Lepidametria commensalis*) is often found in tube. Maine to N. Carolina. Family Terebellidae.

MEDUSA WORM   *Loimia medusa*   **Figs. 114, 115**
Widely distributed in tropics, subtropics. Builds chitinized tube covered with shell fragments, debris, on rocks or buried vertically in sandy mud or gravel. Two body regions: brick-red, thick thorax with *dorsal bundles of setae and ventral pads;* thinner abdomen with reduced parapodia. Numerous white, banded, or purple-checkered feeding tentacles project out of tube. Spaghetti-like *tentacles can spread out over substrate for a meter or more* in search of food particles, which are carried to mouth by way of a ciliated groove. Each tentacle is independent: if one tentacle is touched it will immediately recoil, with no apparent effect on other tentacles. **Similar species:** *Eupolymnia nebulosa.* Family Terebellidae.

ROOFING WORM   *Owenia fusiformis*   **Fig. 120**
Small—to 4.5 cm (1¾ in.) long. Produces a tough tube to 20 cm (7¾ in.) long, covered with overlapping sand grains; tube tapers at both ends. Body consists of 20 segments. Worm extends sticky, *flowerlike feeding crown* of 8 branching, ciliated, mucus-covered lobes to trap plankton. Crown may be placed on sediment near tube to pick up detritus. Red, brown, or green crown also functions as gill. In old snail shells or clean sand in lower intertidal; worldwide; common in Gulf. Family Oweniidae.

BAMBOO WORM   *Clymenella torquata*   **Fig. 120**
To 15 cm (6 in.) long. Orange or green body encircled with red or green rings at joints; body consists of *22 long segments with a jointed appearance, like bamboo.* Lives head down in a straight, thin, fine-grained sand tube 25 cm (10 in.) long. *Hindmost segment (tail) resembles funnel-shaped crown,* closes off top of tube. Prostomium (head) blunt, with eversible proboscis. Eats sediment at bottom of tube, which is so narrow worm is unable to turn around. Lower intertidal; Maine to N. Carolina, Gulf. Family Maldanidae.

Mudworms: Family Spionidae

BLISTERWORM *Polydora websteri*
Small—to 2 cm (¾ in.) long. Flesh-colored. Two long, curled, *purple-spotted palps* project from prostomium. Forms *blisterlike chamber on oyster shells,* from which palps project. Massachusetts to Gulf. **Similar species: Polydora Mudworm** (*P. ligni*) may be reddish; it lives in soft mud tube attached to hard object in shallow water. May be so abundant in oyster beds as to bury oysters in mud tubes. Maine to Florida and Gulf. Family Spionidae.

BEE SPIONID *Spiophanes bombyx*   **Fig. 119**
Small, thin; to 5 cm (2 in.) long. *Prostomium triangular with base of triangle at front,* so that front of worm looks blunt; no palps. Dark eyes near apex of triangle with anterior two wider apart. 3 pairs of short peristomial cirri on either side of tip of triangle. In vertical sand tubes in muddy sand, intertidal or subtidal; Maine to Florida, Gulf. **Related species: Fringe-gilled Mudworm** (*Paraprionospio pinnata,* Fig. 20) also lacks typical pair of anterior palps characteristic of most members of Family Spionidae. Instead, it has a spade-shaped area surrounding the prostomium (head) and *3 pairs of fleshy cirri on segments 2, 3, and 4.* A deposit feeder living in intertidal and subtidal sandy mud; Chesapeake Bay to Florida, Gulf. Family Spionidae.

Tubeworms:
Families Sabellariidae and Ampharetidae

HONEYCOMB TUBEWORMS   **Figs. 115, 116**
Sabellaria floridensis and *Phragmotopoma lapidosa*
Incapable of leaving tubes, these worms depend on water currents to bring them food (small planktonic plants and organic material on particles of sand and shells) and building materials. Bristle-like opercular setae on top of head manipulate food-laden sediment particles. Ciliated feeding tentacles bring food to mouth. Often found near rocks where currents are strong. (1) *S. floridensis* is usually found singly or in small clumps attached to rocks and shells. Long, sinuous sand-grain tube is cemented so securely that worm cannot be removed undamaged. Gulf Coast. (2) *P. lapidosa,* a colonial worm, produces massive intertidal reefs off east coast of s. Florida. Tubes, lined with flat pieces of shell inside and sand grains outside, form dense, strong honeycomb (Fig. 116). Tubes form base of unique community of sessile plants and animals. Family Sabellariidae.

HOBSON'S TUBEWORM *Hobsonia florida*
Small—to 3 cm (1⅕ in.) long. Body inflated anteriorly, with *4 pairs of fingerlike gills* on top of first few body segments. Prosto-

Fig. 116. Chunk of worm reef made by Honeycomb Tubeworm (p. 282).

mium with pair of eyespots on edge. In mucous tubes in brackish to almost fresh water, in marsh tidepools, mud of Widgeon Grass beds. New Hampshire to Texas. Family Ampharetidae.

Errant Polychaetes

Sandworms: Families Nereidae and Nephtyidae

COMMON SOUTHERN CLAMWORM or   **Fig. 120**
LARGE SANDWORM *Nereis succinea*
Large—to 19 cm (7½ in.) long. Head brownish; parapodia with 3 projections on lower lobe, *upper one conical in segments toward front, straplike in segments toward rear;* jaws light amber-colored. Forms U-shaped burrow in muddy sand; tolerant of low salinities and may be found in marsh; intertidal; common on oyster beds. Worldwide; Canada to Florida, Gulf, and W. Indies, south to Uruguay. **Similar species: Small Clamworm** (*N. limbata*), to 15 cm (6 in.) long. Slender, amber-colored jaws. Parapodia small near head, *abruptly becoming longer near tail.* Sandy intertidal; Maine to S. Carolina. Family Nereidae.

CULVER'S SANDWORM *Laeonereis culveri*
Small—to 6 cm (2⅓ in.); half that size in western Gulf. Pink, red, bright yellow or greenish, sometimes with *a red stripe running*

down back on front third of body. 4 dark eyes, horny yellow jaws. In large numbers on salt or mud flats, in perpendicular burrows. N. Carolina to Gulf and W. Indies, south to Brazil. **Related species: Long-palped Sandworm** (*Ceratonereis irritabilis*, Fig. 120). *Light gray at front, with a bluish midregion; brass-colored at rear.* Bases of parapodia green. Mud and sand; Virginia, N. Carolina, Gulf. Family Nereidae.

DWARF SANDWORM *Aglaophamus verrilli* **Fig. 119**
To 4.4 cm (1.7 in.) long, with 50 or more segments. Gray or pearly, with a *red line running down center of back and underside.* Prostomium shovel-shaped, with 2 pairs of short conical palps; first pair at front corners of prostomium. Neuropodia with long, fingerlike erect lobes. Gills, beginning at segments 5–8, are red, inward-curving extensions of notopodia. Eversible pharynx fleshy, tipped with at least *10 pairs of papillae;* 1 pair of horny jaws, usually hidden. Sandy mud of intertidal; Arctic to Chesapeake Bay; also in Gulf. Family Nephtyidae.

Bloodworms: Family Glyceridae

BLOODWORM *Glycera americana* **Fig. 119**
Long — to 20 cm (8 in.). Pinkish white or purplish, with a pink line down back. Thin, with small parapodia; head pointed, with 4 tiny tentacles. Moves quickly, frequently everts pharynx explosively, seizing prey (other worms and amphipods) with 4 black, curved jaws. *Body cavity contains red blood that lacks corpuscles.* Sandy or muddy sand in lower intertidal; Cape Cod to Gulf to Argentina. **Similar species:** *G. dibranchiata* has simple threadlike gills on top and bottom of parapodia; *G. americana* has tree-like gills only on top of parapodia. Family Glyceridae.

Scaleworms, Sea Mouse, and Silkworm: Families Aphroditidae, Sigalionidae, Polyodontidae, and Polynoidae

ROUGH SCALEWORM *Hermenia verruculosa* **Fig. 117**
Lives in crevices in coral. Stout, grub-shaped; flat ventrally, arched dorsally. To 3 cm (1¼ in.) long, with 26 segments. Bilobed prostomium with 4 eyes, anterior pair surrounded by red bands. *Back banded with dark bumps.* Forked, amber-colored setae project conspicuously from body; *dorsal elytra covered with sand.* Possibly commensal with Banded Ophiocoma Brittle Star. Both are transversely banded brown and white with similar papillae, camouflaging worm. S. Florida, Caribbean. Family Polynoidae.

SILKWORM OF THE SEA *Polyodontes lupina*
Large, carnivorous tube-dweller, to 60 cm (2 ft.) long and 2.5 cm (1 in.) wide. Back covered with *brown, opalescent scales* (*elytra*) *with*

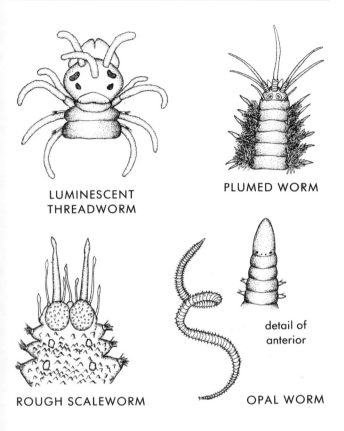

LUMINESCENT
THREADWORM

PLUMED WORM

ROUGH SCALEWORM

detail of
anterior

OPAL WORM

Fig. 117. Heads of shallow-water polychaete worms (1).

white borders. Lives in cocoonlike tube of silky threads secreted by spinning glands in each segment; threads look like coils of stainless steel embedded in worm's parapodia. Worm stays near entrance of 1-m (39-in.) long tube, scans surface with anterior pair of stalked eyes for small prey, which it captures with eversible proboscis armed with powerful jaws. Muddy sand flats; s. Florida, Caribbean. A tiny red parasitic snail, *Conchiolepis parasiticus,* may be attached to gills under elytra. Family Polyodontidae.

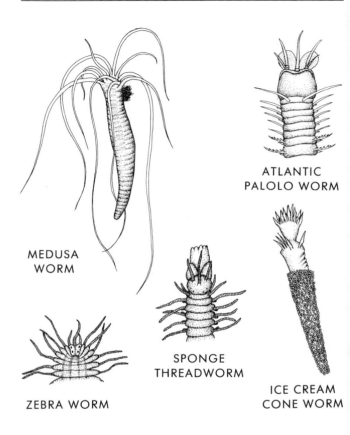

MEDUSA
WORM

ATLANTIC
PALOLO WORM

ZEBRA WORM

SPONGE
THREADWORM

ICE CREAM
CONE WORM

Fig. 118. Heads of shallow-water polychaete worms (2).

GOLDEN SEA MOUSE   *Pontogenia sericoma*
Short—to 4 cm (1½ in.) long. Entire back covered with *hairlike felt* composed of threadlike setae. *Large, golden brown dorsal setae extend up defensively,* curving strongly, almost meeting at dorsal midline, leaving narrow strip covered by felt. *15 pairs of thin, oval, overlapping elytra with concentric rings.* Single median antenna projects between larger lateral palps near pair of stalked eyespots on head. Se. Florida, Caribbean; on rocks or mud flats in shallow water. Family Aphroditidae.

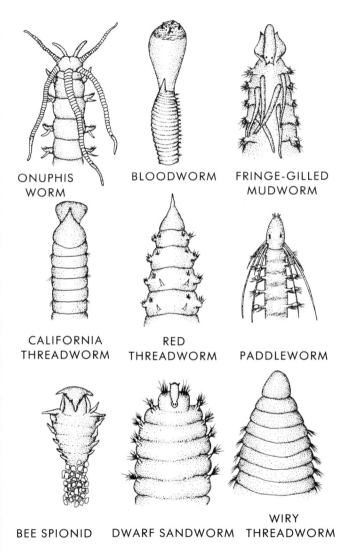

ONUPHIS
WORM

BLOODWORM

FRINGE-GILLED
MUDWORM

CALIFORNIA
THREADWORM

RED
THREADWORM

PADDLEWORM

BEE SPIONID

DWARF SANDWORM

WIRY
THREADWORM

Fig. 119. Heads of shallow-water polychaete worms (3).

TWELVE-SCALED WORM   Fig. 120
Lepidonotus sublevis
Small and broad; to 2.5 cm (1 in.) long with *12 pairs of scales on back*. Brown; camouflaged on mussels, oysters, seaweed, Sea Pansy, in grooves of whelk shells, or living commensally with hermit crabs in snail shells. Often numerous on whelk egg cases. Intertidal and subtidal on oyster bars, and rocky and shelly areas; New England to Florida, Gulf. **Similar species:** *L. variabilis* (Fig. 120) has fringed scales, each with a tuft of hair. Massachusetts to W. Indies. Family Polynoidae.

BOA SCALEWORM   *Sthenelais boa*   Fig. 120
Long—to 20 cm (8 in.)—narrow; covered with over *100 pairs of fringed, mottled brown-gray elytra*. Head with 1 pair of long and 1 pair short antennae; 4 eyes in a square near base of median antenna. Blunt, knoblike pharynx used to capture other worms and small invertebrates. Two anal cirri. Intertidal, burrows in sand or muddy sand; Massachusetts to Florida, Gulf to Texas, Caribbean to Brazil. Family Sigalionidae.

Large, Tube-dwelling Predaceous Worms: Family Onuphidae

PLUMED WORM or PERISCOPE   Fig. 117, Pl. 4
TUBEWORM   *Diopatra cuprea*
Abundant in sand flat-seagrass community: up to 100 worms per square meter of bottom. Look for a small (2.5- to 5-cm—1- to 2-in. high) shell- and debris-covered tube projecting from sand. Inside, worm lies with tips of long tentacles and palps extending outward, testing environment. Body undulates, creating water currents that carry oxygen to *30–40 pairs of miniature red fir-tree-like gills* on dorsum (back). Worm may cautiously creep out of tube to search for food or tube-building material. The slightest disturbance will cause it to immediately retreat to safety of tube, which may extend to 1.5 m (5 ft.) below surface. *Tube ornamented with shells and debris,* which provide a suitable substrate for algae and small epifaunal organisms, attracting worm's prey and protecting worm from predators such as crabs and rays. Lower intertidal and subtidal; Cape Cod to Brazil. Family Onuphidae.

ONUPHIS WORM or SHAGGY PARCHMENT-   Fig. 119
TUBE WORM   *Onuphis eremita oculata*
Long—to 30 cm (12 in.)—and slender. Iridescent, reddish, with *2 short, unsegmented antennae and 5 long, segmented antennae* extending from head. *Two eyes* just behind antennae; 4 long, almost *equal-sized, hairlike cirri* project from hind end. Parapodia lack lower lobe. Thin, membranous, plasticlike tube covered with fine sand in upper portion, smooth and translucent below. Carnivorous, leaves tube occasionally to attack small worms. Lower intertidal and subtidal; Gulf. **Similar species:** *O. magna* and

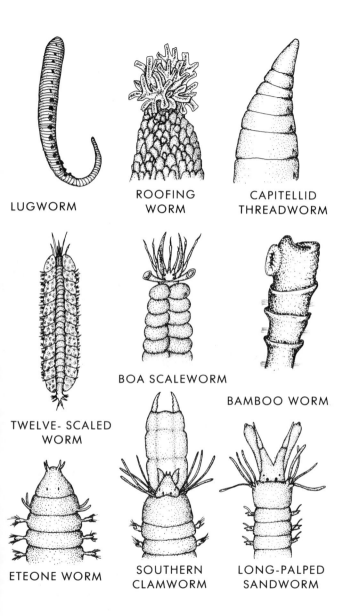

LUGWORM

ROOFING
WORM

CAPITELLID
THREADWORM

BOA SCALEWORM

BAMBOO WORM

TWELVE- SCALED
WORM

ETEONE WORM

SOUTHERN
CLAMWORM

LONG-PALPED
SANDWORM

Fig. 120. Heads of shallow-water polychaete worms (4).

O. eremita have anal cirri of *unequal length* and long, branching, conspicuous gills, especially in midregion of body. They also *lack eyes*. Tube may be covered with pieces of shell, similar to that of Plumed Worm. New York to W. Indies and south to Colombia; *O. magna* is common from N. Carolina to Florida. Family Onuphidae.

Fireworms: Family Amphinomidae

FIREWORM   *Hermodice carunculata*   **Fig. 115, Pl. 26**
To 30 cm (1 ft.) long. *A large, transversely pleated, cushionlike organ, the caruncle,* extends from prostomium to third or fourth segment; used to locate food by tasting water. Large, bushy, *bright red paired branchiae on each segment contrast with bundles of white setae*. Body greenish to chocolate brown. Feeds mainly on corals, sea anemones, hydroids, and other sedentary animals by everting tip of bulbous proboscis over surface of colony. Living tissue is partially digested and sucked off, mixed with mucus and digestive enzymes. **Caution:** *Setae barbed, poisonous, harmful to touch.* In crevices, under rocks, in coral reefs and Turtle Grass beds; s. Florida, Bahamas, Caribbean. Family Amphinomidae.

RED-TIPPED FIREWORM   *Chloeia viridis*   **Pl. 26**
To 30 cm (1 ft.) long; heavy, flattened. *Back striped with red and brown bars.* Gills conspicuous, with fernlike branches; gills contrast with bundles of fine, hairlike, glassy spines along sides. On reefs and rocks, scavenging for food. **Caution:** *Hollow, barbed spines (setae) contain toxin.* W. Indies. Family Amphinomidae.

Long-cirri Worms: Family Hesionidae

STRIPED HESIONE   *Hesione picta*
Active carnivores, able to swallow prey almost as large as themselves. Body to 5 cm (2 in.) long; flattened and rectilinear, with *about 16 segments*. Tentacular cirri and dorsal cirri long and slender, extending far out from sides of body. Heart-shaped prostomium (head) with 4 eyes and 2 small antennae; no palps. Body dark, iridescent, crossed by ivory-colored stripes. Tentacles and dorsal cirri reddish brown. Florida to S. America. Family Hesionidae.

Threadworms: Families Arabellidae and Lumbrinereidae

OPAL WORM   *Arabella iricolor*   **Fig. 117**
Long, cylindrical; reddish brown, iridescent. Lacks visible appendages and *resembles a slender earthworm*. Bluntly rounded prostomium with a row of 4 eyes along rear edge. Proboscis eversible, armed with chitinized jaws, ingests mud. Lacks tube,

but burrows just beneath surface in sand and mud flats, encased in thick coat of mucus. To 30 cm (1 ft.) long, stiff and wiry; *contracts into close spiral coils* when removed from sediment. Massachusetts to Florida, Texas. Family Arabellidae.

TLANTIC PALOLO WORM   **Figs. 115, 118**
Eunice schemacephala
Large—reaches 16 cm (6¼ in.) but only 5 mm (³⁄₁₆ in.) wide. *Head bilobed; peristomium has pair of conspicuous cirri.* Color variable, body usually dark, iridescent reddish brown with conspicuous white bands grading to large white spots on posterior segments. Parapodia thick; from 9th body segment to hind end, *red comblike gills arise from dorsal cirri.* Uses complex jaws to bore through coral, producing galleries of burrows, sometimes damaging living coral. Famous for reproductive habit: epitoky. Hind end of reproducing worm, epitoke, is modified to form a chain of long, narrow segments distended with eggs; each segment has a ventral eye-spot. Eggs are released within 3 days of last quarter of June-July moon. Posterior region of adult is thrust out of crevice, twists counterclockwise, and breaks off, then swims to surface, where eggs and sperms are discharged. Rest of body remains in rock to regenerate new hind end, assuring future propagation. Epitokes swarm, increasing likelihood of fertilization. Swarming has been observed off Dry Tortugas: at 4 A.M. average density was 2 worms per 0.3 sq. m (3 sq. ft.) of ocean surface, but at times wriggling masses formed a thick, vermicelli-like soup. Epitokes of Pacific species are eaten by Samoan natives. S. Florida, Caribbean. Family Arabellidae.

IRY THREADWORM   *Lumbrinereis tenuis*   **Fig. 119**
Elongate, thin, wiry, yellowish or greenish iridescent body, to 15 cm (6 in.) long, with 200 segments and a simple prostomium. Parapodia reduced, with postsetal lobe long and tapered. *Near hind end postsetal lobes become fingerlike and erect.* Eversible pharynx with groups of 4–6 teeth at front and posterior single teeth. Lower intertidal and subtidal, in sandy mud; Maine to N. Carolina, Gulf. Family Lumbrinereidae.

Paddleworms: Family Phyllodicidae

TEONE WORM   *Eteone heteropoda*   **Fig. 120**
Small—to 9 cm (3½ in.) long, with up to 178 segments. Yellowish to greenish. *Parapodia become larger toward hind end,* with last few *darker than body;* dorsal (upper) lobes of parapodia larger than ventral ones. Two long, tapering, fleshy appendages on either side of anus. Low-water line to shallow subtidal; Maine to Chesapeake Bay; Gulf. Family Phyllodocidae.

ADDLEWORM   *Phyllodoce mucosa*
To 10 cm (4 in.) long. Green or brown, with *paddle-like parapodia* and 4 pairs of prostomial tentacles—2 long pairs and 2 short ones.

One pair of anal cirri; 2 large brown eyes. Pharynx eversible, with a *crown of papillae* instead of jaws. Burrows rapidly in sand of lower intertidal and subtidal in Gulf; a related species ranges north to Maine. Family Phyllodocidae.

Syllid Threadworms: Family Syllidae

LUMINESCENT THREADWORM   **Fig. 117**
Odontosyllis enopla
ZEBRA WORM   *Trypanosyllis zebra*   **Figs. 115, 118**
SPONGE THREADWORM   *Haplosyllis spongicola*

Body thin, elongate, with *beaded dorsal cirri projecting from parapodia like strings of pearls*. Found among sponges, ascidians, algae, and other attached organisms, on which they prey, using eversible pharynx armed with 1 or more sharp teeth. Muscular, barrel-shaped organ (proventriculus) located behind pharynx acts as a pump to suck out juices of prey. Some species perform spawning ritual at night: (1) **Luminescent Threadworm** displays striking luminescent pattern of flashes similar to that of fireflies. Females swarming in tight circles on surface light up at intervals of 10–20 seconds, producing a circle of light to which male is attracted (see p. 126). (2) **Sponge Threadworm** lives only in small passageways of sponges, eating tissues of host. Hook-shaped setae adapted for clinging to porous sponge passageways. Tiny—less than 6 mm (¼ in.) long; similar in color to sponge host. (3) **Zebra Worm** is flattened, reproduces asexually; new individuals develop from bud near hind end; as bud matures, it breaks off from parent and swims off. S. Florida and Caribbean. Family Syllidae.

14

Shrimps, Crabs, Lobsters, and Barnacles

Malcolm Telford

Crabs, lobsters, and shrimps belong to the subphylum Crustacea, in the Phylum Arthropoda. They are found in countless numbers on shore and reef, and may be thought of as occupying the marine ecological niches corresponding to those of their terrestrial relatives, the insects.

On sandy shores above the waterline you will find the pale Ghost Crab with black eyes on mobile stalks. In muddy places like salt marshes there will be hundreds of fiddler crabs signaling with their enlarged claws. When the tide is falling you will be able to hear innumerable popping sounds as fiddler crabs push the mud plugs out of their burrows. At night, watch for the red and black Common Land Crab above the beach and the blue-gray Great Land Crab (called Duppy in Barbados) in wetter areas and wasteland. At the surf's edge you may see successive waves uncovering the burrowing mole crabs. Even when they are out of sight you will be able to hear crustaceans: listen for the clicks of pistol and snapping shrimps as you snorkel toward a coral head.

Like that of an earthworm, the body of an arthropod is made up of a series of rings called segments. Many (sometimes all) of the segments have a pair of appendages or limbs. The appendages are modified for different functions: on the head they are sensory (antennae) and feeding structures (mouthparts); in the trunk region they are locomotive (walking and swimming legs), reproductive (copulatory organs), and sometimes respiratory structures (functioning as gills). The body may be divided into head, thorax, and abdomen, but often the head and thorax are fused and the abdomen may be reduced or hidden underneath the rest of the body. In many ways arthropods are the most successful animals in the world, having almost a million species and countless individuals, and occupying every conceivable habitat.

Taxonomy: Two arthropod classes and one subphylum are marine and occur in our region. These are the horseshoe crabs (Class Merostomata), with a single species in our area (Fig. 121); the sea spiders (Class Pycnogonida), and the crabs, shrimps, and lobsters (Subphylum Crustacea).

Table 1. Simplified Classification: Subphylum Crustacea

The sea spiders are small; the slender body joins the long legs together at their bases. The mouth is on the end of a proboscis. Sea spiders feed on hydroids and soft mollusks, which they slurp up by the suction of the proboscis. The greatly reduced body is too small to house the digestive system, which instead branches into each leg: sea spiders literally have hollow legs. There are over 30 species in our region. The commonest is the Purple Sea Spider (Fig. 121) with legs to 8 cm (3⅛ in.) long. It is usually found hidden in intertidal crevices or on pilings.

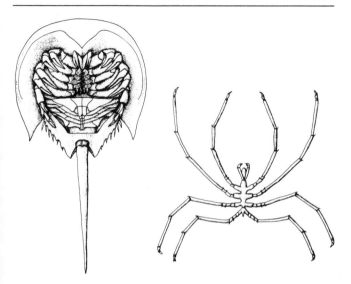

Fig. 121. *Left:* Horseshoe Crab; *right:* Purple Sea Spider.

The crustaceans—crabs, lobsters, shrimps, and barnacles—are a diverse group, with 10 classes (see p. 298). We will use as our example the familiar edible shrimp (Fig. 125). Head and thorax are fused together to form the cephalothorax, covered by a single piece of hardened cuticle or shell called the carapace. The head bears five pairs of appendages, including two pairs of sensory antennae; the smaller, first pair (antennules) is branched, the second pair is not. The next appendages are the mandibles (jaws) flanking the mouth; they crush food before it is swallowed. Following the mandibles are two pairs of maxillae (smaller jaws) with fine teeth and hairs on the edges that help manipulate food. The next eight pairs of appendages belong to the thorax. During the course of evolution the first three pairs have been modified to aid in feeding; these are called maxillipeds (little jaw legs). The third pair of maxillipeds, the largest, covers the mouth area in crabs and is the only visible pair of maxillipeds. The next five pairs of thoracic appendages are the walking legs. The first, second, and third pairs may have claws or chelae. The first pair of claws may be very large; they serve no locomotive function but are used to capture food. The abdomen consists of six segments, usually with appendages. Typically the abdominal appendages are branched and flattened. They may be used for swimming or to carry eggs before hatching. In males the first pair or two of abdominal appendages is modified for copulation. The final pair of abdominal appendages is often large and, with the terminal piece of the body (telson), makes up the tail fan (see Fig. 125).

Growth and development: Crustaceans do not grow continuously, gradually getting larger as time passes, because they live in a hard shell. For growth to take place the shell must be cast off (molted) and a new, larger one produced.

Molting is a hazardous event. Getting out of the old shell must be completed rapidly, in a period of only a few minutes. The entire outer covering of the animal, including the delicate covering of the gills, is changed at the molt. If the process is delayed, a space can develop between the old and new covering on the gills and block respiration. After molting, the animal has no protection from predators until the new shell hardens; it must therefore stay hidden under rocks until the new armor is ready for the world. Anybody who has eaten soft-shelled crabs will agree that newly molted crustaceans are tempting.

Crustaceans may molt continuously throughout their lives, the period between molts becoming ever longer, or they may have a fixed number of molts. However many molts they undergo, there is a progressive development from the larval stage to adulthood. The simplest larva is called a nauplius; it has a nonsegmented body and only three pairs of appendages. The next stage, the zoea, actively swims, and often feeds on the nauplius. The zoea may molt three or four times, getting bigger and more mobile, until it is transformed into a form similar to the adult. A crab, for example, at this stage is called a megalops; it looks like a small crab with its abdomen extended.

The duration of larval life is usually about four weeks, but in some shrimps it is four to five months, and spiny lobsters take even longer to reach adulthood. Motile larval stages help distribute the species and place young animals into an environment with a rich food supply.

Almost all decapods (shrimps, crabs, and lobsters) have separate sexes, but a few shrimps start life as males and after one reproductive period become females. In most instances mating is seasonal and involves elaborate courtship rituals. Many crabs mate when the female is still soft from molting. Premolt females release a pheromone (sex attractant) that summons an eager male. The gentleman may attend his lady for some days before she molts, often carrying her beneath him during this time. After she has molted, the male turns the female onto her back, folds back her abdomen to expose the genital openings, and inserts his copulatory appendages into them. Most crustacean sperms do not have a movable tail and must therefore be placed accurately during copulation. For the Blue Crab this may take as long as three hours. The Shore Crab mates when the female has a hard shell. A wrestling match that looks anything but amorous precedes the climactic moment, which eventually takes place with the male flat on his back. Males of the terrestrial fiddler crabs and Great Land Crabs rely on signaling with their enlarged claws to attract females and entice them into a burrow for mating. Ghost Crabs attract females at night by rubbing one claw against a ridge on an upper leg to produce a cricketlike squeak.

Crustaceans have the ability to break off some or all of their legs voluntarily. This is called autotomy, which literally means "self-cutting," and is performed when a limb is injured, during molting, or as an escape mechanism. When the leg is forcibly raised, it contacts a knob that provides leverage, forcibly breaking the leg off at a special joint. A membrane inside already covers the stump, so little blood is lost and the animal can continue its normal existence. Lost appendages are regenerated at later molts. A crab with an abnormally small leg has probably autotomized that appendage and is regrowing it. Regenerating appendages may require three or four molts to attain full size.

When attacked, the crab autotomizes the leg the predator has grasped, escaping while the predator chews on a fraction of its intended meal. Humans who carelessly grab a crab are in for a second surprise. The animal's claw firmly grasps your finger. You withdraw your hand in pain. The crab autotomizes the claw and runs off. You are left with a pinched finger. Now comes the surprise: when the nerve supplying the claw muscle is severed, the muscle goes into spasm, and the detached claw actually pinches you harder than before and resists opening for two or three minutes.

Symbiotic associations: Many crustaceans live in special association with other animals. In one relationship, known as mutualism, both animals benefit and there may even be a sharing of food. In parasitic associations the crustacean might steal food or even eat the host's tissues. Regardless of the advantages or disadvantages involved, these are both called symbiotic relationships. The literal meaning is "living together."

Some of the best-known symbiotic associations of crustaceans are with mollusks. The Spotted Pea Crab, for example, lives at the edges of the mantle cavity of pen shells. The Oyster Crab steals food from, and occasionally eats the living tissues of, its host. Pea crabs have a variety of hosts. One species, the smallest of all decapod crustaceans, lives on the underside of sand dollars. Several specials of pea crabs infest other sea urchins, including the Sea Pussy urchin. You can even find pea crabs inside the rectums of sea cucumbers.

Several symbiotic crustaceans do not tolerate another adult of the same sex sharing a host. The Oyster Crab is one and the small pea crab hosted by the sand dollar is another.

One of the most obvious associations is that between hermit crabs and snail shells. The crabs do not kill the snails to get the shells, but pick up empty shells from already dead snails. Some hermit crabs choose shells of only one species of snail to live in. The Bermuda Hermit chooses the Magpie shell. This is unusual, because the Magpie snail (West Indian Top Snail) has been extinct in Bermuda for hundreds of years and the crabs have been using the fossilized shells since then. The largest hermit in our area, the Red Hermit Crab, frequently uses Queen Conch or Trumpet Snail (West Indian Triton) shells. This handsome crab itself hosts the tiny Spotted Porcelain Crab, whose colors match those of its hermit host. This porcelain crab may also be found on the finger-shaped operculum of the Queen Conch, but never in association with the closely related Milk Conch, even in mixed herds of both conchs.

Crustaceans frequently form symbiotic associations with corals, anemones, and other cnidarians. The female Gall Crab stimulates the host coral to grow a chamber that eventually encloses the crab. She maintains a flow of water through a hole and uses her hairy maxillipeds to filter out suspended food particles. The tiny male roams around freely and periodically enters the hole to mate with the female in her prison cell.

A dramatic relationship exists between the Star-eyed Hermit Crab and the Tricolor Anemone. The hermit crab deliberately places the anemone on its shell, and when moving from one shell to another, takes its anemones along with it.

Several species of crabs uses sponges to conceal themselves. Sponges often have a terrible smell and/or taste, and contain irritating spicules. The Sponge Crab (Pl. 55) places fragments of sponges on hooklike bristles on its back. These sponges continue to grow until the crab is almost completely covered.

Whenever you examine a coral, anemone, clam, sea cucumber, or almost any other animal, check for the presence of crustacean symbionts.

Taxonomy: There are about 45,000 species of crustaceans placed in ten classes. Species of only two classes are described in this chapter:

1. Barnacles. Class Cirripedia is composed of sedentary animals that attach themselves to a hard surface and remain there permanently. Most species are attached to rocks or wharf pilings, but several prefer to move around attached to ships, turtles, whales, or crabs. All are filter feeders. The body is enclosed in a shell with an opening at the top, through which the legs (cirri) are kicked out to collect food particles.

2. Malacostracans. Class Malacostraca is composed of animals with nine thoracic and six abdominal segments plus the telson. The major group of large crustaceans, with over 28,000 species, arranged in thirteen orders. The commonest species are described beginning on p. 300.

Barnacles

STRIPED BARNACLE   *Balanus amphitrite*   **Fig. 84**
To 1.9 cm (¾ in.) high. Conical, with distinct light *purple vertical stripes* on each plate. On Red Mangrove roots in s. Florida, also pilings, shells, rocks, in estuaries. Massachusetts to W. Indies, Gulf.

IVORY BARNACLE   *Balanus eburneus*   **Fig. 32**
To 2.5 cm (1 in.) high. Conical, white; sides composed of 2 pairs of plates (scutes) overlapping only 1 or 2 unpaired plates. *Two pairs of grooved plates on top.* Most common large barnacle in Southeast and Gulf water, including brackish water. **Similar species: Bay Barnacle** (*B. improvisus*) is smaller—to 6mm (¼ in.) high; sides composed of 2 plates. On oysters, rocks, and pilings, in brackish estuaries; Nova Scotia to Florida, Texas, W. Indies.

CRAB BARNACLE   *Chelonibia patula*   **Pl. 6**
To 1.9 cm (¾ in.), usually smaller. White, flattened cones *on carapace of crabs,* especially Blue Crabs. White plates in opening at top small and *surrounded by fleshy membrane.* **Similar species: Turtle Barnacle** *(C. testudinaria)* lives on sea turtles. Both species Chesapeake Bay to Brazil, Gulf, W. Indies. Both species found only on respective hosts.

FRAGILE STAR BARNACLE   **Fig. 122, Pl. 16**
Chthamalus fragilis
Small and asymmetrical—3mm (⅛ in.) in one diameter, 5mm (¼ in.) in the other—but makes up for its size with great abundance. Forms *grayish crust* in midlittoral zone of rocky shores. Shallow cone composed of 6 overlapping plates. **Related species: Mangrove Star Barnacle** *(C. angustitergum)* forms crust on rocks and Red Mangrove roots in sheltered waters.

Fig. 122. *Left:* Fragile Star Barnacle; *right:* Tropical Goose Barnacle.

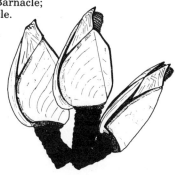

TROPICAL GOOSE BARNACLE *Lepas anatifera* **Fig. 122**
To 5 cm (2 in.) long. Faintly grooved, pearly white plates with brilliant orange edges set in dark purple-brown skin, on *a long, dark, fleshy stalk.* Ancients thought stalked barnacles became geese in spring (since they did not know where geese nested), a legend commemorated in common name of barnacle. Lives on undersides of boats, driftwood, flotsam; cosmopolitan, because it goes wherever its floating home takes it. Never on rocks. Throughout tropical and subtropical Atlantic.

RIBBED BARNACLE *Tetraclita squamosa stalactifera* **Pl. 16**
The large (to 3 cm — 1¼ in.), often solitary barnacle of wharfs and rocky shores in sheltered locations throughout Caribbean. Shell with distinct *ribs sloping to base;* looks like a wrinkled volcanic cone. Tidepools and mid- and lower yellow (intertidal) zones.

Malacostracans

Sideswimmers, Scuds, Beach Fleas, and Skeleton Shrimps: Order Amphipoda

Mostly tiny and laterally compressed (flattened from side to side). First segment of thorax fused to head, other seven segments free. First two pairs of legs on free thoracic segments have clawlike appendages used for feeding; remainder without claws and are used for locomotion. Skeleton shrimps (Suborder Caprellidea) have no other appendages, the abdomen being reduced to a mere knob. Most amphipods, however, have well-developed abdominal appendages, the first three pairs directed forward and used in swimming, the last three smaller and directed posteriorly. Beach fleas use these appendages for jumping. More than 5500 species.

SCUDS *Gammarus, Lysianopsis,* and related genera **Fig. 123**
Small — usually to 1 cm (½ in.) long. Scuds *lie on their sides;* when disturbed, they scuttle along, half jumping, half swimming. Underside of beach rocks often swarming with scuds. **Gravel Scud** (*Lysianopsis alba,* Fig. 123) is abundant in gravel and shells in shallows just below tide line; New England to Florida. *Yellowish white* with short, thick antennules and antennae; second thoracic leg hairy, slender, not as strongly developed as first.

BEACH FLEAS *Talorchestia* and *Orchestia* species **Fig. 123**
To 1.9 cm (¾ in.) or more long. At high-tide line, rarely in water. For respiration these amphipods require moisture-saturated air in heaps of tide-stranded algae. Found beneath debris and in salt

GRAVEL SCUD

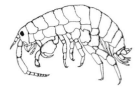

BROWN BEACH FLEA

BEACH SOWBUG

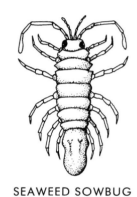

SEAWEED SOWBUG

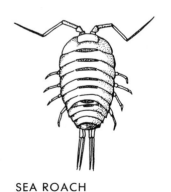

SEA ROACH

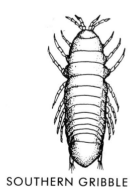

SOUTHERN GRIBBLE

Fig. 123. Amphipods and isopods.

marshes. *Talorchestia* species are usually *sand-colored; Orchestia* species are dark, *usually brown.* Both genera walk with *dorsal surface upward,* they do not scuttle on their sides, as scuds do. Like dog fleas (which are insects), beach fleas will hop away if disturbed. Collect them by dunking stranded seaweed in water— they will swim to surface. **Brown Beach Flea** (*Orchestia platensis,* Fig. 123) to 12mm (½ in.) long, has a stout body. Head and eyes small, black. Second leg has a large claw with an expanded palm and a thin curved finger.

Sowbugs, Pillbugs, Slaters, and Gribbles: Order Isopoda

Usually flattened dorsoventrally (from top to bottom). First segment of thorax fused to head; remaining seven segments free. Unlike amphipods, isopods have seven pairs of legs (attached to free thoracic segments) that are alike except for gradations in length; none specialized for feeding. Abdominal segments frequently smaller than thoracic ones and may be fused together. Abdominal appendages flat, elongate, used as gills. More than 10,000 species, including many terrestrial species.

BEACH SOWBUG *Chiridotea caeca*   **Fig. 123**
To 1.5 cm (⅜ in.) long. Sandy gray. Front of body rounded, to 8mm (⅜ in.) wide. *Abdominal segments fused into a single tapering unit.* Uropods form valves covering gills. These isopods burrow actively, leaving little ridged trails in sand. Sandy beaches, Nova Scotia to Florida.

SEAWEED SOWBUG *Erichsonella filiformis*   **Fig. 123**
Small, slender, elongate—to 1 cm (½ in.) long. *Short antennules;* long, six-segmented antennae. Abdominal segments fused; uropods form respiratory valves. Long Island Sound to Florida and Bahamas; in algae and sand, where its dull greenish gray color makes it inconspicuous.

COMMON BEACH SLATER or SEA ROACH   **Fig. 123**
Ligia exotica
To 4.8 cm (2 in.) long. Long antennae with many small terminal segments. Shiny brown, tapering body with *very long, slender uropods.* Resembles an insect; could be mistaken for a roach. Probably introduced from Europe; now abundant from Georgia to S. Brazil. Nocturnal; remains hidden in wharf crevices and rocks by day, emerging to feed at night, but may be seen by hundreds in shadows during day.

SOUTHERN GRIBBLE *Limnoria tripunctata*   **Fig. 123**
Tiny, almost *cylindrical*—to 5mm (¼ in.) long. Gnaws into submerged wooden structures, especially pilings. Burrows through pressure creosoted wood to reach unprotected timber, where it feeds destructively. Found in riddled driftwood or in

carelessly kept boats; dig culprits out with pocket knife. Rhode Island to Venezuela. **Similar species: Shipworm** (Fig. 107, p. 261).

Mantis Shrimps: Order Stomatopoda

Head unlike that of any other crustacean because it is jointed. Front part, bearing eyes and antennules, moves independently. Carapace covers only rear part of head and first three segments of thorax. Second pair of thoracic appendages greatly enlarged, adapted to seize prey. Mantis shrimps have raptorial legs ending in such a sharp finger that they can cut other shrimps in half. The terminal joint or finger of the second leg may have strong teeth and is *folded along a groove in preceding joint* (see Fig. 124). Some mantis shrimps lurk near entrance to their burrows, others creep up on prey and strike them with an uppercut-like slash, using the

Fig. 124. Mantis Shrimps. *Left:* Common Mantis Shrimp; *right:* Common Rock Mantis Shrimp.

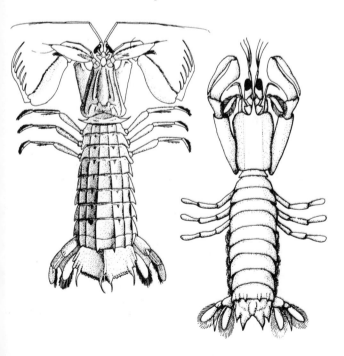

razor-sharp finger. Rapidity of strike resembles that of Praying Mantis, after which they are named. More than 60 species in our region.

COMMON MANTIS SHRIMP   **Fig. 124, Pl. 52**

Squilla empusa

To 20 cm (8 in.) long. Central piece of tail fan (telson) has a *single sharp ridge on midline and 6 large spines on edge;* numerous teeth between 4 innermost spines. Finger of raptorial leg has 6 teeth, including tip; outer edge slightly S-shaped. Whitish, with yellow to orange body ridges and around joints of raptorial legs; eyes green. Cape Cod to Gulf.

ROCK MANTIS SHRIMPS   **Fig. 124, Pl. 52**

Gonodactylus species

To 10 cm (4 in.) long. Species difficult to identify, but any shallow-water mantis shrimp *without teeth on raptorial fingers* probably belongs to this genus. Telson has 3 or 5 longitudinal ridges; 4 ridges on last abdominal segment. **Common Rock Mantis Shrimp** (*G. oerstedii,* Fig. 124, Pl. 52) is variable in color—often dark mottled green to black, but may be cream with green mottling; *base of unarmed finger of claw swollen,* as is *central ridge on telson.* In rock or coral crevices; N. Carolina to Brazil, also Bermuda, W. Indies.

Shrimps, Lobsters, and Crabs: Order Decapoda

The largest and most conspicuous group of crustaceans. All have *ten legs:* five pairs of walking legs on thorax. Often some legs have claws: one pair of claws usually large. Two groups: those with planktonic eggs and nauplius larvae (Suborder Dendrobranchiata) and those that attach their eggs to abdominal appendages (Suborder Pleocyemata). In the latter group the eggs hatch into free-swimming zoea larvae. Suborder Dendrobranchiata contains the commercial shrimps and their relatives. Suborder Pleocyemata comprises Infraorders Stenopodidea and Caridea (shrimps), Infraorders Astacidea and Palinura (crayfishes and lobsters), Infraorder Anomura (mud and mole shrimps, hermit crabs), and Infraorder Brachyura (true crabs).

Caridean Shrimps and Prawns: Infraorder Caridea

Largest group of shrimps. Two distinguishing features can be seen under a hand lens: (1) *first two pairs of legs have claws;* (2) *side plates of second abdominal segment overlap those of first.* About 1700 species. Representatives of three major families described below.

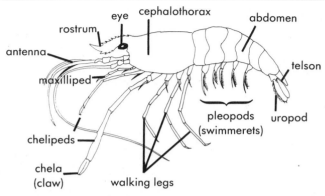

Fig. 125. Anatomy of a shrimp.

STRIPED FRESHWATER GIANT PRAWN   Fig. 126
Macrobrachium carcinus
Large—to 25 cm (10 in.) long. Dark and light greenish brown
stripes along length of body. Chelipeds huge—*length equals body
length.* Awesome claws, nearly equal in size; spiny, with crossed
fingertips. Nocturnal. Florida and Texas throughout W. Indies,
Central America; in rivers, drainage ditches, and ponds. These
prawns spawn in brackish water at mouths of rivers. **Similar
species:** (1) **Swollen-clawed Giant Prawn** *(M. faustinum)* is
smaller—to 10 cm (4 in.) long; *major claw swollen.* (2) **Caribbean
Crayfish** *(M. acanthurus)* reaches 20 cm (8 in.) long. Claws
thinner than in *M. carcinus;* rostrum almost straight, with *2 teeth
behind each eye.* Family Palaemonidae.

COMMON WATCHMAN SHRIMP   Fig. 126
Pontonia mexicana
To 3 cm (1¼ in.) long. A symbiont in pen shells and shells of other
mollusks. *Colorless and translucent,* with large claws (as long as
body). Most often in pairs, lurking just inside opening of host's
shell. Several other species; from N. Carolina to Gulf and Caribbean. Family Palaemonidae.

SNAPPING or PISTOL SHRIMPS   Pl. 51
Alpheus species
One claw grossly enlarged. Movable finger can be locked in open
position while muscles in massive palm contract, creating ten-
sion. Lock mechanism suddenly releases and claw snaps shut
with a noise like a pistol shot. Sound used to warn trespassing
shrimps in territory; also to stun small fishes, which are dragged
into shrimp's lair and eaten. Family Alpheidae. (1) **Common
Snapping Shrimp** *(A. heterochaelis)* reaches 3 cm (1¼ in.) long;
has deep notches in upper and lower margins of palm and grooves
and depressions along its length. Rostrum small; edge of carapace

(beside eyes) rounded, without spines. Reefs and oyster beds; N. Carolina and Bermuda to Brazil, W. Indies. (2) **Red Snapping Shrimp** *(A. armatus,* Pl. 51), to 5 cm (2 in.) long. Lives beneath tentacles of Ringed Anemone, in mated pairs. Pairs stay together for about a month, then switch mates and anemones. (3) **Banded Snapping Shrimp** *(A. armillatus)* is similar to *A. armatus,* but its abdomen is *banded with white and greenish tan.* S. Florida, W. Indies, Caribbean.

SPONGE SHRIMPS   Pl. 51

Synalpheus species

Several species of this pistol shrimp live inside sponges, where they feed on worms, debris, and possibly the sponge itself. Family Alpheidae. (1) **Long-clawed Sponge Shrimp** *(S. longicarpus)* lives in brown sponges from N. Carolina and Florida Keys to Trinidad. Short, broad *rostrum with 3 teeth;* lateral teeth over eyes. Large claw smooth, almost cylindrical, with markedly unequal fingers. To 2.2 cm (⅞ in.) long. (2) *S. minus* is smaller— to 1.2 cm (½ in.), with a less inflated pistol claw; it lives in green sponges. (3) **Short-clawed Sponge Shrimp** *(S. brevicarpus)* is similar but slightly larger and light green; *large, red-tipped claw* (see Pl. 51).

PEPPERMINT or VEINED SHRIMP   Pl. 51

Lysmata wurdemanni

To 4 cm (1½ in.) long. *Translucent with longitudinal red lines edged with white.* Also called Red Cleaning Shrimp. Found among sponges and tunicates, especially on wharf pilings in Florida, Gulf, and Caribbean. This species and others of the genus act as cleaners, picking tissue debris and parasites off surfaces of fishes that actively seek them out. Family Hippolytidae. **Similar species: Red-backed Cleaning Shrimp** *(L. grabhami,* Pl. 51) is *bright yellow* with a *broad red stripe on back* and a thin white stripe along crown of back; long antennae white.

PEDERSON'S CLEANING SHRIMP   Pl. 51

Periclimenes pedersoni

Tiny—to 2.5 cm (1 in.) long. Transparent, with *purplish overtones and dots.* On many species of anemone, especially Ringed and Giant Caribbean anemones. Family Hippolytidae. **Similar species: Spotted Cleaning Shrimp** *(P. yucatanicus,* Pl. 51) is whitish with *brown and black circles and rings;* legs and antennae banded white and brown. S. Florida, Caribbean, W. Indies.

BUMBLEBEE SHRIMP   Pl. 51

Gnathophyllum modestum

Body thick. Rostrum, armed with 5–6 forward-pointing teeth, is short—barely reaches beginning of transparent antennal scales. *Brown body covered with scattered gold dots* and few orange dots. Legs banded with brown or purple. First 2 pairs of legs clawed, second pair longer. Eyes large with conical black protuberance on cornea. On sea urchins and around clumps of coral and sponges in shallow water; N. Carolina to Florida. To 2.1 cm (⅘ in.) long.

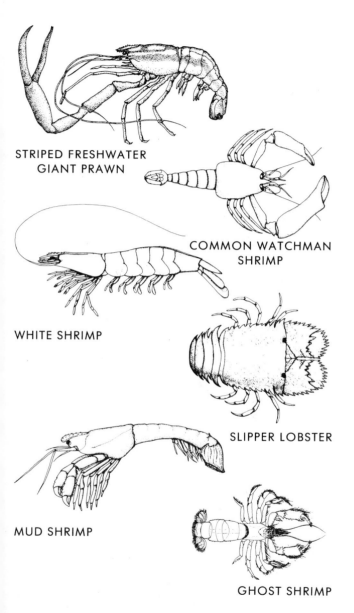

STRIPED FRESHWATER
GIANT PRAWN

COMMON WATCHMAN
SHRIMP

WHITE SHRIMP

SLIPPER LOBSTER

MUD SHRIMP

GHOST SHRIMP

Fig. 126. Shrimps and lobsters.

Similar species: *G. americanum* has a yellow body crossed by broad brown bands. Bermuda to S. America. Family Gnathophyllidae.

BROKEN-BACK SHRIMP *Hippolyte pleuracanthus*

Small—to 1.8 cm (⁷⁄₁₀ in.) long. *Abdomen sharply flexed,* with tufts of hair on back and spines on underside. First and second legs clawed, second claws largest. Color variable, matching seagrass—usually mottled brown-red or bright green. Seagrass beds; Connecticut to Texas. **Related species: Eelgrass Broken-back Shrimp** (*H. zostericola,* Pl. 7) is almost identical; extends range to Yucatan, Brazil, Trinidad, Curaçao, Bermuda. Family Hippolytidae.

GRASS SHRIMP *Palaemonetes pugio*

Small—to 5 cm (2 in.) long. Transparent, with claws on first and second legs; second claws largest. Rostrum tapers to a sharp point, toothed on upper and lower edges; *3 lower teeth. Back straight.* Commonest species in seagrass beds, often in brackish water; Canada to Texas. **Similar species:** *P. vulgaris, P. intermedius,* and **Florida Grass Shrimp** (*Palaemon floridana,* Pl. 7) can be differentiated only by experts.

ARROW SHRIMP   **Pl. 7**

Tozeuma carolinense

Small—to 5 cm (2 in.) long. A well-camouflaged shrimp of seagrass beds. *Rostrum very long—almost twice as long as rest of carapace to abdomen.* Rostrum smooth above and serrated below, inclined slightly upward near tip. Strong spine at either side of base of rostrum. First pair of legs very short. Green, brownish, or reddish, depending on background; may be purple if living on purple soft coral. Swims with body in vertical position. Massachusetts to Florida, Gulf, Caribbean to Brazil. Family Hippolytidae.

Penaeid or Commercial Shrimps: Infraorder Penaeidea

Claws on first 3 pairs of legs; all about same size. Abdomen bent only slightly downward.

WHITE SHRIMPS   **Fig. 126**

Penaeus species

Large, often abundant commercial shrimps. Several species common from Carolinas to Brazil; adults in marine habitats, young in brackish estuaries. (1) **White Shrimp** *(P. setiferus)* largest penaeid—to 18 cm (7 in.) long. Almost transparent, with a bluish tinge; *front half of carapace grooved.* (2) **Brazilian Shrimp** *(P. brasiliensis)* is often found in mixed shoals with White Shrimp. It has lateral *grooves extending entire length of carapace.* (3) **American Pink Shrimp** *(P. duorarum)* and (4) **Brown Shrimp** *(P. aztecus)* are similar commercial shrimp in our area.

Stenopodidean or Coral Shrimps: Infraorder Stenopodidea

Like the penaeids (above), these shrimps have claws on first 3 pairs of legs but *third pair* of legs is *longest*. Commonly called coral shrimps; most often seen around coral reefs, where several species act as cleaners.

ANDED CORAL SHRIMP or BARBER POLE   **Pl. 51**
SHRIMP   *Stenopus hispidus*
To 3.5 cm (1½ in.) long, *whitish, banded with bright red*. On coral reefs, in crevices; s. Florida, W. Indies, Caribbean.

Spiny and Slipper Lobsters: Infraorder Palinura

Well-developed abdomen, which is the part we eat. No transverse lines across outer lobes of tail fan. Front of carapace short; rostrum indistinct or absent. *Walking legs without claws,* but in some species end joint is folded back.

PINY LOBSTER   *Panulirus argus*   **Pl. 51**
To 45 cm (18 in.) long. Unlike northern lobsters and crayfishes, this lobster has *neither pincers nor rostrum*. Carapace cylindrical, armed with numerous strong spines, including a prominent one *bent forward over each eye*. Antennae long, extend back full length of body. Bases of antennae large and spiny; when moved up and down rapidly, produce a rattling or squealing sound that warns other lobsters to stay out of occupied territory. May be brightly colored; carapace yellow and reddish brown, sometimes bluish. Legs lined with yellow; abdomen yellow-spotted. Hides in crevices in reefs by day, feeds at night. N. Carolina to Brazil, but sadly depleted in tourist regions. Several related species.

LIPPER LOBSTERS   *Scyllarides* species   **Fig. 126**
Lobsterlike, but greatly flattened from top to bottom. Bases of antennae enormously enlarged into *flat plates edged with sharp pointed teeth. No claws*. **Slipper Lobster** (*S. nodifer*, Fig. 126) reaches 30 cm (12 in.) long. Sandy colored, mottled with purple-brown. Nocturnal in reef crevices, inshore on fringing reefs; uncommon from N. Carolina and Bermuda southward throughout Caribbean, W. Indies. Several related species.

Mud Shrimps and Hermit, Porcelain, and Mole Crabs: Infraorder Anomura

The crabs have a well-developed asymmetrical abdomen bent beneath them. Uropods usually present, but not always forming a tail fan. Fifth thoracic legs unlike others, are high up on back.

Hermit crabs have an asymmetrically coiled abdomen that fits into an empty snail shell for protection. In porcelain crabs the abdomen is bent beneath the body; tail fan is well developed. Mole crabs, which burrow in sand, have the abdomen bent beneath the body, a long pointed telson, and no tail fan. Mud shrimps resemble true shrimps.

MUD SHRIMP *Upogebia affinis* **Fig. 126**

To 10 cm (4 in.) long; almost pure white. Looks like a miniature lobster with fat abdomen and membranous shell. Almost cylindrical; flattened on front of carapace and on rostrum. Carapace covered with *mat of fine, feltlike hair. Both claws same size.* Eyestalks concealed by carapace. Burrows in intertidal or subtidal sand and mud, often under flat stones; Massachusetts to Brazil. **Similar species:** *U. operculata,* found among algae encrusting dead Staghorn Coral off Barbados and in s. Caribbean. Tail fan and last abdominal segment make a circular plug, used to close tunnels made in algae.

GHOST SHRIMP or BEACH CRAYFISH **Fig. 126, Pl. 6**
Callianassa species

To 8 cm (3¼ in.) long. Carapace about ¼ of animal's length (shorter than in Mud Shrimp). Membranous, smooth, white, glossy; *lacks flattened hairy area in front.* Claws unequal; movable fingers hairy. Like Mud Shrimp, makes extensive burrows in mud and sand, beneath rocks, in intertidal and shallow subtidal zone. Two species along Atlantic Coast: (1) **Atlantic Ghost Shrimp** (*C. atlantica,* Pl. 6) ranges from Canada to Florida, and (2) **West Indian Ghost Shrimp** *(C. major)* from N. Carolina to Florida and Louisiana and from W. Indies to Brazil. *C. major* is larger — to 9.5 cm (3¾ in.) long; males have a large tooth along inner margin of upper, movable finger of claw. *C. atlantica* reaches 6.8 cm (2⅝ in.); male lacks tooth. Gulf of Mexico species, besides *C. major,* include (1) **Trilobed Ghost Shrimp** *(C. trilobata),* which has 3 lobes on lateral margin of telson and a midventral projection (spine) on ischium of major chela, and (2) **Gulf Ghost Shrimp** *(C. jamaicense louisianensis),* which lacks lobes on telson and spines on ischium. Both species are smaller than *C. major.*

SOLDIER CRAB or COMMON LAND **Fig. 38, Pl. 58**
HERMIT CRAB *Coenobita clypeatus*

Carapace to 3.5 cm (1½ in.) long. *Large purple claw* that blocks entrance to shell — because of this feature the crab is called Blue Stone in Jamaica. After a marine larval period, the crab migrates to shore and selects suitable snail shell in which to live. It returns to water occasionally when young, less frequently when older, eventually becoming fully terrestrial, returning to sea only to release new larvae. Adults can be found inland, high on hillsides, sometimes more than 500 m (1600 ft.) above sea level. This hermit occupies a wide variety of shells, especially those of West Indian Top Snail, star snails, and African Land Snail; S. Florida, W. Indies.

WEST INDIAN FLAT-CLAWED HERMIT CRAB   Fig. 127
Pagurus operculatus
Carapace to 1.2 cm (½ in.) long. Width of large claw at least ¾ of its length, with *fleshy frill on lower side of wrist joint.* Brightly colored: legs and small claw orange, large claw whitish, cheliped purple, antennae orange. Shallow water; s. Florida, W. Indies to Barbados.

GRAY'S HERMIT CRAB   *Paguristes grayi*   **Fig. 127**
Carapace to 2.5 cm (1 in.) long, spooned fingertips, inconspicuous hairs on hand that do not conceal spines; carapace *deep wine-red heavily spotted with white.* Florida to Caribbean. Several related species.

THREE-COLORED HERMIT CRAB   Fig. 127, Pl. 52
Clibanarius tricolor
Tiny—carapace to 9 mm (⅜ in.) long. This and related striped hermits live in small snail shells (particularly shells of Four-toothed Nerite and elongate horn and auger snails) in intertidal and shallow subtidal. *Legs blue, but terminal section of each is white, shading to orange-red at joint;* carapace and eyestalks blue, antennae orange. **Similar species:** (1) **Antillean Striped Hermit Crab** (*C. antillensis*) has brownish legs with a wide white stripe. (2) **Green-striped Hermit Crab** (*C. vittatus,* Pl. 52) is large—whole crab may be 7.5 cm (3 in.) long. *Green and white longitudinal stripes* on legs; antennae orange. Claws with *spooned fingers.* In Tulip Snail or whelk shells when adult; in Mud Snail, horn snail, and auger snail shells when juvenile. Tidepools and subtidal shallows. Commonest large hermit crab from Virginia to Florida, Texas; also in Caribbean.

RED HERMIT CRAB   *Petrochirus diogenes*   **Fig. 127, Pl. 52**
Largest hermit in S. Florida, Caribbean waters—carapace to 8 cm (3¼ in.) long. Right claw slightly larger than left. Fingertips hard, stony (*Petro* means "stony," *chirus* means "finger"). Both claws covered by *large granules arranged in groups* separated by *semicircular fringes of flat hairs.* Rusty red; antennae banded with white along filaments and striped at bases. N. Carolina to Brazil, frequently in shell of Queen Conch.

SMOOTH-CLAWED HERMIT CRAB   Fig. 127, Pl. 52
Calcinus tibicen
All hard parts of this little hermit hairless and smooth. Carapace to 1.2 cm (½ in.) long. Left claw much larger than right; fingertips hard and sharp-pointed. Claws reddish, brown, or *maroon with white fingertips;* terminal sections of legs white or yellow, banded with red; carapace red with small white spots. An olive-green variant with pale blue spots is found in some areas. Shallow water; s. Florida to Brazil.

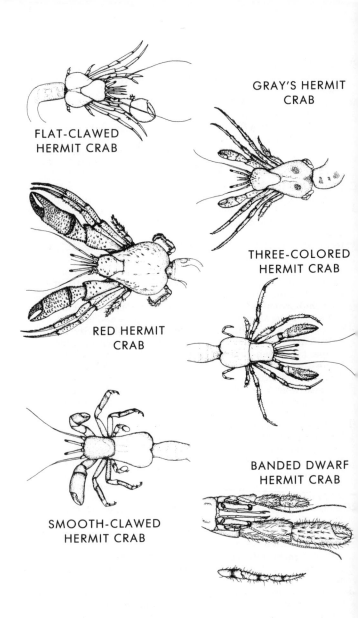

Fig. 127. Hermit crabs.

STAR-EYED HERMIT CRAB *Dardanus venosus* **Pl. 27**
Carapace to 2.5 cm (1 in.) long. Left claw much larger than right, with numerous hair-fringed granules. Pattern of granules outlined by network of fine red lines like blood vessels. *Spooned black and horny fingertips.* Second pair of legs has a longitudinal ridge with granular crossbars on ventral (lower) side. Cornea of eyes greenish blue with a dark central spot and radiating lines, *forming a star.* **Similar species: Bar-eyed Hermit Crab** *(D. fucosus,* Pl. 52) can be identified when alive by the *horizontal black bar* (instead of a star) in cornea. Both species range from Bermuda and s. Florida to W. Indies and Brazil; Bar-eyed Hermit ranges north to N. Carolina.

BANDED DWARF HERMIT CRAB **Fig. 127**
Pagurus annulipes
Tiny—carapace to 1.3 cm (½ in.) long. Claws unequal, right one much larger than left. White to gray with *brown bands on walking legs.* Antennae with broad purple stripes alternating with narrow white bands. Uncommon in northern part of range, from Massachusetts southward; abundant in Turtle Grass beds of Florida and Gulf of Mexico; also found in Cuba and Puerto Rico. **Similar species: Bonaire Hermit Crab** *(P. bonairensis)* may be same species.

LONG-CLAWED HERMIT CRAB **Pl. 7**
Pagurus longicarpus
Small—carapace to 1 cm (⅜ in.) long. Very common, usually in Mud Snail shells. *Right claw narrow and elongate,* nearly cylindrical, hairless, smooth, with median stripe; much larger than left claw. Left claw has spooned fingertips. Active, often aggressive. Just below tide line in sand and in tidepools; Massachusetts to n. Florida, Gulf.

FLAT-CLAWED HERMIT CRAB *Pagurus pollicaris* **Pl. 7**
Large—carapace to 3.1 cm (1¼ in.) long. Large flat claws; right claw larger than left. Major claw *round, has serrated edges, with movable finger quadrangular.* Body and claws tan or light brown in northern part of range; in Florida claws whitish, with dark area near wrist. No stripes on legs. Subtidal to low-tide line; Massachusetts to Florida, Texas.

ROUGH-CLAWED PORCELAIN CRAB **Fig. 128**
Pachycheles ackleianus
Carapace to 9 mm (⅜ in.) long. *Stout, rough claws* with *irregular rows of large, flat, hairless tubercles;* fingers close along their full length. Cephalothorax rich orange-brown, with a broad white stripe on midline; ventral (lower) surface white. On sponges and coral; Tampa Bay, Gulf, Caribbean to Brazil.

LINED PORCELAIN CRAB *Petrolisthes galathinus* **Pl. 52**
Carapace to 1.6 cm (⅔ in.) long. Carapace rough, with small transverse hairy ridges; dark dirty gray, flecked with reddish brown. Legs white with bold brown spots. *Wrist joint of claws*

armed with 4 (rarely 5) teeth. Eyestalks crimson. Shallow water, especially on finger corals; N. Carolina through Caribbean to Brazil. **Similar species:** (1) **Smooth Porcelain Crab** (*P. politus,* Pl. 52) is black-green to copper with blue spots. Along side walls of carapace are *2 brilliant lines, red above, blue beneath.* Joints of legs tinged with crimson, outer segments banded with crimson, tips white; wrist of claws with 3 widely spaced teeth. Under intertidal rocks and in oyster beds. (2) **Square Porcelain Crab** *(P. quadratus)* lacks spines on wrist of claw; drab gray-brown above, cream below. (3) **Van Der Horst's Porcelain Crab** *(P. vanderhorsti)* is rich *maroon with bright blue spots.* Carapace has 3 teeth between eyes. Under rocks or under Red Rock Urchin, intertidal and subtidal; southern Caribbean.

SPOTTED PORCELAIN CRAB   **Fig. 128**

Porcellana sayana

Carapace to 2.2 cm (¾ in.) long; nearly as wide as it is long, with 3 pointed teeth on front. Single spine at terminal joints of walking legs; palms of claws fringed with long yellow hairs. Carapace *orange-red with white and violet spots, each ringed with intense blood-red lines.* Underside white mottled with red. Claws white. Free-living or symbionts of hermit crabs, especially the Red Hermit, with whose color it blends, or on Queen Conch, hiding in snail's shell when disturbed. N. Carolina to Brazil.

SAND or MOLE CRABS   **Fig. 128**

Hippa cubensis and *Emerita* species

To 3 cm (1½ in.) long. Body *loaf-shaped* or almost cylindrical; *second antennae long, plume-like.* Tiny eyes on long, slender stalks. Legs have leaflike, fringed extensions for burrowing, no claws. All 3 crabs described here are purplish, with dashed lines across carapace. Two *Emerita* species—*E. portoricensis* and *E. talpoida*—burrow in sand, face seaward with head and feathery antennae above surface; as waves wash back down beach, antennae sift out particles of food. The **Cuban Mole Crab** *(Hippa cubensis,* Fig. 128) has smaller antennae and is a scavenger. All 3 species live in the swash zone of exposed beaches, moving up and down beach with the tide. **Common Mole Crab** *(E. talpoida)* from New England to Brazil; **Puerto Rican Mole Crab** *(E. portoricensis,* Fig. 40) and **Cuban Mole Crab** *(H. cubensis)* in Bahamas, Gulf, Florida, Caribbean. **Similar species:** (1) **Purple Surf Crab** *(Albunea gibbesii,* Pl. 51) is 5 cm (2 in.) long. Body flattened, elongate, tapering toward rear, with front edge widest; iridescent light purple with white markings. *Eyes on triangular stalks* at center of front margin, with 9 tiny spines on either side of eyes. Long, slender spine at each front corner of carapace. *Small claws on first pair of legs.* Long slender antennae, legs flattened for digging. Sand flats; N. Carolina to Texas, W. Indies to Brazil. (2) **Webster's Mole Crab** *(Lepidopa websteri,* Fig. 12) *lacks spines* on front of carapace. N. Carolina to Florida; Gulf to Mississippi.

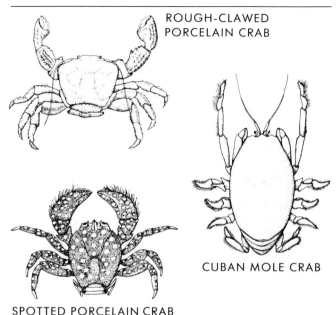

ROUGH-CLAWED
PORCELAIN CRAB

CUBAN MOLE CRAB

SPOTTED PORCELAIN CRAB

Fig. 128. Porcelain and mole crabs.

True, Short-tailed or Tail-less Crabs:
Infraorder Brachyura

The most complex, numerous group of crustaceans, with more
than 4500 species. Abdomen small, thin, folded tightly beneath
thorax, and without uropods. In males, abdomen narrow and
jointed; in females, broad and rounded (Fig. 129). Males have only
two pairs of abdominal appendages, used for copulation; females
have five pairs, used for carrying eggs. The crabs described below
are divided into four groups, based on morphological criteria: (1)
last two pairs of legs reduced, last pair dorsal; (2) mouth area
triangular; (3) mouth area square, with a rostrum; (4) mouth area
square, lacks rostrum.

Sponge Crabs: *Last 2 pairs of legs reduced, last pair dorsal.*
LESSER SPONGE CRAB   *Dromidia antillensis*   **Pl. 55**
Carapace to 7.5 cm (3 in.) long; convex, covered with tan hairs.
Last pair of legs dorsal; these hold sponge on back until it gains
purchase and becomes permanently attached. Robust, crimson-

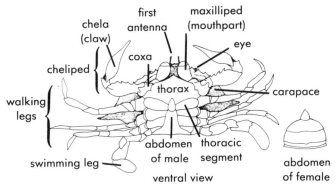

Fig. 129. *Left:* Anatomy of a male crab; *right:* abdomen of a female crab.

tipped claws. Sponges, tunicates, and colonial anemones on back provide camouflage and protection. **Similar species: Sponge Crab** *(Dromia erythropus,* Pl. 12) is larger and wider; covered with stiff, blackish hairs. Tips of legs hairless, light red. N. Carolina and Bermuda to Florida, Caribbean to Brazil.

Purse and Box Crabs: Mouth area triangular.

PURSE CRAB *Persephona mediterranea*   **Fig. 130**
Carapace to 6 cm (2⅖ in.) long; almost perfectly *round,* with a *squared-off cylindrical front and 3 distinct spines at rear.* Gray-brown with dark brown, sometimes reddish spots and reticulated pattern. Innumerable granules, often red-tipped. Next to last segment of abdomen of female becomes an enormously enlarged "purse" for eggs. New Jersey to Florida, Gulf, W. Indies to Brazil.

SHAMEFACED or BOX CRABS   **Fig. 130, Pl. 55**
Calappa species
Flattened claws with a *palisade of teeth along upper surface. One claw has hooked knob* on outer side, a guide when claw is used as

Fig. 130. *Left:* Purse Crab; *right:* Flaming Shamefaced Crab.

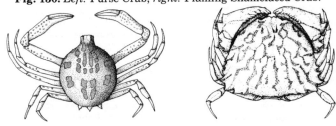

a can opener on a mollusk shell. Usually buried in sand up to eyes. 6 species in our area. **Flaming Shamefaced Crab** (*C. flammea*, Fig. 130) is the commonest; carapace to 8 cm (3¼ in.) long. Sandy white or gray, mottled and streaked with *purple-brown flame-like pattern;* claws striped purple with red streaky patches on inner surface; tips of legs and teeth of carapace yellow. Shallow sand; Massachusetts to Brazil, Bermuda.

GULF CALICO CRAB   *Hepatus epheliticus*   **Pls. 6, 55**
To 6 cm (2⅓ in.) long; tan or gray, with irregular, dark-edged, *red spots scattered over carapace.* Subtidal, buried in sand with eyes showing. May have Tricolor Anemone on back. Virginia, Gulf, W. Indies.

Spider Crabs: *Mouth area square; rostrum present.*

ARROW CRAB   *Stenorhynchus seticornis*   **Pl. 55**
Carapace to 6 cm (2½ in.) long. Long and narrow, with an *elongated, pointed rostrum;* legs long and slender. Beautiful—golden, yellow, or cream, lined with brown, black, or iridescent blue. Slender claws, blue to violet; legs reddish or yellow. Coral crevices in shallow or deep water; N. Carolina and Bermuda to Brazil.

GRAY PITHO   *Pitho aculeata*   **Pl. 55**
Gray, with a *broad, flat front;* eyes on projecting stalks with a *long spine* on either side. Five blunt teeth on lateral margin. Claws stout; fingers of male curved, spooned. To 2.5 cm (1 in.) long. On rocks, coral, seagrass; N. Carolina to Brazil.

GULF ARROW CRAB   *Metaporhaphis calcarata*
Small—to 2.4 cm (⁹⁄₁₀ in.) long, with rostrum occupying at least half of length. Yellow, brown, or gray carapace, covered with round nodules, each surmounted with a hairy tubercle. Eyes project at right angles from head. A *long, sharp, recurved spine*

Fig. 131. Common southern spider crabs. *Left:* Common Spider Crab (*Libinia emarginata*); *right:* Southern Spider Crab (*L. dubia*).

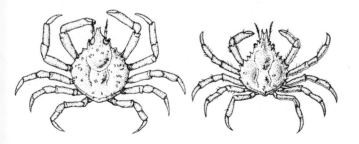

projects upward from merus (third segment) of each walking leg. Turtle Grass beds; hydroid colonies on pilings; N. Carolina to Gulf, south to Brazil.

MOSS CRAB   *Epialtus bituberculatus*   **Fig. 132**

Small—carapace to 1.2 cm (½ in.) long. Rich coffee-brown, chocolate, or orange. Carapace more or less *pentagonal, with 2 often whitish tubercles toward front*. Legs strongly bent, often used as hooks for holding onto seaweed, especially Sea Moss, on wavewashed rocky shores. Three other species from s. Florida to West Indies, south to Brazil. **Similar species:** *Acanthonyx* species may be recognized by subchelate terminal (outer) leg joints.

HUMPBACK or RED-SPOTTED SPIDER CRAB   **Fig. 132**
Pelia mutica

Small—carapace to 1.4 cm (¾ in.) long. A secretive spider crab with a *hairy carapace* raised into a *shallow conical mound* in center. Brown with patches of red. *Red spots on claws;* legs banded with red. Shallow water under stones; Maine (rare) to Gulf and W. Indies.

COMMON SPIDER CRAB   **Fig. 132, Pl. 6**
Libinia emarginata

Large—carapace to 10 cm (4 in.) long; legs to 30 cm (1 ft.) long. Dull brown carapace, often covered with fuzzy growth, spines, and/or tubercles; rostrum bluntly forked. *Median line of 9 spines across back.* Young (less than 1 cm—⅜ in.—long) may be found on bell of Cannonball Jellyfish. **Similar species: Southern Spider Crab** (*L. dubia*, Fig. 132) has row of *6 median spines* and slightly longer fork on rostrum. Both species are sluggish; common on seaweed-covered bottoms in shallow water. Spectacular in home aquaria. Nova Scotia to Gulf; *L. dubia* is more common in South.

Next 7 species: Common Spider Crabs of Genus Mithrax. All *Mithrax* crabs have *spoon-shaped claw tips* and robust legs armed with spines. Carapace has 2 rostral horns and 3–4 lobes on front margin.

BROWN-BANDED CORAL CRAB   *Mithrax cinctimanus*

Carapace to 2 cm (¾ in.) long, longer than it is broad; yellow, with a *large brown spot covering much of center of rear carapace.* Upper arm has 2 or 3 tiny spines on inner margin; claws and feet spotted with brown and white. May have broad brown band across hand of claw. Under rocks, on corals and seagrass; s. Florida, Bahamas, W. Indies.

YELLOW CORAL CRAB   *Mithrax forceps*

Carapace to 2.1 cm (⅘ in.) long; chestnut, terra cotta, yellow-brown, dull yellow, or greenish brown, with *4 teeth along front edge.* Arm has 5 spines on upper margin, 2 long spines on inner margin; legs of young yellow-banded. Intertidal, rocky shores, coral crevices; Bermuda and S. Carolina to Gulf and Brazil.

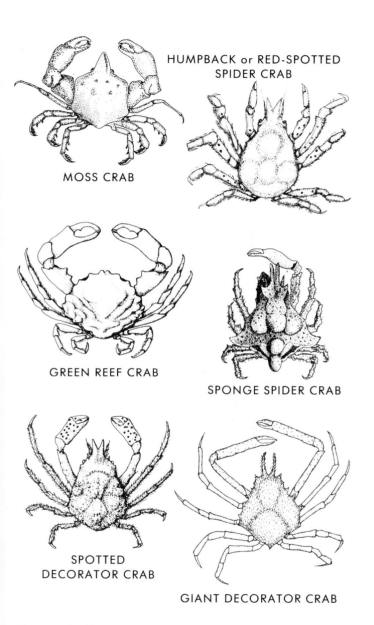

Fig. 132. Caribbean spider crabs.

Similar species: *M. pleuracanthus* (Pl. 53) has 4 lateral spines along edge of carapace; 3 tuberculate, last pointed. Carapace yellowish white, blotched or barred with red; claws light red with pale tips. To 3.6 cm (1⅖ in.) long.

CORAL SPIDER CRAB *Mithrax hispidus*

Large—to 10 cm (4 in.) long. Edge of carapace armed with *4 spines:* first one blunt, often forked; second one longer, sharp and double, curving forward; third and fourth spines more slender and about same length; a tiny fifth spine is higher on carapace. Carapace also has two tubercles in a vertical line from last spine. Cheliped has 4–5 spines on upper margin of first segment; claw has broad low teeth near base of upper finger. Carapace brownish red or terra cotta. Legs red, speckled with pale yellow, often with bright bands at joints; covered with brown hair. Bermuda and S. Carolina to Bahamas and W. Indies, south to Brazil. **Similar species: Knobbed Spider Crab** *(M. caribbaeus,* Pl.54) has *3 spines on edge of carapace;* front edge of upper cheliped has 2 conical spines. Inner edges of claws crenulate (bumpy); in *M. hispidus* they are smooth. W. Indies, S. America.

RED MITHRAX or CORAL CRAB *Mithrax ruber* **Pl. 54**
Carapace to 1.2 cm (½ in.) long; brownish red, bluish toward rear. *Inner arm lacks spines.* W. Indies.

GREEN REEF CRAB *Mithrax sculptus* **Fig. 132, Pl. 54**
Small—carapace to 2.5 cm (1 in.) long. Dark green, with *4 rounded ridges leading to lobes on margins.* Sandy gray legs hairy; wide-gaping claws meet at *deeply spooned tips;* blunt tooth near base of movable finger. Florida, Bahamas, W. Indies to Brazil; on reefs, Turtle Grass beds, shallow finger-coral flats. Almost every stone, shell, fragment of coral seems to shelter one; with each rising tide Bonefishes and other fishes come swarming in to feed on them. **Similar species:** *M. coryphe* is sand-colored and has *3 marginal lobes.*

SPINY SPIDER CRAB *Mithrax spinosissimus* **Pl. 54**
Largest *Mithrax*—to 17 cm (6⅝ in.) long. Carapace hairless, rounded. Carapace maroon or bright carmine; surface rough with short spines: those in center blunt, others sharp; *6 spines along edge of margin, first 2 double.* Chelipeds of male massive; 8–9 stout spines on outer margin of first segment. Fingers of claw curved, leaving wide gape, strong tooth on upper finger. Legs hairy, especially on last 2 segments. Legs brick red; chelipeds rose-red, claws with yellow fingers. Carolinas, Bahamas, s. Florida, W. Indies. **Similar species:** *M. cornutus* is also large—to 9.2 cm (3⅝ in.) long, but carapace yellowish to rose, covered with woolly hairs. Long rostral horns. Florida to Brazil, W. Indies, Bermuda.

RED SPIDER CRAB *Mithrax verrucosus* **Pl. 54**
Medium-sized—to 5 cm (2 in.) long. Back covered with flat-topped granules. Carapace has *8 pairs of spines* along front edge, 9–10 spines from midline to rear edge. *6 sharp spines on outer margin*

of upper cheliped. Claw has large tooth in middle of upper finger; legs covered with coarse hair. Carapace maroon. Claws olive above, lighter below; tips red, teeth white. Nocturnal. Under rocks; S. Carolina to West Indies and Brazil.

SPONGE SPIDER CRAB   **Fig. 132**
Macrocoeloma trispinosum
Carapace to 3.4 cm (1½ in.) long, covered with hooked hairs, into which fragments of sponge are inserted by crab; entire body may be covered by living sponge. Usually yellow, orange, reddish brown beneath sponge. Pair of curved rostral horns; *posterior has 3 conical spines* along rear edge of carapace. N. Carolina to Brazil. Seven other species in our area; *M. subparallelum* (Pl. 55) can be recognized by its U-shaped rostral horns.

SPOTTED DECORATOR CRAB   **Fig. 132, Pl. 55**
Microphrys bicornutus
Carapace to 3.8 cm (1½ in.) long. Also covers its back with living organisms (in this case, usually algae) for protection. Carapace lumpy; grayish white, flecked with brown. Smooth, *whitish claws covered with purple-brown spots.* N. Carolina and Bermuda, throughout W. Indies to Brazil; in tidepools and among beach rocks.

GIANT DECORATOR CRAB *Stenocionops furcata*   **Fig. 132**
Large—carapace to 15 cm (6 in.) long. Rostral horns long, often curved inward. Chelipeds nearly twice as long as walking legs. Carapace with *4 large spines on margin, one on rear edge.* Body and legs covered with dark brown felt, patches of stiff, hooked hairs. Georgia to Brazil.

Next 8 species: *Mouth area square; no rostrum.*
Swimming Crabs (Family Portunidae—next 8 species):
Last pair of legs flat, paddle-shaped.
BLUE CRABS   *Callinectes* species   **Fig. 133; Pls. 6, 53**
Carapace to 9 cm (3½ in.) long; much wider than it is long, with sharp spine at each lateral angle. These, the most pugnacious

Fig. 133. Common Blue Crab.

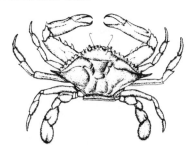

crabs, rear up with claws poised for attack when approached. Six species in our region. (1) **Common Blue Crab** (*C. sapidus*, Fig. 133), the most abundant species, has *2 teeth between eyes;* others have 4. Blue-gray, shading to bright blue on claws; white underneath. Fingers tipped with red; leg joints orange. Commonly found (and eaten) throughout Eastern Seaboard, Gulf to W. Indies. (2) **Ornate Blue Crab** *(C. ornatus)* is similar but has a *greenish* carapace covered with *brown hairs;* walking legs blue with coral tips. (3) **Dana's Blue Crab** *(C. danae)* has an olive carapace that becomes *indigo* on edges of lateral spines; *claws purplish.* N. Carolina, Bermuda, Yucatan; common in Brazil.

PORTUNUS or SWIMMING CRABS   **Pl. 53**
  Portunus species
  Similar in shape and behavior to blue crabs *(Callinectes).* Males can be differentiated by the shape of the abdomen: it is triangular in *Callinectes* and T-shaped in *Portunus.* (1) **Spotted Swimming Crab** (*P. sebae*, Pl. 53) has a tan carapace 7.5 cm (3 in.) long, with *2 distinct red or brown spots, ringed with white,* on posterior. (2) **Sargassum Swimming Crab** *(P. sayi)* is smaller; it lives on sargassum weed, matching its colors. (3) **Iridescent Swimming Crab** *(P. gibbesii)* is small—to 3.7 cm (1²⁄₅ in.) long. Lateral spines curved slightly forward; brownish red ridges cross tan carapace. Front sides of legs look *iridescent purple-red* by lantern light. Massachusetts to Gulf; most common in Gulf Nov.–Jan.

SPECKLED CRAB   *Arenaeus cribrarius*   **Pl. 53**
  Carapace to 5 cm (2 in.) long; gray or tan, with many *small, irregular white spots;* tips of walking legs yellow. *Nine marginal teeth:* last tooth longer than others. Fringe of tiny hairs under spines tends to obscure notches between teeth. Shallow water close to shore, often buried in sand; Massachusetts to Brazil, W. Indies.

LADY CRAB   *Ovalipes ocellatus*   **Fig. 12, Pl. 6**
  To 7.5 cm (3 in.) long; carapace only slightly broader than long, differentiating it from other swimming crabs. Carapace edged with 5 similar teeth; *last tooth not elongated into spine.* Yellow-gray back covered with *leopardlike clusters of purple dots.* Often buried in sand in shallow water; vicious—this is the crab most likely to pinch a wader's toes. Canada to Georgia. **Similar species:** *O. stephensoni* lacks clusters of purple spots on back; Virginia to Florida. Almost identical to **Gulf Lady Crab** *(O. floridanus)* in Gulf of Mexico; nocturnal.

  Mud and Stone Crabs (Family Xanthidae): *Broad-fronted; oval to hexagonal.*

STONE CRAB   *Menippe mercenaria*   **Fig. 134**
  Carapace to 9 cm (3½ in.) long. Smooth, heavy, thick-shelled, with *4 blunt teeth along sides* and stout claws. Dark blue to purple when young; red-brown, spotted with gray or white when older. Legs red, banded or spotted with yellow; fingers of claws dark

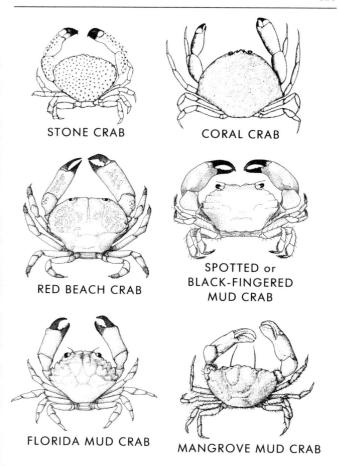

STONE CRAB

CORAL CRAB

RED BEACH CRAB

SPOTTED or
BLACK-FINGERED
MUD CRAB

FLORIDA MUD CRAB

MANGROVE MUD CRAB

Fig. 134. Stone and mud crabs.

brown or black. Commercial, found in fish markets from N. Carolina to Yucatan, Bahamas, and Greater Antilles. Young crabs deeper; older ones migrate into muddy bays and harbors, where they burrow. **Similar species:** *M. nodifrons,* common from Florida to Brazil, W. Indies. Smaller—to 4.8 cm (1⅞ in.) long—redder, with small granular tubercles on front.

CORAL CRAB *Carpilius corallinus* **Fig. 134, Pl. 55**
Largest and one of the most handsome West Indian crabs; carapace to 13 cm (5⅛ in.) long. Carapace smooth, with a *single blunt*

lateral tooth. Entire crab is rich red with fine yellow or white lines and spots; fingers of claws dark red or purple. Once common from Bahamas to Brazil on shallow reefs and Turtle Grass, but overfishing has made it scarce.

RED BEACH CRAB   *Ozius reticulatus*   **Fig. 134**
Carapace to 1.5 cm (¾ in.) long; *rose or wine-colored,* spotted or patched with buff yellow. Fingertips chocolate-brown or black. Among stones on cobble beaches; where wave action is strong, this may be the only crab found. Bahamas, W. Indies to Brazil.

Black-fingered and White-fingered Mud Crabs of the Southeastern U.S., Gulf of Mexico, and West Indies

Richard E. Mulstay

Small oval crabs with 4 teeth along lateral margin of carapace, behind orbit (eye socket). Claws with black or brown fingers (2 species have white fingers). Shallow water, occasionally on land near water.

Next 4 species: *Dark color of lower (fixed) finger extends onto palm.*

COMMON MUD CRAB   *Panopeus herbstii*   **Fig. 135**
Carapace to 4.3 cm (1¾ in.) long; brownish green. Chelipeds darker, sometimes spotted; dark color of lower finger continued for short distance on palm. Claws unequal; enlarged white tooth at base of upper finger of larger claw, *second, third, and fourth marginal teeth large and sharp.* Muddy bottoms, mangrove swamps; Massachusetts to S. America. Common.

BERMUDA MUD CRAB   *Panopeus bermudensis*
Carapace to 1 cm (⅖ in.) long; front dull red. Claws grayish; fingers with tan spot at base, dark color of lower finger continued slightly on palm, fingertips white. All 4 marginal teeth large and sharp. *Raised lines of granules on back.* Chelipeds of male very unequal. Shallow water, including mangrove swamps; Florida to S. America.

SAY'S MUD CRAB   *Neopanope sayi*   **Fig. 135**
Carapace to 2.1 cm (⅘ in.) long. Resembles Depressed Mud Crab (*Eurypanopeus depressus,* p. 325). Bluish green, brown, or buff, with reddish brown spots on yellow background. Dark color of lower finger continues extensively on palm, fingertips light. First marginal tooth rounded and fused with orbit, tips of others angled but *not sharp.* On mud, oyster bars, seagrass beds; Canada to S. Florida. **Related species: Texas Mud Crab** *(N. texana)* in Gulf, Bahamas, and Cuba is slightly larger—to 2.2 cm (⅞ in.) long; often with white fingers on claws. Last segment of last walking

Fig. 135. Black-fingered mud crabs of southern shores. *Clockwise, from top left:* Common Mud Crab, Depressed Mud Crab, and Say's Mud Crab.

legs *longer* than next to last segment (in *N. sayi,* last segment is as long as or shorter).

PACKARD'S MUD CRAB *Neopanope packardii*
Carapace to 1.3 cm (½ in.) long. Dark color of lower finger continued on palm along inner margin, fingertips white. Marginal teeth similar to those of *N. sayi* (above), but *last 3 teeth spiny;* enlarged tooth at base of upper finger. Florida to W. Indies.

CARIBBEAN MUD CRAB *Hexapanopeus caribbaeus*
Tiny—carapace to 8mm (⁵⁄₁₆ in.) long. Dark color of lower finger runs backward and upward on palm, fingertips light. First marginal tooth partly fused with orbit; third tooth largest, *fourth tooth tiny.* W. Indies to S. America.

DEPRESSED MUD CRAB *Eurypanopeus depressus* **Fig. 135**
Carapace to 1.8 cm (⁷⁄₁₀ in.) long; mottled grayish or dark olive-brown. Dark color of lower finger prolonged well back on palm. First marginal tooth forms lobe with orbit; remaining 3 teeth large and sharp. Chelipeds very unequal; fingertips spoon-shaped, *small teeth at base of upper finger.* Shallow water, sometimes in brackish water; Massachusetts to W. Indies.

Next 6 species: Dark color of lower finger does not extend onto palm.

WESTERN MUD CRAB *Panopeus occidentalis*
Carapace to 2.8 cm (1⅛ in.) long. Similar to Common Mud Crab (*P. herbstii,* above). Dull yellow spotted with brown and red; brown dots on chelipeds, brown or rose streaks on walking legs. *4 marginal teeth deeply separated;* first tooth *rounded,* second one

broad and blunt. Enlarged tooth at base of upper finger. Shallow water among rocks, mangrove roots, seaweeds, and pilings; N. Carolina to S. America.

ROUGH MUD CRAB *Panopeus rugosus*

Carapace to 4 cm (1½ in.) long; *hairy and covered with granules.* Second marginal tooth much larger than first, other teeth pointed. Wrist very rough with irregular tubercles, enlarged tooth at base of upper finger. Florida to S. America. **Related species: Hart's Mud Crab** *(P. hartii)* is similar but marginal teeth are very thick and widely separated; fingertips light. To 1.5 cm (⅗ in.) long.

AMERICAN MUD CRAB *Panopeus americanus*

Carapace to 2.4 cm (¹⁵⁄₁₆ in.) long; yellowish or reddish. Upper cheliped purplish, outer claw with spots that are *irregularly shaped,* not round as in Common Mud Crab *(P. herbstii,* p. 324). Carapace squarish, flattened, covered with short transverse lines. Chelipeds very unequal; enlarged tooth at base of upper finger. Florida to S. America.

SPOTTED MUD CRAB *Eurypanopeus abbreviatus*

Carapace to 1.6 cm (⅗ in.) long: yellowish or brownish above. Chelipeds and front margin of carapace reddish or tinged with bluish purple (Brazilian specimens have large dark spots on chelipeds). Front and anterolateral border of carapace rough with granules, smooth elsewhere; marginal teeth blunt and separated by shallow notches. Chelipeds very unequal in males; upper finger of large claw with large basal tooth. Muddy bottoms on oyster beds, under rocks, among sponges; S. Carolina to S. America. Common.

SPOON-FINGERED MUD CRAB

Eurypanopeus dissimilis

Carapace to 1 cm (⅜ in.) long. Marginal teeth large, sharp, widely separated. Chelipeds very unequal; small claw rough and with *spooned fingers,* enlarged tooth at base of upper finger. Florida to S. America.

NARROW MUD CRAB *Hexapanopeus angustifrons*

Carapace to 2 cm (⅘ in.); dark reddish brown or dark gray, often with a light yellow band along front edge of carapace. Hands unequal; upper finger of larger claw has a large tooth at base. First marginal tooth blunt, remaining teeth sharp; second and third successively broader, fourth shorter and narrower. Shelly and soft sandy bottoms; Massachusetts to Texas, Bahamas, Jamaica.

Next 2 species: *Light or white fingers.*

HARRIS' MUD CRAB *Rhithropanopeus harrisii*

Carapace to 1.5 cm (⅗ in.) long, approximately as long as it is wide; bluish above, paler below. First marginal tooth fused with orbit; *line of granules extends across carapace* at level of last marginal tooth. Chelipeds unequal; no enlarged tooth at base of upper finger. Fresh to estuarine water, on a variety of bottoms affording shelter; Canada to Gulf of Mexico. Common.

HEMPILL'S MUD CRAB *Hexapanopeus hempillii*
Tiny—carapace to 7mm (¼ in.) long. Marginal teeth as in Caribbean Mud Crab (*H. caribbaeus,* above), but fourth tooth is well developed; *2 lines of tubercles cross back.* Enlarged tooth at base of upper finger. Shallow water, including mangrove swamps; Florida to W. Indies

FLORIDA MUD CRAB *Cataleptodius floridanus* **Fig. 134**
Carapace to 2.2cm (⅞ in.) long. *Four distinct teeth behind eyes and spooned fingertips;* fourth (most posterior) tooth behind eye is directed obliquely forward. Front of carapace double-edged. Black color of lower (immovable) finger of male's claw continues a short distance onto palm. White or yellowish, with brown legs; a few irregular red or brown spots. Muddy harbors, drainage outlets, and other enriched areas; Bermuda and s. Florida to W. Indies to Brazil. Three related species in same area.

MANGROVE MUD CRAB *Eurytium limosum* **Fig. 134**
Carapace to 2.7cm (1¹⁄₁₆ in.) long; broad, much wider than it is long, smooth; brilliant purplish blue, dark gray, or black. Claws, massive, unequal in size; upper finger curved, round tubercle at base. Fingers white; *upper finger pink or purple near base,* white at tip. Walking legs and margins of carapace hairy; 3 blunt flat marginal teeth; fourth tooth pointed. Burrows in muddy banks, marshes or mangrove swamps, just below high-tide mark; burrows partly filled with water; under rocks in intertidal; on coral reefs; S. Carolina to Brazil.

CALICO CRAB *Eriphia gonagra* **Fig. 136**
Carapace to 3cm (1¼ in.) long; brightly colored—dark brownish green to blue; edge of orbits (eye sockets) and front touched with brilliant yellow. *Claws bluish purple; chrome yellow on inner surface.* Intertidal zone of rocky beaches and breakwaters; N. Carolina to Argentina. Usually in crevices; almost impossible to dislodge. Thoroughly bad tempered, so watch out!

ELKHORN CORAL or GALL CRAB **Fig. 136**
Domecia acanthophora
A small, filter-feeding crab *living in chamber formed by modified growth of coral* around crab. Inconspicuous—to 1cm (½ in.) long, almost colorless, slightly reddish on front with many black spines on carapace and claws. Look for small holes on corals and sponges from N. Carolina to Brazil.

SMALL REEF CRAB *Melybia thalamita* **Fig. 136**
Tiny—carapace to 8mm (⅜ in.) long—and inconspicuous. With a lens a row of spines is visible along top edge of long upper section of legs. Eyes more widely spaced than in Elkhorn Coral Crab (above); *lacks black spines.* On corals and sponges; Florida to Brazil.

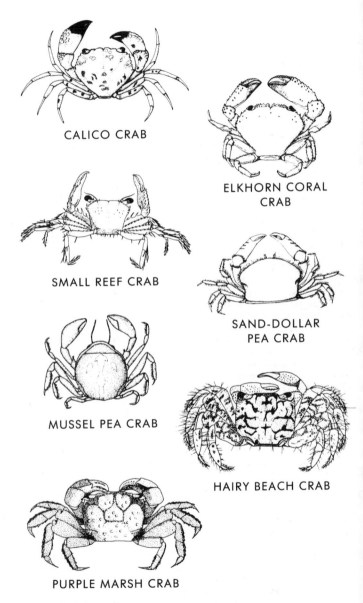

CALICO CRAB

ELKHORN CORAL CRAB

SMALL REEF CRAB

SAND-DOLLAR PEA CRAB

MUSSEL PEA CRAB

HAIRY BEACH CRAB

PURPLE MARSH CRAB

Fig. 136. Reef, pea, marsh, and beach crabs.

HAIRY WHARF CRAB *Pilumnus sayi*

Small oval crab with black-fingered, robust claws; all but rear third of carapace covered with fuzz and/or long hairs. Grayish, reddish brown; *spines black, hairs yellow.* Three pointed spines on edge of carapace. Claws unequal; sharp black spines and yellow hairs on chelipeds. To 2.2 cm (⅞ in.) long. Shelly bottoms, wharf pilings, mangrove swamps; N. Carolina to Florida, Bahamas, Caribbean. **Similar species:** (1) **Florida Hairy Wharf Crab** *(P. floridanus)* is tiny — to 7mm (¼ in.) long, *carapace covered with dense, short hairs, sparser toward front.* Row of *long hairs across front;* upper margin of chelipeds spiny. N. Carolina to S. America. (2) **Brown Hairy Wharf Crab** *(P. dasypodus,* Pl. 56) has carapace thinly covered with hair; upper orbital margin with 3–4 spines. Chelipeds very unequal. Body and claws a brownish wine color; legs much lighter. *Fingers and ends of spines brown.* To 1.1 cm (⅖ in.) long. N. Carolina to S. America.

Pea Crabs (Family Pinnotheridae): *Oval; carapace thin and delicate. Eyestalks small. Symbiotic in mollusks and on sand dollars.*

SAND-DOLLAR PEA CRAB *Dissodactylus* species   **Fig. 136**

Smallest crabs — carapace to 5mm (¼ in.) long; white, commensal or parasitic: live on sand dollars, sea biscuits, and heart urchins. Several species, each host-specific: (1) *D. crinitichelis* is only species on Six-holed Keyhole Urchin. (2) *D. mellitae* lives on underside and in slots of Five-holed Keyhole Urchin.

PARCHMENT-WORM PEA CRAB

Pinnixa chaetopterana

Tiny — carapace to 6mm (¼ in.) long; narrowly ovoid and cylindrical. Mated pairs common in tubes of Parchment Worm (tube, Pl. 4) and other tube-dwelling worms. Feeds on plankton and detritus pumped through tube by worm. Attracted to tube of host by protein exuded by worm. Massachusetts to Brazil. **Similar species:** *P. cristata* and *P. sayana* are almost hairless; free-living. *Large claw of male* has a *C-shaped movable finger;* fixed finger reduced to an almost vertical line. Several other species are commensal with marine worms: *P. cylindrica* lives in burrow of Lugworm and *P. floridana* may live in tubes of Plume Worm.

OYSTER PEA CRAB *Pinnotheres ostreum*

Tiny — to 1.5 cm (⅗ in.) long. Female much larger than male, cylindrical; dark brown with *2 whitish spots on back.* Eyes large and visible on male, concealed by overhang of carapace in female. Carapace smooth, shiny, often soft in females, hard in minute males. Commensal, possibly parasitic at times; lives inside shells of oysters, Jingle Shells, and Blue and Ribbed mussels. Eats mucus string laden with plankton discarded by bivalve; its presence damages gills of host. In extreme cases, where mature crab lives for long time in oyster, host's gills may become completely eroded. Massachusetts to Brazil. **Similar species: Mussel Pea**

Crab (*P. maculatus,* Fig. 136) is brown, hairy, and covered with light spots. To 1.4 cm (½ in.) long. Commensal or parasitic in scallops, pen shells, Jingle shells, mussels, Parchment Worm tubes, even sea stars. Massachusetts to Argentina.

Rock Runners, Spray Crabs, and Marsh Crabs (Family Grapsidae): *Carapace squarish; eyes close to corners.*

HAIRY BEACH CRAB *Geograpsus lividus* **Fig. 136**
Carapace to 2.5 cm (1 in.) long; olive-brown or reddish, with a meshwork of black lines. Legs and claws gingery orange, with a *few long, distinct hairs.* Fast-moving; under rocks near high-water line; Bermuda and Florida to Brazil.

Marsh Crabs

Richard E. Mulstay

Next 2 species: *Square carapace with eyes at front corners; semiterrestrial. Edge of carapace with tooth behind orbit (eye socket).*

PURPLE MARSH CRAB **Fig. 136, Pl. 57**
Sesarma reticulatum
Carapace to 2.5 cm (1 in.) long; purplish to brown with darker speckles, much of claw yellowish. Postorbital tooth not prominent. Last 3 segments of walking legs hairy. Burrows in mud of salt marshes—especially common along banks of tidal creeks, where its larger burrows are intermingled with those of the Mud Fiddler Crab. Massachusetts to Texas.

CURAÇAO MARSH CRAB *Sesarma curacaoense*
Carapace to 1.5 cm (⅗ in.) long; deeply cut postorbital tooth. Under debris among mangroves and on muddy banks of estuaries, sometimes in shallow burrows; Florida to S. America. Sluggish and easily captured.

Next 3 species: *No tooth behind orbit (eye socket).*

MARBLED MARSH CRAB *Sesarma ricordi* **Pl. 57**
Carapace to 2 cm (⅘ in.) long; orange to reddish brown. Legs often marbled. Upper margin of upper finger of claw nearly smooth. Above high water in a variety of shore habitats including debris among mangroves, sometimes in shallow burrows; s. Florida to South America. Common.

GRAY MARSH CRAB *Sesarma cinereum* **Pl. 57**
Carapace to 1.8 cm (¾ in.) long; brown, varying toward olive. Upper margin of upper finger of claw with scattered small tubercles; last segment of fourth walking leg armed with black spines above and below. Above high water in sheltered habitats including among rocks and pilings, sometimes in shallow burrows; Maryland to Florida.

ROBERT'S MARSH CRAB   *Sesarma roberti*
Carapace to 2.7 cm (1¹⁄₁₆ in.) long; tan to dark brown, with
cream-colored spots. Eyes pale green. Claws have a bright red
triangular spot at base of upper finger. Surface of chelipeds and
carapace rough, upper margin of upper finger nearly smooth.
Stream banks to brackish estuarine habitats, including mangrove swamps; W. Indies to S. America.

SALLY LIGHTFOOT   *Grapsus grapsus*   **Pl. 56**
The largest and commonest rock runner from Bermuda and
Florida to Brazil. Carapace to 8 cm (3¼ in.) long; square and flat.
Claws with deeply spooned fingertips. Color variable, often brown
with gray, yellowish, or black striations. On almost all stone
breakwaters and rocky shores in and above spray zone. Runs
rapidly.

COMMON SHORE CRAB   **Fig. 137, Pl. 56**
Pachygrapsus transversus
Small—carapace to 1.2 cm (½ in.) long; khaki-colored, dark olive,
black, with *tan striations across back* and lightly banded legs.
Among rocks, weeds, or mangrove roots, and on pebbly beaches;
Gulf, Florida, Caribbean. **Similar species: Wharf Crab** *(P.
gracilis)* is common in same region on wharves and jetties, but is
pinkish with *convex frontal area between eyes.*

ROUND SHORE CRAB   *Cyclograpsus integer*   **Fig. 137**
Carapace to 1.2 cm (½ in.) long, with *smoothly rounded corners*
(unlike Common Shore Crab). Sand-colored, smooth, shiny. Under rocks in mid-intertidal zone; Bermuda, s. Florida to W. Indies,
south to Brazil.

MANGROVE CRAB   *Aratus pisonii*
Carapace to 2.2 cm (⅞ in.) long; brown, sometimes a dark mottled
olive-green. Brown legs. Tufts of black hairs on claws. *Eyes
widespread, at front corners of carapace.* Tips of legs sharp,
enabling crab to climb up Red Mangrove trees, where it eats
leaves. When pursued, adept at keeping to opposite side of tree
and will, in desperation, run down aerial roots into water. S.
Florida and W. Indies to Brazil. **Similar species: Spotted Mangrove Crab** or **Tree Crab** *(Goniopsis cruentata,* Pl. 22), to 6.3 cm
(2½ in.) long; dark brown with *yellow spots on red legs,* no black
hairs on claw, palms white. Common on Red Mangrove trees in
Caribbean.

SPRAY CRAB   *Plagiusa depressa*   **Fig. 137, Pl. 56**
Carapace to 4.5 cm (1¾ in.) long, with *V-shaped notches in front*
that accommodate folded antennules, and sharp, pointed fingers
of claws, differentiating it from Sally Lightfoot (above), which has
spooned claws. Reddish brown with darker lines and blood-red
spots; yellowish underneath. Scale-like pattern of hairs on carapace. Surf zone of rocky shores; N. Carolina and Bermuda to
Brazil.

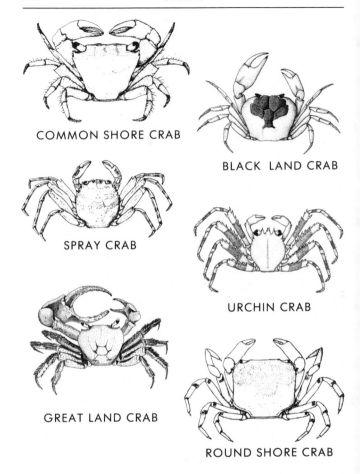

COMMON SHORE CRAB

BLACK LAND CRAB

SPRAY CRAB

URCHIN CRAB

GREAT LAND CRAB

ROUND SHORE CRAB

Fig. 137. Shore, beach, and land crabs.

URCHIN CRAB *Percnon gibbesi*   Fig. 137, Pl. 56
Carapace to 2.5 cm (1 in.) long. Flattened, disklike, brown, flesh-colored or pink, with median blue stripe and iridescent greenish line around front. Legs brown with *golden bands and splotches of gold at joints*. On intertidal rocks, near coral, often hides near or under Long-spined Black Urchin; N. Carolina, Bermuda, Florida, Bahamas, W. Indies to Brazil.

Land Crabs (Family Gecarcinidae): *Gap between outer max-illipeds. Front narrow; sides of carapace strongly arched.*

GREAT LAND CRAB or DUPPY **Fig. 137, Pl. 58**
Cardisoma guanhumi
Huge—carapace to 9.5 cm (3¾ in.) long. Males have vastly unequal claws; *larger claw with slender gaping fingers may be longer than carapace.* Adults pale gray or bluish; young usually blue to violet; very young sandy brown. Common in coconut groves, wastelands, fields, irrigation ditches, marshes, especially close to sea. Nocturnal, sometimes active during day, foraging on fruit and leaves. Constructs large, deep burrows extending to water level; burrows often a nuisance to farmers. Adults mate in male's burrow; females migrate to sea when larvae ready to hatch. Bermuda, Florida, Texas, W. Indies to Brazil. Ingredient of soups and stews throughout Caribbean. **Caution:** If crab has been feeding on poisonous fruit of Manchineel tree, it can cause ulcerous lesions if eaten.

BLACK LAND CRAB *Gecarcinus lateralis* **Fig. 137, Pl. 58**
Carapace to 4.5 cm (1¾ in.) long; dark red-brown, plum, or black in center, shading to bright red around sides and toward rear. Red claws not quite equal in size; sharp-fingered, robust, easily auto-tomized. Legs and underparts sandy or grayish. Last joint of legs has *4 rows of small teeth.* **Similar species: Mountain Crab** (*G. ruricola,* Pl. 58) is larger and has *6 rows of teeth* on last joint of legs. Claws equal. Color variable—carapace often darker than in *G. lateralis,* with yellow areas at rear corners; legs orange. Both species are pests in farms and gardens; both species edible. In underbrush; Bermuda, s. Florida, W. Indies.

Ghost and Fiddler Crabs (Family Ocypodidae): *Eyestalks long and slender; stalks occupy entire front margin of carapace when folded down.*

GHOST CRAB *Ocypode quadrata* **Pl. 58**
Carapace to 4.5 cm (1¾ in.) long. Body and legs pale, sand-colored; sharp claws whitish. *Black eyes project on stalks.* Most active crab of sandy beaches: alert, fast-running; builds burrows just above high-tide line. One of few crabs to stand erect on tips of legs. Nocturnal; a predator and scavenger. New Jersey to Brazil, West Indies, Bermuda.

MANGROVE LAND CRAB **Pl. 58**
Ucides cordatus
Large—carapace to 7 cm (2¾ in.) long. Body oval, lacks teeth at margins. Bluish gray with reddish and purplish blotches, *distinct purple overtones.* Walking legs long, with a *heavy fringe of silky hairs.* Similar to Great Land Crab, but chelipeds distinctly toothed, not smooth, along inner margins; large claw less than twice length of smaller one; enlarged claw of male usually the right claw; and overall color of large specimens quite purple

(carapace not gray or tan, as in Great Land Crab). Lives in wide burrows, often among fiddler and mangrove crabs in muddy areas, primarily in Red Mangrove swamps. Sluggish, may be dug out of burrows easily. Florida to Brazil, W. Indies.

Fiddler Crabs of the Southeastern U.S., Gulf of Mexico, and Caribbean

Richard E. Mulstay

Numerous species at edges of marshes and mangrove swamps and along rivers. Males use huge claw to signal aggressive or amorous intent by waving claw in a distinct pattern characteristic of the species. The characteristics of the male's large claw and the male's coloration during the display phase are given below. Since fiddler crabs are gregarious, females will be found in the same area as the males. Females can be easily identified since they lack the enlarged claw but are usually otherwise similar to males. Carapace lengths are given for large males; females are generally smaller. All fiddler crabs live in burrows above low water; when approached, crabs scuttle to burrows and disappear. Activity rate tied to tides; at low tide, activity peaks as thousands of fiddlers gather at water's edge to feed on detritus.

Next 9 species: *Palm of large claw has an oblique tuberculate ridge.*

BURGER'S FIDDLER CRAB   *Uca burgersi*   **Fig. 138, Pl. 57**

Carapace to 1.2 cm (½ in.) long. Dark mottled brown, often marbled with red or pink on carapace and red on major claw; walking legs usually brown or striped with gray. Upper center of palm of major claw with large tubercles. Lives in habitats sheltered from the open sea—mud or muddy sand near mouths of streams, mangroves; e. Florida to S. America; absent from Gulf. Most common fiddler in W. Indies.

TROPICAL RIVER FIDDLER CRAB   *Uca mordax*   **Pl. 57**
Carapace to 1.6 cm (⅗ in.) long. Similar to *U. burgersi* (above), but fingers of major claw slightly longer and narrower and upper finger slightly thinner. Pile (patches of short hairs) on lower margin of next to last segment of second and third walking legs of *U. mordax* is absent in *U. burgersi*. On mud along banks or mouths of rivers, usually further upstream than *U. burgersi,* occasionally together. Continental Central and S. America from Guatemala to Brazil; not in W. Indies.

RED-JOINTED FIDDLER CRAB   *Uca minax*   **Fig. 139**
Large—carapace to 2.3 cm (⁹⁄₁₀ in.) long. Red bands at joints of appendages. Upper and outer face of large hand with tubercles

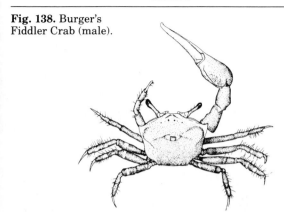

Fig. 138. Burger's Fiddler Crab (male).

diminishing to granules on lower face; upper finger curves down below tip of lower. On mud in cordgrass marshes, among needle rushes, brackish to almost fresh water, upstream in rivers; Massachusetts to n. Florida, Louisiana.

THAYER'S FIDDLER CRAB   *Uca thayeri*
Carapace to 1.9 cm (¾ in.) long. Carapace and claw brown to orange-brown. Lower finger of claw bent down. Muddy banks of mangrove-bordered estuaries and streams; egg-laying females build mud chimneys. Florida to S. America.

MAJOR FIDDLER CRAB   *Uca major*
Carapace to 2 cm (¾ in.) long. Carapace and claw white with purple markings; females dull brown or yellowish. Fingertips sharply pointed, short row of tubercles on inner surface of base of upper finger. On sandy mud flats nearly cut off from open water, near but not among mangroves; Bahamas to S. America. Uncommon.

VE'S FIDDLER CRAB   *Uca speciosa*   **Fig. 139**
Carapace to 1.1 cm (⅖ in.) long. Carapace color seasonally variable, but darker than claw, which is brilliant white. Lower fingertip not as sharply pointed as in *U. major;* slightly curved row of large, uniform tubercles on palm, just behind joint of upper finger. Mud above mid-tide level on sheltered shores near mangroves; Florida and Cuba.

DWARF FIDDLER CRAB   *Uca leptodactyla*
Carapace to 7mm (⁵⁄₁₆ in.) long. Carapace white; claw white with some orange or red. Tooth in middle of upper finger, straight row of tubercles on palm behind and perpendicular to fingers. Tidal mud flats and exposed sandy shores; Florida to S. America.

CARIBBEAN FIDDLER CRAB *Uca rapax*   **Pl. 57**

Carapace to 2.1 cm (⅘ in.) long, light tan; claw light tan, lower palm and finger darker, but never red. Center of palm almost smooth, covered with fine granules, unlike rough palm of *U. burgersi*. Sheltered mud flats near mangroves, flat banks close to mouth of streams; Florida to S. America. This species and *U. burgersi* are the most common fiddlers in Caribbean. **Related species: Long-wave Gulf Fiddler** (*U. longisignalis*) has patches of short hair (pile) on lower surfaces of second and third walking legs. Carapace between eyes bright turquoise, blending into blue-green band toward rear. Muddy substrates; w. Florida to Texas.

MUD FIDDLER CRAB *Uca pugnax*   **Pls. 6, 57**
Carapace to 1.2 cm (½ in.) long. Carapace brown to pale gray, front (between eyes) turquoise (color light or absent in Florida); claw lighter with white tips. Similar to *U. rapax* (above) but center of palm usually has large tubercles. Mud of salt marshes; Massachusetts to e. Florida. Common. **Related species: Gulf Mud Fiddler Crab** (*U. virens*, Fig. 139). Front edge of carapace white, anterior third of carapace with green band. No pile on lower margins of walking legs. Gulf coast from Florida to Mexico.

Next 2 species: Palm of large claw lacks an oblique tuberculate ridge.

LAVENDER FIDDLER CRAB *Uca vocator*
Carapace to 1.7 cm (⅗ in.) long. Carapace dull brownish or grayish; claw yellowish or reddish with white fingers. Tubercles on upper outer surface of hand very small. Partly shaded mud near mouth of streams, close to and among mangroves; W. Indies to S. America.

SAND FIDDLER CRAB *Uca pugilator*   **Fig. 139**
Carapace to 1.4 cm (9/16 in.) long. Carapace almost white with conspicuous pink patch in center; patch brown when not displaying. Claw light, often with pale orange base. Hand has large tubercles (mingled in 2 sizes) on most of outer surface, tubercles near bottom margin abruptly smaller. Sheltered sandy shores; Massachusetts to Florida. The common fiddler of sandy eastern shores. **Related species: Panacea Sand Fiddler Crab** (*U.*

Fig. 139 (opposite). Gulf fiddler crabs. (1) Ive's Fiddler Crab (p. 335); small; male's claw long. (2) Red-jointed Fiddler Crab (p. 334); large; leg joints red. (3) Panacea Sand Fiddler Crab (p. 337); carpus orange or red. (4) Dorsal view of Panacea Sand Fiddler Crab. (5) Sand Fiddler Crab (p. 337); carpus not usually red. (6) Dorsal view of Sand Fiddler Crab. (7) Gulf Mud Fiddler Crab (p. 337); front greenish blue. (8) Dorsal view of Gulf Mud Fiddler Crab.

panacea, Fig. 132) has inner margin of carpus (wrist of cheliped) bright orange or purplish red. Gulf Coast from w. Florida to Texas.

The Distribution of Fiddler Crabs

Using the Atlantic Coast as a starting point, we can view the radiation of fiddler crab species into nearby climatic zones. The three common species of the Atlantic salt marsh have divided their habitat into individual niches: The Sand Fiddler *(Uca pugilator)* dominates the sandy edges of the marsh, the Mud Fiddler *(U. pugnax)* the mud, and the Red-jointed Fiddler *(U. minax)* the upper, low-salinity muddy areas into the marsh's freshwater margins. The three species are easy to differentiate by a combination of habitat preference and appearance. The Sand Fiddler makes characteristic balls of sand and waste that pile up at the entrance to its burrow. The Red-jointed Fiddler is almost twice the size of the other species and has red joints on its legs. A small fiddler crab living in the mud that does not fulfill either description is likely to be the Mud Fiddler.

In Caribbean marshes a similar distribution holds: Burger's Fiddler Crab *(U. burgersi)* occupies the same niche as the Sand Fiddler, and the Caribbean Fiddler *(U. rapax)* is similar to the Mud Fiddler. There does not seem to be a species related to the Red-jointed Fiddler occupying the same habitat, although the Tropical River Fiddler *(U. mordax)* invades brackish and fresh water on Caribbean continental shores.

It is at the juncture of two climatic zones, where the temperate meets the tropical, that speciation of fiddler crabs seems to have flourished. On the Gulf Coast, no less than four new species have been described. The Panacea Sand Fiddler *(U. panacea)* occupies the same habitat as the Sand Fiddler and has the same habits, including manufacture of sand balls, but it has biochemical and minor morphological differences. It is found only on the northern Gulf Coast from Florida to Texas.

The Spiny-fingered or Gulf Freshwater Fiddler *(U. spinicarpa)* and Ive's Fiddler *(U. speciosa),* two very closely related species, apparently split the niche of the Red-jointed Fiddler: the Spiny-fingered Fiddler lives in nearly fresh water and low-salinity areas and Ive's Fiddler occupies more brackish zones. The Spiny-fingered Fiddler has been found only from Alabama to Texas and northeastern Mexico, while Ive's Fiddler inhabits marshes and mangrove swamps from the Florida Keys to Mississippi, skips Louisiana and Texas, and then is found in eastern Mexico and Cuba.

The Gulf Mud Fiddler *(U. virens)* and the Long-wave Gulf Fiddler *(U. longisignalis)* occupy the niche of the Mud Fiddler.

15

Sea Stars, Sea Urchins, Brittle Stars, and Sea Cucumbers

The spiny-skinned animals, Phylum Echinodermata, are fascinating because they present so many contradictions and exhibit such evolutionary conservatism. They have no eyes, yet frequently seek dark areas and shun the light. They have no noses, yet in some cases males can detect the "perfume" of females (pheromones) and will shed their sperms when a far-off female sheds her eggs. They have no fingers, yet are able to probe the sand in search of clams buried beneath the surface. There seems to be no particular need to retain the five parts of the ancestral echinoderm, yet virtually all species have the symbol of the phylum, five grooves radiating out from the animal's center. In many sea urchins the body has evolved so radically that the grooves have no apparent use, yet you will find a pattern of five radiating "petals" on the upper (aboral) surface of these urchins. Whatever the reason, the trademark is retained.

When the ancestral echinoderms were attached to the bottom, it was advantageous to be pie-shaped (radially symmetrical) so that they could catch food drifting from every direction. Now almost all echinoderms are free living, yet they still retain their radial symmetry. One would think, after thousands of years of evolution, they would have discovered the advantage of having a "front." But relatively few species have made the transition from a pie shape to an elongate form.

Two other distinguishing characteristics of echinoderms are an extraordinary ability to regenerate lost parts and a hydraulic system that uses water flowing through radiating vessels to operate a mass of tube feet for locomotion. Thus if a sea star is cut in two, it will become two sea stars; if a predator grasps a brittle star by an arm, it will snap off, leaving the attacker with a writhing arm and the brittle star with its freedom. It will take the animal a few weeks to replace the appendage. A sea cucumber, having no arms to sacrifice, will spew out its innards to distract a predator, and will slink off to regenerate new insides.

Taxonomy: Phylum Echinodermata has five classes:

1. Sea stars: Class Asteroidea. Usually with five more or less rigid arms that merge indistinguishably with central disk. These animals move on hundreds of tube feet projecting through five grooves on underside.

2. Brittle stars or serpent stars: Class Ophiuroidea. These resemble sea stars but have longer, prehensile arms, distinctly separated from disk. Locomotion by sinuous movement of arms; tube feet not usually well developed.

3. Sea urchins: Class Echinoidea. These echinoderms have no arms. Body (test) usually globose, circular, or disklike, covered with long, pointed spines or short, fuzzlike bristles.

4. Sea cucumbers: Class Holothuroidea. These elongate echinoderms resemble an animated salami. Body covered with warty skin, in which tiny (microscopic) spines are invisibly buried. Sea cucumbers move on tube feet; anterior (front) end of body has retractable tentacles.

5. Sea lilies or feather stars: Class Crinoidea. Crinoids have many feathery arms facing upward, which filter plankton from water. Some attached forms have stalks; many species are capable of walking or even swimming. These are deep-water forms, not discussed here.

Sea Stars

Sea stars are predators, feeding primarily on snails and clams found on or under sediment. They capture their prey by attaching to them the suction cups of dozens of tube feet that pull apart the shells of bivalves, or manipulate snails until the aperture is centered under the mouth of the sea star. Then a filmy membrane, part of the sea star's stomach, is extruded through the mouth and inserted into the prey's shell. Enzymes are secreted and the prey's tissues digested. Eventually the sea star drops the now-empty shell, its contents having passed into the stomach as a frothy, partially digested soup. Most sea stars feed this way. However, the spectacular Cushion Sea Star, over 30 cm (1 ft.) in diameter (see Pls. 17, 59), feeds mainly on bacteria it gleans from rotting Turtle Grass. Other sea stars eat urchins, brittle stars, and, it seems, whatever they can catch.

Most sea stars can be found on or under sand in Turtle Grass beds (Cushion, Nine-armed, Beaded, Comet, Limp, and Netted sea stars, for example) or under coral rock and in crevices on finger coral flats (Blunt-armed and Red Spiny sea stars). The Bermuda and Brown Spiny sea stars prefer muddy bottoms, especially in Red Mangrove channels.

All sea stars have an oral surface facing the bottom, which contains the mouth and five radiating grooves, the ambulacra. Each arm contains one ambulacrum, from which protrude hundreds of tube feet (see Fig. 14). The aboral surface, facing upward, is covered with spines. An anus is in the center of the aboral disk; near it is often found a calcareous dot, the madreporite, which acts as a filter, allowing water to pass into and out of the hydraulic (water-vascular) system.

To confirm identification of sea stars, it is useful to compare the length of the rays or arms (measured from the center of the disk to the tip of the arm) with the radius of the disk (measured from the disk's center to the interradial margin—the fork where 2 rays or arms meet). In the following descriptions, **R** = the distance from disk center to ray tip, and **r** = the disk radius. **R = r** means that ray length equals disk radius; **R = 4r,** that ray length is 4 times disk radius.

FORBES' SEA STAR *Asterias forbesi* **Fig. 14**
To 25 cm (10 in.) wide. Purple or brown, with an *orange dot (madreporite) near center of aboral disk.* Subtidal, rarely intertidal under rocks and in tidepools. Eats snails and bivalves, especially oysters. Maine to Gulf. R = 4–6r.

HARTMEYER'S BLUNT-ARMED SEA STAR **Fig. 140**
Asterina hartmeyeri
Small—to 1.2 cm (½ in.) wide. White or pinkish; *rays reduced to rounded bulges on side of disk.* Underside of rocks or coral fragments at or just below low tide, on fringing reefs. W. Indies.
Similar species: Common Blunt-armed Sea Star (*A. folium*) is larger than *A. hartmeyeri*—to 2.5 cm (1 in.) wide. Olive or bluish green; juveniles white. Rays shorter, less distinct than in *A. hartmeyeri.* Bermuda, Florida, W. Indies; common but difficult to find. R = 1.2–1.3r.

BEADED SEA STAR *Astropecten articulatus* **Pl. 59**
To 15 cm (6 in.) across. Color variable: aboral surface brown, purple, or maroon, but regular, beadlike marginal plates always contrasting—usually yellow or tan. *Lacks large erect spines or tubercles* on inner margin of basal superomarginal plates. (If viewed from above, appears not to have marginal spines.) Soft

Fig. 140. Hartmeyer's Blunt-armed Sea Star.

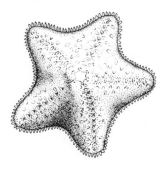

bottoms; Florida, Gulf, W. Indies. R = 4–6.5r. **Similar species: Spiny Beaded Sea Star** (*A. duplicatus,* Pl. 59) is slightly larger than *A. articulatus*—to 20 cm (8 in.) wide. Less flattened, more spiny, with a smaller disk. A *large erect spine* (or at least a tubercle) on inner margin of some or all basal superomarginal plates. Reddish, brown, grayish, or tan, with brown spots. Soft bottoms in shallow water, often in groups; buried when hunting mollusks. S. Florida, Gulf, W. Indies, Cen. America. R = 4–6.5r.

BERMUDA SEA STAR   **Pl. 59**
Coscinasterias tenuispina

To 27 cm (11 in.) wide, usually smaller. Purple, with yellow spines. Reproduces by autotomy, breaking apart into several individuals. Daughter sea stars regenerate new rays in haphazard fashion: some have 5 arms, others *6, 7, 8, or more* (7 arms more frequent than 5). Rays usually at various stages of regeneration, so sizes vary. Soft bottoms in Bermuda; rare or absent elsewhere in our area—probably accidentally introduced from Europe. R = 4–6r.

RED SPINY SEA STAR *Echinaster sentus*   **Pl. 59**

To 15 cm (6 in.) across. Rays short, straight-sided, blunt, covered with *large pointed spines.* Bright or deep red, rarely reddish brown. In finger-coral flats, under shallow coral debris; Florida, Caribbean. R = 4r. **Similar species:** *E. echinophorus* is also red but has slender, tapering rays and smaller, more abundant spines. Jamaica, Brazil, Yucatan. R = 4.5–6r.

BROWN SPINY SEA STAR *Echinaster spinulosus* **Pls. 11, 59**

To 16 cm (6¼ in.) across. Rays long, tapering, not slender. Reddish or greenish brown, often covered with *short, contrasting-colored spines,* sometimes in rows running length of ray. Spines often orange, but may be same color as rest of body, making it resemble the more northern Forbes' Sea Star. Soft bottoms in mangrove channels, especially Florida Keys. In contrast with other sea stars, *E. spinulosus* seeks light and is found in open. Restricted to s. and w. Florida to Alabama. Seagrass beds may be peppered with juveniles the size of a quarter; sometimes intertidal and in tidepools. R = 4–6r.

COMET SEA STAR *Linckia guildingii*   **Fig. 141, Pl. 59**

To 16 cm (6¼ in.) wide. *Rays long and thin; parallel-sided, not tapered,* with blunt tips. Rounded tubercles randomly distributed on aboral surface, but surface feels smooth. Flesh-colored, beige, or tan, rarely reddish. Ambulacra bordered by rows of round granules. On shallow sand bottoms and reef flats, under rocks near low-tide mark; Bermuda, Florida, Caribbean. Adults not as common as juveniles because before adulthood animal may reproduce by autotomy, breaking apart to produce 2 or more daughter sea stars. Often a broken-off mature ray regenerates 4 or more tiny rays (Fig. 141), giving animal a cometlike appearance. Adults can reproduce sexually also. R = 8–12r. **Similar species:**

Fig. 141. Comet Sea Star.

Red Finger Sea Star (*Ophidiaster guildingii*, Pl. 59) is smaller — to 10 cm (4 in.) wide. Usually blotched with purple, pink, or red. Surface similar to that of *Linckia* but with *7 longitudinal rows of smooth tubercles covering aboral surface.* Florida, W. Indies. R = 8–12r.

LIMP or WEAK SEA STAR *Luidia alternata* **Pl. 59**

To 36 cm (14½ in.) wide. Bristling with long (5mm — ¼ in. long), thin, tan spines projecting beyond velvetlike surface. Rays wide at base, bluntly tapered; *limp, easily broken.* Animal sags when lifted; rays easily twisted, giving animal a rag-doll limpness. Blotchy dark brown on tan, or with indistinct black or purple bands; underside tan. Lies buried in sand with outline of body or single ray just visible. Turtle Grass beds, lagoons; Florida, Bahamas, W. Indies. R = 7r.

NETTED SEA STAR *Luidia clathrata* **Pls. 11, 59**

To 30 cm (1 ft.) wide. Covered with *velvetlike spines* characteristic of *Luidia* species. Cream, tan, or bluish gray, with a dark brown or blackish strip down each ray, and *netlike or wavy dark lines* parallel to it. Under sand, in lagoons to deep water; Bermuda, Florida, W. Indies. R = 6r.

NINE-ARMED SEA STAR **Pl. 59**
Luidia senegalensis

Over 30 cm (1 ft.) wide. Aboral surface purple, bluish, or greenish gray; *velvety. Nine long, narrow, sharply tapered rays.* On or under sand in lagoons and Turtle Grass beds, at depths greater than 2 m (6¼ ft.). West Indies; rare in Florida. R = 12r.

CUSHION or RETICULATED SEA STAR **Pls. 17, 59**
Oreaster reticulatus

Huge — to 50 cm (20 in.) wide. Common, spectacular. *Thick, inflated;* height of disk may reach 7.5 cm (3 in.). Walks on thick podia (tube feet) over sand bottoms of Turtle Grass beds. Tips of rays often curled upward. *Disk and rays covered with a netlike array of large, contrasting tubercles.* Juveniles light green; adults variable, often tan or rust with dark brown or red tubercles. S. Florida, Caribbean, W. Indies; has been over-collected by souvenir hunters, so it may be rare in some areas. R = 2r.

Brittle or Serpent Stars

Gordon T. Taylor and Richard D. Bray

Brittle stars, Class Ophiuroidea, may be found under almost any rock or crevice, but their propensity to seek the darkest recesses and their ability to adjust their bodies to the shape of the crevice, together with camouflage coloration, makes them hard to spot. Some species hide under the surface of the sand, with just the tips of their arms visible. At night, when fewer of their predators are active, many brittle stars leave the protection of their shelters to feed.

Brittle stars crawl over the bottom by moving their long, flexible arms in serpentine fashion. Podia (tube feet) are small and lack suction cups; their function is primarily sensory. Arms are clearly differentiated from the body (disk); in the closely related sea stars the arms are merged with the disk.

On the oral surface (bottom side) of the disk are five triangular jaws, each with a central column of teeth. These seize prey (such as larval fishes or invertebrates) or tear tissues from carrion or gather sediment containing microscopic food organisms.

The arms are covered with rows of plates; those on the sides are armed with spines. Tube feet (podia) project from the bottom of each arm and are protected by one or two modified spines called podial scales. There is no ambulacral groove. In some species the podia (tube feet) are used to pass particles of food to the mouth.

Brittle stars have the simplest digestive system of all echinoderms. Above the muscular jaw is the mouth, which opens into a short esophagus, leading in turn to a saclike stomach. There are no intestines, digestive glands, or anus. The stomach does all the digesting, and undigested remains are ejected through the mouth.

Brittle stars feed on a variety of food, ranging from bacteria and microalgae to larval fishes. Many species sift sand and digest out microorganisms, tiny invertebrates, and detritus. Others are predators and feed on small invertebrates and fishes. The Basket Star strains plankton from the water by extending its long, many-branched, mucus-covered arms across the current. Other suspension feeders bury their disks in the sand and extend their arms upward into the water column.

The arms of brittle stars contain neither digestive nor reproductive organs; thus their loss is relatively inconsequential. Once an arm is broken off, regeneration is easily and quickly accomplished.

Major organs of brittle stars are tiny sacs at the base of each arm, called bursae. They open to the exterior through paired openings called genital slits (see Fig. 142). The inner surface of each thin-walled bursa is covered with constantly beating, micro-

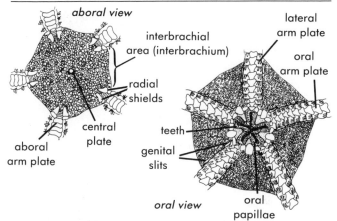

Fig. 142. Anatomy of a brittle star.

scopic, hairlike cilia. These cause a flow of water in the bursa, aiding in respiration and waste removal.

Most brittle stars reproduce during the spring and summer. Most species have separate sexes, but males and females look alike. Gonads line the inside walls of the bursae, facing the body cavity. Sperms or eggs pass through the walls when ripe; the cilia-driven water currents expel them through the genital slits to the outside. Only a small fraction of the millions of gametes meet—the rest are wasted. Each fertilized egg develops into a bilaterally symmetrical larva with long arms, the pluteus. The larvae become part of the plankton, providing food for other organisms. The larvae that survive mature floating near the surface, then sink to the ocean floor, where they become miniature replicas of the adults. Some species brood their young on the walls of the bursae, and release partially developed juveniles through the genital slits.

Descriptions that follow are based on adult specimens; juveniles may differ, especially in color. In general be wary of using color as the sole criterion, as it can vary with habitat, diet, and geographic distribution.

BASKET STAR *Astrophyton muricatum*
Large—when arms are extended at night, width can reach 18 cm (7 in.) or more. Coiled into a flat mass in daytime: expanded into a net at night. *Arms repeatedly branched into many fine tendril-like tips.* Disk, to 3 cm (1¼ in.) wide, five-cornered. Top orange, brown, pink, or tan; bottom lighter. On soft corals; s. Florida, Bahamas, W. Indies, Caribbean to Brazil.

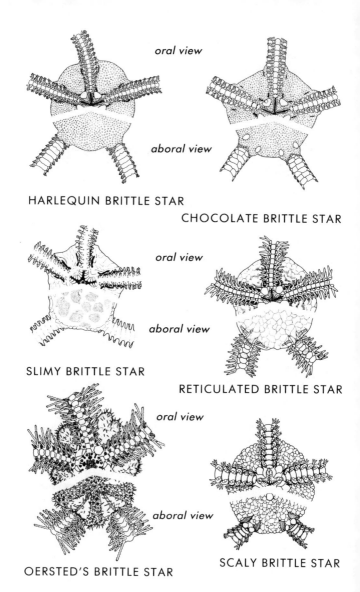

oral view

aboral view

HARLEQUIN BRITTLE STAR

CHOCOLATE BRITTLE STAR

oral view

aboral view

SLIMY BRITTLE STAR

RETICULATED BRITTLE STAR

oral view

aboral view

OERSTED'S BRITTLE STAR

SCALY BRITTLE STAR

Fig. 143. Brittle stars.

FIVE-ARMED OPHIACTIS *Ophiactis quinqueradia*
To 7mm (¼ in.) across disk; arms to 4 cm (1½ in.) long. *Disk and arms covered with thin, transparent skin. Disk appears to be mounted on top of jaw-arm complex.* Radial shields large, blade-like, granular. Arm spines short, flat, conical, granular. Arms long, slender; aboral arm plates ellipsoid, granular. Entire aboral surface usually dark brown or mottled; arms banded; oral surface tan. Usually inside coral crevices, sponges; young in sponges and coralline algae. **Similar species: Savigny's Brittle Star** (*O. savignyi*) usually has 6 arms; green and white. S. Florida, Bahamas, Caribbean.

LOBATE BRITTLE STAR *Ophiocnida scabriuscula*   **Pl. 60**
Disk to 1 cm (⅜ in.) wide, covered with *small scattered papillae;* a series of papillae around perimeter of disk. *Disk appears to be mounted on jaw-arm complex.* Radial shields small, needle-shaped. Arms long, slender; 3 short, blunt, flattened arm spines per lateral plate. Aboral arm plates rectangular. Disk brown, with lighter radial shields; arms tan, banded with brown. Usually buried in sand near shore; s. Florida to Brazil.

MUD BRITTLE STAR *Ophiophragmus wurdemani*   **Pl. 2**
To 1 cm (⅜ in.) across disk; arms long—to 12.7 cm (5 in.). Disk covered with small, even-sized scales, with a ring of bluntly rounded papillae on aboral surface. Radial shields elongate, paired, heart-shaped. Arms flat. *Three pairs of short, blunt arm spines per segment.* Color variable: disk cream, gray, or dark brown, arms barred with cream and gray. Buried in intertidal and subtidal mud, to depth of 12.7 cm (5 in.). N. Carolina to Florida. **Similar species: Caribbean Mud Brittle Star** (*Ophionepthys limicola*) has a yellow or yellow-green disk 1.2 cm (½ in.) wide; arms to 12 cm (4¾ in.) long, each with a *dark longitudinal stripe.* Buried in mud; s. Florida to Caribbean.

BURROWING BRITTLE STAR *Hemipholis elongata*
Disk to 1 cm (⅜ in.) across; threadlike arms to at least 9 cm (3½ in.) long. Disk covered with large scales above; naked below, with prominent radial shields. Disk blue, green, yellow, or tan; arms banded—or sometimes whole animal white; *podia (tube feet) red.* Buried in mud, to depth of 15 cm (6 in.). When tide comes in, it extends arms (which look like stringy plants) from surface of intertidal mud while disk remains buried. *Has red blood* (hemoglobin). N. Carolina to Gulf, south to Brazil.

SPINY OPHIOCOMA *Ophiocoma echinata*   **Pl. 60**
Large—may be over 3 cm (1¼ in.) across disk; arms to 15 cm (6 in.) long. *Spiny, dark brown.* Two genital slits per interbrachium. Spiny arms; *no radial shields.* Oral papillae and dental papillae present. Two podial scales per podium (tube foot). Arm spine closest to mouth club-shaped. Top dark brown, sometimes mottled with tan; arms banded in shades of brown; bottom white. **Similar species:** (1) **Banded Ophiocoma** (*O. pumila*) is smaller—disk to

1.5 cm (¾ in.) across. Arms long, slender. *Spines relatively short,* about 3× length of arm segment; uppermost spines pointed, others blunt. Each podium has a single ovoid podial scale. Disk usually light brown, arms banded in shades of brown; juveniles greenish. In crevices or among coralline algae, close to low-water mark. (2) **Red Ophiocoma** (*O. wendti*) is the largest *Ophiocoma*—arms to 16 cm (6¼ in.) long. Arm spines longest, about 8× length of arm segment. Arm spine closest to mouth not club-shaped. Top black or dark brown; *bottom, especially podia, red;* no white anywhere. All species found under rocks, in crevices in shallow water; Caribbean, W. Indies.

HARLEQUIN BRITTLE STAR   Fig. 143
Ophioderma appressum

To 2.5 cm (1 in.) across disk. Similar to *O. cinereum* but aboral arm plates undivided. Arm spines about ⅔ as long as arm segment and cigar-shaped; one closest to mouth longer and wider than others. Disk usually olive-green; may be brown or gray with white and/or black spots. Arms banded green, gray, or brown and white; *minutely serrated.* Common from Bermuda to Brazil.

CHOCOLATE BRITTLE STAR   Fig. 143, Pl. 60
Ophioderma cinereum

Large—to 3.5 cm (1⅜ in.) across disk. Arms short—only 4× disk diameter. Disk covered with granules; 4 genital slits per interbrachium. *Arms appear smooth*—short, blade-like spines are flattened against them. Oral but no dental papillae. Aboral arm plates divided into 2 or more subplates per segment. Ellipsoid radial shields. Color varies—usually brown, with or without darker specks on disk; arms indistinctly banded. **Similar species:** (1) **Short-armed Brittle Star** (*O. brevicaudum*), to 2 cm (¾ in.) across disk. Radial shields not apparent; divided aboral arm plates thick, irregular in shape. Arms also short, with thick scales at bases. Aboral disk light gray to green; arms lightly banded; oral surface lighter. (2) **Short-spined Brittle Star** (*O. brevispinum,* Pl. 11) is smaller than *O. cinereum*—to 1 cm (⅜ in.) across disk. Aboral arm plates undivided, bell-shaped. Arm spines short (about ½ as long as arm segment) and somewhat cylindrical; at 30–45° angle from arm axis. Two color patterns: (1) light green-and-white mottling on disk, arms banded in shades of green; (2) disk orangish green, arms banded with orange, gray, or green. *Arms appear minutely serrated.* Rare from Massachusetts south, but common in Florida, Gulf. (3) **Black-speckled Brittle Star** (*O. guttatum*) is the *largest W. Indian brittle star*—to 3 cm (1¼ in.) across disk, arms to 15 cm (6 in.) long. Similar to *O. cinereum* but radial shields not apparent. Aboral arm plates thin, divided into interlocking subplates. Disk granules flattened on top. Arm spines flat, blunt, rectangular; *arms appear minutely serrated.* Disk and arms brownish, green, or tan with many small dark spots. All species Bermuda, Bahamas, Caribbean, W. Indies to Brazil; in rubble, under rocks, in shallow water.

RUBY BRITTLE STAR *Ophioderma rubicundum* **Pl. 60**
To 2 cm (¾ in.) across disk. Undivided rectangular aboral arm plates; 2 ovoid radial shields per arm base. *Disk usually solid purplish red* or mottled with white; arms indistinctly banded with same colors. Minute arm spines so arms appear smooth. **Similar species: Smooth Brittle Star** (*O. phoenium*), to 2.3 cm (⅞ in.) across disk, has *minute ovoid radial shields,* sometimes only 1 per arm base. Trapezoidal aboral arm plates. Disk and arms rust-colored or yellowish brown, often disk red, arms green. Arms appear smooth. Both species Bahamas, W. Indies, Caribbean; *O. phoenium* is rare.

SLIMY BRITTLE STAR *Ophiomyxa flaccida* **Fig. 143, Pl. 60**
To 2 cm (¾ in.) across disk. *Disk and arms covered with smooth, opaque skin.* Top of disk has club-shaped radial shields beneath skin and chain of elliptical plates around perimeter. Arms long, slender; with short, pinnate spines. Serrated oral papillae present. No podial scales. Color varies: disk mottled off-white and orange or dark green and gray; arms banded with same colors. *Feels slimy; arms appear smooth.* Back reef; Bermuda, Bahamas, Caribbean.

RETICULATED BRITTLE STAR **Figs. 143, 144; Pl. 59**
Ophionereis reticulata
To 1.2 cm (½ in.) across disk. *Disk covered with budlike papillae; no scales or spines.* Radial shields small, elongate, diamond-shaped. Arms long, slender. Aboral arm plates divided into 3 subplates. Arm spines short, blunt, conical. Ground color bluish or bone-white; *usually a fine brown reticulate (webbed) pattern on disk;* brown bands on arms. Common in clean sand under coral in shallow to deep water; Bermuda and Caribbean to Brazil.

ANGULAR BRITTLE STAR *Ophiothrix angulata*
To 1.2 cm (½ in.) across disk; arms to 7 cm (2¾ in.) long. *Spines on arms glassy.* Disk and radial shields covered with short, two- and three-pronged spines. Arm spines 5 × as long as arm segment; hollow, thin, barbed, somewhat flattened. Color varies: top mottled purple and white, with banded arms or with white radial stripes, or disk and arms tan with radial red stripes. *Usually*

Fig. 144. Reticulated Brittle Star.

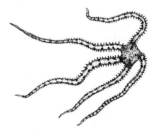

inside sponges; S. Carolina to Brazil; Gulf, Bahamas, W. Indies.
Related species: Striped Brittle Star (*O. lineata*), to 1.2cm (½ in.) across disk; arms to 12cm (4¾ in.) long. Aboral (upper) surface of disk, including radial shields, *covered with short pinnate spines.* Arm spines thick and flattened, about 4× length of arm segment. Top brown or deep purple, with faint radial stripes on arms. A black stripe bordered by white stripes runs down each arm. Bottom off-white. S. Florida, Caribbean.

OERSTED'S BRITTLE STAR   **Fig. 143, Pl. 60**
Ophiothrix oerstedii
Largest *Ophiothrix*—over 1.4cm (¾ in.) across disk; arms more than 8cm (3¼ in.) long. *Spines on arms glassy. Aboral disk covered with long, barbed spines.* Arm spines 4× arm-segment length; lower spines wing-shaped. Each podium has 2 papillae-covered scales. Aboral surface gray or grayish blue on disk; lighter underneath. Fine, zebra-like banding on arms, but *no radial stripes.* Turtle Grass beds; s. Florida, Bahamas, W. Indies to Tobago.

SUENSON'S BRITTLE STAR   *Ophiothrix suensonii*
To 2cm (¾ in.) across disk. Spines on arms glassy. Short spinelets around perimeter of radial shields; long, barbed spines on aboral surface of disk. *Radial shields large, occupying most of disk surface.* Arm spines very long (about 6× arm-segment length), slender, and barbed; lower arm spines hook-shaped. Disk bright red with gray radial shields and bold, black or purple radial stripes on arms. *Inside sponges or on soft corals;* s. Florida to Brazil.

SCALY BRITTLE STAR   *Ophiozona impressa*   **Fig. 143**
Disk to 1.5cm (⅝ in.) across; arms to 7.5cm (3 in.) long. Disk covered with large, irregular, rough scales; no spines. Radial shields triangular; arms short, with a few short, blunt, cigar-shaped spines. Disk bone-white with brown mottling and brown bands on arms; bottom white or cream. In sand or beneath coral rubble; Bermuda to Brazil.

Sea Urchins

According to the fossil record, sea urchins, Class Echinoidea, probably originated as spiny, globose animals that grazed on algae growing on rocks. The Red Rock Urchin (Pl. 62) resembles the ancestral form in appearance and habits. It can be found in depressions in the pitted rock of Caribbean shorelines, just below the water's surface.

But thousands of years of evolution have resulted in a great variety of forms, many of which live on or under the sediment. These species have become modified according to the degree to

Table 2. Common Brittle Stars

Arms extended into elaborate network of tendrils.	Basket Stars, Family Gorgonocephalidae *Astrophyton*, p. 345
Disk and arms covered with smooth *opaque* skin.	Slimy Brittle Stars, Family Ophiomyxidae *Ophiomyxa*, p. 349
Disk and arms covered with thin *transparent* skin. Disk seems to be mounted on jaw-arm complex (see *Ophiocnida*, below).	Family Ophiactidae *Ophiactis*, p. 347
Smooth or minutely serrated arms; 4 genital slits per inter-brachium.	Family Ophiodermatidae *Ophioderma*, p. 348
Large, with long spines on arms. No radial shields.	Family Ophiocomidae *Ophiocoma*, p. 347
Long arms edged with glassy spines. Often inside sponges or on soft corals.	Glassy-spined Brittle Stars, Family Ophiotrichidae *Ophiothrix*, p. 349
Disk covered with large scales. A few spines on arms.	Scaly Brittle Stars, Family Ophiolepidae *Ophiozona*, p. 350
Disk covered with budlike papillae. Arm spines long but pressed to arm.	Family Ophiochitonidae *Ophionereis*, p. 349
Disk covered with small scattered papillae. Disk appears to be mounted on jaw-arm complex.	Family Amphiuridae *Ophiocnida*, p. 347, *Hempholis*, p. 347, *Ophiophragmus*, p. 347

which they penetrate the sand. Sand dollars (keyhole urchins, p. 354) are still circular, but they have become thin and sharp-edged, permitting them to slide under the sand in seconds. Their spines have been reduced to short bristles. They have even developed holes (lunules) in their bodies that interrupt the flow of water, preventing waves from lifting and "sailing" them toward shore. Burrowing forms like the Sea Pussy (Pl. 62) have evolved an arrowhead-like shape, with the mouth moved forward and the anus shifted from the center of the aboral surface, toward the rear. These sea urchins penetrate the sand easily because of their narrow "front."

Turtle Grass beds are an ideal habitat for sea urchins because of the abundance of detritus and living plants. Four species are common there. The Sea Egg and Variable Urchin (Pl. 62) are globose, with short white spines. They are often strewn over the bottom wherever you look. Both species eat detritus, the rotting remains of dead organisms, usually the decaying leaves of sea-grasses. Yet both cannot occupy the same niche. If they had exactly the same requirements, one would outcompete the other, rendering the less fit species extinct. Since this has not happened, ecologists believe that they have precisely split the niche—perhaps one species eats the leaves, and the other the organisms encrusting the leaves.

The Pencil Urchin has a few thick, blunt spines. It hides during the day. Mosslike seaweeds hang from its spines, camouflaging it. The fierce-looking Long-spined Black Urchin (Figs. 61, 62) is sometimes found in abundance in the shallows, but only if there are rocks or corals nearby where it can hide during the day. One would think its 15-cm (6-in.) long, poison-tipped spines would make this sea urchin invulnerable, but a number of animals have been known to prey on it successfully. The Jolthead Porgy and Queen Triggerfish grasp a spine and flip the urchin over, then attack its relatively vulnerable underside. The Emperor Helmet Snail is oblivious to its spines and grinds a hole in the urchin's test (body) with its radula. People, however, manage to become impaled by the spines despite the fact that the urchin is slow moving and obvious. The Long-spined Black Urchin cannot shoot its spines at you; the only way you can become impaled is to accidentally brush by one as you become absorbed in the wonders of the underwater world around you. If that should happen, the barbed spine, covered with toxic mucus, will break off, leaving three or four black dots—the tips of the spines—visible under your skin. The pain will be like that of a bee sting at worst, and usually lasts about half an hour. The best way to obtain relief is to smear meat tenderizer on the wounds. This will digest the proteinaceous toxin, neutralizing it. A topical anesthetic such as Solarcaine might provide relief from the pain. The remnants of the spines will dissolve in a few days. In short, one should no more fear the spiny urchins of the shallows than the bees of the meadow. Besides, an extraordinary epidemic has afflicted the Long-spined Black Urchin. Beginning near Panama, an unknown disease has radiated throughout the Caribbean, decimating these urchins.

The Long-spined Black Urchin has become the protector of a number of animals that hide under or among its spines. The Urchin Crab (Pl. 56) is rarely found far from intertidal rocks unless it is hiding under the urchin's canopy of spines. A number of juvenile fishes similarly find shelter among the spines.

Sea urchins have done the unusual for invertebrates—they have developed "bones." Inside the body, around the mouth, is a complex structure of bone-like struts, Aristotle's lantern. It provides attachments for muscles that move five shiny white teeth projecting from the mouth. Many species use these teeth to almost perpetually scrape rock surfaces, grazing on encrusting algae.

Most of the space inside the test of sea urchins is devoted to storing unfertilized eggs. When the eggs are ripe, a female will shed hundreds of thousands of eggs. These are considered a delicacy in Japan and Greece, and are sold like ice cream on the streets in Barbados. They are reported to be a powerful aphrodisiac by the West Indians.

BROWN ROCK URCHIN *Arbacia punctulata* **Pl. 14**
To 5 cm (2 in.) wide. Spines tan, purple, or reddish black, usually *grayish brown;* about 2 cm (¾ in.) long. Test brown. Similar in habitat to Red Rock Urchin, but lacks red color, smaller, and has 4 periproctal (anal) plates. Commonest in intertidal and subtidal zones; along East Coast of U.S. from Maine to Florida, Gulf, Cuba, Yucatan, but not in W. Indies except Trinidad, Tobago, and others near coast.

INFLATED SEA BISCUIT *Clypeaster rosaceus* **Pls. 62, 64**
Large, thick; a specimen 13 cm (5 in.) long can be 5.5 cm (2¼ in.) high. Covered with short, yellowish, reddish, greenish brown, or brown spines. Body oval, with *5 symmetrical oval petals extending over most of upper surface.* In Turtle Grass beds, on surface of sand or partly buried; often camouflaged with shells, grass. **Similar species: Flat Sea Biscuit** (*C. subdepressus,* Pl. 62) is less inflated than *C. rosaceus*—a specimen 25 cm (10 in.) long may be only 2.5 cm (1 in.) high. Margins rounded; *relatively small petals* extend about ½ length of radius or less. Test widest from posterior to middle. Not as common as *C. rosaceus.*

LONG-SPINED BLACK URCHIN **Figs. 61, 62; Pls. 17, 64**
Diadema antillarum
Length of *needle-tipped black spines* at least 3 × diameter of test, about 15 cm (6 in.) in adults. Spines banded brown and black or brown and white in young. Hides in crevices in coral or aggregates in groups in daytime; feeds on algae and Turtle Grass at night in lagoons, coral reefs. Spines *poisonous.* Bermuda, S. Florida, Caribbean. Test shown on Pl. 64. **Similar species: Magnificent Spiny Urchin** (*Astropyga magnifica,* Pl. 12) also has long spines, but these are *white with ocher, squarish dots,* and are less than 3 × diameter of test. (Thus spines are shorter than those of juvenile Long-spined Black Urchin.) Test to 7.5 cm (3 in.) across. From 0.6m (2 ft.) to deep water; W. Indies to Brazil. Uncommon, but sometimes found in aggregations of 400 or more, especially off Puerto Rico.

RED ROCK URCHIN *Echinometra lucunter* **Pls. 14, 62**
To 6.5 cm (2½ in.) across except off Bermuda and Brazil, where it reaches 8.5 cm (3¼ in.) wide. Spines to 2.5 cm (1 in.) long; red, reddish black, or reddish brown. *Red color almost always visible* at base of spines; rarely animal lacks red altogether, appears pure

black. *More than 4 periproctal (anal) plates.* Rocky shores just below water's surface, under rocks, in tidepools. Caribbean. **Similar species: Reef Urchin** (*E. viridis,* Pl. 62) has *spines with a thin white ring at base, then rose or coral, then green with chocolate-brown tips;* spines finer and longer in *E. lucunter.* Test reddish or maroon. Commonest on coral reef, at 5–12m (17–40 ft.), but can be found near shore. Not usually with Red Rock Urchin.

LITTLE BURROWING URCHIN   **Pl. 63**
Echinoneus cyclostomus
About 2.5cm (1 in.) long, oval; *petals broad and shallow, reach margins.* Cream or reddish yellow, with red tube feet. Four genital plates on middorsal surface look like four-leaf clover. Asymmetrical midventral peristome (mouth), behind which is oval periproct (anus). Buried in sand under rocks on reef flats.

NOTCHED SAND DOLLAR   *Encope emarginata*   **Pl. 63**
To 14cm (5½ in.) long. Flat, oval, with tiny bristles. *Test perforated by 1 oval hole and 5 notches.* Tan, brownish, or greenish brown. Buried in sand off S. America and nearby islands. **Similar species: Michelin's Sand Dollar** (*E. michelini,* Pl. 62) lives in deep water of Gulf.

CLUB or PENCIL URCHIN   *Eucidaris tribuloides*   **Pls. 63, 65**
To 5cm (2 in.) wide, except off Bermuda and Brazil, where it is larger. *Spines thick, cylindrical, blunt-tipped;* relatively sparse — test visible between spines. Test light brown flecked with white. Spines often covered with filamentous algae. Eats sponges, algae, seagrasses. Turtle Grass beds, reefs; Bermuda to Brazil.

SIX-HOLED KEYHOLE URCHIN   **Fig. 145, Pl. 64**
Leodia sexiesperforata
To 10cm (4 in.) long. Round and flat with sharp edges. Tan or gray, covered with fuzzy bristles. Test of this sand dollar perforated with *6 oval holes, 2 in midline.* Abundant beyond breakers on sandy beaches, usually covered with thin layer of sand; can force itself into sediment in 1–4 minutes. **Similar species: Five-holed Keyhole Urchin** (*Mellita quinquiesperforata,* Pls. 62, 63, Fig. 146) *has 5 lunules* in its test. More common off coast from N. Carolina, and less common in Caribbean, rare in Lesser Antilles. Six-holed Keyhole Urchin is more common off Bermuda and Bahamas, and ranges to Uruguay.

VARIABLE or GREEN URCHIN   **Pls. 62, 64**
Lytechinus variegatus
To 7.5cm (3 in.) wide. Profusely *covered with 1-cm (⅜-in.) long, greenish white or white spines* that are sometimes purple-tipped. Specimens off southeastern U.S. may have stout red or purplish spines; individuals from Bermuda have slender, bright purple spines. Test (Pl. 64) light green; podia (tube feet) white. In Turtle Grass beds, often camouflaged with debris; Bermuda, Carolinas to Brazil. **Related species: Williams' Variable Sea Urchin** (*L. williamsi,* Pl. 62) is smaller (to 5.5cm — 2¼ in. — wide), with thinner, longer spines than in *L. variegatus. Podia and pedicel-*

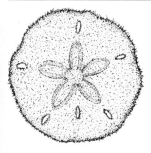

Fig. 145. *Left:* Six-holed Keyhole Urchin; *right:* Five-holed Keyhole Urchin.

laria purple-tipped. Test white or green. On coral reefs, sometimes in shallows.

SEA PUSSY or CAKE URCHIN   **Pls. 62, 64**
Meoma ventricosa
Large—to 12.5 cm (5 in.) long. Four groove-like ambulacra angled from center of dorsal surface. *Fifth (middorsal) ambulacrum an obscured depression* rather than a distinct groove. Mouth on underside projects from anterior (front region) of body as a shovel-like "lower jaw." Reddish brown and bristly, with some anterior bristles to 5 mm (¼ in.) long. Just under surface of sand, creating hillocks. In sand fields of lagoons usually deeper than 2 m (6½ ft.), and in Turtle Grass beds. Ingests sand. Will emerge from sediment at night in response to lowered nocturnal oxygen levels beneath sand. When disturbed it can secrete a yellowish substance that repels predators (stingrays and shamefaced crabs) and can kill small fishes. Test shown on Pl. 64. S. Florida, Bahamas, N. Caribbean. **Similar species: Grooved Burrowing Urchin** (*Brissus unicolor*) is smaller (to 7.5 cm—3 in.—long) but narrower and more elongate than Sea Pussy. Pale brown; 4 groove-like ambulacra radiate from middorsal region—*anterior pair extends at a right angle from center* (in Sea Pussy they point at about a 45° angle toward front). Buried in sand under rocks on reef flats, often in company of Little Burrowing Urchin. S. Florida, Caribbean.

HEART or MUD URCHIN   *Moira atropos*   **Pl. 63**
To 6 cm (2½ in.) long. Ambulacra deeply sunken into test, *appearing as thin slits.* Anterior (front) ambulacrum long; a pair of short ambulacra angle backward but do not reach margin. Pale brown or grayish, covered with thin, furlike bristles. Test inflated, almost spherical; *posterior (hind end) abruptly terminates* —blunt, almost vertical. Buried in mud in shallows; N. Carolina to Florida, Gulf, W. Indies.

GREAT RED-FOOTED URCHIN Pls. 62, 63
Plagiobrissus grandis
Largest urchin—to 23 cm (9 in.) long. Oval; tan or silvery gray. *About 20 anterior dorsal spines*, to 7.5 cm (3 in.) long; spines are raised when animals is alarmed, but always point toward rear. Test covered with thin spines to 1 cm (⅜ in.) long. Bottom surface has a 2.5-cm (1-in.) wide, brushlike tract of long bristles, upon which it walks. Mouth and anus ventral, mouth surrounded by jawlike projection. *Thick red podia concentrated around mouth and anus.* Buried in sand of lagoons—does not come to surface at night, so difficult to find. Test shown on Pl. 63.

SEA EGG *Tripneustes ventricosus* Pls. 17, 62, 64
To 13 cm (5 in.) wide. Profusely covered with 1-cm (⅜-in.) long white spines. *Test (Pl. 64) black, dark purple, brown.* Common on Turtle Grass beds, often covered with debris. Eats algae and Turtle Grass. Eggs eaten by W. Indians.

Sea Cucumbers

In many ways the sluggish, lumpy sea cucumbers, Class Holothuroidea, are the most highly evolved of the echinoderms. Sea cucumbers have even discarded the ancestral radial symmetry and invented a front and back. Unfortunately, sea cucumbers seem not to know what to do with the front and have, instead, lavished much of their creative energy on the posterior. Projecting from the anterior (front) end are a number of thick, often tufted, tentacles. They are used to sweep sand into the mouth and also act as sensory organs. Since the mouth is usually filled with sand and there are no other anterior openings, how does oxygenated water (for respiration) enter the animal? The skin is too thick, warty, and suffused with tiny spines to allow oxygenated water to enter. That leaves only one other possibility, the anus. This richly endowed organ must accomplish a multiplicity of tasks because there are no other openings available. The anus of the Five-toothed Sea Cucumber has 5 shiny white teeth (Fig. 146). No one knows what they are used for, but they symbolize both the number 5—the trademark of all echinoderms—and the importance placed on the multifaceted anus. Inside the anus is a chamber, the cloaca, which receives the feces. Projecting from the walls of the cloaca are a pair of elaborate Christmas-tree-shaped organs, the respiratory trees. Each branch is tipped with tiny bulbs. At frequent intervals the animal relaxes its body wall, creating a vacuum. Water rushes through the anus, which constricts, forcing oxygenated water into the respiratory trees. At the bulbous branch tips, oxygen diffuses into the body cavity. Exhaling is accomplished by contraction of the body wall, forcing the water out in a strong flow. A large cucumber in a gallon container

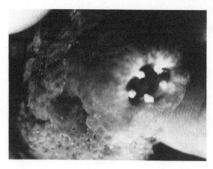

Fig. 146. Anal teeth of Five-toothed Sea Cucumber.

can raise the water level appreciably with each exhalation.

Attached to the respiratory trees are thin tubes called Cuvier's organs. These can be filled with water until they stretch to the breaking point and, like balloons without tied ends, jet out through the anus. They are sticky and/or poisonous, and will immobilize a crab or other predator.

The "secret weapon" of sea cucumbers also depends on the anus. When all else fails, when dull coloration has not provided adequate camouflage, when Cuvier's organs have not deterred a predator, when densely packed spines embedded in a tough skin have not prevented fish or man from shaking the cucumber, it will suddenly eject part of its intestines through the anus. When the Donkey Dung Cucumber does this, it presents the predator with a mass of bright orange delicacies that distract it. The predator munches on the easily accessible internal organs, leaving the cucumber free to crawl off, eventually to regenerate new innards.

The daily routine of a sea cucumber is simple. It crawls slowly on the bottom, using hundreds of scattered podia (tube feet) on its flattened sole. It moves only a few meters a day, shoveling sand

Fig. 147. External anatomy of a sea cucumber (lateral view).

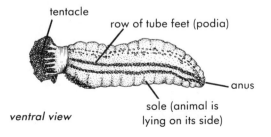

tentacle

row of tube feet (podia)

anus

sole (animal is lying on its side)

ventral view

Fig. 148. Donkey Dung Sea Cucumber with fecal casts near anus. Note Merman's Shaving Brush alga at upper left.

into its mouth. As the sand passes through the intestines the detritus mixed with the sand is digested, and the remaining sand is covered with mucus and released as cylindrical fecal casts. Since cucumbers move so slowly, the curled sand cylinders (fecal casts) are often visible near the posterior (see Fig. 148).

Sea cucumbers are among the largest inhabitants of Turtle Grass beds, and are easily spotted. The Donkey Dung Cucumber is ubiquitous. The Three-rowed Cucumber is the only common form in Bermuda, and the Five-toothed Cucumber is commonest in the Bahamas. If many Five-toothed Cucumbers are available, place several in containers of seawater in the evening. After two hours turn on the lights and quickly peer into the buckets. If you are lucky, a Pearlfish will have appeared (see Fig. 149). This animal lives inside the cloaca and respiratory trees of the cucumber, coming out at night to feed on small crustaceans and return-

Fig. 149. Pearlfish backing into anus of Five-toothed Sea Cucumber.

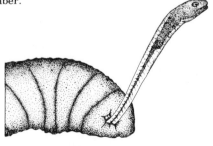

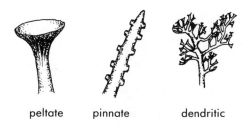

peltate   pinnate   dendritic

Fig. 150. Types of sea-cucumber tentacles.

ing at dawn. It may seriously damage the host. About 70% of Five-toothed Cucumbers harbor Pearlfishes in the Bahamas, while only 2% are infested off Florida.

Examine several Donkey Dung Cucumbers to find a few tiny, white, sharply pointed snails, less than 1 cm (⅜ in.) long, projecting from the pink soles. They are the Cucumber-eating Snail (*Melanella*). In spite of the sea cucumber's thick, ossicle-laden skin, this snail can dissolve the cucumber's body wall. The snail inserts a long proboscis and sucks up the host's body fluid. The snail is so well adapted to a parasitic mode of life that it has completely lost the radula (rasplike tongue). A tiny round parasitic snail that lives in the cloaca of the Brown Rock Sea Cucumber is *Megadenus holothuricula*.

The Beaded Sea Cucumber (Fig. 151) lacks podia (tube feet); it sticks to the undersides of rocks by means of microscopic sharp spines (ossicles) which penetrate its skin. If you pick one up, it will stick to your hand. Be careful not to treat it roughly, as it is easily fragmented.

Tentacles may be used as identifying features. See Fig. 150.

Next 3 species (apodids): No tube feet.
WORM CUCUMBER   *Chiridota rotifera*
Small, wormlike, less than 10 cm (4 in.) long. *Pink or reddish. Has 20 palmate tentacles;* those in inner circle small and easily overlooked. Buried in sand at water's edge and in tidepools, among algae and in dead coral; Bermuda, Florida to Brazil.
Similar species: Seaweed Cucumber (*Synaptula hydriformis,* Pl. 22) has 2 color phases — red-brown or deep green; brown form lives on brown algae, green form on green algae. *A few long, slender, simple digits on tentacles.* Gives birth to live young. Subtidal in tufts of seaweed; green form common in Bermuda, brown form predominates in Jamaica. S. Florida to Brazil.

 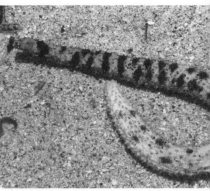

Fig. 151. *Left:* Beaded Sea Cucumber; *right:* double row of dark spots on Burrowing Sea Cucumber.

BEADED SEA CUCUMBER   Fig. 151, Pl. 61
Euapta lappa
Large—to 1m (3¼ ft.) long, but not more than 2.5 cm (1 in.) thick. Body ringed with *thick, squarish, beadlike "segments."* Brown, with thin yellow and black longitudinal stripes; may have white spots. *Thick, long, feathery tentacles.* Ossicles penetrate skin, making animals sticky. Body fragile. Nocturnal; on undersides of rocks in shallow water by day. Bahamas and W. Indies; not in Bermuda.

WHITE SYNAPTA   Pl. 61
Leptosynapta inhaerens
To 15 cm (6 in.) long. Pinkish or yellowish; *wormlike, with 5 white, longitudinal muscle bands* visible through transparent skin. 12 pinnate tentacles. Buried under mud with tentacles extended on surface to pick up detritus. Does not eviscerate (dispel innards); instead it autotomizes, breaking off its hind end. Produces burrows covered by small mounds of fine sand with a central hole 6mm (¼ in.) wide. Lower intertidal or subtidal; Maine to S. Carolina, Bermuda. **Similar species:** (1) **Gulf Synapta** (*L. crassipatina*) lives in a burrow characterized by a depression rather than a mound, and frequents upper intertidal. Adults may swim at night. The tiny reddish Synapta Pea Crab (*Pinnixa leptosynaptae*) lives on its surface. Florida and Gulf. (2) **Red Synapta** (*L. roseola*) is red and has 12 tentacles, *each with 2–3 branches.* Bermuda (under stones), W. Indies.

Next 11 species (Aspidochirotids): *Tube feet and peltate tentacles.*

FIVE-TOOTHED SEA CUCUMBER   Fig. 146, Pl. 61
Actinopyga agassizii
To 30 cm (1 ft.) long. 25–30 peltate tentacles. Color variable—dark gray or brown, spotted. *Five anal teeth visible when animal exhales.* Sole lighter than dorsum (back); numerous pale brown, scattered podia (tube feet). In Turtle Grass beds; most common in Bahamas, becoming rarer going south in W. Indies. May contain commensal Pearlfish in cloaca (see p. 358).

FURRY SEA CUCUMBER   *Astichopus multifidus*
Large and broad—to 45 cm (18 in.) long, 9 cm (3½ in.) wide. Dorsal and ventral surfaces covered with many long (to 1.2 cm—½ in.), soft podia, giving animal a furry appearance and feel. *Dorsal podia pointed, ventral ones with suckers.* Color variable: brown, gray, or mottled; sole may be gray or white, with densely crowded podia. Deep water, rarely inshore; moves rapidly. Anus large, exhales every 10 seconds or so. S. Florida, W. Indies.

BURROWING SEA CUCUMBER   Fig. 151; Pls. 17, 61
Holothuria arenicola
To 25 cm (10 in.) long. Tan or pale gray, sometimes stained with rusty yellow. *Double series of dusky spots on dorsum (back).* Tube feet small, scattered, inconspicuous. Produces large mounds in seagrass beds (see Pl. 17); Bermuda to Brazil.

BROWN ROCK SEA CUCUMBER   Pls. 14, 61
Holothuria glaberrima
To 15 cm (6 in.) long. Smooth skin. Sole covered with many dark brown podia. Color black or dark brown, rarely gray; no spots. *20 bushy black tentacles.* On or under rocks among seaweeds, in surf zone; Bahamas, W. Indies.

GRAY SEA CUCUMBER   *Holothuria grisea*   Pl. 61
To 20 cm (8 in.) long. Gray, deep pink, or mottled; warty skin. Slightly flattened sole, densely covered with yellow podia. 23 bushy yellow tentacles—*11 small ventral ones gradually increasing in size dorsally.* Young among rocks, coral debris; adults in Turtle Grass beds; s. Florida to Brazil.

IMPATIENT SEA CUCUMBER   *Holothuria impatiens*
To 15 cm (6 in.) long. Flask-shaped; mottled gray, brown, or purplish. *Skin feels rough; covered with low rounded warts, some with concentric brown lines.* Anterior (front) end may be darker than rest of body. About 20 tentacles. Under rocks in lagoons, at depths below 2m (6½ ft.). Name comes from readiness to eject sticky white Cuvier's tubules when touched. S. Florida, W. Indies.

DONKEY DUNG SEA CUCUMBER   Fig. 141; Pls. 61, 65
Holothuria mexicana
Large—to 40 cm (16 in.) long. Dark brown or gray, sometimes with sand on dorsum (back). Body often wrinkled, may have few warts. Brown tube feet scattered over *rose-colored sole* (sole may

be white or even brown in older specimens). *22 tan, peltate tentacles.* Commonest Caribbean sea cucumber. Turtle grass beds in W. Indies; absent in Florida, Bermuda. **Similar species: Florida Sea Cucumber** (*H. floridana*) is smaller—to 20 cm (8 in.) long—and more slender. *20 yellow tentacles.* Body usually gray or dark brown; skin thinner and more warty than in *H. mexicana.* Tube feet scattered, *yellow.* Near mangrove swamps in seagrass beds; Florida, Caribbean, Dutch Antilles.

GOLDEN SEA CUCUMBER   *Holothuria parvula*
Tiny—averages 3.5 cm (1¾ in.) long. Golden brown, greenish yellow, or light brown, with numerous bright yellow podia on flattened sole. Dorsum (back) arched, with many low warts. *Fluorescent pigment may be visible on skin.* Readily ejects sticky white Cuvier's tubules when squeezed. Under rocks in reef flats, tidepools; Bermuda, W. Indies.

SURINAM SEA CUCUMBER   **Pl. 61**
Holothuria surinamensis
To 20 cm (8 in.) long. Dark brown, yellowish brown, reddish brown, or purple-brown. May have a series of purple spots on dorsum (back). Cylindrical; covered with small white papillae. *Podia (tube feet) white with yellow tips.* About 20 short, pale, peltate tentacles. Often in algae or among finger corals; Bermuda, W. Indies.

THOMAS' GIANT SEA CUCUMBER   *Holothuria thomasae*
Huge—smallest 1 m (3¼ ft.) long—resembles a vacuum cleaner hose. Yellowish brown to maroon, with brown, light brown, and whitish flecks. Covered with rows of *long, pointed tubercles across dorsum (back), with regions of smooth skin between rows.* Podia short, brown. 20 yellow, pink, or brown, peltate tentacles. Nocturnal; extends from under coral boulders or debris at dusk, remains active at night. Hind end firmly attached to underside of boulder. Lagoons with rubble-strewn bottom, at depths below 2 m (6½ ft.) depth; W. Indies, Caribbean.

THREE-ROWED SEA CUCUMBER   **Pls. 61, 65**
Isostichopus badionotus
Large—to 45 cm (18 in.) long. Large warts on bottom edge of body. Color variable, often brown mottled with orange and black; striped, deep crimson in Tobago. *Three rows of dark brown podia on sole; central row wider and split.* Turtle grass beds, Caribbean and W. Indies; most common species in Bermuda.

PYGMY SEA CUCUMBER   *Pentacta pygmaea*   **Pl. 61**
To 10 cm (4 in.) long. Dorsum (back) has 2 double rows of blunt tubercles. Chocolate-brown, with *4 rows of yellow or pink podia.* 10 tentacles, 2 smaller than others. Shallow rocky bottoms, seagrass beds; Florida, Gulf, W. Indies to Brazil.

Next 3 species (Dendrochirotids): *Scattered podia; dendritic tentacles (see Fig. 150).*

SURINAM PARATHYONE *Parathyone surinamensis*

To 10 cm (4 in.) long. Brown or gray, with *10 dark, dendritic tentacles*. Podia whitish with yellowish tips; numerous, covering body. *Sole lacking*. May be mistaken for the **Brown Rock Cucumber** (p. 361) but has fewer tentacles, no sole, no concentration of podia on underside. Near low-water mark on rocky shores, under rocks; Bermuda, W. Indies.

HAIRY SEA CUCUMBER *Sclerodactyla briareus* **Pl. 65**

To 15 cm (6 in.) long. *Pear-shaped; black or brown*. Saclike, covered with thin, translucent, randomly distributed tube feet. *10 large bushy tentacles, 2 lowest ones smallest*. Lives buried in mud with tentacles and anus protruding — can live in mud so fine other animals would suffocate. Subtidal zone to deep water; Massachusetts to Florida and Texas, rare in W. Indies. **Similar species: Mexican Thyone** (*Thyone mexicana*, Pl. 65) is smaller — to 5 cm (2 in.) long. Grayish; podia scattered over body: those on lower surface have suckers, upper podia do not. Subtidal in seagrass beds; Gulf, Caribbean.

STRIPED SEA CUCUMBER *Thyonella gemmata* **Pl. 11**

To 15 cm (6 in.) long. Elongate; brown, mottled brown, or greenish brown, with 10 dark brown dendritic tentacles, bottom 2 smallest. *Tube feet in double rows,* scattered over body. Lives under surface of muddy sand, with tentacles and anus projecting. Tentacles are laid on sediment surface to pick up detritus, which is sucked from tentacles when placed in mouth. Look for paired holes in mud, about 7.5 cm (3 in.) apart. N. Carolina to Florida, Gulf.

16

Bryozoans, Acorn Worms, Tunicates (Sea Squirts), Ribbon Worms, and Flatworms

In the following section animals of certain phyla, by virtue of their cryptic habits (a tendency to hide), subterranean lifestyle, or small size, will be lumped together as members of "minor phyla." Consisting primarily of worms or colonies of tiny individuals called zooids, each phylum exhibits some uncharacteristically common or relatively large representatives that excite curiosity when discovered washed up on the beach. It is beyond the scope of this book to cover each phylum in detail; only the common or obvious species will be dealt with. The table on p. 365 summarizes the characteristics of each phylum.

MOSS ANIMALS OR BRYOZOANS

Frank J. S. Maturo, Jr.

The phylum Bryozoa is represented by over 4,000 living species, yet they are unknown or unrecognized by most people. The name of the group means "moss animals," but most bear no resemblance to moss at all; instead, they may look like corals, dead seaweed, or gelatinous fingers, or like colored crusts and white lacy patterns on shells, rocks, pilings, and marine plants. They are among the commonest organisms in shallow-water habitats but are usually overlooked by beachcombers. Since each individual of these colonial animals is tiny (about 0.6 mm — $\frac{1}{50}$ in. long), it is only the colony that attracts attention. Also, the planktonic larvae of many bryozoans settle on the underside of submerged objects and complete their development there, thus hiding the growing colony from view. If you turn over submerged shells and rubble or old bottles and cans, you can usually find bryozoan colonies. Some clam shells in favorable habitats have yielded up to 36 species, and a chunk of reef rock about 37cm (14½ in.) long, collected off the North Carolina coast, served as the settlement site for several hundred colonies, comprising an astonishing 77 species! Approximately 300 species occur in eastern U.S. coastal waters from

Table 3.	Minor	Phyla
Phylum	**Common Name**	**Characteristics**
Bryozoa	**Moss animals**	Four types: fist-sized, calcareous colonies, shaped like staghorns or curlicues; large rubbery, branched colonies; tufted colonies resembling seaweed; dime-sized colonies forming scabs on rocks, seashells.
Hemichordata	**Acorn worms**	Long, flaccid worms in burrows; color of head and collar contrasts with body.
Chordata, Subphylum Urochordata	**Sea Squirts, Tunicates**	Three types: sac-shaped individuals about 5 cm (2 in.) long, with 2 "spouts"; colonies of individuals attached by long, rootlike stolons; and gelatinous, encrusting masses with groups of tiny zooids, often arranged in starlike or radiating patterns.
Rhynchocoela	**Ribbon Worms**	Long, flattened, fleshy, unsegmented worms, often with a spatulate but otherwise indistinct head and a long, eversible proboscis, which shoots out to entrap prey. Buried in sand.
Platyhelminthes	**Flatworms**	Mostly parasitic flatworms (flukes, tapeworms), but includes many free-living species. Usually leaf-shaped, with an eversible tubular pharynx extending from center of underside. Under sand or among oysters, under rocks.

Cape Hatteras to the Florida Keys and Gulf Coast. Most bryozoans have a low tolerance for estuarine water and have a patchy distribution wherever there are hard bottoms.

The details of the anatomy of an individual bryozoan, a zooid (pronounced zō-oid), can be seen only with a microscope. With a

$10\times$ hand lens you can make out the gross form of the zooids and even see their funnel-shaped tentacle crowns if you leave them undisturbed in seawater. Ordinary zooids have two basic shapes, boxes or cylinders; the extraordinary zooids (heterozooids) may have several bizarre forms. The box form has many variations, the most common being a roughly rectangular form with a concave end toward the center of the colony and a convex wall at the opposite end. Various rounded, polygonal, and tube-, vase-, and urnlike forms, either symmetrical or flattened on one side, may be encountered. These are the shapes of the exoskeleton, which may be calcareous with a thin outer layer of chitin (cuticle or frontal membrane), or completely chitinous, or gelatinous.

Each zooid has an opening, the orifice, in the body wall through which the tentacles (on a feeding apparatus called a lophophore) are extended. The mouth is located centrally at the base of the tentacles and leads into a U-shaped digestive tract divided into a pharynx, stomach, and rectum. The anus opens at the outside base of the ciliated tentacles, which are stiffly extended during feeding, forming a funnel. The cilia set up currents, drawing seawater into the funnel and out at the base. Unicellular algae are filtered out and directed to the mouth. The stomach is the site for both extracellular and intracellular digestion, and the rectum forms fecal pellets.

The rest of the interior of the zooid is occupied by a fluid-filled body cavity called a coelom. The body cavity lacks organs except during sexual reproduction, when sperms and eggs develop (in that order) from the coelomic lining. Sperms leave the coelom through pores at the ends of certain tentacles; eggs generally leave through a temporary or permanent pore at the base of the tentacles. Fertilization occurs when the egg emerges from the pore. Some species produce eggs with little yolk that develop as they drift in the plankton. Larvae of these species develop a digestive tract and feed for a few days or weeks before seeking out a suitable settlement site. Most marine bryozoans brood their eggs. The resulting larvae have no gut and swim for only a few hours before they must find a suitable substrate or die. Upon settling, the larvae metamorphose into zooids, which bud off additional zooids, forming the colony. The reproductive period for bryozoans from Cape Hatteras to Texas is from late March to late November, but Florida species may reproduce year round.

Besides the feeding zooids, bryozoan colonies may contain non-feeding individuals or heterozooids, which have special functions associated with their shapes. These gutless heterozooids are connected to the feeding zooids and receive nourishment and nerve impulses. The commonest types of heterozooids are keno-zooids, avicularia, and vibracula. Tube-shaped kenozooids form stems that support the feeding zooids. Avicularia are bizarre, appendage-like individuals that have a movable mandible or

Fig. 152. Common Sheep's-wool Bryozoan. *Left:* close-up; *right:* whole colony.

"jaw," which, by frequently opening and closing, probably serves to deter other organisms from settling on the colony. When attached by a short stem to ordinary zooids, the avicularia resemble tiny bird heads. Vibracula have elongated mandibles, each forming a long bristle used to sweep the colony surface clean.

Bryozoans serve as food for fishes, crabs, snails, and sea spiders. Their skeletons are abundant in the fossil record and are useful as indicators for petroleum geologists.

Jetties, pilings, rocks, empty shells, and other hard debris are the best collecting spots for bryozoans, especially the encrusting forms. The larger erect and bushy forms are sometimes washed up on the beach after being torn up by shrimpers' nets. Sargassum Weed washed ashore and Turtle Grass leaves are havens for coral-like bryozoans.

Use a hand lens to examine the colonies. Calcareous specimens may be identified by details of the zooid's orifice. A drop of liquid bleach placed on the colony surface for a few minutes will remove the chitinous covering, revealing the orifices.

COMMON SHEEP'S-WOOL BRYOZOAN   Fig. 152, Pl. 9
Amathia convoluta

Colonies erect, to 7.5cm (3 in.) tall. *Straw or horn-colored; bushy. Each branch resembles elongated spiral.* Branches, composed of kenozooids (internodes), are actually straight but bear cylindrical feeding zooids, which project perpendicularly as a double row spiraling counterclockwise around each kenozooid. **Similar species:** (1) **Alternating Sheep's-wool Bryozoan** (*A. alternata,* Fig. 152) is larger—to 17.5cm (7 in.) tall; its feeding zooids are arranged in a straight line along one side of each kenozooid of branch. *Feeding zooid rows alternate sides from one kenozooid to the next,* though some rows may be rotated not quite 180° from that of adjacent kenozooid. (2) **Delicate Sheep's-wool Bryozoan**

(*A. distans,* Pl. 9) is *more delicate* and densely branched, not as stiff as *A. convoluta;* to 5cm (2 in.) tall. Internodes of branches bear a partially spiraled double row of feeding zooids, which may occupy one-half or two-thirds of the internode (usually the distal or outer half).

MUDDY-TUFT BRYOZOAN Pl. 9

Anguinella palmata

Colonies resemble *tufts of algae or tiny spruce trees;* erect, irregularly branched, to 5cm (2 in.) tall. Zooids tubular, slightly curved inward; *covered with earthy material,* resulting in a dark, muddy gray color.

HAUFF'S ALCYONIDIUM *Alcyonidium hauffi* Pl. 9

Colonies encrust and surround dead stems of sea whips, forming *fleshy, gelatinous, cylindrical masses* with *short, lateral, rounded branches.* Grayish, translucent white, or transparent; sometimes partly dark green, if coated with unicellular green algae.

SAUERKRAUT BRYOZOAN Pl. 9

Zoobotryon verticillatum

Colonies form large, transparent, forked or trichotomously *branching vines,* in which feeding zooids are arranged in 2 rows, one on each side of older internodes, or clustered at tips of younger internodes and growing points. *Colonies flaccid,* can spread out in water—easily confused with a sun-bleached mass of seaweed. Large colonies exceed 30cm (1 ft.) across.

JOINTED-TUBE BRYOZOANS *Crisia* species Fig. 153

Colonies form *tiny white bushy tufts* on rocks and "stems" of large algae. Erect, jointed; each internode composed of tubular, calcareous zooids arranged in 2 rows and alternately. *Orifices elevated slightly and turned forward.* Occasional internodes may have an enlarged, bubble-like zooid, which is a brood chamber for developing embryos. Several species in our area, but they cannot be distinguished without a microscope.

COMMON BUGULA *Bugula neritina* Fig. 30, Pl. 9

Plantlike colonies that form erect *reddish brown or reddish purple bushy tufts.* Zooids arranged in 2 rows and alternately, all facing the same direction. No spines or avicularia. To 5cm (2 in.) tall. **Similar species: White Bugula** (*Bugula* species) is *white;* tips of zooids have 1 or more spines. *Avicularia shaped like tiny birds' heads on lateral margin.* May produce branches with a strongly spiraled pattern. Species cannot be distinguished without a microscope.

COMMON SEA MAT *Membranipora tenuis* Pl. 10

Colony encrusting, calcareous, forming *white lacy pattern* on shells. *Zooids elongate, rectangular or quadrangular* with membranous frontal surfaces. Under frontal membrane is calcareous shelf occupying proximal half of each zooid. Many similar species, but this one most common. **Similar species: Sargassum Sea Mat** (*M. tuberculata,* Pl. 36) grows only on Sargassum Weed and closely related algae. At tip of zooid are *2 blunt tubercles.*

LETTUCE BRYOZOAN
Pl. 10

Thalamoporella gothica floridana

Colonies calcareous; encrusting or erect, the latter forming *fist-size balls of crinkled sheets of zooids* resembling a *head of curly leaf lettuce or ball of cornflakes.* Colonies straw-colored or whitish. Boxlike zooids have a calcareous shelf covering all of area under frontal membrane except at orifice. Look for a *tubercle on each side of round orifice* and a pair of large pits next to orifice. Large avicularia occupy space of feeding zooid, shaped like gothic arches.

VARIABLE CRUST BRYOZOAN
Fig. 153

Schizoporella errata

Colonies form flat crusts on firm substrates. Color variable, *red-orange* more common than white, pink, or orange. Zooids rectangular calcareous boxes; frontal wall appears finely perforated under frontal membrane. Orifice rounded distally with round or U-shaped sinus or notch on proximal border. *A pointed avicularium may be present near 1 side of orifice.* One of the most common encrusting bryozoans of sounds, bays, and estuaries of East Coast.

GULF STAGHORN BRYOZOAN
Pl. 10

Schizoporella pungens

Colonies form erect, *coral-like* growths, typically attached to Turtle Grass or sea whip stems. Live colonies vary in color from bright orange to dark reddish brown or purple-black. Dead colonies turn white if originally orange; may retain color if dark. *Branches of colony cylindrical* when attached to seagrass or a sea whip, but become *tubular and open-ended* where colony grows free from substrate. Tip openings usually occupied by tube-dwelling amphipods and worms. Feeding zooids similar to those of Crust Bryozoan (*S. errata*); large avicularia occupying space of feeding zooids may be scattered about colony. Gulf and Florida Keys.

RED-ORANGE NODULE BRYOZOAN

Stylopoma informata

Zooids similar to those of Variable Crust Bryozoan, but orifice *is a narrow slit or a V-shaped notch.* Colonies form pebble-shaped, multilayered nodules that are vivid *red-orange* when alive.

TEXAS LONGHORN BRYOZOAN
Pl. 10

Hippoporidra calcarea

Colony is established on a snail shell occupied by a juvenile hermit crab, then grows to enlarge shell form so that crab never has to change shells as it grows. Eventually the colony forms *symmetrical lateral projections* that apparently stabilize the colony being moved about by the crab. Vertical projections form on central planospiral axis of colony. Whole colony mimics a piece of coral. All projections are covered with nodules of zooids, perhaps imitating coral polyps. Length of colony, from tip to tip of horizontal projections, reaches 18cm (7 in.).

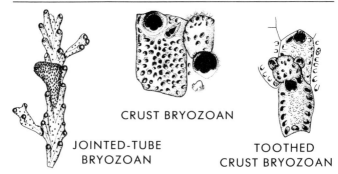

Fig. 153. Encrusting bryozoan skeletons.

TOOTHED CRUST BRYOZOAN *Parasmittina nitida* **Fig. 153**
Colonies encrust firm substrates, forming *pinkish or yellowish
circular patches* on shells, rocks, pilings. Older colonies may
become multilayered and form pebble-sized nodules. Newly dead
colonies are greenish yellow. Zooids are rectangular boxes with
calcareous frontal wall perforated by a row of marginal pores.
Orifice circular, with a median proximal tooth. Oval or pointed
frontal avicularia are located beside orifice. **Similar species:
Spiny Toothed Crust Bryozoan** (*P. echinata*, Pl. 10) is similar
to *P. nitida* but grows as *spiny, spindle-shaped colonies on Manatee Grass.* Colonies to 5cm (2 in.) long in Gulf.

ACORN WORMS

Phylum Hemichordata is a small group of wormlike animals once
thought to be allied to our phylum—Chordata. The similarities
are no longer believed to be significant and this remains a small,
obscure phylum. There are two classes, but only one, the acorn
worms, Class Enteropneusta, is common enough to be covered
here. All acorn worms have a naked, fleshy proboscis and a collar
attached to a flaccid, wormlike body or trunk. The anterior (front)
part of the trunk contains many paired gill slits on its upper
surface. The proboscis is used for burrowing: first the tip is
inserted in the sand, then water is imbibed through one or two
oral pores. The proboscis then swells with water and becomes
turgid, suitable for thrusting into the sediment.

Acorn worms are usually both detritus and deposit feeders.
They pick up tiny pieces of organic matter on the mucus-covered
proboscis and ingest mud, from which detritus is selectively
digested in the gut.

All acorn worms have separate sexes.

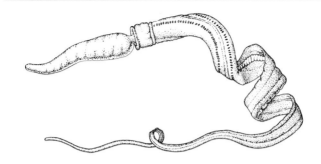

Fig. 154. Northern Acorn Worm.

SOUTHERN ACORN WORM *Ptychodera bahamensis* **Pls. 3, 4**
Long—to 1m (39 in.). Lives in mucus-lined, U- shaped, intertidal
burrows near low-tide mark (see Pl. 4). Posterior of burrow often
marked with coiled fecal casts of gray sand that *smell strongly of
iodine.* Burrow openings may be 1m apart; burrows may be 30cm
(1 ft.) deep. Worm is flaccid, whitish gray with faint white rings,
or yellow; *collar and proboscis white.* Eats mud. In sandy mud
from S. Carolina to Gulf, Bermuda, Caribbean. **Similar species:**
(1) **Northern Acorn Worm** (*Dolichoglossus kowalevskii,* Fig.
154) has a pink or salmon-colored proboscis, a *bright orange
collar,* and a brownish body to 15cm (6 in.) long. Maine to N.
Carolina. (2) **Golden Acorn Worm** (*Balanoglossus aurantiacus*)
has a white or yellowish proboscis and a red-orange collar; trunk
greenish or purplish, with *gold bands. Flattened, winglike
extensions* project from first third of trunk; these contain gonads.
Collar as long or longer than proboscis. Intertidal on mud flats
near low-tide line or subtidal; N. Carolina to Florida.

SEA SQUIRTS OR TUNICATES

Baglike or pillow-shaped, or forming flat, gelatinous crusts on
pilings or Red Mangrove roots, tunicates are hardly identifiable
as animals. But animals they are, complete with a heart that
pumps blood in one direction, then pauses and circulates it in the
other.

Tunicates belong to Subphylum Urochordata of Phylum Chordata. This means that these nondescript animals that spend their
lives straining water through their bodies are our relatives. The
reason they are included in our phylum, Chordata, is that they
have a gelatinous rod called a notochord (in humans this is
associated with the spine). The presence of the notochord has led

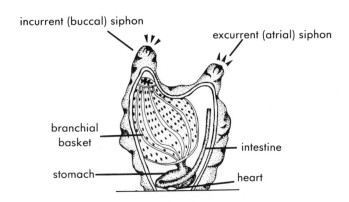

incurrent (buccal) siphon

excurrent (atrial) siphon

branchial
basket

intestine

stomach

heart

Fig. 155. Cut-away view (longitudinal section) of sea squirt.

to the theory that vertebrates evolved from the tadpole-like larvae of tunicates. These larvae, it is suggested, swam up continental streams and, in the process, developed muscles, nerves, and sense organs, thus diverging from their attached ancestors.

All tunicates are filter feeders. They suck water through a dorsal incurrent siphon by beating millions of hairlike cilia on a mucus-covered, sieve-like branchial basket (see Fig. 155). As water flows through this "sieve," microscopic plankton stick to the mucus, and are eventually swept into the intestine and digested. The branchial basket also acts as a gill. The water eventually passes out through the atrial (excurrent) siphon on the animal's side. The tunicate's outer covering, called the test or tunic, is made partially of cellulose—an unusual substance to be used by an animal, since only plants are supposed to be capable of making it.

Tunicates can exist as solitary individuals or as colonies of two types: in the first type each zooid is attached to another by a rootlike stolon but functions independently; in the second, compound type, each individual loses portions of its anatomy and often becomes unrecognizable—just one of a series of dots arranged in a circle around a common excurrent pore. Colonies of compound tunicates resemble a crust or mound, with the zooids functioning communally; often the crowded zooids must lie at an angle or on their sides.

The most distinctive and ubiquitous species in the Caribbean is the Black Tunicate (Fig. 85). This glistening black animal can extend itself to 10cm (4 in.) long. When extended, its siphons look like a pair of long, thin chimneys. When the siphons are not extended it looks like a lump of tar and feels like rubber.

The Pleated Sea Squirt (Fig. 84, Pl. 23) forms tan, rubbery clumps to 5cm (2 in.) tall, in seagrass beds and on pilings, especially in the Gulf. Sometimes whole pilings are obscured by huge colonies of these animals. Look for puckered siphons with four brown lines at right angles at the aperture.

Tunicates, Class Ascidiacea, are a peculiar lot, animals that have chosen, in an evolutionary sense, to live out their lives as scruffy bags attached to Red Mangrove roots or other hard surfaces. But a more daring class has evolved: the salps, members of Class Thalliacea, swim by jet propulsion. They resemble a transparent tube, sometimes containing a black or red dot, the visceral mass. Salps usually live in the open ocean, but sometimes inshore waters abound with them. They resemble the tunicates except that the excurrent siphon (atrial pore) is at the rear of the body, not on the side. This means that water comes in one end and out the other, an arrangement that serves a double purpose. Plankton is filtered out as water passes through the body, and as the water is expelled, it propels the animal forward. Muscle bands run like rings around the body of a salp. As they are contracted, they force the water out and the animal squirts its way through the sea at modest speed.

Reproduction is by budding, so young salps may be attached to the posterior of the parent, forming a chain resembling a four- or five-car train. Each daughter salp is identical to the parent. The most common genus is *Salpa* (Fig. 156). In this group the tube-like body is slightly flattened at top and bottom and is usually partially ringed with 5–9 muscle bands that do not meet on the underside. Internal organs are concentrated in a black dot. Species of *Doliolus,* in a closely related family, have a round, tube-like body surrounded by 8 or 9 *complete* muscle bands. The **Common Doliolid** (*Doliolum nationalis*) reaches only 1.6cm (⅝ in.) in length and has 8 muscle bands. The **Common Salp** (*Salpa fusiformis*) reaches 8.3cm (3¼ in.) in length and is transparent, with a yellowish gut. It has 9 incomplete muscle bands; the first 3 and the last 2 touch each other at the top (dorsal midline). The **Horned Salp** (*Thalia democratica*) reaches 2.5cm (1 in.) long. It has 5 muscle bands and a pair of long horns on upper rear ("tail"). All species live in huge schools near the surface, from Cape Cod to Florida, the Gulf, and W. Indies to Brazil.

The mangrove-dwelling tunicates are discussed separately on pp. 186–190. Species common in seagrass beds, on pilings, or on boat bottoms are discussed on the next two pages.

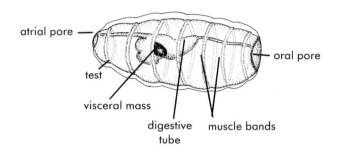

atrial pore

oral pore

test

visceral mass

digestive
tube

muscle bands

Fig. 156. *Salpa,* a free-living tunicate.

SEA PORK *Amaroucium stellatum*   **Pl. 5**
Amorphous, rubbery masses washed up on beaches; to 2.5cm (1 in.) thick and over 30cm (1 ft.) wide. Pink, whitish, dark gray, or bluish. Zooids in circular systems of 6–20, not clearly visible. Seagrass beds; Cape Cod to Gulf. **Similar species: Bermuda Encrusting Tunicate** (Pl. 5) is dark brown, blackish, or deep red. More jelly-like than Sea Pork. Gulf and Caribbean.

SANDY or WESTERN SEA SQUIRT *Molgula occidentalis*
To 4cm (1⅗ in.) long. Sandy or grayish; often fouled with bryozoans, seaweed, or mud. Test feels like sandpaper. Often in colonies of up to 50 individuals, sometimes mixed with Pleated Sea Squirts (Fig. 84), whose shiny exterior contrasts with the muddy appearance of Sandy Sea Squirts. Animals that live on these tunicate masses include the Sea-squirt Flatworm (Fig. 157), pistol or sponge shrimps (Pl. 51), and the Lateral Mussel (*Musculus lateralis*), a light brown, squarish bivalve with fine lines on its shell, reaching 1.3cm (½ in.) long. In the Gulf these mussels are found only on tunicate colonies. Sandy Sea Squirts live in Turtle Grass beds, muddy shallows, and on pilings; N. Carolina to Gulf and south to Brazil. **Similar species: Sea Grape** (*M. manhattensis,* Pl. 19) is grayish, smooth, and bubble-like. Found on boat bottoms, pilings, and seagrass; Maine to S. Carolina. To 2.5cm (1 in.) long.

GREEN COLONIAL TUNICATE or CREEPING   **Fig. 84**
TUNICATE *Perophora viridis*
Tiny—zooid no more than 2mm (³⁄₃₂ in.) tall. Zooids resemble greenish, oval, translucent berries widely separated on creeping

stems. Clusters may be 7.5cm (3 in.) wide. Two siphons and curved gut are visible through test with a hand lens. Forms colonies on pilings, seaweed, and rocks in bays, from low-tide line to deep water; Massachusetts to Florida and Texas; also in W. Indies, especially on Red Mangrove roots.

PLEATED SEA SQUIRT or LEATHERY   **Fig. 84;**
TUNICATE   *Styela plicata*   **Pl. 23**
To 5cm (2 in.) long. Tan, leathery, smooth or with wide wrinkles; siphons become puckered when closed. Siphon opening four-lobed; brown-striped inside. In clumps, sometimes over 30cm (1 ft.) high, in seagrass beds, on pilings, and on mangrove roots; N. Carolina to Florida and W. Indies; abundant in n. Gulf.

RIBBON OR NEMERTEAN WORMS

Phylum Rhyncocoela. Worm-diggers are often startled when they uncover a flaccid, fleshy, flattened worm, sometimes a meter (39 in.) long, while searching for sandworms in the lower inter-tidal zone. Some people call them "tapeworms" because of their flat, white, elongate appearance, but real tapeworms are all parasitic worms that live in the intestines of animals and bear little resemblance to ribbon worms. Nemerteans (ribbon worms) lack segments, or virtually any other surface features, although some have a pair of lateral swellings, called auricles, on the head. Despite their location, the auricles are not "ears"; they contain slits with olfactory receptors, somewhat like elongate nostrils. Eyes may be a few tiny, pigmented dots, grouped on the head or in a row running along edge of body. These primitive eyes can detect light, but cannot perceive images. At night, a ribbon worm emerges from the sand, searching for annelid worms. When it finds one it shoots out a long, threadlike proboscis—often as long as two-thirds of the body—and wraps it around its prey. Then it draws the worm into its mouth, located just below the pore from which the proboscis was everted.

The interior of a ribbon worm is a solid mass of squarish cells with two tubes running through the body: the intestines, which open to the outside of the body via an anus, and the rhyncocoele, the tube containing the proboscis. The ribbon worms are the most primitive animals known to have an anus.

Two common species are found along Atlantic and Gulf coasts, under about 5cm (2 in.) of sand or among rocks or shell debris. It is difficult to dig up a ribbon worm, since it breaks apart so readily. As you enlarge the hole around the worm in an attempt to see a whole one, watch the front end (head) to see the threadlike proboscis shoot out.

MILKY RIBBON WORM *Cerebratulus lacteus* **Pl. 2**
Broad, flat, large, fleshy worm, found under intertidal sand. To
1m (39 in.) long. Whitish, yellowish, or pinkish. When mating,
males become reddish, females brownish. Head spoon-shaped,
with a thin olfactory groove on either side. Mouth under tip of
head, below proboscis pore. **Similar species: Red** or **Leidy's
Nemertean Worm** (*Micrura leidyi*), to 30cm (12 in.) long.
Rounded, triangular, with a head and a tiny, white, pointed tail.
Red, rose, or purplish; paler underneath. Under surface of sand
near low-water mark and below. Both species range from Maine
to Florida and Texas.

FLATWORMS

Phylum Platyhelminthes. These simple animals are low on the
phylogenetic tree — so low that they have evolved few structures
that characterize most other phyla. They have no respiratory
apparatus and must therefore remain paper-thin in order for
oxygen to diffuse from seawater into and through the body. They
have the simplest of excretory systems, actually a series of cells
that beat water out of the body, taking wastes out with the water.
Despite these limitations, the phylum has successfully invaded
many biological niches, the most prominent being other animals'
bodies. Two of the three classes, the trematodes (flukes) and
cestodes (tapeworms), live exclusively inside other animals, usually in the intestines. The third class, Turbellaria, is free-living.
The odd-looking Planaria Worm is a favorite of biology teachers
because of its extraordinary ability to regenerate. Marine turbel-
larians can evert a tube-like pharynx from the middle of the
underside of the body, and use it to suck up oyster spat and other
small invertebrates. Some species cause serious damage to oyster
beds, making it necessary for oyster farmers to suspend juvenile
oysters from rafts above the bottom.
To find free-living flatworms, place a clump of oysters, tunicates, or sponges in an aquarium in a dark room. After a few hours
turn on the lights and examine the surface of the oysters and the
aquarium glass.

HORSESHOE-CRAB FLATWORM Fig. 157
Bdelloura candida
White flatworm, found between flaplike book gills of a live
Horseshoe Crab. To 1.6cm (⅝ in.) long, with 2 black eyes, and a
suckerlike structure at rear. Harmless to host, but worm dies if
removed from Horseshoe Crab. Lays eggs in capsules attached to
gills of host. Easily found if you can concentrate on looking for
them as the gills and legs of a live Horseshoe Crab churn fiercely.

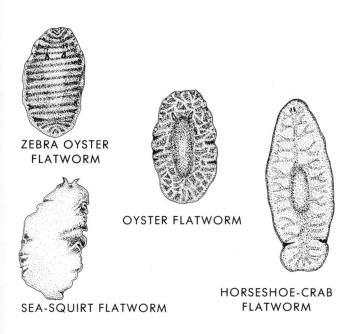

ZEBRA OYSTER
FLATWORM

OYSTER FLATWORM

SEA-SQUIRT FLATWORM

HORSESHOE-CRAB
FLATWORM

Fig. 157. Flatworms.

SEA-SQUIRT FLATWORM   **Fig. 157**
Prostheceraeus floridanus
  To 2.5cm (1 in.) long. Bright orange; complex, multibranched
digestive tract barely visible through skin. Lives among Sandy
and Pleated sea squirts; Gulf.
ZEBRA OYSTER FLATWORM *Stylochus zebra*   **Fig. 157**
  To 3.8cm (1½ in.) long. Oval, with almost parallel sides. Zebra-
like, yellow or white crossbands on a brown background; bands
branch toward edges. Two stubby tentacles near front. Hand lens
reveals two groups of eyespots just forward of tentacles, as well as
marginal eyespots. On oysters and tunicates, also in snail shells
occupied by hermit crabs; Maine to Gulf. Sucks up oyster spat
with its eversible pharynx. **Similar species: Oyster Flatworm**
(*S. ellipticus,* Fig. 157), is pink, brown, or cream. Two pointed
tentacles, 8–12 eyespots along margin of front third of body.
Maine of Gulf.

Fig. 158. Two Crozier's Flatworms on a colony of colonial tunicates.

WAXY TROPICAL FLATWORMS *Pseudoceros* species **Pl. 23**
To 5cm (2 in.) long. Broad—width about ⅓ length. V-shaped pair
of tentacles near front margin. **Crozier's Flatworm** (*P. crozieri,*
Pl. 23) is grayish tan, crossed with thin, wavy, dark brown lines.
Splendid Flatworm (*P. splendidus*) is black, with or without
orange edges. Many other species. In coral rubble, rocks, or sand,
grazing on hydroids or compound ascidians (sea squirts); Bermuda, W. Indies, Caribbean to Brazil.

Glossary
Field Library
Index

Glossary

Aboral: Opposite or away from the mouth, especially in radially symmetrical animals. In sea stars and jellyfishes, the uppermost surface; in polyps, the lower surface.

Aboral arm plates: In brittle stars, a series of calcareous plates forming the upper arm surface.

Alternate leaves: Leaves that extend alternately from the stem, rather than growing opposite one another.

Ambulacral groove: A groove from which protrude an echinoderm's tube feet. All echinoderms except brittle stars and sea cucumbers have five such grooves.

Amoebocyte: An amoeba-like cell that carries food and other substances through the body of sponges and other invertebrates.

Anoxic: Having an oxygen level so low as to be insufficient to support most life.

Aperture: In snails, the large opening in the body whorl of the shell from which the body extends. See Fig. 103, p. 232.

Arm spine: In brittle stars, spines borne by the lateral arm plates.

Autotomy: The deliberate breaking off of an appendage; in crustaceans this is done to deter predators; in sea stars it is done for defense or as a means of reproduction.

Backdune(s) or rear dune(s): The most landward dunes, well vegetated and often merging with the scrub community or maritime forest. See Fig. 5, p. 14, and Fig. 7, p. 16.

Backshore: The flat portion of the beach extending from the crest of the berm to the plant-covered region of permanent stability. See Fig. 11, p. 19, and Fig. 35, p. 79.

Bank/barrier reef: An offshore coral reef running parallel to shore, separated from shore by a shallow channel or lagoon.

Bar: A long, offshore mound of sand lying parallel to shore and almost always submerged; separated from shore by deeper troughs. See **ridge, runnel,** and Fig. 2, p. 11, and Fig. 9, p. 18.

Beach community: The first vegetation zone above the high-tide mark; occupied primarily by pioneering plants. See Fig. 7, p. 16.

Beach scarp: The sharp slope extending from the **berm crest** to the forebeach. Usually no more than 30 cm (1 ft.) high.

Benthic: Bottom-dwelling; living on or under the sediment, pilings, and so forth.

Berm: A flattened region of a beach beyond the intertidal zone where sand is deposited by waves. See Fig. 11, p. 19, and Fig. 35, p. 79. **Berm crest:** The seaward edge of the berm; the sand usually slopes sharply seaward as the **beach scarp** and **foreshore.**

Black zone: The region of a rocky shore just above the yellow (intertidal) zone, wetted by the highest tides. See Fig. 44, p. 92.

Bloom: A sudden abundance of a species due primarily to an increase in its reproduction rate.

Branchiae: Gills; in polychaete worms, the gills may be located on each segment or may consist of a feathery crown at the anterior (front) end.

Byssus: In mussels, ark shells, and other mollusks, a "beard" of threads attaching the animal to the bottom.

Calcareous: Containing calcium carbonate, a chalklike substance.

Callus: In snails, a calcareous deposit extending over a portion of shell, often partially obscuring the **umbilicus.**

Cephalod: A squid or octopus.

Cephalothorax: The fused head and thorax of crabs, shrimps, and other arthropods. See Fig. 125, p. 305.

Cerata: The fingerlike projections on the back of a nudibranch.

Chela: Claw.

Cheliped: A claw-bearing leg. See Fig. 125, p. 305, and Fig. 129, p. 316.

Chenier: In the Gulf of Mexico, a low-lying island or seaside plain, often covered by oaks; formed by the deposition of silt from the Mississippi River.

Choanocyte: In sponges, an internal cell that possesses a flagellum and a sticky, collarlike structure which captures food.

Chromatophore: A pigment-bearing cell in the skin of octopods, fishes, and other marine animals. Used in camouflage.

Cilia: The microscopic hairs found on the surface of corals and other animals. Used for propulsion, for moving food particles, and for removing sediment and debris.

Climax community: A stable, balanced community—the end result of succession.

Cnidarians: Members of the phylum Cnidaria (Coelenterata), including jellyfishes, corals, and sea anemones; the body of these organisms is radially symmetrical and, to a greater or lesser extent, is filled with an acellular, jelly-like material called **mesoglea.**

Cnidocytes: In cnidarians (corals, jellyfishes, and sea anemones), a cell containing a nematocyst.

Columella: In snails, the central core around which the shell develops; also, the inner margin of the aperture of a snail shell. See Fig. 103, p. 232. In corals, a central, stalklike structure at the bottom of the cup, which supports the polyp.

Commensalism: A relationship between two organisms of different species in which one benefits and the other is neither benefited nor harmed.

Compound leaf: A leaf composed of a number of leaflets on a common stalk.

Cord: A raised spiral element in the sculpture of a snail shell, usually a sharply defined, thick, rounded ridge.

Cortication: In seaweeds, an outer covering or layer of cells, common in red algae.

Cryptic: Living in holes, caves, or burrows; hidden.

Cuvier's organs: See **Tubules of Cuvier.**

Deciduous: Leaves shed after one season of growth. Trees that are bare during a season of the year are deciduous.

Dental papillae: In brittle stars, a group of small calcareous plates at the apex of the jaw, below the teeth and above the oral papillae.

Deposit feeder: A sediment-eating animal, such as certain worms and sea cucumbers.

Detritus: Material that is disintegrating or rotting—usually leaves, dead organisms, and so forth.

Dichotomous: In seaweeds, branches or organs that are forked or repeatedly branched.

Disk: In brittle stars, a round, pentagonal, or lobed body containing internal organs; the part to which the arms and mouth frame are attached.

Diurnal tides: Tides that occur once a day—one high tide and one low tide during 24 hours. Compare with **semidiurnal tides.**

Drill(s) or oyster drill(s): Snails, including *Thais, Urosalpynx,* and others, which prey on bivalves and barnacles by drilling a hole in the shell.

Dune community: A plant community bordering the beach where plants stabilize mounds of sand; just inland from the beach community. See Fig. 7, p. 16.

Elytra: In polychaete worms, scales covering the body.

Endozoic: Living inside an animal.

Epibiont: A plant or animal that lives on the outside of another plant or animal.

Epiphyte: A plant that grows on the surface of another plant but is not a parasite.

Epitoke: In polychaetous annelids (worms), either the whole worm or the posterior (rear) half, modified for reproduction.

Epizoite: An animal that lives on the surface of another organism.

Errant polychaetes: Marine segmented worms (annelids) that move about and often do not live in burrows or tubes. Compare with **sedentary polychaetes.**

Euryhaline, eurythermal: Capable of surviving a wide range of salinities (**euryhaline**) or a wide range or temperatures (**eurythermal**). From the Greek *eurys,* meaning "broad."

Exposed beach: A beach which is unprotected from the full brunt of the sea; this type usually has high surf.

Feeding polyp: In cnidarians, a specialized polyp used to obtain food. Also called a gasterozooid.

Filamentous: In seaweeds, the thallus (body) of an alga consisting of a chain of individual cells attached end to end; to the naked eye the series of cells can appear as threads, sheets, or cottony masses.

Filter feeder: An organism that filters food, usually plankton or bacteria, from the water. Also called a **suspension feeder.**

Foraminiferan: An amoeba that produces a microscopic test that often resembles the shell of a snail.

Foredune(s): The most seaward dunes, usually covered with grasses and other pioneering plants. See Fig. 5, p. 14, and Fig. 7, p. 16.

Foreshore: The seaward, sloping portion of the beach extending from the intertidal zone to the point where the beach levels off. See Fig. 11, p. 19, and Fig. 35, p. 79.

Fringing reef: A coral reef contiguous with the shore; this type lacks a lagoon. Compare with **bank/barrier reef.**

Gastropod: A snail, limpet, nudibranch, or sea slug.

Gastrovascular cavity: In cnidarians (corals, jellyfishes, and anemones), an internal chamber in which food is digested and from which nutrients are transported throughout the body of the polyp or medusa.

Genital (bursal) slits: In brittle stars, narrow openings on the oral (lower) surface of the disk, on each side of the arm bases. See Fig. 142, p. 345.

Girdle: In chitons, the fleshy border of the body, which may be naked (unscaled) or covered with scales or bristles. See Fig. 108, p. 263.

Gorgonians: Soft corals of Order Gorgonacea: sea fans, sea whips, and branching soft corals.

Gray zone: The widest region of rocky shore above the intertidal zone (see Fig. 44, p. 92). Wetted infrequently, only by storm tides. Often flat, gray, pitted.

Halophyte: A plant adapted to a highly salty environment.

Hermaphrodite, hermaphroditic: Having both sexes contained in one animal.

Hinge: In bivalve mollusks, a brown, plasticlike structure holding the two shells together. See Fig. 106, p. 253.

Holdfast: In seaweeds, a rootlike structure that serves as an organ of attachment.

Inferomarginals: In sea stars, beadlike plates along the oral (lower) margins of the rays (arms).

Interbrachial area: In brittle stars, the area of the disk between the arms. See Fig. 142, p. 345.

Intertidal zone: The region of a shore that is inundated daily by tides. Also called the **yellow zone.** See Fig. 44, p. 92.

Lagoon: A body of water separated from the sea by banks or coral reefs. The region between a shore and a bank/barrier reef or inside the ring of islands composing an atoll.

Lateral arm plates: In brittle stars, calcareous plates bearing arm spines, lying between the oral and aboral arm plates. See Fig. 142, p. 345.

Lower platform: The region of rocky shore just below the intertidal zone; rarely exposed, even by the lowest tides. See Fig. 44, p. 92.

Lunule: In bivalves, the heart-shaped area in front of the umbo, or beak (see Fig. 106, p. 253); in sea urchins, oval perforations through the test (shell).

Madreporite: In echinoderms, the opening of the water-vascular system. A sievelike valve; often appears as a bright dot near the center of the aboral (upper) surface.

Manus: The next to last segment of a crab's walking leg. Also called the propodus.

Matted felt zone: An algal plant community above the intertidal zone, consisting of short-cropped filamentous algae.

Medusa: A jellyfish: it has a bell-shaped body and a downward-facing mouth.

Megalops: The final larval stage of a crustacean; the stage that begins to resemble the adult.

Mesoglea: The acellular, jelly-like material composing much of the body of a jellyfish.

Mesotidal: Having a tidal range between 2–4 meters (7–14 feet).

Microtidal: Having a tidal range of less than 2 meters (7 feet).

Mutualism: A relationship between two organisms of different species in which both benefit.

Nacreous layer: In mollusks, the smooth, iridescent inner layer of the shell, often called mother-of-pearl.

Nauplius: The first larval stage of a crustacean; it has three pairs of appendages, no segments, and either one or no eyes.

Neap tide: A period of minimal tide movement, occuring for a few days twice a month. During this period low tides are not very low, and high tides are not very high. Compare with **spring tide.**

Nematocysts: In cnidarians (jellyfishes, corals, and anemones), the microscopic dartlike structures that are sticky, poisonous, or otherwise entrapping; used to capture plankton (food) and for defense.

Oolitic limestone: Rock composed primarily of petrified corals and the skeletons of other calcareous organisms.

Operculum: In snails, the "door" used to close the aperture of the shell. See Fig. 103, p. 232. Any doorlike or lidlike structure closing off a shell or tube.

Opposite leaves: Leaves attached directly opposite one another on the stem. Compare with **alternate leaves.**

Oral arm plates: In brittle stars, a series of calcareous plates forming the oral surface of the arms. See Fig. 142, p. 345.

Oral disk, oral end: In radially symmetrial animals such as sea stars or sea urchins, the region around the mouth. In sea anemones, the oral disk is the flattened part of the tentacle-fringed upper portion of the body.

Oral papillae: In brittle stars, calcareous projections of the various shapes, lying around the edge of the lower surface of the jaw.

Oscules: In sponges, large excurrent holes.

Ostia: In sponges, the incurrent holes or pores that permit the entrance of water.

Palps: In errant (free-living) polychaetes, paired sensory projections extending from the ventral surface of the prostomium (head) which aid in feeding; in sedentary polychaetes, the palps are dorsal, grooved, and adhesive, and are used to carry food to the mouth.

Parapodia: Soft, paired appendages or folds running the length of the body of polychaete worms, sea slugs, and other animals. See Fig. 19, p. 38.

Parasitism: A relationship between organisms of different species in which one benefits and the other is harmed.

Parietal wall: In snails, the portion of the body wall bordering the inside wall of the aperture; it covers the **columella.**

Pedicellaria: Tiny, three-jawed, often stalked appendages, scattered over the surface of sea stars and sea urchins. Used primarily for defense against small organisms that might settle on the surface, and sometimes for cleaning the surface.

Pelagic: Swimming or floating above the bottom; living in open water.

Periostracum: The hairy or horny outer layer of a seashell.

Periproct: In sea urchins, the anus.

Peristome: In sea urchins, the mouth.

Peristomium: In polychaete worms, the first segment, just behind the head. See Fig. 113, p. 273.

Petals: In sea urchins, ambulacral grooves in the aboral or dorsal surface that often look like a five-petaled flower.

Petiole: In plants, the leaf stalk.

Pharynx: The throat region; in polychaete worms it is eversible and toothed, and is used for capturing prey.

Pheromone: A substance released into the environment by one animal which affects the behavior of another of the same species. For example, a sex attractant released into the air or water by a female moth or crab will attract males.

Phytoplankton: Usually microscopic, often one-celled plants drifting in the water column.

Pink zone: The region of rocky shore below the lower yellow (intertidal) zone, encrusted with pink algae such as *Porolithon* or *Goniolithon*. See Fig. 49, p. 102.

Pioneer plants: Plants characteristic of the first stage of succession. Colonizers of bare sand.

Pinnate: Resembling a feather; having opposite projections from a central stalk. In plants, having leaflets on each side of a common petiole (leaf stalk). **Twice-pinnate** means that each leaflet is further divided into smaller leaflets.

Plankton: Organisms that cannot swim against wind-driven ocean currents; drifters. May range in size from tiny larvae and eggs to huge jellyfishes. See also **zooplankton** and **phytoplankton.**

Planula: The ciliated oval larva of cnidarians.

Pneumatophore: An air-containing organ. In the Black Mangrove, it is an extension of the root that absorbs air; in the Portuguese Man-of-War, it is an air-filled bladder.

Podia: In echinoderms, tube-like projections of the water-vascular system, often called tube feet because sea stars, sea cucumbers, and some sea urchins walk on them. The podia are used primarily to carry food in brittle stars and crinoids.

Polychaete: A class of annelid worms with distinct parapodia and setae (bristles) on most body segments.

Polyp: An attached animal with a columnar body topped by a ring of tentacles; a sea anemone, for example.

Polysiphonous: In seaweeds, this refers to filaments that comprise elongate cells parallel to each other, as in a bundle; a common arrangement in red algae.

Primary consumer: A plant-eater.

Prismatic layer: In mollusks, the middle layer of the shell.

Producer: A green plant that produces food through photosynthesis.

Prop root: In Red Mangrove trees, adventitious roots that extend from the trunk and arch into the water.

Prostomium: In polychaete worms, the head, bearing the mouth, eyes, and so forth. See Fig. 113, p. 273.

Protandrous hermaphroditism: In certain bivalves (such as oysters), some species of fishes, and other taxa, a type of reproduction or condition in which an animal is first a male and then becomes a female.

Protected beach: A beach in the lee of an island or behind a barrier reef; this type is exposed to little wave action.

Pulmonate: Air-breathing; for example, a group of air-breathing snails that must live above water in salt marshes and tidal flats.

Pygidium: In polychaete worms, the last segment, bearing the anus. See Fig. 113, p. 273.

r: In sea stars, the distance from the center of the disk to the interradial margin—that is, from the center of the disk to the point of the V between two rays.

R: The distance from the center of the disk to the tip of a ray, or arm of a brittle star or sea star.

R = 4r: This means the length of a ray is approximately four times the radius of the disk. **R = 12r** means that the arms are very long compared to the diameter of the disk.

Radial shields: In brittle stars, five pairs of calcareous plates found on the aboral surface of the disk, near the arm base.

Radially symmetrical: Symmetrical around a central axis, so that cutting along any plane through that axis produces mirror-image halves. Radially symmetrical animals are round and lack distinct heads.

Radula: The file-like "tongue" of a snail. See Fig. 100, p. 228.

Raptorial legs: Appendages for capturing prey.

Ray(s): The arms of sea stars or brittle stars.

Reproductive polyp: A polyp specialized for reproduction; a gonozooid.

Repugnatorial glands: In sea slugs, glands which secrete an unpleasant (usually bad-tasting) substance; a defense mechanism.

Rhinophore(s): The paired, tentacle-like olfactory (smelling) organs on the head of a nudibranch or sea slug.

Ridge: An elongate mound of sand which runs parallel to the beach and projects from water at low tide. Separated from shore by a depression called a **runnel.** Ridges usually coalesce with the shore over time. See Fig. 9, p. 18.

Rostrum: The knife-like, often serrated structure projecting like a horn from the center of the head of a shrimp or crab.

Runnel: A shallow depression separating a ridge from shore. See Fig. 9, p. 18.

Saltbush community: A plant community found at the landward edge of some southern salt marshes, dominated by Marsh Elder (Pl. 21) and Groundsel Tree (Pl. 21).

Scrub and thicket community: The most landward of the plant communities bordering the beach; characterized by woody shrubs and trees.

Secondary consumer: A carnivorous animal that eats herbivorous animals (**primary consumers**).

Sedentary polychaetes: Polychaetous annelids (segmented worms) that live in tubes and burrows.

Semidiurnal tides: Tides that recur twice a day—two high tides and two low tides every 24 hours.

Septum: A calcareous partition inside the cup of a coral; in cephalopods, a partition between the chambers in the shells of *Spirula, Nautilus,* and others.

Sessile: Attached to the bottom or to rocks, pilings, and so on.

Setae: The bristles extending from the parapodia of polychaetes or from the appendages of many tiny arthropods, such as amphipods and isopods.

Siphonal canal: In snails, the fold extending from the aperture at the front of the shell. This canal contains the siphon tube when the animal is alive. See Fig. 103, p. 232.

Sole: The flat ventral surface of a sea cucumber or sea slug.

Spring tide: The period of greatest tidal range, occurring twice each month; the period with the highest high tides and lowest low tides. Compare with **neap tide.**

Stenohaline, stenothermal: Having a limited tolerance for variations in salinity (**stenohaline**) or temperature (**stenothermal**). From the Greek *stenos,* meaning "narrow."

Stolon: In seaweeds, a horizontal, stemlike structure or filament growing close to and often attached to the substrate (bottom). Erect portions of an alga are usually attached along a stolon.

Substrate: The bottom, which may be muddy, rocky, or sandy; called the substratum by specialists.

Succession: The evolutionary sequence whereby plant and animal communities replace one another until they reach a stable climax community.

Succulent: A plant with water-storage tissue in the stem and simple, thick leaves.

Superomarginals: Beadlike plates along the aboral (upper) margins of the rays (arms) of sea stars.

Suspension feeder: See **filter feeder.**

Suture: In snails, a thin groove between any two whorls of the shell. See Fig. 103, p. 232.

Swale: A valley between the foredunes and rear dunes. Also called the **interdune meadow.** See Fig. 7, p. 16.

Swash: The feebly moving thin sheet of water that flows up and down the beach as the last remnant of a wave after it has crashed on the shore. See Fig. 10, p. 18.

Symbiosis: Any relatively long-term interdependence between two species. **Parasitism, commensalism,** and **mutualism** are subsumed under this term.

Teeth: In brittle stars, broad, calcareous plates forming a column that projects into the jaw cavity at the jaw apex.

Tentacle or podial scales: In brittle stars, one or two scales at the base of each podium.

Tentacular cirri: Elongate appendages rising from the peristomium of a polychaete; sensory organs. See Fig. 113, p. 273.

Terete: In seaweeds, the round appearance of the body of the plant, in cross section.

Tertiary consumer: A carnivore that eats **secondary** and **primary consumers.**

Test: In an aquatic animal, the outer covering made of a nonliving substance; it can be shell-like, capsular, or rubbery. Echinoderms, tunicates, and foraminiferans have tests, for example.

Thallus: In seaweeds, the body of the alga (may include leaflike, stemlike, and rootlike structures).

Tidepool: A small body of water containing animals and plants, trapped between rocks or in depressions in the sand. The pool is replenished intermittently or daily with seawater at high tides.

Trade winds: Relatively constant winds originating at the equator; they blow from the east in the tropical northern hemisphere.

Tubules of Cuvier (Cuvier's organs): White or pink, sticky tubules or threads ejected from the anus of sea cucumbers as a defense mechanism.

Umbilicus: In snails, a hole at the base of the body whorl. See Fig. 103, p. 232.

Umbo (plural, umbones): The pointed portion, or "beak," of a bivalve shell. See Fig. 106, p. 253.

Uniseriate: In seaweeds, cells or structures that appear in a single row, line, or series.

Upper platform: The portion of a rocky shore that extends from the strandline to the region that is almost perpetually submerged; includes the **intertidal zone.** See Fig. 44, p. 92.

Valves: In bivalves, the two shells (see Fig. 106, p. 253); in chitons, the eight plates.

Vanishing tide: In the Gulf of Mexico and other confined embayments, a low high tide and a high low tide sometimes succeed each other so that the normal tidal sequence "vanishes." See Fig. 26, p. 55.

Veliger: In mollusks, the actively swimming larval stage, characterized by a ciliated collar or velum.

Washover fan: The fan-shaped, flattened area behind the dunes resulting when the sea broaches the dune line during a storm and deposits sand landward of the dunes. See Fig. 5, p. 14.

White zone: The region of a rocky shore extending from permanently dry land to the strandline; wetted only a few times a year by storms. See Fig. 44, p. 92.

Yellow zone: The region of a rocky shore bounded by high and low tides. Also called the **intertidal zone.** See Fig. 44, p. 92.

Zoea: The second larval stage of a crustacean; it has swimming appendages and large eyes.

Zooid: Each individual in a colony or compound organism; arises through asexual reproduction.

Zooplankton: Drifting or floating aquatic animals—fish eggs, microscopic larvae, jellyfishes, and so forth.

Zooxanthallae: Microscopic dinoflagellates; one-celled organisms living in the tissues of corals and other organisms. The zooxanthellae produce food by photosynthesis that can be shared with the host organism (see p. 202).

Field Library

The publications listed below can be taken with the serious naturalist and used as supplements to this Field Guide. An asterisk means that the book is an inexpensive paperback. A square means that the book was written for laymen.

Abbot, R. T. 1974. *American Seashells*. New York: Van Nostrand.
* Amos, W. H., and S. H. Amos. 1985. *Field Guide to Atlantic and Gulf Coasts*. New York: Alfred A. Knopf.
  Bond, J. 1980. *Birds of the West Indies,* 4th ed. Boston: Houghton Mifflin.
* Bullard, L. F., and J. B. Harrell. 1979. *Coastal Plants of Florida*. Tallahassee: Florida Dept. of Agriculture.
* Chaplin, C. G., and P. Scott. 1972. *Fishwatcher's Guide.* Valley Forge, Pa.: Harrowwood Books. (Printed on plastic, can be taken under water.)
  Colin, P. 1978. *Caribbean Reef Invertebrates and Plants.* Neptune City, N.J.: T. F. H. Publishing Co.
* Emerson, W. K., and M. K. Jacobson. 1976. *The American Museum of Natural History Guide to Shells.* New York: Alfred A. Knopf.
* Forman, R. T. T. 1974. *An Introduction to Ecosystems and Plants on St. Croix, U.S. Virgin Islands*. West Indies Laboratory, P. O. Box 4010, Christiansted, St. Croix, U.S. Virgin Islands.
* Fotheringham, N. 1980. *Beachcomber's Guide to Gulf Coast Marine Life.* Houston: Gulf Publishing Co.
  Fox, R. S., and E. E. Ruppert. 1985. *Shallow-water Marine Benthic Macroinvertebrates of South Carolina.* Columbia, S.C.: University of South Carolina Press.
* Fox, W. T. 1983. *At the Sea's Edge.* Englewood Cliffs, N.J.: Prentice-Hall.
* Gosner, K. 1978. *A Field Guide to the Atlantic Seashore.* Boston: Houghton Mifflin. (Covers more northern waters but includes some southern species.)
* Greenberg, I., and J. Greenberg. 1977. *Waterproof Guide to Corals and Fishes.* Miami: Seahawk Press.
* Hanlon, R., and G. Voss. 1975. *Guide to Seagrasses of Florida, the Gulf of Mexico, and the Caribbean Region.* Coral Gables, Fla.: Sea Grant Public Information Services, University of Miami. Also available in this series are guides to *Mangroves and*

Poisonous Trees, Lobsters and Lobsterlike Animals, Common Gorgonians, Large Marine Gastropods, and Octopods and Squids.

▪ * Heard, R. W. 1982. *Guide to Common Tidal Marsh Invertebrates of the Northeastern Gulf of Mexico.* Ocean Springs, Mich.: Mississippi-Alabama Sea Grant Consortium.

▪ Humfrey, M. 1975. *Seashells of the West Indies.* New York: Taplinger.

▪ * Kaplan, E. 1982. *A Field Guide to Coral Reefs of the Caribbean and Florida.* Boston: Houghton Mifflin.

▪ * Leatherman, S. P. 1982. *Barrier Island Handbook.* Available from U.S. National Park Service, Cumberland National Seashore, P. O. Box 806, St. Mary's, Ga. 31558.

▪ * Lipson, A. J., and R. L. Lipson. 1984. *Life in the Chesapeake Bay.* Baltimore: Johns Hopkins University Press.

* Little, E. L., and F. H. Wadsworth. 1964. *Common Trees of Puerto Rico and the Virgin Islands.* Washington, D.C.: U.S. Department of Agriculture, Forest Service; Government Printing Office.

▪ * Meinkoth, N. A. 1981. *The Audubon Society Field Guide to North American Seashore Creatures.* New York: Alfred A. Knopf.

▪ Randall, J. 1983. *Caribbean Reef Fishes.* Neptune City, N.J.: T. F. H. Publishing Co.

▪ * Rehder, H. A. 1981. *The Audubon Society Field Guide to North American Seashells.* New York: Alfred A. Knopf.

▪ Roessler, C. 1979. *The Underwater Wilderness.* New York: E. P. Dutton.

▪ * Rudloe, J. 1971. *The Erotic Ocean.* New York: World Publishing Co.

Rützler, K., and I. G. Macintyre. 1982. *The Atlantic Barrier Reef Ecosystem at Carrie Bow Cay, Belize, I. Structure and Communities.* Washington, D.C.: Smithsonian Institution Press.

▪ * Sefton, N., and S. K. Webster. 1986. *Caribbean Reef Invertebrates.* Monterey, Calif.: Sea Challengers.

▪ Silberhorn, G. 1982. *Common Plants of the Mid-Atlantic Coast, A Field Guide.* Baltimore: The Johns Hopkins University Press.

▪ Smith, F. G. W. 1971. *A Handbook of the Common Atlantic Reef Corals.* Austin: University of Texas Press.

▪ * Spitzbergen, J. M. 1984. *Seacoast Life: An Ecological Guide to the Natural Seashore Communities in North Carolina.* Chapel Hill: The University of North Carolina Press.

▪ * Stephenson, T. A., and A. Stephenson. 1972. *Life Between Tidemarks on Rocky Shores.* San Francisco: W. A. Freeman and Co.

Sterrer, W. 1986. *Marine Fauna and Flora of Bermuda.* New York: John Wiley (expensive).

Taylor, W. R. 1972. *Marine Algae of the Eastern Tropical and Subtropical Coasts of the Americas.* Ann Arbor: University of Michigan Press.

Thresher, R. 1980. *Reef Fish*. St. Petersburg, Fla.: Palmetto Publishing Co.

* Voss, G. 1976. *Seashore Life of Florida and the Caribbean*. Miami: Banyan Books.

* Warmke, G., and R. T. Abbot. 1975. *Caribbean Seashells*. New York: Dover.

* Welkerling, W. J. 1976. *South Florida Benthic Marine Algae*. Miami: Comparative Sedimentology Laboratory, Rosenstiel School of Marine and Atmospheric Science, University of Miami.

Williams, A. B. 1984. *Shrimps, Lobsters, and Crabs of the Atlantic Coast of the Eastern U.S., Maine to Florida*. Washington, D.C.: Smithsonian Institution Press.

Index

Page numbers in *italics* refer to illustrations.